ARIZONA

The Grand Canyon State

A STATE GUIDE

*Compiled by Workers of the Writers' Program
of the Work Projects Administration
in the State of Arizona*

Completely revised by Joseph Miller
Edited by Henry G. Alsberg

AMERICAN GUIDE SERIES

ILLUSTRATED

Sponsored by The Arizona State College at Flagstaff

HASTINGS HOUSE · Publishers · NEW YORK ·

FIRST PUBLISHED IN APRIL 1940
COMPLETELY REVISED EDITION 1956
REPRINTED APRIL 1959

Foreword

THE ARIZONA GUIDE seeks to tell the story of the wide-open spaces, the color that nature has generously splashed, of towns continuously inhabited prior to the coming of the white man, and of the missions. It contrasts the air-cooled-by-nature, pine clad northern area with the air-cooled-by-man desert area of central Arizona. It gives credit to the dry farmer raising beans and corn, to the farmer in the irrigated citrus, lettuce, cantaloupe, and alfalfa belt, and to the miners of gold, copper, and other minerals. The dude ranch and the cattle ranch, the modern city and the primitive Indian village, the public school, climaxing in the colleges of higher learning, and the private school are portrayed. Tales of the old west are presented as mention is made of modern writers. The pictograph receives attention and so does modern art. Arizona is a delightful haven for the retired, an opportunity for the ambitious young. Arizona is a study of contrasts, and this GUIDE is your guide so that you may know Arizona.

THOMAS J. TORMEY
*Former President, Arizona State
College at Flagstaff*

Preface

This book is dedicated to everyone who has had a part in its making. Of the shortcomings of the volume we are aware. For the merits it possesses, we offer our thanks to all who have lent a hand.

Woven into the book are many accounts of vivid incidents in Arizona history—many of them of a controversial nature. In the controversial material we have simply stated, "This is one version." Since the word "version" is unfamiliar to some of our old timers, many are likely to say, "That ain't the way I heard it!"

We are especially grateful to numerous consultants, specialists in branches of learning, also Federal, state and local governmental agencies and civic associations, and others whose names are too numerous to mention.

THE EDITORS

Foreword to the Revised Edition

ARIZONA has enjoyed a most remarkable growth in the past decade, necessitating a general revision of this volume. Aside from being the nation's fastest growing state percentage-wise, the population having doubled since the 1940 Census, it ranks first in rate of income growth and bank deposit growth. The state also ranks second in both passenger car and truck registration growth. The population of both Phoenix and Tucson has greatly expanded, due not only to vigorous annexation programs, but also to a great influx of new residents, many of them former GI's and Air Force personnel, who were trained on Arizona's sun-drenched desert terrain, and who decided, when ready to make a home, that this was the place.

Arizona began its great expansion shortly after Pearl Harbor in 1941. Due to the almost perfect year-round flying weather in southern Arizona, several airfields "sprang up" practically over night, and three of the larger fields are still operating on a permanent basis, Luke Air Force Base, and Williams Air Force Base near Phoenix, and Davis-Monthan Air Force Base near Tucson. The Naval Air Facility, huge storage depot, continues at Litchfield Park. Old Fort Huachuca, near the Mexican border, has been reactivated as a U. S. Electronics Proving Ground.

About the same time the airfields began to dot the landscape, the aircraft manufacturing industry made inroads on the desert, to make parts and various assemblies. Among these new installations were those of the Goodyear Aircraft Corporation, AiResearch Manufacturing Company, Aluminum Company of America, and later, the Hughes Aircraft Company. The great power dams on the Colorado River stepped up output of electrical energy to meet the challenge of the new war industries, and the airfields. The mining industry began to work at capacity.

With the closing of the historic Jerome copper mine, due to depletion of ore reserves, which also necessitated the shut-down of the nearby Clarkdale smelter, development began at the new Lavender Pit at Bisbee, and the new copper camp of San Manuel. The latter is a boom town in the desert northeast of Tucson, a new city of 2,000 model homes with a population of some eight thousand.

Uranium has been found in several sections of the state, and the Navajo Indian Reservation has been revealed as the No. 2 source of the nation's supply. Several major oil companies and others are pacing a state-wide, drilling-for-oil wave.

Arizona continues to grow at a rapid pace in the post-war era. The huge airfields stay on, training fighter and bomber personnel for the national defense, and the skies are punctuated with zooming jet planes. The great manufacturing plants continue to produce not only for air-force requirements, but also for many needs of the domestic market. The state leads the nation in farm income growth, and aside from the lettuce, melons, grapefruit and oranges, and numerous other crops, Arizona produced over one million bales of cotton in 1953, the highest in its history. The total livestock and agricultural income for the year was almost $400 million.

To augment the state's economy, in addition to the above mentioned, there is the increasing number of tourists who find the state's climate and varied scenic attractions unsurpassed. The northern section is especially agreeable in summer, and southern Arizona in "winter."

Phoenix, Tucson, Mesa, Scottsdale, are the spring (February) training grounds for four major league baseball clubs, the New York Giants, Cleveland Indians, Chicago Cubs, and Baltimore Oreoles.

Arizona's future seems unlimited. Much depends upon an adequate water supply from the Colorado River to irrigate more of the rich desert land which produces such fabulous crops and needs only the magic touch of water, together with the brilliant sun, to produce an expanded acreage for an ever growing population.

Arizona now has the largest Indian population in the United States, with 65,761, to 53,769 for Oklahoma, according to the 1950 Census. While there are additional school facilities being added on the reservations, many of the Indian children are being assimilated into the public schools. The demand for school facilities far exceeds the expanding capacity of the elementary, the high schools, and the colleges. Segregation in schools has finally come to an end with desegregation in the Phoenix Union High School System. Another step forward in Arizona is the right to vote granted to Indians who can meet state educational requirements.

The revision of this volume was accomplished through the facilities of the Department of Library and Archives, Phoenix, and aid given by the Director, Mulford Winsor, and Librarian, Alice B. Good. Valuable aid was also forthcoming from the University of Arizona, and its President, Dr. Richard A. Harvill, and various department heads; the Arizona State College at Tempe, and Dr. Rufus Kay Wyllys, Head of the Department of History; the State Highway Department for aid in checking highway status and mileages; various governmental agencies, custodians of national monuments, national forests, Grand Canyon National Park, as well as chambers of commerce, postmasters, and various individuals, for whose cooperation we express our gratitude.

JOSEPH MILLER

Contents

Part III. Tours

Part IV. Appendices

Illustrations

xiii

THE DESERT—*continued*

TERRITORIAL DAYS   *Between* 128 *and* 129

THE MOUNTAINS   *Between* 222 *and* 223

Maps

General Information

Railroads: Southern Pacific Lines (SP), Atchison, Topeka & Santa Fe Ry. (SF). (See Transportation map.)

Bus Lines: Greyhound Lines, Santa Fe Trailways, American, Continental, and numerous smaller lines connecting principal points.

Motor Vehicle Laws: Hand signals must be used. Headlights or spotlights that dazzle not permitted. Personal injury or property damage over $50 must be reported to some civil authority.

Prohibited: Coasting in neutral; parking on highways and bridges; passing a vehicle going in the same direction at an intersection; inadequate brakes.

Proof of car ownership required of out-of-state motorists. Visitors' permit should be obtained from the inspection station or any highway patrol officer by nonresident motorists who wish to remain in the state more than ten days. Operators' licenses from other states honored, but visitors without licenses must get them from the county assessor's office after 30 days from the time of entering state. Copies of the Arizona Motor Vehicle Code of Traffic Laws can be obtained from the State Highway Department at Phoenix.

Warnings for Motorists: Do not leave trunk highways without a full supply of gasoline and oil, and without information on distance to the next filling station. It should not be assumed that every settlement shown on map has these supplies. When leaving main highways it is advisable to have a few yards of stout rope for towing purposes and in sandy country, a couple of burlap bags to give traction in getting out of ruts. On narrow mountain roads keep close watch for cars coming in opposite direction and, if one appears, draw into the first possible passing place. The up-car has the right of way. Avoid parking in washes or dry stream beds, as sudden rainfall often fills them to impassable depth.

Motor Inspection: State officers examine baggage to prevent importation of diseased citrus fruit, cotton pests, or other things likely to endanger Arizona agriculture. State border stations maintained by Highway Department to give information and levy 5¢ per gallon tax on fuel in excess of amount carried in standard tank.

Airlines: American Airlines Inc. (coast to coast): Phoenix, Tucson, Bisbee-Douglas. Trans World Airlines (coast to coast): Phoenix. Bonanza Air Lines: Yuma, Ajo, Phoenix, Prescott, Kingman, Las Vegas-Boulder City for Boulder Dam. Frontier Airlines: Clifton, Safford, Tucson, Phoenix, Prescott, Flagstaff, Winslow. Grand Canyon Airlines Inc.: North and South Rims (summer only).

Poisonous Snakes and Plants: Poisonous plants in Arizona are so rare as to be negligible. Cactus thorns are never poisonous. In summer rattlesnakes, Gila monsters (world's only poisonous lizard), scorpions, and a few stinging insects may be encountered; however, only ordinary precaution is necessary.

Climate and Equipment: Tourists should have clothing and equipment to suit wide divergence of temperature. In camping carry plenty of bedding. Containers of drinking water are advisable when traveling in the state. In the southern part water is usually available every few miles, in the northern Indian country stations are many miles apart. The summer sun is intense but never dangerous if hats are worn and water is available. Guides may be hired and camping equipment may be rented by hunters or explorers in almost any vicinity.

Fish and Game Laws: There are specific open and closed seasons and bag limits for various game and fish. Local inquiry is essential. License is required for each sportsman, and limit laws are rigidly enforced.

Licenses (hunting and fishing): Residents (persons who have lived in Arizona at least one year): Fishing, $3.50; hunting, $4; general hunting and fishing, $7. Nonresidents: fishing, $10; small game, $20. Special elk, antelope, and bighorn hunting licenses may be secured from state game warden (Phoenix) as well as other special licenses and general information.

Camping: Guard against careless fires; extinguish campfires before leaving camp by covering with dirt or water. Arizona has many thousand square miles of national forests, carefully patrolled. It is illegal to cut trees, to remove plant specimens of any nature without state permit, or to pick wild flowers near any roadway; also to dig in or otherwise disturb any archeological site, ruin, national monument, or other public property.

Alcoholic Liquors: Sold except between 1 a.m. and 6 a.m. weekdays, and from 1 a.m. to 12 noon Sundays.

Recreational Areas: Grand Canyon National Park and Boulder Dam recreational area are renowned vacation regions. Kaibab, one of Arizona's seven National Forests, is famous for big game hunting. There are sixteen national monuments. Outstanding recreational areas are Papago State Park, South Mountain Park, Horsethief Basin, and Apache Trail, near Phoenix; Oak Creek Canyon, Northern Lakes area near Flagstaff; Granite Dells, Garden of the Gods, near Prescott; Mount Graham, near Safford; Santa Catalina, Sabino Canyon, Tucson Mountain Park, Colossal Cave Park and Saguro Forest State Park near Tucson; Ferndale and Pinal recreational area, near Globe; Hualpai Mountain Park, near Kingman.

Accommodations: Main highways are dotted with tourist cabins and hotels—from the luxurious to the rustic. Dude ranches are numerous, but seldom near main highways. In northeastern Arizona and in many hunting areas accommodations are limited. Inquire locally. Northern resorts may be closed in winter, and southern ones in summer. Trailer camps are available in the larger centers. Other camping facilities are abundant throughout the state.

Suggestions for Visitors to Indian Reservations: The carrying and sale of liquor is forbidden by the Federal Government; hunting and fishing are subject to special regulations—information available at Indian agency offices. Visitors should keep in mind that the Indians have the same rights as other property holders in deciding under what conditions outsiders may visit their lands and their homes; they should not attempt to photograph Indians or enter their homes without asking permission. Fees are usually asked for admission to dances and for permission to photograph the Indians, their homes and ceremonies.

Never assume that an Indian does not understand remarks made about him in English and do not use pigeon-English in speaking to him, no matter how badly he seems to understand when addressed. Any courteous person is safe in Indian country.

For Motorists Entering Mexico: No passport required for United States citizens. No formality necessary for stay of less than 24 hours. For longer stay procure tourist card ($3) from Mexican consulates or at border. Temporary permit (3 mos.) for car is obtainable at border from Mexican Customs. Carry identification cards and certificates of car registration. It is advisable to bring certificate of smallpox vaccination for the American Sanitary Authorities on return trip. Fire arms prohibited except for hunting when special permit is required. U. S. Customs admit, duty free, articles purchased in Mexico, not for resale, to a total value of $200 (U. S. currency) for each person.

Admission fees to National Monuments are generally $.25 per person. Admission and guide fees are not applicable to children under 12 years of age or to groups of school children 8 years of age or under, when in charge of a responsible adult.

Calendar of Annual Events

Exact dates not always fixed. Persons interested in certain events should correspond with various Chambers of Commerce for latest information.

JANUARY

First week	at Phoenix	Salad Bowl Parade and Football Game. Select teams.
First week	at Phoenix	Arizona National Livestock Show
Second week	at Flagstaff	Ski Carnival
Third week	at Phoenix	Open Golf Tourney; national PGA circuit
Fourth week	at Wickenburg	Gold Rush Days

FEBRUARY

Second week	at Yuma	Silver Spur Rodeo
Second week	at Phoenix	Major League Spring Training (N. Y. Giants)
Second week	at Tucson	Major League Spring Training (Cleveland Indians)
Second week	at Mesa	Major League Spring Training (Chicago Cubs)
Second week	at Scottsdale	Major League Spring Training (Baltimore Orioles)
Third week	at Tucson	La Fiesta de los Vaqueros (Championship rodeo)
Fourth week	at Phoenix	Cactus Show. Desert Botanical Gardens.

MARCH

First week	at Phoenix	Dons Superstition Mountain Lost Gold Mine Trek
Third week	at Phoenix	World's Championship Rodeo
Fourth week	at Tucson	Livestock Show
Fourth week	at Mesa	Rawhide Roundup

APRIL

First week	at Douglas	Rodeo
First week	at Wickenburg	Caballeros Desert Horseback Ride
Second week	at Tucson	Festival of Fine Arts
Easter	at Grand Canyon	Sunrise Service at Shrine of the Ages, South Rim
Easter	at Guadalupe, near Tempe	Yaqui Indian Easter Rites (five days ending Easter morning)
Easter	at Pascua, near Tucson	Yaqui Indian Easter Rites (five days ending Easter morning)
Fourth week	at Phoenix	Masque of Yellow Moon Pageant

MAY

First week	at Parker	Inboard Regatta (boat races)
First week	at Nogales	Fiesta de las Flores. Cinco de Mayo (5th of May) Bull Fight and celebration.

JUNE

Fourth week	at St. Johns	St. Johns Day (rodeo)

JULY

First week	at Flagstaff	All-Indian Pow-wow (rodeo and tribal dances)
First week	at Prescott	Frontier Days Rodeo
First week	at Springerville	Round Valley Rodeo
First week	at Show Low	Rodeo
Second week	at Glendale	Melon Festival
Fourth week	at Mormon Settlements	Pioneer Day Celebration

AUGUST

First week	at Prescott	Smoki Ceremonials and Snake Dance
Third week	at Payson	Rodeo
Fourth week	at Hopi Villages	Snake Dance
Fourth week	at Bisbee	Serbian Festival

SEPTEMBER

First week	at Williams	Rodeo
First week	at Benson	Rodeo
First week	at Kingman	Mohave County Fair
Second week	at Window Rock	Navajo Tribal Fair
Third week	State-wide	Fiesta; anniversary of Mexican Independence
Third week	at Prescott	Yavapai County Fair

OCTOBER

| Fourth week | at Tombstone | Helldorado |

NOVEMBER

| Second week | at Phoenix | Arizona State Fair |
| Fourth week | at Florence | Junior Parada (junior rodeo) |

DECEMBER

| First week | at Tucson | Feast of St. Francis at San Xavier Mission |

Horse and dog racing fall and winter season at Phoenix and Tucson. (pari mutuels)

PART I
Arizona's Background

Contemporary Scene

LAND of extremes. Land of contrasts. Land of surprises. Land of contradictions. A land that is never to be fully understood but always to be loved by sons and daughters sprung from such a diversity of origins, animated by such a diversity of motives and ideals, that generations must pass before they can ever fully understand each other. That is Arizona.

Organized as a territory in 1863, admitted to the Union in 1912, Arizona is the nation's youngest state, and alive with the spirit of youth. Yet if we count the aeons through which it has been inhabited by man, civilizations that have come and gone, Arizona is an ancient and venerable land.

Arizona has been the home of hairy aborigines who stoned to death the giant sloth, the mammoth, and many another beast now extinct; of nomads little more advanced who huddled in natural caves, hunted with spears and bows, yet developed an art of basketry not surpassed today; of cliff dwellers who built shelters of stone, learned how to shape clay into pottery, but did not practice even the rudiments of agriculture; of pastoral tribes who built pueblos, planted corn and cotton beside irrigation canals; of fierce raiders who preyed upon their peaceful neighbors; of swashbuckling *conquistadores* and gentle priests who strove to impress the faith and culture of Spain upon the natives they found here; and last of these modern interlopers, the Yankees, who leveled mountains for their copper, laced the face of the land with ribbons of concrete, dammed rivers to make the deserts bloom, and in less than a century worked changes vaster than their predecessors had wrought in thousands of years.

Arizona is a land of contrasts geologically, racially, socially, and culturally. Its mountains tower a mile or more into the air; the rivers have cut miles deep into the multicolored earth. Snow lingers on the peaks while the valleys are sweet with the fragrance of orange blossoms. Here are sere deserts and the largest pine forest in the world. Here are fallen forests turned to stone, and forests of trees that have survived the slow change from jungle to desert by turning their leaves to thorns. Modern transport planes fly on regular passenger and mail routes, while Hopi grandmothers scatter sacred cornmeal on the newborn infant and pray to the sun for blessings.

Arizona's settlements vary from trading posts to cities. Here are sprawling cow towns with false fronts and most of the other attributes of Wild West fiction except lawlessness; mining camps crouched on mountain ledges; Indian pueblos whose architecture was ancient before Columbus sailed; farming villages where practically all inhabitants are pious members of one church; reservation stores where Indians exchange their blankets and jewelry for phonographs and silk headbands; tourist towns built around natural wonders such as the Grand Canyon; palatial resorts where wealthy seekers of health and recreation gather; lumber camps where the roar of the sawmill is heard day and night; ghost towns where bats and ground-squirrels flit through cobwebby ruins; and lastly, the cities of Phoenix and Tucson, with air-cooled buildings, landing fields, broadcasting stations, country clubs, all the other trappings of modernity.

And what of the people who dwell amid these contrasts? Can we give a true picture by describing a typical, or average, Arizonan? No, for there is no such person. Arizona is too new as an American state to boast of a homogeneous population.

When one speaks of an Arizonan, does he mean one of the 70,000 Indians whose ancestors were here first? Does he mean one of the 150,000 Mexicans, who may be descended from seventeenth century invaders or have crossed the international line only yesterday as an immigrant? Does he mean a grizzled pioneer who may have come half a century ago to fight Apaches and brave the other dangers of a perilous frontier? Does he mean one of the 500,000 or so who have come in every country on the face of the earth?

With a few rare exceptions which may arise from sheer lack of time to welcome all newcomers, Arizonans are warm-hearted and hospitable. Beyond this, it is unsafe to make any statement without many qualifications. They subscribe to a wide variety of political and religious beliefs, are cynical about all politics and passive toward religion. They are volubly proud of their state; they are indifferent to its rich history and color. Every one of these assertions can be easily proved by pointing to numerous specific instances.

There has been indifference, yes, but it is passing. It arises from the attitude of the first Yankee to venture in after Arizona was acquired from Mexico. They, and others who followed up to the end of the last century, came mainly hunting gold or to win by farming, cattle raising or trade, quick fortunes that would enable them to live in ease amid more civilized surroundings. Even yet, the propensity to regard Arizona as only a place to abide temporarily until arrangements can be made for moving on to California, has not entirely died.

It was later arrivals who told Arizonans, and finally convinced them, that they had a state of unsurpassed charm and grandeur, a romantic history stretching back into the mists of antiquity, and extraordinary opportunities. They looked around and saw for themselves the beauties and marvels that hordes of tourists were swarming here to see. Unconcern was gradually transformed into jealous pride. Better transportation facilities, modern comforts, more material prosperity, all aided in bringing Arizonans to this new appreciation of their own state.

Still it must be admitted that all but a handful of Arizonans have only the most hazy knowledge of the details of their state's history, and little inclination to learn. Coronado, Kino, Anza, are to them but names about which they have scant curiosity. But the "another-redskin-bit-the-dust" type of reminiscence offers unfailing delight. An Arizona newspaper sponsors an annual pioneer reunion and makes it the occasion for publishing many tales of the state's turbulent beginnings as told, and perhaps embellished, by early settlers. These stories are placed on file by the Arizona Historical Society, ultimately to comprise a unique, if not altogether accurate chronicle.

Arizonans are likely to greet each other with a *"Como esta, amigo?"* (How are you, friend?) and part with an *"Adios"* (Go with God); but few are more than vaguely aware of the state's Spanish heritage. Yet, pageants depicting the mission and aboriginal periods seldom fail to draw enormous audiences. Museums are well supported with public funds, and many groups receive encouragement in their efforts to keep alive the traditions and flavor of the past.

Somewhat self-consciously, Arizona tries to live up to its cowland reputation for the benefit of tourists. As part of his new business of attracting and entertaining guests, a stockman turned "dude rancher" or guide will don bright silk shirt, sombrero and chaps far more showy than anything he ever sported at the stern tasks of rounding up steers, wear them shamefacedly for a time, then glory in their splendor.

Part of the atmosphere, too, is a common tendency to speak of the state in superlatives. Few are long immune from the infection. For the first few weeks the "tenderfoot" may sneer at "Arizona bragging," but soon he finds himself defending his new home against the skeptic as jealously as any old-timer who has been here all of a year. As stoutly and as loudly as any he will maintain that Arizona has the most spectacular scenery, the finest climate, the most fertile soil, the deepest canyons, the biggest dams, the richest mines. He can prove it about the canyons and the dams, feels no less positive about other points which are necessarily matters of opinion.

This is a marked change from pioneer days, when boasting was usually confined to accounts of personal exploits. But one custom of those times that has not changed is to judge every man by what he is and does, rather than by what he owns. If one does not work and contribute to the general welfare, he is scorned as a drone, or worse, ignored.

A fourth of Arizona's inhabitants are Indians and Mexicans, unassimilable into an Anglo-Saxon population, and there are many reasons why the Caucasians have attained only a limited degree of homogeneity. There has not been time, distances are great, and white men were brought to Arizona by a wide range of interests which militated against a common understanding. Dr. E. D. Tetreau, University of Arizona sociologist, partially lists these interests as "the desire for gold and other forms of wealth; the passion to spread Christianity among the natives; political ambition; the pursuit of scientific and technological interests in relation to the development of communication facilities, irrigation, and the extraction of minerals; the quest for health; and the urge to find adventure in forest and desert wilds."

Along political and economic lines, a great majority of Arizona people are liberal minded almost to the "try anything once" point. Dr. Tetreau comments: "There is considerable evidence that earlier tendencies to exploit natural resources, to take all that could be taken and move on, are being tempered by the development of new interests and corresponding politico-economic philosophies." He finds them "keenly alive to questions of employment and wages, the control of immigration, the increase of the purchasing power of the laboring man, and the encouragement of quality as well as quantity in the products of the farm. . . ."

One direction their liberalism takes is toward provisions for popular education that might seem almost extravagant, considering population and taxable wealth. Arizona people insist that Arizona schools be of the best, regardless of cost. Parents who never went beyond the grammar grades are determined that their children shall have university diplomas. Arizonans are generous in providing libraries, recreational facilities, especially anything that promises to help children enjoy childhood and become better equipped to meet the battles of later life.

The liberal spirit was at its height when Arizona adopted a state constitution, embodying such advanced ideas for 1911, as the initiative, referendum, and recall. Followers of U'Ren of Oregon, and other "radical" thinkers of the time, predicted that the "God-given document" was to create a new heaven here on earth. Yet those instruments of popular government have been little used, the recall scarcely at all. It is difficult to persuade voters to read initiated and referred measures; they don't take the time to understand them and commonly vote "no" on what they do not understand. This does not mean, however, that they would be willing to surrender any of the privileges guaranteed by their constitution. Any serious suggestion of that nature would be smothered under a storm of protest.

Registered voters are preponderantly of the Democratic party but "straight tickets" are few and party fealties are held anything but sacred. Now and then Arizona elects a Republican governor, and since statehood it has gone Republican in four national elections. Usually, though, the candidates successful at the Democratic primary are success-ful at the general election.

In territorial days, Arizona's sympathies were all with Democracy, not only because so many of its settlers were from the South but also because so many of its silver mines naturally swung it to the doctrine of free silver. Since statehood, immigration from the Solid South has continued to be more heavy than from any other section. In addition, many a newcomer who was a Republican in his former home decides to turn Democrat here because that appears to be the only way to exercise any wide choice among candidates, or to get anywhere politically.

Arizona owes much of its color and individuality to the Mexicans, who largely retain their own culture and customs in an environment constantly growing more alienized. Almost every city and town of any size has its Mexican quarter—squalid, for most of its inhabitants are laborers in the lower wage brackets, but picturesque withal. The drowsy plunk of a guitar, strings of red peppers drying against brown adobe walls, are part of the exotic charm that is Arizona's. Such quarters have their own stores where native foods are sold, restaurants, moving picture theaters, even weekly newspapers.

Few Mexicans are of pure Castilian descent; they are mainly a fusion of Spanish and Indian blood and proud of their ancestry, whether they are immigrants or the progeny of pioneers. History is filled with the names of Mexicans who played a prominent part in the development of the first settlements. Their descendants are respected, prominent, and in some cases well-to-do. In Yuma, Nogales, and Tucson especially, are to be found many families of Spanish extraction enjoying friendly business and social relationships with Anglo-Americans.

Most of the people spoken of as Mexicans, however, are mine and farm laborers, often performing menial work that no Yankee can be persuaded to undertake. The Mexican has been called "the chore boy of Arizona." His economic status is such that he has little opportunity to adopt the modes of life followed by the lighter-skinned people who employ him, but it is also true that he has slight inclination to change his ways.

All Mexicans cling passionately to the musical Spanish tongue. Some live here for decades without learning a word of English, but have no objection to their children attending English-speaking schools, where they learn fast and sometimes rank as star pupils. Yet the children, dismissed from school in the afternoon, will immediately fall to chattering among themselves in Spanish.

Spanish interpreters are provided in the courts and *"Se Habla Espanol"* (Spanish Spoken) is a sign displayed in many American stores. Many pretty senoritas and young men find employment as salespeople because of their bilingual ability.

The Indians also afford a bright and novel note for the Arizona scene. There are seventeen different reservations and fifteen tribes, some of which are hereditary enemies; so there is even less unity among them than some whites, though their forbears have dwelt here much longer.

More than the Mexicans, the Indians are reluctant to assume the features of American life, although this reluctance is in a measure overcome among Indian children educated in boarding schools maintained by the Great White Fathers. They are distinctly foreign to the cities, where they squat along the sidewalks to sell their pottery and baskets; and become natural to their surroundings only on the reservations. There they work at cattle and sheep raising, or farming; wear a bastard dress half Indian and half western; speak usually in their tribal tongue; and many still faithfully observe the rites and taboos of native religion.

Indians, Mexicans, pioneers, engineers, cowpunchers, ranchers, miners, tourists; ruins that crumbled when Rome was young, mighty dams not yet complete; forests, deserts, mountains, mesas; mines, farms, orchards. These are Arizona, land of contrasts and contradictions, never to be fully understood by the most understanding, always to be loved by those who know the state.

Natural Setting

WITH an area of 113,956 square miles, Arizona is the fifth largest state in the union. Utah lies along the full extent of its extreme northern boundary; on the south it is bordered by Mexico, on the east by New Mexico, and on the west by Nevada and California. Its extreme length is 400 miles; its extreme width, along an east-west line between New Mexico and California in the southern part of the state, is about 335 miles. The northern border adjoining Utah is approximately 280 miles long.

The state comprises three distinctive physical areas, each with its own more or less individual climate, flora, and fauna. The northern section, particularly in the northeast, contains loftly plateaus gashed by huge canyons; in the central section, high mountain ranges extend diagonally in a general northwest-southeast direction; the southern section consists largely of low and level river plains in the east, and of a great desert traversed by the Gila River in the west.

The northern part of the state, an area of approximately 45,000 square miles, lies within the Colorado Plateau region and is distinguished by its remarkable canyons, including the Grand Canyon of the Colorado River. Two immense contrasting forces, volcanic and erosive, have played important parts in determining the physical characteristics of this area. The San Francisco Plateau, the portion of the Grand Canyon region lying south of the Colorado River, comprises from two to three thousand square miles with Flagstaff near its center. The region is covered with lava flows and dotted with several hundred volcanic cones. Above the surrounding tableland rise the San Francisco

Mountains with Humphreys Peak, an extinct volcano, which has a height of 12,670 feet and is the highest point in Arizona. From the base of the plateau there is a rapid descent to the south. The area is drained by the Colorado, Little Colorado, and Verde rivers, together with a number of smaller streams. The northeastern section is a canyon-cut, broken tableland, studded with hills, buttes, and mesas; the average elevation is about five thousand feet. One of the most interesting features is the Painted Desert, a wild plateau destitute of water and vegetation, its surface broken by columns, lone peaks, and buttes of remarkably colored sandstone eroded into fantastic shapes. The famous Petrified Forest is within the desert.

The mountain region of Arizona, lying between the plateau and plains sections, comprises the lower half of Mohave County, all of Yavapai, Gila, Greenlee, Graham, Cochise, and Santa Cruz counties, the western half of Pima and Pinal counties, and the northwestern part of Maricopa County. The general elevation of the entire area is higher than that of the plains district but lower than that of the Colorado Plateau. This region, a part of the Mexican Highland division, contains thirty mountain chains of the Basin and Range type. The mountain tops are generally from about four thousand to six thousand feet above the valley bottoms; several peaks, however, rise to elevations of about eleven thousand feet. The region is rich in mineral resources, principally gold, silver, and copper. The broad ridge that forms the edge of the Colorado Plateau narrows in this mountain region to the Mogollon Rim, or Mesa; and along this ridge lies a great unbroken stretch of pine forest.

The plains district, comprising about 35 per cent of the state's area, lies partly in central, but mostly in southern, Arizona. The district is well irrigated and contains the Gila and Salt River valleys, two of the most fertile areas in the United States. The greater part of the southwestern section, lying within the Sonoran Desert of the Basin and Range Province, has a comparatively low elevation. It consists largely of vast stretches of desert plains, broken by short mountain chains from one thousand to three thousand feet in height, trending in a northwesterly or southeasterly direction. The mountains are seldom heavily forested, and the plains and broad level valleys maintain characteristic desert flora or are destitute of vegetation.

Most important of Arizona's rivers is the Colorado, which flows through the northwestern part of the state and forms the state's western boundary for nearly all of its remaining course. With its numerous tributaries, chief of which are the Gila, Little Colorado, and Williams rivers, the Colorado drains almost the entire state. Along its upper course within Arizona is the magnificent Grand Canyon.

The Gila, the second largest river, crosses the state from east to west and flows into the Colorado near Yuma. Its most important tributary is Salt River, formed by a union of the Black and White rivers in the Mongollon Mountains. The Salt joins the Gila about twelve miles southwest of Phoenix. Others of the Gila's tributaries, the Santa Cruz and San Pedro, flow only at flood time. The Verde River, tributary of the Salt, has its source in a series of springs in Chino Valley in the great Colorado Plateau. The Little Colorado rises in the Sierra Blanca range near the eastern boundary of Arizona, only a short distance from the sources of the San Francisco, Black, and Salt rivers, and enters the Colorado at the Grand Canyon. Most of its course is northwesterly. Its first important tributary is the Zuni River; further on it is joined by the Rio Puerco; and about ten miles from this junction it receives the Lithodendron Creek, on the banks of which is the Petrified Forest.

CLIMATE

The important determinants of climate in Arizona are altitude, interfering mountain ranges, and distances from large bodies of water. In general, rainfall is light and humidity low, making for clear air and a very dry atmosphere. This results in a wide variation between day and night temperatures; in summer the mercury may soar during the daylight hours, but night brings a refreshing coolness.

The mean monthly temperature in Phoenix ranges from a low of about 51 degrees in January to a high of about 90 degrees in July, the annual mean being about 70 degrees. But temperature variations incident to elevation are considerable throughout the state. Over the mountain plateaus, summer temperature seldom exceeds 90 degrees; but extremes of 100 to 106 degrees in the Painted Desert, of 100 to 125 degrees in the Colorado River Valley in Mohave County, and of 115 to 119 degrees in the southern part of the state are recorded nearly every summer. In winter, night temperatures range from 32 degrees above to 25 degrees below zero over most of northern Arizona.

Total annual rainfall varies between the two extremes of 2 to 5 inches in the lower Gulf valley and from 25 to 30 inches in the mountains. Phoenix has an annual precipitation of about 8 inches, while the average fall in northern Arizona is from 8 to 15 inches. Rainfall is heaviest from July to September, and a season of lighter precipitation occurs from December to March. Rain and snow usually come from clouds blown northwest from the Gulf of Mexico and the Gulf of California. Only the greater altitudes have any considerable snowfall. In northern Arizona the winter fall varies from a trace at the bottom of the Grand Canyon to more than 70 inches on the Kaibab and Coconino Plateaus.   These mountain snows feed the Colorado, Little Colorado, and Gila rivers.

Sunshine is one of Arizona's greatest assets.   The amount of possible annual sunshine enjoyed in different parts of the state ranges from 73 to 90 per cent, with an average for the state as a whole of about 80 per cent.   Phoenix has an annual average of 235 clear days.

In general Arizona has little wind, the highest mean annual velocity locally recorded being that of 8 miles an hour at Flagstaff.   Destructive winds are of occasional occurrence, however; a velocity of 58 miles an hour has been reported at Clemenceau, and a storm at Mesa and Tempe in 1919 resulted in a crop loss of half a million dollars.

The northern and more elevated parts of the state have a growing season only about one-third as long as that of the southern lowlands. On the average, an increase of a thousand feet in elevation shortens the growing season by about three weeks.

Relatively speaking the humidity in Arizona is very low.   This tends to mitigate the extreme summer temperatures, and accounts for the small number of heat prostrations recorded in the state.   Annual humidity reaches its highest point in January and its lowest in May and June.   The highest daily point is in early morning, the lowest in late afternoon.

GEOLOGY AND PALEONTOLOGY

The Grand Canyon of the Colorado, one of the world's most impressive natural wonders, affords a remarkable picture of geologic changes during hundreds of millions of years.   Along the canyon walls are series after series of rock terraces, each portraying a separate geologic period.   Deposited in these rock layers are fossil remains of countless varieties of former living creatures, from minute organisms to great animals.

The granite and gneiss of the lower gorge are part of the original earth crust, of Archean time. The limestones, sandstones, and red shales above the granite are of the Algonkian era.   The Unkar and Chuar groups (named for the places where they are seen) were laid down partly in the sea and partly on beaches and along streams and estuaries to a thickness of many thousand feet on the granite surface.   To the most recent period of earth history, the Cenozoic era, belong the two great uplifts that raised the present plateau, the formation of canyons, the volcanoes, and the remarkable sculpturing of the Grand Canyon country.   The process of erosion, the gradual modeling of the canyon, continues today.   (See Grand Canyon.)

At the beginning of the Cambrian period, the first division of the Paleozoic, or old life era, nearly all of what is now Arizona was dry land. An area from the sea in the north reached down into this part of the continent and inundated the northern end of the state. At the bottom of the shallow waters were deposited the sediments that later formed what are known to geologists as Tapeats sandstones of the Grand Canyon, Bright Angel shale, and Muavlimestone. Marine organisms, the most numerous of which were trilobites, throve in the waters unmolested. The sea continued its expansion into the continent, and during the later Cambrian period water entirely surrounded an area comprising at present about half of Utah, a part of New Mexico, the southern portion of Colorado, and southeastern Arizona.

The trilobites, the creatures that dominated the Cambrian period and the succeeding Ordovician, resembled flattened small lobsters without claws, crawling in the bottom of the water.

Generally, trilobites were made up of three portions, the head part, the body which is composed of joined segments, and the tail part called pygidium by scientists. One of the best known genera of the race of trilobites is Neolenus.

The principal event during Ordovician time was the emergence of the continental land. No doubt an inland sea covering the present Clifton-Morenci region and the Dos Cabezas Mountain area—most of southeastern Arizona and extending into New Mexico—must have remained throughout the early Ordovician period. The walls of the Grand Canyon show no trace of this period or the succeeding one, the Silurian. The Devonian, the age of fish, is well represented. Work on Devonian fauna has only begun; proper excavation and collecting on a large scale should enrich museums with exceptionally well-preserved specimens, especially of the armored fish Arthrodira.

Stand, in imagination, during the Devonian period on ancient Mazatzal land, a large strip of land located in what is now the central part of the state. No blade of grass grew on the bare rock; not a wing flitted in the air, although the climate was equable. The sun shone bright and hot. All around the bleak land was shallow sea. From the shores the ocean bed sloped northeast and northwest. For fifty miles from the northwest side of Mazatzal land near the present site of Payson to the region of Lake Roosevelt, low land lay grey under high tides. To the southeast, coral reefs and atolls rose in broad masses above the water on the site of the Santa Rita Mountains and of the Picacho de la Calera hills. Where Tucson now stands lay a wide lagoon.

The sea floor was covered by thick beds of Spirifer clams that would have made good chowder. The heaps of their remains hardened into limestone; and today, when Tucsonians construct house foundations and plaster their houses, they buy lime burned from this limestone. These Spirifer clams (brachiopods) throve so plentifully in the Devonian sea that covered Arizona and adjacent regions that they constitute a good horizon indicator to geologists.

Northeast of Jerome where the Island Mesa is, the variegated faunal inhabitants of north-central Arizona ranged in abundance. The Cladopora and Stromatopora reefs extended as far as today's site of the Perkins and King ranches on the Verde River. Fossil beds in this district are very rich. Toward the San Francisco Mountains and Flagstaff the Devonian deposition thins out, due either to erosion or to temporary existence of land. The slope of Mount Elden, an igneous intrusion breaking through the Devonian strata, is highly fossiliferous.

In the Grand Canyon a large Devonian river meandered along a channel that cut into the Muavlimestone. This river, together with other natural forces, eroded the Devonian deposition to such an extent that there is scarcely a Devonian stratum in this area. When later erosion sculptured the earth's surface into the deep chasms and mesas of the Grand Canyon, the course of this ancient river was completely effaced.

Lungfishes, found in Mount Elden beds, indicate a step toward terrestrial life; and it was during Devonian time that the first animal crossed to the land, leaving its footprints in the mud. This early animal was an amphibian resembling a salamander. Throughout the following geological periods, animal life went through numerous changes and developed a skeleton. The reptile, a new class of vertebrate, came into being and from this predecessor arose the dinosaurs and other mighty animals that dominated the earth for possibly millions of years. The reptiles became rather numerous in the Permian, the last period of the Paleozoic era, and were rulers of the Mesozoic era.

In the course of the Permian period, changes in the earth's surface were taking place. Regions that were under water became land. The Appalachian ranges came into being. The sea receded to the south of North America. An arm of this sea cut northwestward to the Arctic seas across what is the United States, and separated from the continent a long strip of land constituting the southwestern part of North America today. Northern Arizona was a swampy part of this large island. The region now included in the Fort Apache Indian Reservation was intermittently exposed and submerged, while southwestern Arizona remained under deep sea. Consequently there are in the state three areas of Permian deposition.

In the northern area a young Permian forest was growing. The spores and twigs that were carried from the coast of Gondwana land across the sea to the south and from Angara land in the region of the Ural Mountains began to sprout on the swampy shores of ancient Arizona. That bleak Mazatzal land resounded with the croak of amphibians and reptiles and with the splash of these creatures gamboling in the swamps. Their numerous tracks and the impressions of their bodies left in the mud are preserved in rock.

Gradually the sea covered this region, a reptilian paradise, and sands buried the bones and covered up the tracks of the reptiles. Their remains hardened into the Coconino sandstone that underlies all of the plateau region of northern Arizona. The Coconino formation of the Grand Canyon is famous for its amphibian tracks.

The sea deepened; for a long period the northern area of Arizona remained under water. The deposition that accumulated forms the Kaibab strata of the Grand Canyon country. Here, today, stand the Kaibab forests.

The famous Petrified Forests, the beautiful "chalcedony forests," are found embedded in deposits of the Triassic period, the first of the Mesozoic era. Triassic strata are also picturesquely exposed in the Painted Desert.

The plateaus of northern Arizona, rising from 5,000 to 7,500 feet, show a vast series of Carboniferous and Mesozoic marine strata covered by Tertiary lacustrine and terrestrial formations, originally some 15,000 feet thick. The surface of the land was formed by a huge uplift in Eocene time, the first period in recent geologic history. Afterward the action of water and other erosive forces cut the gorges and molded the buttes and mesas. During Miocene time there was a second uplift and, while the Colorado River was at work cutting the Grand Canyon, molten masses broke through and flowed on the plateaus. The rocks of this region tell of three periods of such volcanic activity, the largest and most striking record of which is the San Francisco Mountain.

In southern Arizona geologic changes are less marked and less picturesquely revealed than in the plateaus of the north. The Paleozoic rocks are extensively exposed in this southerly mountain area. Cambrian sandstones overlie the Pre-Cambrian and, succeeded by limestones of Cambrian to Mississippian age, are followed by Pennsylvanian and Permian limestones. The Cretaceous strata of the Mesozoic era are largely made up of earlier rocks.

NATURAL RESOURCES

Minerals: Since 1907 Arizona has led all the states in the production of copper. It had produced 27,771,000,000 pounds by the end of 1953, and still probably has ore containing 18,000,000,000 pounds of copper capable of being recovered at a cost of from sixteen to twenty-four cents a pound at present day prices. Gold and silver (usually found in association with copper) and lead and zinc also are important; there are barite, molybdenum, tungsten, feldspar, flourspar, gypsum, manganese, mercury, asbestos, clay, coal and iron. With exception of coal and iron, these have been partially exploited; most of them are being produced today.

Following is a condensed tabulation of Arizona's production of five principal metals from 1860 to the end of 1953: Copper 13,885,631 tons; Lead 535,487 tons; Zinc 645,172 tons; Gold 11,641,760 ounces; Silver 326,564,730 ounces.

Non-metallic mineral production in Arizona has exceeded $85,000,000 in total value. Gila county is the principal source of asbestos in the United States. Because of its long fiber and iron-free quality, Arizona asbestos is valuable to the electrical appliance industries.

Gold and silver were the first metals mined extensively, and search for them was a major factor in the Territory's development. Placers were worked in Yuma County along the Colorado and in the Bradshaw Mountains of Yavapai County. Important lode gold mines were developed near Prescott and Wickenburg. In the nineties, Congress, Octave Mines, the Fortuna and Harqua-Hala, all enriched their owners. Earlier, the silver mines of Superior (Silver King) and Tombstone were famous producers. In the early 1900's extensive production of gold came from the Oatman district in Mohave County. The gold mine closing order of 1942 shut down most of the gold mines of the state, but because many copper, lead and zinc ores contain appreciable amounts of the precious metals, Arizona is still an important producer.

Copper is distributed among nine large and many smaller districts. The major copper-producing districts have been Clifton-Morenci, Ajo, Globe, Miami, Ray, Bisbee, Superior, and Jerome (until 1953). From these districts two very different grades of ores have been mined in great quantities: high-grade deposits of 5 to more than 20% copper; and later, low-grade disseminated or porphyry ores averaging less than 1%.

Equally important are the smelters, concentrators, and leaching plants that make the ore into crude copper to be shipped to other states for refining. The rich ore is usually smelted, and the low-grade ores are concentrated and then smelted, or leached and deposited on plates by a process of electrolysis. Some towns with little mining of their own are important to the industry because of the mills and smelters established in them. Chief among these are Douglas, near Bisbee, and Hayden, near Ray.

At the beginning of the 20th century, it was believed that most of Arizona's high-grade deposits had been found. Only two, the Magma, at Superior, and United Verde Extension, at Jerome, have been discovered since, and that was over forty years ago. However, in 1905, D. C. Jackling found the solution to mass production of low-grade copper ore at Bingham, Utah. He applied his discovery to the Ray ore and thus started the mass-exploitation of low-grade copper ores. Today over 90% of Arizona's copper production is from ore-bodies with less than 20 lbs. of recoverable copper per ton.

No outright statement of economic reserves of copper ore is possible.

For that reason many larger mines avoid statements of ore reserves. Physical measurement of ore deposits is only part of the problem of determining economic reserves. A greater difficulty is estimating the economic basis. Not only do the commercial reserve totals fluctuate with changes in the price of copper, but also inflationary cycles can raise cost of production and wipe out otherwise economic reserves. Since 1930, American copper producers have been squeezed by a relative decrease in the purchasing power of copper compared with other commodities.

The major producing districts now in operation, according to conservative estimates may on the average continue producing for the next fifteen years; new developments should not only extend the life of copper producing mines, but actually raise annual production from the present 390,000 to 450,000 or 500,000 tons, beginning in 1955 or 1956.

The largest of these developments is San Manuel Mine of the Magma Copper Company. This company plans to spend over 100 million dollars to create a producing capacity of 140 million lbs. of copper a year, together with some production of molybdenum. Lavender Pit at Bisbee will produce 75 million lbs. annually by next year (1955). Silver Bell Mine of the American Smelting and Refining Co. will produce 36 million lbs. annually beginning in 1955. Bagdad is expending millions to double its present capacity of 20 million lbs., and Miami's Copper Cities development will replace Castle Dome production now exhausted.

Until 1952 when this country was flooded with enormous imports of lead and zinc, the lead-zinc industry in Arizona had been showing a healthy growth. Annual lead production had increased from an average of 7,500 tons for 1911-1942, to 22,770 tons for 1943-1952. Annual zinc production increased from 3,870 tons to 44,443 tons for the same periods.

Today, annual lead production has dropped to a 9,500-ton-rate, and zinc to a 25,000-ton-rate. Nearly all the major producers have ceased production, due to the disastrously low prices of the two metals.

Principal producers of lead and zinc have been the Iron King at Humbolt, Trench Mine at Patagonia, Republic-Mammoth Mine near Dragoon, Cochise County, Aravaipa Group in Graham County, Hilltop Mine in San Simon district, Copper Queen Mine at Bisbee, and Magma Mine at Superior. A great number of lead and zinc deposits throughout the state cannot operate at present prices.

Manganese, molybdenum, asbestos, barite, lime, gypsum and perlite have become substantial factors in Arizona's economy. Tungsten would also become important if a convenient buying depot could be established in Arizona. Uranium is being produced but production figures are not published.

Forests: Arizona's forests are a valuable natural asset, providing lumber, protection for water resources, a home for wild life, and areas for recreation.

Forest country is found at altitudes of from 5,000 to 11,500 feet. The mountain region contains the largest area of yellow pine timber in the United States. Eight national forests, with a combined area in 1952 of 11,429,948 acres, contain nearly three-fourths of the timber within the state. The total stand in these national forests is estimated at about 16,270,000,000 board feet of saw timber, and about 175,500,000 board feet was cut during 1952. The total production of lumber for the state as a whole was 275,600,000 board feet in 1952. Flagstaff, Williams, Winslow, Fredonia, Springerville, Heber, and McNary are the chief centers of sawmill operations.

Water: Water, vital not only to agriculture, which is virtually 100 per cent irrigated, but to mining and industry, forms the fluid but nevertheless firm foundation for Arizona's prosperity. In no state are water resources any more important; and no state could grow more if the water supply were unlimited.

Arizona's irrigated acreage stabilized itself in the 1930's at more than a million acres, expanding somewhat under the pressure of World War II and the rise in farm prices but always feeling the limitation which surface and ground supplies of water placed on it. This irrigated acreage produced a variety of crops (see Agriculture).

Arizona has been a leader since prehistoric times in the use of water resources. The civilization of the now-disappeared Hohokam was based on a system of canals along the Salt and Gila Rivers. In modern times the Salt River Project, the key dam of which was named for Theodore Roosevelt and which was completed in March 1911, proved to be the pattern for Western Reclamation development. The Salt River Project was the first major multiple-purpose project authorized under the 1902 National Reclamation Act, and has proved probably the most successful. The original investment has been repaid many times, and Arizona has grown to where the direct income tax revenues accruing to the Federal Treasury (in 1953) were more than twelve times the full original Federal investment in the Salt River Project. This is not an unjust comparison because the development of the Salt River put Arizona into its present forward economic position.

Major Arizona reclamation dams, all storage unless indicated otherwise, are: Roosevelt, Horse Mesa, Mormon Flat, Stewart Mountain, and Granite Reef (diversion) on the Salt River; Horseshoe and Bartlett on the Verde; Coolidge on the Gila; and Lymans on the Little Colorado. Partly in Arizona and partly in other states are Hoover (Boulder) Dam and these others below it on the main stream of the Colorado River: Davis, Parker, Laguna, and Imperial.

Development of the groundwater supply has taken place throughout Arizona, but the agriculture of the Safford Valley on the Gila River and of Pinal County, also in the Gila River System, is particularly dependent on pumped water. Groundwater tables dropped alarmingly in the decade and a half prior to 1953, and the state made efforts, most of them apparently futile, to regulate pumping.

The state also has been striving for some years to obtain additional water from the Colorado River, and this fight was carried to the Supreme Court of the United States in 1952.

The state's population growth has accentuated the general water problem, which experts believe eventually will be solved satisfactorily but a solution to which does not appear easy.

Arizona has many mineral springs, the most notable ones being at Agua Caliente, southwest of Phoenix; at Tonopah, west of Phoenix; at Clifton, in the eastern part of the state; at Castle Hot Springs, northwest of Phoenix; at Soda Springs Ranch, near Rimrock in Yavapai County; at Buckhorn Mineral Springs, east of Mesa; and elsewhere. These springs are all privately owned and most are maintained in connection with resorts.

Use of water to develop electric power has increased vastly since the early 1930's, principally along the main stream of the Colorado River. The general policy of using a portion of hydroelectric power revenues to finance reclamation works has been followed—a policy virtually as old as the Reclamation Act itself.

PLANT LIFE

The popular conception of Arizona is of a barren desert country, yet the flora ranges from the subtropical to the subalpine. Strange and unusual plant types are found from mountain peak to desert floor. As the altitude varies, so does the vegetation, and seasonal conditions determine largely the abundance of flowers and the length of the blooming season. Good rains in November, December, and January bring a gorgeous spring blooming, spreading colors with a lavish hand on mountains, mesas, and deserts. Miles of golden poppies and countless Mariposas of varying color carpet the foothills and mesas; in the mountains, the air is filled with the scent of pine and the fragrance of flowering shrubs; and the desert is spread with a tapestry of innumerable blossoms.

Southern and northern Arizona differ greatly in altitude and climate. Among the subtropical plants in the lower Sonoran Zone near Yuma and Ajo, where the altitude is almost at sea level, is the organ pipe cactus. This is one of the finest of the cactus family, having a striking appearance and bearing flowers and fruit. The fruit is valued by both Indians and Mexicans as a source of supply for conserves and wine. On the other hand, a fine example of the subalpine growth is found on the San Francisco Mountains near Flagstaff where, at an altitude of more than twelve thousand feet, the snowbank primrose blooms in the snow.

Even were it not for the myriad growth of flowers, the word "desert" as applied to Arizona would be misleading, for there are always green shrubs and cacti to add color and variety to the landscape. Arizona leads in the number and diversity of cactus plants, and while most of them grow on the desert, some are found high on the mountains, surviving low temperatures.

An excellent example of the manner in which plant life changes with the altitude is revealed on Bright Angel Trail in the Grand Canyon. At the rim altitude, 7,000 feet, the snowberry, fernbush, and other high altitude plants are found. As the trail winds down into the canyon, the change in vegetation is pronounced. Plants growing near the river altitude of 2,400 feet are similar to the vegetation growing at that altitude in other parts of the state.

Growing in the high altitudes of Arizona are: geraniums, sedums, saxifrages, mimulus, lathrus, gentians, violets, veronica, ranunculus, gnaphalium, emmenanthe, tradescantis, hesperidenthus, aguilegias, artemisia, artennaria, anemones, areabromo, hypericum, and many others. On the mesas are found: lesquerella, gaura, menodora, gomphrena, kallstroenua, hedeonia, gilias, arenaria, callomia, wedeliella, porophyllum, grindelia, senecios, linums, evolvulus, and others. In spring, after a "wet" winter, the upper mesas are golden carpets of baeria with purplish pink splashes of Owl's clover.

Near Superstition Mountain is a gorgeous flower garden of desert plants and shrubs, the colors and arrangement a source of delight to travelers. Many interesting and unusual plants distinguish this part of the Arizona desert; the most outstanding is the saguaro or giant cactus, the state flower of Arizona. The largest tree growing on the American desert, it is ranked as one of the most remarkable plants in the world. At the age of ten years, it is only four inches high; after thirty years, it is only three feet high. It is more than one hundred years old when full-grown, attaining a height of forty or fifty feet. In May and early June the exotic white flowers of the saguaro blossom. The fruit, several inches long and of a purplish hue, has been used by the Indians as food for centuries. Each year, the Papago collect quantities of the sweet and juicy pulp.

The jumping cholla, feared by man and beast because of its almost impenetrable masses of stout sharp spines, is the spiniest of all the cholla cacti and grows in the hottest of the most arid foothills and deserts. The barrel cactus, from the trunk of which candy is made, grows in the hot rocky foothills of southern and western Arizona. The top of this cactus may be cut off, the pulp crushed, and water secured, thus often proving a lifesaver to wanderers on the desert.

The weirdly beautiful Joshua tree, theme of superstitious beliefs and legends, is the largest of the yuccas, and has grotesque branches usually pointing all in one direction. The yucca known by the Mexicans as Our Lord's Candle, on the other hand, has no trunk at all but sends up wonderful clusters of cream-colored flowers from a large bunch of dagger-like leaves. The sunlight on these blossoms produces a startling illusion of candles. The ripe fruit is highly prized by Indians as a food; strings and ropes are made of the fibers of the trunk and leaves. Sandals made of these braided yucca fibers are found in ancient cliff dwellings.

One of the loveliest of desert flowers is the night blooming cereus, (see TOUR 1c), an exquisite white blossom with a spicy fragrance, that blooms only one night in the year generally the latter part of June. The flowers open at sunset and are closed by seven-thirty o'clock the next morning.

The temperate zone of northern Arizona is well timbered and abounds with the common varieties of wild flowers such as: lilies, iris, flag, buckwheat, pigweed, buttercups, mustard, strawberry blossom, wild rose, sunflower, monkshood, primrose, milkweed, phlox, sweet peas, honeysuckle, larkspur, and bleeding heart. Most of these bloom in July and August although a few appear in June and September. Among varieties of flowers and grasses readily observed from the highway are: false needle grass, blue gramma, salt grass, sand dropseed, wild foxtail, Indian grass, Texas crab, Texas timothy, winter fat, wild millet, wild phlox, Mexican cliff rose, western thoroughwort, and Wright's Muhlenberg grass.

A flowering tree found on the desert is the ironwood, a small spiny-branched tree bearing in May and June an abundance of lavender and purple flowers. The wood is remarkably heavy and hard and is valued as a material for handicraft and for fuel. The beautiful misty-green palo verde tree adds distinction to the desert. Its bright green coloring in bark and branches and the brilliant yellow blossoms that appear in April and May radiate beauty. The genus is also valued for erosion control in gullies, as honey plants, and as food for birds. It has been said that the mesquite is the most useful of the desert trees. It furnishes food and shelter for men and livestock; its wood is used for fuel and fence posts; and the juice and gum of the inner bark are used medicinally. The palatable and nutritious pods of the mesquite have always been used as a staple food among the Mexicans and Indians.

Since early settlers were isolated so completely, and therefore dependent upon their own resources in time of sickness or when wounds required treatment, the use of home remedies and native herbs became widespread. Many of the remedies still receive the approbation of modern medical science. Usually the knowledge of herbs and plant properties was obtained from the Indians and the Spanish-speaking people, who had been using them for centuries. Among the Arizona plants acknowledged to have at least some medicinal value are: the root of the ocotillo or "slim wood," the root and stem of the clematis, the leaves and twigs of the juniper, the antiseptic gum of the pinon, the creosote bush (the leaves of which are heated and used as poultices), the dogbane, the root of the jujube, the gumweed, the blue verbena hastata, wild lettuce, the root of dogwood, and the inner back of service berry.

Near Pine Creek (see TOUR 10), where the hills are covered with poppies, lupines, phacelias, golden gilia, creamcups, anemones and covenas, there grows a plant called hill tea. From the leaves a brew is made by old-timers, which is supposed to have much medicinal value. Another well-known plant used medicinally by the Mormons and other natives of the state is called Mormon tea.

A plant growing in moist places in the canyons of the Huachuca Mountains is the chuchupate. It is used medicinally several ways, but it is supposed to be especially beneficial in cases of asthma. Teas made from mullein and hoarhound were used by early settlers and thought to have excellent medicinal properties. Two of the sages, the pearly everlasting and the false tarragon, are thought to be valuable medicinally. It is said that the Indians used the powdered dry berries of the lemonade sumac for medicinal purposes. The bark of the bitterbark or cascara is in great demand in Europe and eastern United States for medicinal use. In Arizona the tree is found in the Grand Canyon and the Chiricahua Mountains.

While poisonous plants are not abundant, there are numerous species, including the hairy loco, arrowgrass, mountain lupine, whorled milkweed, tall larkspur, scarlet lobelia, poison ivy, sleepy grass, mountain loco, Colorado rubber plant, and death camass.

Among the trees found at high elevations are white and silver fir, Douglas fir, one-seeded juniper, Ponderosa pine, narrow-leaf cottonwood, black cottonwood, native walnut, post oak, western birch, western box elder, Lowell's ash, and western black locust. These regions are thickly wooded and a startling contrast in character to other parts of Arizona.

ANIMAL LIFE

Animal species unknown elsewhere, and many common to other sections, are found in Arizona. Altitudes varying from a few feet above sea level to nearly thirteen thousand feet are a major factor in the distribution of these widely differing types.

Big game was abundant when trappers traveled across Arizona's deserts, mountains, canyons, and plateaus but the large species were subsequently depleted and in some cases exterminated. Since game refuges have been established, however, some species have increased beyond their former numbers. Arizona's game refuges number 15; national parks, monuments, and federal game refuges number 7; totaling 22.

White-tail deer, Rocky Mountain mule deer, desert mule deer, and Coey's black-tail deer, number hundreds of thousands, and show a trend toward increase; northern elk, imported from Yellowstone region, have become so numerous they are subject to annual hunting season; pronghorned antelope, at one time believed headed for extinction, are now regaining their former numbers; desert bighorn sheep, the Nelson and Gaillard species are found in remote ranges.

About two hundred buffalo (*see TOUR 1a*) still range free in northern Arizona, their number kept more or less stationary by an annual buffalo hunt, in which a specified number of hunters are each allotted one buffalo. Black and brown bear are plentiful; mountain lions, enemies to deer and domestic livestock, are numerous; and the Mexican jaguar, similar to the leopard, is sometimes found in the southern mountains. Coyote are present everywhere in large numbers. Of these the Great Basin species is the largest, weighing thirty pounds or over. The big-eared swift, or desert species of fox are widely distributed. Likewise badgers, beavers, ocelots, otters, raccoons, ring-tailed cats, muskrats, and weasels find suitable haunts in Arizona, although the otter has become rare, and the beaver and muskrat are no longer numerous.

In southern and western Arizona, Bailey and desert bobcats are found, most numerous where small game is plentiful. Great-eared antelope jackrabbits skim the southern plains, and the black-tailed jackrabbits leap high above the desert brush, their range where the terrain is least rough. Also having a generous distribution are the three species of skunk, the common striped skunk, the hog-nosed or badger, and the small spotted or hydrophobia skunk, which is dreaded as a carrier of rabies.

Several varieties of tree squirrels, including the Abert tassel-eared species, inhabit the wooded mountain and plateau regions. The small chickaree, or American red squirrel, in the north and the fox and grey squirrels in the east, southeast, and central sections all show dissimilarities appropriate to their habitat. The Kaibab white-tailed squirrel, a magnificent species of the squirrel family found only on the Kaibab plateau, boasts tasseled ears, a black breast, and a white tail; it is so highly valued by the state, none is permitted to be killed or removed from its forest home.

Among the small mammals found throughout the state are cottontails, chipmunks, ground squirrels, rock squirrels, meadow mice, shrews, cooton-rats, pocket mice, deer mice, grasshopper mice, and harvest mice. Prairie dog towns are common in the northern regions. Wood rats, known also as pack and trade rats, build their nests chiefly in the canyon forests. Usually thrown up in the scant shade of some desert bush or cactus, the mounds of the kangaroo rats dot the arid valleys.

In many of the southern mountains and valleys, rattlesnakes exist in great numbers; but despite their deadly venom and their numerous population, deaths resulting from rattlesnake bites are infrequent, the average mortality being less than one victim yearly.

The king snake, itself a nonpoisonous species and immune to the venom of the rattlesnake, frequently attacks and devours it. Harmless species include the bull or gopher snake, several forms of racer, four ground snakes, the western water snake, the tiny California blind snake, the rosy boa, the rock snake, the dog-nosed snake, LeConte's snake, the hog-nosed, and the ring-necked snakes.

Three varieties of freshwater or mud turtles—the keeled musk turtle, the Arizona mud turtle, and the yellow-necked mud turtle—live in the ponds, the rivers, and the dams. The desert tortoise wanders about the arid plains during the warm months and seeks shelter in deep burrows from the winter's chill or the scorching sun of mid-summer.

About the much-feared Gila monster (*see TOUR 1c*), Professor Charles Taylor Vorhies, University of Arizona, makes the following interesting comment:

"To begin with, it is the largest lizard native to Arizona and, while recorded from Nevada, Utah, and Sonora (Mexico), it occurs more commonly here than elsewhere. It is a true lizard but belongs to a particular family called beaded lizards on account of the beadlike character of the scales. To this family belong two, and only two, species. These are *Heloderma suspectum,* the Gila monster of our state, and *Heloderma horridum,* which occurs in Mexico and is far removed from the Arizona form; the latter is much larger and is quite distinct in appearance from the former. These two are the only poisonous lizards in the world."

An edible lizard found in rocky desert regions is the chuckwalla, which subsists on tender leaves, buds, and flower petals. Entirely harmless, with no defense but a flailing tail, it is easily captured by the Indians and used by them as an epicurean delicacy. Certain lizards have the peculiar habit of rising upon their hind legs and running in the manner of bipeds when alarmed. Probably the most frequently noted is the beautiful collared lizard, so named because of its black, or sometimes yellow and red, collar; its diet consists of insects and smaller lizards. The small banded gecko darts from cover as twilight settles upon the desert and, like a tiny tiger, stalks and pounces upon its prey. Among the many other species found in Arizona are the desert iguana, the blue-spotted skink and the Sonora skink; the tesselated, the kings, and the leopard lizards, and several forms of swift.

About four hundred varieties of birds are found in the state, and of these nearly one hundred and fifty are permanent residents; more than fifty are casual visitors; about sixty are winter sojourners; and seventy-five or more spend only the summer months. In addition to these are the migratory birds that merely linger a time on their southerly or northerly flights.

The California condor once stretched its wings above the deserts and mountains of western Arizona and is thought perhaps to exist still in high isolated ranges. A familiar sight is the turkey vulture wheeling against the skies to the north; the black vulture sails less expertly over the southern plains. Golden eagles still hunt along the mountain chains, and the bald eagle, fast becoming rare, perches wherever there is opportunity to rob the fishhawk of his prey. The wild turkey is still found in moderate numbers in Arizona's timbered mountains. Other interesting birds are the falcons, grouse, white pelicans, great-horned owls, ibis, egrets, sandpipers, mocking birds, and even large thick-billed parrots, flaunting their gaudy plumage in the Chiricahua Mountains in company with the exotic coppery-tailed trogons.

The Indians

THE INDIAN tribes of Arizona belong to three large linguistic families: the Yuman, the Athapascan, and the Uto-Aztecan. The Yuman group occupy a region along the Colorado River and the lower reaches of the Gila; as a result of continuous contact its tribes possess certain cultural resemblances. The Athapascan family, represented by the Apache and Navajo tribes, probably had much in common at the period of their arrival in the Southwest, but have become differentiated, especially since white American occupation. The third group, the Uto-Aztecan, belong to one of the most widely extended language families in America. They range from western Wyoming through the Great Basin down into Mexico. The tribes of this group in Arizona, unlike the Athapascan and Yuman tribes, are unaware of their relationship to one another.

The Yuman Family: Little is known of the origin of the Havasupai (blue or green water people), but linguistic evidence and their present territory suggest that they may be an offshoot of the Hualpai. Their dialect resembles Hualpai speech, but their culture to a limited extent is similar to that of the Pueblo. They mingle freely with the Hualpai and acquire wives from them.

The Havasupai are a tribe of about two hundred, and are believed never to have been much more numerous. They live at the bottom of Cataract Canyon within Grand Canyon National Park (*see Park Tour 3*), where they possess agricultural lands. Their chief support and interest is agriculture, based on irrigation, but although they own 50,000 acres within the park, little of it can be cultivated and they possess no livestock. Throughout the growing season they live in the village. When the harvest has been gathered and an annual dance of rejoicing has been held (often with the collaboration of the Hualpai, Navajo, and Hopi), they leave the canyon and build camps on the plateau. Here much of the time is devoted to gathering seeds and to hunting, but the chief source of food is the surplus of corn from the previous season's crop.

The Hualpai (pine tree folk) live on a reservation south of the Grand Canyon (*see TOUR 2c*). Within its relatively large area are only a few cultivable spots near streams and springs, and the small crops of corn and beans are soon exhausted. Their main food supply is the fruits, berries, and nuts gathered by the women; and the deer, antelope, mountain sheep, rabbits, and other game hunted by the men. Their number is steadily declining and now amounts to about four hundred. The Hualpai, as a rule, have failed to profit by efforts intended to educate them and improve their health, and they cling to their ancient superstitions and customs.

The Mojave (three mountain), once largest and most warlike of all Yuman tribes, live in two groups; about 1,175 on Colorado River Reservation south of Parker (*see TOUR 3B*), and 374 in the environs of Needles. These areas are approximately the same regions that they inhabited before they were confined to reservations. The Mojaves who live at Needles support themselves by work in the railroad shops, by fishing, beadwork, a few raise cattle, and some do laboring and some skilled work in Needles. Though their income is very low, they are good citizens.

The Chemehuevis are Southern Paiute, and number over 350. Many live on Colorado River Reservation. They do irrigated farming of alfalfa or cotton, railroad, and other work.

The Federal Government has expended $15,000,000 in the clearing, leveling, and subjugation of some 34,000 acres on Colorado River Reservation, and some 56,000 acres still remain available for subjugation, all of which will fall into the gravity irrigation system created by building of Headgate Rock Dam. Many Navajo and Hopi families have also colonized here.

For the Mojave, warfare was not the economic asset it was for such marauders as the Apache, but rather a means for acquiring power and prestige within the tribe. Frequently they fought with a shorthandled club as well as with bows and arrows, and they were eager to engage in personal combat. Their mythology is concerned largely with two deities, Matavilya and Mastamho, who caused the creation of all natural life. Today contact with the supernatural is obtained through dreams. Great importance is attached to them, and in large part they are held to determine an individual's vocation and career.

The Yuma (son of the captain) occupy a reservation just west of the town that bears their name, but some of them live on the Arizona side of the Colorado River. They formerly held an extensive territory around the confluence of the Gila and Colorado rivers. Extension of irrigated lands and development of industry, supplying urban employment, have in large measure caused the disappearance of their native crafts. The Yuma still practice their old religious and ceremonial rites, despite a nominal acceptance of Christianity; many of their beliefs and observances are akin to those of the Mojave.

The Cocopah, a division of the Yuma, numbering about three hundred, live on a reservation near Yuma (*see TOUR 4*). The summer houses of this tribe are brush arbors; the winter houses are wattled huts, coated with plaster inside and out. Their mortuary observances include the sacrifice of all the belongings of the deceased immediately after death; personal possessions are distributed among non-relatives in order of arrival and claimed property is burned with the body.

The Maricopa, a combination of five Yuma tribes which have gradually become distinctive in speech and customs, are found in two communities. About three hundred live at the junction of the Gila and Salt rivers in the Gila Indian Reservation; the rest are at Lehi on the south bank of the Salt. Before 1800 the Maricopa held the country along the Gila above Gila Bend and along the Kaveltcadom downstream halfway to the Colorado. After 1800 they moved eastward to become neighbors of the Pima, and by 1830 were joined by the Halchidhoma. Later remnants of the Kohuana and Halwikyamai fled from the region of the Colorado and became a part of the group now called Maricopa. Close association with Pima in recent years has led to the assumption that the Maricopa resembled that tribe, but actually they show far greater signs of kinship to their Yuman-speaking relatives. Even today the three hundred Maricopa on the western side of the Gila River Reservation form a distinct unit and mingle very little with their Pima neighbors. In common with Yuma of the Colorado River, they practice agriculture, growing corn, beans, melons, and cotton, and their food is supplemented by wild cholla beans, berries, and saguaro fruit. Hunting, largely confined to deer, mountain sheep, and rabbits, is less important to them than to most other tribes. Their religious practices bear much similarity to those of the Mojave and other tribes to the west of them.

The Yavapai (sun people), both linguistically and in their nomad life are much like the Hualpai and Havasupai, before the latter turned to agriculture. They claimed the region of the Rio Verde Valley as their territory together with Black Mesa. Within this range, from the Pima and Maricopa country to the south and the Hualpai lands to the north, they lived almost entirely by hunting and gathering wild plants. Placed on the San Carlos Reservation in 1875, they drifted back gradually to their old habitat, and now live on their reservation within the Fort Whipple military compound (*see TOUR 1b*). They number only fifty.

The Athapascan Family: Represented by only two tribes, this is the largest Indian group in Arizona, numbering more than sixty thousand. Of these more than fifty thousand are members of the widely scattered Navajo tribe, the remainder are Apache. Really a group of tribes, some Apache live on the White River and San Carlos Reservations in Arizona, others on two reservations in New Mexico. Since the other Athapascan-speaking peoples are found in the Mackenzie River Valley and on the coast in northwest Canada, and in northern California and Oregon, it is believed that the southwestern representatives of the family are immigrants to this region, though the time of their arrival is a matter of speculation. The Navajo and the Apache, now differentiated, were probably closely similar at the time of their first contact with the Spaniards. The latter, indeed, called the Navajo "Apaches de Nabaju."

The Apache (enemy) call themselves *dine, inde, tinde,* words that in various dialects signify "the people." Until they were at last subdued they were the most warlike tribe in the Southwest. Their fighting spirit was especially evident in the period 1870-1900, when the encroachments of white settlers roused them to fierce resentment.

When in 1870 the Chiracahua band was placed on the Ojo Caliente reserve in New Mexico, the leader, Cochise, made raids that caused the authorities to move them to Tularosa. Cochise escaped with a group of followers, but returned to his band when it was established on the Chiricahua Reservation in 1872.

The Chiricahua Reservation was abolished in 1876, and the Apache were moved once more, in accordance with the policy of concentration. In 1877 Geronimo, together with other chiefs, joined by members of the tribe from Mexico, began a series of raids in southern Arizona and New Mexico. In 1882 he surrendered to General George Crook, but three years later assembled another band and once more terrorized the settlers of southern Arizona. He and his band finally surrendered in 1886 and imprisoned at Fort Pickens, Florida. Geronimo died in the military prison at Fort Sill, Oklahoma in 1909.

Another group of Chiricahua, under the leadership of Victorio, resented their transfer from the Mescalero Reserve in New Mexico and twice escaped from San Carlos, only to be returned. When they had gone back to Mescalero for a third time, arrangements were made for them to be permitted to remain there. Indictments against Victorio and some of his followers, however, led him to flee and take up raiding again. Often opposed by troops outnumbering them four to one, Victorio's band of three hundred warriors inflicted more damage than they received. When, in 1880, he was killed in a fight with Mexican troops, the rest of the group surrendered. In 1900 the Apache's last foray took place, when a group in Chihuahua raided a Mormon settlement.

Even after the Apache were at last restricted to their settlements, the white man persisted in his encroachments. Early in the 1890's a cattle company was allowed to graze a herd of 2,000 cattle on the Apache reserve. Several years later, an Indian complained that the company's cattle were trespassing on his land. Investigation revealed that the company was pasturing 12,000 head instead of 2,000 on the reserve, and was paying no grazing charges. The company agreed to a lease, and other big cow outfits moved in later. The income from grazing rights was an easy solution to an Apache's living problem, although it amounted to no more than $40 yearly for each Indian.

The Indians' employment by the ranchers made them expert cowhands, and they decided that what they had learned to do for the white men they could do for themselves. They applied to Washington for the recovery of their lands, and in 1923 a sympathetic Indian commissioner ordered the cattle companies off the reserve. The Indians were the final victors in the long struggle for possession; the last company left their land in 1936.

Originally a nomadic people, the Apache, whose numbers in Arizona are about ten thousand, were little given to agriculture. But today they grow garden vegetables and are supplied with meat from their fine herds of cattle. These are a highly important factor in Apache economy. On the San Carlos Reservation (*see TOUR 8*) are 18,000 cattle, valued at about $1,800,000. Approximately 18,000 head are on the Fort Apache Reservation (*see TOUR 8*). These reservations occupy a mountainous area about a hundred miles square in east-central Arizona.

The religion of the Apache is noteworthy for its great number of rituals. There is a ceremony for almost every event life may afford, and dances or songs are a part of certain ceremonies. The Apache conception of the deity is Usen, a being without sex or place, that cannot be approached directly, but whose influence must flow through such an object or phenomenon in nature as the sun, lightning, the owl, or the snake.

Like most of the Athapascans, the Navajo, (*see TOURS 2, 5, 6*) call themselves *dine,* "the people." Among several theories concerning the application to them of the tribal name Navajo, the most probable is that it is derived from the Tewa word *Navaju,* meaning cultivated land in a canyon. The Navajo, like the Apache, to whom they are closely related, are believed to have come into the Southwest five or six hundred years ago.

Before sheep, horses, and cattle were introduced into America in the sixteenth century by the Spaniards, the Navajo were a small unimportant tribe that got a living from agriculture, and by hunting, raiding, and gathering roots and seeds. They took a highly important step when they stole their first sheep from those left among the Pueblos by the Spaniards, for instead of immediately eating their booty, as other tribesmen did, they bred them, tended flocks, and developed to some extent into a pastoral people.

Until the conquest of New Mexico by the United States in 1846, the Navajo preyed persistently on the Pueblo Indians and the Spanish settlements. Two treaties of peace were made with them, but their raids continued until Kit Carson led an expedition against them in 1863. He killed many of the sheep on which they depended for a livelihood, and captured about eight thousand of the tribe, who were sent to Bosque Redondo on the Pecos River in New Mexico and held there until 1867. In that year they were restored to their own country and given a few head of sheep apiece by the Government.

Since that time the Navajo have increased from the captured eight thousand to more than seventy-five thousand and have proved themselves an uncommonly adaptable people. Though their culture has been largely borrowed from neighboring tribes, its components have been blended into something distinctive.

Agriculture and the raising of sheep and goats are the basis of Navajo economic life. They move their herds as the needs of grazing and watering make necessary, but they are not true nomads, for each family moves within a limited area. The Navajo live in widely scattered hogans (houses) instead of in villages. In summer the log hogans give place to brush shelters, but each type of house is a temporary structure, partly because of the necessity of moving several times a year, partly because of the Navajo belief that a hogan in which death has occurred must be immediately abandoned or burnt. Women as well as men are fine riders, the children are taught to ride almost in infancy, and horse racing is a popular Navajo sport.

Among both Navajo and Apache the odd custom of the "avoidance relation" is still widely observed; a married man must never look at or speak to his mother-in-law. Religion is a highly important part of Navajo life. There are many nature gods, animal gods, and local gods, a vast store of religious legend and myth, innumerable ceremonial songs, prayers and dances.

The Uto-Aztecan Family: This, the most widely distributed language family of Indian tribes, is represented in Arizona by three tribes —the Kaibab Paiute, the Hopi, and the Pima-Papago.

The Northern Paiute of Arizona, who now occupy a small reservation west of Fredonia (*see TOUR 1a*), were formerly the southernmost of many groups scattered over the Great Basin from southern Idaho to the Grand Canyon. Others of the tribe are in Nevada and Utah. The Arizona group, numbering less than one hundred and administered from a Utah agency, depends primarily on its cattle for a livelihood.

The Hopi (peaceful ones), the only Pueblo Indians in Arizona today, numbering more than four thousand, were first mentioned by the Spaniards of Coronado's expedition in 1540. In their villages (*see TOURS 2, 5*), perched on the tops and slopes of high mesas, life has not been greatly affected by modern civilization, though its adjuncts—beds, stoves, trucks, canned goods—have become familiar things. But the essential pattern and structure of Hopi life have not changed. The raising of corn, beans, and squash, grinding the corn into powder-fine meal for *piki* (paper-thin cornmeal bread), making pottery and baskets, and conducting the year-round cycle of ceremonies for rain, health, and long life, as had been done for centuries before the white man's coming, go on unaltered. Corn is the principal Hopi food. All the grinding is done by women and girls, who develop a rhythmic precision of motion and almost machinelike skill. The weird song of the grinders and the rumble of the mill are characteristic sounds of Hopi villages.

From 1540 on the Hopi were visited several times by the Spaniards, whose coming they received peacefully until 1680. In that year they destroyed the missions that had been established in their villages, and killed the priests who had attempted to convert them to Catholicism. The Spaniards made no efforts to re-establish control.

Despite the relatively brief period of their contact with the Spaniards, the Hopi acquired from them many things that vitally affected their economy. Livestock (including sheep, horses and burros), wagons, metal tools, the beehive oven, and the chimney still bear Spanish names in Hopi speech. The Hopi also got peach and other fruit trees from the Spaniards, and continue to cultivate these fruits successfully.

This tribe retains its ancient organization into clans in which property is held by the female line and descends from mother to daughter. When the Hopi took over livestock from the Spanish, however, they adopted the Spanish pattern of ownership, so that today cattle and sheep, one of the chief sources of tribal wealth, are owned by the men. Rich in an ancient inheritance of mythology and folklore, the Hopi's religious life resolves itself into an annual cycle of ceremonies that occupy the forefront of their thought and conversation. The rites are based on a few simple but all-important wishes—for long life, healing, rain, and fertility.

The Pima ('no') and the Papago (bean people), who number about 13 thousand, live today on the Gila River and Salt River Reservations and on the Papago and San Xavier Reservations (*see TOURS 4B and 4C*). These peoples regard themselves as a single family rather than as kinsmen, and seem to have had a common origin. The Pima on their irrigated lands, are farmers and stock raisers, but many of the

Papago, in their desert country to the south, pursue a more primitive way of life than the more highly developed branch of the family. Some of the Papago have acquired a considerable measure of civilization, and have proved excellent farmers, miners, and railroad workers. Others, for whom the desert has long supplied most of their simple needs, continue the old nomadic way of life, getting food and medicine from its weeds, weaving baskets from its grasses, building homes from its soil. The Papago were the guardians of the San Xavier Mission and other historic shrines. The lands of American settlers, to whom they were faithful friends, were often the Papago's only shelter in time of danger.

During the Apache troubles, the Papagos lived in eleven large villages, but after 1880 they spread out into a pattern of small agricultural villages in the valleys where rain floods provided a certain amount of irrigation, and winter camps at the base of the mountains near a well or spring. After the drilling of deep wells at the field villages by the Government in the 1930's, the hill villages were largely deserted, and are now used mostly during the cactus fruit harvest.

Archeology

THE SOUTHWEST is one of the best known and most intensively investigated archeological areas in the United States. The region is covered with the remains of earlier civilizations, and in the pueblo section enough work has been done to permit a relatively complete reconstruction of the history of its culture, although one that is being constantly modified by new discoveries. Archeologists working in the field build up their reconstructions on masses of detailed evidence. The very brief outline presented in this article ignores local differences.

Early Indian cultures in the Southwest are classified in three main groups—Basket-maker, Pueblo, and Hohokam, the first being the oldest in Arizona.

THE BASKET-MAKER CULTURE

In the northeastern part of Arizona and adjacent areas, hunters settled in the caves of that region and built storage pits lined with stone slabs. Pottery was not known to these people until toward the end of their time, but they made finely coiled baskets. This culture is divided into three periods, designated for the archeologist's convenience as Basket-maker I, Basket-maker II, and Basket-maker III.

Subterranean dwellings, called pit houses, came into use among these people after they outgrew caves. But although it first occurs in association with Basket-maker culture, the pit house cannot be considered a distinguishing feature of that culture, since this type of dwelling continued to be used until the Great Pueblo Period.

The principal characteristics of the Basket-makers, as indicated by their existing remains are as follows: they were a long-headed people; they had no pottery until late in this period; they did not possess bows and arrows, but used the *atlatl* or spear thrower to hurl darts; they made square-toed sandals from yucca and other fibers, twine-woven bags, cord and rabbit-fur robes, slab-lined storage cists, and pit houses; they exhibited fine workmanship in stone, shell, and bone; and developed an agriculture in maize, squash, and beans.

THE PUEBLO CULTURE

The Pueblo people either conquered the Basket-makers or amalgamated with them. They were a round-headed people, who deformed the skull artificially by flattening the rear portion, probably by using a hard cradleboard.

One of the greatest aids in the study of Pueblo culture has come from Professor A. E. Douglass of the University of Arizona, who discovered a method of dating pre-historic ruins by a study of the growth of tree-rings in beams taken from ancient buildings. The growth is slight in dry years and greater in years of considerable rainfall, and on this basis Professor Douglass has constructed a chart which enables him to determine dates accurately as far back as 700 A.D.

The first period of Pueblo culture dates from about 800 to 900 A.D., the second from about 875 to 950 A.D. As contrasted with the limited area over which Basket-maker remains are found, those of the early Pueblo culture are distributed from the Colorado River on the west to Texas on the east.

In the south and west, the pit-type dwelling continued but the pits were dug deeper. Entrance was gained by means of a ladder through the smoke hole. The homes of pit-house people are found scattered from Monument Valley on the Arizona-Utah boundary to the Mexican border on the south. The most notable sites known are the circular pit pueblo, Juniper Cove ruin, eight miles west of Kayenta; the transitional rectangular pit houses near Flagstaff; and villages of the latter type in the Gila Bank ruin near San Carlos Reservoir, at Martinez Hill, and in the University ruins near Tucson.

Cotton was added to the list of cultivated plants, and was woven into cloth garments. Cooking utensils of black pottery seem to have been common over the entire area at all periods. They were made by building up successive coils of clay, which in most cases were afterwards smoothed off so that all evidence of the coiling process was obliterated. However, in one type of pottery the sides were not smoothed, leaving a rough spiral finish. This type is known as corrugated ware; it was first made during the earliest Pueblo period, and continued in use until about 1400 A.D. Another type of pottery is a black-on-white ware, found all over the area and made from the first period to the close of the third. There are local differences in design and form, but a common characteristic is the use of a white or grey slip over the entire surface, on which were painted designs in black.

Houses built above the ground were a development of the second period. Of stone or adobe, one story high and containing from 6 to 14 rooms, they were L-shaped or U-shaped in structural plan, and were called clan houses.

The third period, known as the Great Pueblo Period, was characterized by the building of large pueblos and cliff dwellings. In Arizona the best existing examples of this period may be seen in the Segi Canyon near Kayenta. The largest structures are Keet Seel and Betatakin, now part of the Navajo National Monument.

The Great Pueblo Period waned toward the end of the thirteenth century, and eventually all the great villages were abandoned. Authorities generally attribute the exodus to a twenty-three-year drought (1276-99), probably caused by the denuding of forest lands around centers of population. That the people migrated southward rather than toward the streams of the Rockies may have been owing to the arrival from the north of fierce marauders—such as the Navajo and the Apache.

Examples in Arizona of the fourth period, ending with the initial phase of Spanish contact, are found in the Hopi country. The sites of Sikyatki and Awatobi on the Hopi Reservation belong in part to this period. The historical connection between certain characteristics in their architecture and pottery indicate that the contemporary Hopi Indians are the carriers of this earlier civilization.

One of the most striking archeological features of the Southwest is the *kiva* or ceremonial chamber, usually a subterranean affair but sometimes built above the ground level. First occurring in the early Pueblo period, *kivas* are always present in subsequent sites and even in the villages of the modern Pueblo Indians. They are both round and square in outline, and access is always provided by means of a ladder through the smoke hole.

THE HOHOKAM CULTURE

During the years that cover the origin and growth of the northern or plateau cultures, a distinct and unrelated people was colonizing southern Arizona. The Hohokam or desert people are not so well known as the Basket-makers and Pueblos, for intensive study of their

Indians

Forman Hanna

HOPI DOORWAY

WALPI, THE SKY VILLAGE

STREET, HOPI PUEBLO

Max Kegley

NAVAJO CAMP, WINDOW ROCK FAIR

NAVAJO GIRLS

"Frashers"

APACHE WOMAN GRINDING CORN

NAVAJO HORSEMEN

TYPICAL SAN CARLOS APACHE TEEPEE

Max Kegley

NAVAJO WEAVER

LAST OF THE LONG HAIRS—A PIMA INDIAN

Photo Shop

Max Kegley

**PREHISTORIC CITY NEAR CLARKDALE,
TUZIGOOT NATIONAL MONUMENT**

**"KEET SEEL", GREAT CLIFF DWELLING,
NAVAJO NATIONAL MONUMENT**

WOVEN DESIGNS IN COTTON CLOTH, FOUND IN PREHISTORIC
MONTEZUMA CASTLE NATIONAL MONUMENT

PREHISTORIC BURIAL EXCAVATION,
BESH-BE-GOWAH, NEAR GLOBE

HOPI KATCHINA DOLL

Joseph Miller

archeology has only recently begun. Hohokam is a Pima word denoting "the ancient ones."

The plateau cultures are considered to be largely of local development, but the Hohokam, often called Canal Builders, are supposed to have entered the southern region with a relatively well developed culture and continued their growth there.

The earliest stage of their occupancy shows a widespread distribution of small villages in the broad semiarid valleys of the region. This is known as the Colonial Period. The people lived in shallow rectangular pit houses, the walls of which were constructed of poles, brush, and mud plaster. They cremated their dead in pits. They made pottery of two types—red-on-buff, and plain brown; the distinguishing traits of this phase of ceramic development are the bowl form with wide flaring rim, decoration in naturalistic symbols, and the repetition of small design elements.

The next stage, known as the Sedentary Period, showed a greater concentration of settlements and a withdrawal from the outlying districts. Houses were either of the pit type or built above the ground, and the village was surrounded by a wall. The pottery is buff with red design, or plain red; and it lacks the characteristic bowl shape of the earlier period.

The invasion of people from the plateau region, as mentioned above, is believed by some to be responsible for the typical pueblos of the following or Classic Period, placed at from 1300-1350 to 1400-1450 A.D. Notable in this period was the development of the great compound type of dwelling, of which Casa Grande is one of the best existing examples. Casa Grande consists of a number of houses surrounded by a wall of solid construction. Apparently the houses and wall were built by packing adobe into a sectional frame and allowing it to set, and then superimposing another section, much after the fashion of modern concrete construction. There were also cliff dwellings, such as those that may still be seen at the Tonto National Monument, and extensive irrigation works in the Gila and Salt River valleys. Los Muertos, a city of thirty-six communal buildings nine miles southeast of Tempe, was supplied with water from the Gila River by a large canal, thirty feet wide at the top, four feet wide at the bottom, and seven feet deep at the center. Many side canals led off from this and provided for the irrigation of large tracts in the valley. Some of these old canals are now being used in connection with modern irrigation systems.

In the succeeding or Recent Period houses were built of poles, brush, and clay; with the compound and pueblo continued in some sections. The modern pottery is supposed to be represented by the culture of the Pima and Papago Indians, but whether these latter are actually descendants of the Hohokam is a moot question.

ARCHEOLOGICAL SITES

The areas listed below, containing many of Arizona's most significant archeological remains, are now maintained as national monuments. Fuller descriptions of these sites and descriptions of numerous other sites are to be found elsewhere in this volume. (*See Index for page references.*)

Navajo National Monument. In this tract of 360 acres in northeastern Arizona, within the Navajo Indian Reservation, are the remains of three exceptionally large and interesting cave pueblos—Betatakin, Keet Seel, and Inscription House. Betatakin (Navajo, houses in the rock shelves), in a branch of Segi Canyon, is 450 feet long and 150 feet deep; it contained 150 ground-floor rooms. Keet Seel (Navajo, broken pottery), is in another branch of Segi Canyon; this cave, 350 feet long and 50 feet deep, had more than 250 rooms. Inscription House (so called because of a carved inscription, "S-hapiero Ana Domo 1661") in Nitsie Canyon contained 50 rooms (*see TOUR 6*).

Canyon de Chelly National Monument. Near Chinle, in northeastern Arizona, within the Navajo Indian Reservation, Canyon de Chelly (the latter a Navajo word denoting "place among the cliffs") and the neighboring Canyon del Muerto (Spanish, canyon of the dead) contain remains of some of the largest cliff dwellings in Arizona. More than 300 sites are scattered over an area of 83,840 acres. The largest of the 138 major ruins is the so-called White House (*see TOUR 5A*).

Wupatki National Monument. North of Flagstaff many interesting ruins are scattered over this area of 35,865 acres. The principal groups are Wupatki, Teuwalanki, and Nalakihu. Wupatki (Hopi, tall house), from which the monument takes its name, dates from the eleventh or twelfth century and is remarkably well preserved; this red sandstone structure contains 125 rooms, and below the pueblo to the east is a large circular amphitheater. Teuwalanki (Hopi, citadel), the principal group of ruins, occupies a commanding position on the top of a small mesa. Nalakihu (Hopi, house alone), at the foot of the hill, has been partly restored and consists of several rooms (*see TOUR 1a*).

Walnut Canyon National Monument is an area of 4,750 acres near Flagstaff, including a village of about 300 cliff dwellings built under the sloping canyon walls. Unlike the communal type, these cliff houses contain from six to eight rooms each and were apparently intended for separate families (*see TOUR 2a*).

Tuzigoot National Monument. The Tuzigoot (Tonto Apache, crooked water) ruins, 42 acres, about two miles east of Clarkdale near Peck's Lake, consist of three large pueblos, one of which has been excavated, exposing more than 100 rooms. The excavations yielded large quantities of pottery, beadwork, and other forms of handicraft (*see TOUR 2A*).

Montezuma Castle National Monument. A tract of 521 acres near Camp Verde, contains the remains of ancient cliff dwellings, chief of which is a five-story structure of adobe brick reaching to the top of a natural cave high up in the cliffs (*see TOUR 2A*).

Tonto National Monument. At the junction of the Tonto and Salt Rivers, 1120 acres, near Roosevelt Dam. The two principal ruins are adobe dwellings of the early fourteenth century, the lower a two-story structure of twenty-nine rooms and the upper (originally three stories high) a house of about seventy-five rooms (*see TOUR 3A.*).

Casa Grande National Monument. An area of 472 acres a little to the north of Coolidge, originally containing at least six separate and distinct villages of the Hohokam culture. The monument takes its name from a four-story building constructed of subsoil from the region; it was thirty-eight feet high and undoubtedly served as a watch tower (*see TOUR 4C*).

Other important archeological remains within the state are Kinishba Ruin, four miles east of Fort Apache; Elden Pueblo, five miles east of Flagstaff; University Ruins, eight miles northeast of Tucson; Pueblo Grande, five miles east of Phoenix; and Gila Pueblo and Pesh-Ba-Gowah Pueblo, near Globe; Point of Pines, 60 miles east of Globe on San Carlos Apache Indian Reservation.

MUSEUMS

Large and interesting collections of pottery, textiles, basketry, and other material produced by or relating to the Indians of Arizona will be found in the following institutions: Museum of Northern Arizona, at Flagstaff; Heard Museum, Arizona Museum, and Pueblo Grande Museum, at Phoenix; Museum of the University of Arizona, at Tucson; Gila County Museum, at Globe; museums at Pesh-Ba-Gowah Pueblo and Gila Pueblo, near Globe; and Casa Grande National Monument Museum, at Coolidge; Montezuma Castle National Monument near Camp Verde; Tuzigoot National Monument near Clarkdale; Tumacacori National Monument near Nogales.

History

THE FIRST known inhabitants of the region that is now Arizona were the ancient house and canal builders of the desert and the cave and cliff dwellers of the upland country. Archeological remains indicate that these people of an age of stone attained a high degree of civilization.

Just who was the first white explorer to enter the region is a matter of conjecture and controversy. According to some accounts, one of Cortes' lieutenants, Jose de Basconales, came up from Mexico early in 1526 and penetrated the country as far north as Zuni. A better case, though by no means a conclusive one, has been made out for Alvar Nunez Cabeza de Vaca, his two companions, Castillo and Dorantes, and the Negro slave known as Estevan or Estevanico. They were the sole survivors of the expedition led by Panfilo de Narvaz, which in 1528 landed at Tampa Bay on the coast of Florida with the intention of conquering and colonizing the vast inland country. The rest lost their lives at the hands of hostile Indians, or through privation, disease, and shipwreck. During eight years of hazardous adventure, Cabeza de Vaca and his followers worked their way towards the Pacific. They had come as far west as the San Pedro River in present Arizona before they turned southward, reaching Culiacan, Mexico, in 1536. De Vaca's stirring narrative of his odyssey is necessarily vague as to the specific route followed.

Although two Franciscan priests, Juan de la Asuncion and Pedro Nadal, are mentioned in some sources as having traveled from Mexico northward to the upper Colorado River in 1538, the first white man definitely known to have explored the region that is now Arizona was another Franciscan, Marcos de Niza, an Italian in the service of Spain. Early in 1539 he was sent from Mexico City into the northern country by the viceroy of New Spain, Antonio de Mendoza, to search for the legendary "Seven Cities of Cibola" (Zuni villages occupying sites near the present town of Gallup, New Mexico), which were rumored to have streets and walls adorned with gold and precious jewels.

From Culiacan in March 1539, De Niza continued northward accompanied by another friar, Onorato, and by the Negro slave, Estevan, who had accompanied Cabeza de Vaca in his wanderings. At the Indian village of Petatlan, Onorato fell ill and De Niza was forced to proceed without him. He crossed the Rio Mayo, and reached the Indian village of Vacapa, where he awaited news from Estevan whom he had sent ahead to explore the country to the north. Estevan, meanwhile, had made his way across the desert and through mountain passes, unharmed by the superstitious Pima Indians, who were awed by his brilliant attire, feathers, and bells. When he reached the Cibola city, however, the Zunis were not impressed by his costume and soon put him to death. De Niza learned of the Negro's fate as he neared the native stronghold and decided not to enter this place of stone houses. From a distance, however, it appeared to be all that rumor had depicted. After raising a cross and claiming the region in the name of the viceroy, he hastily retraced his steps to Mexico.

In 1540 the Spanish nobleman, statesman, and soldier, Francisco Vasquez de Coronado, led a large force of cavalry and foot soldiers on an expedition from Mexico City to the "Seven Cities," with De Niza as guide. Several priests intent on converting the Indians were in the company. Coronado's route followed the San Pedro River to the Gila, then north to the sources of the Little Colorado and into the Cibola country. After a short but vigorous fight, he captured and entered one of the seven cities, which he renamed Granada.

Coronado's report to Mendoza, written at Granada, August 3, 1540, condemns the report De Niza had made in the previous year. Coronado assured the viceroy that Marcos had "sayd the trueth in nothing that he reported, but all was quite contrary, sauing onely the names of the cities, and great houses of stone: for although they bee not wrought with Turqueses, nor with lyme, nor brickes, yet are they very excellent good houses of three or foure or fiue lofts high . . . The seuen cities are seuen small townes, all made with these kinde of houses that I speake of: and they stand all within foure leagues together, and they are all called the kingdome of Cibola, and euery one of them haue their particular name: and none of them is called Cibola, but altogether they are called Cibola. And this towne which I call a citie, I haue named Granada."

Coronado made his headquarters there for several months. Shortly after his arrival, he sent Pedro de Tovar with an escort of cavalry into the Hopi country, of which he heard much from the Cibolans. Another party was dispatched under one of his captains, Garcia Lopez de Cardenas, to search for the great river of which they had heard. After a march of twenty days, the party sighted the Colorado from the high walls of the Grand Canyon. They explored the rim for several days, vainly trying to find a trail leading down to the river, and then they returned to Cibola.

After two years of fruitless searching for treasure, during which time extensive territories were claimed by him as possessions of Spain, Coronado returned to Mexico City in 1542 with the remnants of his once formidable army. Exhausted and believing that his efforts had been futile, he retired to his estate, never to reappear in the history of New Spain. He died about 1549.

While Coronado was marching to Cibola, Hernando de Alarcon and his men sailed up the west coast of Mexico, entered and explored the Gulf of California, and ascended the Colorado River in small boats for some distance. He was, so far as is known, the first white man to navigate the river.

Coronado's failure to discover gold put an end to extensive explorations in the Southwest for a period of forty years. In 1580-81 Spanish soldiers escorted Fray Agustin Rodriquez into the Cibola region, but deserted him and another priest when they found rich silver ore on the Gila. Antonio de Espejo led a small expedition into New Mexico in 1582 to rescue the missionaries and also to search for precious minerals. It has been said that Rodriguez and his soldier-guard settled on the site of Tucson, but Espejo found that Rodriguez had been killed by Indians near the site of Bernalillo. Espejo marched into what is now Arizona as far as the Bill Williams' Fork, west of Prescott, before he found silver ore; he then returned to Mexico, taking ore samples with him. His reports to the viceroy probably stimulated Spanish interest in Mexico, but sixteen years passed before Juan de Onate, under contract with the viceroy, led an expedition of several hundred colonists north from Mexico City and formally took over the vast territory of New Mexico in the name of the King of Spain.

Spanish missionary activities among the Indians began early in the seventeenth century, when Franciscan priests from colonies along the Rio Grande built chapels and baptized converts among the Hopi pueblos. In the Pueblo uprising of 1680 the priests were killed and the churches burned. According to Hopi legend, their death paid for a gift of Hopi maidens offered by the priests to Spanish soldiers. Thereafter, the Hopi consistently refused to have anything to do with the religion of the white man.

Among the Indians to the south, where the priests were more successful, mission work was begun in 1692 by the Jesuits, foremost among whom was Padre Eusebio Francisco Kino, a native of Trent, Austria. From his headquarters at the mission of Nuestra Senora de los Dolores, in the Mexican Province of Sonora, Kino made many journeys among the tribes of Pimeria Alta—the upper country of the Pima Indians, comprising what is now northern Sonora and southern Arizona. Alone or accompanied only by friendly Indian guides, he journeyed up and down the Santa Cruz, San Pedro, and Gila rivers, preaching to the Pima, Papago, Cocopa, Maricopa, and Yuma tribes, giving them new varieties of grain and vegetables and helping them to raise cattle, sheep, and horses. Kino's visit of 1694 to the ruins of Casa Grande on the Gila River was probably the first made by a white man. Seven of the twenty-four missions that he established in Pimeria Alta during his twenty-four years of service were within the present boundaries of Arizona, although only three—Guevavi, Tumacacori, and San Xavier del Bac—were known to be in full operation at the time of his death in 1711. The ruins of Guevavi (founded 1692), about eight miles north of Nogales, are barely traceable today. Tumacacori (1696), about eight miles northwest of Nogales, is in a state of semiruin but is now protected as a national monument. San Xavier del Bac, the most noted of all, was founded in 1700 on a site nine miles south of Tucson; as rebuilt by the Franciscan Order between 1784 and 1797, it is said to be the finest example of mission architecture in the United States. After Kino's death, missionary work ceased for the most part until 1792, when the Franciscans made San Xavier a permanent mission.

During Kino's administration, there was no Spanish garrison north of Fronteras near the San Pedro River in northern Sonora, and the missions were virtually unprotected from the raids of hostile Indians. The Apache had come down from the north about a century earlier and had committed so much murder and thievery that their name was a terror. In 1751 the Pima and Papago joined in an uprising throughout Pimeria Alta. Priests who failed to escape to southern Sonora were killed, and silver-mining equipment (according to some accounts, the Spaniards had begun mining operations as early as 1736) was destroyed. In the following year a *presidio,* or garrison, was established at Tubac in the Santa Cruz Valley, and in 1753 the priests returned to the missions.

When the Jesuits were expelled from all parts of the Spanish dominions in 1767, the mission property in New Spain was transferred to the royal *comisario.* The viceroy appealed to the Franciscan College at Queretaro, Mexico for priests of that order to conduct the missions in southern Sonora and Pimeria Alta. Among the fourteen assigned to this work, Padre Francisco Tomas Garces was sent to San Xavier del

Bac, with the little neighboring village of San Cosme as *visita,* or clerical outpost. In 1772 San Xavier boasted an adobe church and two hundred parishioners. Guevavi had eighty-six inhabitants, and Tumacacori ninety-three. There were two hundred persons at the *visita* of San Jose del Tucson, a small unfinished church at Ignacio just east of Guevavi, and the near-by *visita* at Calabasas. The *presidio* at Tubac was removed to the present site of Tucson in 1776.

In 1774 Padre Garces and Padre Juan Diaz accompanied an expedition led by Captain Juan Bautista de Anza, later (1777-88) Governor of New Mexico, to lay out an overland route between the missions of Pimeria Alta and those of California. The trail led from Tubac to the Gila River and west across the Colorado River to San Gabriel on the Pacific.

On a special mission to the Hopi Indians in 1776, Garces pushed his way north along the Colorado River. He met Mojave and Chemehuevi Indians who received him hospitably. Entering the region of present-day Prescott, he persuaded friendly Yavapai to accompany him as guides to the Hopi pueblos. On the way they visited the Havasupai Indians, who were living then, as now, in the depths of the Grand Canyon. Garces remained three days at Oraibi, the cliff city of the Hopi, but his gifts were rejected and he was not allowed to remain. Disheartened by his failure, he returned to San Xavier. In his eleven months' journey of some twenty-five hundred miles, he had visited nine tribes and met approximately twenty-five thousand Indians.

Later Padre Garces visited the Yuma along the Colorado River, considered among the most dangerous Indians of that region. The first year of his work in the Yuma country was promising; but in the following year a party of soldiers and colonists with their wives and families, arrived and appropriated land belonging to the Indians. In June 1781 a detachment of soldiers led by the lieutenant governor of Lower California stopped and pastured their horses and cattle on the fields of mesquite beans which provided the Yuma with their chief source of sustenance. Indian hatred, long simmering, reached the boiling point. Padre Garces was clubbed to death while celebrating Mass; another priest, the *commandante* of the village and his corporal, and all the soldiers were killed. When news of the massacre reached General Teodoro de Croix, *commandante* of the Mexican military forces, he at once planned the severest measures of reprisal, but it was more than a year before the necessary forces could be spared. In September 1782 he sent an expedition of one hundred and sixty soldiers, assisted by allied friendly Indians from California; they made war against the Yuma, killing one hundred and ten and taking eighty-five prisoners.

Following a vigorous campaign begun in 1786 to curb the Apache, whose continuous raids had made life unsafe for the colonists, a treaty was concluded which gave the Indians the benefit of a rationing system, at a yearly cost to the Spanish Crown of from $18,000 to $30,000. Immigrants came in increasing numbers from old Mexico to farm, prospect, and raise stock.

During the Mexican wars of independence (1811-22) mission work languished, northern settlements were neglected, and thousands of lives were lost in Pimeria. Ranchos, haciendas, mining camps, and other settlements were destroyed by Indians. Even the Pima and Pagago tribes became hostile. In 1827 the new republic of Mexico expelled the Franciscans and the era of missions soon came to an end.

Upon winning independence from Spain in 1822, Mexico proclaimed General Augustin de Iturbid emperor but banished him in the following year. A republic was founded in 1824; the ousted Emperor who had meanwhile returned to Mexico, was tried for treason, condemned, and put to death on July 14, 1824. In that year the Territory of Nuevo Mexico was formed, including what are now the states of Arizona and New Mexico. The capital at Santa Fe had about 4,500 inhabitants. The eastern portion of the territory had a population of about 20,000 whites and 8,000 friendly Indians; and the ranches along the upper Rio Grande were rich in cattle, horses, and sheep. In marked contrast, all the ranches in the western portion—the present Arizona —had been abandoned, leaving only two settlements, Tubac and Tucson, each protected by a small garrison.

Americans began to arrive in the New Mexico settlements, as reports of the territory's rich resources spread throughout the East. Enterprising frontier merchants sent in great caravans of freight drawn by mule and ox teams. The value of merchandise carried over the trail between Independence, Missouri, and Santa Fe increased from $15,000 in 1822 to $450,000 in 1844. By 1824 a few of the bolder traders had pushed their way farther west into the Apache country of Arizona. American trappers explored along the Gila, Salt, and Colorado rivers, and found an abundance of beaver and game. Probably the most picturesque of these early trappers was Bill Williams whom Will H. Robinson, Arizona historian, has described as follows:

"Long, sinewy and bony, with a nose and chin almost meeting, he was the typical plainsman of the dime novel. He always rode an Indian pony, and his Mexican stirrups were big as coal scuttles. His buckskin suit was bedaubed with grease until it had the appearance of polished leather; his feet were never encased in anything but moccasins, and his buckskin trousers had the traditional fringe on the outer seam. Naturally, Indian signs were an open book to him, and he was even readier to take a scalp than an Apache, who preferred to crush the heads of his victims and let the hair stay."

In the 1820's there were some fourteen tribes of Indians in this western portion of the territory, among them the friendly and hospitable Papago and Pima, the hostile Mojave and Yuma, and the Apache, who were always at war with neighboring tribes or with the whites.

Few of the events connected with the acquisition of the present state of Arizona from Mexico by the United States were enacted within the territory itself. By proclamation of May 13, 1846, President Polk announced the existence of a state of war with Mexico. In carrying out the plan for the invasion of New Mexico and California, an Army of the West was organized under the command of Colonel Stephen W. Kearny. The diplomat James Magoffin, sent on a secret mission to the governors of Mexico in their various provinces, was so successful that the Mexican forces had faded away by the time Kearny and his army reached Santa Fe. On August 18, 1846 without any opposition, the Americans entered the town, where they were cordially received by Lieutenant Governor Vigil and given a salute of thirteen guns; then the American flag was raised over the *palacio* of the Spanish governor. Kearny immediately began work on the construction of a military post and on September 22 inaugurated a plan of civil government for the territory.

For Arizona, significant events during the Mexican War were Kearny's later expedition across Arizona to California and the cross-country journey of the so-called Mormon Battalion. Kearny and his men crossed the Gila River near Florence, came upon the Casa Grande plain, and were amazed at the prosperity of the Pima and Maricopa Indians. One of the men wrote: "To us it was a rare sight to be thrown in the midst of a large nation of what are termed wild Indians surpassing many of the Christian nations in agriculture, little behind them in the useful arts and immeasurably before them in honesty and virtue. During the whole of yesterday our camp was full of men, women and children who wandered among our packs unwatched and not a single instance of theft was reported."

The Mormon Battalion was organized as a unit of the Army of the West. Anxious to find a region in which they could live without persecution, the Mormons had agreed to enlist for one year provided they would be discharged on the Pacific coast. In July, 1846, the five companies of untrained recruits and their wives started west from Council Bluffs, Iowa. At Santa Fe the unfit were weeded out, together with most of the women, and the battalion continued on its journey under the command of Lieutenant Colonel Philip St. George Cooke. The troops had a two months' allotment of rations and supplies, carried in wagons over country which up to that time had never been traversed by a vehicle. Cooke led his forces southwest into the Mexican state of Sonora, then north along the San Pedro River and by way of Tucson through the Pima country to the Colorado River. Tucson was captured on December 16, 1846, and in January, 1847, after many adventures but no fighting, the battalion reached the old San Diego Mission, having accomplished the work of marking a wagon road from Santa Fe to the Pacific.

The Mexican War ended with the Treaty of Guadalupe Hidalgo, signed in February, 1848. This treaty set the southern boundary of Texas at the Rio Grande and ceded to the United States the future states of Nevada, Utah, most of Arizona, a large part of New Mexico, parts of Colorado and Wyoming, and all of California. The southern boundary of New Mexico, which included the present Arizona, was fixed at the Gila River.

It soon became evident that a favorable right of way should be secured for a southern transcontinental railroad along the route marked by the Mormon Battalion, and that the numerous Mexican claims arising from disputes about the newly-created border line should be settled. To this end negotiations were completed in 1853 for the purchase by the United States from Mexico of the strip of land between the Gila River and the present southern boundary of Arizona and New Mexico. This was the Gadsden Purchase, so called because it was negotiated for the United States by James Gadsden, minister to Mexico at the time; the land acquired comprised more than 45,500 square miles, for which the United States paid $10,000,000.

In 1853 the War Department ordered surveys to be made for a possible transcontinental railroad approximately along the course of the thirty-fifth parallel. The survey party, headed by Lieutenant A. W. Whipple, crossed the north central portion of Arizona westward from Zuni, New Mexico, to Cajon Pass, California. The Atlantic and Pacific Railroad, forerunner of the present Santa Fe line, later followed closely this course. A party under Edward F. Beale, using camels for pack animals, surveyed the route in 1857-58 for a wagon road along the thirty-fifth parallel. The camels were later turned loose—to the terror of other pack animals and the occasional wreckage of pack trains—roamed over the desert until they were finally exterminated by mule drivers.

After the close of the Mexican War, overland travel to California through Arizona increased rapidly. It has been estimated that by 1851 more than sixty-thousand persons had passed through the territory. Many others had stopped at various points along the Gila River and established farms and ranches. Although cut-offs were sometimes used, the route generally followed the old wagon road blazed by the Mormon Battalion. Indians frequently attacked wagon trains and killed many of the emigrants. Best known among hundreds of such raids was the Oatman massacre, in which the Oatman family, moving by wagon to California, was set upon by Apache in 1851. Oatman, his wife, and an infant were killed, a son was left for dead, and two daughters were taken as prisoners. The younger daughter died in captivity from brutal treatment. Years later, the older girl was ransomed from some Mojave Indians, who had purchased her from the Apache. Lorenzo Oatman, the son, recovered from his wounds, and he and his sister were reunited.

In 1857 the San Antonio and San Diego Stage Company began to operate the first stage line through the region. Six-mule coaches were used, but for a hundred miles of shifting sand the traveler was obliged to exchange his coach seat for a saddle mule. Through Indian territory the coaches were accompanied by an armed escort. The line later gave way to the Butterfield Company, whose route extended for 2,759 miles from San Francisco to St. Louis, by way of Los Angeles, Yuma, Tucson, and El Paso. Mail was carried twice a week under contract for a trip that took twenty-five days.

From 1852 until the Southern Pacific Railroad from the west coast to Yuma was completed in 1878, many passengers and quantities of freight were brought in sea-going vessels through the Gulf of California to Puerto Ysabel, at the mouth of the Colorado River, where they were transferred to light steamers bound for ports along the river. Yuma, 175 miles up the Colorado, was the disembarking point for southern Arizona; passengers and freight bound for Prescott, Wickenburg, or other places in central Arizona were unloaded at La Paz or Ehrenburg. Hardyville, now a ghost town 337 miles up the river, was then considered at the head of navigation on the Colorado.

Among the earliest pioneers who came from the east immediately after the Gadsden Purchase was Charles D. Poston, who played an active part in the territory's development. With Herman Ehrenberg, a mining engineer, Poston spent the winter of 1854-55 prospecting in the hills above Tubac. In 1856 he headed an expedition sent out by the Sonora Exploring and Mining Company (of which he was one of the organizers) to develop the Heintzelman mine, 30 miles from Tubac. The first run of ore, smelted in an adobe furnace, produced 2,000 ounces of silver and 300 pounds of copper; 600 hours were required for the run. Improved apparatus was gradually introduced, and in 1859 the mine produced about $100,000 worth of silver. Meanwhile the Arizona Mining and Trading Company, organized by Poston, opened the first copper mine at Ajo in 1854; the ore was shipped to Wales where it sold for $360 a ton. Following the discovery in 1858 of gold placers along the Gila River some twenty-five miles above Fort Yuma, a community of about one thousand persons quickly grew up in this region and was christened Gila City. While at first some prospectors panned as much as $100 worth of gold a day, the deposits were rapidly exhausted and Gila City became the first of Arizona's numerous ghost towns.

In 1858 Tubac had a population of eight hundred, of whom five-sixths were Mexican. Each family possessed peach and pomegranate orchards. Poston wrote of the community: "We had no law but love, and no occupation but labor; no government, no taxes, no public debt, no politics. It was a community in a perfect state of nature. As syndic under New Mexico, I opened a book of records, performed the marriage ceremony, baptized the children, and granted the divorce." In thus assuming the duties of church and state, Poston brought much trouble on his head. The vicar apostolic from New Mexico arrived on the scene and pronounced Poston's marriages, baptisms, and divorces spurious. However after considerable persuasion the vicar became reasonable and sanctioned the marriages for a fee of $700. Paper money of local issue, known as *boletas,* redeemable in silver, was the medium of exchange in Tubac. As few of the Mexicans could read, the different denominations of the *boletas* were indicated by pictures of animals on the currency. Thus the likeness of a pig denoted a value of one "bit" (twelve and a half cents); a calf, two bits; a rooster, four bits; a horse, six bits; and so on through the various denominations. The territory's first newspaper, the *Weekly Arizonian,* began publication at Tubac in 1859.

It had become apparent early in the 1850's that the territory of New Mexico was too large and unwieldy for efficient administration, and that a division should be made. Tucson, the largest city in the Gadsden Purchase area, was 250 miles from the county seat at Mesilla, and more than 500 miles by stage from Santa Fe, the territorial capital. Consequently the citizens of the Santa Cruz Valley for the most part made and administered their own laws. In 1856 Congress was petitioned to set up a separate territory of Arizona, comprising the land included in the Gadsden Purchase. Several bills introduced toward this end failed of passage, and separate territorial status was not achieved until early in the Civil War.

Since most of the American settlers in the Gadsden Purchase area had come from the south, conventions held in 1861 at Tucson and Mesilla declared this area to be Confederate country, and Tucson citizens elected Granville H. Oury a delegate to the Confederate Congress. In the same year lieutenant Colonel John R. Baylor, commanding a company of Texas Confederates, defeated Union forces in the Rio Grande Valley and organized the territory of Arizona, comprising all that part of the territory of New Mexico south of the thirty-fourth parallel. The Confederate Congress passed an enabling act on January 18, 1862; and on February 14 of the same year, President

Jefferson Davis proclaimed Arizona a territory of the Confederacy with Mesilla as the seat of government.

At the outbreak of the Civil War most of the Army officers in the region joined the Confederate forces, and many military posts were abandoned. The Apache again raided the white settlements, and Cochise, chief of the Chiricahua Apache, was on the warpath. The white population of Tubac and all the miners in the territory fled to Tucson. In February, 1862, a troop of Texas Confederate cavalry under Captain Sherod Hunter reached Tucson and was welcomed by the inhabitants. By April of the same year, California infantry and cavalry under Colonel James H. Carleton were concentrated at Fort Yuma. Meanwhile, Hunter had advanced with his command to the Pima country, where he confiscated 1,500 sacks of flour intended for the Union forces at Fort Yuma, and his pickets captured without bloodshed a squad of nine Unionists under Captain William McCleave. A stronger Union force started east and was informed by Indian scouts that Hunter's command was just ahead, on its way back from Tucson. A detachment of cavalry under Lieutenant James Barrett made a wide detour and attacked on the Confederate flank while the main column attacked simultaneously from the rear. Barrett reached the Texans in Picacho Pass and engaged them before the supporting column arrived. He and two of his men were killed, and three others were captured. This was the only engagement between Federal and Confederate forces in what is now Arizona.

The most important battle on Arizona soil between whites and Indians occurred in July, 1862, when eleven companies of Union infantry, two companies of cavalry, and two batteries of artillery, on their way from Tucson to New Mexico, were attacked in Apache Pass by Chiricahua Apache and Mimbres (Warm Spring) Apache under Cochise and Mangas Coloradas. The soldiers were surprised by a musket volley fired by Indians hidden behind rocks and trees on the steep sides of the canyon. The men, who had marched many miles without water, and were trying to reach a spring, brought their howitzers into action and the Apache fled pell-mell.

At this time the United States treasury was greatly depleted, and the Congress at Washington suddenly awoke to the fact that the gold fields of Arizona were receiving wide publicity. On February 24, 1863, it passed an act to create a separate territory of Arizona with boundaries approximately as they are today except that they included a part of lower Nevada. The first territorial governor, John N. Goodwin, arrived in the following year and fixed the temporary seat of government at Fort Whipple in Little Chino Valley. Soon, however, this army post was moved eighteen miles south to Granite Creek; so the gubernatorial party packed its belongings and followed the soldiers, who provided protection against the Apache. About a mile upstream from the military camp, the Governor and his staff established their second capital and erected Arizona's first Governor's Mansion, a two-story structure that was rather imposing in its day. The present town of Prescott grew up around this mansion. In 1867 the capital was moved to Tucson, but was returned to Prescott ten years later. It remained there until 1889, when Phoenix became the permanent seat of government.

After formation of the territory as authorized by the Federal Congress in 1863, Charles D. Poston, who had served as a colonel in the Union Army, was elected territorial delegate to Washington. The first territorial legislature, sitting from September 26 to November 10, 1864, issued licenses for the construction of toll roads and franchises for ferries on the Colorado River. It also authorized a bond issue of $100,000 to equip a body of militia to control the Indians. When the bonds failed to find purchasers, the territory was obliged to depend on the services of four companies of volunteers.

In 1870 Arizona and southern California were garrisoned by a joint military department with headquarters at Fort Whipple. General George Stoneman, in command of the department, adopted a policy of exterminating lawless Apache and rewarding with rations and blankets those who were peaceful. However, many Arizonans considered that he was too lenient, and took matters into their own hands. Several citizens of Tucson, leading a band of Mexicans and Papago, attacked a large number of sleeping Apache and killed eighty-five, most of them women and children.

General George Crook, who succeeded Stoneman in 1871, followed the general policies of his predecessor but displayed much better judgment and won the respect of the peaceful Apache, who even helped to capture their lawless tribesmen. General Crook used the same methods of warfare against other recalcitrant tribes—the Tonto, Hualapai, and Yavapai—who surrendered to him in 1873. The lessening of danger from Indian raids encouraged many new settlers to come to Arizona.

In the 1860's a colony of Mormons founded Walnut Grove in Yavapai County, Fredonia in what is now Coconino County, and Callville in what was then Pah-Ute County, now part of Nevada. In 1873 Jacob Hamblin, friend of Brigham Young, laid out a wagon road from Lee's Ferry southward to hasten colonization. During the 1870's Mormons established the permanent northeastern towns of St. Joseph, Snowflake, and Show Low; and, in the Salt River Valley, Jonesville (later renamed Lehi) and Mesa City. The largest Mormon district in the state eventually developed from settlements made in 1879 along the upper Gila River in Graham County.

During the same decade the population of the territory increased from 9,658 to 40,440. Many settlers in the Santa Cruz Valley, in the fertile areas about Prescott Basin, and in the Salt River Valley were carrying on extensive agricultural operations. With the exhaustion of the rich surface placers, lode mining had begun in various sections, and in 1877-78 came the mining booms at Bisbee and Tombstone. The Southern Pacific Railroad of California was extended eastward to Yuma in 1878, and by the early 1880's all the principal towns of the territory were connected by stage service. During 1881 the Atlantic and Pacific Railroad, now the Santa Fe, pushed west from Albuquerque as far as Winslow and in 1883 was completed across the territory. The Federal government granted the railroad alternate sections of land, amounting to more than ten million acres.

The office of superintendent of public instruction was made an elective office by legislative act of 1879, and Moses H. Sherman, who had been appointed by Governor John C. Fremont, was elected superintendent in 1880. To his successors, however, William B. Horton and Robert Lindley Long, belongs the credit for bringing together the unorganized schools of the territory into a unified system during the five year period, 1883-1887. Normal school training began in 1885 when the legislature made provision for the territorial normal school at Tempe; the state university at Tucson was authorized by the same legislature. In 1889 the Northern Normal School of Arizona was opened at Flagstaff.

A law was passed in 1885 forbidding polygamists and bigamists from voting or holding public office. The first move to preserve Arizona's rich archeological remains was made in 1889, when the ruins of the ancient city of Casa Grande and several hundred surrounding acres were set aside as a National Monument. In the same year the seat of government was moved from Prescott to Phoenix. By 1890 the territory's population had increased to 88,243.

In the twenty years following the Civil War about fifteen army posts for the protection of settlers were established in the territory, and the reservation plan of dealing with the Indian problem was slowly and with great difficulty put into effect. Early in the 1880's the famous Indian chief Geronimo with a band of Chiricahua Apaches left the White Mountain Reservation in Arizona, and for several years wrought havoc among the ranches and settlements of Arizona and New Mexico. After a strenuous army campaign, Geronimo and his band surrendered in 1886 and were imprisoned at Fort Pickens, Florida.

In the Spanish-American War (1898) Arizona contributed three troops to the first United States Volunteer Cavalry—the famous Rough Riders—and three companies to the First Territorial Infantry. Arizonans with the Rough Riders fought throughout the Cuban campaign, notably at Guasimas and San Juan Hill.

The wealth of Spanish and pioneer Arizona was not entirely in its soil and rich veins of ore. It was also in its people, and in the leaders who have left honored names in the historical records of the state: Father Kino, no less zealous as a geographer and explorer than as a priest; Juan Bautista de Anza, captain and colonizer of New Spain; Padre Garces, carrier of the Cross to the pueblos; Pauline Weaver, trapper, scout and guide; Charles D. Poston, known as "the father of Arizona"; Mangas Coloradas, Apache chief who died resisting the white man's invasion of his native region; Major John W. Powell, conqueror of the Colorado River; Jacob Hamblin, fearless Mormon trail-blazer; Al Sieber, a scout whose cunning exceeded that of the Indian; Ed Schieffelin, prospector and discoverer of the Tombstone Bonanza; and John P. Clum, Indian agent respected by the Indians because he respected them.

As early as 1892 a bill providing for Arizona's admission as a state was passed in the United States House of Representatives but was killed in the Senate. In 1902 a senatorial committee on statehood, on a tour of inspection in the southwest, raced through the territory in three days and returned to Washington with a proposal for admission of the territories of New Mexico and Arizona as a single state. Arizonans almost unanimously opposed this plan and defeated the proposed jointure by popular vote. In June, 1910, the Congress passed the enabling act authorizing Arizona to frame a constitution.

Provisions for the initiative, referendum, and recall were included in the constitution, but President Taft refused to approve statehood unless the clause providing for the recall of judges was omitted. This was done and on February 14, 1912, President Taft signed the proclamation that made Arizona the forty-eighth and last state to be admitted into the Union. At the first state election, however, the provision for recall was restored. George W. P. Hunt, who had come to Arizona in 1881 from Missouri, was elected first state governor, and served seven two-year terms before his death in 1934.

When Arizonans formed their state government they planned to make it one that would always be under the control of the people. The terms of the more important state officers are for two years only. The people reserve the power—independent of the legislature—to propose laws and constitutional amendments and to enact or reject laws and amendments.

The legislature, convening annually the 2nd Monday in January, is bicameral; each county has 2 senators; the number of representatives from each country apportioned according to population, total limited to 80, since 1953. The judicial structure consists of these various units:

there is a supreme court, superior court, and several lesser courts. The supreme court has 5 judges, elected for 6-year terms on a staggered basis; each serves part of his term as chief justice. Besides the governor and other executive officials, there are over 100 commissions and boards for law enforcement and administration of state institutions.

When the original constitution was drawn up, it was considered by some to be too liberal, and even radical. But Senator George E. Chamberlain of Oregon, speaking in the United States Senate on April 17, 1911, in defense of the initiative, referendum, and recall in the Arizona constitution said "the three in combination are a perfect safeguard to the rights of the people and an absolute check upon maladministration of affairs." Most of the provisions to which objection was made are now regarded as matters of course and have been adopted by other states.

A pension plan for teachers who have taught for twenty-five years in Arizona public schools was adopted in 1912, and free textbooks were provided for school children in the same year. Gambling was outlawed in 1907, woman's suffrage came in 1912, and prohibition in 1914. (Repeal of the prohibition act was voted in 1932.)

With the entry of the United States into the World War in 1917, thousands of the state's citizens enlisted in the army and navy. (The first native Arizonan to die in France was Mathew Rivers, a Pima Indian youth.) Many new farms were developed to produce wheat, and Arizona mines were worked to capacity. Labor difficulties in the mining industry reached a climax in 1917 when members of the International Union of Mine, Mill, and Smelting Workers struck in the Warren County district. The Bisbee Deportation resulted from this strike.

Arizona has made the most notable advances in its history in the period since the World War. Its population increased from 334,162 in 1920 to 749,587 in 1950, a gain of more than 100 per cent for the decade. A modern system of paved highways now connects all the more important centers and gives access to the state's principal scenic and recreational areas. Completion in 1929 of the Marble Canyon Bridge over the Colorado River provided the connecting link in a main arterial highway for traffic between Arizona and Utah. Legislation during this period included a workmen's compensation act and provision for a state industrial commission in 1920, and the adoption of a state-wide sales tax in 1933.

There has been a phenomenal development of Arizona's great natural resources—minerals, grazing lands, vast acreage fertile under irrigation, lumber, and water power. Roosevelt Dam on the Salt River, completed in 1911, and Boulder Dam on the upper Colorado, 1936, Coolidge Dam on the Gila, 1930 both give irrigation and power to undeveloped areas.   Bartlett and Horseshoe Dams on the Verde River, completed 1939 and 1944 increase water storage for the Salt River Project.   Reservations for the maintenance of the Indian population (which is the largest of any state) have been extended and improved; and conservation agencies to protect and develop the state's forests and animal life have been established.   The scale on which land is being brought into use through irrigation may be judged from the fact that a total of 326,159 acres in Arizona were (1940) under the jurisdiction of the U. S. Bureau of Reclamation in the Salt River Project, the Yuma Project and the Yuma-Mesa Project, and supplemental projects.

The decade 1940-1950 saw a startling growth of Arizona's population, largely due to the federal government's wartime activities and demands and war-stimulated business and industry.   World War II launched the state's first really big industrial boom, as the prices and production of cotton, copper, aluminum, cattle, and foodstuffs soared. Phoenix and Tucson sprouted factories and nearly doubled in size, and several new towns mushroomed.   All over Arizona's broad lowlands army training camps sprang up, together with military depots and hospitals, aviation fields, prison camps for enemy aliens and settlements for relocated Japanese Americans.   Many of the civilians and soldiers brought or attracted to the state in this period became permanent residents.

This sudden expansion, after the depression decade, brought several problems to Arizona.   Numerous changes had to be made in governmental machinery.   A new social difficulty came with an influx of Negro and Mexican labor.   The educational system and administration of social welfare called for expensive reforms and rising taxes, as did efforts to maintain the highway system and the valuable tourist trade.

Increasingly important was the problem of conserving and utilizing the precarious water supply.   Though the state's government agreed in 1944 to abide by the Santa Fe Compact of 1922 for distribution of Colorado River water among the Basin states, how to determine and apply Arizona's share led to heated argument.   The Central Arizona Project, for irrigation and power in the Gila and Salt River valleys, caused a bitter dispute with California, both in Congress and the U. S. Supreme Court.   There was no doubt that Arizona needed an assured and regulated supply of water and power, if her enlarged population and economic life were to be maintained during the second half of the twentieth century.   But on the whole the state had reason to be optimistic about the future.

The Sunburnt West of Yesterday

ARIZONA life overflows all categories. To suggest the flavor of its past, much of which still can be tasted today, we must draw upon the reminiscences of those who were ranch cooks three or four decades ago and of those who frequented the saloons in territorial days; we must celebrate the stubborn little burro, friend of the prospector, and remember the wild horses descended from the stallions and mares brought to America by Spanish explorers; we must even eulogize the western saddle, most prized of all a cowboy's possessions. Let us return to the sunburnt west of yesterday which casts so deep a glow over the Arizona of today.

THE "ARIZONA NIGHTINGALE"

For a century the burro and the prospector have made history in Arizona. Together this inseparable pair has shared hunger and thirst. Together they have known the scorching days and the lonely nights of the desert. Cities have sprung up and flourished upon the sites of their discoveries. Bonanzas they uncovered have changed political and industrial destinies.

The burro is a stubborn, lazy, contrary little animal; at the same time he is particularly well fitted by nature to serve the needs of the prospector. He is tough and sure-footed on the trail; he can do with less food, less water, and less rest than the horse, mule, or ox; he can subsist equally well on succulent green grasses or dry bark and weeds.

Known commonly as the jackass, this long-eared little creature is respected throughout the southwest—roundly cursed yet respected—and here he is usually referred to by his Spanish name, burro. Because of his extraordinary bray, he is sometimes ironically called the "Arizona Nightingale."

Prospectors claim that without the burro the discovery of important mines and the development of the southwest might have been delayed for many years. Some aver that occasionally the burro has assumed the role of prospector; at times, in his independent search for food the burro has discovered mineral deposits for which men had searched for years.

Henry Wickenburg's burro is said to have been directly responsible for the greatest gold discovery in Arizona. The burro wandered from camp, and when Wickenburg sought him in surrounding hills, the animal, with proverbial contrariness, attempted to elude his master. Wickenburg, becoming angry, threw stones at the stubborn little burro. The stones were heavy and fell short of their mark, for they contained gold; the famous Vulture Mine at Wickenburg was thus discovered.

A native of Andalusia and Barbary, the burro was first brought to this country by the Spaniards. Missionaries and treasure seekers for the Crown found the enduring little animals useful in exploring the new country; and later both mule and burro were used by Spanish colonial miners to pack ore and to operate the *arrastra,* a primitive ore-crushing mill.

Though his services are not so necessary now, the burro's share in the economic development of the southwest will not soon be forgotten. In the days of the first white settlements, when there were no wagon roads, burro trains were used to bring in supplies necessary to the settlers. A train of a hundred or more burros brought flour to Wickenburg and Prescott from Pima Indian villages, grain from Ehrenburg, Colorado River port, and salt from Zuni salt wells across the New Mexico border.

A large proportion of the burro population, no longer needed, has been turned loose to become a part of the wildlife of the west. Thousands of the tough-skinned little beasts now exist in a wild state throughout Arizona and below the Mexican border. The typical herd of wild burros consists of fifteen or twenty jennies and a jack, who rules the herd. In order to maintain his position as ruler the jack must be able to defeat all comers. When two burros fight for supremacy the struggle may last for days. The loser, finally overcome with exhaustion, must quit the herd.

The panther or mountain lion, Arizona's worst predator, constantly kills deer, antelope, horses, and cows, but the little wandering burro has been known to escape the panther's ferocious spring from ambush. The usual easy movement of the burro changes to a whirl-wind of teeth and hoofs. His skin, tough and protected with heavy hair, makes it more difficult for the lion to slash and kill with his customary dispatch. There are exceptional instances where the little "trail blazer" has stood his ground even against the lion.

Some prospectors believe that the burro is a sacred animal—that Jesus placed a cross upon the beast's shoulders as a reward for its service. In proof they will show a more or less distinct cross on every burro. They also claim that a burro never dies of natural causes. "Did you ever see a dead burro?" they challenge the skeptical, and the answer is usually, "No."

The burro has his place in southwestern literature, appearing as an inconspicuous but important character in many western stories. And Ferde Grofe immortalized him in one movement of the noble *Grand Canyon Suite*.

The little burro is still useful to man. He is used as a pack animal by both Americans and Mexicans; he is employed in lieu of a truck to carry chickens and hay to market and to pack wood and water for family use. Children have pet burros to ride. And the prospector and his burro are still familiar sights in Arizona, as they travel across deserts and dim mountain trails in the search for the rainbow's end.

BLOOD AND THUNDER DAYS

The following account of the killing of Jack the Ripper was written by an eye witness.

It was on the day before Thanksgiving in 1906 that I reached Benson from Boston on my way to Mazatlan, Sinaloa. As the northern terminus of the railroad to Guaymas, the only gateway into Old Mexico on the west coast, Benson's trade with Mexico was enormous. Cowboys, miners, Mexicans, and Chinamen filled the town streets. Saloons abounded, and gamblers were plentiful.

All the railroad trains to Mexico were tied up. At the time I arrived there was a strike on the line. As a result of this delay Benson hotels had filled up with bankers, drummers, mining men, and Mexicans bound southward. Since there were no theaters, automobiles, movies, or Y.M.C.A. building, these strangers, in accordance with the custom of the day, naturally gravitated to the saloons. One such place opposite the railroad station was the principal gathering point. Its bar was on the left as you entered. On the right was a roulette wheel, next a big cast-iron stove, then a couple of card tables, and at the far end an old piano. An immense coal-oil lamp suspended from the ceiling near the front of the room was the main source of illumination. A small oil lamp on the piano relieved the darkness of the rear.

The place was owned by Jesse Fisher and the principal bartender, who also acted as croupier and card dealer in emergencies, was a character well known in southern Arizona as Jack the Ripper. His real name was unknown to most people. If you wished to attain a ripe old age, you did not ask people questions concerning their names. The etiquette of those days was very strict on this point.

Each new train left additions to the stranded crowd, and Thanksgiving Eve found a hilarious bunch recklessly playing the games and drinking in Fisher's place. Several "hostesses," a common saloon feature of the times, added to the liveliness. Thanksgiving Day came, and still no Mexican train service. Jack the Ripper ran the roulette wheel that morning. The play was quite heavy but about one in the afternoon most of the patrons left to enjoy their Thanksgiving turkey, and the games closed temporarily. I remember Fisher and Jack checking up the roulette wheel then. First they put the money representing the bank—in other words, the money backing the table—into one canvas sack. The rest was the house winnings or profit for the morning. This counted up to $612. Fisher put this into another sack, except for the odd $12, which he shoved over to Jack as a tip or extra fee for his expert handling of the crowd and table. Jack was dissatisfied. "Hell, twelve dollars is dam little for making you six hundred dollars in only a few hours—you're stingy," he said to Fisher. He repeated this several times, but otherwise did not seem very sore, and a few hours later he and Fisher left together for their Thanksgiving dinner, leaving a bartender in charge. They returned around six o'clock, both very friendly, although it was apparent that they had taken some liquid refreshment with their meal.

More trains had passed through in the meantime. The crowd was larger, all the games were running, someone continually banged on the tinny piano and some of the hostesses tried to sing. It rapidly developed into a large night. Spurred and armed cowboys entered, just arrived from their ranches, and in accordance with the Arizona law that required guns to be removed within thirty minutes after reaching town, they gave their forty-fives to the bartender and then danced with their spurs on. Arizona-wise drummers drank just enough to get comfortably litup in a sociable way, and then drank enough to stay in that mellow condition. One immaculately dressed Easterner held aloof from the rest of the crowd, drinking only a little wine occasionally. We thought him somewhat snobbish, and speculated whether or not he were a preacher, until he suddenly slapped a couple of twenty dollar gold pieces on the bar, collected all the hostesses, and invited the whole house up to have a drink. Gold and silver were the only mediums of exchange in those days, and anything smaller than a two-bit piece was absolutely unknown in these parts.

I sat on a stool in back of the roulette wheel taking it all in. It was vastly different from anything I had ever seen or heard of in Boston. Occasionally I bought a cigar or put a few chips on the roulette game to pay the house for the space I was occupying. It was a bitterly cold night outside, and the hotel rooms were bare and cheerless. Everyone was in a good-natured mood. Several rich landowners from the interior of Mexico were present. They seemed to turn up their noses at our American whisky. Not being able to get their native *mescal,* anything short of sulphuric acid was tasteless to them. Fisher, the owner, drank but little. He had to keep order. I remember his telling one of the girls she had better wear longer dresses when she appeared on the streets, lest she get the whole outfit in bad with the law. I looked—the girl's dress was actually a full five inches from the floor! The only discordant element was Jack the Ripper. Every time he passed near Fisher, he would mutter "stingy."

The drinks flew around faster. Soon a rather large hostess was sitting on the knees of a little bandy-legged cowpuncher, telling him her troubles. The Mexican grandees started playing the wheel in a big way. They selected a few numbers and piled the limit on each. Had any of those numbers ever come up the Mexicans would have been the new owners of the saloon, wheel and all.

At last I decided to retire. Everyone was getting woozy and the hour was late. As I started for the door I was startled by seeing Jack the Ripper produce the house gun, a big forty-five, from behind the bar. Like a chump I stopped to see what he was going to do. A few others saw him at the same time. They were more experienced. Those that could threw themselves down in front of the bar out of his sight. "Bang" went the Colt. The bullet shot out the big coal-oil lamp, causing semi-darkness. I made one grand dive for that cast-iron stove. If there had been anything larger near, I would have selected it. As fast as I was, a New York drummer was faster. He got there first and calmly tossed me back. One glance at the doorway showed me I was too late there also. It was jammed to the top. About twenty men had tried to go out at once, and they appeared piled up there like cord wood. "Bang" went the Colt again, and the chimney of the small lamp at the rear crashed. I made a second dive for the stove, but the big-nosed drummer repelled me. Again the Colt spoke, then a man yelled and another gun joined in. It spat a fusillade, and by the sing of its slugs I knew it to be a Luger automatic, a new type of gun just appearing in Arizona at that time. Burnt powder smoke filled my nostrils. This was plainly no time to fool around without cover. Remembering my football training, I tackled low and hard and heaved the drummer into the open where he began to squeal like a stuck pig. Then I took his place behind the stove. Unless you have been in a similar situation, you will never appreciate the beauty and advantages of a big old-fashioned coal-oil burner over the little tin heater of today.

The Colt spoke again, and the Luger soon answered with a second volley. Evidently its owner had slipped in another clip. Then I noted that each "zing" of the Luger was accompanied by an ominous "zip," sounding pretty much like when you shoot into a wild bull.

By the noise from the rear I knew the door there was also jammed. There was no more shooting and the front door was soon cleared of its human dam. Not knowing exactly what might happen next and fearing the guns were simply being reloaded, I leaped outside and then stopped, standing as close to the building as I could and right beside the doorway. I correctly guessed that the near-by doorways were already filled with my late companions, who would probably welcome me much as the drummer had.

From the time the Colt was first fired, until the last Luger slug "zinged," I do not think more than twenty seconds elapsed. There must have been a full moon, for outside it was almost as light as day. There was no more shooting. Everything grew deathly quiet. I was the only person in sight on the main street. Soon a few cautious heads appeared above a stone wall across the road that separated the highway from the railroad grounds. The doorways around disgorged their occupants. Townspeople appeared and soon a great crowd collected. I turned my head before they arrived and cautiously looked inside. The interior was quite dim. The crazy little lamp on the piano was smoking badly and giving a little light, its smashed chimney strewn over the top of the piano. The moonlight helped me to see that Jack the Ripper was still at the bar, seemingly leaning over it on both elbows. As I looked, he slumped over backward to the floor.

It happened that Harry Wheeler, then a lieutenant of the Arizona Rangers, was in town. He appeared and took charge of the proceedings. An inquest was immediately held. Then we learned that the user of the Luger automatic was Jesse Fisher. With his left hand he was holding on to the place below and behind his left hip where Jack's third shot had punctured him. It was only a flesh wound, though rather inconvenient. Jack the Ripper was dead. Fisher stated that when the Ripper shot out the lights he thought it was simply friendly fun, but when the third shot stung him where it did he felt he must stop the racket lest Jack hurt some one else. Of course all the other witnesses corroborated Fisher and he was freed on the spot. All the Luger slugs hit Jack's breast and a silver dollar would have covered the place where most of them entered. They made one big hole right through his body. Pretty good shooting in the dark!

Late the next morning I went down town—to find business going on as usual. A new bartender was on duty in Fisher's saloon. Hardly a word did I hear anywhere about the shooting of the night before. The Benson of those days had seen too many saloon killings to become excited over this little affray.

CATTLE ROUNDUP

This account of a range roundup in Arizona a third of a century ago is in the words of a "greenhorn" ranch cook.

Down in the corrals a cloud of dust heavy with alkali and profanity filled the air. Suddenly over the top bars shot the head and forelegs of a bronc. As he landed and kicked his way to freedom his rider somersaulted in the air, then landed face-down in the dirt.

I ran to help the fallen rider, but he arose and looked at me blankly. "What's the matter? I'm not hurt." Then he roared to his pardner in the corral. "Ketch that hammer-head, I want my saddle back." This seemed an ordinary incident in a bronc-fighter's daily life.

I was the newly hired cook for the outfit and it was my first day at the ranch. Only yesterday I had been touring America in a box-car. Ditched by the freight crew in Willcox, I was hired by the foreman as a roundup cook, although I assured him I had never cooked outdoors over an open fire in my life. "You'll make out all right," he said. Roundup cooks were hard to find in 1906.

That afternoon I drove the big wagon loaded with supplies to the ranch on the San Pedro about twenty-five miles away. The boss started me on the right road, but never having seen so much open country before I thought seriously at times of turning back. There were many faint wagon tracks called roads. I was afraid of getting lost. However the mules picked their own route. They paid no attention to me and late that evening we arrived at the ranch.

It was typical of others in the valley. The main building was of adobe with tremendously thick walls. The roof had been made by laying heavy round poles close together and covering them with dirt. Above the roof rose parapets with spaces to shoot through. It had been built in the early Indian days; and as it was directly in the path of hostiles favored between the San Carlos Indian reservation and Old Mexico, it had been the scene of many stirring happenings. Its few windows were mere slits through which a rifle could be fired. One small room served as the office and quarters of the boss, another small room was the kitchen, and a still smaller one was for the cook. The rest of the building was one immense room with ten built-in bunks, each large enough to accommodate two men if required, and a long table that made it a dining room at meal times.

One feature that interested me was the rack of twenty old-time single-shot Springfield army rifles of 45-70 caliber. They had been furnished by the government in the days of Geronimo and Cochise, and remained a mute reminder of the past. Numerous small gouges on the outside walls showed where hostiles had taken shots at the house; while inside, bullet holes in the woodwork and a pock-marked ceiling indicated a desire on the part of its occupants to shoot up something.

Outside was a barn used as a storage place for grain and ranch supplies, with a lean-to at one end that served as a saddle room. Two small sheds helped keep the sun off the wagons. An immense corral with thick adobe walls, now crumbling away, told eloquently how cattle were protected from Apaches in the old days. It had been replaced by pole corrals, all of which were grouped around a windmill and a well.

Most of the punchers were Texans. I soon learned that personal questions were taboo. If a man wanted anything known concerning his past he volunteered the information. The punchers ranged in age from sixteen-year-old Bud, a wrangler, to Old Buck with snow white hair, who rode with Forrest's cavalry in the Civil War. Later Buck had fought Comanches in Texas and hunted buffalo, and had been up the trail to Abilene and Dodge City when there wasn't a wire fence from the Gulf of Mexico as far north as a man could ride.

The punchers were gathering horses and shoeing-up the night I got in, and over two hundred saddle horses were penned at the ranch corrals. Between roundups the ponies ran unshod, but when the work was on every horse and mule was plated. Each puncher shod his own string, although they helped one another. If a horse was inclined to kick too much, they tied up one hind foot. The shoes were put on cold; they simply rasped the hoof down, and after fitting the shoe they tacked it in place. Each puncher had ten head of horses in his string to use as he saw fit. Some in each string were gentle but any horse that was bridle-wise was classed as a gentle pony. Two bronc-fighters, or peelers as they were often called, were breaking horses at the ranch. On the roundup they rode the rough string made up of broncs (young half-broken horses) and old outlaws that were too tough for the average waddie.

Feeding this outfit would have been easy for an old hand, but it was far from simple to me. We had meat at every meal. A fat heifer was killed at sundown and hung outside to cool. Before sunup I cut off enough for the day's needs, then wrapped the rest in a meat tarp and put it in the shade. After sundown I removed the tarp and hung the meat out again. It is surprising how well a beef will keep when handled in this manner. Frijole beans, potatoes, and hot biscuits were served at every meal. Lick (syrup) took the place of butter. Dried fruit cooked with plenty of sugar was the usual dessert. Canned milk was bought in town. The outfit was running around 20,000 head of cattle on its range, but there wasn't a single milk cow in the lot. Most of the punchers were good cooks, and since they had to eat my cooking they helped me in every way. But it was some time before my biscuits were fit for a dog to eat. The coffeepot was always busy when the punchers were at the ranch. In those days coffee was called "jamoka." Tea was never used.

I had been at the ranch about a week when the roundup really started. A big wagon was brought to the kitchen door and the chuck box put in place. It was fitted with shelves to hold all the small supplies, while other compartments were fitted to hold the bulky articles. One end, which also served as a lid for the box, was hinged, and when it was let down it was my working table. Everything in this box was so compact that no matter how often we plunged down into arroyo beds or rumbled over rocky ledges the contents were always safe. A beef was killed and placed in the wagon box, together with several sacks of beans, potatoes, and onions. Then came the huge dutch ovens used for outside cooking. Next the bedding was rolled and corded. Each man carried a huge waterproof tarp inside which he spread his blankets; and between his blankets he placed his extra clothes—if he happened to have any. The war bag in which a puncher carried his tobacco, cartridges, and other odds and ends usually served as a pillow.

It was my job to drive the chuck wagon from one camping spot to another, as well as to feed the crew. Since I wasn't familiar with the range a puncher acted as pilot. Two wranglers drove the *remuda,* as the bunch of horses was called, and herded it during the day. At sundown the wranglers were relieved by two nighthawks, who herded the ponies at night.

Our first camp was on the river about twenty miles from the ranch. Here we met a neighbor from the south with an outfit just like ours, along with several stray men (small owners from along the mountains). The stray men worked as regular hands and ate with us at the wagon. In addition to looking after their own animals it gave them a chance to keep an eye on the other outfits in their neighborhood. For at this time the big outfits, and the small ones too, had an unholy reputation for branding everything they could, regardless of ownership. While the men spoke politely and softly to each other most of them wore hardware.

Every morning at daybreak the *remuda* was driven in. By holding a lass-rope in each hand the men made a rope corral while their ponies were roped out. As soon as each horse was saddled his rider topped him off. To me it was like watching a wild west show as even a gentle cowhorse is apt to pitch on a frosty morning.

The men were divided into two groups which rode in opposite

directions of the circle to be worked. As soon as the ponies were un-cocked they left camp on a trot, dropping men at regular intervals until the last two men had met. Every gully and every clump of brush was worked, as the cattle were driven in toward a designated spot at the center of the circle. It was usually around two o'clock before the drive was finished.

Now the *remuda* was driven in again and fresh horses were caught and saddled, as the ponies used in the morning had been going at top speed over the roughest kind of country. A quick lunch at the wagon and the evening work began. Punchers were stationed around the herd to keep the cattle bunched properly and to hold the various cuts. By the time the ropers rode into the herd the branding irons were hot. Unbranded calves were cut out with their mothers. It was necessary to have the mother as her brand proved ownership of the calf.

With a flick of his rope a calf was heeled by a roper and dragged out to the fire, where the bulldoggers slipped the rope after flanking him, and held him down until he was earmarked and branded. The bull-doggers usually worked in pairs, although there were always men who preferred to work alone. When a grown animal was found un-branded one puncher roped him around the horns while another heeled or roped the critter by both hind feet and stretched him out between them. A few good calves were usually kept for bulls and the other bull calves were castrated.

After all the calves were branded, the steers, fat cows, and strays were boosted out of the drag into one of the three small herds, and the work was through for the day. Every night a few stray men cut out their animals and started for home, while new men came in as the roundup neared their range.

The last thing done each day was to drive the *remuda* in again and rope out the punchers' night horses. Each puncher took his turn at standing guard. The men usually worked in pairs. Two hours on guard was the usual time but occasionally when trouble arose a man would be out all night. At night around the fire the men relaxed. Horses, men, and cattle made up most of their talk. By nine o'clock they were all asleep or blinking up at the stars.

In this manner the range was worked. Although the work was mostly routine it never dragged and no two days were alike. It was not unusual for a bronc to buck through camp, knocking the pots and pans four ways at once, to the amusement of the punchers and my discomfiture. Horses running at top speed often fell and men were hurt. There was always some excitement. The work climaxed at shipping time with the usual bust in town. When the last steer had been prodded into the car, the extra hands were paid off.

Back at the ranch the old hands were scattered in line camps over the range, living much like coyotes. Except for occasional trips to headquarters for chuck, they seldom saw one another. They were keeping an eye on the water, tending the hospital bunch, branding the slicks (calves that had slipped through the roundup) on their part of the range, and above all watching the neighbors and knowing where they rode. Riding alone from daybreak till dark, there was always plenty to do.

At headquarters only three punchers rode from the ranch. Two extra men were sweating (working without pay). The chuck wagon had been put away until spring. I cooked on the stove in the house. Down at the big corrals clouds of alkali dust and profanity hung heavy again, where two peelers were breaking horses.

WILD HORSES

Arizona's wild horses are disappearing from the box canyons and open grasslands, where once they roamed unrestricted and multiplied by the thousands. Like the Indians they have been forced on to the high mesas and into the roughest country, and even here they are meeting a terrifying end. They are chased and hunted like predatory animals, trapped or shot to become chicken feed, fertilizer, dog food, or even steak. Stockmen say that wild horses eat too much grass, drink too much water.

History records that after the prehistoric American horse had become extinct there were no horses in America until 1519 when Hernando Cortes came on his first voyage of conquest, bringing with him eleven stallions and five mares of Arabian stock. Frightened by the strange animals, the Aztec of Mexico made no attempt to capture the few that escaped when Cortes' soldiery fled from attack. These beautiful horses were never seen again by white men.

In 1540 other horses escaped from Hernandez de Soto's camp on the west bank of the Mississippi. At some spot westward from the Gulf plains and northward from Mexico the descendants of these two bands, in all likelihood, met, probably in the region that is now Mexico or Arizona. When the Spanish padres treked across Arizona some rode horses brought from the homeland to New Spain. It is probable that many of these animals broke their hobbles and joined their wild cousins in the open.

When Zebulon Pike and his company traveled through Colorado and New Mexico and as far north as Nebraska in the early eighteenth century, they found thousands of wild horses and many half-wild ponies used as mounts by the Indians. All these animals, undoubtedly, were descendants of the score or so of horses that escaped from the Spanish expeditions. The pioneers in New England and the Northwest had

The Desert

Buehman

SAGUARO CACTI

DESERT FLORA

SUNSET, PHOENIX
SOUTH MOUNTAI
PARK

Jerry McLain

PHOENIX AT NIGHT
FROM SOUTH MOUNTAIN PARK LOOKOUT

Jerry McLain

Frank H. Tillotson

MIRAGE

SUPERSTITION MOUNTAIN, APACHE TRAIL

McCulloch Bros.

METEOR CRATER, NEAR WINSLOW

"PETRIFIED PUMPKIN" PATCH, NORTH OF CAMERON

Joseph Miller

THE PAINTED DESERT

"OLD FAITHFUL", THE LARGEST LOG IN
PETRIFIED FOREST NATIONAL MONUMENT

Marshall Beauchamp
ORGAN PIPE CACTUS

Tom Imler, Jr.
CHOLLA, "JUMPING" CACTU▮

SAGUARO CACTUS BLOSSOM, ARIZONA STATE FLOWE▮

Norman Wallace

YUCCA, "SPANISH BAYONET"

Max Kegle

SHIP ROCK, BELOW FREDONIA

"TOTEM POLE",
MONUMENT VALLEY

Max Kegley

to cope with red men who slipped through the forests afoot, but two generations later the first settlers of the west battled with Indians who were expert horsemen. The Indian bands swept over the hills on their fleet little ponies and wiped out emigrant wagon trains—thus, incidentally, setting free more horses of varied breeds to roam at will.

It was not until the Mormons moved into their empire in Utah that the white men fully realized how extensive were the herds that thundered across the valleys. The Mormons in northern Arizona saw Indian mounts that were small and unkempt, often not weighing more than 800 pounds. But these ponies had great endurance and could carry 180-pound braves for many hours in country that exhausted the heavier horses of the white men.

Big cow outfits moved into the virgin grasslands of Arizona and increased their *remudas* from the wild horse herds. From the Indians they learned that the best way to capture the horses was to run them down. Cowboys worked in relays to keep the wild animals moving day in and day out over many miles of territory, changing mounts frequently so that their own anmials would not be killed by the pace the rugged mustangs set. The cowboys worked through long shifts and finally found it possible to haze entire herds into corrals, where the best horses were cut out from the exhausted band. Because the range riders, with their love for horses, were reluctant to kill the inferior animals, these were turned loose to run the range again.

In dry country it was much simpler to build a fence around faraway water holes and await the arrival of the animals. Because the odor of man is a danger signal for horses, at times the trappers had to stay away from the corral for several days until the wind carried off their scent. The horses entered the trap through a gate that could not be opened from the inside.

The wild stallions and their mares lived and fought with the wolves and panthers, but man on foot terrified them. Sometimes the horses would turn and run recklessly against the corral or pasture fence, often smashing the fence and escaping to the range once more. Entire herds have been known to stampede, breaking barbwire fences by sheer weight of numbers, leaving behind a few dead and torn mustangs, the first to hit the barrier. One western writer tells of a wild horse, corraled on the rim of the Grand Canyon, that chose to plunge to death over the precipice rather than await capture by a man coming toward him afoot.

In terror, the wild horse seems to lose possession of his senses and plunges ahead regardless of obstacles. But once he is caught and handled, he soon loses his fear of human beings. One of the quickest ways to gentle a wild horse is to feed him.

In the summer of 1927 a wild horse movie was taken in Arizona.

Local punchers were paid a dollar a head for each horse they brought in. More than a thousand wild horses were gathered in a big corral and for a week were fed and watered. One scene called for a stampede of the entire herd, but the wild horses refused to be stampeded. By some chance two Shetland ponies had been penned with the bunch, and when the corral gates were opened the Shetlands came out in the lead! The director was the wildest thing on the lot.

The stallion must fight for life, mates, and herd leadership. He is also the guardian, directing the band to water by running behind his mares, nipping the flanks of any who would turn from the desired course. It is the stallion who keeps watch until his band has watered out. Only then will the leader drink. At any sign of danger he breaks the mares into flight, and takes the lead in headlong flight for some refuge he knows in mountain or valley.

The day always comes when the leader's place is challenged by some stallion of a smaller band that wants more mares, or by a young stud that does not yet possess mates. Then there is no flight but a battle which the mares watch with interest. They are willing to belong to the stallion that survives the kicking, biting, and striking bloody encounters that sometimes end in death. Because leadership passes by might from stallion to stallion, the rulers are not usually the glossy-coated and beautiful animals sometimes seen posing on bluffs, but more often are scraggy and battle-scarred old veterans of countless battles. At times hunters find a youngster in command of a band, and often—though this is disputed by some men who profess to know wild horses—a wise old mare actually directs the movement of the herd and is its watchman, relinquishing only the breeding rights to a stallion. The females, as well as the males, can and do fight chiefly to protect the colts from wolves and panthers.

Sometimes the wild horses welcome the gelded cow horses that stray into their herd from a near-by ranch. But more often the stud drives the visitors away. It is not uncommon to see a gelding following at the outskirts of a wild herd and giving affection and motherly care to a spindle-legged colt.

The thousands of wild horses that roamed the valleys have ruined much of the forage for stock and saddle horses and, it is also charged, have ruined waterholes and polluted water by playing in the streams. Cattlemen and speculators have carried on a relentless warfare against them. Driven together in huge roundups, the best horses are broken and shipped away as saddle mounts. Many went to the British Government for use of soldiers in Africa during the Boer War. The unsatisfactory, the smallest, and the old horses are killed for dog and chicken feed—hence the term "chicken horses," used in many localities. Undersized and often underfed, these light-bodied wild horses still possess remarkable endurance and can travel many miles in a day. But their number has grown pitiably small, and they have been driven into mountains where grass is sparse and springs are few. So starved have they been in recent years that many horse hunters swear by all that is holy that wild horses have changed their food habits, that today they will ignore oats and alfalfa hay for the dry range grass and browse that is their steady diet. The hunted wild beasts can live on scanty rations, going for days at a time without a mouthful; still more remarkable, lack of water for one to three days seems no great hardship. After longer periods without water they sometimes become frantic. They have been seen, after a long run to a water hole, pawing viciously into dried ground, digging and churning the earth to get water.

Driven hard across land where feed is scarce, inbred with inferior animals, and with the best blood of the range cut out, the bands of wild horses have become weakened and subject to disease. Many are found, clean-picked skeletons, in lonely spots far from water and forage. In the hot months blowfly eggs laid in scratches on their hides torture them and often result in death. In summer hunters drive them from the high mountains to the barren lands below. When blizzards blow in winter the horses are forced to remain on the high mesas, away from the valleys where cowboys would run them down. It is estimated that fifty thousand wild horses still live in the north and northeastern sections of Arizona, hunted and frightened. They are totally without the glamour the movies have given them for there are no currycombs in the wild country to remove dried blood, burrs, and thorns.

Only the Indians are vitally interested in the preservation of wild horses. They want to be able to capture the best for mounts and to sell others for a few dollars, with which to buy a bright velvet jacket or a silver-mounted bridle. Then, too, the Navajo have no objection to horse stew. A few nature lovers also seek to prevent the extermination of the horses but with little success. Hunters, disease, hardship, and the demands of cattlemen and sheep-raisers are powerful forces allied against the once thundering herds.

THE ARIZONA COWBOY AND HIS SADDLE

In "Wild West" fiction and films the Arizona cowboy moves in an aura of frontier romance, his six-shooter constantly flashing from its low-slung holster to deal justice to some double-crosser. A reckless, devil-may-care individual who is ready for trouble, even looking for it, his advent into town is usually heralded by pistol shots and the splintering of glass.

The cowboy is and always has been a colorful figure in real life as well as in the realm of imagination. But the veil of romance in which he has become enveloped through exaggerated characterization, is the principal reason why visitors to Arizona are disappointed by their first sight of a real cowboy. With reference to the cowboy of even forty years ago, the conventional characterization of story, screen, and stage is far from the truth.

There were those in the territory in the eighties who would fire a few shots or let out a few wild yells as they rode into town after a two months' stay on the range; and sometimes a cowboy a bit the merrier for alcohol would ride his horse through the swinging doors of a saloon and order drinks for the house. The history of the cattle industry in Arizona is frequently illuminated by flashes of gunplay. One particularly bloody page has to do with the Tewksbury-Graham feud, the famous Pleasant Valley war, in which at least nineteen men were killed in a range quarrel. Cattle thieves and marauding Apaches also were often the cause of warfare.

But such things were the exception rather than the rule even in the 1880's. Quarrels that fifty years ago might have been shot out on ranch or range are now settled prosaically in the courts. And when the Arizona cowboy comes to town today, he is noticeable for his high-heeled boots and big hat, or perhaps for his peculiar walk, his slightly-stooped shoulder, and the squint in his eyes resulting from years of looking into the sun.

For the most part the life of an Arizona cowboy today consists of hard outdoor labor under conditions only partly civilized. He is up long before the sun rises and works until dark. He is his own black-smith, doctor, tailor, and sometimes cook. Nearly all his day is spent in the saddle, with intervals of branding calves and dosing cattle for every sort of sickness. He must endure blazing heat in summer, snow and cold rain in winter. His holidays are few and far apart—the Fourth of July and Christmas. His pay will run from $30 to $75 a month with "chuck"; or he may simply sweat, that is, work for bed and grub. His food will not vary much; plain grub and lots of it—beef, potatoes, beans, sourdough biscuits with "lick" (syrup). His big meals come in the morning and in the evening when he gets in from riding.

After supper the cowboy enjoys his only leisure time on work days. Then the bunch will sit around the fire swapping stories and smoking cigarettes. If the boss is away they may play cards; but since it encourages late hours and is sometimes the cause of serious quarrels, card playing is frowned upon in most cowcamps.

In a roundup the punchers ride out on the range to bring in the scattered herd for shipping, and to brand new calves. The chuck wagon goes along if the country is not too rough, otherwise the kitchen is packed-in on horseback; and in either case that usually salty individual, the range cook, accompanies the outfit. Until the roundup is finished, the cowboy lives out-of-doors, sleeping on the ground in a bed-roll.

Cowboys are seldom tophands in all departments of the range business. Some can handle horses expertly but are not so good with cattle; others know every steer in a herd but cannot break a horse. So most cowboys are either "peelers," who specialize in breaking horses, or punchers, who spend most of their time with the cattle. In addition to these, there is the wrangler, an inexperienced hand who takes care of the *remuda,* or herd of saddle horses and pack stock.

Usually, the peeler gets better pay than the puncher, but the physical strain is so great that few peelers last more than ten years in riding unbroken horses. Since the cowpony is an essential factor in the cattle business, it is important that the peeler know his work. He must be able to subdue a horse sufficiently for safety and dependability without breaking the animal's spirit.

For every cowboy who is unnecessarily cruel to a horse, there are five who will whip the man for his brutality. Cowboys swear that a well-broken horse usually knows more than the man riding him. Strong and enduring, the cowpony may be trained for special work such as roping and cutting animals from the herd, or may be developed into an "all-round cow hoss." These animals are quick to realize what is wanted and need little encouragement. They know what to do and are almost human in their disgust with a rider who does his work poorly.

Most of the early Arizona "cowpokes" came from Texas, and the equipment and clothing of their present-day successors are Texan in character, having little in common with the ornate regalia of the California *vaquero.* The Arizona cowboy uses a hemp rope rather than a braided rawhide *riata,* and his saddle is of the "double-rigged" type with two cinch-straps, instead of the center-fire with a single cinch-strap. His costume consists of high-heeled boots, chaps, big hat, shirt, blue Levi overalls in summer and Oregon breeches in winter. When he goes to town he leaves the chaps at home. He pays more for his hat and his boots than for any other articles of clothing. He usually carries a pistol in a holster or tucked inside his belt or pocket, and often when on the range a short-barreled carbine as a saddlegun to protect the stock against predatory animals.

The colorful speech of the present-day cowboy is a mixture of hybrid Spanish and English shaped to his own purposes. Many of his songs were composed during night guard on the range, when the puncher sang so that his cattle would know where he was and would not be "spooked" by his sudden appearances as he rode among them.

In camp the punchers play practical jokes on each other which may be rather rough and dangerous—especially if the cook, who somehow never learns to appreciate the cowpoke's brand of humor, is the victim. They may get together with ranchers' families for dances and parties. That distinctively western entertainment, the rodeo, was originally an exhibition of cowboy skill in the regular activities of cattle ranch and range. But today it is largely commercialized and many of its features are of the circus type, remote from the cowpuncher's everyday life. While most professional rodeo performers were once punchers, they have long been unaccustomed to routine ranch duties. The first public rodeo in the United States was held at Prescott in 1888, and Prescott's rodeo has been an annual event ever since.

Although the gun-slinging, wild-eyed type of western cowboy has passed—if, indeed, he ever existed as a representative type—the quiet and industrious cowboy is still with us and will be as long as beef is eaten. He needs no notched guns and daredevil deeds to make him a colorful figure; his life of hard work and outdoor living contains sufficient excitement and danger. The part played by the early cowboy in the development of the new southwest, when less hardy men would have failed, is history; and the picturesque traditions that he established are worthily maintained by the cowhand of today.

The Western Saddle: The Spanish-Mexican saddle of early California was a thing of beauty. The quality of its material and workmanship, and especially its richness of ornamentation, determined the social status of the *caballero* who, mounted astride it, competed in feats of horsemanship. It resembled the western stock saddle used by cattlemen of today in its high, padded pommel and round-headed projecting cantle (the projection being known as "the bucking rim"). Of the Spanish-American *vaquero,* Abbe Domenick wrote: "He is content with a wretched hut for his residence—while he decorates his saddle and bridle with gold and silver ornaments."

Texas claims to be the birthplace of the modern cowboy saddle, and it is true that much of the evolution of the western saddle took place in that fenceless empire of a century ago. The elaborate, top-heavy affair of Spanish type was modified in detail and stripped of its superfluous features until it became a saddle of service, with decoration a secondary consideration.

Perhaps no other man-made device is more thoroughly adapted to the needs of its user than the western or Texas saddle. Spending the greater part of his working hours between pommel and cantle, the cowboy has fashioned his saddle to meet every requirement of his trade. Vanity, love of display, and pride of possession may account for much of the ornate frequently found in its make-up, but fundamentally it is built to stand the strain of one of the most precarious of occupations. Although primarily designed for the cattleman it has been adopted by nearly all classes of riders throughout the west, despite its apparent clumsiness and excessive weight. This is proof of its thorough practicality.

The cowboy prizes his saddle above all his other possessions. He may display interest and pride in such parts of his equipment as boots, hat, chaps, and spurs; but his saddle is the one really important consideration. His mount, due to the killing pace maintained in a day's work, is frequently changed, for in every outfit of size, each cowboy has his own string of saddle horses. But it is different with the cowboy's saddle. Where he goes it goes. He has been known to part with his boots, his bankroll, and even his best girl; but no cowboy in his sober senses would consider parting with his saddle. It is to him a badge of honor and a stamp of royalty. Take away his saddle and he is but a man; with it and his mount he is a veritable centaur. A western schoolboy when asked who Benedict Arnold was, replied: "He was a man who sold his saddle."

In making a saddle, from the shaping of the tree or frame down to the finishing touches, every detail calls for an unusual degree of skill and artistry. As a rule, the tree is made of Oregon pine, a wood noted for its lightness, elasticity, and strength. It must be carefully shaped to conform to the requirements of both rider and horse. An ill-fitting shoe may pinch, but an ill-fitting saddle may really torture.

After the tree has been tooled and shaped, the various structural parts such as cantle, seat, side-boards, pommel, and horn are attached by mortising and bolting. It is then covered with rawhide put on wet and allowed to shrink, after which several coats of waterproof varnish are applied to insure complete protection against extremes of moisture and dryness. The tree is now ready for the addition of such details as centuries of experience have demonstrated to be comfortable and useful.

First comes the building of a foundation for the seat. A strip of galvanized iron called the strainer is placed over the middle of the tree to cover the open space between the side-boards, and upon this is laid a piece of soft and thick leather shaped to the form of the rider. Next the skirts, cut from the best grade of selected hide, are attached to the tree; and these are followed by the rigging—the leather straps at the sides of the pommel, to which the girth rings are attached. Where two girths are used, a flank rigging is placed over the sideboards at the rear of the cantle.

Then comes the covering of pommel, seat, and cantle with leather, an operation calling for the highest degree of skilled workmanship. Next are attached the stirrup straps and the fenders, the latter serving to protect the rider's legs from the sweat of the horse. Then upon the under part of the skirts is glued and sewed a layer of sheepskin with the fleece side out.   Tie strings are affixed here and there; jockeys (leather pieces serving no other purpose than to trim the saddle) and tapaderos (a protection in riding through brush) are set in place; stirrups, with or without leather foot guards, are set in their straps; girths or cinches of leather, horsehair, or cowtail are attached to the tree; and with a few finishing touches the western saddle is ready for long and faithful service.

Agriculture

NEWCOMERS to Arizona often ask why more of its broad deserts and valleys are not brought under the plow. The uncultivated land, they say, must be as rich as the land that is being farmed. The answer is: lack of water. Even in prehistoric times Arizona's agriculture, and hence its population, suffered on this account. Pastoral tribes dug canals to lead water from streams to their fields, and traces of their irrigation systems constitute interesting archeological remains. Indeed, some of those canals were reconstructed and enlarged by the white pioneers who took possession of the land in the nineteenth century.

The areas where crops are produced without applying water from streams, artificial reservoirs, or wells are small and relatively insignificant. In other words agriculture in Arizona means irrigation agriculture. Of the 1,365,000 acres harvested in 1952 over ninety-five per cent was irrigated. Because of light rainfall, dry farming is confined to the higher elevations where some crops, principally beans and potatoes, will thrive.

But when water is added to rich soil under the Arizona sun, the results are astonishing. It is irrigation that makes possible the bounteous yields of cotton, alfalfa, small grains, sorghums, melons, lettuce, dates and citrus fruits for which the state is noted. "Man-made oases," they are called—the fertile farm districts known as Gila Valley, Salt River Valley, Casa Grande Valley, and Yuma Valley, and the smaller sections where persistence, ingenuity, and industry have made the desert blossom. Their total acreage is by no means inconsiderable, and their per-acre yield, both in quantity and value, is among the highest in the nation.

The irrigation farmer almost never has a crop failure. Storage and wells have almost entirely removed the hazards to which pioneer agriculture was subjected. When unregulated streams were the only source of irrigation water, freshets often washed out the crude brush dams, and fields parched while floods raced away to the sea. By the time the dams could be repaired the river or creek might have shrunk to a trickle. Except in Mormon communities held together by religious ties, the result was a more than ordinarily transient agricultural population with discouraged settlers constantly "pulling up stakes" and drifting on to regions where they hoped conditions would be less difficult and uncertain.

The Mormons were the first modern irrigators in Arizona. In the 1860's they settled the fertile areas of Mesa, Lehi, the Safford, Thatcher, and Franklin districts, and others. A fundamental idea of the Mormon Church was that its members should live by and upon the soil. In the valleys of the Gila, the Salt, the Little Colorado, and the San Pedro where the white man had previously failed, the Mormons set their stakes, cleared the land, dug ditches and dammed unruly streams.

After many discouraging attempts at irrigation, and a controversy with Mexico over the waters of the Little Colorado—finally compromised on the basis of granting three-fifths to the Mormons—a large dam known as the Slough Reservoir was built in 1886 at a cost of $200,000. It was washed out in 1903 and later rebuilt more elaborately under the name of the Lymans Project. In 1915 it was again washed out. Another $200,000 was spent but the dam failed to meet the needs of the fast-growing settlements. State aid eventually led to expenditures totaling $800,000 and a flood-resistant structure was finally built.

One of the first practical irrigation ditches constructed in Arizona carried water from the Salt River through a region between Phoenix and Tempe. As at the time no crops other than grain and forage were contemplated, only the flooding method was used. The water was released from headgates and allowed to flow out over the land. This same method is used for alfalfa and forage crops in general, and for all grain.

The beginning of pioneer agriculture in Salt River Valley is fascinating. In the sixties some pioneers were attracted here by the lush wild hay, with high prices paid for it at nearby military posts, they set up a hay camp. Later a pioneer prospector, noting the lay of the land, with water from Salt River easily available by utilizing ancient canals found here, realized its possibilities. A canal company was formed, supplies brought in, and within six months several miles of canal were completed.

Within a year crops were harvested; ranches established; the fabulous Phoenix area was born.

The other method of irrigation, used largely for cotton, fruits and vegetables, is the furrow method. This consists in releasing water through flumes, then along furrows or rills, to reach the vegetation. All grain crops are irrigated up to the time of harvest as otherwise the crops would shrivel. Care is taken not to use water too generously since much damage may be done to fruits and vegetables if irrigation is excessive. Unless the irrigation of fruits ceases at just the proper time before maturity the product will be watery and unfit. Too much water also causes damage to vegetable crops, rotting the roots and growing too much top.

It is the duty of ditch bosses, or water distributors, to measure the allotment of each water user, the miner's inch being the standard used. At the same time the individual user must see that he gets his full quota when the water comes down.

Spraying the fruit trees and vegetables crops, required as a precaution against scale, grasshoppers and other bug menace, must be done between those periods when water is due to come down the flumes, as the water is released promptly on schedule and may not be deferred. At such times all other work ceases until the water has passed. Spraying and tree pruning are not long delayed, however, as the porous soil and the sun's intense heat soon absorb and evaporate the moisture, the soil hardens, and the work of actual cultivation may proceed.

Gophers and other ground rodents were a constant menace to an irrigation system, often destroying ditches and flumes by drilling holes and passages under the ditch banks. For this reason dogs and cats were allowed to overrun the country and poison was also used in the campaign against the rodents. However these menaces have been reduced to a minimum in Arizona by the constant vigilance of those who cultivate the land.

Now the floods that were once a menace are impounded in immense reservoirs or lakes and permanent concrete diversion dams have been constructed. Salt River and Casa Grande valleys are dotted with pumps that augment the gravity water supply and also control the underground water table, which under constant irrigation may rise and drown out the roots of plants. Electricity to operate these pumps is generated as the stored water is released from reservoirs. On some years more than half of the irrigation water for the entire state is pumped. The era of pump development began after World War I and reached its height in 1953.

In the Arizona climate assured water means assured production. This certainty has given the state a stable agriculture and has made a tremendous difference in the attitude of its farmers. No longer subject to the vagaries of floods and rainfall, they are permanent citizens instead of being (as was all too often the case in earlier times) temporary dwellers whose main ambition was to get away. Electrified farms, radios, automobiles and good roads that make it possible to reach the centers of population in a short time, have all added to their contentment and their pride in the state they call home.

By 1930 practically all the gravity water in Arizona, except of the Colorado River, had been put to beneficial use. In 1936 the State Planning Board reported that the only possible expansion of agricultural acreage lay in making use of Colorado River water. A start has been made in this direction by a system now under way to serve the 580,000-acre Gila project near Yuma; and by the construction of the Headgate Rock Project to irrigate 80,000 acres of the Colorado River Indian Reservation near Parker.

Wells have added greatly to the area of crop land yet the underground water within economical pumping distance is definitely limited, and at the present time is lowering alarmingly. This is the answer to the question of why more of Arizona's deserts are not supporting happy farm families such as are found in the irrigated districts. It should also be explained to the uninitiated that the rights to water are well protected by laws under the doctrine of "prior appropriation." Water belongs to the land on which it is first applied, and no more may be applied than is reasonably necessary to produce maximum crops.

Before the completion in 1911 of the Roosevelt Dam, Salt River Valley's first storage dam, Arizona's place in national agriculture was small indeed. With a dependable water supply farmers began to realize the possibilities of their soil and subtropical climate. The Yuma reclamation project—not involving water storage, since there was always plenty in the Colorado—was finished in 1912. Coolidge Dam, impounding the Gila for Casa Grande Valley, was dedicated in 1929; the Bartlett Dam on the Verde River, completed in 1939, has increased water storage for the Salt River Project. Each of these stabilized the area served, brought large increases in population and production, made modern cities of what had been frontier towns, and brought new towns into existence. Crops that had been grown only for local or state consumption were soon moving by rail to markets outside Arizona. New crops were introduced.

With the decline of copper mining for several years after 1930, agriculture took first place among Arizona's economic activities both in value of product and in percentage of total taxes paid. Since 1935 mining production has been substantially increased and in good years again tops the value of agricultural products. However, as agriculture is no longer very far behind mining in annual cash value of products and employs a much larger percentage of the state's population, its economic importance is generally considered to be equal to that of any other basic Arizona industry.

In 1953 the cash income from Arizona farm and ranch production was $370 million, $40 million less than 1952. The commodities marketed and their value for 1953 were as follows: cotton lint and cottonseed, $200,000,000; cattle and calves, $60,000,000; lettuce and other vegetable crops, $45,000,000; commercial hay and alfalfa seed, $22,000,000; dairy products, $15,000,000; sheep, lambs and wool, $5,000,000; eggs, chickens and turkeys, $5,000,000; citrus fruits, $5,000,-000; miscellaneous crops, livestock and livestock products, $13,000,000.

Though less than two per cent of Arizona's seventy-two million acres are cultivated, eighty-five per cent produces good natural pasturage. Beef production is consequently one of Arizona's major industries, and has been important since the Spanish missionaries brought to the territory some of the first herds ever seen in what is now the United States. The climate in general is so mild that cattle owners do not have to winter feed; the practice is to graze livestock on the range throughout the year. Cost of production is therefore lower than in sections where it is necessary to supplement free grazing with harvested feeds.

In the days of the Spaniards longhorn cattle roamed at will over a fenceless wilderness. The *vaquero* rode with a running iron (an all-purpose branding iron) on his saddle. Beef for local consumption was abundant and cheap; only the hides and tallow could be marketed "outside." After the Civil War Americans began to drift great herds into Arizona, mostly from Texas, and they found markets at the military posts and the mining camps. By the time the railroad came, in the early 1880's, the industry had attained such size that cattle were available for shipment to other sections.

Range land adjacent to points of water supply was, of course, the most desirable, and the early outfits were situated along streams or near springs and natural tanks. Pastures were unknown; corrals and ranch houses were few; cattle were held constantly in day and night herds from the time a roundup started until they were delivered at the railroad. Although cattle were cheap and the annual loss of a few hundred was not a serious matter, conditions demanded men of the most rugged type and daring nature for range work. The cowboy had to be *mucho hombre,* literally much man, versatile and adaptable; and the operator of an outfit had to be pretty much of a he-man to carry on his business.

Anything that had four feet and horns was a cow. No attention was paid at first to quality of beef produced, or to breeding animals especially adapted to the conditions under which they must live. Some progressive cowmen, under the stress of competition, finally began to buy shorthorn bulls and then Herefords. Eventually the short, blocky Hereford became the predominant breed through its ability to withstand hardships in bad seasons and its size, and because it "dresses out" the greatest quantity of meat in proportion to total weight.

In the mid-nineties it became evident that the limit of stocking had been reached on the range land then in use. This brought about an effort to open new grazing lands through the development of water in surface tanks and wells. Cattlemen already in business then began to control their ranges through rights to the more important watering places, and in general to protect themselves against the invasion of newcomers. This they accomplished by homesteading, obtaining control of land through water rights, and acquiring title by filing scrip purchased from railroads. Whenever possible a cattleman fenced his holdings.

In 1906 the United States Forest Service began to establish recognized grazing rights on specified areas. When Arizona was admitted to the Union in 1912 it was granted 10,685,000 acres of public land, and as practically all this soil was suited only to grazing, it was leased to stockmen and fenced by them. Another chapter in land control was written with enactment of the Taylor Grazing Act, 1934, which laid the groundwork for erosion control and rehabilitation of Federal lands. Four grazing districts have been established with a gross area of more than 18,000,000 acres.

Roundup time on the range is a season of great activity, much of it still picturesque despite the passing of free range and all that went with it. Many producers work their cattle twice a year. It is not uncommon for those operating in the same vicinity to combine their forces into one rodeo outfit. When this is done the interests of each one—branding, earmarking, working the cattle back to their own—are looked after by all.

Arizona ranges are primarily breeding ranges where the cows live and raise their calves. Little "grass beef" is marketed. The increase, baby-beef calves or yearlings, is driven or shipped to the farms of Salt River, Casa Grande, and Yuma valleys, to be fed out for market. If thin, they may be placed on pasture for a time; if in fair condition they go directly to the feed lots for 90 to 120 days. About one fourth of the cattle raised in Arizona is slaughtered in the state; though many thousand head are shipped out, many thousand are shipped in. The traffic in and out of Arizona is by rail and truck. The Arizona Livestock Sanitary Board reported an outward movement of 395,000 head in 1952, and 97,000 head slaughtered within the state, and 225,000 head shipped in. Net marketing of Arizona-produced cattle for 1952 was 267,000, though in 1938 the number net marketed was 418,000 head.

The sheep industry is also dependent on the range. Sheep-raising first came to Arizona from Spain, by way of New Mexico. Because of climatic conditions it was at first largely confined to the Hopi and Navajo Indians of the north, and the Navajo still own approximately half the sheep in Arizona. The sheep of non-Indian owners have always been run in large units, and the little fellow has never played a very important role in this industry. Since 1930 there has been a marked tendency toward consolidation of flocks under corporation ownership.

The Bureau of Agricultural Economics estimates about 430,000 sheep in Arizona in January 1953. A considerable number of these are owned by the Navajo and range on their reservation. The balance graze on the national forests in summer and are driven south to the valleys at the beginning of winter. It is estimated that 100,000 sheep are pastured in the Salt River Valley, every winter, several thousand more in Casa Grande Valley, and some in Yuma Valley. Trainloads of spring lambs are shipped out to the eastern markets, principally in midwestern large cities. Arizona fat lambs are the earliest in the United States and usually bring profitable prices.

More than 2,300,000 pounds of wool were produced in Arizona, in 1952. Some came from Indian reservations. Indian sheep, first third of the 20th Century, were of poor quality and yielded average fleece of less than 4 pounds yearly, while average fleece from non-Indian owned sheep was over 8 pounds.

While both cattle industry and sheep industry are primarily based on range grass, the products of the irrigated farm districts are also important to them. In 1952 the estimated value of hay feed by meat producers to their stock was $7,000,000 and of grains $3,000,000; this was, of course, exclusive of cash income from these commodities.

The old standby of the Arizona farmer is alfalfa. It produces little pasture or hay without plenty of water, but is drought-resistant to a high degree; a stand is not killed out though it may be without water for months or even years. In no important farm section of Arizona are winter temperatures severe enough to affect alfalfa. When water is abundant, from five to eight crops are cut annually, and a ton to the acre at each mowing is not unusual. In their search for water, alfalfa roots go to incredible depths, open and aerate the soil, and prepare it for perfect moisture penetration. A common procedure is to grow alfalfa on a piece of land for three or more years, then plow it up and grow such soil-depleting crops as cotton, sorghum, small grains, melons, and vegetables for an approximately equal period.

With adequate water, Salt River Valley was soon shipping baled alfalfa hay as far away as New York, although the best markets were found on the Pacific Coast and in the Midwest. Yuma Valley and then Casa Grande Valley began to do the same. Gila Valley has long been noted for the fine quality of its alfalfa hay. Yuma and Buckeye valleys found that they could grow alfalfa seed that often commanded a premium.

Next in importance to alfalfa as a forage crop is the sorghum group, including hegari and milo maize. Hegari is especially popular for grain, for pasturage, and for silage. Thousands upon thousands of tons are chopped and packed in pit silos, which are merely holes scraped into the ground. A pit silo near Mesa is said to be the largest in the world. It is on a large "feeder ranch" of which dozens are found in Salt River, Casa Grande, and Yuma valleys. At these ranches range cattle from within the state, from Mexico, and occasionally from other states are fattened on alfalfa hay, silage, and cottonseed cake for Arizona and Los Angeles slaughterhouses. Winter pasturing of sheep also consumes much of the forage.

Arizona's main cash crop is cotton. First grown commercially in 1912, it became important by 1917 when the World War brought on a cotton boom. Originally Arizona grew only American-Egyptian long staple cotton—first the Yuma variety and later an improved selection called Pima, with lint averaging one and nine-sixteenth inches in length. The lint is extra fine and strong, with many other qualities that set it apart from ordinary cotton.

In 1953 the principal cotton was an Upland strain developed by the Arizona Agricultural Experiment Station, called Arizona 44. The average length is near one and one-sixteenth inches. During World War I, American-Egyptian sold for one dollar a pound. Salt River Valley farmers went Pima crazy. Every possible acre was planted to cotton. Most of the valley's 60,000 dairy cows were sold. Again in World War II the demand for production of American-Egyptian cotton rose. A 1953 crop of 990,000 bales short-staple and 33,000 bales long-staple cotton was indicated as of January 15, 1954.

In 1937 Arizona grew 268,000 bales of short-staple cotton on 261-000 acres in five counties, and 12,000 bales of Pima on 21,000 acres in Casa Grande and Salt River valleys. The Pima growers began making an effort to advertise the quality of Pima fabrics for fine shirtings and dress goods, and thereby increase the demand for their lint, all of which is taken by domestic spinners. From ninety to ninety-five per cent of the short-staple production had been exported to foreign countries, principally Japan.

In 1938 and 1939 the cotton situation was considered the most serious part of the Arizona farm problem. The supply of American cotton for 1938-1939 reached an all-time peak; cotton exports decreased rayon competition was effecting the domestic market, and prices were low. Arizona farmers consequently reduced their 1938 short staple acreage to forty-four per cent under the 1937 acreage, and substituted alfalfa, flax, American-Egyptian cotton, and other products, or did not seed their land at all. The cash income from Arizona cotton was nearly 200 million dollars in 1952, and only eleven million in 1938.

Gins are scattered through all the agricultural districts where cotton is grown, and cotton-oil mills are located at strategic points. The oil is shipped to Los Angeles and other manufacturing cities; the residual cake or meal brings good prices as stock feed.

Cantaloupes and lettuce are among the crops that an assured water supply made possible. Production of both was started soon after completion of the Roosevelt Dam, but did not gain full momentum until the 1920's. From early December until late April much of the head lettuce on American and Canadian tables comes from Yuma and Salt River valleys. In 1952 winter lettuce at Yuma produced 2,900,000 crates on 14,000 acres; early spring lettuce in the Salt River Valley produced a little more than 2,000,000 crates on 14,000 acres; and late fall lettuce in the Salt River Valley produced 2,800,000 crates on 14,000 acres.

The Arizona cantaloupe crop is important. In 1952, 3,400,000 crates were produced on about 23,000 acres. In recent years carrots have become of considerable importance. In 1952, 2,700,000 bushels were produced on 6,800 acres. Cantaloupe shipments begin at Yuma in the latter part of May and end in the Salt River Valley eight or ten weeks later.

Arizona is famous also for its citrus and dates which come from Maricopa and Yuma counties. The first commercial orange grove was planted in 1891 at Ingleside, northeast of Phoenix. Before the end of the century it had been demonstrated that soil and climatic conditions approached the ideal for both grapefruit and oranges. Sunshine and freedom from frost combined to produce a high sugar content and a superior flavor. Another great advantage was the absence of insects and scales, the control of which in other citrus regions forces growers to make heavy outlays. No fruit is admitted to Arizona without inspection, and no nursery stock at all. For many years every citrus tree planted in Arizona, every bud used, has been propagated within the state.

With no pests to fight, no grove heating necessary, cheap water and high average production, costs of citrus growing in Arizona have always been held to a low level.

Heavy planting of groves began in 1930, when a series of profitable seasons created an unprecedented demand for suitable land and young trees.

The University of Arizona's publication *Arizona Agriculture* reported, 1952, 20,000 acres of citrus in Arizona: oranges, Maricopa county, 9,000 acres; oranges, Yuma county, 450 acres; grapefruit, Maricopa county, 7,500 acres; grapefruit, Yuma county, 1,200 acres; lemons,

Maricopa county, 1,000 acres; lemons, Yuma county, 400 acres. Arizona's 1951-52 main citrus crop production was about 2,140,000 boxes of grapefruit, and 730,000 boxes of oranges, considerably below normal. A principal reason for the smaller crop was the cyclical nature of citrus production. Valencias constituted one-half of Arizona's orange crop. Lemon production continues to gain with extensive new plantings on the Yuma Mesa.

Perhaps Arizona's most picturesque crop is dates. Commercial date production is confined to Yuma and Maricopa counties, although there is plenty of irrigated land elsewhere in the state that is excellent for the purpose. Palms are much less susceptible to cold than citrus trees. Most of the gardens are small, but some growers have as many as fifteen or twenty acres. Varieties grown are "soft dates," very different in texture and flavor from imported pressed dates. Packed in attractive containers, they bring fancy prices locally and in most of the larger cities of the United States where they are being shipped to expanding markets from year to year as their fame spreads.

Superb apples and peaches are grown in the mountain valleys, but the orchards are so widely scattered and many of them are so far from transportation facilities that little of the fruit is sold outside the state. In the warm southern districts, deciduous fruits are produced for local consumption only, with the exception of seedless grapes. About 2,800 tons of grapes were shipped from Arizona in 1952 in an early July "spot" when few if any grapes are moving from other producing areas. They had a value of more than $600,000.

Both dairying and poultry production are unstressed enterprises in Arizona, although feed is cheap and the climate is such that a minimum of housing and equipment is required. The state produced only a little of all the butter and cheese it consumes and only part of the poultry and eggs. One reason for this is that the products of other states within trucking distance are often dumped upon the Arizona markets with demoralizing effect. Another is that a large percentage of the Arizona farm population originated in areas where the one-crop system predominates, and therefore is not of a temperament to "fool with cows and chickens."

The unprecedented advance of farming in Arizona in the decade ended with 1953 was the result of a combination of forces according to Dr. George W. Barr, Head of the Department of Agricultural Economics, University of Arizona. He points out: "In this period the farmers took advantage of findings of many years of research which gave them more productive varieties, better insect control, improved water penetration, and more and larger machines precisely adapted to their needs. In the later years of this decade, Arizona became the fifth State of the Union in cotton production and for several years first in yield per acre."

Machine farming has been adopted widely in Arizona, and this has an inevitable effect of increasing the size of the farm unit and decreasing the number of owner-operators. To farm most efficiently, a farmer must have tractors and other expensive equipment. Once he has acquired such equipment, he naturally wants to expand his acreage sufficiently to keep it busy and reduce his overhead; so he is in the market to buy or lease more ground.

The harvesting of Arizona's cotton crop constitutes a gigantic task. Aside from the 50,000 laborers employed to pick the 1952 crop, a force of nearly 2,000 mechanical pickers was in operation. Approximately 500 of these mechanical pickers were custom operators and during the first half of the season the supply of custom machines was larger than the demand.

The land area of Arizona is reported by the Census of 1950 as 72,688,000 acres of which 55 per cent is reported to be land in farms which farms number 10,412. Of course these units which the census calls farms include many very large cattle ranches where a section of land supports very few cattle. Actually, in 1942, there were only 1,300,000 acres irrigated. The latter constituted practically the only land where sufficient water was available to grow crops.

Farmer's selling, buying and service associations are not numerous. For the 1935-36 marketing season there were thirteen listed, with a membership of 1,240, doing an estimated business of $1,340,000.

Arizona has an excellent agricultural extension service, functioning as a part of the University of Arizona College of Agriculture. In 1952 all counties but two had agricultural agents or farm advisers. Specialists of the extension service and college are constantly traveling through the farm districts, assisting farmers to solve their problems of irrigation and culture, and working toward a general betterment of crops and animals. A crop improvement association, formed in June 1933 at Yuma, encourages the production and planting of pure seed and aids in introducing better varieties. Its work has materially raised the quality and per-acre volume of crops. It is a non-profit farmer's organization.

The College of Agriculture maintains experimental farms in the Salt River Valley, in Yuma county, in Pima county and in Graham county. Dedicated in September 1953 was a modern research building located on the University's College of Agriculture 160-acre farm west of Mesa. This new facility provides laboratories and offices where the intricate problems of irrigation farming can be solved.

From the facts and statistics presented in this essay, it will become abundantly apparent that, despite large as yet uncultivated areas, Arizona is one of the most productive regions in our country, speaking from the agriculturist's point of view. Visitors to the State, especially those

from the well-watered eastern seaboard, who at first glance are struck
by the great expanses of uncultivated lands, will soon be convinced as
they travel about, of the State's extraordinary fertility.

Industry, Commerce, and Labor

THE PEOPLE of Arizona rattle off a number of words beginning with "C" to summarize their economic life—"cotton, cattle, copper, citrus and climate"—thus indicating that the state's wealth is based on agriculture, mining, and the tourist trade. To these should be added the lumber and manufacturing industries.

Pioneers came to Arizona to find metals; some of them drove cattle and sheep into the tall grass, and began to plant in the fertile valleys. Since then, agriculture and mining have developed together; forts, towns, dams, railroads, and highways have been built to serve them. Gradually, as transportation and accommodations for visitors improved, the influx of part-year residents, vacationists, and health-seekers assumed large proportions. The tourist trade is comparatively new, but it doubled during the last decade while the value of mining production has more than doubled.

Nevertheless, the total value of all minerals mined during the state's history is still much greater than the aggregate income from any other one source. Since 1858 Arizona mines have produced more than three billion dollars worth of metals, of which nearly 85 per cent was copper. Gold accounts for five per cent, silver for four per cent, and the small remainder is made up of lead, zinc, manganese, tungsten, and molybdenum. Considerable uranium is now being mined in Arizona.

Other mineral deposits are known to exist in the state, but most of them have little present commercial value. The one exception is in the United States. Because of its long fiber and iron-free quality, Arizona asbestos is valuable to the electrical appliance industries.

Gold and silver were the first metals mined extensively in Arizona, and the search for them was a major factor in the territory's development. The Spaniard, Antonio de Espejo, conducted the first recorded gold and silver prospecting trip into what is now Arizona in 1582. On the Bill Williams Fork, west of the site of Prescott, he found silver ore so close to the surface it could be dug by hand. These deposits were rediscovered by Juan de Onate, another Spanish explorer, early in the seventeenth century, but apparently no mining resulted from either expedition.

Although little is known about early Spanish and Mexican mining in the state, most of it appears to have been for silver in the south, near the missions established by Father Eusebio Francisco Kino from 1692 until his death in 1711. There are many legends about the silver which the mission padres are said to have taken from the mountains around Tucson; one of them is that the altar of San Xavier Mission was once adorned with silver objects worth $60,000. Americans also located and worked some silver mines near Tucson and Tubac soon after the United States acquired the territory in 1853. The Cerro Colorado Mine, forty miles southwest of Tucson, was one of the extensive producers.

The first gold rush started in 1858 when rich placers were found near the Colorado River at Gila City. A few years later the placer mines at La Paz and Ehrenberg in central Yuma County were discovered, and at about the same time other placer fields were worked in central Arizona at Rich Hill, Lynx Creek, and Hassayampa in the Bradshaw Mountains of Yavapai County. Important lode gold mines were also developed at this time near Prescott and Wickenburg, the Vulture probably being the richest.

During the Civil War, the territory was often without troops, and the people were usually too busy defending themselves from Apache and outlaws to do any prospecting. Post-Civil War conditions, among them the relatively low value of gold resulting from high commodity prices, turned the prospectors' interest to silver. In 1876, the Silver King, a highly productive mine, was located near the present town of Superior, and the silver deposits in the vicinity of Globe caused a stampede across the Apache Indian reservation. Three years later the Tombstone district in southern Arizona was an even greater bonanza. However, the silver boom was unable to survive the deflation period, 1884-1893, which again made gold the most profitable metal. Most of the silver deposits had thinned out, silver was demonetized in 1893, and miners once more turned their attention to gold. Only Tombstone was able to return to silver mining for a few years after 1900.

the asbestos found in Gila County, the principal source of this mineral

In the final decade of the nineteenth century, Arizona had the last gold-mining revival it was to see until the depression of 1929. In the nineties, new gold deposits were discovered in Yuma and Yavapai counties; the Congress and Octave mines in Date Creek and Weaver Mountains, and the King of Arizona, Fortuna, and Harqua Hala in the Yuma County desert, all enriched their owners. The Mammoth, north of Tucson, also became important at this time. New milling methods and development of the cyanide process aided production in the new mines as well as in the old.

But when commodity prices rose once more near the end of the century, copper became the dominant metal of the state's mining industry. The only exclusively gold-producing district that has remained more or less constant in production is Oatman, in the northwestern part of the state; extensive development took place here after output was curtailed in most of the older lode gold mines. Nevertheless, Arizona's production of gold and silver increased with the development of the large copper mines, due to the fact that many copper ores contain large amounts of the precious metals. Ores of copper, lead and zinc have yielded the greater portion of the silver since 1903, and most of the gold since 1923.

The increase in the price of gold in 1933, plus depression conditions and their effect on copper, resulted in a renewed interest in the gold fields and prospecting. However, while production from these sources has increased, lode gold mining is still a minor industry in Arizona, and placer mining is no longer considered even mildly profitable by most miners.

Arizona's deposits of copper were developed during the decades when the consumption of electricity was doubling every few years. The world demand for copper, though experiencing periodic slumps, seemed almost unlimited following 1880. During this period Arizona's annual production grew from 800,000 pounds valued at $90,000 in 1874 to the peak of 831,740,000 pounds valued at $201,281,000 in 1951.

Copper is distributed among seven large districts and eleven or more smaller ones. The major copper-producing districts have been Globe-Miami, Warren-Bisbee, Clifton-Morenci, Ajo, Jerome, Ray, and Superior. From these districts two very different grades of ores have been mined in great quantities and at a large profit: high-grade deposits of from 5 to over 20 per cent copper; and later, the low-grade disseminated or porphyry ores averaging less than one per cent.

Equally important are the smelters, concentrators, and leaching plants that make the ore into crude copper to be shipped to other states for refining. Every district has always had one or more costly reduction plants managed by metallurgical experts, for the profits of mining have depended, in the last analysis, on getting the most copper and other metals out of the ore at the least cost. The rich ore is usually smelted, and the lower-grade ores are concentrated and then smelted, or leached and deposited on plates by a process of electrolysis. Some towns with little mining of their own are important to the industry because of the mills and smelters established in them. Chief among these are Douglas near Bisbee, and Hayden near Ray. San Manuel, new copper city, will have a smelter by 1956.

Copper mining in the state began with the high-grade deposits. The first incorporated mining company in the territory was formed about 1855 to mine copper at Ajo, where a huge low-grade ore body was streaked with a small amount of 50 per cent "ruby" copper. The rich ore was mined, hauled three hundred miles across the desert, and shipped via the Gulf of California to Swansea, Wales, where it brought $360 a ton. This rich ore may have been sold at a profit, in spite of the heavy transportation costs, but there was not enough to maintain long-time production. Furthermore, the Mexican Government claimed the property as part of the land south of the Gadsden Purchase and sent 110 cavalrymen to order off the American miners. A battle followed which the Americans are said to have won, but the low-grade copper and the desert apparently defeated them in the end.

But there were other copper fields in the territory far richer than Ajo, and in the 1870's the need for copper, plus the government's partly successful attempts to pacify the Apache, encouraged mining men to take a chance on Arizona. Within a few years four of the most valuable high-grade copper districts in the world were discovered in mountainous parts of the territory: at Clifton and Morenci in the eastern part of the state; at Globe some hundred miles west of Clifton; at Bisbee in the south near the Mexican border; and at Jerome in central Arizona. Copper mines sunk in all these districts despite the problem of transportation and the menace of the Apache, each had an early period of struggle and slow growth. But by 1900 all were in full production, with millions of dollars invested in them.

Arizona copper mining has always required the investment of large initial capital, but in the early years each of the important districts had more than one company operating in it. The field was large, the risks great, and in the beginning there was room for everybody with money to buy and work a prospect. The pioneers at Clifton and Morenci, the first important district to be mined, were the Leszinsky brothers, New Mexico frontier merchants, whose company later became the Arizona Copper Company; and Captain E. D. Ward, one-time Army officer and Indian fighter, who organized the Detroit Copper Company. At Bisbee two large companies and two smaller ones survived from the many started in the area. Phelps Dodge, the eastern metal company which developed the Copper Queen under the management of Dr.

James Douglas, was the largest of these. The Calumet & Arizona organized by Captain Jim Hoatson, Michigan mine foreman, had holdings almost as valuable around Warren and Bisbee. The Globe area had one large company, the Old Dominion Mining & Smelting Company, and several smaller ones. The United Verde at Jerome was developed by Senator W. A. Clark, Butte copper magnate; and the United Verde Extension at Jerome was brought into production in later years by James S. Douglas, son of the pioneer Phelps Dodge executive.

All of these companies had periods of remarkable prosperity and paid large dividends to their stockholders, but none were as aggressive and successful as the Phelps Dodge interests. This corporation gradually acquired ownership or control of all the large companies named above and most of the smaller ones. Today it is the most powerful corporation in Arizona, one of the largest copper producers in the United States.

At the commencement of the twentieth century, it was generally believed that most of the world's high-grade deposits had been found. Both production and consumption of copper were increasing at a great rate, but the discovery of reserve supplies of rich ore was not keeping pace. Prospectors found large new deposits in western states, but these were chiefly low grade. One or two companies had experimented on a small scale with processes for concentrating this disseminated ore, and their failure to make a profit convinced the industry that low-grade bodies could not be made commercially important. However, J. C. Jackling, a young engineer who worked for years on this problem, finally found the solution in mass production. His experiment with concentrating 2 per cent ore at Bingham, Utah, was on a large scale instead of a small one, and he made it pay.

Development of the low-grade copper districts in Arizona began in 1906, when Jackling purchased the mines at Ray, east of Phoenix, for the Nevada Consolidated Copper Company. Miami, six miles west of Globe, quickly followed. A few years later the large low-grade deposits at Ajo, became the first in the state to be mined by open pit. In addition to these three new districts, low-grade deposits in the high-grade districts of Bisbee and Clifton-Morenci also became valuable.

Only very large companies undertook to develop the low-grade deposits, as the huge mills that had to be constructed, and capital equipment installed, cost a great deal, at least ten or twelve million dollars. The Ray mines are being operated by the very important Kennecott Copper Corporation, and the Inspiration Copper Company works somewhat extensive mining property at Miami and is a subsidiary of the great Anaconda Company which has the distinction of being the world's largest producer of the metal. The other Miami concern, Miami Copper Company, was financed by the Lewisohn interests. The New Cornelia property at Ajo was developed by the Calumet & Arizona Company of Bisbee and later absorbed by Phelps Dodge. Phelps Dodge also exploited low-grade deposits in Bisbee at Sacramento Pit and, in 1939, began to equip the Clifton-Morenci area for handling porphyry ores.

The copper-mining district, Superior, is a high-grade deposit west of Miami across the Pinal Mountains. Its one big producer, the Magma, has been developed since 1914 from the old Silver Queen not far from the famous Silver King. The Magma ore is very rich in copper, gold, and silver.

The Magma and the low-grade copper districts of the state came into full production during World War I when the need of the metal for war purposes shot the price up. The output of the new mines, added to that of the higher-grade developments, made Arizona the world's major source of copper. Profits and dividends exceeded the expectations of the most optimistic copper magnates, even after the Government fixed the price at thirty-five cents a pound, and production was pushed to the limit.

In 1921, however, the copper industry suddenly found itself with a large oversupply, and the price dropped to twelve and one-half cents. Production was curtailed, and the copper companies began a campaign to educate the public on the manifold new uses of copper. This campaign, coupled with the low copper price, increased the consumption of copper both in building construction and the electrical field. The mines reopened, the steady price of about fourteen cents between 1923 and 1928 permitted the companies to make a profit, and production soon became greater than during the war. The Arizona mines were not the only ones to take advantage of the prosperous years. This state's deposits were among the last in the United States to be discovered, and all the big new copper fields found after 1913 were in other countries. Gigantic supplies of South American, African, and Canadian copper flowed into the market, and Arizona mines lost their dominance in the world market.

When the depression of 1929 abruptly decreased the consumption of copper 25 per cent a year, the market became hopelessly glutted, sending copper down to less than six cents a pound by 1932. Most of the Arizona mines were shut down, or nearly so, between 1931 and 1933, but in 1934 the price went up to eight cents and production began to increase. It gained generally until 1938, when it was once more curtailed, but since World War II has maintained a high level.

Arizona maintains its place as the largest copper producer in the United States and it still has important supplies of unmined ore, though of increasingly lower grade. Of the state's copper mines, the New Cornelia at Ajo was the largest producer in 1938, followed by the Copper Queen at Bisbee, United Verde at Jerome, Miami Copper at Miami,

Inspiration at Miami, Magma at Superior, Nevada Consolidated at Ray, and last the Morenci properties.

For 1953, according to preliminary figures of the U.S. Bureau of Mines, Arizona's copper production was 784,600,000 pounds, value $224,395,600. Almost 85 per cent of this came from six open-pit mines, situated at Morenci, Ajo, Ray, Miami (Castle Dome), Inspiration, and Bagdad. Production of zinc decreased from 47,143 tons in 1952 to 27,300 in 1953, lead production from 16,520 tons to 9,300 for same period, both due to price decline.

Arizona's income from agriculture (crops and livestock) for 1952 was $410,000,000; from manufacturing (excluding smelter operations), $292,000,000; 1952-53 fiscal year income from mining was $193,176,000; estimated income from tourist trade for 1952 was $135,000,000 and is increasing at an amazing rate. While most visitors stay only a short time, a considerable number settle down for a season or longer, and many in recent years have built homes and have settled here permanently.

Northern Arizona's cool forests and mountains are popular in the summer time; and southern Arizona, warm and sunny when the north is under snow, gets the winter trade. The Phoenix and Tucson areas are the centers for visitors in winter; Flagstaff and Prescott are the summer capitals. No count is kept of the people coming to Arizona by train, plane and bus, but out-of-State automobiles (passenger cars) entering Arizona in 1952 numbered just short of 2,000,000.

Supplying visitors with the things they want is in many respects no different from supplying local needs. Travelers naturally do much roadside purchasing, and there is a surprising number of gas stations and eating places in small towns along the main highways. Interest in art and western curios, gifts, and smart vacation clothes is always evident in the city shops. But, in general, the trade of out-of-state persons has affected Arizona wholesale and retail businesses principally by adding greatly to their volume during the tourist seasons.

Of businesses dedicated exclusively to the tourist trade, the lodging of visitors is probably the most important; and of the thousands of tourist courts, fine hotels, sanitariums, and guest homes, the guest ranches are regarded as most characteristic of the state. There are more than three hundred dude ranches in Arizona. Some have large herds of ranging cattle and only a few guests, others have many guests and just enough cattle to keep the visitors entertained. Still others dispense entirely with the cows and specialize in swimming pools, tennis, and relaxation in the sun. But since guest ranching has developed more or less fortuitously from a combination of bad times in the cattle business and the eagerness of visitors to live on a real ranch, many dude ranches still retain the cowboys, horses, and atmosphere of the old-time western ranches.

Crossing Arizona by the much-used southern routes, one hardly sees enough real timber to make a box of matches. It is not easy, then, to realize that above the cactus and bunch grass sweeping up the mountain sides there are high wooded areas, and that farther north stands one of the largest unbroken stretches of western yellow pine timber in the United States.

Most of the forests of Arizona—about 20,000,000 acres—are set aside as national forest land. They are invaluable to the state for recreation and for the conservation of water, soil and game; in addition they yield between 18 and 20 million dollars in lumber annually. Practically all of this wood is taken from the 2,774,000 acres of commercial saw timber—97 per cent of all there is in Arizona—owned by the Federal and state governments, and by the Indian people who offer for sale units ranging from fifty million up to one hundred and twenty-five million board feet of ripe timber, and the standing trees are purchased by lumber companies who log and mill them.

There are more than 130 different species of trees in the State, but the saw timber stand consists mainly of four—ponderosa or western yellow pine, Douglas fir, white fir, and Engelmann spruce. Of these about 82 per cent is ponderosa pine, a soft fine-grained inexpensive wood in demand for sashes and doors, flooring, and general millwork. The largest forest of this pine, about three hundred miles long and between twenty and sixty miles wide, begins north of the Grand Canyon and extends through the central part of the state into New Mexico. The most important logging operations are concentrated in this area, with the biggest lumber mills located at Winslow, Flagstaff, McNary, and Fredonia.

The transcontinental railroad race to the Pacific gave impetus to the lumber industry in Arizona. When the Atlantic and Pacific lines were being pushed toward Flagstaff on their way to California, the company had difficulty obtaining crossties. Edward E. Ayers, who had a contract to supply the Mexican Central at El Paso with ties, offered to provide them also for the northern railroad. He established his mill at Flagstaff in 1881 and, in 1882, the first train rolled into Flagstaff over ties hewn from Arizona forests. Mr. Ayers' salesmanship may have sold these first Arizona ties, but the enduring quality of the logs soon convinced the railroads that they should be used in preference to others in the Southwest.

The success of the Ayers enterprise, which became the Arizona Lumber and Timber Company, attracted additional mills. Two other sizable companies, the Saginaw Manistee Lumber Company originally at Williams, and the Southwest Lumber Mills, Inc. at McNary, were established. More recently the Winslow Timber Company and the Nagel Lumber & Timber Company have built mills at Winslow and

Whiting Brothers have started a large operation at Fredonia. There were 37 smaller sawmills in the State in 1953.

Because of Government stewardship of Arizona forests, conservative management practices were started early in the twentieth century and have prevented "cut out and get out" treatment which had ruined many forests in other states. Lumber business expanded rapidly during the first decades of the century and boomed during World War I. Like other industries it was seriously affected by the 1929 depression but recovered in the late 1930's and made substantial contributions to national wood requirements during World War II and the post war construction period. At present cutting proceeds in Arizona forests at about maximum sustained yield capacity and the industries and communities which are dependent upon the forests for their economic well-being are prosperous.

In view of Arizona's dependence on agriculture, mining, lumber, and visitors, it may seem strange that manufacturing volume has doubled (1953) since 1950, tripled since 1946. Total output was worth $292 millions in 1952, employing over 30,000 people. Dollar volume of manufacturing in that year was about equal to agricultural crop income, and now tops mining by a wide margin in value of output as well as in employment furnished. More than half the working population is engaged in other trades and professions, such as wholesale and retail trade, building, mechanical industries, professional and semi-professional occupations, and in transportation.

Since World War II the great airfields in Arizona have added impetus to the State's economy. The air conditioning and cooling innovation had its birth in Arizona and today large manufactories furnish this equipment not only to the Southwest, but many other states in the nation.

Primarily a vacation land and a producer of raw materials, a large part of Arizona's energy has always been spent in maintaining its life lines, the channels of interstate traffic and commerce connecting it with the rest of the world.

Nevertheless, as will appear from the data given above, Arizona, in the past fifteen years, has undergone considerable economic tranformation. Its economy is no longer as one-sided as in 1940. There has been a marked trend toward industry, which will, doubtless, continue in the coming decades, and an increasing percentage of the population will be employed in manufacturing.

Labor: The Constitution of the State of Arizona incorporates not only those markedly democratic measures for which labor organizations have fought on principle, such as the initiative, referendum, and recall, but also many provisions directly concerned with the interests of workingmen. Most of these provisions—for example, strict prohibition of the use of a labor blacklist and provisions for employers' liability and workmen's compensation—were designed to regulate the practices of employers. This constitution encountered powerful opposition, both at the time it was written and during the course of ratification. Arizona nevertheless became a state under it in 1912, a clear indication that the workingmen of the territory were represented by articulate and effective organizations.

In territorial days, the largest groups of Arizona wage earners were the Mexicans, European-born immigrants, and native whites engaged in agriculture, mining, and transportation. As a general rule, the Mexicans were rated as unskilled labor, while the skilled and semi-skilled work was done by native and European whites.

The early unions were organized by the white workers to improve their standards of living and working conditions, but they made little effort to include the Mexicans. In fact, the general policy of most unions, before statehood and even later, was to discriminate against Mexicans and to bar their penetration into any trade or occupation considered desirable by the better-paid workingmen. This attitude of the white men, partly race prejudice, was primarily due to their fear that, given the opportunity, their employers would replace them with cheap Mexican labor. The employers' practice of paying lower wages to Mexicans than to white persons doing the same work was established early. It was claimed that Mexican laborers were less efficient, but it was also contended that their lower standard of living enabled them to work for less pay. Be that as it may, large numbers of Mexicans continued to migrate into the state until after the World War. As the trade unions failed to organize the lower-paid workers, the outstanding problem of labor was the existence of two competing classes of workingmen, each a threat to the aims and security of the other.

The skilled railroad workers were the earliest to organize in Arizona. The engineers and trainmen established the first lodge of the Railroad Brotherhoods in Douglas about 1900, and branched out rapidly until they represented practically every member of their craft in the territory. The Arizona Brotherhoods developed with their national organizations into well-organized and powerful unions, which the railroad operators soon recognized and bargained with. Once their strength was built up in the territory, they never lost it.

The objectives of the Brotherhoods sprang from their determination to secure safety, tenure, and increased wages; and their program to decrease the large number of accidents on the railroads brought them into active participation in Federal, and sometimes state, politics. In 1903 they succeeded in getting the Arizona Legislature to pass an act forbidding the working of trainmen for more than sixteen consecutive hours. But, generally speaking, prior to the Constitutional Convention in 1910, the railroad workers gained little through territorial legislation.

The miners' unions, which sprang more or less spontaneously out of the dangerous and semi-feudal conditions existing in most of the early mining camps, had neither the influence nor the central organization of the Railroad Brotherhoods. Most of them were connected with the Western Federation of Miners, but they functioned as independent unions. Strikes were frequent and were characterized by the militancy of the miners and the refusal of the operators to bargain with their employees in any way except as individuals.

The first local of the Western Federation of Miners was formed at Globe in 1896 in protest against a wage cut and the employment of Mexicans in the Old Dominion mine. Instead of striking, the miners presented their demands to the mine superintendent and told him to grant them or be escorted out of town. The Old Dominion owners closed the mine, but the union survived the shut-down and grew until Globe was labelled the "center of labor agitation in the Territory."

In 1903, when the territorial legislature passed a law making eight hours instead of ten a legal working day underground, the miners and operators in practically every camp disputed over whether wages were to be cut accordingly. At Clifton and Morenci the mine employees had no organization, but they rejected the operators' offer of nine hours pay for eight hours work, and went on strike. The Governor sent the rangers, and later the U.S. troops, into the district to establish order; and the strikers were restrained by court injunction from interfering with the company mines and plants.

In 1907, the Bisbee miners, who had voted the previous year not to organize a union, struck for higher wages. They were enjoined by injunction from picketing incoming trains bringing men to work in the Bisbee mines, and from using the mails to send out strike notices. They organized a local of the Western Federation of Miners at that time, but 1907 was a depression year, and the strike failed. In 1909 the union at Globe demanded an increase in shaftmen's wages, and the Old Dominion Company refused to allow the union's walking delegate (the dues collecting agent) to enter company property. The walking delegate continued his collecting at the mouth of the shaft. The Old Dominion and all other mines in the district closed down in protest and remained closed until the union removed their delegate.

Unions attracting less attention than that of the miners, but influential in their trades and localities, were organized in the printing and building trades and among the barbers, bartenders, gas and steam fitters, boiler makers, and other skilled workers. In agriculture—where the farm field workers were nearly all Mexicans, and the range hands were cowboys with a tradition of individual action and loyalty to the "old man"—there was no organization.

In 1910, when the bill enabling Arizona to draft a constitution and form a state government was signed by President Taft, the labor organizations were determined to "write the Constitution." Their combined membership by no means represented a majority of the territory's voters, but the unions based their hope of dominating the Constitutional Convention on the belief that the majority of voters disapproved of corporation control in government. It had been frequently charged that the mining and railroad companies controlled the territorial legislatures. The small property owners and business men were anxious to deprive the corporations of their political power so that the large companies might be taxed more and the small owners less.

Both the Democrats and the Republicans were aware that this economic issue would probably decide which party elected the most delegates to the Constitutional Convention. When several labor unions, whose members usually voted Democratic, met at Phoenix on July 11, 1910, and formed a Labor Party, the Democrats incorporated labor's planks into their own program rather than allow this new party to split the Democratic ranks. In exchange the unions promised to support the Democratic ticket. When the Constitutional Convention convened October 10, 1910, the Democrats were in the overwhelming majority and all the forces of labor were united within that party.

At this convention the trade unions achieved, for the first time in Arizona history, recognition as a dominant factor in political affairs. As long as the Republicans and other Democrats did not combine against them, the labor delegates held the balance of power. George W. P. Hunt, a Democrat friendly to labor, was elected president of the convention. With his help, the representatives of organized labor did, to a great extent, "write the Constitution," but their success was by no means complete. They lost an anti-injunction measure designed to curb the injunction powers of the courts, and a provision listing judges under the elective officers subject to recall; the latter, however, failed only through veto by the President of the United States. Also lost were most of the measures aimed at Mexican labor, as for example, an alien labor law which would have prevented the employment of non-English-speaking persons in hazardous industries and would have required employers to hire no more than 20 per cent alien labor.

With statehood, the unions consolidated their gains and entered on a period of rapid growth. The years between 1912 and 1918 were the most active, and probably the most decisive, in the history of Arizona labor. The Arizona State Federation of Labor was organized on January 20, 1912, through a meeting of forty-seven representatives; practically all the unions in the state, except the Railroad Brotherhoods, were soon affiliated with it. (The Western Federation of Miners had affiliated with the American Federation of Labor in 1911, and in 1916 the name of the union was changed to International Union of Mine, Mill and Smelter Workers.)

The Industrial Workers of the World also were active in the state during these years, chiefly in the mining towns and among the Mexican agricultural workers. But compared with the state federation, the I.W.W. had few members. The size of the State Federation of Labor increased with every annual convention, until in 1917 it had a larger membership in proportion to population than any other state in the union.

But as it grew, the Federation's strength was repeatedly being tested by strikes in the copper camps during the World War period. In 1915, the two large districts employing Mexican miners—Clifton-Morenci and Ray—struck for higher wages and a greater degree of comfort and safety. Contrary to the general opinion of the time that Mexicans would not join labor unions, these two camps seem to have been well organized. Governor Hunt kept both troops and strike-breakers out of Clifton and Morenci, and the state federation gained a wage increase for the miners. The strike at Ray was settled with both sides making concessions. In 1916 Ajo miners struck, with moderate success; and the same year the Jerome miners went out, and the operators met their demands.

In July, 1917, the long struggle of the miners reached a climax when members of the A.F. of L's International Union of Mine, Mill and Smelter Workers—some of them also members of I.W.W.—struck in the Warren district. More than fifteen thousand men were affected. Sheriff Harry Wheeler, former captain of rangers, deputized two thousand armed men to protect the properties of the mining corporations. Then followed the famous Bisbee Deportation. The sheriff's deputies arrested 1,186 people, most of them strikers but some storekeepers and bystanders, and loaded them into boxcars. After a train trip of three full days under armed guards, they were unloaded in the desert near Hermanas, New Mexico. Although President Wilson's Mediation Commission, meeting several months later, obtained some concessions for the miners and although the mine operators were rebuked by the President, still the miners' unions were crushingly defeated.

Their defeat is sometimes attributed to activities of the I.W.W., whose lack of agreement with A.F. of L. policies tended to split the unions into two factions. The U.S. Department of Labor, commenting on these strikes in *Bulletin No. R.817*, says: "The issues of radicalism and sabotage were raised, but the Mediation Commission, appointed in 1917 by the President of the United States, found that 'neither sinister influences nor the Industrial Workers of the World can account for these strikes.' Although the operators agreed not to discriminate against the International Union of Mine, Mill and Smelter Workers, they announced that they would employ 'only such men whose character and past record is such as will insure their being loyal to American principles.' They refused entirely to tolerate the more militant and independent unions."

Many of the union men could not or would not work in these camps after the strikes, and their jobs were taken by Mexicans and a new type of Arizona workingman—young men from the agricultural and mining districts of the Middle West. For two decades following, the mines of the state remained virtually unorganized.

The depression of 1921 was another setback for labor, but by 1925 the Federation of Labor was again making gains in many trades. In agriculture, effective A.F. of L. unions were formed among the fruit and vegetable packers, the aristocracy of labor in this field. But 1929 brought retrenchment again, and for several years unemployment overshadowed all other problems. Organizations unaffiliated with the A.F. of L. began to grow among the unemployed. In 1934, a hunger march on the Capitol at Phoenix, followed by a strike among relief workers for more nearly adequate relief, received much publicity and met with drastic opposition from civil authorities.

By 1935, union activity had again increased, and since that time has continued to show substantial results. One of the A.F. of L.'s outstanding accomplishments is the solid organization of the lumber workers around Flagstaff, McNary and Williams, where the industry employs Mexican, Negro, and white workers.

Since 1935 the Congress of Industrial Organizations has also been active in Arizona. Many of the fruit and vegetable workers withdrew from their A.F. of L. union to form branches of the United Cannery, Agricultural, Packing and Allied Workers of America, a C.I.O. organization which is making a determined effort to organize all agricultural workers. Of the farm laborers in Arizona, some twenty thousand are Mexicans, migratory workers, and dispossessed farmers from the Middle West, who are seasonal workers earning an average annual income estimated at $259. The C.I.O. also took over two miners' locals, at Bisbee and Oatman, and at the present time (1940) is carrying on a vigorous organizing campaign in most of the mining and smelting towns of the state.

In 1939, Arizona labor was again contemplating united political action. In May, delegates from the Brotherhoods, A.F. of L. and C.I.O. unions met in Phoenix and formed the Arizona League for Better Government, an organization which they hope will become powerful enough to elect local and state representatives friendly to their interests.

Their aims are much the same as those of labor in 1910, and their effectiveness in 1940 and thereafter, as in 1910, probably depends on their unity and ability to enlist the support of other groups willing to declare common cause with them.

From 1940 till 1946 state labor unions showed a tremendous gain. In 1946 a constitutional amendment prohibiting unions from signing contracts requiring union membership was adopted. In 1947 the state legislature adopted a bill implementing the amendment. Labor unions, by circulating petitions, referred the measure to the people; it was adopted. That act served to slow up membership in the unions temporarily, but membership has since increased steadily, despite another attempt to halt labor by adoption of a measure referred to the people by a group of employers, known as the "anti-picketing" law. It prohibits picketing of any employer unless there exists between the employer and the majority of its employees a bona fide dispute regarding wages and working conditions.

Almost all Arizona labor unions accept both Mexican and colored members; thousands of them are in the unions now.

Transportation

LESS than a century has passed since a weary Quaker forty-niner, driving his oxen day after day over the only wagon trail in Arizona, cried in despair: "I can't see what God Almighty made so much land for!" Less than a hundred years ago camels trekked across Arizona wastes to Colorado River steamers; and scarcely fifty years ago the creaking log wheels of *carretas,* the crude Mexican carts attached by long poles to the horns of half-wild oxen, announced to Tucson and Phoenix the approach of Mexican traders.

The trails on which pioneer wagon trains crawled through Arizona have become paved highways, frequently paralleled by railroads, and above them flies the speedier traffic of the air. The sound of the *carretas* has long been silenced, the camels have been hunted down by cowboys, and the steamers have rusted and rotted in the red river silt. The stage coaches, mule teams, and pony express have also disappeared. The burro and the horse alone remain, supreme on remote mountain and range trails. Men in other places worked a long time to develop modern techniques for transporting commodities and people across "so much land," but the task of applying those techniques to Arizona has been accomplished in about fifty years.

First Trails and Wagon Roads: Until the last decade of the nineteenth century, when Arizona agriculture and mining became important, the major driving force behind the development of transportation in the territory was the desire to establish satisfactory routes to California. For many years, most of both Spanish- and English-speaking travelers coming into Arizona were merely passing through on their way elsewhere; and their governments—Spain, Mexico, and United States in succession—were chiefly concerned with the area as an obstacle to transcontinental transportation.

Even Father Kino, the courageous missionary who loved Arizona and labored to spread Christianity among its Indians, was vitally interested in a trade route from Sonora, Mexico to the Pacific. In his missionary work from 1692 until his death in 1711, he made fourteen journeys into southern and western Arizona from Mexico, and his maps and observations were a great aid to the Spaniards in establishing overland connections between Mexico and California.

Through Father Kino's trips and the missions he established, the area along the Santa Cruz, San Pedro, and Gila rivers in what is now south-central Arizona became the most accessible part of the territory for settlers and traders from Mexico, and *carretas* and burro trains ventured into it early. The San Pedro and Santa Cruz rivers, running from south to north almost parallel to each other into the Gila River, were natural courses for travelers. The Gila River could be followed westward through otherwise waterless country to the great Colorado River. These three rivers were the basis of early travel in southern Arizona not only from Mexico but from eastern United States to the west.

The most famous road—and the worst—opened to white men by Father Kino was *El Camino del Diablo* (Devil's Highway), across the extreme southwest corner of Arizona. *El Camino del Diablo* stretches from Sonoita, Mexico, on the border, to the mouth of the Gila on the Colorado River where Yuma now stands. With about one hundred pack animals and a party including Lieutenant Juan Manje and several Indians, Father Kino set out in 1699 on this route to explore the unknown country toward California. The trail led through arid lifeless country, fairly level but with no certain supply of water between the Sonoita River and the Gila, a distance of about one hundred and thirty-five miles. There were no streams, and what water there was had been stored in natural rock cavities by infrequent showers. This area was described about two centuries later by a traveler as "a land of 'silence, solitude and sunshine,' with little to distract the eye from the awful surrounding dreariness and desolation except the bleaching skeletons of horses and the painfully frequent crosses which mark the graves of those who perished of thirst."

Father Kino's party did not go as far as the Colorado on this first attempt, but later the padre reached the big river by following the Gila down to its mouth. He then returned via *El Camino del Diablo*, and afterwards used it several times as the shortest route between Sonora and the Colorado.

After his death in 1711 *El Camino del Diablo* was neglected for more than sixty years. Captain Juan Bautista de Anza, commandante of the Tubac presidio, and Padre Francisco Tomas Garces, the zealous Franciscan missionary, were responsible for opening it up again. They marched westward in 1774 over *El Camino del Diablo* under orders from the Spanish government to break a road from Sonora to the West Coast. Their expedition was successful, and the Devil's Highway was subsequently much used. Spaniards and Mexicans going from Sonora to California preferred it, in spite of the heat and lack of water, to the longer route north and west along the Gila River, which was infested by Apaches.

Most of the Spanish-speaking travelers along this desolate trail were aware of its dangers and prepared for them, but the gold rushes to California and the Colorado River between 1849 and 1865 brought hundreds of immigrant parties to *El Camino del Diablo* who knew nothing about the terrors of the passage. The report of the Boundary Commission issued in 1857 states that "during the few years that this road was much traveled, over 400 persons were said to have perished of thirst between Sonoita and Yuma, a record probably without a parallel in North America."

The first wagon road across Arizona—Cooke's Road through southern Arizona and along the Gila River—resulted from the joint desire of a group of Mormons to reach the Pacific Coast and of the United States Government to break a road through to California for military purposes. The Mormons, organized as the Mormon Battalion in the Army of the West, started out from Santa Fe under the command of Lieutenant Colonel Philip St. George Cooke in 1846. They laboriously pushed their wagons across the eleven hundred miles of little-known wilderness to San Diego in 102 days. At times they were without water and short of rations, with men and mules almost too exhausted to move. They let their wagons down the steepest descent of the Continental Divide at Guadalupe Pass by ropes, forced the Mexican troops in the Presidio of Tucson to retire before them, and hewed their way through a chasm of rock narrower than their wagons. Their route from the east was along the northern border of Mexico to the San Pedro River and then north along that stream to what is now Benson. At this point they went west to Tucson, and from there traveled northwest to the Gila and down it to the Colorado.

Cooke's Road was followed by many immigrant trains, but many varied the route somewhat by extending it along the northern border of Mexico as far west as the Santa Cruz River—almost to Nogales—and following that river north to Tucson and the Gila.

Not long after the entrance of California into the Union, the people of California began to press Congress for overland mail and stage service. In 1857 appropriations were therefore made for building roads across the western territory to the Coast. One of these was Leach's Road from El Paso to Fort Yuma, named for James B. Leach who superintended construction. This road, completed in the autumn of 1858, followed Cooke's Road—except that it entered Arizona at a point farther north, on a line with Tucson and Benson, but missed Tucson by turning north at Benson to follow the San Pedro to the Gila.

The other important Arizona road in the direction of California, broken at this time by the government, crossed the territory in the north. This was Beale's Road, from Fort Defiance, New Mexico to the Colorado River, on a course near the thirty-fifth parallel. This route had already been explored by the Sitgreaves expedition and surveyed by Lieutenant A. W. Whipple for a railroad route. Beale's route of 1857 was later followed by the Santa Fe Railway line and U.S. Highway 66.

It was on this northern road-opening expedition that camels were introduced into Arizona. Edward F. Beale, who superintended the project, had long believed that it was logical to use camels as beasts of burden in the western desert; at length he succeeded in convincing the War Department and Congress of the plan, and the storeship, *Supply,* made two trips to the Orient to obtain the animals. According to Beale's reports, the camels did remarkably well on the journey across Arizona and back again. They carried their heavy loads easily, needed water only at long intervals, and lived on desert bushes that mules and horses refused. It was Beale's dream that regular camel caravans would be developed from this excellent beginning, but only a few attempts were made after this expedition to use camels in the Southwest.

Another important early wagon road was the Mormon Road running south from Utah through the extreme northern part of Arizona to Beale's Road. This thoroughfare was marked out by the Mormon, Jacob Hamblin, who began his missionary work with the Hopi in 1858, and thereafter made repeated trips back and forth from Utah. He frequently crossed the Colorado River at the Crossing of the Fathers on the Utah line, but in 1864 ferried across a little farther down at the mouth of the Paria River. By 1872 this new crossing was called Lee's Ferry, after John D. Lee who operated the ferry there. Hamblin's Mormon Road was traversed for the first time by wagons in 1873 by a group of his kinsmen. They followed it from Lee's Ferry through the Painted Desert to Grand Falls and then along Beale's Road to Winslow.

Stage Coach and Mule Skinner Days: The first regular stage line in Arizona was operated by the San Antonio and San Diego Stage Company, beginning in 1857. It received $149,000 a year from the mail contract and this enabled it to build up satisfactory service. Stage coaching was an expensive business requiring much capital investment in draft animals, coaches, and fortified stations in Indian country; and revenue from passengers was never sufficient to maintain a line. It is said that the cost of early mail delivery across the continent averaged about $65 a letter.

The San Antonio and San Diego Company sent the mail through on horseback before stage service was established. The first rider to carry the mail into Arizona from the west rode the 110 miles from Carrizo Creek, California, to Yuma in thirty-two hours without changing horses. Soon afterward, three passenger coaches followed the mail riders eastward, and regular semimonthly service was inaugurated. The route was over Cooke's Road up the Gila and south to Tucson, thence east to Benson and approximately along Leach's Road out of the territory by way of Apache Pass and Doubtful Pass.

An advertisement of this company dated Oct. 1, 1858, reads: "Passengers and Express Matter forwarded in NEW COACHES, drawn by six mules over the entire length of our Line, excepting from San Diego to Fort Yuma, a distance of 180 miles, which we cross on mule back. Passengers GUARANTEED in their tickets to ride in Coaches, excepting 180 miles, as above stated. . . . An armed escort travels through the Indian country, with each Mail Train, for the protection of the Mails and Passengers." Passenger fares from San Diego were $40 to Fort Yuma, $80 to Tucson, $125 to El Paso, and $200 to San Antonio.

About a month before this advertisement appeared, however, the government had signed a six-year contract with John Butterfield, of Utica, New York, to carry the mail through St. Louis to San Francisco twice weekly at $600,000 a year. Consequently in December 1858 the original company, having lost the vital government subsidy, withdrew from Arizona.

The Butterfield line, which afterward became the Overland Mail Company, represented the height in stagecoaching efficiency. It had 100 Concord coaches, 1,000 horses, 500 mules and 750 employees, and operated between San Francisco and Tipton, Missouri, at the western end of the Missouri Pacific Railroad. The contract with the government required the line to make the 2,759 mile trip in twenty-five days; but the usual time was twenty-three days, and once it was even cut down to sixteen days.

Although it provided the best service possible, the Butterfield Line was noted more for speed than comfort. The heavy Concord coaches were drawn by teams of four broncos, which were changed at stations scattered along the route. There was an exciting interval of bucking and stampeding when a fresh team was harnessed, and throughout the journey the coach often lurched dangerously on and off the road.

In spite of the fortitude required of their passengers, the number of stage coaches increased in the territory and many short lines were operated. Mail and passenger lines ran between Ehrenberg on the Colorado River, Wickenberg, and Prescott—all gold-mining camps— between Phoenix and Florence, and other points.

The Civil War disrupted means of communication in the Southwest and transportation in Arizona suffered a setback from which it was long in recovering. Some of the stock and other property of the Butterfield Line were confiscated by the Confederates in Texas in 1861, and the lack of military protection in Arizona against the Indians and road agents was an added reason for discontinuing the service. A few stage-coach and horseback mail lines were operating in the late 1860's and early 1870's, and there were steamboats on the Colorado River, but in the main Arizona was virtually cut off from adequate communication with the outside world. There was little intercourse even between points within the territory during this period.

In 1874 the Texas and California Stage Company was organized to operate between Fort Worth and San Diego, and about 1875 established daily service. The main route was 1,700 miles long, and 1,200 horses were used. Company headquarters were moved from San Diego to Yuma and then to Tucson as railroads encroached upon the shrinking field. The route was abandoned when steel rails finally ran along every mile of the way between Yuma and the Texas terminal. Nevertheless, stage coaches continued to operate in Arizona for a good many years, connecting the railroads with towns they had not yet reached.

The stage lines, which charged a dollar a pound for excess baggage, had little effect on freight transportation. According to a pioneer account, the typical old-time freighting outfit that served Arizona settlements was made up of "twenty- to twenty-four mules or horses and a large wagon, to which was attached at least one trailer wagon and frequently two, operated by two men, the driver and a helper called a 'swamper.' Both were proficient in profanity beyond all other men. Both took their whisky straight and did not limit the quantity. Both wore red flannel shirts summer and winter. Freighting was no easy job even if for hours at a time both driver and swamper might be seen sleeping peacefully on top of one of their loaded wagons when traversing a level stretch of road. Taking care of a dozen span of mules or horses, cooking meals by the roadside, and sleeping on the ground in all sorts of weather called for men of the most rugged type. To drive a team of twenty-four mules over a mountain road, turning sharp corners and yet so managing the long line of animals as to maintain a steady pull on the wagons, was an art."

Steamboating on the Colorado: While overland transportation was at its crudest in Arizona, river traffic was at its height. Nearly the entire commerce of the territory until the coming of the railroads in the

1880's was by water communication. The silt-laden waters of the West's longest river formed the highway that carried the trade, not only of Arizona and southeastern California, but of Utah whose freight wagons received their burdens at the highest point of navigation.

Ocean going steamers and sailing vessels navigated to the head of the Gulf of California and there discharged their cargoes into shallow draft steamers and barges for transportation up the Colorado River. Yuma was Arizona's principal port and supply depot. Almost daily long wagon trains of freight left its warehouses for forts, towns, mines, and ranches in various parts of southern Arizona, and barges and steamers were always at her docks.

Before the development of river traffic, the supplies for Fort Yuma were landed near the river's mouth and then brought overland to the fort. The high cost of this land transportation—$75 a ton for the 175 miles—induced the government to seek a cheaper way of bringing supplies up the river. In accordance with this idea, a topographical engineer, Lieutenant D. H. Derby, was dispatched to make a survey of the Colorado from its mouth to Fort Yuma.

Lieutenant Derby arrived at the head of the Gulf in late December 1850 in the schooner, *Invincible,* and early in January 1851, succeeded in sailing the schooner some twenty-five miles up the river. Since this was the low water season and the boat drew eight to nine feet, further progress was made impossible by the shallow water. Leaving the schooner, Derby traveled sixty miles farther up the river in a small boat, and here he encountered a detachment from the post coming down stream to meet him. River traffic was begun shortly afterward.

About the time of Derby's expedition up the river, the government gave a contract to George A. Johnson for transporting supplies from San Francisco, California to Fort Yuma. Johnson carried his cargo to the head of the Gulf of California in the Schooner, *Sierra Nevada;* there he constructed flat boats on which he piled the freight, dragging them upstream to Yuma by hand with ropes and poles.

The next record of river navigation is an account given by Captain James Hobbs who lived in Yuma in the year 1851. He records seeing a stern-wheel steamer, the *Yuma,* and states that the Indians were so frightened upon seeing the boat that they ran for their lives, yelling that "the devil is coming, blowing fire and smoke out of his nose and kicking the water back with his feet." Strangely enough, the Indians who lived in the fertile bottom lands of the Colorado had no canoes.

It is the *Uncle Sam,* however, that is usually credited with being the first steamer to navigate Colorado waters. This boat had been built in the East by Captain Turnbull who succeeded Johnson in the contract for transporting army supplies to Fort Yuma. In 1852 it was brought, knocked down, to the delta near the river's mouth, and there assembled and launched. It proved the utility of steamboats on the river, but lacked sufficient engine power to master the stream's swift current during high water season. The *Uncle Sam,* a twenty horsepower side-wheeler, with sixty-five foot keel, fourteen-foot beam, and twenty-two inch draft, operated until June 22, 1854, when it foundered at its moorings at Pilot Knob, a few miles below Yuma.

Captain George A. Johnson, who later became the most noted and principal navigator of the river, then appeared in Yuma, bringing a 104 foot side-wheeler of seventy horsepower known as the *General Jessup.* It carried a sixty-ton load on two feet of water and was the first steamer to ascend to the head of Black Canyon. This was early in 1858, a short time before Lieutenant Ives covered the same route in the *Explorer.*

On this trip the *General Jessup* made contact with the road-surveying expedition of Beale, which was traveling back east over the new Beale's Road to test its practicability during winter. Beale's account of their meeting, dated January 23, 1858, is as follows: "We reached the Colorado River early in the morning, having encamped in a rain storm the night previous a few miles from it. Shortly after leaving camp, my clerk, F. E. Kerlin, who with two of my party had been dispatched the day previous in order to have my boat ready for crossing, was seen returning. Various surmises were immediately started as to the cause, and as soon as he was within speaking distance he was questioned eagerly for the news. He gave us a joyful surprise by the information that the steamer 'General Jessup,' Captain Johnson, was at the crossing waiting to convey us to the opposite side. It is difficult to conceive the varied emotions with which this news was received. Here, in a wild, almost unknown country, inhabited only by savages, the great river of the West, hitherto declared unnavigable, had, for the first time, borne upon its bosom that emblem of civilization, a steamer.

"In a few minutes after our arrival the steamer came alongside the bank, and our party was transported at once, with all our baggage, to the other side. . . . I brought the camels with me, and as they stood on the bank, surrounded by hundreds of wild unclad savages, and mixed with these the dragoons of my escort, and the steamer slowly revolving her wheels preparatory to a start, it was a curious and interesting picture."

On its voyage down river the *General Jessup* struck a submerged rock at Picacho, fifty miles north of Yuma, and sank. It was later raised, brought to Yuma and repaired, but the following summer its boiler exploded, killing two men and again sinking the craft. Johnson then secured another vessel and from this time forward traffic on the Colorado was continuous until the coming of the railroads.

Johnson soon organized a company and held control of the river transportation with little opposition until 1878, when his company, the Colorado River Navigation Company, disposed of its holdings to the Southern Pacific Railroad Company. In 1864 the steamer, *Esmeralda,* owned by Thomas E. Trueworthy, and the *Vina Tilden* of the Philadelphia Mining Company offered some competition to the Johnson line. Two years later a new navigation company bought these boats, but it soon failed, leaving Johnson clear sailing.

Considering the difficulties of river navigation and the cost of transferring cargo to and from ocean steamers, the price of freight was not excessive. Merchandise from San Francisco to Yuma was carried for $40 a ton and ore from Yuma to San Francisco for $10 a ton, with rates rising proportionately to and from points farther up the river. Cabin passenger fare from San Francisco to Yuma was $40 in 1874 but was raised the following year to $90. Each river town was a terminus of a freight route; the principal points above Yuma were Ehrenberg for shipments to and from Wickenberg, and Hardyville for Prescott. Callville, the Mormon settlement on the Colorado a few miles below the Virgin River, was first reached by barge in 1866. The settlement was near the head of summer navigation and good wagon roads led from there into Salt Lake City.

Upriver traffic carried general merchandise, mining and milling machinery, mine supplies, food stuffs and miscellaneous items, passengers, troops and military supplies. The downriver loads consisted of bullion, ores, hides, pelts, wool and miscellaneous items, passengers and troops. There was always considerable downriver travel in row boats to Yuma and from all upstream points.

River nagivation was a matter of skill and experience, since there were constant difficulties and dangers to be overcome. At the mouth of the river great tidal waves called "bores" or "burros" raged at times through the delta, foaming and roaring like a Niagara. Where the insurging waters of the tide met the flowing river water, a ridge arose, growing until it broke into a wave ten feet or more in height that crashed northwards. Other menaces in the lower river were shallows concealing mud and sandbars and snags; farther north in the river bed lay pebble bars and submerged boulders. Sometimes a boat would be grounded an hour, sometimes for days. The river steamers all used wood as fuel, and the Indians cut this near the river and piled it on the banks.

Some small flat-bottomed sailing craft were also in use on the river. There was no room for tacking, but this was unnecessary, as the wind generally blew either up or down stream—and when the wind blew wrong there was nothing to do but tie up until its direction changed.

The railroads put an end to steamboating and transcontinental stagecoaching at about the same time. But while the old overland routes have become great avenues of smooth traffic, the river highway has shrunk to an unnavigable flow. Great dams have harnessed the Colorado's strength and hold back her water to irrigate the fertile desert land, and today the once wild and majestic stream dribbles past Yuma half hidden, most of the year, in the sands and mud.

The Iron Horse: The railroads, no less than the early roads and stagecoach lines, were built across Arizona as avenues between the East and the West. In rapidly-developing California and more so in the East transcontinental railroads were vital issues several decades before they were built. The people of Arizona, of course, had an even more intense interest in communication across their territory, but their needs and opinions had little influence on the forces at work to bring them the steel rails. By 1850 leaders in both the South and the North realized that political control of the West depended to a very great extent on which section developed efficient transportation connections with the new area. As a result of this political rivalry and the pressure from railroad companies and other economic groups both in the East and West, railroad surveys were made before there was a single stage line across the territory.

In 1853 Congress appropriated $150,000, to which other sums were added later, "to ascertain the most practicable and economical route for a railroad from the Mississippi River to the Pacific Ocean." Lieutenant A. W. Whipple was appointed by Secretary of War Jefferson Davis to make the survey from Fort Smith, Arkansas to the Colorado River, along the thirty-fifth parallel later followed by Beale's Road. During the same administration James Gadsden was appointed ambassador to Mexico and negotiated the famous purchase bearing his name, chiefly in order that a railroad might be run through country less mountainous than that along the northern route. In 1854 and 1855 railroad surveys were made across southern Arizona, one for the Texas Western Railroad Company along approximately the same line subsequently followed by the Southern Pacific.

The Civil War checked the activities of ambitious southerners and kept northerners busy with matters outside Arizona, but by 1868 several corporations were vigorously promoting railroads across the territory. All were asking and expecting government aid. Congress had already granted authority to two companies for lines across Arizona—one in the south along the thirty-second parallel, and the other in the north along the thirty-fifth parallel—and had given to each grants of alternate sections of land for forty miles on either side of the lines. The Texas-Pacific Railroad Company, holding the franchise for the southern route, was unable to raise the necessary capital to proceed with the work, and the Atlantic and Pacific Railroad was slow in its westward approach to the territory's north route. Years passed with no rails laid in

Arizona, and in 1877 a California railroad, the Southern Pacific, approached the territorial boundary from the west and asked to come in.

The Southern Pacific received its charter from the Arizona legislature October 8, 1878, after much delay and deliberation. James H. McClintock in *Arizona—The Youngest State* says: "There was a good deal of log rolling over the Southern Pacific Railroad franchise and a strong lobby to push its passage was established in Tucson. . . . It may be worthy of note that in later years C. P. Huntington, head of the Southern Pacific, set the 'value' of an Arizona Legislature at the ridiculously low figure of $4,800. But he may not have referred at the time to this particular franchise grant." This railroad failed to obtain the land subsidy originally offered the Texas company.

The Southern Pacific arrived at the west bank of the Colorado opposite Yuma in the spring of 1877, and spent all summer building the bridge across the river. But when it was finished, the Federal government, which had given the company permission to build the bridge, refused to allow trains to run over the Federal stream or across the military reservation on its east bank. The first crossing onto Arizona soil was therefore made surreptitiously, while the garrison at Fort Yuma was asleep. Southern Pacific engineers, unable to resist the temptation of forbidden ground, took an engine quietly across the Colorado. When they were safely past the fort, "the engineer tied down the whistle valve and used all the steam he had in celebrating the advent of the iron horse into new territory." The awakened soldiery soon chased the trespassers back into California, but Arizona had seen its first train. After the granting of the franchise, construction proceeded eastward, booming the little towns along the way—particularly Maricopa, thirty-five miles south of Phoenix.

The first locomotive reached Tucson in March 1880, amid the roar of cannon and martial music. The citizens of the Old Pueblo could scarcely control their elation, and sent telegrams to the President, the Governor, the officials of several large cities, and other prominent persons. One of these triumphant messages was as follows:

> Tucson, Arizona, March 17, 1880
>
> To His Holiness, the Pope of Rome, Italy. The mayor of Tucson begs the honor of reminding Your Holiness that this ancient and honorable pueblo was founded by the Spaniards under the sanction of the Church more than three centuries ago, and to inform Your Holiness that a railroad from San Francisco, California, now connects us with the Christian world. R. N. Leatherwood, mayor. Asking your benediction, J. B. Salpointe, Vic. Ap.

It seems that three old-fashioned Tucsonians looked with some embarrassment on what they evidently considered the rather over-effusive display of pride on the part of a pioneer-hardened community. When they heard about the telegram to the Pope, they immediately hunted up the telegraph operator and bribed him to follow their orders: The telegram was not sent, but that evening, when the celebration banquet was at its height, this "reply" was read:

> His Holiness the Pope acknowledges with appreciation receipt of your telegram informing him that the ancient city of Tucson at last has been connected by rail with the outside world and sends his benediction, but for his own satisfaction would ask, where in hell is Tucson?
>
> [Signed] Antonelli.

It is said that the mayor and many of his fellow-banqueters had by this time reached such a state of mind that, while their feelings were hurt, they did not question the authenticity of the wire.

The Southern Pacific continued eastward through Benson, Bowie, and Willcox and connected with the Santa Fe at Deming, New Mexico, in 1881.

The Atlantic and Pacific Railroad Company, with a land grant subsidy of more than ten million acres along the thirty-fifth parallel in Arizona, began to lay its tracks westward across the territory in 1882. It encountered many difficulties along this mountainous northern route, but completed the line to the Colorado late in the summer of 1883. This road was absorbed later by the Atchison, Topeka & Santa Fe Railway.

Once the cross-country lines were built, the question of branch railroads into the central regions became tremendously important to the towns along the main roads. Each railroad town hoped to tap the mining and agricultural wealth of the surrounding area by becoming its transportation center; and as competition was intensified, several communities undertook to subsidize local railroads, in order to get in ahead of rival towns. Tucson was worried both by the ambitions of Benson and by two proposed lines south from the Atlantic and Pacific Railroad to Globe, Prescott, and Phoenix. The urgency of the situation caused Tucson to involve Pima County in the Arizona Narrow Gauge Railroad proposition, which resulted in nothing except ten miles of unused track and a debt of $319,000, finally assumed by the state.

Yavapai and Maricopa counties also subsidized railroads, and though their lines were built, the state eventually had to assume responsibility for the several hundred thousand dollars of county bonds issued on them.

But in spite of these costly mistakes, the steel rails gradually reached southward and northward from the main roads. In 1895 the Santa Fe, Prescott, and Phoenix Railroad was finished, and provided efficient service connecting the northern cross-country route with the southern one. By 1900 or soon afterward all the important mining centers had railroads. In 1912 Arizona had 1,678 miles of railroad, and statehood accelerated the building of branch lines; by 1916 there were 2,144 miles of track, and the tonnage carried had been tripled.

Railroad development in Arizona, as elsewhere in the United States, reached its peak in the 1920's, and has since suffered from sharp competition with newer forms of transportation. Considerable retrenchment has taken place since 1930, and some of the branches are no longer being operated.

The railroads of this state have been regulated both by Federal and state laws. Some laws were passed to benefit the railroad employees, such as the long-contested law prohibiting more than seventy freight or fourteen passenger cars to a train in Arizona. Others, such as the Interstate Commerce Act forbidding the railroads to charge a higher freight rate for a short haul than for a longer one, greatly benefitted the wholesalers and general public in Arizona and other mountain states. Prior to the passage of this act, rates from the East to the Pacific Coast were lower than to Arizona, and in many cases the tariff to California and back to Arizona was less than to Arizona direct.

Highways: At the turn of the century, when there were still plenty of people in Arizona who had never seen a railway train, an automobile was unloaded at the Southern Pacific depot in Tucson. Dr. Hiram W. Fenner, who had ordered it, fiddled with the contraption until it got up steam, and finally drove gingerly through the tremendous crowd in the first automobile to enter the territory. Not long afterward, Globe also had a horseless carriage, though they do say it spent less time getting stalled on the steep mountain grades than in the machine shop of the Old Dominion Mining Company, where high-priced engineers constantly tinkered with its nuts and bolts.

Arizona was slower than some eastern states in accepting the motor car as a reliable form of transportation, because for many years it lacked improved roads. However, with the close of World War I, motorists both inside and outside the state clamored for better highways, and the road-building program of the state was begun in earnest.

In 1952 Arizona had 3,962 miles of state roads and 16,148 miles of county roads. The network includes portions of transcontinental highways and traverses the fourteen counties. The Arizona Highway Department maintains the state roads and is constantly improving them.

Transcontinental bus and truck lines serve the principal Arizona cities and intermediate points; and independent lines reach the more remote towns.

State border inspection stations are maintained by the Arizona Highway Department at Apache, San Simon, Duncan, Springerville, and Lupton on the eastern border; at Kingman, Parker, Ehrenberg, and Yuma on the western border; and at Fredonia on the north. The officials at these stations have two principal duties: to welcome visitors and furnish them with desired information; and to check commercial vehicles, especially in regard to excess motor fuel brought into the state. Since the enactment of the gasoline tax law in 1933, motor vehicles are required to pay a tax of 5 cents a gallon on all motor fuel in excess of that carried in the standard factory tank equipment of their particular models. On gasoline carried through to out-of-state destinations reimbursement of the tax is made when the fuel leaves the state.

Plant inspection stations are maintained by the Bureau of Entomology and Plant Quarantine at San Simon, Gripe, Globe, and Holbrook on the east; at Kingman, Parker, Ehrenberg, and Yuma on the west; Fredonia on the north. Cars are stopped and inspected for fruits, plants and other materials (such as honey) in order that Arizona may be kept free from insect pests. Busses, trucks and noncommercial vehicles are all stopped for this purpose.

Air Travel: In January 1910, eleven planes, three dirigible airships, and several free balloons were exhibited at Los Angeles at the first international meeting of fliers on American soil. The following month three of these aviators came to Arizona on a barnstorming tour. The "Men-Birds," as they were called, made their first flights in the state at Phoenix, and thousands of awe-stricken Arizonans crowded into the capital city to see them. Tucson, not to be outdone, also arranged for a Man-Bird exhibition by Charles K. Hamilton, one of the three performing in Phoenix. Tickets were sold for the spectacle, and in order to prevent gate crashing, Aviator Hamilton was required to take off and land in a very small field surrounded by a high board fence. In his flimsy and awkward ship, Hamilton accomplished this feat, which modern airmen would pronounce absolutely suicidal, three times; and the newspapers reported that "despite a stirring breeze he attained the terrific speed of 40 miles per hour."

In 1911 Robert G. Fowler broke the world's sustained flight record by flying from Yuma to Maricopa without stopping—165 miles in 206 minutes—and Cal P. Rogers, trying to top the transcontinental flight record, reached Tucson twenty-seven days after he left New York. Both of these flyers had difficulty in landing at Tucson; and as the word was passed among aviators, the airships that visited other southwestern towns passed right over the Old Pueblo. But Tucson was air-minded enough to establish the first municipal air field in the United States— one of such dimensions that Tucsonians could say in triumph, "If that isn't big enough for them to land, we'll rent the county."

In 1927 Commander Francesco de Pinedo, the Italian who traveled by seaplane to six continents, landed the first seaplane in Arizona— where it burned up while refueling on Roosevelt Lake. Commander Pinedo flew into the state from the lake of Elephant Butte Dam in

New Mexico. He called Arizona "this corrugated inferno of boulders, cliffs, and canyons so deep that they look black from far above," and said: "To ride a seaplane across a desert hunting a lake was like flying an airplane over the ocean seeking an isolated island on which to land."

Regularly scheduled passenger and express plane service into Arizona was begun late in November 1927, when the Aero Corporation of California inaugurated a tri-weekly line between Los Angeles, Phoenix, and Tucson. The schedule became a daily one about a year later. Phoenix, Tucson and Douglas now have daily transcontinental plane service. Planes also stop at Prescott, Flagstaff, Winslow, Douglas, Ajo, Yuma, and Kingman.

Education and Religion

FOR NEARLY a century and a half education and religion in what is now Arizona were closely associated. The Jesuit missionaries who came up from Old Mexico and established religious centers in this region taught the friendlier Indians something of secular learning as well as the elements of Christianity.

From the time the mission schools were abandoned in 1827 until the organization of the territory in 1864, there was no educational advancement. The pioneer settlers, thinly scattered over an immense area of arid and mountainous country, were too occupied with securing a foothold and defending themselves against the Indians to do anything towards establishing schools.

But with the coming of more stable times and a more rapid growth in population, the need for some sort of public educational facilities began to be generally recognized. The first territorial governor, John N. Goodwin, urged the legislature to establish elementary schools, high schools and a university, and recommended that part of the funds raised by taxation should be set aside for educational purposes. But the legislators decided that the territory was still too unsettled to justify the establishment of a public school system. At this time a free school for Mexican and Papago children was being conducted at San Xavier del Bac Mission, and the legislature granted the school $250. Small amounts were also voted for prospective schools at Mohave and Prescott.

According to the 1870 census there were more than nineteen hundred children of school age in the territory; but there was no public school. From 1869 to 1877 Governor A. P. K. Safford worked to found an educational system, and because of his efforts became known as "Father of the Public School System in Arizona." He believed in free schools, and saw the need of education in a territory that had recently been transferred from the government of one country to that of another. He sympathized with the predicament of a people who could not read the language in which their laws were written.

Governor Safford proposed to appropriate funds from the territorial revenues and divide them among the counties in proportion to the number of children of school age in each county. Counties were to be divided into school districts, and taxes levied on all property to support one or more schools in each county for a six-months term annually. This plan at first met with bitter opposition in the legislature, but the governor was so successful in securing public support for his proposals that they were finally adopted.

The first school, opened by John Spring at Tucson in 1871, was a crudely-furnished adobe building with dirt floor and roof. The pupils were 138 boys, nearly all Mexicans, and the teacher not only taught them but also washed, combed, and brushed the untidy ones. It was difficult to get well-trained teachers in a frontier town where an Indian raid might break up a school session at any time. In 1873 Governor Safford secured the territory's first experienced teachers—two California women for the school in Tucson and a man at Prescott.

The legislature of 1879 created the office of state superintendent of public instruction. By 1880 the school enrollment had increased to ten times that of 1873, and there were 101 teachers.

Bisbee's first school opend in 1881 in a miner's shack with a dirt floor and no windows. Slates were sold to the pupils at 75¢ each and pencils at 25¢. A Mexican boy was paid one dollar a month to deliver each day a bucket of drinking water which he brought to the school on a burro. The schools held Indian drills similar to the fire drills of today.

The legislature of 1885 established the Arizona Territorial Normal School at Tempe. An appropriation of $5,000 was made for the erection of a building and twenty sections of rich land were granted as an endowment. The school opened its doors to students in February 1886.

Provision for a territorial board of education, to be appointed by the governor, and for a public university at Tucson was also made in the legislative session of 1885. The people of Tucson had hoped to secure the capital as a political plum, and were not enthusiastic upon receiving the university instead. The legislature voted $25,000 for buildings and equipment, with the proviso that forty acres of land in or near Tucson be privately contributed as a site for the university. At the last moment three prominent Tucson gamblers donated the land.

The Northern Arizona Normal School at Flagstaff was established by the legislature in March 1899, after attempts to set up first a reform school and then an insane asylum in the town. The institution opened on September 11, 1899 with twenty-three pupils and two teachers.

Eastern Arizona Junior College had its beginning in 1888, when the president of the St. Joseph Stake (the stake is a territorial unit of the Mormon Church) was authorized by his church to establish an academy to be known as the Latter Day Saints' Academy of St. Joseph Stake. It was opened in 1891 at Safford but was moved to Thatcher in the following year. Its name was later changed to Gila College.

In the state public education system of today, each elementary and high school district is governed by a board of three members, serving three years. Union high school districts have boards of five members, serving five years. All district boards are under the jurisdiction of county school superintendents, who hold elective office for a term of two years. The county superintendents are collectively supervised by the state superintendent of public instruction, who is elected for a two-year term. He is a member of the state board of education, as are the governor, the presidents of the university and teachers' colleges, a city superintendent, a county superintendent, and a high school principal.

Elementary and high school districts range in size from five to one hundred square miles. A union high school district is composed of two or more adjacent elementary districts, and two counties in the state have a county form of high school district. Temporary "accommodation schools" may be established in regions not yet organized into school districts. Bus transportation is provided for pupils in the larger districts. Children from eight to sixteen years old are required to attend school for not less than eight months of each year.

Elementary teachers must have had four years, and secondary teachers five years of college work, to qualify for teaching in the public schools. Although Arizona has many sparsely settled areas, elementary and secondary schools are available for all of its children. In 1930, ninety-one per cent of the children between seven and thirteen years of age, were actually enrolled in public schools, as compared with seventy-nine per cent in 1920.

Following 1930 came one of the darkest periods in the state's educational history. Arizona's public school enrollment, which in 1930 was 103,806, decreased during the next few years. The enrollment in the state's private and parochial schools (nearly all elementary or secondary in character) is about five per cent of that in the public schools. The number of public school teachers was 3,273 in 1930; but during the difficult depression years it declined seriously, until in 1934 there were only 2,834. These teachers received an annual average salary of $1,637 in the former year and $1,309 in 1934. According to the biennial report made by the state superintendent of public instruction July 1, 1934 to June 30, 1936, there was a gradual betterment of public school conditions during this period.

The amount spent upon public school education in Arizona was $46,518,435 in 1952, representing (with respect to total public school population in average daily attendance) a per capita outlay of $270.62. The Federal government contributed a little less than three per cent of 1952's total, the state government 27.7 per cent, the counties nearly nine per cent, and the school districts the remainder. The state supplies free textbooks for pupils in the elementary schools.

Courses in home economics, agriculture, trade and industry are provided in a considerable number of the state's fifty-nine public high schools. The total enrollment in such courses was 4,335 in 1936. Vocational instruction in rural areas is supplemented by the work of county farm and home demonstration agents. Technical training in law, engineering, agriculture, music, and education is offered by the three institutions of higher education, which had a combined enrollment of 3,157 in 1934. Because of the large percentage of Mexicans and Indians in Arizona's population, "Americanization" work is an important part of the school programs.

The education of Indian children in Arizona is under the jurisdiction of the Office of Indian Affairs, of the U. S. Department of the Interior. For the year ending June 30, 1938 there were 13,000 Indian children, six to eighteen years of age, in the state, of whom 8,000 were enrolled in Indian schools. There are several types: Federal day schools, reservation boarding schools, and non-reservation boarding schools; mission, private, and state day schools and boarding schools. A small number of Indian children are also cared for in the regular public schools. This is in line with the Indian Office policy of transferring educational functions of the Indian Bureau to the public school systems as rapidly as adequate, mutually satisfactory plans can be developed and worked out.

RELIGION

The first attempts at Christianization of the Indians in what is now Arizona were made by missionaries of the Franciscan order early in the seventeenth century. The sword and the cross went side by side in exploring the great Southwest, the sword acting as guardian for the cross in the conquest of new lands and the search for gold. The Pueblo uprising of 1680, during which priests were killed and churches burned, marked the end of Franciscan activity, but ten years later the Jesuits began to establish missions in Pimeria Alta. Coming from the mission at Dolores in Sonora, Father Eusebio Francisco Kino, beloved Jesuit priest, preached to the Pima, Yuma, and other tribes.

For twenty-four years Father Kino worked indefatigably as a missionary, traveling afoot and alone over great stretches of arid country, braving hunger and thirst in the scorching heat of summer, or the cold of winter as he converted thousands of Indians. He taught the natives to plant crops of wheat, maize, beans, and melons, and introduced domestic animals and stock raising. Seven of the twenty-four missions established by Father Kino in Pimeria Alta were in what is now Arizona. Three of them—San Gabriel Guevavi, San Jose de Tumacacori, and San Xavier del Bac—were known to be in full operation when Father Kino died in 1711. The Pima Indians eagerly accepted the teachings of the Jesuits. But the fierce Apache were a constant menace, and in 1751 they destroyed the mission at San Xavier. It was rebuilt in the following year, but abandoned after an Indian attack in 1763.

In 1767 the Jesuits were expelled from New Spain, and missionary work was again taken up by the Franciscans. Foremost among them was Father Francisco Tomas Garces, a simple man who came to be deeply loved by the Pima and Papago, and who like Father Kino, cheerfully endured hardships of every sort in his missionary work among the Indians. The most famous of his many and far-flung journeys was the special mission to the Hopi Indians in 1776, when he traveled twenty-five hundred miles and saw twenty-five thousand Indians. In 1781 he met a tragic death at the hands of the Yuma.

The heroic and germinal period of the missions in Arizona ended with the massacre of Garces and the reprisals which followed it. The Franciscans were expelled by the new republic of Mexico in 1827, but the Roman Catholic Church was firmly established and has never since lost ground.

According to the last Federal religious census (1936), of the 165,020 Arizonans who were church members, 94,043, or fifty-seven per cent were Roman Catholics. As the state's population has more than doubled since this census, it can be assumed that the church populations have also doubled.

The Mormons or Latter Day Saints numbering 22,331 members, comprised the largest non-Catholic religious group in Arizona (1936). Mormons seek guidance by adherence to the precepts of the Bible as interpreted in the Book of Mormon and in revelations which come to their apostles and members. Their temples are not meeting places but are used for sacred rites of the "Celestial Marriage" and the "Baptism for the Dead." They have developed a missionary program of wide scope.

Protestant churches were slow to develop in Arizona. There was no Protestant church in Tucson until 1878, when a Presbyterian mission was built there and used by all non-Catholic denominations. In 1881 various other denominations began building churches of their own. The Methodist with 11,489 members, the Presbyterian with 6,746 members, and the Baptist with 9,032 members were the principal Protestant denominations, according to the 1936 Religious Census.

Religious beliefs and practices among the Indians are too complex a subject for consideration here. The Hopi have responded least of all to the white man's religion, and retain their ancient dances, including the weird ceremony in which live rattlesnakes are held in the dancers' mouths. While the Yuma were willing to accept some of the tenets and ceremonial forms of Christianity, many remain faithful to at least some of the most important of their old rituals. Each Easter in the Yaqui village near Tucson, and in Guadalupe village not far from Phoenix, the Yaqui Indians stage their Passion Play. The Papago, who were among the first to accept Christianity, perform their ancient rites each March at San Xavier. The *Chilt-ko,* or harvest ceremony, and various bird songs give thanks to the gods and ask for further beneficence. The sacred songs are handed down from one generation to another.

Newspapers, Radio and Television

THE STORY of newspaper pioneering in Arizona is the absorbing tale of editors who had to be tough, who "confronted the desert and walked in the shadow of death . . . their hourly associates horned toads, rattlesnakes, burros, Gila monsters, and bad men red and white."

Half a century ago Arizona editors could shoot and write with equal facility, and frequently did. Such versatility was a necessity, for many of the pioneer newspapermen were called upon to defend their personal honor and their sometimes too "candid" opinions on local happenings by duels. There appears to be no record that any one of the antagonists was killed, for they generally "shot wide." In less formal differences, however, they were known to defend themselves effectively.

And well they knew when to duck. As exponents of law and order, the editors would condemn the practice then in vogue of "shooting up the town." Immediately cowboys in their cups and the wilder element in the vicinity would show their disapproval of such editorial views by riding down the main street and firing into the newspaper office. The entire newspaper staff would drop to the floor, hiding under the press or anything else which offered shelter from the flying bullets. The bombardment over, the staff got up and work was resumed. But for the most part the community gave the editors support and a certain homage bordering on hero worship.

The printing press in early Arizona often preceded the pick and shovel. The first newspaper, the *Weekly Arizonian,* appeared in Tubac in the spring of 1859, when that town was only a handful of white settlers, many of them cutthroats from Sonora, and outcasts from Texas and San Francisco.

There was no lack of live news for the ambitious editor in those days, for every man was a law unto himself, and the leading citizen was frequently the one "whose trigger finger was nimble and whose knife was sure." But, contrary to present-day ideas of news value, the more prosaic occurrences usually took precedence over the almost daily deeds of violence. Death was familiar, and a new shipment of supplies for the general store was more interesting and unusual news.

The *Prescott Miner's* report of an Indian attack is typical:

"Charlie Genung is in from Peeples Valley to buy some bacon. The weather is cold in his locality and there is little of news. He says that he and his neighbors were annoyed last week by a bunch of Yavapais, who came into the valley and ran off a couple of mules. Genung and several other ranchers pursued and killed several of the redskins. George Brown got a bad arrow wound in the shoulder."

The crude little Washington hand press on which the *Weekly Arizonian* was printed was the first press in Arizona. It came by sailing vessel from the East, around the Horn to San Francisco, and from there it was laboriously freighted to Tubac. Nearly twenty years later it was used to print the *Tucson Star,* and in 1879 it was moved to Tombstone for the *Nugget,* first newspaper in that famous town. The little press, which also printed the Tombstone *Epitaph,* recorded the thoughts of some of the keenest minds and the most able writers of that day. Among the noted contributors to these first newspapers, particularly the *Epitaph,* were John P. Clum, Pat Hamilton, Harry Brook, John D. Dunbar, Sam Purdy, Charles D. Poston, Harry Wood, Dick Rule, William O. O'Neill, O'Brien Moore, and many others; men who knew the business of writing and whose work was well done even in the light of journalistic standards today.

The *Arizonian* moved from Tubac to Tucson, thence to Prescott and back to Tucson, and finally folded up in 1871. It was the first paper to try to convince the authorities in Washington of the need for greater military protection and to support the idea of a territorial government separate from New Mexico.

The *Arizona Miner* appeared on March 9, 1864 at Fort Whipple, seventeen miles north of Prescott; the first copies were printed on single sheets of colored mapping paper, twelve by twenty inches. Launched by Richard C. McCormick, an experienced newspaper man from New York, then secretary of the territory, it was edited by Tisdale A. Hand, and wielded a strong political influence in the territory. When the seat of territorial government and its protective force of soldiers at Fort Whipple moved to Prescott, the *Miner* went too, and with it went McCormick. The first number issued at Prescott was eagerly welcomed.

"There was a deep pride in the Arizona hamlet as its entire population gathered around the little hand press," reads a contemporary account, "to welcome the birth of a journalistic babe of promise that would carry afar the story of its greatness. The only compositor was the pressman; across the iron press bed the 'devil' energetically distributing ink on a composition roller, but none too skillfully. The paper had been 'wet down' the day before and lay in smooth dampness. The forms being linked, the printer thrust a piece of paper upon the typon points, slowly unhooked the swinging frisket and brought it down to protect the margins of the paper, rolled the bed under the platen, heaved away on the 'devil-tail' lever that gave the pressure, and rolled back the bed. Then there was deep sensation among the bespurred spectators. Possibly a few relieved their feelings and spread the glad tidings of joy by shooting through the roof or the door."

In 1867 the territorial capital was moved from Prescott to Tucson, and again the *Miner* moved. But this time the newspaper went with McCormick, for he had been elected governor of the territory. His paper became the *Tucson Citizen* in October 1870, and was used as a political organ by the administration.

Many noted Arizona pioneers were connected with the *Miner,* and through some stroke of fate most of its publishers and editors came to a tragic end. Tisdale A. Hand died of tuberculosis; Meacham, one of its earliest editors, died of wounds received in an Indian fight; Charles W. Beach, who was its publisher for years, was assassinated in 1889; S. N. Holmes, another editor, met his death in a hotel fire; and William "Bucky" O'Neill, also an editor, was killed in battle while serving with Theodore Roosevelt's Rough Riders in the Spanish American War.

The independent and outspoken *Arizona Sentinel* was established at Yuma in 1871 by C. S. Miner, and lays claim to being the oldest paper continuously published in Arizona. In March 1877, the *Daily Bulletin,* first of dailies, began publication in Tucson with four four-column pages. The *Tri-Weekly Star,* which soon succeeded it, was edited by L. C. Hughes, who later became governor of Arizona. It had a news service over a "fearful and wonderful telegraph line, strung for much of its course on giant cactus or mesquite trees, its wires frequently utilized by unfeeling teamsters for wagon repairs." The paper's name was later changed to the *Arizona Daily Star.*

The first newspaper in Phoenix was the *Salt River Valley Herald,* started in January 1878 by Charles E. McClintock. In September 1880, it became the *Phoenix Herald* and eventually was absorbed by the *Arizona Republican.* Among the most interesting newspapermen of the eighties was Judge James A. Reilly, who wrote cleverly in the vernacular and was a well-known character in the Southwest. Speaking his thoughts too freely, however, lost the judge the Democratic county printing, and he finally left for Tombstone during the early days of the camp. In Tombstone he practiced law with a humor and sagacity that became legendary.

A story, typical of southwestern pioneer journalism, is told of the *Daily Arizona Silver Belt,* which was established at Globe in 1878 by Judge A. H. Hackney, an outstanding and greatly beloved newspaper man. When Judge Hackney was ready to print the first issue he found he had no type large enough for the masthead; so he carved one out of a block of wood sawed from a well-seasoned ox yoke.

The first number of Tombstone *Epitaph* was issued on May 1, 1880, and was printed in a tent. When the *Epitaph* appeared there were only six counties in the territory and ten other newspapers printed in the English language: the *Nugget* at Tombstone; the *Record,* the *Citizen,* and the *Star* at Tucson; the *Silver Belt* at Globe; the *Salt River Herald* and the *Weekly Phoenix Herald* at Phoenix; the *Enterprise* and the *Miner* at Prescott; and the *Sentinel* at Yuma. Before the close of 1880 six new papers were started: the *Bullion* at Harshaw, the *Chronicle* at Globe, the *Drill* at Pinal, the *Gazette* at Phoenix, the *Enterprise* at Florence, and the *Miner* at Mineral Park.

The old *Arizona Kicker,* famous Tombstone newspaper, had a wide circulation because it expressed the attitude of the West and of westerners. Outspoken to the point of humorous offense, it was often in deep water, and fought its way out, answering all charges in its columns with bravado. The *Kicker's* modern counterpart is found today in the *Brewery Gulch Gazette* published at Bisbee.

Claiming the first "Associated Press" service in Arizona, Perry Williams, first experienced telegrapher in the territory, was located at Maricopa in the 1880's and from there supplied citizens and newspapers with news from the outside world. In later years, Mr. Williams would chuckle as he confessed that he frequently "faked the news" when he was short. The invention of a telephone by Samuel Lount of Phoenix was reported by local newspapers in the early eighties. Mr. Lount made no effort to promote his invention, merely using it for communicating between his place of business and his home. Old-timers in Phoenix claim that it worked as well as the present day system.

During this period newspaper editors in Arizona might continually differ on personal or political matters and the majority of them had at one time or another been jailed or fined for libel or slander, but on one problem they were in accord and stood together in a solid phalanx—Indian atrocities and the manner in which they believed the situation should be handled.

It was apparently impossible to make the authorities in Washington realize the true and frightful condition; and newspaper editors to a man were fiercely antagonistic to what they called "weak-kneed policies of military authorities" in dealing with the Indians. In 1871 the *Prescott Miner* published a list of four hundred victims slaughtered by the Apache. It was reported that between March 1864 and the fall of 1871, at least four hundred pioneers had been murdered; two were known to have been burned alive, fifty-three had been wounded and crippled, and five had been carried into captivity.

When Geronimo was at the height of his power in 1885, editorials in every newspaper pressed the fight against the Indians. The *Phoenix Herald* wrote: "There is only one course to pursue with these San Carlos Apaches, and that is to transport the entire gang. Till that is done, the Southwestern part of the Territory will never be safe. As to where they should be taken, there is not much hesitation on the part of Arizonians in saying that it should be to a graveyard, but in deference to the 'eastern notion' we will be satisfied with the Dry Tortugas or some island on the Pacific coast or Boston."

The fantastic story of the "Baron of Arizona" merits mention here because it was through the alertness of a "stammering printer," who worked for Tom Weedin on the *Florence Citizen,* that the most tremendous fraud in the history of the West was exposed.

In 1887 the claim of James Addison Reavis was established on the basis of ancient Spanish documents recognized by the government as legitimate, and he was granted a tract of land in Arizona 236 miles long and 78 miles wide. Editor Tom Weedin was chief exponent for all doubters, but his violent editorials contending that the Baron and his lordly ways were the very epitome of "fakery" were drowned out by the overwhelming news that Robert G. Ingersoll, the great lawyer, had pronounced the claim flawless. From 1887 until 1893 the bizarre existence of the Reavis-Peralta family proceeded with pomp and splendor.

Then Bill, Tom Weedin's printer, shattered the Baron's Utopia. Phoenix had wrested the capitol site away from Prescott, and Bill on a "postman's holiday" in Phoenix had a hankering to look over the printing exhibited in the old documents filed there. Naturally he was interested in the Baron's famous papers. His interest heightened when he discovered that one very "ancient" document was printed in a type that had only been invented a few years previous to the filing of the claim in 1887. Feverishly he examined the rest, and discovered the startling fact that one of the documents plainly bore the mark of a Wisconsin paper mill that had only been in existence ten or twelve years. Bill became a bashful and reluctant hero; the judgment of Tom Weedin was vindicated; and the Baron was convicted in January 1895 and sentenced to six years in prison at Santa Fe.

In lusty pioneer Arizona, newspapers arose on every hand; some of them gained strength and lasting leadership, and many others were short-lived. In the development of this frontier journalism "local patriotism was the only cult. Each editor believed in his heart that his own village was destined to become the center of the great Southwest. On that subject he lied to himself and the world alike. In the riot of his imagination, every nearby hill had the mineral treasures of Golconda, and in every little valley he saw the budding promise of a modern Eden."

The publications of this period which are still in existence today are numerous, and include the *Arizona Citizen,* now the *Tucson Citizen* (1870); *Arizona Sentinel,* now the *Yuma Daily Sun* and continuing *Sentinel* (1872); *Arizona Star,* now the *Arizona Daily Star* (1877); *Arizona Silver Belt,* (Globe)-Miami (1878); *Arizona Gazette,* now the *Phoenix Gazette* (1880); *Tombstone* Epitaph (1880); *Winslow Mail* (1880); *Prescott Courier* (1882); *Mohave County Miner,* Kingman (1882); *Coconino Sun,* Flagstaff (1882); *Arizona Range News,* Willcox (1884); *St. Johns Herald,* now the *Apache County Independent News* (1885); *Tempe News* (1886); *Arizona Republican,* now the *Arizona Republic* (1890); *Williams News* (1891); *Florence Blade-Tribune* (1892); *Winslow Mail* (1893); *Graham County Guardian,* Safford (1895); *Arizona Orb,* now the *Bisbee Daily Review* (1896); *Copper Era,* Clifton (1899); *Douglas Daily Dispatch* (1902).

In the two most populous cities: in Phoenix the *Arizona Republic* absorbed the *Phoenix Gazette* in 1930 as morning and evening newspapers, respectively; separately edited yet singly owned and directed. At Tucson, the *Arizona Daily Star* and the *Tucson Daily Citizen,* are also published as morning and evening newspapers, respectively.

Territorial Days

FLAGSTAFF IN 1882

WASHINGTON STREET, PHOENIX (1905)

ROAD SIGN

Opposit
(*above*) YUMA ABOUT 188
(*center*) OLD STAGE AT TOMBSTONE (c. 1880)
(*bottom*) SALOON AT GILA BEND (c. 1880)

STREET SCENE IN OLD TOMBSTONE

Joseph Miller

OLD FORT MISERY, PRESCOTT

PIONEER SCHOOLHOUSE, PHOENIX

OLD GOVERNOR'S MANSION, PRESCOTT (1864)

RUINS OF
TERRITORIAL
PRISON, YUMA

Joseph Miller

GERONIMO, APACHE RENEGADE

GERONIMO AND NATCHEZ (*Mounted*) ; SON OF GERONIMO (*Left*) (c. 1885)

FFICERS AND SCOUTS,
RT APACHE (1875)

AL SIEBER, CHIEF OF SCOUTS
(*Seated*) (1881)

S.S. *SEARCHLIGHT*, COLORADO RIVER, YUMA (1909)

PRESIDENT TAFT SIGNING STATEHOOD BILL (1912)

Carson

RADIO AND TELEVISION

Radio found immediate and enthusiastic acceptance in Arizona. The topography of mountain and desert resulting in isolation of remote settlements, made the miracle of radio a welcome antidote for either enforced or chosen solitude. Men still live in Arizona today who watched the smoke signals of hostile Indians; rode the narrow twisting roads along sheer canyon cliffs in stage coach or on horseback; watched the slow, tedious transformation of barren deserts into fertile valleys and gem-like cities. To these survivors of a primitive yesterday, Arizona has bridged two separate eras; and by no means the least of the changes they witnessed was the coming of the radio.

In awed respect, Arizona's old-timers watched the conquest of space . . . the treacherous vastness of space, which well they knew required strength, courage, endless and arduous journeys to conquer. Suddenly, miraculously, fearful vastness was dwarfed to virtual nonexistence . . . the still air made vibrant and alive with human voice.

Although Arizona cannot claim any part in the initial discoveries of radio, its subsequent interest has been ambitious and aggressive. Licensed on June 21, 1922, KFAD in Phoenix, now KTAR, was the thirty-sixth station in the entire country, and was the first to be licensed in the state. Soon after, KFCB also in Phoenix, now known as KOY, which had been broadcasting for some time as an amateur station, was also licensed to operate. For many years these two stations were without competition in Arizona.

They were, however, not the only pioneers in radio; for as the "hams" elsewhere contributed greatly to the success of broadcasting, so the amateurs of Arizona assisted in radio development in the state. These amateurs were the only ones who could build or repair or understand the earlier "contraptions," and the "tinkerers" who knew the intricacies of the subject were men set apart and admired. From 1922 to 1924 more than 75 per cent of the sets used were built by amateurs. Practically all of the radio receiving sets were crystal sets. Headphones were the thing and no sets had loudspeakers.

Station KTAR, started as KFAD by MacArthur Brothers, as a 1,000 watt station, is now a 5,000 watt station and operates a minimum of eighteen hours per day. The station passed into the hands of Electrical Equipment Co. of Phoenix in 1925. In 1929 this company was joined in its ownership, operation and management by the Arizona Publishing Company, publishers of the *Arizona Republic*.

KTAR became an associate member of the NBC network in 1930, first station in Arizona to broadcast regularly programs on a national network. One of KTAR's outstanding programs is the annual Easter Morning sunrise service from the rim of the Grand Canyon, initiated in 1934. The service is released over a nation-wide network. In 1944, ownership passed to John J. Louis, originator of "Fibber McGee and Molly" and "Great Gildersleeve" radio programs. KTAR is the key station of the Arizona Broadcasting System.

Radio station KOY, the first to broadcast in Arizona, began as a tiny amateur station in the back of a local radio and sporting goods store, conceived by the proprietor as a business promotion for radio equipment. The little station grew steadily, however, and in 1936 was purchased by Burridge D. Butler and the Salt River Valley Broadcasting Company. It is now a 5,000 watt station, member of the Mutual-Don Lee Broadcasting System, and key station of the Arizona Network.

Arizona's pioneer television station, KPHO-TV, began operations on Channel 5 in Phoenix, December 4, 1949. At that time there were less than two thousand television receivers in the state. With 5 to 6 hours daily telecasting, as affiliated station of CBS, NBC, ABC, and DuMont networks it serviced with live network programs when the transcontinental coaxial cable began feeding them to Phoenix audiences in 1952. KPHO-TV expanded its program schedule and in 1954 telecasted 14 hours daily to an audience of more than 80,000 families. Purchased by Meredith Publishing Company in 1952, it was a Basic Affiliate of CBS, but later CBS moved to KOOL-TV, Channel 10.

Phoenix' second television station took to the air October 24, 1953, with a unique share-time operation on Channel 10. KOY and KOOL, long-time radio rivals, agreed to share time equally alternating weekly for daytime and nighttime telecasting, thus avoiding the expense of costly competitive hearing for the channel. Later, however, KOOL bought out KOY'S share and now the station is KOOL-TV.

Meanwhile, Arizona's other radio pioneer, KTAR, continued to fight a three-cornered battle with two rivals for Channel 3, the fourth and last channel available in the Valley. They finally purchased KTYL-TV. Mesa, Channel 12, and the call letters were changed to KVAR. Thus ended the Channel 3 battle, which is now KTVK Television, an ABC affiliate.

Tucson has two stations, KVOA, Channel 4, and KOPO, Channel 13; Yuma has one, KIVA, Channel 11. Several Arizona communities are served television by means of booster facilities.

Sports and Recreation

AS A NATURAL locale for sports and recreation Arizona leaves little to be desired, for its wide range of temperature and elevation and its varied topography provide activities to suit practically all tastes. In winter, for example, skiing and tobogganing may be enjoyed in the northern mountain area while—by traveling a few hours to the south—one may "drop down" to a sun-drenched desert playground.

With the great majority of visitors and permanent residents alike, the favorite outdoor pastime is riding—a year round activity in southern Arizona. Cow ponies are generally used, although almost any other kind of mount suited to the experience and desires of the individual rider may be obtained in the larger communities. Mule and burro pack trips, with or without the services of a guide, are especially popular in the mountain and desert sections. A bit of amateur prospecting for gold or silver commonly adds to the interest of such trips.

Guests at dude ranches often accompany the cow hands on spring and fall roundups and exhibit their skill in horsemanship at the amateur rodeos staged by many of these ranches. The amateur or professional rodeo with its bronco busting, calf roping, and steer bulldogging, is a prominent sporting event in nearly every community or resort in the state. Most important of these exhibitions are the one staged annually ever since 1888 at Prescott, as part of the Frontier Days celebration in the first week of July, the Phoenix Jaycee Championship Rodeo, and *La Fiesta de los Vaqueros* (Festival of the Cowboys) held at Tucson.

The sportsman finds a plentiful supply of big game, and the popularity of hunting is indicated by the number of licenses—about one hundred fifty thousand—issued yearly. Seasonal and bag limits are designed to conserve the supply of game and vary from year to year. Bison or buffalo, brown and black bear, mountain lion, deer, elk, and other species of big game are found in certain sections of the state, and may be hunted in season; also antelope, bighorn sheep, javelina or wild pig, tree squirrel. Grouse, and pheasant, are at present (1954) protected by closed season.

The mule deer, so called because of his long ears, is the principal big-game animal of Arizona and is found nearly everywhere in the state except in the Navajo country in the northeastern section. More than fifty thousand (comprising the largest single herd of mule deer in the United States) roam the Kaibab forest, north of the Grand Canyon. The largest bucks weigh up to two hundred and forty pounds dressed and carry antlers with a spread of from thirty to forty inches. The little Arizona whitetail, seldom weighing more than a hundred pounds, is more numerous but also more elusive, and is found only in rough brush country. Certain Arizona business firms offer prizes to the hunter bringing in the first deer as well as the heaviest buck of the season.

Of the six indigenous species of cloven-hoofed animals found in Arizona by the first white settler, the elk alone became extinct; but imported stock, preserved through supervision and protection, are now to be found on the Mogollon Plateau. Additional stock released in the Hualpai and Bill Williams mountain areas have brought the number of elk in the state to between three and four thousand head. Elk hunting was revived in 1935 and during the 1952 open season, 1,693 elk were taken. Special permit is required for elk hunting. The elk is the largest round-horned deer in the world, the bulls sometimes weighing as much as 1,700 pounds.

The only wild bison or buffalo in Arizona today are found in Houserock Valley, and Raymond's ranch. A short hunting season is permitted under closely restricted conditions.

The state's most predatory animal, the lion, may be hunted the year around. The great cats are usually found in the roughest and most brush-covered country, where deer are plentiful. Since a lion will commonly destroy no fewer than fifty deer in a year, the killing of one lion means saving the lives of hundreds of deer. Occasionally the jaguar, called *el tigre* by the Mexicans, drifts in from Sonora; but unlike the mountain lion the jaguar can seldom be treed. Many hunters seek bear as well as deer on the Mogollon Rim. A black or brown bear is always a fine prize, often weighing as much as six hundred pounds. Hunting lion and bear on horseback, with a well-trained pack of dogs, is a sport that is truly western; the hunter, riding at breakneck speed over rough and broken ground with the roar of the dogs in his ears, experiences an unforgettable thrill.

Numerous species of smaller game attract the sportsman. The wild turkey, largest of American game birds and classed as big game in Arizona, is found throughout the northern pine and oak area. Because the bird is so wary that one slight awkward move or careless crackle of brush may ruin any chance of a kill, the hunter regards the taking of a wild turkey as something of a feat. Various species of duck, goose, snipe, and other waterfowl inhabit the lakes and streams, including the green-winged and blue-winged teal, mallard, widgeon, redhead, and wild goose. White-wing pigeons, quail and doves may be hunted in season, as well as jack rabbits on which there are no closed season or bag limit. The coyote, while not a game animal, provides occasion for many a sporting shot.

With an increasing number of artificial lakes—impounded waters of mighty reclamation projects generously stocked from the state's numerous hatcheries—and with its many mountain streams and natural lakes, Arizona has much to offer the fisherman. The White Mountain district in particular lures the sportsman to try his skill in its cold waters for rainbow, German brown, and other trout, which are plentiful there. The string of beautiful lakes below Flagstaff and the big bodies of water in the Salt River irrigation system provide good fishing for bass as well as numerous other varieties. Coolidge Lake, near Globe, contains fine bass, crappie, and bluegill. Bright Angel Creek at the bottom of the Grand Canyon offers perhaps the best fishing in the state; the trout grow large in its icy waters and are full of fight.

The larger communities offer the usual recreational opportunities available to city dwellers elsewhere in the United States. But unlike those in most other parts of the country, the golf links, tennis courts, and swimming pools of southern Arizona can be enjoyed throughout the year. Phoenix has each winter a season of horse-racing and dog-racing, with pari-mutuel betting permitted. Automobile races are held at Phoenix, Flagstaff, Douglas, and a few other cities. There are several ski runs in Arizona's high country. The most popular ones are located at the Arizona Snow Bowl near Flagstaff; in Rustler Park in the Chiricahuas; and a third near Prescott.

School and college athletics play a prominent part in the recreational activities of the state. The University of Arizona and the two state colleges are represented in the Border Conference Intercollegiate Athletic Association, the other members of which are institutions in New Mexico and Texas. The major sports sponsored by this organization are football, basketball, and track events; with baseball, boxing, tennis, and golf occupying a minor position.

High school teams compete in events sponsored by the Arizona Interscholastic Athletic Association, which is divided into five districts—the Northen, Southern, Eastern, East Central, and West Central. Football, basketball, and track events constitute the major conference sports. Phoenix Union High School is an associate member of the California Interscholastic Athletic Association and competes with several Coast schools, as do teams from Mesa, Yuma, and Tucson. Some Arizona high school gridiron elevens meet teams from Texas and New Mexico. The annual Greenway Track and Field Meet offers classified competition to athletes from elementary schools, and there are state track meets held annually for high schools. With many golf courses in the southern part of Arizona, and inspired by the annual appearance of the nation's top golfers at Phoenix and Tucson, golf is gaining among the high schools and the public at large. Swimming also holds high interest in the southern section, while skiing flourishes in the north.

The Arts

CENTURIES before the discovery of America, the first Indian story-tellers chiseled on smooth rock surfaces tales of the villages, the exploits of warriors, and the achievements of the hunt. These pictographs—men and animals and strange geometrical designs—constitute Arizona's first written literature.

When the Indians were segregated on reservations, the younger generations, school-trained and under the influence of the white man's civilization, lost interest in the tribal legends. Many tales disappeared completely, while others were preserved only through the efforts of white collectors. J. William Lloyd gathered the legends of the Pima Indians under the title *Aw-Aw-Tam Indian Nights*. A self-schooled carpenter, physician, cowpuncher, and colonist, Lloyd wrote down the legends "in the manner in which they were told." Frank G. Applegate showed his sympathy with and understanding of the Hopi in his simple and often humorous *Indian Stories from the Pueblos,* which retain much of the flavor of the original narratives.

Stories of Indians and of Indian life make up a large bulk of the state's literature. In recent years the dime-novel redskin, cunning and murderous, has been replaced by Indian characters sincerely studied as representatives of a unique culture and social life. Several painters have lived among the tribes and learned their language, and their pictures of Arizona Indians are in the world's leading museums. Mary Russell Colton, artist, and her husband, Dr. Harold S. Colton, are directing the revival of Hopi arts and crafts at the Museum of Northern Arizona. Oliver La Farge, who came to Arizona as an archeologist, traversed hundreds of miles of Indian country and made extensive observations of Indian manners and customs before writing his Pulitzer Prize winner, *Laughing Boy,* and his later *Enemy Gods.*

The Spanish strain survived throughout Arizona's development and appears side by side with other elements in the state's literature and art. A number of powerful chronicles were compiled by Spanish explorers of the sixteenth century. The earliest of these was Marcos de Niza's *Descubrimiento de los siete Ciudades,* one of the world's famous narratives of discovery, giving an account of the so-called Seven Cities of Cibola. Coronado's noted expedition, started in 1540, was chronicled by Pedro de Castanedo in his *Relacion de la Jornado de Cibola.* Antonio de Espejo also explored this region and composed a chronicle of his experiences; and the expeditions of Juan de Onate were the subject of an epic poem by Gaspar de Villagra (or Villagran). Father Eusebio Francisco Kino, the Jesuit missionary, introduced Catholic church music into the missions he established early in the eighteenth century, teaching the Pima and Papago sacred songs. In the missions, too, appeared the first Arizona painting executed under European influence. Indian neophytes under the direction of the padres, decorated the walls of the missions in pigments derived from vegetable substances. Father Kino was the author of a travel narrative, *Historical Memoir of Pimeria Alta,* which gave a close description of Arizona's physical appearance, its plant and animal life, and the character and customs of the natives.

The valuable diaries of Father Francisco Tomas Garces, the Franciscan missionary who made several expeditions to the Gila and Colorado Rivers, are contained in Elliott Coues' *On The Trail of a Spanish Pioneer.*

Travelers, trappers, and pioneers from the United States introduced their customs and manner of life into Arizona in the nineteenth century, and writers and artists among them recorded the territory's appearance and characteristic happenings from a new perspective. James O. Pattie, a trapper of the early days, described his adventures in *The Personal Narrative of James O. Pattie;* and J. Ross Browne in the drawings and sketches of his adventures in the Apache Country, left a picture of hardships encountered by settlers in pioneer Arizona. In the seventies Frederic Dellenbaugh went into the Grand Canyon with the second Powell Expedition and painted the first oil landscapes of Arizona, one of which is in the Arizona Museum in Phoenix. Thomas Moran, famous for his painting of the grandiose scenery of the West, also went into the Grand Canyon with the expedition of Professor F. V. Hayden, and took the hard voyage down the Colorado River with a party led by Major Powell. In the nineties Moran lived and painted on the rim of the Grand Canyon; his *The Grand Canyon of the Yellowstone* and *The Chasm of the Colorado* are in the National Capitol. Frederic

Remington is another nationally known artist who spent much time in Arizona in the eighties and nineties and left many canvases expressive of its vitality and color. These early paintings and illustrations gave the world its first visual conception of Arizona.

The cowboy, introduced to millions of readers through the pulp magazines, came to have the reputation of being a simple, horse-loving individual, brutal and quick on the trigger. The late Zane Grey, a native of Ohio, did nothing to change this false impression in his many novels of the west, and often sacrificed artistry and truth to gunplay. Nevertheless his novels, especially *The Call of the Canyon,* give a vivid impression of Arizona landscape, and his first book *The Last of the Plainsmen,* a nonfiction work, has a striking picture of the upper Grand Canyon country. Ross Santee writes of the real cowboy. His stories deal with simple and normal themes: the rodeo, the roundup, and the struggle of ranchers against drought. Usually accompanying the stories are the author's own illustrations. Santee, a native of Iowa, spent many years in the saddle in Arizona before he became known as an artist and author. His *Cowboy* is an authentic story of life on the open range.

Other writers have treated Arizona either realistically or with romantic simplification. In *Arizona's Dark and Bloody Ground,* Earle Forrest tells the story of the Pleasant Valley War, the tragic feud between the Graham and Tewksbury clans. William H. Robinson, born in Illinois, has written many books covering different phases of early Arizona days. In *Thirsty Earth,* he tells of the settler's struggle for water and the building of the first irrigation canals. His novella, *The Witchery of Rita,* is a story of the San Xavier Mission. Jack Weadock's *Dust of the Desert* is an authentic and picturesque story of life on the border. Adolph Bandelier's *The Delight Makers,* a fictionalized account of prehistoric Arizona, is one of the finest novels of ancient life in America. Stewart Edward White's *Arizona Nights* is a collection of descriptive short stories.

Dick Wick Hall—rancher, mine promoter, homesteader, garageman, and postmaster—is Arizona's most notable humorist. In the early 1920's he began to issue a mimeographed sheet, *The Salome Sun,* distributed free for the purpose of agitating for better roads through Salome, where he had established a "laughing gas" station. The *Sun* contained humorous sketches of local characters and was full of puns, exaggerations, and crackerbox philosophy. Hall's sheets reached such success among tourists that the author and his hometown became known in distant parts of the country and his contributions were solicited by the nation's largest magazines.

The poet, Sharlot Hall, who came to Arizona in a covered wagon when she was twelve, has endeared herself to the state through her writings and her devotion to the preservation of historical mementoes.

Her poems, celebrating her adopted state, appear under the title *Cactus and Pine*. Eminent among Arizona poets is Edward Doro, whose work deals with universal rather than local themes; his *Shiloh* is a powerful poem about Jesus saved by Judas after a sham crucifixion. Doro has received the Russel Loines Memorial Award and a Guggenheim Fellowship.

Among the many contemporary writers are: Nora Laing, whose *Desert Ships* is a story of health seekers; Mary Kidder Rak, telling in *Cowman's Wife* of life on a small ranch from a woman's point of view; Hilda Faunce, portraying in *Desert Wife* a white woman's loneliness on an Indian reservation; Jack O'Connor, who in a swashbuckling romance, *Conquest*, paints the early exploits and rise to power of an Arizona pioneer; Oren Arnold, feature writer and journalist; Stuart David Engstrand, author of *The Invaders*, a novel about economic struggle on the farm; Frances Gillmore who in *Windsinger* wrote of the Indian's spiritual life and his awareness of beauty; Laura Adams Armer, winner of the Newberry Prize for her children's story, *Waterless Mountain;* and Charles G. Finney, author of the fantastic story, *The Circus of Dr. Lao,* which was conceived in China and written in Tucson.

The Grand Canyon, the Petrified Forest, the Painted Desert, and the brilliant skies and mountains of Arizona continue to be celebrated by visiting and native artists, writers, and musicians. Francis McComas of California, and Albert Groll of New York, have done many water colors and oils of Arizona's canyons and deserts. George Elbert Burr of Phoenix has contributed etchings and paintings to the world's foremost museums: his *The Sand Storm in the Little Colorado* and *Moonlight Near Holbrook* are in the Phoenix Municipal Collection. Harold Bell Wright, nationally popular author, lived for many years near Tucson, and Owen Wister also spent some time in the state. The English novelist J. B. Priestley came to Wickenburg in 1935-36 to complete a novel, and while here gathered the material for his autobiographical study, *Midnight on the Desert*. Robert Sherwood's play *The Petrified Forest* found a symbolic meaning in this dry land. Ferde Grofe's *Grand Canyon Suite,* Victor Young's *Arizona Sketches,* and Cadman's *Land of the Sky Blue Water* are musical compositions inspired by Arizona subjects.

Many fine books have been published on Arizona since 1940 and space does not permit comment here on some of the outstanding volumes. There is a selective list, however, on pages 511-13.

Architecture

THE EARLY Indians of Arizona built no permanent structures, but lived in natural caves or brush shelters and under overhanging cliffs. Descendants or successors began to sink circular pits into the ground, covering them with roofs constructed of cedar cross-beams and branches crisscrossed and matted with bark and earth. These were supported by posts and extended a little above the ground. The subterranean walls were usually faced with rocks, and earth was banked around to form a wall aboveground. Entrance was made by a hatchway cut through the wall.

First round-cornered and then rectangular pit houses evolved from the circular habitations. Greater structural strength resulted with the development of square corners and solid walls of stone. The dwellers walked upon the roofs, entered through trapdoors, and descended by ladders.

As the natives learned to fit rocks and chink them with mud, the pit type of structure was gradually abandoned and surface structures were built. These were widely scattered, according to the availability of materials, and consisted of six to fourteen rooms, one story in height.

The necessity for common protection against marauders influenced the building of pueblos or communal structures on high mesas, in valleys, or in recesses in cliff walls; these structures housed entire clans.

Stone was most frequently employed, though several ruins reveal the use of adobe or sun-dried mud blocks, the materials readiest to hand. The edges of the mesas, like the walls of the cliffs, furnished an inexhaustible supply of building stone, often of the proper size for masonry and requiring little or no dressing. The general plan of these pueblos usually included a central courtyard around which were built the series of dwellings.

Temporary shelters were erected near the fields during the agricultural season, and deserted for the pueblo or cliff house, which overlooked the fields, when the season was over.

The front and sides of cliff dwellings were sometimes built several stories high to meet the roof formed by the overhanging cliffs. Montezuma Castle in the Verde Valley is illustrative of this type. Each of the cubical rooms had a single opening barely large enough to permit entrance, a feature designed as a measure of protection.

The pueblos on the mesas of approximately the same period were quite similar though more extensive. The rooms were cubical and were arranged without any inner passageways. The roofs of the first-floor rooms formed the floors and porches of those above. Additions were made as needed. The upper stories, terraced back, were reached with portable ladders. The upper and inner rooms served as living quarters, the lower and outer ones for storage. No semblance of order or alignment was adhered to. The idea of camouflage may have influenced the builders, for the pueblos blend admirably with their surroundings. The Hopi Villages on the high mesas in northeastern Arizona are examples of this type.

The *kivas,* ceremonial chambers, an integral part of all pueblos, were built as separate units in the central courtyards. These were sunk into the earth or rock and were circular in form. The roofs, built flush with the surface, were constructed of cedar poles matted with branches, bark, and mud. Entrance was made by a ladder extending through a hatchway. The kiva is still found in practically all pueblos, modified to some extent; the circular form still survives, contrasting with the cubical design of the dwellings.

The pueblos of the people known as Canal Builders in the semiarid valleys of southern Arizona developed into great compound types consisting of a number of cubical structures with walls built of packed mud or huge mud blocks made from caliche, the subsoil of this region. A large main superstructure, apparently used as a watchtower and fort combined, was erected in the midst of these villages, as at Casa Grande.

Casa Grande itself was erected between the years 1300 and 1400 A.D. It was built of huge mud blocks and stood four stories high. The first story with the exception of one room was filled in with dirt, and an extra room was built on top of the third story, thus achieving a four-story structure with the strain of only three stories on the walls. This device permitted greater height for more effective observation.

Wooden poles were extended through the structure at the several story levels, covered with sticks, and filled in with mud smoothed to a fine finish to form the floors. Miniature doorways, a feature of pueblo architecture, were the only openings, with the exception of tiny holes here and there that served for ventilation and possibly other purposes.

Though evidence of a number of similar units has been discovered in the vicinity, there remain only the stately ruins of Casa Grande's watchtower, the foundations of several of the dwellings, traces of the protective wall that surrounded the unit, and the almost obliterated network of an ingenious canal system.

The first Spaniards invading the area of Arizona found most of the villages of the Hohokam culture in ruins. The occupied dwellings were dome-shaped mud and brush huts (hogans) as well as rectangular mud and brush houses and open-sided shelters. These were all constructed over a makeshift framework of cedar poles—a type of building still used by most tribes. Except for a few pueblos on the mesas in the Hopi country, the cliff dwellings and great pueblos were likewise deserted. The Indians at this time were building huts similar to those in the southern valleys.

When the Spanish padres came into southern Arizona and constructed missions in the last years of the seventeenth century, they encouraged the Indians to build their villages about the newly constructed mission houses. They taught them to make adobe brick by churning a mixture of mud and straw with their bare feet, forming blocks by hand, and setting them in the sun to bake.

The varied styles of mission buildings can be traced to Mexico, itself an architectural melting pot. But the padres in Arizona, too distant to duplicate these missions in any precise manner, contented themselves with imitating them as best they could. Few artisans could be found able to create in the styles familiar to the padres, and the individual ideas of the architect-builders gave added variation to mission architecture. For these reasons and because of topographic and climatic conditions the missions of Texas, California, and Arizona differ considerably except in certain general features, such as the patio, low shaded cloisters, and massive walls. Although the plans of mission churches were in general rectangular, there were exceptions, notably San Xavier del Bac, which was cruciform.

The distinguishing features of the California missions were massive round arches, pitched roofs of red clay tile, and ornamental ironwork and grillwork, sometimes imitated in wood painted black when metal was not available. Arizona's missions had high arches, vaulted and domed ceilings, and usually two bell towers on the front, each surmounted by a small dome. These well-proportioned towers, with their octagonal and arcaded belfries flanked with graceful flying buttresses, put the Arizona missions in a class by themselves.

San Xavier del Bac and San Jose de Tumacacori are noteworthy examples of the mission style in the Southwest, which represents a combination of many influences. San Xavier, completed in 1797, best preserved of the missions and the only church still in use, perhaps more completely embodies all the elements that enter into the mission architecture of this region, and remains the most perfect example in the country of the combination of Byzantine, Moorish, Spanish, and Mexican Aztec influences that characterize this style.

Strikingly beautiful in its desert setting nine miles south of Tucson, San Xavier is notable for its construction and design. The church and its dependencies are designed largely in the late Spanish Renaissance or Churrigueresque style borrowed from the contemporary architecture of viceregal Mexico. San Xavier is built entirely of burned brick with molded brick cornice, even the upper floors and roof including the dome, being carried completely on arches. The ceiling of the nave and transepts is formed by a series of flat domes between transverse brick ribs. The dome over the crossing is supported on a high octagonal drum, pierced with medallion windows.

The brick walls are coated with a white lime plaster, except the ornamental brick, which is highly colored to represent glazed tile. The entrance facade, elaborately decorated in the Spanish baroque style, is adorned with pilasters and panels and enriched with low plaster relief. The interior with its high altar and side chapels is richly embellished with carvings and painted ornament. Little timber is used in its construction. Only the doors with their frames and the spindles before the windows, the three front balconies, and some interior details are of wood. The foundation is of rubblestone, well cemented, extending from five feet below to two feet above the surface.

Tumacacori Mission, located ten miles north of Nogales, was finished early in 1800 and shows the Spanish influence characteristic of all missions built in the Southwest. Its construction for the most part is of sun-dried adobe bricks laid in mud mortar, which accounts for its semiruined condition, though completed later than San Xavier. It is rectangular with a massive square corner tower, and the general design tends very much toward a pseudo-classic treatment. The front facade, though typical of mission architecture, suggests with its superimposed columns the earlier and more classic tradition established in Spain by Juan de Herrara.

The walls of the church are six feet at the base and are offset on the outside to a thickness of three feet at the top. Where greater weight was to be carried, as in the three-story bell tower at the east front corner of the building, the walls are nearly ten feet thick. Burned brick coping was applied in places where erosion might affect the softer mud bricks. The flat roof, which has been reconstructed, was originally covered with cement and tile.

Native materials and frontier needs dictated the types of the first structures built by early Mexican settlers in southern Arizona. Pioneers from the American states to the east imitated the simple adobe box-type of the Mexicans, pierced with a doorway and window openings. The roofs were of round logs or *vigas* covered with sticks and brush and plastered with mud. Adjoining was an open lean-to covered with branches and supported by posts. The lean-to protected the house from the intense sunlight and served a more general use than the house proper, functioning somewhat in the manner of a loggia in Italian and Spanish types of houses.

Adobe buildings are especially suited to the southwestern climate, for adobe not only keeps out the extreme heat of summer but retains the warmth of the house against winter cold. From primitive days when huge mud blocks were formed of the subsoil of the region, through the mission period when padres taught the Indians to mix it with straw, and grass, mold it into bricks, and set them in the sun to dry, this crude, strong, earthen material has played a highly significant part in building construction in Arizona. With the importation of materials, adobe was sometimes denied its true character, hidden beneath a veneer or false front of wood. Stores, and the typical old saloon, for example, had a shiplap front facade a story-and-a-half high, behind which adobe served to support the roof. Improvements in the method of manufacture and a wider appreciation of its insulative qualities, however, has increasingly revived the use of adobe as a building material.

As pretentions grew with bank accounts, adobe was neglected. People desired "better things" and this often meant the abandonment of the original lean-to. An instance where it was not forgotten is represented by the old Thalheimer house, at Fourth and Jefferson Streets in Phoenix. This typical house is completely surrounded by a porch which protects the walls from the intense heat, as well as diffusing the glare of the sun. It is a story and a half high, and has a storage attic under the low gable roof which insulates the living quarters of the house. A large wide screened hall running through from east to west literally divided the house into two parts, and served as a suitable place for dining, living, or sleeping.

A commendable start toward a well-integrated architecture was made in the old main building at the University of Arizona, Tucson, though not developed in the later buildings. Here the double-deck gallery is structurally integrated, serving the same purpose as the porch in the Thalheimer house, and also as replacing the hallway in gaining entrance to the rooms of the north and south wings. The dryness and the type of soil at Tucson permitted the raised basement plan for the main floor.

Arizona has suffered importations of every type and style of architecture. If popular elsewhere they became popular here. Rather unsightly houses and school buildings in Victorian Gothic, Italian Renaissance, and neo-classic styles were imposed on the landscape—none of which has contributed to an indigenous architecture.

Then, too, there was the extremely ornate "gingerbread" architecture of the eighties and nineties, when fanciful scrollwork trim, cupolas, and brackets were in vogue. Many of these old structures of the horse and buggy days still stand in striking contrast to simpler buildings of contemporary design. Examples are seen at Monroe and Third Streets, and Adams at Eighteenth Avenue, Phoenix.

In the early nineteen-hundreds the *Ladies Home Journal* began a campaign for more sightly homes, which had an effect upon the Far West and abated somewhat the tidal wave of Victorian and General Grant alterations. With their passing came the bungalow with its low sweeping lines and wide veranda, a derivation of the East Indian bungalow popularized in California. Residences of this type were designed with more ample fenestration, and their simple lines were essentially organic. Overhanging eaves served as roof for the surrounding porch. Their floor plans, while unimaginative, were direct and compact and the houses were comparatively inexpensive. When built as a story-and-a-half house, the lower floor was well insulated, but the upper half-story was uninhabitable in the summer.

The forms of mission architecture embodying a noble tradition served as precedent for churches, schools, and public buildings. In many examples the arcade across the front connects the extended wings of the U-shaped structures to form a patio; this is exemplified in the Brophy Chapel on north Central Avenue, Phoenix, designed by John R. Kibbey of Los Angeles. The Pima County Court House, Tucson, by Roy Place, is Spanish in design, and the new post office at Phoenix, by Lescher & Mahoney, Phoenix, is Spanish Renaissance.

Other notable examples of traditional architecture in Arizona—all showing Spanish Colonial influence—are the Cathedral of St. Augustine, Tucson, by Henry O. Jaastad; Methodist Church (North), Tucson, by Thoralf Sundt; Trinity Episcopal Cathedral, Phoenix, by Shepley, Rutan, and Coolidge of Boston; and Pioneer Hotel, Tucson, by Roy Place of that city.

The veterans' hospital group south of Tucson, planned by the Veterans Bureau, Washington, D. C.; Grunow Memorial Clinic, by Fitzhugh and Byron, and the Orpheum Theater, Phoenix, by Lescher and Mahoney, are of Spanish Colonial design. The Phoenix Country

Club, by Lescher, Kibbey and Mahoney, Phoenix, is a modern adaptation of a Spanish ranch house.

Influenced by Italian Renaissance is the Security Building, Phoenix, by Curlett & Beelman of Los Angeles. Several of the new buildings at the University of Arizona, Tucson, designed by Roy Place, including the auditorium, women's gymnasium, science, and administration buildings are Lombard Romanesque.

The Yavapai County Courthouse, Prescott, by W. N. Bowman; liberal arts building in the Phoenix Union High School group by Lescher and Kibbey, and the Tucson Senior High School by Roy Place, are all classical in design.

Throughout the semitropical southern section of Arizona modern domestic architecture presents a hodgepodge of numerous influences with a definite trend similar to the California-Mission or Monterey style at Santa Barbara, California. This is much in evidence, alongside of Cape Cod, French Provincial, English, and other styles.

The Pueblo style is adapted in the design of many structures. A good example is the Hopi House, at the South Rim of the Grand Canyon; the Pueblo home, near McDowell and Seventh Avenue, Phoenix, and the Heard Scout Pueblo on the slope of Phoenix South Mountain.

There is a trend toward the modern in new homes and commercial buildings especially in Phoenix and Tucson. These structures, quite severe in design, are constructed mostly of steel, concrete, and glass.

The construction of skyscrapers in Phoenix and Tucson is said to be the result of high land values, which necessitated concentration within the business areas. Notable examples of these in Phoenix are the Luhrs Tower, by Trost and Trost of El Paso, one of the tallest setback structures in the Southwest, and the Professional Building, by Morgan, Walls and Clements, and the Title and Trust Building, by Lescher and Mahoney. Designed with sharp vertical lines, they are seemingly out of place in a country of vast distances and great spaciousness.

The Arizona Temple of the Latter Day Saints in Mesa is considered by many architectural experts one of the most beautiful ecclesiastical edifices in the nation. By Young and Hansen of Salt Lake City, its design follows an original plan supposedly based on that of Solomon's Temple. The exterior is neo-classic in treatment. Unlike other temples built by the Mormons, the Mesa Temple has no towers or spires but a striking central mass with slender colonnades and flat roof. Perfection of masonry, honest sincerity of line, and elegant simplicity characterize this impressive shrine.

In recent years architects have been called upon to plan guest-ranch and resort hotels of types peculiar to the Southwest. Many of the resorts carry out the plan of a central main structure surrounded by a number of separate units such as the San Marcos at Chandler, and the Camelback Inn and the Arizona Biltmore Hotel, north of Phoenix.

The Arizona Biltmore, luxurious resort at the foot of Squaw Peak, is an example of the use of modern materials in harmony with desert surroundings. The original scheme of the hotel is the work of Frank Lloyd Wright, but the building was erected under the supervision of Albert McArthur, a former apprentice of Wright. The cement blocks, held together with steel interlacing set into the poured joints between them, are in an openwork design. This feature of construction gives the surface a richness of pattern comparable to that of the Spanish style.

Frank Lloyd Wright and the Taliesin Fellowship, a group of student-apprentices under his tutelage, are building (1939) winter quarters on a tract of Arizona desert located about twenty-six miles northeast of Phoenix at the foot of McDowell Mountain. The building group is being solidly constructed of concrete and native stone, with redwood beams and trusses, and canvas roofing with air spaces between. The group will consist of living and working quarters for the Fellowship and residence for Mr. Wright. Here the Fellowship will spend four or five months of each year in residence and carry on its work in architecture exactly the same as at its permanent home at Taliesin in Wisconsin, but with special attention to the Arizona region.

Many of the resort dwellings in the northern part of the state are constructed of locally available materials, as, for example, the log cottages of one and two stories with foundations of boulders at the Hassayampa Mountain Club just south of Prescott. El Tovar Hotel at the South Rim of the Grand Canyon is unusual: a long, low structure of native boulders and pine logs. The interior like the exterior is rustic, the rough natural logs forming the principal element in its design and finish, in contrast with the Bright Angel Lodge, alongside, which is entirely constructed of hewn logs.

A trend toward large-scale planning is in process in Indian reservation architecture. The New York firm of Mayers, Murray, & Phillip has been commissioned in connection with the Indian Service Public Works Program to design structures in harmony with the architecture of each particular area. Near Phoenix, at Sacaton and Salt River in particular, the Spanish-Pueblo style is followed. Long low buildings with wide overhanging eaves and tile roofs harmonize with the surrounding landscape, which is characterized by growths of palms and other tropical plants. At Salt River, where sand and gravel are plentiful, a cement block has been manufactured for building construction and is proving quite satisfactory.

In the Navajo country, particularly at Window Rock, the recently constructed buildings of the Navajo Central Agency are of stone laid in adobe mortar. The ancient method of insulation used by the

Navajo has been applied, even with the flat roof construction, the device of a built-up roof of logs covered with six inches of adobe. The octagonal council-house is especially interesting.

On the San Carlos Reservation the buildings are of tufa stone quarried in the vicinity. At Shonto in the Navajo country the Day School and Community Center are based on the design of the hogan. These buildings, with interesting domed roofs, seem an integral part of the landscape, which is dotted with native hogans.

Arizona boasts of the world's four highest reclamation dams of their types, each architecturally significant. Boulder Dam, the highest, is a huge steel-and-concrete barrier connecting Arizona and Nevada. Wedged between the walls of Black Canyon and rising from bedrock to the height of a seventy-two-story building (727 feet), it is 600 feet thick at its base, tapering up to 45 feet at its crest, which is 1,282 feet wide. Boulder Dam's functional beauty makes it a distinguished architectural achievement. Roosevelt Dam is the highest masonry dam, built entirely of rubble stone, horizontally arched in form. Coolidge Dam is the highest of the multiple-dome type. The symmetrical conception relieves the massiveness ordinarily displayed in this type of engineering monument. Bartlett Dam is the highest multiple-arch impounding barrier. It rises from arches seven feet thick at the bottom to something more than two feet thick at the top.

The aesthetics of bridge design is receiving increasing attention. One of the country's beautiful bridges is that at Tempe. It is of concrete construction and is supported by a series of arches in a structurally decorative design. At intervals are lighting standards and pergolas that serve as resting stations for pedestrians. Navajo Bridge, spanning the Colorado in Northern Arizona, is the highest steel-arch bridge in the United States, with a span of 616 feet, 480 feet above the water. The structure itself is 115 feet high. Another bridge spanning the Colorado is the steel suspension bridge at the bottom of the Grand Canyon on the Kaibab Trail. Aside from the fact that it was transported to its location on mule-back piece by piece, it is of definite architectural significance. It is 440 feet long, suspended from eight 1½-inch steel cables, and provided with a structural steel truss which serves both as a stiffening member and as guard rails.

Indian Arts and Crafts

INDIAN art in Arizona is a very wide subject, associated with many cycles of historical, cultural, and ethnic development. The art of the Indians of this region ranks with the richest and most highly perfected of any of the North American tribes. Basketry, pottery, weaving, metal craft, leather tanning, painting, costume designing and ornamentation, and the making of ceremonial dolls are traditional arts still practised among the native peoples of Arizona.

Although Indian basketry has many variations in size, shape, design, color, and decoration, there are but two basic techniques—coiling and weaving. In the former, the basket is sewed around a foundation, each successive coil being linked to that underneath. In the woven type, there is a warp and weft, the strands of the weft passing under and over the warp, or being wrapped around it. Examples of both types of basketry dating from before the Christian era have been found in the caves inhabited by the Basket-makers in the northeast corner of the state; since that time there has been no fundamental change in basket technique.

Hopi women make baskets of plaited fibers from yucca leaves identical with those found in prehistoric ruins. Using the sewing method the women of the middle mesa build baskets from thick foundation coils of grass stems bound with split yucca leaves. Their designs comprise geometrical patterns and representations of animals, butterflies, and clouds. The Navajo weave baskets of sumac twigs, the designs being worked in with dyed twigs. A typical pattern is a band, three to six inches wide, woven with zigzag edges in black and with a red line running through the center, set on a light background of twigs in natural color. It was a tradition that every design be broken or intersected by a line of uncolored twigs—a "Way Out" to act as a relief for the sewer's eyes.

Pima women still make excellent baskets, including huge storage baskets, of finely split willows. In ancient times, the Pima also produced sleeping mats, cradles, baskets for "medicine" use, and the beautiful *kiaha* or carrying basket in loose-lacework (these are to be seen now only in museums). The *kiaha* was made, too, by the Papago, who skilfully looped a strong but delicate fiber cord into a texture that can only be described as lace. Women used the *kiaha* to carry their babies and for a hundred other purposes, but since the introduction of horses and wagons it has all but disappeared from use. Today when baskets are made primarily to trade, two forms predominate, the flat tray and the bowl-shaped vessel, the decorations serving to identify the work of the different tribes.

Pottery was widely distributed in the Southwest in prehistoric times. The earliest corrugated ware is found in post-Basket-maker sites. Later wares with a white slip and decorated in black were made; and these were followed by work in a great variety of styles and decorative patterns in which traditional textile designs were adapted to the new medium. There was a remarkable uniformity in the ancient black-on-white pottery, but, with the emergence of the new styles, forms belonging to a number of distinct regions became recognizable: the mugs of the Mesa Verde, the long-necked jars of the Chaco Canyon, and the more globular jars of the upper Gila with their handles moulded in the form of animals. Especially distinctive are the food bowls of the Mimbres region, painted with amazingly intricate geometric designs and a profusion of forms from life.

The diversification of styles increased until at some prehistoric time misfortune overtook the pottery makers. Oppressed perhaps by roving tribes or reduced by famine and drought, they abandoned much of their ancient range and withdrew into a smaller area. Here the Spaniards under Coronado found them in 1540 still plying their ancient crafts in approximately seventy-five villages or pueblos.

Within historic times pottery has been made by the following tribes: Hopi, Havasupai, Hualapai, Mojave, Maricopa, Cocopa, Yuma, Pima and Papago. Among these tribes, vessels for cooking and storing water, parching pans, ladles, and other utensils were all made of pottery; with rare exceptions they have been replaced by the more efficient metal wares brought in by traders.

Pottery in aboriginal America can be differentiated from that of the Old World in one important particular: the potter's wheel was unknown, and the vessels were, and are today, shaped entirely by hand.

This permits a greater variety of forms, including square shapes, which are still seen occasionally. The usual procedure is to build upon a small base by adding coil upon coil of clay, each pinched on to the coil below, until the desired size is obtained. Then the vessel is thinned, either by scraping or rubbing with a stone or by using a paddle and anvil. This thinning obliterates the marks left by the coiling process. The paddle and anvil method prevailed throughout the Hohokam archeological area and is used by the Maricopa and other tribes who live there today. The scraping technique belongs to the Pueblo area and is still used by the Hopi. After being rubbed smooth with a stone, the vessel is set aside to dry. When dry it is generally painted before firing. Designs are made by incising as well as by painting.

Hopi pottery has an interesting history. The earliest Hopi pottery found at sites like Awatobi and old Shungopavi is a black-on-white ware decorated with geometric figures. Later, this was replaced by a red ware decorated in black. In the Jeddito Valley is found a special type of pottery with a clear yellow base decorated with brown geometric patterns. This type seems to have changed gradually into that known as Sikyatki, from the ancient village of that name about three miles from Hano on the First Mesa; it, too, has a yellow base but is decorated in brown and red, in conventionalized representational forms. After this phase, Hopi pottery retrogressed—as indicated by examples found at Awatobi, a village destroyed about 1700 A.D. Up to 1900 Hopi pottery was white or yellow and decorated in black and red.

The Museum of Northern Arizona at Flagstaff has been working to preserve the artistic traditions of the Arizona Indians, principally the Hopi; great progress has been made in reviving the best in their arts and crafts. Several Hopi craftsmen have also struggled to keep the native arts alive. Among these the name of Nampeyo (Nam-pay-oh), the Tewa potter of Hano, occupies a leading place. (The Tewa originally came from New Mexico and settled among the Hopi at about 1700 A.D.) Throughout her long life—she is probably more than seventy years old—Nampeyo has toiled to restore the art of pottery to the high position it held in pre-Spanish days. She has worked at the sites of pre-Spanish villages excavated by the Smithsonian Institution, making drawings in crayon of the forms and decorations of the work produced during the golden period of Pueblo culture. She has imitated in her own work the color of the slip, the style of decoration, and the shapes of the older vessels, and has influenced other potters to return to these models.

Unfortunately, however, when the superiority of Nampeyo's work began to attract the attention of collectors and the demand exceeded the supply, a great flood of inferior pieces issued from imitators and the production of spurious pottery became an active industry.

Weaving, principally of native grown cotton, was practiced in the ancient Southwest. Today the most celebrated Indian weavers are Hopi men and Navajo women. The Hopi is the only tribe in North America in which weaving is a man's art. Of the various cotton garments now made by the Hopi the best known are the white wedding robes woven by every groom for his bride, the women's ceremonial robes (similar to the wedding robe but with red border), and the dancing kilt and sash. The kilt is woven in white cotton and then embroidered with colored Germantown yarns. The sash has a cotton warp throughout, but the weft, with a central section of cotton, has colored woolen yarns at both ends, which are decorated with designs representing squash blossoms, rain, and other fertility symbols.

The Hopi men also weave in wool striped blankets, leggings, and garments, including a black dress for women which covers the right shoulder but leaves the left shoulder bare. The dress is secured by a tightly woven belt of red cotton with designs in black.

Despite the wide variety of their work the Hopi are perhaps less famed as weavers than the Navajo, whose looms produce only rugs and blankets. The history of Navajo weaving is a very complex one. It is believed that the nomad Navajo learned the art from their more sedentary neighbors. The people themselves attribute its origins to a Kisani woman who, according to the Navajo legend, received her instruction from the spider. Until recent years it was the custom among Navajo weavers to leave, as a tribute to the Spider Woman, a little hole in the center of each blanket, like the hole in a spider's web. The custom was abandoned when traders refused to accept "defective" blankets. The Spider Hole survives today in the Navajo ceremonial basket.

It is estimated that Navajo weaving is about one hundred and fifty years old, the oldest written record of it dating from 1780. Like so many things in modern Navajo life, the art of weaving was borrowed from two sources, Spanish and Pueblo—the Spaniards supplying the wool, the Pueblo the loom. The first Navajo products were blankets for their own use; later these were bartered to the Spaniards. From the beginning of the nineteenth century until their captivity in 1863, they wove what is known as the bayeta blanket. Bayeta is Spanish for English baize, a red-dyed product of finely spun wool, which the weavers unravelled and respun to make the weft for their blankets. Sometimes it was mixed with native woolen yarn, sometimes used alone in the weft strands. After the invention of aniline dyes in the Old World inferior yarns were supplied to the weavers, and this was reflected in the quality of the later blankets.

When the flocks of the Navajo were destroyed and the tribe moved en masse to Bosque Redondo, weaving ceased. Upon their return to the old territory they were furnished new flocks of sheep, government issues of cotton clothing, cheap cotton twine, Germantown yarns, and aniline dyes. At the same time traders entered the reservation. Thus weaving became an industry, its products made for sale rather than for use by the tribe. Traditions in weaving yielded to the need to "fill orders," and between 1890-1900, when the market demand first made itself felt, some very poor work was done. Later, standards were fixed with regard to the quality of dyes, weave, and materials.

The weavers' desire to please their white customers has at times resulted in grotesque inventions; the pattern on a soap wrapper, a linoleum design, the trader's name, and the price of the rug, have been incorporated into Navajo rug designs.

The earliest blankets were striped, as are many of the Pueblo blankets of both prehistoric and historic times. During the second period (1800-63), in addition to the stripes, the design showed a series of zigzags running horizontally, sometimes meeting in a diamond in the center. After the return of the tribe from captivity—the period of Germantown yarns—the diamond design rapidly displaced the terraced and striped. The fourth style, that having a border, dates from 1900 to the present time. Within each style there are many variations in color and composition, but almost all of the patterns are of a geometric character.

In recent years a moderately successful attempt has been made to revive some of the older patterns and colors. There has also been a tendency to reproduce in weaving the figures and colors used in sand painting. Today it is possible to obtain almost any size and quality of rug, varying in price from two or three dollars to more than a thousand. The value of the Navajo weavers' products amounts to hundreds of thousands of dollars per year; yet the individual artist's return for her labor has been estimated at about five cents an hour.

Another art still practiced by both the Hopi and the Navajo is sand painting. These paintings, however, can rarely be seen, since they are used only in secret ceremonies. The artist paints by spreading sand evenly upon the earth, and then upon this background working out his symbols in differently colored sands. The Hopi sand paintings are always made in the kiva and contain many fertility symbols. Navajo paintings are much larger and are an important part of the chants held to cure the sick. The painting is destroyed as soon as it is finished, since the patient is laid on it, and sands from different parts are rubbed on his feet, knees, abdomen, and head. Water color reproductions of sand paintings may be seen in books and museums.

An interesting development in American art is the work in water color and gouache being produced by native Hopi who make use of the old designs and motifs for paintings in a modern decorative style. Fred

Kabotie is a leading Hopi artist whose favorite subject is Indian dancers in traditional costume; his painting of the Hopi snake altar is on display at the Watch Tower in Grand Canyon National Park.

Silversmithing was learned by the Navajo and Hopi from the Mexicans and Spaniards. The tools used today are few and very simple, as compared with those of the accomplished metal worker of the sixteenth and seventeenth centuries. The Indian craftsmen produce mainly necklaces, belts, bracelets, rings, buckles and ornamental buttons. The Mexican silver dollar was formerly much used for raw material, but in recent years sheet silver is procured from the traders.

The more valuable pieces are set with turquoise ("Indian diamonds"). Lately polished petrified wood has been used as a substitute for turquoise but this is only for the tourist trade, for the Indians value only turquoise. The work is done entirely by hand, and the stamped designs are made with a die or with the round end of a file. They use no calipers or dividers to find the center of a piece, but depend upon the accuracy of the eye. A favorite Navajo product is a leather belt strung with flat oval-shaped disks called conchos. The disks measure four or five inches in diameter and are handsomely engraved. The belt is fastened with a large buckle and will usually contain about $50 worth of silver. Jewelry of silver and turquoise is the Navajo's proudest possession, and it is this, rather than money, that he saves for the future. All traders accept the family jewelry in pawn, knowing that it will be redeemed as soon as the shearing season arrives. The ornaments worn by the Navajo consist of flat beads and turquoise strung together in artistic style. The flat beads, made of shell from the Gulf of California, were used as a medium of exchange in early days.

The Hopi, who are the only wood carvers among Arizona Indians, produce each year thousands of kachina dolls in connection with the ceremonial dances. These dolls, carved and painted in the likeness of the masked gods, are distributed to the children by the kachina dancers when they first come to the village during the Bean Dance in February and again when they return to their ancestral home in July. They are carved from soft cottonwood roots, or willow roots, with the aid of a rasp and a knife. Then they are painted and decorated with feathers, flowers, corn husks, dyed horsehair, woolen yarn, and deer skin in the same way as are the masks of the kachinas.

Folklore and Folkways

MOST of the songs, sayings, habits, and customs that belong to Arizonans as a people were bequeathed to them by widely varying and often sharply conflicting cultures. The first Arizonans were Mexicans and Mormons, cowboys and prospectors, miners and soldiers, Serbians, Confederates, Yankees, Italians, English, Spanish—and Indians. They lived in Arizona as groups of strangers— more or less isolated from each other by barriers of nationality, creed, or geography—fighting for life and property in a grim but promising wilderness. And there was not one of them who did not try to pass on to his children both his conception of the new land and the most vital elements of his native culture. Today it seems that none of them quite succeeded in this and that none of them completely failed.

The present people of Arizona are separated from their pioneer predecessors by very few generations, and they are remarkably aware of certain aspects of their frontier heritage. The drama of the pioneers is the classic saga of the state. In one way or another—with fiestas and pageants, Spanish and Indian place names and architecture, and the cowboy regalia they encourage dudes to wear on the city streets— current Arizonans express their determination to remember the way of their grandparents (or their neighbors' grandparents).

But the present generations are separated from the earlier ones by forces more powerful than time—by the million miles of rails, roads, wires, and air waves that bind them to the ideas and activities of their contemporaries in every other near and far part of the world. The effect of radios, modern machinery, and neighbors from New York and Oklahoma is not to be denied. Today prospectors and real cowboys are rare. The children of Mexican citizens who can truthfully say "No sabe" to an English sentence are forgetting their Spanish. A Missouri-born coffee shop proprietress in Bisbee, the mining camp that was once a Cornish stronghold, will tell you that she is the only person in town who bakes Cornish pasties "like the Cousin Jennies used to make for the Cousin Jacks." An Arizona poultry farmer says: "Now, you take my grandfather. He was a strict Mormon—very strict. Never got near a stimulant and believed in polygamy. And there was my father. He was a pretty good Mormon, always paid his tithes— only he had to have his coffee so some called him a Jack Mormon. And me. My wife is a Baptist from Texas but I'm still a Mormon. Don't drink and I don't smoke. But now you take that long-legged college kid of mine. Course he ain't got sense enough yet to pound sand in a rat hole, but you know what he claims he is?—a Pantheist!"

The traditions of the old, small, closely-knit groups of Arizonans are not entirely lost, although the social-economic patterns which fostered them are nearly all broken. Religious ties, family loyalty, and long habit still keep much of the lore and many of the customs of the older generations alive. And if these guardians of the past must give ground before an intruding world, some of the strictly local ways and beliefs may survive even that loss finding expression in the lives of future Arizonans who, carelessly and without thought, keep contact with the earlier people through the hard bright desertland that is their home.

Indian Folklore: The Indians possess the richest and only wholly indigenous folklore of the state, and they have kept it largely to themselves. The white men have taken the land of the natives and admired their handicraft, but they have seldom been tempted by the Indian's traditional way of life. Exchange of lore and beliefs between the two races has consequently been largely one-sided, with the white people determinedly spreading their own culture among the Indians but generally uninterested in Indian folklore except to undermine and destroy it.

Legend, ritual, and superstition once governed the daily routine of the Indian down to minute details: the systems and seasons of planting and harvest, the rules of warfare and the hunt, birth and death customs, government, religion, dancing and song. Along prehistoric trails, in tepees, caves, and rock shelters whose ruins still remain, the folklore of the Indians was fabricated of fact and fancy. Subsequent generations added to the beliefs and stories and perpetuated them by word of mouth. Legend explained the origin of all things and became the cornerstone of law. Myth upheld and enforced mandate.

It is impossible to deal adequately with the folklore and folkways of the several Arizona tribes within the limits of this essay, but the following examples will suggest their nature and scope.

Songs are called upon to effect treatment of disease, assurance of crops, rain, and good weather. Animals are credited with causing ailments and cures. The medicine man is still largely preferred to the physician. Old men among the Hopi have always been the tribal heroes, and to this day they are depended upon to direct the people in all matters.

When a son is born to an Indian couple, the celebration is greater than for a daughter. Twins are considered a special favor of the gods. A Navajo child born during the winter is rolled in the snow to give it strength and bravery. Should a child die the cradle board is immediately burned; if it lives, the board is considered lucky and is used for the next child. The Hopi smear a newly born child's face with a clay and ash mixture to insure a ruddy complexion.

A most interesting ceremony of the Mojave takes place over their dead and during cremation. The body is taken to what is known as the Cry House, where the people congregate and sing. The body is then carried to the cremation grounds, placed upon a pile of logs, and burned at sunrise while the tribesmen sing, dance, and wail. Many prized possessions are thrown on the burning pyre as a special honor to the dead, some even sacrificing clothing torn from their persons. The Navajo remove the dying from the hogan whenever possible. However if death occurs inside, the body is dressed in its best and buried, and then the family burns the hogan and leaves never to return. The Havasupai avoid community graveyards, each family having a separate burial plot. Each year the Hualpai have a "big cry," when all members of the tribe gather and the year's dead are collectively remembered.

Nature is the altar of the deeply religious Apache's spiritual devotions. Earth, air, and water are his Holy Trinity. The animals are his little brothers, the birds his next of kin. All Indian tribes hold that animals have the gift of speech. The Apache have a legend that the coyote brought them fire and that the bear in his hibernations communes with the spirits of the "overworld" and later imparts the wisdom gained thereby to the medicine men. An Indian asks forgiveness from the animal he is about to kill—solemnly assuring it that a happy future awaits it in the life to come, and that hunger has made his action necessary.

Christianity, brought to the Indians of Mexico and Southern Arizona in the sixteenth and seventeenth centuries, has been neatly blended with some of the oldest native ritual. The religion of the Yaqui Indians, political refugees from Mexico who now live in villages near Tucson and Phoenix, is mainly Catholic. However it is a Catholicism mixed with many pagan beliefs and rites. Some of the dances celebrating Easter are performed by painted men dressed in breech cloth, mask and headdress. Pagan evil spirits are one with Pharisees tormenting Christ. In the Easter pageants Christ comes to His death by being shot with a popgun, Judas is burned in effigy, and Christ is raised from the grave—all to the accompaniment of gourd rattles and little copper bells.

The Lore of the Spaniards: The impression made on the Southwest by soldiers, missionaries, and civilians from Old Spain has been a lasting one. Wherever they touched Arizona soil they left something—name or building or legend—to memorialize their presence; and sections of the state they never saw have been partially Hispanized by the Indians called Mexican who have the language, religion, customs, and some of the blood of their Spanish conquerors.

The Spanish were the first white men to know Arizona. They came into the territory in the sixteenth century, laid the basis for a colonial empire in southern Arizona, and lost it all to the Mexicans early in the nineteenth century. Few pure Spaniards remained but the Mexicans and Anglo-Americans were reminded of them by hundreds of legacies, both material and intangible.

Every generation has been interested in the legends of mines lost and treasures buried by the Spanish padres. The old Spanish mission at Tumacacori lies in ruins partly because of the tunnels and holes dug under its foundations by treasure seekers who believed the legend of its padres' buried gold. There are similar stories about the mission of San Bernardino just across the Arizona boundary in Mexico. Those who search southern Arizona for the Taiopa Mine, where the San Bernardino priests are supposed to have mined their gold, sometimes look for a fire always kept burning in the mountain fastness; they believe that the Indians faithfully tend this guiding light under orders from the padres of two centuries ago to keep it burning in front of the mine until they return.

The most interesting legends of Spanish colonial life, as well as the most beautiful building, have been preserved by the native Arizona Indians whose ancestors worked for the Spaniards and were Christianized by them. Most of the Spanish missions were built in the land of the peaceful good-natured Papagos. These were the Indians who built the mission of San Xavier del Bac under the direction of the priests and took care of it voluntarily after the Spanish had been driven from the country.

In order to construct its great dome, according to legends of the Papagos, the padres filled the church with earth and fashioned the dome over the firmly rounded pile of dirt. Then when the work was done, they informed their Papago laborers that scattered through the earth in the church were many gold pieces, and the Indians quickly cleared out the dirt to find the coins. San Xavier is unfinished—one of its two towers lacks a dome. The Papagos say that on the day the church was to be finished Padre Baltaser Carillo climbed to the top of the tower to lay the bricks of the last dome—work which would put the final touches on a church fourteen years in the building. In his eagerness to have the long task over, Padre Baltaser lost his balance and crashed to his death through the tower well. And so the tower was left as Padre Baltaser had last seen it, in order that all who looked at it might be reminded of him.

Stories of the Blue Lady, probably the most mysterious legend of the Southwest, are also told by the Indians of southern Arizona. *La Senorita Azul* is, according to widespread accounts of native tribes in Texas, New Mexico, Arizona, and northern Mexico, a beautiful young woman dressed in blue. She came to their ancestors of the seventeenth century to tell them of the Christian God, and she still appears occasionally, usually to women or children, to bring them some great gift of Heaven. Some of the first white men to explore the southwest—Fray Alonso de Benavides, Ponce de Leon, and Padre Eusebio Kino—heard accounts of the Blue Lady from tribes who, though without any previous contact with missionaries, professed Christianity because of her visits.

It is a matter of history that Marie Coronel de Agreda, one of the most devout women of Spain and, between 1629 and 1665, head of a religious order with robes of blue, claimed to have made repeated visits to the Indians of the New World. She gave detailed and accurate descriptions of what she saw there, and some of the tribes she describes were not seen by white men until a quarter century after her death. Yet it has been ascertained beyond the possibility of doubt that Marie Coronel never in her life left Spain. And it is equally certain that no woman, setting out from any American port to travel into the desert alone, afoot, and without provisions—as both she and the Indians described her journeys—would have escaped notice completely. Yet the Blue Lady was never seen by any eyes except those of the tribes she visited.

The Mexicans: Arizona belonged to Mexico before it became a part of the United States, and there was a period in its history when its population, except for the native Indians, was overwhelmingly Mexican. The Mexicans of this state are as much at home in it as the Anglo-Americans; and the most superficial observer is aware of them as an integral part of Arizona's heritage. Arizonans consume the spicy Mexican-Indian dishes—tacos, enchilladas and tamales—as midwesterners eat hot dogs and hamburgers. They say *muy coyote* to describe an individual who is wily or dangerous; *mucho hombre* to express admiration for manly characteristics; and have long since forgotten that such slang as *loco, pooch, palaver,* and *hoosegow* was acquired from the foreign language spoken across their southern border. Some of their newest houses are Mexican ranch style, with Mexican tile and Mexican richness of color; and there is scarcely a novelty shop in the state which does not sell something decorated with that familiar symbol of Old Mexico—the sombrero and serape-clad peon sleeping in the shadow of a giant saguaro.

But in spite of their willingness to borrow local color from neighboring Mexico, the Anglo-Americans of Arizona have usually made a conscious effort to avoid the adoption of the more fundamental traditions and characteristics of the Mexican people. In general the Arizona Mexicans have been segregated from more fortunate Arizonans, both as strangers belonging to an alien race of conquered Indians, and as persons whose enforced status in the lowest economic level made them seem less admirable than other people. They have consequently retained a firmer hold on their native customs and folklore than have other groups of foreigners less discriminated against. However a large percentage of Arizona's people of Mexican descent are United States citizens, well educated and undeniably American, who have never been to Mexico in their lives, and most of these are not vitally concerned with the traditions of any country except the United States.

Among the customs common to every Mexican community are the fiestas—patriotic and religious celebrations as gay and important as the Fourth of July. *El Cinco de Mayo* (May 5), anniversary of Mexican victory over French armies in 1862; and *Diez y Seis* (September 16), anniversary of Grito de Dolores, the proclamation of Mexico's independence from Spain in 1810, are two of the annual *fiestas patrias*. But there are many other occasions, chiefly religious, which call for commemoration and festivity. The entire Mexican community participates in most of these, and the towns are filled with Spanish-speaking visitors from the rural districts. There are parades, queens, speeches, songs, dancing, feasting, and sometimes fireworks. There is also some wine and *mescal* (for the men—Mexican women never drink in public and seldom in private) and a spirit of relaxation and general good will.

In the old days when entertainment was none too plentiful, the fiestas were popular with Anglo-Americans as well as Mexicans. Nowadays the Mexican people have their fiestas practically to themselves, though these celebrations are among the most colorful in the state. Most communities have only one large fiesta annually, usually September 16, and the others are *fiestas caseras* (home parties), which attract little attention from outsiders.

La Fiesta de San Juan, one of the most important holidays of the Mexican Catholics, is celebrated in the homes of all those persons bearing the name of Juan, Juana, or Juanita. This holiday comes on the 24th of June and in every town with a river or canal, it begins at four o'clock in the morning when all the young folks go for a swim—probably commemorating the baptism of St. John. Later all the Juanitas and Juans are serenaded and given presents just as if it were their birthday; and in their homes there is plenty to eat and drink, with music and dancing which may continue all night.

The belief that it always rains on St. John's Day is quite general among Mexicans everywhere. It is said that if it does rain on this day the rest of the summer will have plenty of rainfall, but if the day should pass without any rain at all, there is sure to be a drought for the remaining summer days. There is also a belief that hair trimmed on San Juan's Day will grow more abundantly afterwards, but though most Arizona Mexican girls know of this old hair-trimming custom, few of them admit following it nowadays.

Many Mexican people are deeply religious, and at the same time subscribe to beliefs which, though now invested with some aspect of their religion, have a pagan rather than a Christian origin. Most of them profess not to believe in the superstitions of their fathers, but stories of *espantos* (ghosts) and *las animas* (the souls of dead people come back to this world) are still quite common. *Las animas* are usually doing penance for having broken a promise of a gift or mass to some saint while they were alive, or perhaps they put money or valuables in some secret place and must stay in purgatory until this treasure is recovered and put to some good use. In either case they come back, sad and despairing, to communicate with some relative or friend and cause him to fulfill the unfinished mission. The souls of murdered men invariably return to torment their assassins into confessing.

Buried riches are the theme of countless *espanto* tales, and in many of them the treasure is spirited away after the finder catches only a glimpse of it. To recover a buried treasure without having it disappear miraculously in the process, one must be entitled to it, and also be willing—really willing deep in his heart—to share it with the poor and helpless. Buried money, especially silver, gives off a bright glow which comes right up through the earth and can be seen as a dim light on nights when the weather is misty or there is a gentle rain.

Belief in the evil eye, the ability of certain people to harm others by looking at them, is still fairly common even among young Mexicans. Usually this strange power is adjudged the gift of the devil and may be detected by a peculiar look in the eye of the possessor, but sometimes it is said to be a power which most people may exercise at times. The strongest individual of twins is generally considered the most likely possessor of the evil eye. The sickness of people who have been *danado* (harmed) cannot be cured by doctors, and the curse on them can be lifted only by the person who put it there. This usually means that the possessor of the evil eye is called to touch the afflicted part of the sufferer or nurse him, and if this service is not forthcoming, the stricken person dies. The school of thought holding that everybody has the ability to harm another by wishing for his possessions has developed a rather charming custom—that of touching a thing admired in order to remove any possible curse from the admiration. Well-meaning possessors of this eye power invariably go through this touching ritual, even with strangers they meet on the street and even if the thing admired is the stranger's eyes or hair, and it is to be considered a compliment.

One of the pleasantest gift-giving customs in the world, and one which no person of Mexican heritage is ever too rich or too poor to forget, is the breaking of the *pinate.* It takes the place of the Christmas tree in Mexico, and in the United States climaxes many holiday and birthday parties. A *pinate* is a large pottery jar filled with sweets and presents and elaborately dressed up in bright tissue paper and streamers to resemble a doll either comic or beautiful. The *pinate* is hung high in the patio and, one by one, the children are blindfolded and given three chances to break it with a long pole.

All Mexican people sing a lot whether their voices are good or bad. They sing naturally and with spirit all the songs that their parents knew and all the late ones that they hear. In the United States, of course, they like the popular dance songs too, and there are some older Mexicans who say gloomily that these American tunes are destroying their countrymen's love of music. Whether this is true or not, the Mexican flair for composing original songs seems to be disappearing in Arizona. *Corridos,* those spontaneous ballads through which the Mexican singers dramatized and commented upon the happenings and heroes of the moment, are not so common now. A few on Arizona themes are heard occasionally, but they are usually inferior to the old Mexican *corridos,* which have such rhythm and lustiness that even persons knowing no Spanish can listen to them with pleasure. However the story is the backbone of a *corrido,* and some local ones have survived because of perennial interest in their subject matter.

For example, the only two Arizona *corridos* well-known among the Mexican population of Bisbee were composed about twenty years ago. One, *El Corrido de Guillermo Daniel,* was composed by a young Bisbee Mexican sentenced to hang as a confessed murderer. Although Guillermo does not so state in his song on the subject, he is said to have been innocent, confessing to the crime to shield the real murderer, a close friend or relative who had a wife and many children. Guillermo was incarcerated in the Tombstone jail, and wrote the first part of what he supposed to be his last *corrido* there. However a few days before the date of his execution, the other prisoners in the Tombstone jail found a way to break out, and Guillermo went with them, consequently having the opportunity to complete his song while in hiding at Bisbee. He was never recaptured, and is said to be alive and happy today in Mexico. *El Corrido de Guillermo Daniel* deals with its author's emotions rather than deeds, although it records carefully all the dates connected with his unfortunate situation.

The other Bisbee *corrido, El Corrido de la Quemazon de Bisbee,* is the story of Bisbee's great fire on Chihuahua Hill, the Mexican section of the mining camp. It was composed by Senor Francisco Chavez who with his guitar and fine voice was much in demand at parties and dance halls as an entertainer. The opening lines of this song, in literal translation, are:

The year, nineteen hundred and seven, and who would have thought it possible?
At about eleven o'clock at night half of Bisbee went to burn.
Americans and Negroes and a part of Mexicans
Were running frantically with cans of water in their hands.
And all the firemen didn't know what to do—
They said, "The water has given out. Now Bisbee is going to burn."

The *corrido* ends:

This song is composed, was composed by surprise,
I would sing it over again for a glass of beer.
To all my friends I give notice, if they don't know,
This song was composed by Senor Francisco Chavez.

The Lore of the Mining Towns: There was a time when the Arizona definition of a mine was "a hole in the ground owned by a miner." Those were the days when prospecting was a dynamic occupation; when the best mining men in the territory were searching the hostile glaring desert for gold, silver, or copper; and when each visualized a 150-foot gallows frame for a mining camp of twenty thousand people rising on the ground around every ten-foot hole he dug in a mountainside "ninety miles from nowhere."

Nowadays in the spots where these prospector dreams proved up, the mines are gigantic underground factories, too impressive to be called holes, and the miners all say, "Prospectin's dead and gone to hell." But a mining-town storyteller can still talk all evening on the subject of prospectors.

The Arizona term "Hassayampa," which means somebody very old and out-of-date, or a liar, or both, was originally coined to apply to the territory's first gold rushers, the prospectors who ventured into southwestern and central Arizona in the 1850's and 1860's. The Hassayampa River was one of their best camping places, and because of the prospector's traditional evasiveness to questions, the reputation already distinguishing one or two other western rivers was applied to it: "He who drinks of the water Hassayampa can never again tell the truth."

The hundreds of stories about Arizona prospectors cover every aspect of their profession—their eccentricities, burros, town sprees, lucky strikes, and especially their hardships. However the most popular of them belong to one of two types: tales of prospectors' lost mines and legends or anecdotes in which the famous men of Arizona mining history are characters.

There is a saying in the Southwest that "the mines men find are never so rich as those they lost." To prove it, Arizona's folklore is filled with stories of fabulous deposits of precious metals found, and then lost, and searched for diligently through two or three generations. Every section of the state has its share of lost mines, but probably the most famous one is the Lost Dutchman Mine in the Superstition Mountains about thirty-five miles east of Phoenix. The long series of very interesting legends dealing with this rich gold mine begins with a young Mexican lover fleeing the wrath of his sweetheart's father and seeking refuge far north in the forbidding Superstitions. He is supposed to have found the great gold deposit when its location was still a part of Old Mexico, but the Gadsden Purchase was about to take place, so the young man's entire Mexican community formed a great expedition and made the long march into the Superstitions. There they mined as much of the gold as they could carry and set out jubilantly for home. But the Apaches ambushed them, and killed the entire party—four hundred men—except two young boys concealed under a bush. These two children found their way back home, and grew up with the knowledge that they alone knew the location of the mine. When they were old enough they took a third partner and went to the Superstitions, finding the mine without difficulty. They had hardly begun to dig, when the Dutchman came along.

The Dutchman was a prospector with a long white beard, and his name was Jacob Wolz, or Walz. He had been prospecting in the Superstitions, and a band of Apaches had driven him into a part of the mountains he had never seen before. He stumbled into the camp of the Mexican boys and became friendly with them and they told him about their mine. Wolz killed the three Mexicans and from about 1870 until his death the mine was his.

As stories of the Dutchman's gold ore spread around Phoenix and Florence, many prospectors tried to trail him into the mountains but he outwitted them, or killed them. Wolz is said to have admitted killing eight men because of the mine, including his own nephew. He died in Phoenix in Oct. 1891, with a shoe box of the beautiful ore under his bed. Almost with his last breath he gave a friendly neighbor directions to the mine, saying they must be followed exactly as the mine entrance was concealed under ironwood logs covered with rock. Unfortunately the most important landmark in Wolz's directions, a palo verde tree with a peculiar pointing branch, could not be located then or later.

Since then, literally thousands of prospectors, both professional and amateur, have searched for the Lost Dutchman Mine, and their luck has been uniformly bad. Some have never come back at all, others have returned with pieces of human skeletons and accounts of almost dying of thirst, and still others have been mysteriously shot at in the wild canyons. The tragedy and violence connected with the Lost Dutchman have added to the strong conviction of Arizonans that the Superstition Mountains are cursed. Some people say that pigmies guard the mine; some think it possible that a few wild Apaches still live up there; and others believe that some prospector has found the Lost Dutchman and shoots to kill any who approach the bonanza. Of course, there are some who say Dutchman Wolz "never had nothin' up there nohow," but judging by the number of prospecting expeditions into the Superstitions annually, these skeptics can never command as large an audience as exponents of more exciting theories.

Prospectors are traditionally free men, unhampered by family, but Ira B. Jarolemon in *Romantic Copper* records this tribute of an old sourdough to his wife: "I got a good woman, too. She's a hard worker, and a good cook, and she ain't so good lookin' so that any other fellar besides myself is likely to get stuck on her."

The miners of Arizona's great copper districts belong to many different nationalities. Most of them, and particularly those who worked as miners in their Old Country, brought their mining superstitions and customs with them. The belief that mines are inhabited by impish "little people"—called *kobolds* by the Germans, *duendes* by the Mexicans, and *tommyknockers* in English—has been one of the oldest and strongest of these beliefs. These eery creatures, inclined to mischief rather than malice, often carried off small tools and played pranks, and long ago it was the custom to keep them in a good humor with offerings of food. While it is now almost impossible to find a hardrock miner who professes belief in them, the "little people" still appear in stories and songs. The following verse from the old Hardrock Hank ballad is an example:

> "I'm a hardrock miner an' I ain't afeard of ghosts,
> But my neck hair bristles like a porcupine's quills
> An' I knock my knuckles on the drift-set posts
> When the tommyknockers hammer on the caps an' sills
> An' raise hallelujah with my pick an' drills."

Among the superstitions which many present-day miners at least halfway subscribe to is the belief that accidents occur in threes; when one happens, two more will follow in rapid succession. Miners also say that accidents are most frequent at midnight, and men on the night shift always feel safer when that hour is past. A woman, it is said, will invariably bring bad luck into any mine; and the resulting taboo, whether it serves as a real or convenient excuse, makes it very difficult for women to visit an Arizona mine today. Miners have a saying that "if your lamp don't burn bright, your woman's steppin' out with another fellow;" and while it usually results merely in jocular comment, a faulty carbide lamp can sometimes cause a suspicious man to knock off in the middle of a shift.

Most mining men are subject to strong hunches which they seldom disregard. Almost any old miner has a story like the following: "I was working in a stope one day and all at once a funny feeling struck me and I yelled to my partner 'Beat it, Jim. Get out of here quick!' and I ran and climbed up the manway, and just as I reached the top of the ladder the entire stope caved under me. The foreman ran up and said, 'What's going on, Mark?' and I said, 'I don't know. All I know is that something told me to get out of there.' "

Mine rats are liked rather than otherwise by miners, as the men believe the rats will give warning of impending cave-ins and bad gas. Miners do not regard this as a superstition, as they say that the rats notice the slightest movement of the surrounding rock and scamper to places of safety. It is bad luck to kill a mine rat and a miner who does it is in the same category as a man who, above ground, mistreats a dog. The underground rats live from the scraps tossed them from the miners' dinner buckets, and they become very accurate timekeepers, appearing at the exact moment the lunch hour begins, even before the miners sit down and open their pails. Miners who work for a long time in the same mine get to know the rats as individuals and naturally give them names such as "Old Gramp" or "Mike."

Nowadays the nationality differences between miners have little significance underground, but above ground they may be noted by the particular foods and holidays, and sometimes by special musical instruments, customs, and habits of thought. Each nationality group is regarded as more or less clannish by the others; but as a matter of fact, none of them have been clannish enough to retain more than a fragment of their native customs.

The Slavic groups, more than any of the others excepting the Mexicans, have clung to their native culture. The Slav citizens of Arizona came originally from many different parts of southern and central Europe—Austria, Jugoslavia, Montenegro, and other countries—and they are divided by religion into two groups: those of the Greek Orthodox Church and those of the Roman Catholic Church. The Slavic Christmas celebrations (the Orthodox commemorate the day on January 7) are big events in every mining town in the state. All Slavs take seriously both their hospitality and their cooking, and the Christmas season means open house with an abundance of holiday food and wine available all day and night long. The center piece of every table is a roasted suckling pig with a red apple in its mouth and a string of cranberries around its neck. As many Slav families are receiving at the same time, the crowds move from one home to another with the singing and dancing growing progressively gayer.

One of the native musical instruments of the Montenegrins and Serbians is the *gusle,* something like a mandolin, with goatskin across the sounding box and strands of horsehair for strings. The *gusle* is handmade, ornately carved and embossed with mottoes and honored names, and is played with a bow. Its range is limited, but a skilful player (always male—women do not touch the *gusle*) can make its music the perfect accompaniment for emotional Slavic songs. Most of the songs sung with the *gusle* are old European ones but a few have been composed in this country. One of the best of these is "Underground in America" by Lazar Jurich, which records in practiced rhythm and rhyme the lament of the Serbian miner. The following extract is translated literally.

> "For the mine is a tragic house,
> It is the worst of all prisons—
> In bitter stone excavated
> In barren depths located—
> Where there is no free breath,
> With a machine they give you air.
> By you always burns a lamp,
> And your body struggles with the stone.
> Hands work, never do they stop,
> And your chest sorrowfully heaves,
> For it is full of poisoned smoke
> From gelatin's powder white.

> "We, miners, sons of sorrowing mothers,
> Look like men from the wastelands.
> In our faces is no blood
> As there is in other youth.
> Many poor souls their dark days shorten,
> Many poor souls and with their heads do pay.
> There is no priest or holy man
> To chant the final rites."

Mormon Folkways: In addition to the distinct groups resulting from various nationalities and occupations, Arizona has also had communities of native Americans with background and customs different from their neighbors. Most important of these are the Mormons, who came to Arizona as pioneers in search of religious liberty and settled in agricultural sections chiefly populated by members of their own faith. The Mormon communities of today—chief of which are Snowflake, Joseph City, St. John, and Egar in northern Arizona, and Mesa and St. David in the south—are not greatly different from other towns except for the large number of fine old trees surrounding them.

But the Mormons have cultivated for several generations an unusual spirit of group unity, and this is obvious now in some of the customs and activities peculiar to their communities A dance in a Mormon town is usually a community affair held either in the school building or the church. It may be a high school party or a farewell for a missionary. (Mormon boys, upon reaching manhood generally serve two years or more in the United States or in a foreign country as missionaries for the Church of the Latter Day Saints.) But whatever the occasion, everybody attends, from the oldest to the youngest. The Mormons, unlike some other religious groups, see no harm whatsoever in dancing and lively music, and their children receive very early training in the polka, schottische, and modern steps, as well as in playing musical instruments. The Mormons are very fond of family reunions, and as the genealogy of every member is carefully recorded by the church, the Mormons are aware of even the most distant relatives. Their reunions are consequently enormous, with one hundred to three hundred people attending, and they are held out of doors like a huge picnic.

Every year before Thanksgiving Day the men and older boys of a Mormon community cut and haul wood to all the widows of the town; and usually in addition, beeves are killed and distributed among them. The widows and other women prepare a special dinner, which may be so elaborate as to become a banquet, and afterward there may be a dance or party.

The Cowboys: The folklore of the cowboys is better known than that of any other Arizona group, and much of it has found its way into fiction. The stories of the Pleasant Valley War and the Earp-Clanton feud, while still recent, have taken on the rich flavor of legends.

Besides contributing to the lore of the state, the cowboy has given many idioms to the language. From the range came many catch-phrases which have been added generally to the modern American vocabulary. High-tailing it, hoofing, outfit, layout have a direct cattle lineage, as have worn down to a nub, taking the hide off, and bed down. Such slang as plumb locoed, panhandler, strays, and mavericks, hog-tied, and runt came from the range as did rustler, roundup, cowed, roping them in, riding herd, and throwing the bull. By an agile feat of the imagination it is possible to trace necking to a similar origin: on the roundup, when a steer was unruly, his neck was tied with a short rope to that of a gentler animal to quell the disturbance—and that was necking.

Many legends which have grown around the cowboy vary with the geography. Some are true, others only partly true. A cowboy's affection for his saddle is almost legendary. A notorious bandit of early Arizona, his horse shot from under him, was escaping afoot. Hoofing it for about a mile, he met a young horse wrangler and when he told the boy he wanted to use his outfit, the lad said, "Sure, I know you. You are Black Jack. You can have this outfit, and welcome. But please, mister, send the saddle back because it is my own." The saddle was returned.

On the trail and around the chuck-wagon, the cowboys developed storytelling into a high art, and no other folk tales have more humor or suggest more clearly the distinctive and colorful character of the tellers and their background. Cowboy stories are of several types: those dealing with actual experiences of the teller or other cowboys; legends; and the tall tales which the cowboys label just plain lies. The cowboys' songs are even better known than their stories, and probably no other type of American folksong is better liked and more often imitated.

Perhaps the nearest approach to an Arizona Paul Bunyan would be the cowboy's High-Chin Bob, Badger Clark's hero of "The Glory Trail." The poem passed from mouth to ear until its fireside version was printed in *Poetry* as authentic folklore. Cowboys from the Mogollons will tell you that even now, on certain nights when the wind sings through the pines and the moon is high, a ghost lion can be heard rattling over the stone and through the brush trying to throw off the loop that a ghost rider on a ghost horse, true to the glory of his profession, will never turn loose.

Here are three stanzas of the cowboy's version, as given by John Lomax:

Way high up in the Mokiones, among the mountain tops,
A lion cleaned a yearling's bones and licks his thankful chops;
And who upon the scene should ride, a-trippin' down the slope,
But High Chin Bob of sinful pride and maverick-hungry rope.
"Oh, glory be to me!" says he, "an' fame's unfadin' flowers;
I ride my good top hoss today and I'm top hand of Lazy-J,
So, kitty-cat, you're ours!"

*   *   *

'Way high up in the Mokiones that top hoss done his best,
'Mid whippin' brush and rattlin' stones from canon-floor to crest;
Up and down and round and cross Bob pounded weak and wan,
But pride still glued him to his hoss and glory spurred him on.
"Oh, glory be to me!" says he, "this glory trail is rough!
But I'll keep this dally round the horn until the toot of judgment morn
Before I'll holler 'nough!"

*   *   *

'Way high up in the Mokiones, if you ever camp there at night,
You'll hear a rukus among the stones that'll lift your hair with fright;
You'll see a cow-hoss thunder by—a lion trail along,
And the rider bold, with his chin on high, sings forth his glory song:
"Oh, glory be to me!" says he, "and to my mighty noose.
Oh, pardner, tell my friends below I took a ragin' dream in tow,
And if I didn't lay him low, I never turned him loose!"

PART II
Cities

Bisbee

Railroad Station: Southern Pacific Station, Bisbee Junction; ticket office, Galena Townsite.
Bus Station: Southern Pacific Station, Main St., for Pacific Greyhound Lines and Nogales-Bisbee Stage Line.
Taxis: Bisbee to Lowell, 50¢; Bisbee to Warren, $1.

Accommodations: Four hotels, four tourist camps.

Information Service: Chamber of Commerce, Copper Queen Hotel, 11 Howell Ave.

Motion Picture Houses: Three.
Swimming: Municipal Pool, Locklin Ave., free.
Hunting and Fishing: Deer, quail, bear, and duck in season.
Tennis: Five courts, free; Garfield School, Tombstone Canyon; St. Patrick's Church, Tombstone Canyon and Quality Hill; Central School and High School, School Hill; Vista Park, Warren.
Golf: Warren District Country Club, 8 *m.* SE. on Naco Rd., greens fee $1; Holidays, $3.
Radio Station: KSUN (1200 kc.)

Annual Events: Pageant of Progress, July 4; Good Neighbor Day, Oct.; Night in Belgrade, Serbian Festival, Aug.

BISBEE (5,300 alt., 6,000 pop.), seat of Cochise County, and center of one of the richest copper districts in America, is the principal town of a large community—the Warren Mining District with a population of 12,000—built in or near a canyon called Mule Pass Gulch. The gulch, about six miles long and bordered by high hills, begins above Bisbee on the west and winds downward in an easterly direction, through Bisbee and then Lowell, to the sloping foothills around Warren. Bisbee occupies approximately two miles of the upper and steepest section of this gulch, its houses clinging to the slopes of two long, narrow canyons, terraced tier upon tier. Flights of stone and wooden stairs, dirt trails and casual uneven streets reach the uppermost dwellings, their foundations often level with the roofs of the houses below. It is an old saying in the town that "most any fellow with a chaw in his jaw can sit on his front porch and spit down the chimney of a neighbor's house." Bisbee is proud of the fact that it is the largest town in the United States without house-to-house mail delivery. Its citizens trudge down the hills to the post office every day, taking pride in the knowledge that the U. S. Post Office Department considers their town too exhausting even for postmen on their appointed rounds.

US 80 follows the floor of Mule Pass through Bisbee and Lowell, and provides the only route for automobile traffic across the Mule Mountains. Lowell and Warren must be identified as separate towns, but in fact and appearance they are residential suburbs of Bisbee. For some reason, Bisbee has chosen to call its part of US 80 by four names. This two-mile-long main thoroughfare is divided arbitrarily into four sections: West Boulevard, Tombstone Canyon, Main Street, and Naco Road.

The upper and western end of the street, slanting sharply, is known as West Boulevard and is lined with tourist courts and small houses clustered in ravines. Then the highway takes a turn, and at that point it becomes Tombstone Canyon, the longest segment of the street and the best residential section of Bisbee. In Tombstone Canyon, the downward grade of the highway is somewhat less noticeable, but the hills and bluffs on both sides are high and abrupt, with houses built all over them. In spite of their seemingly precarious location, the residences in Tombstone Canyon have an appearance of permanence that most mining camps lack. Bisbee is a town in which many families have lived for more than thirty years; it has good schools and churches, and almost as many solid, brightly painted houses as mining-camp shacks. In Tombstone Canyon are old and carefully repaired homes with pretty flower gardens fronting those fortunate enough to have yards.

Tombstone Canyon ends—and Main Street begins—at Castle Rock, a limestone bluff with tower-like formations on top. Main Street is the shopping section. It sweeps downhill bordered by two blocks of busy stores, cafes, and banks, makes a jog around the Post Office Plaza, and stops at old Southern Pacific site a few hundred yards east of the plaza. The highway from that point is called Naco Road. The eastern boundary line of Bisbee is less than a quarter of a mile past the depot.

Even though it is near the outskirts of town, Post Office Plaza serves as the center of Bisbee. Most roads, streets, and trails lead—in however devious a manner—to the plaza, a small flat of almost-level ground between Bucky O'Neill and School Hills. The post office is directly west on Main Street, and the plaza itself is occupied by the large company store of the Phelps Dodge Corporation. Across the street to the north are the park-surrounded general offices of Phelps Dodge. The plaza is the point around which the town grew, and not far from it are old mine workings and buildings—landmarks of boom days. The old Copper Queen Mine and others of the first mines in the district are to the south above the post office, near the cavelike glory hole in the side of Bucky O'Neill Hill. Across the street northeast of the plaza, Brewery Gulch and O K Street—at one time the most thickly populated thoroughfare in Arizona—meet Main Street.

Brewery Gulch, Bisbee's second important canyon, is approximately a mile long and comes down from the north to join Mule Pass Gulch at a right angle. Chihuahua Hill rises above it on the east, and School and Miller Hills border it on the west. The street along its floor is well paved inside the Bisbee city limits, and inclines steadily upward in a south-to-north direction. O K Street is a narrow paved trail, almost parallel with Brewery Gulch, which takes a steeper course up the side of Chihuahua Hill. Along these two streets still stand musty hotels with rusted grille balconies; old miners' boarding houses with such names as "The St. Elmo" or "The Bonanza" in faded lettering; and saloons with glazed windowpanes and ice-cream parlor stools at the bars.

Brewery Gulch, once the stronghold of mining-camp revelry, is now law-abiding, though an occasional Johnson Day picnic (Bisbee slang for saloon brawl) keeps its bad reputation alive. Farther up, Brewery Gulch becomes a residential section. Most of the houses are weathered stone, wood or adobe, some very narrow and tall, others long and flat, all of them built on high rock or cement platforms or naked stilts. People of many nationalities live in Brewery Gulch, and their children play football in front of the houses of the former red-light district, talk border Spanish spiced with mule-skinner American, and greet all passers-by in courteous English.

Where the pavement of Brewery Gulch ends, say the Mexicans who live in it, begins the town of Zacatecus. The usual attributes of a town are not present in Zacatecus, its one store having been torn down. It has, in fact, the distinctly rural flavor of a remote Mexican roadway. Each house has an old-fashioned well, numerous friendly dogs and children, and a fenced-in rock platform confining burros, rabbits, chickens, and pigs—one or many.

The Phelps Dodge Corporation, producer of approximately half of Arizona's gold, silver, and copper, owns most of the productive area of the Warren District and employs the majority of its men. The Shattuck-Denn Mining Corporation, a small independent, is the only other sizable company in the district. Phelps Dodge ownership of Bisbee's largest hotel, hospital, department store, library, and other enterprises, in addition to the Copper Queen mining properties, causes Bisbee people to speak of it as "The Company."

The price of copper is accepted in Bisbee as the determining factor of its economic life. A stranger can learn about the copper market by asking any Bisbee citizen whether the mines are hiring men or laying them off. A mining camp measures prosperity in terms of miners working, and Bisbee knows from experience that a rise or fall in copper can bring in thousands of families or send an equal number away. After a nine-year period of serious unemployment, most of Bisbee's miners were working again in 1939. But the people of Bisbee do not say whether they think this means the return of the old prosperity. They know that the ore is down there under the ground—enough of it, they believe, to keep Bisbee thriving for another fifty years. Technological development, however, has cut down the number of men needed to mine a ton of metal, and production, therefore, must go very high to fill the town's rooming houses to capacity again. As to how much the district's unmined wealth may mean in pay roll cash for Bisbee—"Well, that depends on the price of copper."

Bisbee's history is essentially the story of its mines. The first discovery of minerals in Bisbee occurred in 1875, when Hugh Jones came into the region searching for silver. He was disgusted because the ore showed only "copper stains" and left without establishing his claim. In 1877 three Army scouts camped in Mule Pass and one of them, John Dunn, found samples of ore. Unable to turn prospector himself, Dunn grubstaked George Warren and sent him into Mule Gulch. Warren staked several claims, brought in other prospectors and named the vicinity the Warren Mining District.

In 1880 Phelps Dodge and Company, then a small eastern firm, sent Dr. James Douglas, a minister and physician, to buy some good copper prospects in Arizona. Dr. Douglas is said to have turned down the United Verde claims at Jerome, from which millions of dollars of ore have since been taken; but he bought property near the Copper Queen in the Warren district. A huge ore body, which eventually yielded a hundred million dollar profit, was discovered on the line between the Copper Queen and Phelps Dodge properties. Instead of wasting their time and money in the courts, the two companies merged as the Copper Queen Consolidated Mining Company.

By 1898 this copper country was attracting miners and mining men from all over the world, and prospectors were asking fortunes for their claims in the district. When Captain Jim Hoatson, one of Michigan's best copper-mine foremen, came to Bisbee on a vacation, he hurried back to Calumet, raised $550,000, bought fifteen acres of land west of Sacramento Hill, and put down the Irish Mag Mine, which paid more than $15,000,000 in dividends.

Hoatson's Calumet and Arizona Company soon became a strong rival of Phelps Dodge for possession of all the ore-bearing hills around Bisbee. One or the other of these two companies finally bought all of the property considered valuable in the district, with the exception of 108 acres owned by the Shattuck Mining Company and the Denn Mining Company, comparatively small concerns. In 1925 the small companies merged into the Shattuck-Denn Mining Corporation. In 1931 the Phelps Dodge Mining Corporation bought the Calumet and Arizona, thus achieving, through ownership of 9,100 productive acres, unquestioned dominance of the district.

The mining camp of Bisbee, named for Judge DeWitt Bisbee, shareholder in the Copper Queen, followed the pattern of life laid down by the development of its mines. When the mines were merely claims the camp was a raw settlement of prospectors, burros, and saloon-keepers. In the early 1880's, with mining on a small scale, Bisbee attracted the tough hombres from Tombstone and other gun-totin' communities on both sides of the Border. Hundreds of burro- and axe-owning Mexicans swarmed in to haul wood for the small smelter.

The camp became a colony of frame shacks on rough streets hacked into the slopes of the hills. After a heavy rain in the mountains, the main street was flooded and muddy for days. The first school was a miner's shack above Castle Rock, with packing boxes for desks and brown wrapping paper to write on. Whenever the camp was threatened by an Apache raid, a whistle was blown four times—two shorts, one long, and one short—and the teacher led her pupils, trained by frequent Indian drills, to the nearest mine tunnel for protection.

Whisky, known as "bug juice," was responsible for much of the violence in early Bisbee. The first hanging occurred in 1882. A drunken Mexican strolled into camp, killed one man and wounded another, then ran up into a canyon and hid in a cabin. The murderer was caught, and the miners took a day off from their work to attend to their "public duty." Without any trial the Mexican was marched up the canyon and hanged to a tree near Castle Rock. The body was still swinging when the Reverend Prichard rode by. "Something must be done to civilize these savages," he said; after his return to New York he sent Bisbee a collection of "well chosen" books.

Around 1900 Bisbee became one of the liveliest boom towns of the West. Enterprising eastern engineers brought their wives out and built fine homes. Professional miners from England, Spain, and other European mining sections came in. The strong young Irish, Finnish, and Slav peasants arrived, learned to be miners, and sent money home to bring their relatives. Bisbee called itself a "white man's camp;" Mexicans were not allowed to work underground, and Orientals were told to get out of town before nightfall. For this reason Bisbee had none of the Chinese laundries and restaurants common to other frontier mining towns. In 1902 the town was incorporated, and by the first ordinance women were not allowed to serve as bartenders or entertainers in local saloons. Nevertheless the riotous dance halls, boarding houses, and saloons of Brewery Gulch flourished and overflowed. In 1908 streetcar service was established between Bisbee and Warren. In the same year a fire destroyed about half-a-million dollars worth of property in Bisbee.

There was steady growth in the years before the World War. Streets were paved and deep drainage ditches were dug to carry away dangerous flood water; churches and schools were built. The smelter, with its sulphur smoke that had kept the town barren of almost all green life, was moved to Douglas, and plant-hungry householders were able to cultivate vines, flowers, and small vegetable patches on their sloping grounds. The town lost much of its rough mining-camp appearance.

The population shifted constantly as restless miners migrated from one camp to another. Two of the largest foreign-born groups, Mexican and Slav, celebrated their national festivals and holy days, and still do so today. On the third of May, the Day of the Holy Cross of the Catholic Church, the Mexicans march in costumed procession up Brewery Gulch to a cross on the farthest hill. The Serbians and other Slavic members of the Greek Orthodox Church hold open house on January 7, their Christmas. They also commemorate, on January 27, the anniversary of the birth of St. Savo, the eleventh century father of Slav education; and on December 4 they celebrate the birth of Yugoslavia.

Unionization of miners reached its height during the World War when the copper mines were running at capacity production. In Bisbee the strike of the members of the International Union of Mine, Mill and Smelter Workers in July 1917, culminated in the Bisbee Deportation, during which more than a thousand persons were loaded into boxcars and deported to the desert. The case aroused nation-wide attention.

Following passage of the Workmen's Compensation Law in Arizona, the big companies worked vigorously to remove health hazards underground. The Phelps Dodge Corporation installed modern ventilation systems in their Copper Queen branch and cut their accident rate 96.5 per cent between 1925 and 1934. In 1930 at the beginning of the depression, thousands of Bisbee workers lost their jobs, others took drastic wage cuts since it is the general practice in the copper industry to gear wages to the price of copper, and copper prices declined more than 70 per cent from 1929 to 1932. In June 1935, the Bisbee Local of the International Union of Mine, Mill and Smelter Workers called a strike against the Phelps Dodge Corporation, during which the secretary of the union was shot. The National Labor Relations Board held hearings on this strike in Bisbee in 1938.

In the state that ranks first in the United States in copper production, the Copper Queen branch of the Phelps Dodge holds third place as producer of copper and first place as producer of gold and silver. Output rises and falls with the demand for copper, but the district around Bisbee continues to be, as it has been for almost fifty years, one of the most important metal producers in the country.

POINTS OF INTEREST

1. COCHISE COUNTY COURTHOUSE (*open 9-5, workdays*), Quality Hill on US 80, a four-story concrete structure designed with deeply set vertical window lines, was built in 1931. It crowns an artificial plateau fringed with trees, and has a garden and a bronze

---

BISBEE-WARREN MINING DISTRICT. Points of Interest

1. Cochise County Courthouse
2. Miners' Monument
3. Copper Queen Mine Glory Hole
4. Observation Point
5. Brewery Gulch Gazette
6. Old Custom House

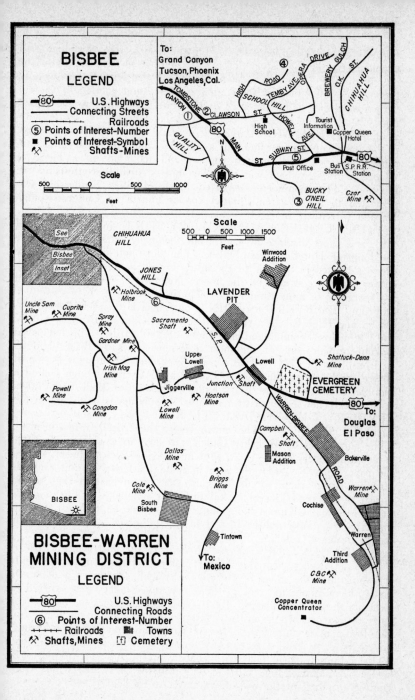

BISBEE
LEGEND

- 🛡️80 U.S. Highways
- —— Connecting Streets
- —— Railroads
- ⑤ Points of Interest-Number
- ■ Points of Interest-Symbol
- ⚒ Shafts-Mines

Scale

500 0 500 1000

Feet

To:
Grand Canyon
Tucson, Phoenix
Los Angeles, Cal.

QUALITY HILL

① TOMBSTONE CANYON
② CLAWSON

HIGH SCHOOL ROAD
TEMBY AVE
OPERA DRIVE

④

HOWELL AVE
High School

BREWERY GULCH
O.K. ST.
CHIHUAHUA HILL

Tourist Information
Copper Queen Hotel

MAIN ST.
SUBWAY ST.
⑤

N

Post Office
Bus Station
S.P.R.R. Station

80

③ BUCKY O'NEIL HILL

Czar Mine

CHIHUAHUA HILL

See Bisbee Inset

Scale

500 0 500 1000 1500

Feet

JONES HILL

Holbrook Mine

⑥

Uncle Sam Mine
Cuprite Mine
Spray Mine
Gardner Mine

Sacramento Shaft

Winwood Addition

LAVENDER PIT

Irish Mag Mine

Powell Mine

Congdon Mine

Upper Lowell

Jiggerville

Junction Shaft

Lowell

Lowell Mine

Hoatson Mine

S.P.

Shattuck-Denn Mine

EVERGREEN CEMETERY

WARREN-BISBEE ROAD

80 To:
Douglas
El Paso

Campbell Shaft

Mason Addition

Dallas Mine

Briggs Mine

Cole Mine

South Bisbee

Bakerville

Cochise

Warren Mine

Warren

Tintown

To:
Mexico

Third Addition

C&C Mine

Copper Queen Concentrator

BISBEE

BISBEE-WARREN MINING DISTRICT
LEGEND

- 🛡️80 U.S. Highways Connecting Roads
- ⑥ Points of Interest-Number
- ┼┼┼┼┼ Railroads
- ⚒ Shafts, Mines
- 🏠 Towns
- ⊞ Cemetery

fountain on the lower front level. On the foyer walls are eight plaster panels portraying the history of Cochise County and Arizona. Modeled in relief by R. Phillips Sanderson, they are gilded with a thin spray of bronze. A relief map of the county, modeled and painted by George Sellers of Bisbee, is on the wall of the staircase leading to the second floor.

2. The MINERS' MONUMENT, foot of Quality Hill on US 80, is the figure of a miner holding a hammer and chisel. It is cast in cement, sprayed with molten copper, and mounted on a block of Colorado granite which was used for miners' drilling contests in the nineties. The monument, executed by R. Phillips Sanderson, was dedicated to the Warren District copper miners by Congresswoman Isabella Greenway in 1935.

3. COPPER QUEEN MINE GLORY HOLE, in Bucky O'Neill Hill, is a short distance by trail from the upper parking lot opposite the Johnston Hotel on Main Street. The glory hole is a large cavelike opening blasted in the side of the hill. Jagged boulders streaked with copper stains are strewn on the floor. Near the base of the back wall are entrances to mine tunnels closed by iron bars.

4. From OBSERVATION POINT, on School Hill, reached via Clawson St. and High Rd., is a view of Tombstone Canyon, Brewery Gulch, and Chihuahua, Youngblood and Bucky O'Neill Hills. This flat paved lookout provides one of the most accessible views of Bisbee and its environs. Bucky O'Neill Hill, Castle Rock, and the business section of Bisbee are below to the south. Lowell and Warren, hidden behind a shoulder of hill, are below Black Knob Peak south of Mule Pass Gulch.

5. A weekly newspaper with a national circulation is published in the BREWERY GULCH GAZETTE BUILDING (*open 9-5 weekdays*), 33 Subway St. The motto below the *Gazette's* masthead is, "The sun shines on Brewery Gulch 330 days in the year, but there is moonshine every day." F. A. McKinney, editor and publisher, started the paper in 1931 "with the idea in mind that in a mining camp as large as Bisbee there should be some sort of publication that would appeal to the mud diggers by talking their language." The *Gazette* prints informal columns and comment on Bisbee happenings, western affairs, and national politics in a style that preserves some of the flavor of old Brewery Gulch.

6. SACRAMENTO PIT (*open all hours*), SE. Post Office Plaza, is a hole 435 ft. deep, cored out of Sacramento Hill. In 1911 a shaft was sunk into the slopes of the high east wall. In 1917 a dynamite charge blew off the top rock of the crown, and dredges were worked to excavate the pit's ore bodies. By 1931 the pit floor was too narrow for dredges to work in; the ore was taken out by caving-in the walls into the lower mine tunnels. Between 1917 and 1931, the pit, which covers 35 acres, yielded 20,843,667 tons of ore. Today the abandoned pit is a funnel-shaped hole with copper, green, and rust-colored rock walls. A narrow-gauge railroad, cut into the pit walls, winds from the highest shelf of the man-made crater to its floor.

7. OLD CUSTOMHOUSE (*open workdays*), E. on Naco Rd., a one-room adobe building to which a wing has been added, was one of the first structures in the Warren District, and is now used as a gasoline station. Loopholes through which customs officers fired at raiding Apaches are filled with plaster.

8. LAVENDER PIT, a tremendous new open pit operation is underway in Bisbee and will cover an area approximately four times the area of the old Sacramento pit. This development is named for the late H. M. Lavender, who was Vice-President and General Manager of Phelps Dodge Corporation. The pit operation is a $25,000,000 project, where an estimated 41,000,000 tons of concentrating ore is hidden. Waste rock is being removed at the rate of about 60,000 tons daily. A portion of the old Sacramento pit is being filled with waste. The mine is so extensive that entire businesses and residential areas in the Bisbee district have been relocated to make way for the project. Highway 80 is to be rerouted and will traverse one of the benches in the pit. The Lavender Pit will be more than two-thirds of a mile long and about one-half mile wide at its greatest dimensions, and from the highest point to the bottom of the finished excavation, the depth will be approximately 1,000 feet. It is expected the pit will be fully developed by the end of 1954 and new plant facilities completed for the treatment of low grade ore.

POINTS OF INTEREST IN ENVIRONS

Divide Monument, 3.2 *m.;* Naco, Sonora, Mexico, 11.6 *m.* (*see TOUR 4b*).

CORONADO NATIONAL MEMORIAL, 26 *m.,* established in 1952 by Presidential Proclamation, commemorates the entrance of the Coronado Expedition into this area in 1540. Located between Bisbee and Nogales on the southern slope of the Huachuca mountains, it is reached via State 92, paved from Bisbee to Montezuma Canyon entrance road, 19 *m.,* thence 7 *m.* (2 *m.* paved; 5 *m.,* graded forestry road) to park headquarters (*parking and picnic areas*). The Pass is 6,300 ft. alt., and Coronado Peak, overlooking Mexico and the United States, is 6,800 ft. alt. This site affords a spectacular view.

Douglas

Railroad Station: 16th St. and Railroad Ave., for Southern Pacific Lines.
Bus Station: Greyhound Bus Depot, G Ave., for Pacific Greyhound Lines.

Airports: Bisbee-Douglas International Airport, 8 *m.* N. on US 666 for American Airlines; Municipal Airport, 4 *m.* E. on 10th St. for Charter Service and Flying School.

Accommodations: Six hotels; six tourist courts; four near-by guest ranches.

Information Service: Chamber of Commerce, and Climate Club, 10th St.

Motion Picture Houses: Two; one drive-in operating summer only.
Swimming: Municipal Swimming Pool, 17th and Estrella, adults 50¢; YMCA Swimming Pool, 10th St. S. and Railroad Ave.
Tennis: High School Courts, 12th St. and D Ave.; Park Court; 15th St. Park, free.

Golf: Municipal Golf Course, 2.3 *m.* NE. on Leslie Canyon Rd., 9 holes, greens fee, $1.50 weekdays, $2.50 Sun. and Holidays.
Shuffleboard: Tenth St. Park, 10¢ per game.

DOUGLAS (3,990 alt., 9,828 pop.), home of the Phelps Dodge Copper Queen Smelter, is near the southeastern corner of the state, and just across the line from Old Mexico. To the east are the tawny slopes of the Pedrogrosa and Perilla Mountains, and to the north are the Swisshelm Mountains.

On G Avenue, the main street, the commanding height of the Gadsden Hotel breaks the facades of the two-story brick and frame office buildings. Mexican cafes and saloons, off Tenth Street, operate among vacant offices and stores which still bear the faded scroll signs of once lively enterprises, but are now rented to working families. In the dusty streets west of G Avenue red brick and adobe barracks are occupied by a few Negro families and the large Mexican population. The drab barracks are brightened by painted screen doors and brightly colored shawls hanging in the windows.

Three parks in the residential area east of G Avenue and green lawns, flower gardens and chinaberry trees brighten the town's appearance. Yet, to Douglas residents, the prettiest sight is the spirals of twisting, rolling smoke that lift from the great smelter with a smelting capacity of 100,000 tons of copper ore per month, and jobs for 800 men—for the smelter smoke means life itself to the town.

In 1900 the Phelps Dodge Company of Bisbee sent representatives into the Sulphur Spring Valley to look for a site on which to set up a Copper Queen smelter. The company had just acquired mines at Pilares and Nacozari, Mexico. Because the smelter at Bisbee could not be enlarged, and because loaded ore wagons could be braked down the Mule Mountains, the site of present Douglas was selected. Alfred Paul, Park Whitney, C. A. Overlock, and J. A. Brock, who had heard of the intentions of Phelps Dodge, hurriedly staked their claims in this region, and beat the company to the land office. They commissioned the International Land and Improvement Company to survey and sell lots, and by the time workmen flocked in with their families to build the smelter, the found tents, houses and shacks occupied by gamblers and prostitutes awaiting their arrival.

The town was named for Dr. James Douglas, then president of Phelps Dodge. Dust was so thick in the streets that "one sank to his shoe-tops just walking through it," and heavy planks were laid across each corner crossing. In 1901 a depot was built for the El Paso & Southwestern Railroad and a branch line was started to Nacozari.

The first cafe, made of railroad ties, was opened on Tenth Street. In the Cattle Exchange, Waldorf, and White Horse gambling palaces dancing girls sang the latest ragtime tunes from Herald Square and the Barbary Coast. One well, from which water was carried in barrels, supplied the booming settlement; the only available bathtub was in a barber shop.

In 1904 the stack of the Copper Queen Smelter was blown in; the town was incorporated the following year and the children of its new citizens packed the large room of the only schoolhouse. After the inauguration of a public utility and trolley car system the voters cast ballots in a lawyer's derby hat for municipal officials.

Completion of the Calumet & Arizona Smelter, a few years later, brought new workers to Douglas. More than 50 per cent of Arizona's copper was processed in the two smelters, and before the World War they had a $500,000 monthly pay roll.

Agua Prieta, the companion town in Mexico, grew from several adobes clustered around a spring and flourished on the export of copper ores from the Nacozari mines. In 1904 Americans and Mexicans swapped slogans and cheers at the bull ring at Agua Prieta. The brother of Admiral Cervera, who commanded the Spanish fleet at Havana, was presented as the prize toreador of the premiere bull fight to the governors of Arizona and Sonora.

Seven years later, the same citizens fled from bullets exchanged between the federal troops of Mexico and Captain "Red" Lopez' volunteer soldiers. A military adventurer born of American and Mexican parents in Tucson, Arizona, Lopez cornered the federal troops in trenches dug along the International Line, and his soldiers' bullets spattered houses and stores in Douglas. Captain E. J. Gaujot, stationed with the 1st United States Cavalry at Douglas, observed the fighting from the flat roof of a two-story building on G Avenue. Later to protect American citizens from gunfire across the border, Captain Gaujot persuaded federal troops to surrender Augua Prieta to Lopez.

On November 2, 1915, Pancho Villa laid siege to Agua Prieta. He threatened, in case of American interference, to storm Douglas. Major Frederick Funston, commanding American troops, countered with a threat to assist Calles' federal army if shells from Villa's guns landed in the United States. For five days guns east and west of the adobe houses exploded shells in the sandy streets of Agua Prieta. When Villa retreated toward Chihuahua he told reporters he had been defeated by Major Funston and the American troops. He later made a retaliatory assault on Columbus, New Mexico.

Because of the World War, and resulting high copper prices, Douglas boomed. When the United States entered the war 25,000 National Guardsmen were stationed in long frame barracks on the flat plains north of the city limits. New homes were built and streets were paved. Range cattle were driven into corrals near the depot and slaughtered to feed the thousands of soldiers and smelter workers.

National Guardsmen, enlisted soldiers, and many families left town after the war, and Douglas was paralyzed by the post-war depression. It was not until 1923 that smoke lifted again from the smelter chimneys. During prohibition tourists came to Douglas and jammed into taxis for the White Horse Cabaret and the Club Social at Agua Prieta.

In 1931 the Calumet & Arizona Smelter merged with the Phelps Dodge Mining Corporation. Workers from the Copper Queen Smelter, which was abandoned, joined the large number of applicants for Federal relief. This crisis lasted until a rise in the price of copper caused the Phelps Dodge Corporation to open the Bisbee and Nacozari mines. In 1938 many workers left relief rolls to return to the enlarged Calumet and Arizona Smelter. The Chamber of Commerce encouraged the construction of a new automobile highway to the Angostura Dam, ninety miles south of Agua Prieta, hoping that the opening of a large recreation area in Mexico, with fishing and big game hunting, would make Douglas an international tourist attraction.

POINTS OF INTEREST

The CALUMET & ARIZONA SMELTER (Copper Queen) 1 *m.* W. on Highway 80, is an orderly arrangement of low black buildings, covering an area of 300 acres. Black and yellow slag and tailing dumps lead from the buildings into the sandy plains.

The Phelps Dodge Mining Corporation acquired the smelter in 1931 and has added to it $2,500,000 worth of new equipment and buildings. Eight hundred men are employed in average production years, and the plant has a monthly smelting capacity of 100,000 tons of ore.

The buildings are connected by a continuous conveyor belt which carries the ore through the separate processes of manufacturing. When the ore has been crushed in huge revolving barrels it is screened and bedded in acid tanks. The pulverized product of the tanks is roasted to a calcine concentrate and finally in four reverberatory furnaces converted into slag and copper mattes. Two anode furnaces produce a 99-60 anode copper, with traces of gold and silver, which is shipped for further refinement to a plant at El Paso, Texas. The plant also produces 6,000 tons of sulphuric acid every month.

The MUNICIPAL AIRPORT, on E. 10th St., has a three-quarter mile runway, part of which is in the United States and part in Mexico. East of the field is the running profile of Chevrolet Hill, College and Saddlegap peaks merging into the plains; and the rounded dome of Niggerhead Mountain in Mexico can also be seen from here.

The UNITED STATES BORDER STATION AND SUB-PORT, S. on G Ave., is a concrete, brick, and tile structure, housing the Customs Offices and the Immigration and Agricultural Quarantine Stations. In 1937 it handled exports amounting to $1,741,380 and imports, especially cattle and copper ores, amounting to $2,108,425.

The COMPANY OF MARY NOVITIATE (*open 9-5 daily*), 10th St. and Ave. A, is the only novitiate of the International Institution of the Company of Mary in the United States. It is governed by a mother general in Rome. Each year twenty girls from Mexico, Cuba, and the United States are trained here for missionary and educational work. In the summer months local Mexican boys are taught primary subjects. The novitiate was established in Douglas in 1926, the year the Institution was expelled from Mexico. The principal building, a large cottage, adjoins several dormitory additions. A chapel, decorated with statues from Barcelona, Spain, and the grottoes of Our Lady of Lourdes and Our Lady of the Sacred Heart are in a garden dotted with fruit trees, flower and vegetable gardens.

CHURCH PARK, E. 10th St., is a square block of green lawn with Episcopal, Presbyterian, Baptist, and Methodist Churches at its four corners. The congregations hold a non-sectarian service in the middle of the lawn on Sunday evenings.

The BISBEE-DOUGLAS INTERNATIONAL AIRPORT, 8 *m*. N. on US 666 was formerly the Douglas Army Air Base of World War II. Its 28,000 acres has multi-direction runways 7,500 feet long. American Airlines planes land here daily but the large hangars and barracks, formerly used by the Army, stand vacant. Many planes are cleared here each month for fishing trips to Angostura dam and most of the Mexican ranchers use the facilities for the clearance of private planes.

The TENTH STREET PARK, 10th St., is centered by a visitors clubhouse and winter visitors to Douglas form their own club and provide their own entertainment. Shuffleboard courts are located in the park and are in almost constant use.

The FIFTEENTH STREET PARK, 16th St. and Carmelita Ave., is lined with benches under mulberry, chinaberry, and ash trees. Walks and automobile drives lead to baseball and football fields, lighted for night games.

POINTS OF INTEREST IN ENVIRONS

Geronimo Monument, 38.9 *m.;* Skeleton Canyon, 44.4 *m.;* Crystal Cave, 62.2 *m.;* Chiricahua National Monument, 65 *m.* (*see TOUR 4a*). Stronghold Canyon and Cochise Memorial Park, 64 *m.* (*see TOUR 7c*).

Agua Prieta, Mexico

The earth-colored adobe house of AGUA PRIETA (3,980 alt., 8,000 pop.), are arranged in almost continuous one-story rows on dust-filled streets; painted door and window frames or an occasional tilted roof relieve the monotonous succession of low house fronts. Behind ocotillo fences and high mud walls with looped arches are intimate family patios filled with flowering oleanders.   South of the last single adobes the wide Bavispe River valley is cut by wavering sandy roads and fringed with distant purple ranges.

Avenida 3, the main commercial and entertainment street, begins at the customs gate on the International Line.   Emblems of national beers and imported liquors are stamped across the crimson or whitewashed facades of *cantinas* and cabarets, which have lost some of their trade since repeal of American prohibition.

Many Americans and visitors from other lands enjoy the entertainment and hospitality offered in the *cantinas,* curio shops and restaurants in Old Mexico, just across the line.

The gas station in the middle of the short block of stores is studded with three polished pumps.   Around it automobile stages advertise passenger trips to Nacozari, copper mining town across the mountains, and to Angostura, where the largest irrigation dam in northern Mexico is located.

West of the railroad tracks on Calle 5 was the *ranchita,* corral of brothels and saloons.   Between walls decorated with huge nude paintings, girls dressed in pink, red, blue, and purple gowns danced all night long to the music of a Mexican band.   Hungry parrots squawked at strange young men, and a cageful of singing canaries on the bar could be heard between popular song numbers.

The town's social life is organized around the family, school, and church.   Mothers chaperone daughters at Saturday night dances in the Club Social, Calle 2; fathers play endless billiard games in small pool halls and wind up the night at Sonora Cantina, Calle 6.   The elementary school facing the concrete walks of the public park, Avenida 4 and Calle 6, is packed with children. Older women, carrying black umbrellas, stroll to vesper services in the adjoining Catholic church.

There are no monuments to commemorate historical incidents that have given Agua Prieta the national nickname, "Cockpit of Mexico." In 1911 Captain "Red" Lopez, with volunteer soldiers, stormed and sacked stores, houses, and the local branch of the Sonora State Bank. Lopez took advantage of the unsettled state of Mexico after the electoral defeat of President Diaz and seized cash revenue collected for the export of fat cattle from ranches near the Bavispe River and copper ores from the Nacozari mines.

Four years later Pancho Villa and his army finished the long march from the state of Chihuahua and laid siege to Agua Prieta. His Krupp guns exploded shells inside adobe houses and damaged the black silos of the local flour mill. *Soldaderas* ran through the streets carrying water, food, and ammunition to soldier husbands in both armies. When Villa retreated toward Chihuahua he left a half-standing border town and burning pyres of dead soldiers.

Agua Prieta does not boast of these events; they have happened because of its geographical situation, its wealth, and its military importance. The town is connected by railway with the rich Nacozari and El Tigre copper mining districts. East of Niggerhead Mountain, which rises from the plains south of the Arizona line, a small depression in the contour of the distant mountain range marks the only practical pass into the state of Chihuahua. Agua Prieta has no connection by railroad, by highways, or even by desert roads with any other Mexican state. Since 1910 Mexican rebel armies have frequently confiscated revenues collected at the local customhouse.

In 1920 Alvaro Obregon, president of Mexico, and Plutarco Elias Calles, his successor, drafted the Agua Prieta Plan, model of the present social and political constitution of Mexico, in the Curio Cafe, Calle 5. The event is commemorated by a bronze plaque over the door of the cafe.

In 1929 General Yocupicio, present governor of Sonora, commanded a rebel army in Agua Prieta. His soldiers mingled with curious and unmolested American tourists seeking liquors and wild-game dishes at cabarets and saloons. This bloodless incident was almost forgotten when Aimee Semple McPherson, Los Angeles evangelist, told a crowd at the Brookhill Restaurant, Avenida 3, that she had been kidnaped by Mexican bandits. Townspeople looked at her dancing pumps and wondered why the thin soles had not disappeared during the fifteen-mile hike from Niggerhead Mountain.

POINTS OF INTEREST

The CUSTOMHOUSE, NW. corner, Calle 2, Ave. 3, is a red brick building with a square tower flanked by tall decorated windows and a four-columned portico bearing a carved inscription below the pediment: *Aduana Fronteriza de Agua Prieta,* the Customs House of Agua Prieta.

The CLUB SOCIAL, NW. corner, Calle 2, Ave. 4, is a white stone building with a domed Moorish tower surrounded by a high wall and is a social club and cabaret in which Americans and Mexicans mingle on Saturday and Sunday nights. In American prohibition years it catered exclusively to American and European visitors. For March 5, 1932, the club register reads: "Will Rogers and wife (honest she is). Local residence, Naco. Introduced by Senor Calvin Coolidge. Remarks: Play that there 50 cent slot machine. There is plenty in there."

The BROOKHILL RESTAURANT, SW. corner, Calle 2, Ave. 3, is noted for wild game, deep-sea fish dinners, and a varied European cuisine. It is a favorite rendezvous for stage and screen celebrities.

NACOZARI RAILWAY DEPOT, W. on Calle 2, is a simple red-brick structure with a peaked roof and an outside *ramada* shelter waiting-room in which native travelers sit among huge bundles and cackling chickens. The autovia, a two-decked automobile bus on the railroad track, leaves for Nacozari Tuesday, Thursday, and Saturday at 1 p.m. The one-way fare is 3.80 pesos and the round-trip fare 7.60 pesos; in American money 75¢ and $1.50. The local train leaves for Nacozari Monday, Wednesday, and Sunday at 1 p.m. One-way and round-trip fares are 10.10 and 10.75 pesos; in American money, $2 and $2.10.

CURIO CAFE, NE. corner, Calle 5, Ave. 2, now called El Rancho Grande, is the tavern in which Calles and Obregon drafted the Agua Prieta Plan. Above the front entrance a bronze plaque reads: "Dedicated by the 2nd Company of the 18th Battalion to the leaders of the Revolution. The Agua Prieta Plan was signed in this house April 23, 1920." The former proprietress, Mrs. Catliff, rented rooms to visiting generals and statesmen for almost twenty years. On the barroom walls are rifles, sombreros, and Krupp shells of Villa's army. Other relics are on display in the National Museum, Mexico City.

The ALAMEDA MUNICIPAL, Calles 5-6, Ave. 4, Agua Prieta's park, has an oval bandstand in the center of its sandy lawn planted with Bermuda grass, and is crossed with dove-colored concrete walks lined with concrete benches. Under small trees concession stands offer soft drinks and Mexican foods.

The CATHOLIC CHURCH, Calle 7, Ave. 7, a squat adobe structure, resembling a Russian church, is topped by a steeple and gilded cross. Mexican boys in black suits and girls in white dresses and thin head shawls attend communion services on Sunday mornings. Weekday vesper masses are thronged with old women wearing black shawls over black flowing dresses.

The CRUZ GALVEZ, Calle 7, Ave. 7, is a crude cluster of obelisk grave shafts inscribed with the names of the soldiers who died fighting Captain "Red" Lopez in 1911 and Pancho Villa in 1915. Two large mass graves of unidentified soldiers stand at the corner of the street-crossing.

Flagstaff

Railroad Station: Santa Fe Ave. and Leroux St. for Atchison, Topeka & Santa Fe Ry.
Bus Stations: Railroad station, Santa Fe Ave. and Leroux St., for Santa Fe Trailways; 118 W. Santa Fe Ave. for Pacific Greyhound Lines.
Taxis: 60¢ anywhere in the city.
Airport: 5 *m.* S. on US 89; taxi $1.75; limousine 90¢.

Accommodations: Six hotels, forty tourist courts, nine guest lodges.

Information Service: Chamber of Commerce, Santa Fe Ave. and Beaver St.

Motion Picture Houses: Two.
Swimming: Arizona State College Pool, on campus, Humphrey St. and Dupont Ave., students only.
Tennis: City Park Courts, Toltec St. and Aspen Ave., free.
Skiing: Arizona Snow Bowl, 13 *m.* NW. on Fort Valley Rd.
Golf: Flagstaff Country Club, 3 *m.* N. on Shultz Pass Rd., greens fee $1.
Hunting and Fishing: Duck, bear, deer, elk, bass, trout in near-by lakes and streams, guides and equipment available.

Annual Events: Powwow with 7,000 Indians participating, July 4th weekend. Hopi Craftsmen Exhibition at Museum of Northern Arizona, 1st week in July; Northern Arizona Square Dance Festival; Navajo Craftsmen Exhibit; All-star Football and Basketball Games, coaches clinic; all in August.

FLAGSTAFF (6,907 alt., 7,663 pop.) is on the high Coconino Plateau. Southward are the gorges and canyons of Oak Creek, rimmed with painted mesas. Eastward extend painted deserts. Mars Hill, a low mesa running north to south, is a green backdrop on the west, and on the northwest Mount Elden (9,280 alt.), dark green and oval-shaped, rises above the town. Northwest of Mount Elden the blue dome of the sky is pierced by the San Francisco Peaks, consisting of Humphreys Peak (12,611 alt.), Agassiz Peak (12,300 alt.), and Fremont Peak (11,940 alt.). The Hopi name for the San Francisco Peaks is translated as "High Place of the Snows"; they were said to be "so high that when the sun shines on one side, the moon shines on the other."

Flagstaff with its Indian, white, Mexican, and Negro population, is a town of traditional, ethnic, and occupational contrasts—exemplified by the cowboy's spurred boots, the lumberjack's hobnailed shoes, and the Indian's moccasins, worn on the streets. In summer the days are warm, the nights are cool, and a pungent pine scent drifts in from the surrounding woods.

One- and two-story business houses of red Coconino sandstone line Santa Fe Avenue (US 66), running east and west, and San Francisco

Street, running north and south. The whir of the lumber mills at the western end of Santa Fe Avenue and at Mogollon Avenue and Clark Street can be heard downtown. Small buckboards and wagons drawn by scrubby Indian ponies rattle into town from the Navajo reservation 43 miles away, and rattle out again loaded with flour, cloth, potatoes, and shiny tin dishes. Dudes gather in restaurants and feed nickels into juke boxes. Papooses peep from cradleboards on their mothers' backs as vividly dressed Navajo and Hopi women sell pottery and blankets, silverware and baskets along the curbs.

Mexican and Negro mill workers live across the tracks between South Beaver Street on the west, Grant Avenue on the south, and Verde Avenue on the east. Little Mexico is approximately twenty square blocks of unpainted and unadorned one- to four-room frame dwellings, Mexican stores, restaurants, and pool halls. The Mexicans cling to their own customs and foods, and the older women still wear *rebozos,* or shawls, over their heads. Northeast of Little Mexico is a section of small unpainted, smoke-blackened frame houses, occupied by Negroes brought from Louisiana to work in the lumber industry.

North of the business section is the Flagstaff residential area with neat frame, sandstone, and brick houses surrounded by well-kept lawns and shaded by towering pines.

The Nahohi (powwow), held each year at Flagstaff on July 3, 4, and 5, transforms the town into an Indian village with the residents and tourists as onlookers. Seven thousand Indians, representing twenty tribal nations from seven southwestern states, take part in ceremonials and present an all-Indian rodeo, which is held in the afternoons. Indian handlers swarm over the chute as a Navajo eases himself into the saddle and feels for his stirrups. As he adjusts the hackamore and sets himself to meet the first big jolt, the chute gate opens. The bronc, a wild horse from the Painted Desert, will not weigh 900 pounds soaking wet, but he comes out bucking. The crowd roars as the rider "goes for leather" and comes up with both hands full of dust. Another chute swings open before the first rider has dusted his pants, and the show goes on. Bulldogging, team-tying, calf-tying, relay and squaw races follow. A relay race awaiting the flag at the starting line is scattered from hell to breakfast as a Supai rider on a bucking bull comes out unannounced. How the contests are judged is a mystery to most of the spectators, but there are no complaints from the Indians; they take it all with a laugh. Excitement runs high, though winners seldom set fast records.

As night falls, hundreds of campfires glow from the pine-clad slopes. Indian women are laden with silver and turquoise, children are in costume no less colorful, papooses slumber in cradleboards, and men move about in the half-light wrapped to their eyes in vividly colored blankets. Little groups form about fires for their own miniature powwows, and individuals visit from one fire to another, pausing to watch dancers moving to the rhythm of the drums.

There are fifteen to twenty tribal dances each night and the ceremonials are broadcast. In the Kiowa Eagle Dance chanters wearing the buckskin of the Plains Indian form a half-circle and chant the eagle song to the muffled beat of drums. Three young men dance to the front, rows of eagle feathers fastened to their arms and legs; the feathers in close-fitting headpieces tilt with every movement, and bells jingle from leg bands and moccasins.

The Indians depict the peaceful life of their villages with the Yeibetchia Prayer Dance of the Navajo children, the Navajo Red Ant Dance, singing of the "Great Warrior," and the Zuni Water Carrier's Song, Hopi Buffalo Dance, Chant of the Water Hole, Navajo Fire Dance, Zia Crow Dance, Apache Devil Dance, Zuni Rainbow Dance, and the Hopi Clown Dance. Navajo women dance each night until dawn, their shrill voices rising in crescendo.

Ancestors of the Tonto Apaches and Navajos who take part in the powwow were the first known inhabitants of the Flagstaff area. Permanent settlement by whites was begun in 1876, when F. F. McMillan built a corral and shack on a site that is now near Flagstaff's northern city limits. He selected the site because of its fine spring, already well known to couriers, surveyors, and trappers. A few months after his arrival, McMillan was joined by a group of scouts, who camped here to await prospective settlers sent out from Boston by the Arizona Colonization Company.

In celebration of the Fourth of July 1876, the scouts stripped a lofty pine of its branches, and "with suitable ceremony," bound an American flag to the tree with rawhide strings. Later they laid out a townsite here, but when the rest of the group arrived, they were so disappointed at not finding the promised fertility and mineral wealth that the whole party moved on to Prescott. The following year John Clark settled in Clark's Valley and "shot a great bear right where Flagstaff now is"; it took twelve bullets from a new Henry rifle to kill the bear. In 1881 Edgar Whipple, who "drove a six-horse outfit," opened a store and saloon at the spring. The camp began to grow and a group of settlers, including Whipple, established a larger store.

Meanwhile the gigantic flagpole had become known from Santa Fe to San Francisco: "Travel straight west, stranger, until you come to that flagstaff. There's a good spring there and the water is the best you ever tasted. It's warm, too, alongside that mountain and a good place to camp." Trappers, travelers, and cowboys moving their herds west from Texas looked towards the San Francisco Peaks as they eased from sweaty saddles at the end of a day's ride.

During construction of the Atlantic and Pacific Railroad (later the Santa Fe), which arrived here in 1882, Fort Moroni was established seven miles northwest of Flagstaff. The fort, a log house sixty feet in length, was used as headquarters for the Moroni Cattle Company, controlled by John W. Young, son of Brigham Young. As one of the railroad contractors Young needed beef and rail ties. Edward E. Ayer, an expert timber man, contracted to supply the ties and bridge timber, and soon Flagstaff had a sawmill.

In this era, when Flagstaff's one street was lined with wide-open saloons and gambling houses, there were events challenging the wildest fiction. Railroad foremen paid in cash, usually gold. If the money was not forthcoming, railroaders showed a pugnacious spirit, lynching one contractor for failure to meet a pay roll on schedule. At another time a section hand absconded with a $10,000 pay roll. In his haste, a sack containing $6,000 slipped from his saddle and was lost. Later the man was caught, and because he was unable to tell where the money was hidden, the posse decided upon an immediate hanging. The victim made his last requests, watched the noose fitted to his neck, and prepared to die. The rope was cast over a tree limb and, while the man awaited the jerk of the rope, a lightning bolt struck the tree. Believing the interference an act of God, the posse reconsidered hanging and put the man in jail. Five years later the sack of money was found and he was freed.

With the coming of the railroad the town grew as the lumber industry developed, and sheep and cattle raising expanded in the surrounding country. In 1891 Flagstaff was made seat of Coconino County, which with an area of 18,623 square miles is the second largest county in the United States. Because of favorable atmospheric conditions the Lowell observatory was established just outside of Flagstaff in 1894. Five years later the Arizona State Teacher's College opened its doors. The census of 1900 showed 1,271 as the population of the town, and this number was increased by the arrival of quarrymen who came to work local deposits of red sandstone. Manufacture was begun of fire brick from volcanic tufa found in large quantities near by.

Flagstaff obtained its water supply from the spring near the old flagpole until 1914, when the town installed a system that brought water from the San Francisco Mountains fifteen miles away. By 1920 Flagstaff had a population of 3,186, and in 1928 it was incorporated as a city.

Tourists are a major source of income for Flagstaff and the town has many auto camps. Bus companies maintain touring services to many points of interest, including the Grand Canyon and the lakes on the southeast. Further trade comes from the many ranches in the vicinity, and from Hopi and Navajo reservations, but the lumber mills, operating the year round, employ almost one-third of the population.

ARIZONA STATE COLLEGE

Arranged in a circle on the northern portion of a campus of more than 160 acres, beautifully situated alongside US 66 and 89, on the southwest outskirts of Flagstaff, are most of the principal buildings of Arizona State College.

Completing the circle of buildings on the front of the campus is the student center, built in 1951-53, which houses a student union, auditorium, and dining and banquet halls.

In 1893 the 17th Territorial Legislature voted to levy a half-mill tax on each dollar of assessed valuation to create a boy's reformatory. Flagstaff was selected as the site, a building contracted for, and exterior walls and roof constructed. Then came a period of waiting. No incorrigible boys came to Flagstaff to be reformed. The legislators then decided in 1897 an insane asylum was needed.

In 1898 there was $17,000 in the building fund set aside for the public building at Flagstaff. This building still stood vacant and only partially constructed. It was decided to use part of the money to install windows and doors, paint the roof, and to provide proper grading and drainage around the walls.

As time drew near for the 20th Territorial Legislature to convene in January, 1899, pressure groups and newspapers of the territory voiced opinions on what should be done with this unoccupied and unfinished building at Flagstaff. In his message to the Legislature the governor recommended that the building be sold or be used as a normal school. A bill was introduced, passed, and late in the same month, signed into law.

A. N. Taylor of Jamestown, N. Y., former schoolmate of A. A. Dutton, was first principal of the new Northern Arizona Normal School. He and Miss Frances Bury of Tempe made up the entire faculty when the school opened its doors on September 11, 1899. Professor Taylor traveled by train and by horse and buggy to tour the northern part of the state in search of students for the new school. On opening day there were only twenty-three enrolled. Ten more were expected the following Monday.

Nevertheless, the college grew; during 1938-39 the student body numbered 465. In the fall of 1947, enrollment jumped to 776. The college now has a plant and equipment valued at more than five million dollars. It offers five years of standard college work, and, in 1952, began offering a sixth year of advanced work acceptable toward a Doctor of Education degree.

In the spring of 1925, the legislature changed the status of the institution from a normal school to a teachers college authorized to grant the Bachelor of Arts in Education degree. In 1937 the legislature authorized the college to offer courses carrying graduate credit which would permit the conferring of a degree of Master of Arts in Education. In 1946 the Board of Regents of the University and State Colleges authorized the college to confer the degree of Bachelor of Arts, Bachelor of Science in Education, and Master of Arts in Education.

Since 1947 new buildings and other major improvements had, by the close of 1953, reached a total value of over $3,000,000. New construction completed in that six-year period included a science building, men's gymnasium, student union, dining and banquet halls, auditorium, stadium, and central heating and maintenance plant. Late in 1953 the Board of Regents voted to request the legislature appropriate another million dollars for continued plant expansion and improvement on the spacious campus.

Old Main, original building constructed under the act of 1893, continues to be the chief classroom building. Adjoining it to the west is Ashurst Auditorium, built in 1917-19, remodeled in 1953-54 into a modern department of music building. The original gymnasium, built in 1925, south of Old Main, was remodeled in 1952 into a physical education building for women. In the basement is a swimming pool. Hanley Hall, built in 1912 as a dining hall, was remodeled in 1937 into a science building and again in 1951-52 as a men's dormitory.

In 1952-53 an astonomical research observatory was constructed in order that the college could carry on a research program for the U.S. Air Force under direction of a member of the college science department.

Dormitories include Hanley, Taylor and Bury Halls for men, and the Women's Quadrangle, made up by Campbell, Morton, North, and Morton Annex Halls, for the women. In the south portion of the campus is Cottage City, providing modern cottages and apartments for married students.

The pine-shaded CITY PARK, W. end of Cherry Ave., has a campground, race track, an artificial lake providing swimming in summer and skating in winter, a baseball park with a grandstand seating 2,500, and rodeo grounds. City Park is the scene of the annual Indian Powwow.

POINTS OF INTEREST IN ENVIRONS

Sunset Crater National Monument, 17.5 *m.;* Wupatki National Monument, 23 *m* (*see TOUR 1a*). Elden Pueblo, 6 *m.;* Walnut Canyon National Monument, 12.8 *m.* (*see TOUR 2a*). Lowell Observatory, 1.4 *m.;* Museum of Northern Arizona, 3 *m.;* Government Cave, 31.9 *m.* (*see TOUR 2b*). Oak Creek Canyon, 13.4 *m* (*see TOUR 2A*).

Globe

Railroad Station: S. Broad St., for Southern Pacific Lines.
Bus Station: Corner Oak and Pine Sts. for Pacific Greyhound Lines, White Mountain Passenger Line, Payson Stage, and Pleasant Valley Stage.
Taxis: 50¢ within city limits.

Accommodations: 5 hotels, 6 tourist courts.

Information Service: Chamber of Commerce, Dominion Hotel.

Motion Picture Houses: Two.
Swimming: School Hill for school children only.
Tennis: Globe High School courts, E. Ash St.
Golf: Cobre Valley Country Club, 4 *m.* W. on US 60-70, nine holes; greens fee $1.
Hunting and Fishing: Deer, bear, and quail in season. Trout and bass in San Carlos Lake at Coolidge Dam, 32.4 *m.* NW. on State 88.
Radio Station: KWJB (1210 kc.)

Annual Events: Arizonac Club Junior Round-up rodeo, June; State-Invitation Golf Tournament, May 10; Globe Jubilee, Oct. 20-22.

GLOBE (3,509 alt., 6,419 pop.), set against the background of the Apache Mountains to the northeast and the Pinal Mountains to the south and west, is still an old-fashioned western mining town. It appears to be a solid town, standing up as few other mining camps ever have without the mines that made the big boom, and evidently destined to live long as Gila County's main residence and trading town.

But on a green and rose-colored hillside at the northern limits the remains of a great copper mine stand as the landmark of a famous old mining camp. Below the dark skeletons of the abandoned buildings lie the black slag dumps and the weathered tailings dumps (gigantic accumulations of copper ore residue). The tailings, leached to colors as fine as those of the surrounding mountains, occupy the creek valley like mellow sand dunes. They make a pleasing picture, but to the old-timers of Globe the Old Dominion Mine is not part of the scenery. It is a gravestone, harsh-looking and sad, commemorating Globe's career as a great Arizona copper camp—one that flourished with the Old West, and, so they say, died with it.

Although cross-country highways have brought Globe into close contact with the rest of the world, the town's appearance has never changed much. Its young men still carry dinner buckets; and on Saturdays, at least, its crooked Broad Street is crowded with cowboys, Apaches, and old prospectors with drooping mustaches and sharp faded eyes. Its buildings huddle in the canyons and line neat streets over the rolling hills, looking much the same as they did when automobiles were still the doubtful gadgets of the rich. Its houses were built with a mixture of hasty mining-camp planlessness and the ornate stiffness of early twentieth-century architecture. When they were new they must have appeared raw and out of place against the tremendous backdrop of the Pinal and Apache Mountains. But now they have the quaintness of outmoded things, and are as much at home below the purple-blue peaks as the venerable tailings dumps.

Broad street, the town's main thoroughfare and only business street, is a paved ox-and-mule trail, winding and uneven, that casually follows Pinal Creek through a canyon dividing the foothills on which the town is built. The street was never straightened because of concessions made by the town surveyors to early settlers who—with six-shooters on their hips—lived in shacks on the twists of the original trail. Pinal Creek is a dry wash now, its waters having seeped underground to flood the Old Dominion, but the big sycamores and cottonwoods on its banks give the street's bridge crossings a pleasant sylvan touch.

The buildings along Broad Street are the prim brick and stone of 1908, painted to look like new, and tired frame boarding houses, too worn to carry date inscriptions and too empty to care. The chain stores, movies, and smart shops have no more individuality in Globe than elsewhere, but the restaurants and saloons are as western as an old cow pony. The most interesting restaurants follow customs that have satisfied generations of plain-thinking ranchmen and cowboys. They have liquor licenses, Chinese cooks, tables as large as they can find, and private dining rooms with the doors torn off. They serve a baked potato with homemade rolls on the bread plate, beans with every dinner, and specialize in steaks, extra large, at a dollar each.

Invariably, and not excepting even the range-garbed cowmen, the most genuine westerners on Broad Street are the Apache Indians from the near-by San Carlos Reservation. It is a very bad day indeed— and bad weather is rare in the Globe vicinity—when the Apaches are not conspicuously present, stoically feeding their nickels into juke box machines, or clustered in dime stores looking at the shiny pots and pans. Apache men have long since adopted the practical apparel of the cowboys, but women still wear gaudy flowing skirts and carry papooses on their backs.

The different residential sections of Globe used to be an index to the many nationalities living in the camp, but today only two groups—the English from Cornwall, and the Mexicans—still have particular neighborhoods. The Italians and Slavs, the other two well-represented nationalities, live, as they say, "all over." Some still own picturesque adobes or flimsy frame houses along the narrow canyons and hills west of North Broad Street, where all of their countrymen once lived. Others, especially among the Italians, left the mines as young men to go into business for themselves, and can afford to live in East Globe, the nicest part of town. East Globe's tree-named streets—Oak, Ash, Sycamore—run straight up a wide hill; here nearly all the homes have pretty yards, copper roofs, and other evidences of prosperity.

The three hills—Noftgers, Pascoe, and School—are said to be Cornish territory. Noftgers Hill, crowned by one of the town's four large grade-school buildings, is one of several hills in the area east of Broad Street, north of East Globe. Pascoe Hill, also in this section, is separated from Noftgers Hill by a deep steep-sided canyon approximately a block wide and crossed by long bridges. School Hill, west of Broad Street, is also dominated by a school building, and has a large G (said to have been laid to help air pilots identify the town) on its side in white-painted stone. Noftgers and School Hills share the nickname of Cousin Jack Hill, with occupants of School Hill applying the title to Noftgers Hill, and vice versa. The Cornishmen have been known as "Cousin Jacks" so long that they are also called "Cuzzie," and both the name and the diminutive displease them. Pascoe Hill has been corrupted to "Pasty" Hill, in honor of the Cornish delicacy, meat and potato pie.

Ruiz Canyon, the Mexican section of Globe, is one of the brightest Spanish-speaking neighborhoods in Arizona. Situated at the extreme south end of Broad Street, it winds upward between high green hills— and the sun shines down into it with special diligence. Some of the adobe houses must be fifty or sixty years old, but few things look decrepit in Ruiz Canyon. The homes are long and L-shaped, with steepled red or green roofs; and the yards are artfully fenced and ingeniously gated with discarded bedsteads perfectly balanced and latched. The yards contain flower beds bordered with dun-colored beer bottles; black wash tubs set over primitive fire pits; rabbit pens, wood piles, children and their little red wagons—and yet they are neat and orderly. It is very peaceful in Ruiz Canyon, and the common sounds are those made by canary birds, turkey gobblers, an old man sawing wood, or a brown child chasing a maaing white goat over a mesquite-covered hilltop.

Globe was first settled in 1876 as the result of a silver-strike boom, but its greatest wealth and later prosperity were due to the rich copper deposits found beneath the surface silver. The silver stampede that brought the pioneers invaded the San Carlos Reservation, territory set aside under solemn treaty for the exclusive use of the Apache, wildest and most desperate Indians in the Southwest. It was country so ringed around by impenetrable mountains, and so well defended by the Apache, that it had been considered worthless for any other purpose. For five years before 1876, the military authorities had been busy driving 4,500 sullen Apaches onto it.

A globe-shaped boulder of almost pure silver, with surface scars said to resemble the continents of the earth, was found on the reservation just inside its western boundary. There Globe was begun, forty miles west of the old San Carlos agency headquarters which, as the center of the conflict connected with Apache pacification, was called

"Hell's Forty Acres." Besides the "globe" which named the new camp, so much other silver was discovered within a twenty-mile radius around it, that men rushed in to gather riches regardless of all hazards. It was not long before the twelve-mile strip containing the precious metal was taken away from the Indian reservation and given to the whites. Even today, Apaches questioned regarding the infringement of their rights sometimes grow profane over whites who stole Besh-ba-gowah. *Besh* is the Indian word for metal, and *Besh-Ba-Gowah*—the metal village—is the only name by which Globe has ever been known to the Apache.

In the beginning, Globe was a few tents and shacks on the east bank of Pinal Creek, and its greatest problem was its isolation. For twenty-two years there were no rail facilities nearer than 120 miles. Mules and burros toiled over the most difficult mountain passes in the territory carrying ore west to San Francisco, and ox teams creaked laboriously through Apache land bringing general merchandise from Silver City, New Mexico, on the east. One of the first Silver City residents to travel the trail to Globe did so with a load consisting of a hogshead of whisky and a sack or two of potatoes. Sale of liquor on an Indian reservation was illegal and, besides, the newcomer had no liquor license under which he might dispense his stock anywhere in Arizona. Under the circumstances, he sold potatoes at one dollar each and threw in a pint of whisky as a good-will offering.

The silver around Globe lasted only about four years, but before it was exhausted the incredibly rich copper ore under it was found to be almost as valuable. In 1881 when copper capitalists were getting interested in the district, the Apache revolted as a result of mismanagement and broken promises, and began to murder every white man they met. Globe appealed frantically for soldiers to protect it, received none, and organized the Globe Rangers, an effective home guard that kept the camp from being attacked. Nevertheless until the surrender of Geronimo in 1886, the trails to the mining camp were so dangerous as to discourage all but the most adventurous, and development of the district's copper mines proceeded very slowly.

In 1882 John Hays Hammond came to Globe on mining business, and was unable to find a room anywhere in the camp. Finally a boardinghouse keeper agreed to let him use a room whose occupant was known to be temporarily out of town. Hammond went to sleep, but was soon disturbed by a man who loudly demanded the return of his bed. Luckily Hammond was able to offer the stranger a drink of whisky, and its powers of appeasement were such that the two men shared the bed for the rest of the night. Hammond left Globe early the next morning, and was gone for several days. When he returned, he saw two bodies hanging from a sycamore tree on Broad Street, and one of them was the stranger with whom he had recently shared bottle and bed!

The hanging which occurred during Hammond's brief absence was one of the most dramatic in Arizona's frontier history. On August 23.

1882, the carrier on the mail route across the Pinal Mountains dashed into town shouting: "Apaches have taken the mail train. Andy Hall is dead!" and told of being fired upon by hidden assailants. Hall was the express messenger traveling with the mule train to bring in a box containing $10,000. The posse which followed the mail carrier back to Hall's body on the mountain trail, also found the mules dead, the express box missing, and Dr. Vail of Globe dying of bullet wounds. In his last words the doctor told of meeting two white men who had inquired if he had heard shots, and who, when he replied in the affirmative, shot him.

The next day John Hawley, Lafayette and Cicero Grime, well-known men of Globe, were arrested. Cicero confessed that he was only a scout to find when the money was coming. That night Hawley and Lafayette, hoping to escape, consented to go with a body of men to the place where the loot was hidden. In the Grime cache was two-thirds of the money, which indicated to the men that Cicero was equally guilty with his brother. When the two murderers and the dozen armed men returned with the money, the express agent, J. J. Vosburg, read to them a telegram that he had just received from the superintendent of the express company: "Damn the money. Hang the murderers. [Signed] Valentine." Opinion seems to have been divided on the guilt of Cicero Grime—or possibly the men of Globe pitied his wife and large family. He was held for trial but the other two were told to make their wills. It was a little past two o'clock in the morning when they finished, and someone at the Methodist church began tolling a funeral knell. With the entire male population watching silently, the prisoners were marched to the large sycamore tree standing in the middle of Broad Street near the bend in Pinal Creek. A clergyman stepped forward to "do his office for those about to die" and was gruffly refused by Hawley. Grime said bitterly, as his hands were about to be tied behind him, "Damned if I'll die with my boots on!" and he sat down in the muddy street and removed them. A hundred men pulled on the ropes which soon afterward sent the murderers up to the branch of the tree.

During this period, when Indian scares kept competition at a minimum, the Old Dominion Copper Company established itself with a small smelter and the acquisition of the best copper prospects in the vicinity. Its expenses were heavy—shiploads of coke from Wales docked at San Francisco with furnace fuel for the Old Dominion smelter at Globe, and the haulage cost on coke from the Coast to Globe was sixty-five dollars a ton. But the copper was rich enough to stand the high cost of production, and in 1886 the camp bragged that all the copper coins minted by the United States Government were being made from bullion extracted at Globe.

Globe was not very important as a copper producer, however, until after 1895, when the Lewisohn Brothers of New York bought control of the Old Dominion and invested millions of dollars in it. A new smelter was built and a branch railroad line from the south into Globe was completed in 1898. For the next twenty-five years the Old Dominion was one of the greatest copper mines in the world. It had many difficulties—underground water, heat, inadequate ventilation, and decreasing returns from lower-grade copper found at greater depths. Eventually the Lewisohns sold control to the Phelps Dodge interests, whose improved methods kept the mine producing on a gigantic scale.

Globe shared in the Old Dominion's glory, and even surpassed it. Other mines were developed not far away; the fine grazing country of Gila County fattened countless head of cattle, and much of the income from them was spent or invested in Globe. In the early 1900's Globe called itself the "Capital City of the County with a Copper Bottom." It was, in fact, a metropolis of the wild west, where people and influences from the world beyond the imposing mountains were as important as those of the isolated frontier. The "Cousin Jacks" and other hardrock miners brought into Globe the idea of collective bargaining for working men, and the union they formed was the strongest and most militant miners' local in Arizona. From the windows of their new union hall they could watch spreeing cowboys compete in impromptu rodeos down Broad Street, with an occasional wild-eyed steer crashing through the plate-glass window of an up-to-date saloon. When Mrs. Minnie Maddern Fiske and her company were brought to Globe in the early 1900's, the famous actress did not arrive until twelve o'clock on the night of the performance. She found the Globe opera house packed with people in their best clothes who had waited patiently for four hours. The show went on at midnight and lasted until 4 A.M., and the audience received it with such enthusiasm that twenty years later members of Mrs. Fiske's company still remembered Globe as one of their greatest triumphs.

Globe in its prime had fifty restaurants and saloons that never closed, and most of them were gay with dance-hall music and the voices of the women, who, 150 in number, were segregated in the trim shacks lining the creek bed of North Broad. As late as 1916 a girl running a soft-drink stand on Broad Street witnessed three murders in one week.

The events which changed Globe, and broke its spirit, did not all happen at once. The first came in 1909, when the camp of Miami was established seven miles west beside low-grade copper developments very much larger than the Old Dominion. The merchants of Globe saw the new camp rise to challenge their exclusive possession of the county's business. Though they hurried to establish branch stores in Miami, their fear and bitterness gave a note of uncertainty to Globe's triumphant prosperity.

In July 1917 seventeen-hundred union miners struck against the Old Dominion company for a closed shop. Strikes were not new in Globe. The camp had had several, the first in 1896; sometimes the union won, and sometimes the operators shut down the mine "to show who was boss." But the strike of 1917 occurred during war time, and was complicated by a jurisdictional dispute between the Western

Federation of Miners and the International Workers of the World. Each of the unfriendly unions put a picket line around the properties of the company, and an organization called the Home Guard armed against both of them. Martial law was declared, and troops of the Seventeenth Cavalry arrived and instantly dispersed all crowds. Sturdy barracks were built on the slag dumps in front of the Old Dominion, and when the cavalrymen moved out of them after a month or so, infantrymen took their places and stayed for nearly two years. The grip of the powerful trade unions in Globe was completely broken, and a large number of skilled hardrock miners left the town forever.

Eventually the great cattle ranchers also felt the pressure of misfortune. Overgrazing and drought made the range poorer every year. Finally the San Carlos Reservation, for many years grazed by the cattle of white men, was restricted to Apache stock only. Ranchmen around Globe had to cut their herds drastically.

When the nation-wide depression reached Globe in 1931, the Old Dominion was closed down with other mines in the district. Its equipment was out of date and its ore very low grade. Its pumps were stopped and the big mine filled with water. The people of Globe knew then that the Old Dominion was abandoned.

For two years nearly all the men of Globe worked for the W.P.A. Then the Miami mines reopened, and many of the town's young miners were able to find work there. Tourist traffic increased, and business became better.

Today, Globe is getting used to being a quiet county seat town. For every old-timer who looks at the Old Dominion and strokes his whiskers and says, "There's as good copper in her as has ever been mined. She'll come back," there is somebody younger who smiles and says, "Well, even if she doesn't, we'll get along."

POINTS OF INTEREST

On the flattened crown of a hill, 1 m. N. on US 60-70, is the OLD DOMINION MINE AND SMELTER, fronted by old slag dumps of the smelter and sandlike tailings dumps of the concentrator mill that push out on flat plateaus into the gulch of Pinal Creek. The road winding up the hill past the partly destroyed plants provides an excellent view of Globe.

The mine's only present function is to furnish water for the town. This water supply is obtained from underground springs on the twelfth level, one-half mile from the main shaft, where the flow was so great that it prevented mine development in that direction. The pure spring water, not contaminated by mine workings, is held back by a dam and pumped up into the town reservoir.

Beside the mine stands the OLD DOMINION LIBRARY, on Smelter Rd., a two-story stucco building erected as a memorial to three miners who lost their lives in the fire at the Interloper Shaft of the Old Dominion, February 20, 1906. The employees of the Old

Dominion each contributed a day's pay to build it, and the library was financed until 1931 from a trust fund of the Old Dominion interests. It contains about 18,000 volumes, among which are many books on mining and history, and a large collection of western stories. Since 1931 the library has been kept up by the city of Globe and Gila County and managed by voluntary workers of the Women's Club of Globe.

GLOBE CEMETERY, S. end of Hackney Ave., occupies several slopes of a foothill of the Pinal Mountains. Names have disappeared from the wooden markers over the graves of early settlers. Thomas P. Hammond, "murdered by Apaches September 1, 1876," is buried under a chinaberry tree.

To Al Sieber, famous Indian Scout, the Territory of Arizona erected a shaft here in 1907. Sieber was chief of scouts at San Carlos when that post was the most dangerous in America, and campaigned with General Crook and General Miles against the Apache chief, Geronimo. He was killed in 1907 by falling rock while supervising Indian labor in the construction of Roosevelt Dam (*see TOUR 10*).

GILA COUNTY COURTHOUSE, S. Broad St. between W. Cedar and W. Oak Sts., built in 1907, is a box-like three-story structure of large blocks of basalt chopped out of the near-by hills. The courthouse is ledged into a hill and is fronted on Broad Street by a flight of stone stairs rising to a porch with benches. The banisters of the stairways inside are sheeted with copper from the Old Dominion Mine.

After 1909 THE LODGE, S. Broad St., a saloon and card room across from the courthouse, had been a hangout for pioneers, cow punchers, prospectors, and miners. Games of poker, hearts, and rummy were usually in progress at the card tables. The fixtures at the bar, the huge wall-glass behind the counter, and the samples of ore in mahogany chests were reminders of the early life of Globe. (Now closed.)

IRENE VICKREY MEMORIAL COLLECTION, Dominion Hotel lobby, is made up of several cases of artifacts from Besh-ba-gowah ruins, 1 mile S. of Globe. The display includes pottery, stone and bone implements, and many other items from the vicinity. The shell jewelry and one of the pottery jars, in the shape of an effigy, were traded probably from Indians off the shores of the Gulf of Lower California and Mexico, in the early 14th century. The late Irene Vickrey, an archaeologist, spent many years working at Besh-ba-gowah; except for this special collection, the artifacts found there have been placed in the University of Arizona Museum.

The FORMER RESIDENCE OF GEORGE W. P. HUNT, 548 S. East St., a plain frame house, was occupied by him until 1912, when he was elected first governor of the state of Arizona. From then until his death in 1934, Hunt was Globe's most widely known citizen and, during the greater part of that time, the most influential man in Arizona's political life. He was elected governor for seven terms, and during the Wilson administration was Minister to Siam.

Hunt came into Globe in 1881 driving a burro. He worked as a waiter in a Chinese restaurant and shoveled muck in the Old Dominion's Yuma stope, which he said was so hot and ill-ventilated that candles would scarcely burn there. In the next thirty years he became Globe's leading merchant and banker and was active in the territorial legislature. While he was governor he fought for good labor legislation and the abolition of capital punishment—and every man in Arizona was either very much for him or emphatically opposed.

POINTS OF INTEREST IN ENVIRONS

Besh-ba-gowah Pueblo Ruin, 1 *m.;* Gila Pueblo, 3 *m.* Here is headquarters for all National Monuments in Arizona and New Mexico as well as of several other National Monuments. Now a Museum (open); San Carlos Indian Reservation, 4.1 *m.;* Ferndale Recreation Area, 17 *m.;* Coolidge Dam and San Carlos Lake, 26.5 *m.* (*see TOUR 3a.*). Roosevelt Dam and Lake, 32.4 *m.* (*see TOUR 3A*).

Miami

Railroad Station: Keystone and Railroad Aves., for Southern Pacific Lines.
Bus Station: Miami Ave. and Live Oak St., for Pacific Greyhound Lines; Keystone Ave. and Sullivan St., for Consolidated Stage Lines.
Taxis: Rate 12½¢ a mile.

Accommodations: One hotel; three tourist courts.

Information Service: Junior Chamber of Commerce on Keystone Ave.

Motion Picture House: One.
Swimming Pool: Y.M.C.A. pool, 42 Miami Ave.; adults 25¢.
Tennis: Lower Miami courts, 1 m. E. on US 60-70; Miami High School courts.
Golf: Cobre Valley Country Club, 2 m. E. on US 60-70; 9 holes, greens fee $1.
Hunting and Fishing: Deer, elk, bear, turkey, and quail in season; trout in near-by streams and lakes.

Annual Events: Miners' Celebration, Mar. 22-24, drilling contests and fandango features, field sports; Labor Day, drilling contests and field sports; Mexican Independence Day, Sept. 16, parade and ball.

MIAMI (3,408 alt., 5,000 pop.), which owes much to the American copper industry's revolutionary discovery of large-scale milling processes for the cheap reduction of very low-grade ores, occupies a small valley at the foot of the Pinal Mountains. In every direction from the town the hills roll back to green and blue ranges, banked one against the other until sharp outlines are softened by the distant haze. On the high hills to the north are the company villages and huge plants of the Inspiration Consolidated and the Miami copper companies. Beyond them are the cavings—great jagged canyons sunk by the removal of copper-bearing earth from under the hills and mountains that formerly stood there. These man-made canyons are too high up to be visible from Miami, but the smelter's coal-black slag dumps and the cement-colored tailings from the concentrators stretch for miles over the heights and down into the flat alongside the town. At night, when the smelter is working, the mounds of slag glow red with streams of molten rock dumped from the furnaces.

The town's business section is laid out on the valley floor, called Miami Flat, and on both sides of it are the alternate hills and canyons where most of the residents have their homes. Straight through the middle of Miami Flat runs Bloody Tanks Wash, which for centuries spread over the entire flat whenever it received the flood waters from the surrounding mountains. Today the wash still carries the floods, but it does so under the name of the Canal, a dredged and concreted channel crossed by arched concrete bridges. The back ends of buildings on Sullivan and Live Oak Streets face each other across the Canal. Their second stories are built to hang over it, and the watercourse is a

202

convenient depository for their used tin cans and other debris. Once inside the limits of Miami, Bloody Tanks Wash is stripped of all the characteristics of a dangerous mountain freshet, and usually looks tame.

Sullivan and Live Oak Streets follow straight courses on either side of the Canal. Sullivan is the main business street; and Live Oak, traversed by US 60-70, usually introduces the community to visitors.

As it enters Miami on the west, Live Oak Street is lined by beautiful new homes, near which stand some fine school buildings. As in most mining camps, nearly all the houses in Miami were flimsy; they were built for a shifting population and at a time when two houses were more valuable than one, even if they both fell down in a few years. At its eastern end Live Oak Street passes the large electrical plant of the Miami Copper Company, and the big white house surrounded by trees and lawns that was home of Cleve Van Dyke, the real estate man who founded the town. On the highest hill to the south is Buena Vista Terrace, one of the uniformly well-groomed and prosperous residential sections.

Sullivan Street indicates even more clearly than Live Oak the various stages of Miami's fluctuating career. Banks, smart haberdasheries, and taprooms with chromium-trimmed bars are housed in good-looking brick and concrete structures put up around 1915. Next door to them stand the boom-day structures of 1909-12—bleached false-front shanties, looking like fugitives from a ghost-town movie set. These are soft-drink parlors, Mexican cafes, tortilla factories, and barber shops displaying such signs as *El Fenix Barberia y banos* and *Casas for Renta.* One of these shacks is the office of the *Silver Belt,* the newspaper that Cleve Van Dyke purchased and transplanted from Globe. Some of these old buildings have been torn down.

The miners and mill-workers of Miami have always congregated on Sullivan Street where they come to trade, and on the side-street bridges over the Canal where they sit on the concrete railings and sun themselves. The people of Miami are of a dozen different nationalities, the largest groups being Mexican and Slavic. Although cowmen are not strangers in town, they are sufficiently alien to arouse philosophical comment. A cow poke passing a group of miners is sure to inspire such observations as "take those thirty-dollar boots away from him and he wouldn't live thirty minutes."

Before 1907 the Miami district was almost uninhabited by white men, and was chiefly noteworthy for its scenery and for vast deposits of copper ore of too low a grade to be profitably mined. Up to that time its most exciting event was the Bloody Tanks Massacre of 1864, when Colonel King S. Woolsey and his party, who had been sent in to "pacify" the Indians, had attacked a band of Apache. The blood of Apache dead and wounded colored and named the mountain stream that bisects the town. According to a less reliable version of the massacre, Woolsey invited the Indians to a feast, then poisoned them with strychnine.

A group of Globe businessmen bought most of Miami Flat—so

named by early settlers for Miami, Ohio—with the idea of getting rich. They learned at once that their new townsite had few friends and a good many impressive enemies. Other Globe businessmen violently disapproved—a new town meant the loss of most of the valuable new trade. But what was even more serious, the Miami and Inspiration companies also frowned on the venture. They preferred company-owned towns, in which their employees lived in company houses, traded in company stores, and—when they were no longer employed—did not remain in the vicinity to become problems. The new owners of Miami Flat, convinced that their project was doomed to failure, abandoned it.

Cleve Van Dyke, fresh from the successful development of Warren townsite near Bisbee, came to Globe and acquired title to Miami Flat for $25,000. Van Dyke ignored the dissenting voices, bought the *Silver Belt,* and promoted Miami as an enterprise inspired by social idealism. He advertised the new town as a place that would encourage home building, relaxation from the restraint of living twenty-four hours daily "on the works," and the exercise of personal choice in dealing with independent trade concerns. Globe merchants boycotted the *Silver Belt,* mine companies planned attractive company villages, and Miami came in with a boom.

Inspiration began the construction of its huge reduction plants in 1912 and the Miami Copper Company, begun in 1907, was developing on a large scale. For years Miami building could not keep pace with the demands of the workers for places to eat and live. The railroad from Globe, the smelter, the company buildings and towns, the mines —all needed construction workers and miners. There was a standing order in the employment agencies of a dozen large American cities for "1000 men wanted at Miami, Arizona." They came—and the town could not take care of them. Hundreds slept in the open or on the floors of saloons. Beds and cots were occupied in shifts, day and night. Restaurants and boarding houses were always filled, and lines of hungry men stood in front of them waiting their turn. In a few years company pay rolls rose to $750,000 monthly.

During the World War years, the "Concentrator City" lived up to its title. The mining companies' huge plants, built at such staggering cost by brilliant engineers, were ready to profit from the high copper price of 1915. During the next five years the whole district produced to the limit of its capacity. Miami was a flushed mining capital, spreading out into the suburbs of Lower Miami and Claypool with a population growing larger than its rival, Globe.

The big wartime strike of 1917, which was duplicated in every copper district in Arizona, hit Miami hard. But when the strike was lost Miami almost forgot it. Its effects were not noticed until after the post-war depression of 1921, when it was apparent that the racial composition of men on the mine pay rolls was changing from a mixture of many nationalities to a majority of Mexicans.

The slump of 1921 was followed by eight good years. The Canal, the schools, and a modern sewage disposal plant were built. Good fire-fighting equipment replaced the old hand-drawn hose cart. The streets were well paved and lighted, even some of those in the steep dead-end canyons. Influence was exerted to bring a local highway over the mountains; completed in 1922, it is now a segment of US 60-70.

In the 1920's Miami was the storm center of Arizona politics. Cleve Van Dyke, growing richer and more powerful every year, had not made peace with the groups originally opposing him. The breach between his forces and those of the mining companies widened, and Miami and Globe took sides in the quarrel. In a dispute over how much mining property should be subject to city taxes, Miami was incorporated, disincorporated, and reincorporated. When Globe would have forgotten its boycott of the *Silver Belt,* Van Dyke remembered and refused all advertising from its merchants. This led to the establishment of rival dailies in both towns.

By 1923 the feud had completely outgrown Gila County, and the two factions were opposing each other as leading forces in the Arizona gubernatorial election. Former Governor Hunt, leading citizen of Globe but nevertheless Van Dyke's candidate in this campaign, won the election; he was also elected for the two succeeding terms, and again in 1930. The *Silver Belt* effectively claimed Hunt's triumph as its own, and everybody conceded that Van Dyke's forces had scored a victory. Eventually, though, Hunt's Miami supporters were used against him, for in the 1932 campaign he was defeated on the sarcastic slogan, "Let's move the state capital from Miami back to Phoenix, where it belongs!"

Miami was not prepared for the terrible slump of 1931 which deprived almost its entire population of employment. Miami Copper curtailed production and the Inspiration shut down almost completely.

During World War II, Miami district's mines produced copper to capacity but were handicapped by labor shortages. The government thereupon released several hundred men from the army for service in the mines. In this period the Castle Dome property, to the west (now inactive), was brought into copper production.

After the war production continued at high level, and with outbreak of hostilities in Korea, the metal again was placed on the critical list of materials and its distribution was controlled by the government. Mining operations, 1953-54, continue active.

POINTS OF INTEREST

The SILVER BELT BUILDING (now demolished) was at 709 Sullivan Street. One of the oldest shacks in Miami, it housed the newspaper that Cleve Van Dyke purchased and transplanted from Globe, the town of its origin. This pioneer sheet, once a strong daily and an important factor in promotion of the new Miami townsite, was a struggling weekly in 1939. The unpainted shack, bulging at the sides and with a wooden awning extending over the sidewalk, retained all the atmosphere of an old-time country newspaper. But in its front wall was an enormous plate glass window, and behind it, looming large and efficient, was the up-to-date press purchased just before the 1930 depression.

Securely anchored above the building's false front was a weather-beaten electric baseball scoreboard—invented and put together in 1915 by the staff of the *Silver Belt*. For many years it was the only one of its kind between El Paso and Los Angeles, and until 1930 it gave a play-by-play description of all the World Series games. When it was operating, hundreds of miners and mill workers deserted their shifts and filled the street in front of the *Silver Belt*. Lucky ones rented chairs from the second-hand store across the way, the owner of which then closed up so that he also could enjoy the occasion.

The *Silver Belt* was first published in Globe in 1878 by Judge A. H. Hackney, one of the first and best-known newspapermen of the Territory. The Judge described the celebration of his first issue of May 2 in the second issue as follows: "On Thursday last when our first issue was being 'struck off,' Mr. Barnes of the firm Kerr & Barnes entered the office evidently carrying something and followed by a procession of wide-awake citizens, and after spreading a sheet of paper on the floor and putting his hat upon it, he opened his Pandora's box, which was quickly followed by the popping of corks from bottles bearing the impress 'Sparkling Catawba' and Yankee Doodle's bird of universal freedom roosting on North America's coat-of-arms. Upon the glasses being filled and lipping over, Barnes and the rest of us drank to the Arizona Silver Belt."

The *Silver Belt* has had many editors since Judge Hackney's time, all of whom have managed to retain some of the old western editor's flair for plain speaking and direct action.

INTERNATIONAL TORTILLA FACTORY AND STORE, 719 Sullivan Street (now demolished), housed in a reddish-brown wooden building, specialized in making and retailing Mexican foods. Bundles of dried red peppers hang from pegs on the wall, and the top shelves were crowded with Mexican pottery painted in bright designs.

In the show cases were Mexican candies: *Pilonsillos,* brown, cone-shaped, and made from pure cane sugar; and *tuna,* made from the strained juices of the prickly pear cactus fruit and bearing a close resemblance in flavor and consistency to the sweet potato. Also for sale were *guajes ciriales,* tan-colored gourds about the size of an ordinary grapefruit, imported from Mexico because the Mexicans believe the gourd has medicinal properties beneficial to those suffering from respiratory ailments.

The tortilla factory was at the rear of the store. Tortillas are corn cakes, very thin, about the size and shape of pancakes. Indian in origin, they are eaten by Mexicans and Indians as bread, and are also used to make *enchiladas, tocos, tostados,* and *chilacas*—the Mexican equivalent and variations of the sandwich. Tortillas sell for a penny each and can be eaten plain or fried crisp; when fried they have a flavor similar to popcorn.

The corn from which tortillas are made is cooked in lime to crack the skin which is then pressed off by hand. After being rinsed in two or three tubs of water to complete removal of the skin, the corn is ground into dough, patted into cakes, and toasted on a flat hot griddle. This factory has an electrically-driven grinder and a machine resembling a miniature printing press to roll and cut the tortillas. It also has an old-fashioned Indian *metate,* a small inclined table on three short legs, cut out of a solid piece of stone, with the top nicked to afford a grinding surface. Another stone, nicked on four sides, is used to grind the corn by pounding. Mexican women refer to this *metate* as "three legs and one hand."

The HOME OF CLEVE VAN DYKE (*private*), founder of Miami, a large three-story white house on East Live Oak Street is surrounded by eight acres of lawns, shrubbery, shade trees, and orchards. Van Dyke homesteaded the land around 1908, erecting a cottage for his young bride when it seemed that a town the size of Miami could never exist here except in a mirage. As copper soared and Miami boomed, the bungalow was remodeled and added to until it grew to its present size. This house was for many years the finest dwelling for miles around. Although overshadowed in newness and grandeur by the Spanish-type home built at Inspiration for the general manager of the mining corporation, the Van Dyke house is still the largest in Miami.

The MIAMI POST OFFICE, Sullivan and Cordova Sts., a one-story concrete structure, was erected in 1926. In the early days this institution was referred to as the "rolling post office." It operated in leased buildings while land was sold in that vicinity, then moved to another location where property was being sold. Miami citizens were continually in search of their post office, and never certain that it would stay put once they had found it. The post office (1954) is now in the Craig Bldg., Live Oak St., as is the Arizona Silver Belt.

POINTS OF INTEREST IN ENVIRONS

Bloody Tanks, 1.9 *m.;* Old Dominion Mine 6 *m.;* Pinal Ranch House, 11.1 *m.;* Thompson Southwest Arboretum, 24.8 *m.* (*see TOUR 3a.*). Tonto National Monument, 31 *m.* (*see TOUR 3A*).

Nogales

Railroad Station: Grand and International Aves. for Southern Pacific Lines.
Bus Station: Grand Ave. for Citizens Auto Stages, and Nogales-Bisbee Stages.
Taxis: 25¢ within city limits.

Accommodations: Seven hotels; eight tourist courts; numerous guest ranches in near-by Arizona and Sonora, Mex.

Information Service: Chamber of Commerce, 101 Grand Ave.

Radio Stations: XEAF (900 kc.), in Nogales, Sonora; KNOG (1340 kc.), in Nogales, Arizona.
Motion Picture Houses: Two.
Swimming: Karns Pool, 861 Grand Ave., and City Pool in Civic Bldg.
Hunting and Fishing: Wild game, trout, in Sonora, Mex.
Tennis: High School court, Sonoita and Plum Sts.
Golf: Nogales Golf Club Course, 3 *m.* W. on Harrison Ranch Rd.

Annual Events: Rodeos, spring and fall; Anniversary of French defeat at Puebla, Mex., May 5; Mexican Independence Day, Sept. 16.

Russet hills roll gently into NOGALES (3,689 alt., 6,500 pop.), from the east and west; velvety knolls, undulating in great dark waves, are mantled with a sparse covering of yellow desert grass, yucca, and an occasional mescal. They parallel the business districts of Nogales, Arizona, and Nogales, Sonora, and form a pass through which the towns extend north to south, a street ending abruptly here at the foot of a tall slope and there at a sheer red cliff.

With the first light of morning the flat roofs of the business buildings and the housetops on all the hills glisten in the strong sunlight; the faint noises of the Mexican town and the bustle of the American town merge into early morning activity. A gentle breeze moves through the pass. On International Avenue, at the foot of Morley and Grand Avenues, hundreds of Mexican employees of American establishments file past the customs officers through the two *garitos,* passenger gates. Produce trucks and jitneys rattle through the streets, carts and burro trains of wood haulers go by.

International Avenue parallels the ornamental wire fence between the United States and Mexico, extends to an abrupt hill on the east, and on the west runs along the residential quarter of Crawford Hill. The gayly colored curio shops, the delicious smell of dozens of *cantinas,* Mexican restaurants, a hotel with tiny iron grilled balconies, stores, narrow winding streets, and the low adobes of Nogales, Sonora, are on the south side of the street. On the American side there is an unbroken row of brick office buildings, hotels, and stores. Atop Crawford Hill are unpretentious one- and two-story frame, brick and adobe houses, most of them brightened by terraced lawns and flower gardens that look out over the pass into the Mexican hills.

North from International Avenue, Morley and Grand Avenues, the two principal streets, extend along the east and west sides of the Southern Pacific tracks which bisect both the Arizona and Mexican towns. The business and shopping district of one- and two-story brick buildings lies within an area of four or five blocks. The city park, with green lawns, small shade trees, benches, walks and a central bandstand, fronts on Morley Avenue.

North on Grand Avenue is Cemetery Hill, the Negro district, where retired officers and soldiers from Fort Huachuca live. Across the arroyo to the west is Nogalitos, a Mexican colony, and on East Street, toward the International Line, is a larger Mexican settlement of low rambling adobes, with narrow alleys twisting up-hill.

Mexican and American national celebrations are holidays for the people of both towns. Spanish, as frequently as English, is heard on the streets.

Because of its position on the border Nogales is called the "Key City to the West Coast of Mexico." It is the largest Arizona port of entry on the Mexican border, and the trading and banking point for the rich region to the south consisting of the states of Sonora and Sinaloa and Nayarit. Seventy-five per cent of the total volume of business is selling merchandise to Mexico, and handling and warehousing the products of Mexico's west coast.

This large area with more than 500,000 inhabitants is isolated from the rest of Mexico by the high almost impassable Sierra Madre mountain range from Nogales to Guadalajara—a region noted for its winter vegetables, principally tomatoes. About 5,000 carloads were shipped into the United States in 1939, destined for Canadian and eastern markets. Most of the money from these shipments finds its way back to Nogales.

The town lies within a rich mineral area, with approximately three hundred partly developed mines—gold, silver, copper, lead and molybdenum—in a radius of thirty miles. It is also the focal point for shipment of cattle. However Nogales reflects little industrial and commercial activity. In addition to the depression, which touched most towns in much the same way, Nogales has had a more difficult problem. The Tariff Act of 1930 raised duties to a point of practical embargo on many important commodities, and Mexico immediately declared a retaliatory tariff.

These, with subsequent tariff acts and the depreciation of the Mexican currency in relation to the American dollar, cut international trade to a minimum and crippled Nogales. Failing to obtain favorable tariff changes the town is turning its attention to the surrounding rich mineral districts, herds of purebred Hereford cattle are increasing on the lush grass ranges, and thousands of tourists are being attracted to the real charm of Mexico "just across the street."

In 1880 Jacob Issacson, San Francisco merchant, reached Arizona's "last frontier" on the southernmost point of the Arizona-Old Mexico Border. In a grove of black walnut trees in Nogales Pass—the short-cut on *El Camino Real* between Guaymas, Sonora, and Tucson—he erected a trading post and a resting place for passengers of the Tucson to Guaymas stage. The store was made of mud-plastered oak timbers and was surrounded by a mud-plastered ocotillo fence which protected him from prowling beasts and marauding Indians. Outside the fence, and on the flats close to the approximate markers of the boundary line fixed by the Gadsden Purchase of 1854, grew a small settlement of tent-roofed shacks and adobe huts—known as Issactown. As the settlement grew, rude dusty streets were laid out among the hills and other settlers arrived to build shacks and tents on the flats within the pass.

In 1882, two years after Issacson's arrival, the Southern Pacific laid a track from Moreno, (forty miles north of Guaymas, Sonora) to Benson, Arizona. The railroad passed through Issactown, which was renamed Nogales for the trees growing on the original site.

With the coming of the railroad the settlement "attained its majority" and was described by a contemporary writer as "quite a camp, with a box-car railroad station, one adobe house, and several frame shacks built in part from drygoods boxes, with tents stretched over the wooden walls, the latter about four feet high." Another account (1884) reported that the town had grown to "a double row of slab shanties and mud huts, the former being American, the latter Mexican."

One of the early buildings was erected by John Brickwood, who ventured into the settlement shortly after Issacson. It is said that when the final boundary survey was made by a joint American-Mexican commission, it was necessary to cut a niche in the south wall of Brickwood's building to allow the placing of a line monument. Several fugitives chased by the Mexican officials found sanctuary in the niche. Brickwood's house was a saloon and it was so located on the International Line that he could sell his drinks on the American side of the bar and his cigars on the Mexican side, avoiding payment of duties.

The small border town boomed on the prospects and proceeds of the new railroad, and became a supply base for ranchers and miners in the vicinity and a refuge during Apache raids. The buildings on the American side abutted on the line and all of International Avenue was in Mexico. The town was "wide open," with three or four saloons on the west side of Morley Avenue and several on the other side. Decoys were hired to drink, dance, and gamble with patrons. Occasionally there was a shooting.

Nogales was incorporated in July 1893, a year before the opening of the Mexican customhouse. Until 1894 there were only nine young women in the town; they formed a dramatic society and presented *Ten Nights in a Barroom*.

During the following years, as the town grew, it was involved in a series of revolutions across the border. Yaqui Indians, in 1897, built a fort on Chureas Hill, on the Mexican side. After the Indians had raided Nogales, Sonora, the Americans formed a militia and joined Mexican townspeople in storming the fort. Twelve Yaquis were killed before the rest of the band escaped into the arroyos and mountains south of Nogales. American soldiers in 1911 moved into Camp Little to defend Nogales from the guerilla bands of Madero rebels, who had captured parts of Sonora in 1910. In February 1913, Generals Obregon and Cabrel, Madero rebels in command of Yaqui Indians, attacked the Mexican town held by Mexican federal troops. Bullets flew across the border, hitting buildings and breaking windows as Obregon forced the federal troops into Arizona.

The Mexican border town remained in control of Madero forces until 1916, when it was captured by Pancho Villa and his peon army. Villa's threat to shoot up Nogales, Arizona, resulted in closing the International Line to all traffic. Nogales was quickly organized into defense zones, barricades were erected on International Avenue, and 10,000 National Guardsmen arrived by train. One train of Villa's troops moved south into Sonora, but the remaining soldiers threatened to blow up the American barricades. Colonel Sage, commanding the 12th Infantry, gave the order to fire. Many Villa soldiers were killed, others retreated south into Sonora, and the International Line was again opened.

On August 26, 1918 a Mexican ammunition smuggler, caught crawling under the fence of the International Line, was killed by an American customs guard. The incident strained relations between the American and Mexican townspeople to such an extent that, two days later, an American and a Mexican customs guard shot at each other; firing by civilians on both sides of the Line grew into a general battle between the townspeople of the two cities. It lasted from two o'clock in the afternoon until seven o'clock that night, and there were many casualties on both sides.

General Calles arrived from Hermosillo, Sonora with troops that night. General Cabell, at the same time, brought American troops from Fort Huachuca and El Paso. Captain Lungerford was killed while leading Negro cavalry across the Line. Civilians of Nogales, Arizona, opened a protective fire from the windows of the Southern Pacific depot while American troops drove the Mexicans from buildings and streets next to the border. American and Mexican commanders declared an armistice on August 29. Between seventy and eighty Mexicans, including the Mayor of Nogales, Sonora, were killed in the battle; American casualties numbered thirty-two. In September 1918 Governor Hunt of Arizona and Governor Calles of Sonora fixed a "permanent" armistice.

This armistice endured until the Manso-Topete rebellion in March 1929 in Sonora against the federal government of President Calles. Nogales, Sonora, was bombed twice by Mexican federal airplanes, and the Mexican citizens moved into the Arizona town. Later a body of unnamed American citizens arranged for the peaceful surrender of rebel troops to the Mexican federal army.

POINTS OF INTEREST

SANTA CRUZ COUNTY COURTHOUSE (*open 9-5 weekdays*), Morley Ave. and Court St., erected in 1904 on a terraced slope overlooking Nogales Pass, is a square granite building with an aluminum gilded dome. In front of the courthouse, on several flat terraces, is a native cactus garden.

IMMIGRATION INSPECTION STATION, International and Terrace Ave., is a stuccoed concrete structure with a red tile roof; the front porch is an arcade of romanesque arches overlooking the International Line. It houses the Bureaus of Immigration, Naturalization and Plant Immigration, and the Offices of the United States Commissioner, United States Customs, and Customs Agency. The customs offices for the fiscal year ending June 30, 1953, handled imports from Mexico worth $35,956,960 and exports to Mexico worth $37,507,858.

The UNITED STATES CUSTOMS PATROL (*open 9-5 daily*), Morley Ave. between Wayside Dr. and Washington St., a white plastered Mexican adobe with a veranda porch on a landscaped knoll, is the official station of Company D of the Southwest Division of the United States Customs Patrol, with headquarters at El Paso. The patrol consists of one captain, one lieutenant, three sergeants, and eighteen patrolmen, whose duty it is to detect and prevent smuggling of all kinds. Company D patrols the Arizona-Old Mexico Border from New Mexico to California and during one week of 1939 four units rode horseback 280 miles in sixty hours. The structure housing the patrol has been a residence, brothel, gambling palace, and undertaking parlor.

The CHURCH OF THE SACRED HEART, Arroyo Blvd. and Walnut St., is Romanesque in style with a square bell tower. During the period of church suppression in Mexico the citizens of Nogales, Sonora, attended this church.

CAMP LITTLE, Grand Ave. at the north entrance of Nogales, was established in 1911 and abandoned in 1931. The barracks, dining halls, workshops, and recreation centers, formerly used by the Twelfth and Twenty-fifth Infantry, are closed.

POINTS OF INTEREST IN ENVIRONS

Ranch House of Pete Kitchen, 8 *m.;* Calabasas, 12.1 *m.;* Tumacacori, 18.1 *m.;* Tubac, 21.8 *m.;* San Xavier Indian Reservation, 63 *m.* (*see TOUR 1d*). Site of Fort Crittenden, 26 *m.* (*see TOUR 4A*).

Nogales, Mexico

Tourists and visitors may pass freely back and forth across the International Line without interference and in perfect safety. The traveler desiring to go beyond the confines of Nogales, Sonora, must comply with immigration and customs regulations. American citizens need no passports to go anywhere in Mexico. Instructions for border traffic plainly indicated at International Line.

NOGALES, SONORA (25,000 pop.), lying quietly between the warm brown hills of the pass, is basically a Sonoran community vibrant with Mexican life. Most of its houses are compact plastered adobes, simple and colorful, suited to the climate, society, and customs.

The scene varies only in details during the day when all is comparatively quiet on Calle Elias. At the south end of the street where the low adobes melt into the brown hills an old Mexican with rusty gray hair, flowing mustache and beard, dressed in tattered khaki, a sombrero slanted over his eyes, leans against a mud wall as though sleeping in a standing posture. A Mexican woman wrapped in the folds of a black *rebozo* slips quietly along the narrow walk. The voices and laughter of young girls in Paris frocks and of young men merge with the cries of children selling sugar-coated cigarettes, and the hawking of sidewalk vendors displaying handmade leather belts, holsters, spurs, saddles, bridles, and other handicraft goods.

The gay pink, orange, gray, and white adobes of Calle Elias contain curio shops with leather goods, glassware, earthenware, weaving, basketry, carved wood, and wearing apparel from Sinaloa, and imported Paris perfumes; the air is pungent with the smell of Carta Blanca, Monterey, and other Mexican beers and liquors from the scores of *cantinas,* and of the appetizing foods from the restaurants, decorated with colored paper cut-outs.

If it is evening there will be *charra* orchestras and singers in the *cantinas,* singing and playing the *corridos,* ballads and folksongs; and over glasses of beer, mescal, or mixed drinks the occupants of a *cantina* will join in the refrain.

Across the railroad tracks to the west is the Plaza of the Thirteenth of July, a landscaped park with small trees, benches, and the inevitable bandstand in the center. The little stands on the west side are used for brightly colored cold drinks, ice cream, candies, Mexican pastries, hot *tortillas, tamales,* and cigarettes. Mexican men and boys, as though conforming to a ritual, stroll up and down the crowded walks returning flirtatious glances of the girls passing in the opposite direction; old men and women loll on the benches beneath the shade and talk with *compadres.*

The tiny balconies, with ornamental iron grillings, across the facades of the rooming houses, hotels and residences on International Avenue, Calle Campilla, Calle Obregon, and the dark and narrow dusty streets jutting off them are deserted and appear as unhappy afterthoughts of a nostalgic architect. The aroma of oleander blossoms comes from the patios on Calle Obregon where most of the Mexicans live and work.

Calle Obregon runs north and south through the town's center. The blank compact walls of the low plastered adobe business houses and residences hug the narrow walks from International Avenue to the smooth rolling *lomas* (hills) on the southern outskirts. It is a completely Mexican community with its markets, theaters, lotteries, vendors, wood haulers, and water carriers.

There are many residences between the business buildings, but it is often difficult to distinguish one from the other except for scrolled signs and an occasional display window. At dusk, however, the difference is apparent. Residential doorways are open to the refreshing night breezes, for Mexicans live much of the time in their patios, secluded behind blank adobe walls. These vary from small bare areas to lovely flower gardens with whispering fountains; the scent of honeysuckle or oleanders and the cadence of soft singing voices escape through half-open doorways.

Business during the day is carried on by the *mestizos,* small shopkeepers found on Calle Obregon and on practically all the other streets of Nogales. Trucks with cornhusks for *tamales,* with produce and various other supplies, automobiles and passenger busses roll up and down the streets; burro trains of the wood haulers amble silently along dusty hill trails and roads into the town; men and women carrying great baskets of groceries balanced on their heads are a common sight.

Because Nogales is dependent upon international trade, its officials and citizens in June 1939, petitioned President Lazaro Cardenas for a ten-year reciprocal trade agreement between the United States and Mexico. The agreement, which both towns have sought since 1930, would make the town a free port of entry. It is now (1954) a free port of entry.

POINTS OF INTEREST

The CAVERN, 27 Calle Elias, is a cafe known for the variety of its fresh wild game, deep sea fish dinners, and its imported wines and liquors. It is a cave (originally a gold mine) fifty-seven feet under the slopes of Chureas Hill. In the early 1880's it was the jail from which Geronimo, the Apache Indian chief, escaped. During the Calles administration prohibition was declared and the large stocks of wine and liquor stored in the vaults were seized and emptied into Calle Elias. The street was flooded with barrel after barrel of wine. Two Mexicans who had dropped to their knees and imbibed until too full to rise, were shot by federal soldiers and died with their lips in the rich red wine.

MERCADO MUNICIPAL, 424 Calle Obregon, supervised by the Sonora Sanitary Department, is a large gray stucco one-story building filled with stands of fruits, vegetables, meats, sea foods, candies, pastries and household utensils. It also contains a *tortilla* factory where a dozen girls bake thousands of *tortillas* daily. The interior is filled with all the sounds, smells, and sights of the typical Mexican market place.

The SOUTHERN PACIFIC OF MEXICO DEPOT, opposite Plaza of the Thirteenth of July is a Spanish colonial structure of white plastered adobe from which trains leave daily for Mexico City and other points in the interior.

The MEXICAN CUSTOMHOUSE AND REVENUE OF-FICE (*open 9-5 weekdays*), a white-plastered building with romanesque columns and a square clock tower, is predominantly Moorish in style.

ADMINISTRACION DE CORREOS Y TELEGRAFOS, (*open 9-5 weekdays*), Calle Campillo and Calle Juarez, is Moorish in style with Doric columns and great wide windows partly enclosed by ornamental iron grilling. The telegraph and postal systems are operated jointly by the Mexican government.

The SACRED HEART CHURCH, Calle Juarez, a gray sandstone structure with a square tower, is the only church in Nogales, Sonora. Owing to the ban on churches in Mexico it had been closed, but in 1939 was allowed to reopen.

TWENTY-EIGHTH OF AUGUST MONUMENT, Calle Obregon, is a stone shaft on a cleared drive, with an inscription recording the names of the Mexican citizens killed in the battle between the two towns on August 28, 1918.

Phoenix

Railroad Station: Union Station 4th Ave. and Jackson St.; for Southern Pacific Lines and Santa Fe Ry.

Bus Lines: Greyhound Lines and Sun Valley Bus Lines depot located at NE corner Van Buren and First Sts.; American Trailways and Continental Trailways bus depot at SW corner Van Buren and First Sts.

Airport: Sky Harbor, 4 *m.* E. on S. 24th St. for American Airlines, Trans World Airlines; Bonanza Airlines, and Frontier Airlines. Downtown ticket offices, Adams Hotel; Limousine $1.25.

City Busses: Fare 15¢; Metropolitan busses, zone rates to outlying areas.

Traffic Regulations: Parking meters 1¢ for 12 min.; 5¢ per hr.; 10¢ for 2 hrs.; 8 to 6 daily except Sun. and Holidays.

Street Order and Numbering: Central Ave. divides E. and W. segments of named streets. Washington St. divides N. and S. portions of numbered thoroughfares, which are streets east of Central Ave. and avenues west of Central Ave.

Accommodations: 60 hotels; 10 winter resort hotels; auto courts and camps; rates generally higher during winter and early spring.

Information Service: Chamber of Commerce, 124 N. 2nd Ave.; AAA., 748 E McDowell Rd.

Radio Stations: KOY (MBS); KTAR (NBC); KPHO (ABC); KOOL (CBS); KIFN; KRIZ; KTYL; KRUX; KONI.

Television Stations: KPHO-TV, Channel 5; KOOL-TV, Channel 10; KVAR, Channel 12.

Theaters and Motion Picture Houses: Little Theater (Civic Center) 10 E. McDowell Rd.; 22 motion picture houses; two shows Spanish pictures exclusively. Numerous drive-in theaters throughout area.

Swimming: University Park, Van Buren St. and 10th Ave.; Coronado Park, 12th St. and Palm Lane; Encanto Park, 2700 N. 15th Ave.; Eastlake Park (colored), 16th and Jefferson St.; Grant Park (Mexican), 2nd Ave. and Grant St. Pools generally open from June 1 to Sept. 15.

Golf: Municipal links, 15th Ave. and Encanto Blvd., 18 holes, 9 holes; Phoenix Country Club, N. 7th St. and Thomas Rd., 18 holes; Arizona Country Club, Scottsdale, 18 holes. Other 18 hole golf courses in area, San Marcos, Arizona Biltmore, Wigwam (Litchfield Park), Paradise, and Sundown. For locations and fees inquire of Chamber of Commerce, Phoenix.

Tennis: At all city parks. No fee except for metered light, night.

Baseball: Phoenix Stars of Arizona-Mexico League.

Annual Events: Salad Bowl Parade and Football Game, Jan. 1; Arizona National Livestock Show, Jan.; PGA Golf Tourney, Jan.; Major League Spring Training (N.Y. Giants) Feb.; Cactus Show, Feb.; Dons Superstition Mt. Lost Gold Trek, March; World's Championship Rodeo, March; Masque of Yellow Moon Pageant, May; Arizona State Fair, Nov.

PHOENIX (1,080 alt., 150,000; met. area, 300,000 pop. 1955 est.), capital of Arizona, is a desert metropolis in the approximate center of the Salt River Valley—a rich irrigated agricultural area. The valley, roughly an oval forty miles east and west by twenty miles north and south, slopes generally to the southwest. The floor of the plain is remarkably smooth and the city's streets appear uniformly level; the view down any street reveals mountains on the horizon. The valley reaches far into the north to Squaw Peak and Camelback mountains etched against the horizon. To the east, though more than fifty miles distant, the Four Peaks, a noted landmark, are clearly visible.

The mountains, seen from South Mountain Park Lookout (*see TOUR 3b*), melt into the dry desert yellows and browns; saguaro like giant needles rise from the desert floor, and merge in turn with the rich colors of the valley—solid squares of blue—green alfalfa, green citrus groves, and golden fields of ripened grain. From the lookout the city's residential sections are obscured by trees, and the tall down-town buildings resemble toy blocks stacked high on a velvet carpet.

The climate is semitropical though there is far less rainfall than is usual in semitropical regions. The mean annual precipitation is 7.8 inches, the heaviest rainfall coming from sudden showers in July and August, with other rains in December. The coolest month in Phoenix is January with a mean temperature of 51 degrees. The monthly mean rises steadily up to July, when it often exceeds 100 degrees.

In winter thousands of visitors from other states and Europe crowd the streets and speed up the tempo of the town. Highlighting the tourist season is the Salad Bowl Parade and Football Game, the morning parade of beautiful floats, beauty queens, high school and college bands from over the state vie for prizes, and the New Year's Day game is between teams of national prominence. Also a highlight is the World's Championship Rodeo and Parade in March, when the top professionals compete for rich cash prizes during three days of competition. The town goes "Western" for this event, and almost everyone, locals and visitors alike, don Western garb in three days of revelry. The rodeo parade, on opening day, is one of the finest, with no motorized equipment. From early morning until parade time a continuous stream of hundreds of horsemen move into the city from all directions to participate.

In these busy months stores display windows full of Indian blankets, silver and turquoise jewelry, beadwork, and Mexican wares; Indian women squat on sidewalks at the busiest corners with their handmade pottery spread around them, silently waiting for a buyer; dude cowboys parade in and out of the best hotels wearing spotless ten-gallon hats and polished high-heeled boots; rents are high and living quarters scarce. After the visitors have fled before the summer heat, residents move slowly and tarry in the shade of an occasional awning over the sidewalk. The true cowboy loafs unnoticed in his weather-stained Stetson, his boots with rundown heels and his desert-colored work clothes. All through the year a few Indian women with their pottery sit stolidly on the sidewalks.

Climate and cultural heritage have influenced the architecture of Phoenix. Modified Spanish Colonial and Indian pueblo types are widely used. The former is generally a low rambling structure of painted adobe brick with red tile roof and patio, while the latter follows the traditional form of an irregular two-story structure with set backs, walls of adobe and roof supported on *vegas* (rafters).

The better residential sections of Phoenix—Encanto, Palmcroft, Country Club Manor, Biltmore, and Arcadia—have green lawns and flowers throughout the year. The many cottonwood trees that shade the lawns and walks are never completely bare, for new leaf buds are formed before all of the winter-killed leaves have fallen. Palm, tamarisk, eucalyptus, olive, and citrus trees also provide shade. On spring nights the sweet heavy perfume from outlying orange groves floats over the city, and in late spring oleander hedges burst into white and pink bloom.

The majority of Mexicans and Negroes live south of the railroad tracks. At Jackson and South 16th Streets and at Grant and 5th Streets, are the homes of many of the more well-to-do Negroes. Here dwellings are neat and attractive with lawns, shade trees, and flowers. The Negroes have their own churches, hospitals, newspapers, and social activities.

Farther east is the "shack-town" of the poorer Mexicans, and "7-Up Camp," a block of shacks along the north side of the railroad tracks housing hundreds of Mexican families. The houses are nondescript in materials and appearance with bare unshaded yards. The more prosperous Mexicans live between Second and Fourth Avenues south of Madison Street, in rows of well-kept homes with landscaped lawns. From Seventh Avenue westward is the poorer Negro section with living conditions similar to that of the poorer Mexican sections.

Mexican residents comprised about half the population prior to 1900 despite the fact that Phoenix always prided itself as being a "purely American town." In 1938, however, they numbered less than 10 per cent, and the Negro population was less than 2 per cent. This is not a decrease in the number of Mexican and Negro residents but a larger proportionate increase in the white population. Many Indians, educated at the Indian school, have settled in Phoenix; they have a social life of their own, seldom mixing with other racial groups.

During the last few years air-conditioning has brought greater summer comfort to residents of Phoenix, most of whom were accustomed to spending their nights on lawns or porches. Thousands of houses are equipped with inexpensive homemade excelsior window-box coolers, while others have more expensive factory-made types. Business houses, offices, and public buildings are cooled by elaborate refrigeration plants and artificial cooling in Phoenix is now the rule rather than the exception.

Phoenix is generally known as the air-conditioned capital of America, where this innovation was born, and where, in extensive plants, various types of air-conditioning and cooling equipment are manufactured and distributed throughout the country.

The great air fields in the Phoenix area, Luke Air Force Base, and Williams Air Force Base, as well as the Naval Air Facility, add thousands of military and naval personnel to the local scene. Luke is an advanced fighter training base, where pilots are trained in gunnery, skip-bombing and rocket firing, while Williams is also a training base; both for jet fighters. Naval Air Facility is a storage station for naval aircraft.

On the side of modern Phoenix an ancient people, the Hohokam (people who have gone), at one time erected buildings, dug canals, prospered at farming, and, at an unknown date, disappeared. Reminders of these aborigines are constantly being discovered within the city limits. Workmen have unearthed pottery and human bones dating back many centuries. Fragments of pottery and an ancient clan house have been found at La Ciudad (the city), a mound within the city.

Pima and Maricopa Indians inhabited this area when the white man arrived and may still be seen on the city streets. They were a peaceful people, hence the traditional Indian warfare was not a major problem for white settlers.

The present city was founded and has developed within the span of one human life. Mrs. Adeline Gray, who arrived in 1868, and was one of the first white women in this area, died in 1936. The first white American to pitch his tent in what is now Phoenix was John Y. T. Smith, who in 1864 established a hay camp and contracted to supply forage to Camp McDowell, an army outpost about thirty miles distant. In 1867 Jack Swilling, a pioneer prospector from Wickenburg, stopped for a few days at the hay camp. He noticed the lay of the land, with water from the near-by Salt River easily accessible by utilizing the ancient canals, and realized its agricultural possibilities. Upon his return to Wickenburg he interested others and formed the Swilling Irrigating Canal Company with a capital of $10,000. Supplies were hauled with an eight-mule team from Wickenburg, a distance of fifty-four miles, and within six months several miles of the canal were completed. Within a year crops were harvested and several ranches established.

Among the canal builders was "Lord" Darrel Duppa, English adventurer, scholar, and inebriate. Seeing the prehistoric mounds and canals, he suggested that the village be named Phoenix for the mythical bird that was consumed by fire every 500 years and immediately arose resplendent from its ashes; he predicted that "A city will rise Phoenix-like new and more beautiful from these ashes of the past." The name was made official when an election precinct was created.

Hancock's Store, a crude one-story adobe, was the first building constructed on the townsite, which approximated the business district of present-day Phoenix. It served as a store, courthouse, justice's office, and butcher shop. The proprietor killed a beef, quartered it and hung it up. Customers cut off what they wanted with their own knives and paid from twenty-five to thirty-five cents a pound for it. One beef a week usually supplied the demand.

Mike's Brewery was the next house completed; others quickly followed and soon the main street was lined with buildings on both sides. The Phoenix Hotel, a one-story structure in the form of a hollow square, stood on the northwest corner of Washington and Third Streets; it had a swimming pool covered with a canvas roof, which afforded the luxury of a cool plunge in summer. The water was turned in from an irrigation ditch near by.

A Phoenix correspondent wrote the following optimistic prophecy for the *San Diego Union* of March 5, 1872: "This is a smart town which had its first house completed about a year ago. Now it contains many houses, also stores, work shops, hotels, butcher shop, bakery, courthouse, jail, and an excellent school which has been in operation for months. Lately hundreds of ornamental trees have been set out which in a few years will give the town the appearance of a forest city and will add to its beauty and comfort. When it has become the capital city of the Territory, which it will, undoubtedly, at no very distant day, and when the 'iron horse' steams through our country on the Texas Pacific road, Salt River Valley will be the garden of the Pacific Slope, and Phoenix the most important inland town."

In 1878 Charles E. McClintock started weekly publication of the *Salt River Valley Herald,* the town's first newspaper. A complete history of Phoenix, of its irrigation projects, and of some of the early pioneers, appeared in the first issue. Ice was manufactured in 1879 and delivered in a wheelbarrow at seven cents a pound—a milestone in the progress of a city with high summer temperatures.

Phoenix was now the supply point for the north-central Arizona Territory, which included rich mining districts being explored by hundreds of prospectors. Large freighting outfits drawn by several teams of oxen, horses, or mules, came in loaded with lumber or other merchandise and carried out flour, grain, and other farm products. Stagecoaches rolled in from Prescott and Maricopa Wells. Where prominent business houses now stand were large corrals, said to have had a capacity of 2,000 head of stock. Soldiers from Camp McDowell and miners and cowboys from the surrounding hills congregated in saloons and gambling palaces.

The Southern Pacific Railroad had suspended construction at Casa Grande, forty miles away, and many of the workers gravitated to Phoenix. The town had 1,500 inhabitants—about half of them Mexicans. Outlawry was rampant during this period, and disputes between Mexicans and Americans flared openly.

Following nine violent deaths, including the murder of two prominent citizens, a vigilante group was formed. The leaders forced the jail, grabbed two suspects, and hanged them publicly. Troublemakers were rounded up and forced to witness the executions, after which each was given a canteen of water and told to "get plumb out of the country." So Phoenix "moved into the new century with all the routine, rip-snortin' wildness of a Sunday school convention."

The city was incorporated in 1881. An electric plant, one of the first in the West, operated by steam engines burning cordwood, was installed here in 1886 by a Japanese; but the process was too expensive for electricity to be commonly used at that time. The first railroad, the Maricopa and Phoenix, entered in 1887 and the same year a narrow-gauge street railway system was opened, using light open cars drawn by mules. An electric system was installed six years later. In 1888 the first city hall was built on Washington Street on the site of the present Fox theater building.

In 1889 the territorial legislature, meeting at Prescott, passed a bill removing the seat of government from that city and locating it permanently in Phoenix. Money was subscribed in Phoenix to pay the expenses of moving all of the legislative equipment. The "legislative solons packed their gripsacks and, scorning the humble stage line from Prescott to Phoenix, which went rocketing over the mountains on the old Black Canyon Road," they pulled out for the new capital in Pullman coaches, it being beneath the dignity of legislators in those days to travel other than by rail. The trip was made by way of Los Angeles, California, thence to Yuma and Phoenix. The first thing most of the members did upon arrival in Phoenix was to buy shining silk hats and proper accessories; legislative duties were then resumed in the new City Hall.

Phoenix was becoming quite an attractive town of about 2,000 when the devastating floods of 1891 imperiled the community. Warm rains falling on the deep snow-covered Tonto country turned the Salt River Valley into an inland sea. Washing the none too sturdy dams before it, the entire southern section of the town was swept away by the raging torrent, with more than a hundred adobe houses melting away like lighted candles. The Salt River rose so high the water reached the center of town, over a mile from the river bed. Rowboats plied up and down the business streets; water covered the tops of desks in offices. Human lives were imperiled south of the main street— many Mexicans clinging to treetops were rescued by horsemen. The waters subsided, but heavy rains fell again, and the scenes of four days previous were repeated. Two days later the river began to recede again, ending the greatest flood in the annals of Phoenix. Reclamation dams have removed the flood menace, and since the completion of Bartlett Dam, the Salt River has ceased to exist in the Phoenix area.

A ten-acre plot one mile west of the center of town was donated for a new capitol. The legislature appropriated funds and the capitol was dedicated and formally occupied in February, 1901.

The population in 1910 had grown to 11,134 and the following year street paving was begun in the downtown section. When Arizona became a state on February 14, 1912, a holiday was declared under the title of "Admission Day." Governor-elect Hunt, inaugurated on the same day, asked for a simple ceremony in keeping with his campaign policy of a simple administration. He refused transportation from his hotel to the capitol and walked the dusty mile, followed by a large procession of perspiring political friends.

What is thought to be the first 5-cent auto fare in the United States originated in Phoenix in 1913, when the original "jitney bus" was started. Similar systems were soon adopted in Los Angeles, Kansas City, and many other American cities.

By 1920 the population had grown to 29,053. The most important increase came after the completion of the first main-line railroad, the Southern Pacific, into the city in 1926. Reclamation dams made possible further development of rich irrigated areas in the vicinity of Phoenix, and agriculture, together with the other main sources of revenue, mining and climate, transformed the town into a metropolitan city. Phoenix is increasingly important as a Southwest distributing center. The Salt River Valley Water Users Association is a co-operative farmers' organization for irrigation in the valley. The city's industries include creameries, dairies, citrus packing plants, lettuce, melon, and mixed vegetable packing houses, a flour mill, broom factories, a brewery and distillery, meat packeries, and cotton gins.

The population increased to 106,000 in 1950; and with a vigorous annexation program under way and several additional square miles being taken in, the population of the city proper is 150,000, and in the metropolitan area, 300,000, with about a half million people living in the Valley of the Sun, within a 25 mile radius.

POINTS OF INTEREST

1. The CITY HALL AND MARICOPA COUNTY COURT-HOUSE, W. Washington St. between S. 1st and S. 2nd Aves., is a modern structure of modified Romanesque and Italian Renaissance design. Occupying the major portion of an extensively landscaped square, the building is constructed in the form of an "H." The central portion, or bar of the "H," is seven stories in height, while the east and west wings are four.

The exterior and finish is of terra cotta made to simulate stone in variegated shades of tan with first story walls of rusticated finish. Texas pink granite is used around the entrances of the east, or court-house wing of the building. Two huge eagles are carved in the upper corners of the west, or city hall entrance portico. The roof of the central portion of the building is covered with variegated tile in seven colors, shading from tan to red.

The bronze entrance doors to the first floor foyer of the courthouse, from Washington Street, have grilles of wrought iron and thresholds of cast brass. Granite steps with two landings lead to the foyer. Another flight of marble steps leads into the lobby. The wainscot in the foyer, lobby and corridors on the first floor is Italian Montenelle marble with a black and gold base. The wainscot in other corridors and on the stairways is of pink Tennessee marble with base of Belgian

The Mountains

BOULDER DAM, WORLD'S HIGHEST BARRIER

SAN FRANCISCO PEAKS, NEAR FLAGSTAFF

Marshall Beaucham,

CANYON DEL MUERTO "NARROWS",
CANYON DE CHELLY NATIONAL MONUMENT

GRAND CANYON FROM POINT IMPERIAL, NORTH RIM

RED ROCKS, OAK CREEK CANYON, NEAR SEDONA

BRIGHT ANGEL POINT, NORTH RIM, GRAND CANYON

GRANITE DELLS, NEAR PRESCOTT

CANYON DE CHELLY NATIONAL MONUMENT

DOWN THE TRAIL, SOUTH RIM, GRAND CANYON

DERLAND OF ROCKS,
RICAHUA NATIONAL
MONUMENT

Marshall Beauchamp

MULE DEER AND FAWNS

KAIBAB SQUIRREL

SNOW ON PINAL MOUNTAIN

Forman Hanna

black marble. A circular stairway with wrought iron railings, leads from the first floor to the fourth.

County and city offices occupy the entire building, with jail facilities on the sixth and seventh floors. Edward Neild of Shreveport, designed the courthouse portion and Lescher and Mahoney of Phoenix, the city hall section. The building was constructed in 1928 at a cost of $1,200,000.

2. The LUHRS TOWER, S. 1st Ave. and W. Jefferson St., a thirteen-story office building, is of modern design, and has a lofty set-back tower adorned with slender buttressed piers. Trost and Trost of El Paso were the architects.

3. The PROFESSIONAL BUILDING, E. Monroe St. at N. Central Ave., designed by Morgan, Walls and Clements of Los Angeles, is a modern eleven-story building, asymmetrical in plan, with a thirteen-story tower-like wing at one side. The lower stories are Indiana limestone and the upper portion is cement jointed and colored to simulate limestone. The building houses medical and dental offices, clinics and laboratories.

4. The TITLE AND TRUST BUILDING, N. 1st Ave. between W. Adams and W. Monroe Sts., designed by Lescher and Mahoney, is a modern U-shaped structure rising eleven stories above the first floor shops. The main entrance is flanked by massive pylons.

5. The SECURITY BUILDING, N. Central Ave. and W. Van Buren St., is an eight-story structure of modified Italian Renaissance design, the top story being in the form of an arcaded gallery set behind a roof balustrade. The most striking feature of the exterior is a tower rising like a lofty penthouse from the roof of the main structure. Surmounting the penthouse is a slender cupola.

6. The UNITED STATES COURTHOUSE, N. 1st Ave. between W. Monroe and W. Van Buren Sts., constructed in 1912, was recently remodeled. The U. S. District Court, Federal Bureau of Investigation, Secret Service, and other governmental agencies occupy the building. Designed by Lescher and Mahoney, the building is constructed of grey cement precast to simulate stone.

KEY

1. City Hall and Courthouse
2. Luhrs Tower
3. Professional Building
4. Title and Trust Building
5. Security Building
6. United States Courthouse
7. Phoenix Post Office
8. Westward Ho
9. Trinity Episcopal Cathedral
10. First Presbyterian Church
11. Arizona Museum
12. State Capitol
13. Phoenix Union High School
14. La Ciudad
15. Heard Museum
16. Third Ward Chapel of the Latter Day Saints' Church
17. Encanto Park
18. United States Indian School

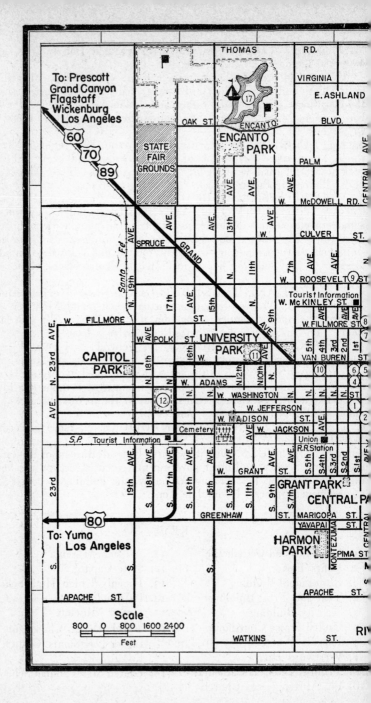

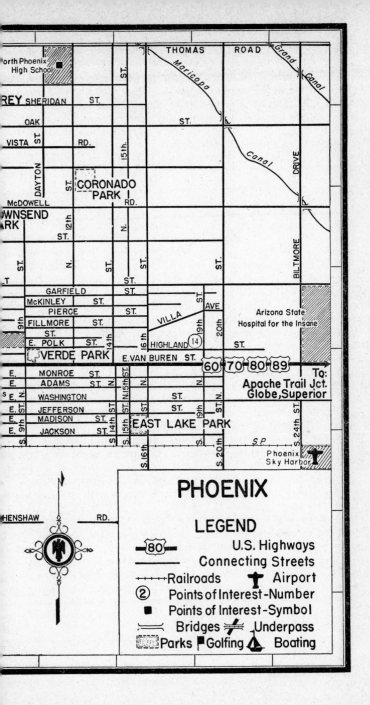

PHOENIX

LEGEND

—{80}— U.S. Highways
Connecting Streets
++++Railroads   ✈ Airport
② Points of Interest-Number
■ Points of Interest-Symbol
Bridges   Underpass
Parks Golfing Boating

7. The PHOENIX POST OFFICE, W. Fillmore St. between N. 1st Ave and N. Central Ave., is a two-story Spanish style structure. The exterior is of cream colored stucco and the roof is of tile. The windows are heavily grilled in the manner of early Spanish Colonial architecture. The building, designed by Lescher and Mahoney, stands well back from the street and the grounds are beautifully landscaped. The main entrances on Central and 1st Avenues lead to a broad lobby which extends the entire length of the building from east to west. At each end of the lobby are murals depicting Western and Indian scenes: those on the east end are by Laverne Black and those on the west by O. E. Berninghause.

8. WESTWARD HO, N. Central Ave. and W. Fillmore St., is a 15-story hotel dominating the northern skyline of downtown Phoenix. It is an impressive cruciform building with a lofty central setback tower capped by a red tile roof, above which rises a red neon warning light for airplanes. The exterior detail is Mediterranean, a combination of Spanish and Italian Renaissance decorative forms. The architect was L. L. Dorr of Los Angeles and Phoenix.

9. TRINITY EPISCOPAL CATHEDRAL, 100 W. Roosevelt St., designed by Shepley, Rutan and Coolidge of Boston, is a modern example of Spanish-Colonial architecture. The walls are native tufa stone and the tile roof is supported on exposed timber trusses. The exterior is dominated by a graceful campanile which forms a pleasing architectural transition between the church and the parish building.

10. The FIRST PRESBYTERIAN CHURCH, W. Monroe St. between N. 4th and N. 5th Aves., is designed in a modified Spanish Colonial style. Precast stone was used in the construction of the exterior. The architecture of the red tile-roofed building seems particularly well adapted to the environment.

The lofty interior of the East Wing or auditorium is spanned by six massive hand-adzed timber trusses. The interior decorations are in harmony with the exterior. A huge art glass window, set in the south wall, depicts Christ at Prayer, after Hoffman's "Gethsemane." The seating capacity of the main auditorium is 1,200 with 300 auxiliary seats in the arcaded aisles.

The extensive building with many offsets fronts the entire city block. A loggia connects the auditorium with the chapel, or west wing, across the Monroe Street front, forming an open court. The church tower, rising more than a hundred feet at the front of the auditorium, is topped by an illuminated cross and contains the Deagon chimes, made of tubular bells electrically operated from the organ console. By means of an automatic clock connection, the chimes strike the hour and each fifteen-minute interval. The architect was Norman F. Marsh of Los Angeles.

11. The ARIZONA MUSEUM (*open 2-5 daily, excepting Mon.*), 1002 W. Van Buren St., is a one-story structure of Spanish-Pueblo architecture, resembling some of the early missions of the Southwest. A twin-tower entrance portico extends from the west front of the

building which is generally rectangular in shape. It is constructed of unfinished adobe brick with *vegas* extending at the roof lines. The museum was built in 1927 with funds raised through public subscription, and most of the collections were donated by pioneer families.

Outside, at the east end of the building, stands an old locomotive used in the early days. To the left of the portico at the museum entrance are the grinders of the Bichard flouring mill, the first steam mill in the Salt River Valley. In 1869 when this set of grinders was considered the most improved machinery available, it was shipped from the West Coast at great expense and set up on the block where the Luhrs Tower now stands.

The front room of the museum houses relics of Arizona pioneer days. The mode of Arizona home life in the nineteenth century is shown in exhibits of pioneer kitchenware, costumes, and exquisite old needlework and crewelwork. The oldest dress made in Phoenix is preserved here. Other relics of the Arizona frontier are powder horns, sabers, old pistols and rifles, a sidesaddle used by Mrs. Adeline Gray, the first white woman in Salt River Valley, branding irons, jail leg irons, and stones from the adobe corral that served as the first jail.

A pair of ox shoes is reminiscent of the period when heavy freight into this territory was drawn by oxen from Yuma. Camel hair from the Florence herd recalls the ill-starred attempt of the government to form an Army Camel Corps. A display of ostrich eggs is from one of the several local ostrich farms that prospered during the 1890's when plumes were the height of fashion. Pioneer farm implements include an old plow made from the rim of a wagon wheel and a cradle for harvesting grain.

Mining history of the state is represented by a dry washer from Quartzsite. A collection of mineral specimens, started by Dr. Joseph Munk, and cases of native flora and fauna are also features of the first room.

In the second room, used on occasion as an auditorium, are Indian displays, including pottery, ranging from shards to perfect specimens of bowls and burial urns, well-preserved skeletal remains, figurines, arrows, sandals, and remnants of old basketry. There is also pottery, weaving, and basketry of the modern valley tribes; the last bridle used by the Apache chief, Geronimo, Pima war shields, masks, burden baskets, and bows and arrows.

The museum has a small art collection, mostly old and contemporary Arizona scenes. The most noted painting publicly owned in Arizona is a large altar-piece, "The Madonna Enthroned with the Child and Four Saints," by the Italian painter Girolamo Genga (1476-1551), given to the museum by Samuel Henry Kress in 1933. The collection also includes a painting of the Grand Canyon by Frederic S. Dehlenbaugh, who accompanied Major Powell on his trip down the canyon in 1872. A small reference library and some original manuscripts complete the collection.

During the winter season free lectures are given on Arizona history and other related subjects of popular interest.

12. The STATE CAPITOL (*open 9-4:30 Mon.-Fri., 9-12 Sat.*), W. Washington St. and 17th Ave., is centrally located in a ten-acre park. Through all seasons the extensively landscaped grounds are kept fresh and green. The principal trees are Arizona ash, Russian mulberry, umbrella, Mexican chino, eucalyptus, elm, and citrus; there are also blue Japanese fan, royal, date, and various other palms. Flanking the south entrance to the building are two banana plants. In the southwest corner of the grounds is a cactus garden containing prickly pear, saguaro (giant), barrel, cholla (jumping), hedgehog, organ pipe, night blooming cereus, and other varieties of cacti. Two large petrified wood pedestals from the Rainbow Forest of the Petrified Forest National Monument flank the east entrance.

The building is Neo-Classic in design. Its first or basement story walls are of granite and the superstructure of tufa, both native materials. The original central section of the building, four stories in height and designed by J. Reilly Gordon, was completed in 1900. It is rectangular in shape, and is surmounted by a dome topped with a statute of a winged female holding a torch aloft in the right hand, typifying liberty, and bearing in the left hand a wreath, signifying peace. The central feature of the interior is a large rotunda, the circular opening or well of which, twenty feet in diameter, reaches from the first to the fourth floor. The rotunda is lighted by a series of openings around the base of the dome. Set in the floor is the Great Seal of the state, a huge mosaic of colored tile. In the north and south wings are the halls and galleries of the house of representatives and the senate, occupying the third and fourth floors respectively. The building also houses various other state offices.

In 1918 a wing, designed by A. J. Gifford, was constructed extending west from the center of the main building. Another wing, designed by Orville H. Bell of Phoenix, was added in 1938, and the entire building is now in the form of an "H," the center wing forming the bar, and the original building and new wing forming the east and west staffs. In their exterior architecture the two later additions conform generally with the parent structure.

The new wing was constructed chiefly for the Arizona Department of Library and Archives, which occupies the north half of the second floor, and all of the third and fourth floors. In the main administration offices on the third floor is a set of eight murals by Jay Datus, entitled *Pageant of Arizona Progress*. The four principal panels depict ancient (or prehistoric) civilization, the missionary era, the pioneer era, and the modern era. Four narrow panels flank the large paintings on the north and south walls, and tell the story of Arizona's progress from the Indian point of view. A principal feature is the reproduction of four prominent Arizona peaks, from which aboriginal inhabitants transmitted smoke-signal messages from tribe to tribe and group to group.

The main reading room, on the third floor south of the administration offices, with eight large windows facing south and west, is finished in oak paneling, separated by fluted Corinthian columns. Mezzanine balconies overlook the reading room on the east and north. Under the north balcony is the genealogy room and under the east balcony are two rooms containing Arizoniana. Adjoining these rooms on the east are newspaper file stacks, four decks high.

The library division of the Department of Library and Archives contains approximately 307,000 titles. The law library consists of about 40,250 volumes and is notable for the completeness of its collection of reports. The Arizoniana section, containing 20,000 volumes, in addition to pamphlets, manuscripts, maps and pictures relating to the history of Arizona, is outstanding. It includes what is thought to be the largest collection of files of Arizona newspapers in existence. Other major collections are: American history and geography, political and social science, United States and state documents, geology, general reference, and legislative reference.

The FRANK LUKE, JR. MEMORIAL, on the capitol grounds fronting 17th Ave., an impressive monument erected to Arizona's heroic World War I aviator, stands in a landscaped lawn panel which leads to the capitol entrance.

The oversize bronze likeness of the aviator stands on a huge granite base. Embedded in the base are replicas of five medals of honor awarded for valor, including the Congressional Medal of Honor and the Distinguished Service Cross (with oak cluster). On the reverse side of the pedestal is a bronze tablet bearing the names of Arizona men who died in World War I. The monument is the work of Roger Noble Burnham of Los Angeles, and was erected with an appropriation of $10,000 by the state legislature for that purpose and unveiled on Armistice Day 1930.

Known as the "Balloon Buster," Luke, just twenty-one years of age, was credited with twenty-one official victories in his thirty-nine days of actual combat service. Having utter disregard for military regulations and discipline Luke fought as a lone eagle; many of his victories were achieved single-handed. His plane riddled with bullets and his engine dead, Luke was forced down and killed behind the German lines.

13. GRAND CANYON COLLEGE, 3222 W. Camelback Rd., on a 160-acre campus, has 12 buildings, incl. dormitories. Founded at Prescott in 1949 by the Baptist General Convention it later moved to Phoenix. Offers courses in Business Administration and Economics, Education, English, Foreign Languages, Music, Physical Education, Religion, Mathematics, Science and Social Science. Fully accredited by the University of Arizona; approved by the State Board of Education for the certification of elementary teachers; approved by the Veterans Administration for veterans education and by U.S. Dept. of Justice for nonimmigrant alien students.

14. LA CIUDAD (the city), a fenced enclosure at 400 N. 19th St., is in a residential district within walking distance of the business section.

Here with streetcars and motor cars and all the noise and bustle of modernity around them, are thick adobe walls that were dwelling places of people who lived at least 1,500 years ago.

La Ciudad is a semi-pueblo type structure, unearthed in 1927. Two test pits were sunk which showed the original building level, and revealed that room after room had been abandoned for some unknown reason. Some believe that after one tribe of people had abandoned their dwelling, another followed and built upon the former dwelling which had probably been reduced by that time to a mere mound with each room filled in, thus making a several deck affair. Access to each room was gained through an opening in the roof by means of a ladder. La Ciudad, after hundreds of years of erosion, still stands 19 feet high, 110 feet wide and 170 feet long.

The burial area for this ancient city extends a quarter of a mile to the east and west. Many human remains were uncovered, most of them inhumations, while a very few were cremations. The custom of providing the departed spirit with various articles was always followed; bowls, water jars, and food were often buried along with the body. Among the specimens found are various types of pots and jars, some of them shaped to represent animal and human figures. Carved shell frogs, about half natural size covered with pieces of turquoise to resemble the animal's color, shell carvings of road runners, rabbits, butterflies, snakes, and many other unusual designs were found. Many of these artifacts are on display in the Heard Museum.

15. The HEARD MUSEUM (*open 10-4 daily except Mon.*), 22 E. Monte Vista Rd., contains a large collection of prehistoric relics. The Indian and Spanish exhibits were gathered by Mr. and Mrs. Dwight B. Heard, who built and endowed the museum. The structure is of Spanish Colonial design, with red tile roof, archways, grilled windows, and balconies, a patio paved with colored stones, and a beamed ceiling.

One room is devoted to artifacts and shards from La Ciudad. Among these are charred remains of fires and of cooked foods from the ancient clan-houses.

Navajo and other Indian weaving from the earliest times to the present are shown. There is an extensive collection of blankets, some made prior to 1850. Most striking for their delicate beauty are blankets from the Chimayo village in New Mexico, and those from Saltillo in Old Mexico. Developments in the Navajo and Hopi methods of selecting patterns, dyes and sizes can be traced. The designs themselves are usually symbolic, representing to the Indians elemental forces of nature—sky, clouds, the rainbow, birds, and animal deities.

One room shows primitive work done by the Pacific Coast Indians, from southern California to Point Barrow, and a case is devoted to beadwork and buckskin garments by the Thompson and Frazier River Indians of the northern interior. The second floor holds specimens of ancient European, Asian, and African cultures.

The entire north end of the museum is an auditorium. Its furnishings, however, are largely museum pieces, mostly Spanish in origin, including a massive central table, obviously from the home of a don, and intricately carved desks, chests, and chairs. In the same room is a richly embroidered silk wall hanging from China, recording in ideographs the history of a Chinese family. It is said to be one of three of its kind in existence.

16. The THIRD WARD CHAPEL OF THE LATTER DAY SAINTS' CHURCH, N. 3rd St. and E. Ashland Ave., is an imposing structure dominated by a square tower 85 feet high, the upper section of which is walled with glass blocks and illuminated at night.

17. ENCANTO PARK, N. 15th Ave. and Encanto Blvd., is a 227-acre municipal park. Although in 1934 this tract was under cultivation, in five years it has been transformed into a highly developed park and recreational center, with extensive grounds landscaped with many palms and other shade trees, shrubs and flower gardens. A two-mile boating lagoon, an innovation in a desert country, winds in and around the picnic area and golf course. Swans and wild ducks live on two islands in the lagoon. Stocked with bass, crappie and perch, fishing is free and exclusive to children under sixteen years of age. An 18-hole golf course flanks the east, west, and north sides of the park. Outdoor concerts are held occasionally at the band shell where the terraced lawn provides seats for large audiences. The Clubhouse at the 15th Avenue entrance is a two-story structure of Spanish design, which also serves as a public dining room. Motorboats and canoes may be rented at the boathouse southeast of the clubhouse.

The playground area includes facilities for tennis, basketball, croquet, shuffleboard, horseshoe, roque, and archery.

18. The 90 buildings of the UNITED STATES INDIAN SCHOOL (open 8:00-5:00) N. 3rd St. and Indian School Rd., occupy a forty-acre campus of extensive lawns with a profusion of palm, chinaberry, orange and olive trees. Only forty-two pupils attended the boarding school in 1891, the year is was founded by Dept. of the Interior. In 1954, its 63rd year of operation, it had 700 students, 90 per cent of whom were full-blooded Indians belonging to approximately twenty different tribes. The school is open to Indian children from the states of Arizona, western New Mexico and Utah. Instruction is offered to students beginning at grade seven and continuing through grade twelve. Emphasis is placed upon those experiences and activities which will enable young Indian boys and girls to make a living and adjust socially to that environment which they will become a part of. (Few if any of these students according to very accurate follow-up records go back to the reservation.) Preparation is also provided for professional work beyond high school level to those students who are qualified. A very extensive vocational program is provided for all students because so many are placed in this field.

THE PHOENIX UNION HIGH SCHOOLS and PHOENIX COLLEGE system is composed of eight schools. PHOENIX UNION

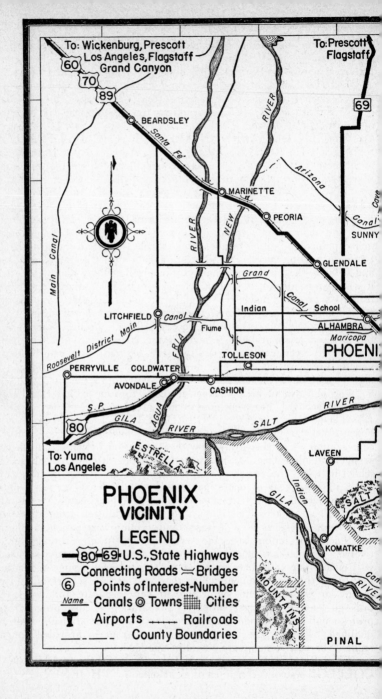

To: Wickenburg, Prescott
Los Angeles, Flagstaff
Grand Canyon

To: Prescott
Flagstaff

60
70
89

69

BEARDSLEY

Santa Fe

RIVER

Arizona

MARINETTE

Cave

PEORIA

Canal

RIVER

NEW

RIVER

SUNNY

GLENDALE

Main Canal

Grand

Canal

School

Indian

LITCHFIELD   Canal

ALHAMBRA

Roosevelt District Main

FRIA

Flume

Maricopa

PHOENI

TOLLESON

PERRYVILLE   COLDWATER

S.P.

AVONDALE   CASHION

AGUA

GILA   RIVER

SALT   RIVER

80

To: Yuma
Los Angeles

ESTRELLA

LAVEEN

GILA

Indian

SALT

KOMATKE

Can

RIVER

MOUNTAINS

PINAL

PHOENIX
VICINITY
LEGEND

—80—69— U.S., State Highways
— Connecting Roads ⇌ Bridges
⑥ Points of Interest-Number
Name Canals ◎ Towns ▦ Cities
⊤ Airports ⸺ Railroads
— · — · — County Boundaries

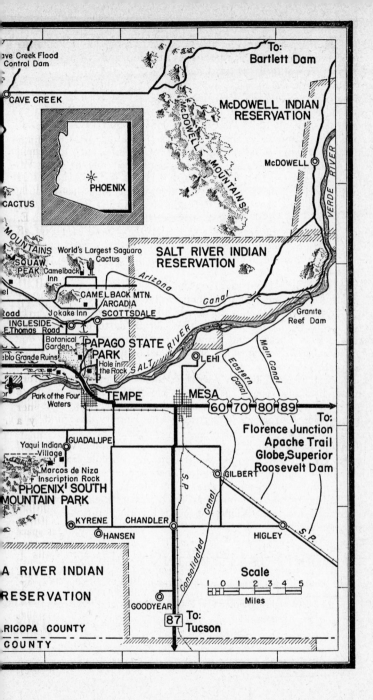

Cave Creek Flood
Control Dam

CAVE CREEK

To:
Bartlett Dam

McDOWELL INDIAN
RESERVATION

McDOWELL MOUNTAINS

McDOWELL

VERDE RIVER

PHOENIX

CACTUS

MOUNTAINS

SQUAW
PEAK

World's Largest Saguaro
Cactus

Camelback
Inn

SALT RIVER INDIAN
RESERVATION

Arizona

Canal

CAMELBACK MTN.
ARCADIA

Jokake Inn   SCOTTSDALE

Road

INGLESIDE
E. Thomas Road

Botanical
Garden

blo Grande Ruins

PAPAGO STATE
PARK

Hole in
the Rock

SALT   RIVER

Granite
Reef Dam

LEHI

Eastern Canal

Main Canal

Park of the Four
Waters

TEMPE   MESA   60 70 80 89

Yaqui Indian
Village

GUADALUPE

Marcos de Niza
Inscription Rock

PHOENIX SOUTH
MOUNTAIN PARK

S P

Canal

GILBERT

To:
Florence Junction
Apache Trail
Globe, Superior
Roosevelt Dam

KYRENE   CHANDLER

HANSEN

HIGLEY

S.P.

A RIVER INDIAN

RESERVATION

RICOPA COUNTY

COUNTY

Consolidated   Canal

GOODYEAR

87

To:
Tucson

Scale

1 0 1 2 3 4 5

Miles

HIGH SCHOOL, 512 E. Van Buren St., est. 1895, has 12 buildings on a 13-acre campus, incl. a 15,000-seat stadium and 3,500 seat field house, 1953-54 enrollment 3,505. PHOENIX COLLEGE, 1202 W. Thomas Rd., est. 1920 on a 49-acre campus, 11 buildings, and 1953-54 enrollment 960. NORTH PHOENIX HIGH SCHOOL, 1101 E. Thomas Rd., est. 1939, on a 30-acre campus with 7 buildings and 2,528 students, 1953-54. WEST PHOENIX HIGH SCHOOL, 2910 N. 19th Ave., est. 1949 on a 40-acre campus has 9 buildings with a 1953-54 enrollment of 2,636. CARVER HIGH SCHOOL, 415 E. Grant, est. as a separate school 1922, has been abandoned due to desegregation of schools 1954. PHOENIX SOUTH MOUNTAIN HIGH SCHOOL, 5401 S. 7th St., est. 1953 on a 37-acre campus has 10 buildings and 500 students 1953-54. PHOENIX CAMELBACK HIGH SCHOOL, 4612 N. 28th St., est. 1953 on a 40-acre campus has 11 buildings and 514 students 1953-54. PHOENIX TECHNICAL SCHOOL (High School Division), 525 N. 7th St., began operation 1935 and has 4 buildings of Spanish Colonial design and 1,496 students 1953-54.

CIVIC CENTER, Central Ave., and McDowell Rd., with its LITTLE THEATER, and new million dollar PUBLIC LIBRARY, opened in 1952. The first unit, the Little Theater, graces the NE corner of the property. The second unit, the Library, is to be joined by a ramada with the Theater and proposed Art Museum, the third unit. The ramada also will serve as an outdoor auditorium for 4,000 persons at patio performances.

In addition to usual library facilities, there are, on the main floor, three music listening rooms. Also there are special Braille rooms for sightless recordings of selected fiction and non-fiction book narration, provided by the Library of Congress. The Library has more than 150,000 books.

Green and white asphalt floors, woodwork of blond maple and birch, soundproof ceilings and recessed fluorescent and incandescent lighting, and thousands of square feet of window space are construction features. Gigantic windows on the north and south sides typify light and space facets of Valley of the Sun building design, entirely eliminating commonly accepted ideas of drabness associated with libraries. Leslie J. Mahoney, architect.

POINTS OF INTEREST IN ENVIRONS

Papago State Park, 7.8 *m.;* Phoenix South Mountain Park, 7 *m.;* Pueblo Grande Ruins and Laboratory, 5.6 *m.;* Guadalupe Indian Village, 14.4 *m.* (*see TOUR 3b*); Frank Lloyd Wright Architecture Foundation, 26 *m.* (*see* Architecture).

Prescott

Railroad Station: Cortez and Sheldon Sts. for Atchison, Topeka & Santa Fe Ry.

Bus Station: W. Gurley and Montezuma Sts. for Continental Trailways and Greyhound Lines.

Airport: 7.5 *m.* NE. of Prescott, 0.3 *m.* E. off US 89; Bonanza and Frontier Airlines.

Taxis: 50¢ for 10 blocks; trips by zone.

Accommodations: Eleven hotels; 22 tourist courts and lodges on principal highways; 20 guest ranches in environs.

Information Service: Chamber of Commerce, 102 E. Union; Immigration Commissioner, Courthouse.

Radio Station: KYCA (1500 kc.).

Motion Picture Houses: Two.

Swimming: Granite Dells Recreational Area, 5 *m.* N. on US 89, then 0.5 *m.* E. on an unnumbered dirt road. Arizona's Garden of the Gods, 5.1 *m.* N. on US 89, then 0.2 *m.* W. on an unnumbered dirt road. Fees for both pools: adults 35¢, children 25¢.

Hunting and Fishing: Trout in near-by streams; deer, bear, turkey, and duck in season.

Tennis: City Park and Athletic Field, Gurley and Washington Sts., free. Hassayampa Mountain Club, 1 *m.* S. on US 89, free.

Annual Events: Smoki Dances, 1st week Aug.; Annual Frontier Days Rodeo, July 2, 3, and 4.

PRESCOTT (5,347 alt., 7,654 pop.), seat of Yavapai County, in the mountainous section of west-central Arizona, is hemmed in on three sides by ranges rising to Granite Peak, Spruce Mountain, and Mount Tritle. The rocky outline of a great lion that dominates the western skyline is Thumb Butte. Granite Creek meanders through the dense pine forests of the serried mountains encircling Prescott and, after seasonal rains, flows through the town, partially substantiating northern Arizonans' boast that "Our rivers have water in them!" The smell of pines is one of the first sensations of the visitor to Prescott, especially if he has crossed a desert before arriving. The site of "The Mile-high City" was at one time covered with a forest of pines; similar forests with boulder-strewn creeks, immediately south and west of town, contribute to Prescott's growing popularity as a summer resort.

The broad business streets, running north and south and east and west, wind into the bordering hills, and the Plaza, a shaded park two blocks long and one block wide, with the massive classical courthouse at its center, is surrounded by commercial buildings. The Spanish-Mexican influence common to much Arizona architecture is absent here; since timber and granite boulders are available in abundance there are no adobe structures as in the southern desert valleys.

Prospectors in typical garb, miners who work scores of small dig-

235

gings in the surrounding hills, Yavapai Indians from the reservation that borders the town, cowboys who "ride herd" on the 60,000 head of cattle in the county, and sheepherders who tend the "woolies," give a flavor of the old West to the town.

For three days each summer Prescott is given over completely to the Frontier Days Rodeo, an annual event since 1888, when the first public rodeo in the United States was held here. Cowboys from ranches in the surrounding hills are on hand; punchers from the desert and mountain reaches in distant parts of the state drift in to compete; and professional "waddies" from bordering states arrive, set on lifting the prize money, or selling their saddles to get home. For three days they bust broncs, bucking bulls, or, perhaps, their own backs, and compete in the bull-dogging, team-tying, and calf-tying contests, and the races. The celebration ended, they return to their "leppies" (dogies) in Arizona's "back countries," or go on to contests in other parts of the state where "a cowboy's luck oughta be better."

Members of the Walker party, prospectors for gold who arrived in this vicinity in 1863, were the first white campers on Granite Creek. The first families joined the Walker encampment in 1864; some came from California and some from New Mexico. Joseph Ehle and his family started from New Mexico with 200 head of cows, but by the time they arrived at Prescott the herd had been reduced to four, most of them having been killed by Indians.

Alarmed by the influx of Confederate sympathizers, among whom the Walkers were counted, Congress passed a bill, signed by President Lincoln in 1863, creating the Territory of Arizona. In 1864, after three months of travel by wagon and horseback over settled parts of the territory, Governor John N. Goodwin and a group of Washington-appointed officials arrived at Fort Whipple in Little Chino Valley, seventeen miles north of the site of Prescott, where they fixed the temporary capital. The decision was based on the presence of timber and wild game, the possibility of gold, the fact that several American settlers were already there, and the supposition that the seat of government would not be welcome in the cities of Tucson and La Paz, farther south, where the officials had found Confederate sympathizers. When, in the same year, Fort Whipple was moved to Granite Creek, the capital and the legislature moved with it. The new site was named for William Hickling Prescott, the historian, and the streets were given the names of Cortez, Coronado, and other persons prominent in history.

The first house in Prescott, a two-room log cabin, was used as a courthouse and as a residence for the judge; it later became a boarding house, known as Fort Misery. Logs were hewn on the site and drawn by ox team to build the capitol and the governor's mansion, across Granite Creek in West Prescott. Workmen had to be armed against Indian attack, and fabulous prices were paid for trim and nails. The two-story, eleven-room Governor's mansion was finished first, at a cost of $6,000. Though the capitol was still under construction, the legislators assembled there in September, 1864, but were driven out by an early rain and snow storm. They adjourned to the Governor's mansion where the first legislation was formulated before a roaring fire.

In 1867 the capital was moved to Tucson, where it remained for only ten years, despite the fact that in 1875 the legislature voted to make Tucson the permanent seat of government. Prescott lost its position as territorial capital and the population fell to less than 500; the mines, which had attracted many settlers, were on the eve of failure owing to the high cost of transportation and supplies and to the persistent hostility of the Apache Indians. Promoters in the East, however, were busy luring new settlers to Prescott, promising them a life similar to that in a New England village. Newcomers were quick to recognize Prescott as a frontier post when they saw the houses of unpainted logs and rough lumber encircling the plaza, and realized that white-painted schoolhouses and churches, thriftiness and respect for law were even more elusive than the "gold aplenty" to be picked up on the hills. Prescott had ten saloons and more than a dozen gambling halls and the citizens indicated their fondness for peace by robbing and beating a squad of United States soldiers who had been sent to protect them from the Indians. "Last night I was in a billiard saloon here," one early-day arrival is said to have commented, "a game of monte was going on in one corner, brag-poker in another, and a couple of dogs were having a free fight under the billiard table. I lived in Boston once for some time, but have no recollection of seeing anything exactly like that!"

In 1870 there was a revival, due to the introduction of machinery and more modern methods of mining; miners came in on all trails, new strikes were made, and by 1873 some 7,300 gold mines, among them the Congress and the Crown King, were recorded in the vicinity of Prescott. In 1877 the capital was temporarily moved back to Prescott. There followed twelve years of wrangling; the capital was placed on the auction block at every session of the legislature, with Prescott and Tucson the chief bidders, either fighting to hold it or to get it. The first act passed by the legislators and signed by the governor in 1889 provided that the capital be permanently and immediately established at Phoenix. By that time all the territorial plums had fallen and Prescott's basket was empty.

Meanwhile mining was supplemented by a thriving stock-raising industry, and the frontier town had grown into a city with a sash, blind, and molding factory, several sawmills, a planning mill, brick yards, and lime kilns, two public halls, two newspapers, two hotels and several boarding houses, twenty-five stores, twenty saloons, three breweries and more than twenty lawyers. The population had increased from 500 to 4,000 and Prescott firms were doing the largest business in the territory. The coming of the railroad from Ashfork to Prescott in 1893 and its extension to Phoenix in 1895 provided inexpensive transportation, and Prescott continued to thrive.

In July 1900, the business section of Prescott and the area around

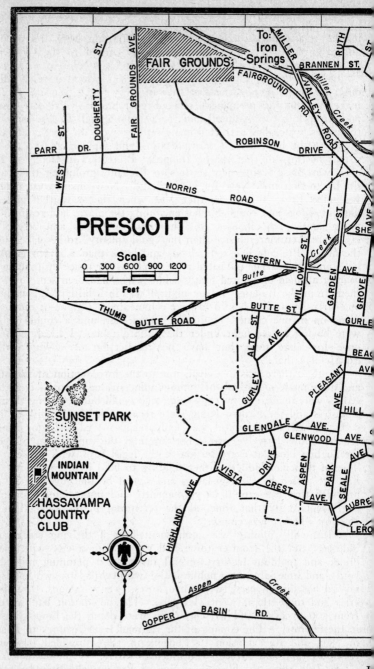

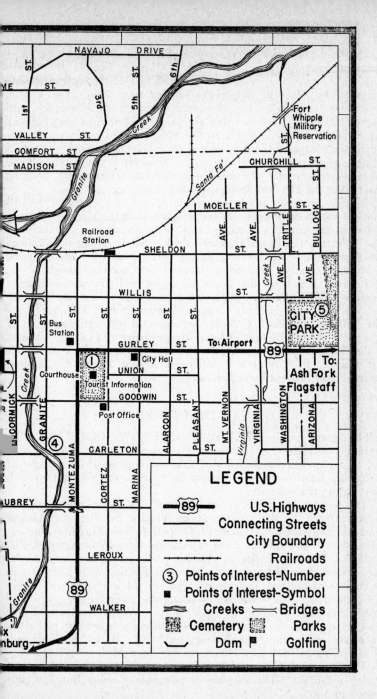

ers' Home 4. First Schoolhouse 5. Smoki Pueblo and Museum

the courthouse and plaza were swept by fire, caused by a drunken miner overturning a kerosene lamp in one of the lodging houses. The flames completely demolished "Whisky Row" and part of the wall of the old capitol. Only two of the town's saloons were left. The firemen were almost helpless because of scarcity of water, and it was not until a space had been dynamited that the progress of the fire was checked. Meanwhile the saloon-keepers moved their salvaged equipment to the courthouse plaza, where they continued in operation, with the sheriff acting as treasurer. Property owners immediately began to rebuild, and the following year, the city installed an adequate water system, bringing water from the Del Rio Springs, nineteen miles away.

Mining for gold, silver, copper, lead, and zinc is still Prescott's principal means of support. A fair proportion of the city's retail trade is due to the county's ranchers, who maintain about sixty thousand head of cattle, nearly all Hereford stock. Sheep raising has declined considerably, many of the sheep having been replaced by Angora goats. In 1936 the county's production of mohair was 500,000 pounds.

Prescott has been the home of many well-known personages: Fiorello La Guardia (b. 1882), mayor of New York, who spent his boyhood here while his father was bandmaster at Fort Whipple; Captain William (Bucky) O'Neill, organizer of the Arizona unit of Roosevelt's Rough Riders; Ottmar Mergenthaler (1854-99), inventor of the Mergenthaler linotype; Earle Sande, jockey, who received his first training in Prescott's Frontier Days; and Henry F. Ashurst, United States Senator from Arizona since 1912.

POINTS OF INTEREST

1. The gray granite YAVAPAI COUNTY COURTHOUSE (*open 9-5 workdays*), Montezuma St. between Gurley and Goodwin Sts., on the green, tree-shaded PLAZA, was built in 1917 at a cost of $250,000. Band concerts and community sings are held on the north lawn during the summer.

The equestrian STATUE OF "BUCKY" O'NEILL stands at the north entrance to the courthouse on Gurley St. between Montezuma and Cortez Sts. William O. O'Neill (1860-98), editor, lawyer, judge, sheriff, and soldier, came to Arizona from Washington, D. C. in 1880. He became one of Arizona's beloved characters and was known throughout the state as a "first-rate fighting man," happiest in the pursuit of outlaws, and always ready to risk a chance with either bullets or cards. His nickname, "Bucky," was given him because of his predilection for "bucking the tiger" at the West's favorite old-time game, faro. The first man in Arizona to enlist when the call came for volunteers in the Spanish-American War, "Bucky" O'Neill was killed leading his men in a charge up San Juan Hill.

The base of this bronze statue is a massive granite boulder from a near-by mountain. The monument, executed by Solon Borglum, was erected in 1907.

2. PIONEER SQUARE (*open 9-5 daily*), Capitol Drive between W. Gurley and Beach Place, surrounded by a stockade partly covered with vines, is a group of pioneer structures dating back to Prescott's earliest days. A few old-timers in Prescott recall lookouts posted on the hill directly north of the enclosure to guard against Indian attacks.

The GOVERNOR'S HOUSE, facing the Capitol Drive entrance, is a sturdy log structure built in 1864, in which early sessions of the legislature were held. Except for its pioneer appearance the building bears few signs of age. In the house is a collection of frontier household utensils, firearms, and furniture, the property of Sharlot Mabridth Hall (b. 1870), Prescott author and poetess.

Back of the Governor's House in The SHARLOT HALL MUSEUM, a large masonry structure with a flagstone floor, which houses Sharlot Hall's library of early printed matter, books, and historical documents relating to Arizona. The main room contains an exhibit of pioneer articles.

The LOG CABIN (R), built in 1937, is a replica of a typical pioneer ranch house, and is equipped with old utensils and tools.

FORT MISERY (L), a two-room log structure, is a reproduction of the first house in Prescott, built the winter of 1863-64 by Manuel Yeserea who arrived with Governor Goodwin's escort. The first court in Prescott convened in this hut. One morning during court term an alarm sounded warning of an Indian attack. The court, officers, and prisoners, rushed out and joined in the defense of the settlement. After the fight there were no prisoners. Typical of the times, the court, in appreciation of the prisoners' services, wrote "case dismissed" into the records.

Fort Misery seems to have gained its name from the meals provided by "Virgin Mary," who in 1864 converted the cabin into a boarding house. There was venison, however, and, rarest of pioneer delights—*café-au-lait*—the *au lait* provided by two goats tended by the proprietress. Known by no other name, "Virgin Mary" was noted for her kindness and generosity, and any other identity she may once have possessed she carried into an unmarked grave.

THE GRAVE OF PAULINE WEAVER, NE. corner of the enclosure, is marked by two large boulders and a bronze plate. Weaver, son of a pioneer father and a Cherokee mother, came to Arizona in the early 1830's as agent for the Hudson's Bay Company. A hunter, trapper, scout, and guide, he was noted as a peacemaker between the whites and the Indians. On one scouting occasion he was asked why he was wearing two guns. "Well," he said, "I might be doing something else with one of my hands at the time."

3. The ARIZONA PIONEERS' HOME (*open 9-5 daily*), S. end of McCormick St., a substantial three-story brick building, a city block in length, is the only institution of its kind in the United States. It is state-maintained, with the official name of Home for Arizona Pioneers and State Hospital for Disabled Miners. Authorized by the legis-

lature in 1909, it was occupied in 1911. Aged and infirm pioneers are admitted to the home if they are at least sixty years old and if they have resided in the state for thirty-five or more years. The average age of the residents is eighty years. In 1936 a guest died at the age of 108; another claimed 104 years, and several others more than ninety. Each guest receives a yearly birthday cake and personal congratulations from the governor.

From the seat among the granite boulders in front of the home, the Loma Prieta (dark earth) Mountains are seen to the southeast. Slightly to the northeast is the rocky bulk of Granite Mountain; and the dark ranges reaching into the northeast distance are the Black Hills, part of the Mingus Range; in pale but clear outlines beyond are the San Francisco Peaks, highest mountains in Arizona, sixty-five miles away.

4. The FIRST SCHOOLHOUSE, NE. corner of Granite and Carleton Sts., reconstructed as a residence in recent years, was built of logs in 1864. It was maintained by private donations and operated for several years with volunteer teachers, before public provision could be made for a paid teacher. The first class, numbering six pupils, was taught for a short time by Miss Fannie B. Stephens, who gave up her job to get married, because, as she later said, "Women were few and wives were in demand in those days." Moses H. Sherman took over the school and later drew up the first state school laws. Sherman became the first Arizona state superintendent of public instruction.

5. The SMOKI PUEBLO AND MUSEUM (*open by appointment —see Russell Inslay, 208 W. Gurley St.*), Arizona Ave. between Gurley and Willis Sts., two pueblo-type structures, were built as a site for the annual Smoki Dances and to house ceremonial costumes and paraphernalia. In the museum are many objects of Indian arts and handicraft, Indian relics, and a library on Indian history.

The "Smoki People," a group of business and professional men and women of Prescott, perpetuate the rituals, dances, music, and folklore of the Indians of the Southwest. A day in August is set aside each year for the ceremonials, and many weeks of practice precede the production, resulting in a conscientious fidelity to detail.

Most noted is the Snake Dance, patterned after a Hopi ceremonial, with writhing reptiles, chanting "snake priests," tom-toms, and swaying bodies. The Eagle Dance is distinguished by its melodious music and feathered regalia. The dancers attempt to convey the eagle's cunning and stamina, and to explain the meaning of his various gyrations in flight. The Corn Grinding Song, a dance to the music of the flute and tom-tom, depicts the Indian maiden's daily task.

POINTS OF INTEREST IN ENVIRONS

Fort Whipple and Yavapai Indian Reservation, 1 *m.;* Hassayampa Mountain Club in Prescott National Forest, 3 *m.;* Granite Dells, 5.4 *m.* (*see TOUR 1b*).

Tombstone

Railroad Station: Toughnut St. for Southern Pacific Lines.
Bus Station: Crystal Palace, 5th and Allen Sts., for Greyhound Lines.
Accommodations: Three hotels, numerous motels and apartments.
Information Service: Chamber of Commerce, Schieffelin Hall, 4th and Fremont Sts.
Motion Picture Houses: One.
Swimming: 5th and Fulton Sts., open summer only, adults 30¢, children 10¢.
Tennis: High school grounds, free.
Hunting: Deer, quail, ducks and doves, in season.
Annual Event: Helldorado Day, October (see below).

TOMBSTONE (4,539 alt., 849 pop.) lies on desert hills between the San Pedro Valley on the west and the Dragoon Mountains on the north and east. The climate is typical of the high desert, with warm summers and winters bright with sunshine.

The first impression of Tombstone is that of a bygone period. Almost all the buildings were erected between 1879 and 1882, when the site was a cactus- and brush-covered hillside. Some new homes and business structures have been added in recent years.

Benches, scattered along the main street in the shade of roofed sidewalks, contribute to the old town's hospitable atmosphere. Old-time miners and cattlemen, now retired, loiter on the streets and talk of the early days. There is no hurry, no nervous spasm of industry, and although it is still a mining center, Tombstone is only a ghost of the roaring camp it used to be.

"Instead of a mine, you'll find a tombstone," said a fellow-soldier to Ed Schieffelin in 1877, as he set out from Fort Huachuca, regardless of danger from the Apaches, to "look for stones." Schieffelin remembered the warning, and when he came across some rich-looking ore, said to himself, "Here is my tombstone." He gave that name to the place, recorded his claim, then went to the northern part of the territory. There he obtained funds by persuading his brother, Al, and Richard Gird, assayer and influential mining man, to join him.

Al Schieffelin and Gird were disappointed when they arrived at Tombstone, and called the place the "Graveyard" because it was here that "they buried their hopes." Soon after they had established camp, Ed Schieffelin struck it rich. "You're a lucky cuss," said his brother, and he was indeed, for the Lucky Cuss turned out to be one of the richest mines in Arizona. Other mines were staked out in the vicinity, among them Tough Nut, Goodenough, East Side, and West Side.

The town of Tombstone was laid out in 1879, about a mile from the first Schieffelin camp, and was incorporated and made the seat of

Cochise County in 1881. As the immense riches of the locality became known, men of all professions flocked in. By the end of 1879, there were forty houses, cabins, and tents in Tombstone, and a population of about one hundred permanent residents besides the thousand and more miners who camped outside the town. The population in 1881 is believed to have increased to about seven thousand, though doubtful sources estimate it as high as twice that number.

Experts from the waning gold fields of California and Australia, in many cases booted out by vigilante committees, arrived to open gambling halls; two out of every three buildings in the business district were saloons and gambling dens. The gamblers of Dodge City, at that time an infamous hell hole, moved in en masse; an immense red-light district sprang up simultaneously with church spires, and the first cemetery encroached so rapidly on the residential district that a bigger burying ground had to be laid out. The sole support of the school system was derived from a tax on saloons and bagnio dance halls where reckless men nightly matched their speed on the draw with shifty tin-horn gamblers, knowing well that some one would pass out with his boots on. Tombstone became synonymous with everything wild, reckless, daring, and novel.

The turbulent side of Tombstone's history reached its height with the Earp-Clanton feud of the early 1880's. The Earp clan sought to shield their dealings with shady characters behind their official positions of city marshal, deputy sheriff, or United States marshal. The Clantons and McLowerys, a group of cowboys, became unfriendly to the Earps when Doc Holliday, a member of the Earp clan, was accused of a stagecoach hold-up and the killing of Bud Philpot, a cowboy and member of the Clanton-McLowery group. The climax came with a gun fight at the O K Corral in 1881. Ambush warfare continued until the remaining Earps had killed several men and fled to Colorado. The governor of that state refused to sign the extradition papers, saying: "It was not safe to turn the men over to anyone who came for them."

Tombstone, thereafter, with John Slaughter as sheriff, was a comparatively peaceful community. The most imminent danger was from the Apache chief Victorio, whose headquarters were in the Dragoon Mountains. Slaughter was a cattleman who came in contact with rustlers and border bandits while protecting his cattle interests. He saw no advantage in going to great expense to track down a bad man, arresting him at the risk of his life, and taking him to Tombstone with a possibility of gang rescue en route. When he ordered crooked gamblers, saloon hangers-on, bandits, cow thieves, and other hard characters to leave the country, many went, at once, but others, relying on their own speed with a forty-five, stayed. When offense occurred, Slaughter took the trail, and seldom returned with a live prisoner. Usually he reported that he had chased the suspect "clean out of the county;" these suspects never reappeared in Tombstone—or anywhere else.

The camp had only ten years of highly active life and only half of these were eventful. By 1890 the population had dwindled to 1,875, and has not exceeded 2,000 at any time since.

Underground water, found at a depth of 500 feet, sounded Tombstone's death-knell as a prosperous mining community. Two companies put in pumps, but found that they were draining the entire district and doing so at an enormous cost. The other companies refused to share in the expense, though they benefited from the drainage system. In 1886 and 1887 the surface works of the Grand Central and Contention burned, making it impossible to combat the flow of water, and practically closing down the mining district.

In 1901 the mines were consolidated into the Tombstone Consolidated Mining Company, and another effort was made to pump out the water. A shaft driven down 1,080 feet uncovered good silver and copper ore; Tombstone seemed about to experience another boom. Disaster came in 1909 when the workmen failed to drain the oil tanks properly. Water got into the fuel pipes beneath the boilers, extinguished the fires, and flowed into the shafts. New pumps were lowered and an effort was made to continue the work, but the cost was prohibitive, and in 1911 the company declared itself bankrupt. The property was sold to the Phelps Dodge Company in 1914.

Tombstone was "too tough to die," however, and mining operations on a moderate scale are still carried on. It is estimated that about $80,000,000 worth of minerals have been taken from the Tombstone mines.

POINTS OF INTEREST

1. The BIRD CAGE THEATER (*open 8 a.m. to 6 p.m. daily; 60¢ adm. includes guide*), 6th and Allen Sts., is an oblong adobe building having three plain front doors with fan windows and red-brick Romanesque arches above. Built in 1881, it was the town's variety house, saloon, gambling house, and brothel. The theater was named for its bird cage-like boxes in its small auditorium. On each side is a row of eight boxes, one of which is level with the stage. During the first three years of its operation, the theater never closed its doors. The respectable folk of Tombstone shunned the Bird Cage, which very early acquired the reputation of a temple dedicated to the diversion of the lusty unattached, but the town's officials, notables, and local desperadoes could generally be found here when inquiries failed elsewhere. Marshal Wyatt Earp and his clan usually occupied the boxes on the left, while the Sheriff John H. Behan faction settled on the opposite side. Acts that were vociferously cheered by one side were immediately considered poison by the other, an aggressive partisanship said to have instigated several shootings within the little theater. This partisanship was probably intensified by the refreshments served on small tables in the boxes and on the main floor. There was also a room backstage where admirers were permitted to toast their favorites. Famous variety artists of the day appeared here.

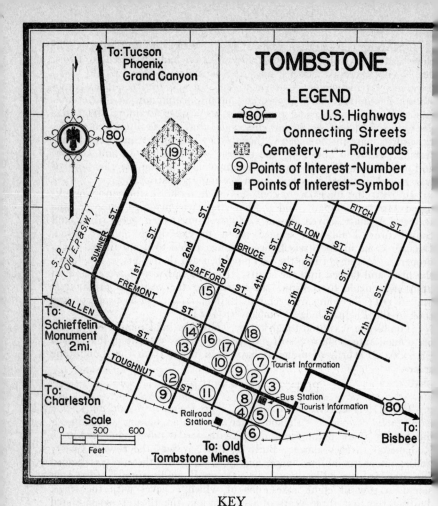

KEY

1. Bird Cage Theater
2. Crystal Palace Saloon
3. Oriental Bar
4. Russ House
5. Million Dollar Stope
6. Large Ore Dumps
7. Office, Tombstone Epitaph
8. Wyatt Earp Marker
9. Morgan Earp Marker
10. Can Can Restaurant
11. Rose Tree
12. Courthouse
13. Site of an old Blacksmith Shop
14. Wells-Fargo Office
15. Episcopal Church
16. OK Corral site
17. City Hall
18. Schieffelin Hall
19. Boot Hill Graveyard

The Bird Cage ceased to be a theater in the 1890's, and is now a very interesting museum of early Tombstone history. Although the bar is comparatively recent, the wallpaper, lithographs, and oil paintings were part of the original interior decoration. A large oil painting of nudes that hung in the saloon, pictures of variety artists, an organ from the Episcopal church, a square piano from Schieffelin Hall, and dice and faro tables are among the articles exhibited.

2. The CRYSTAL PALACE SALOON, NW. corner 5th and Allen Sts., is a gray frame building with overhanging eaves that protect lolling inhabitants from the summer sun. The Crystal Palace with its many well-designed French windows, doors, and trim was one of the most luxurious and famous of Tombstone's early-day saloons and gambling houses. For many years its doors were closed, but in 1902 it was reopened, bringing memories of past glories to many old-timers still living in Tombstone. Walter Noble Burns in *Tombstone* recalls it as "resplendent with oil paintings, mirrors, brass and mahogany, three bartenders—sometimes five—always on duty. . . . Night and day, the gambling tables girdling the saloon walls were surrounded by tense throngs. Gamblers dealt or sat lookout with their sombreros on and their six-shooters buckled around them. Monte tables were stacked with gold and silver money. Faro was played in feverish silence. . . . The little ivory ball in the roulette wheels and the dice in the chuck-a-luck boxes rattled noisily. . . . In the small hours, the sirens of the resorts drove in cabs and barouches to the Crystal Palace . . . swarmed in with gusts of tipsy laughter—pompous old mesdames, reckless young beauties in paint and finery, low-cut gowns, and satin slippers—and drank with the men at the bars or bucked the games until morning."

The Crystal Palace, again a favorite gathering place, contains a fine collection of early-day ore specimens of the Tombstone district.

3. The ORIENTAL BAR, NE. corner 5th and Allen Sts., across from the Crystal Palace, was famous as the hang-out of U. S. Deputy Marshal, Wyatt Earp. It is now a drug store. Earp and Sheriff John Behan took great care never to stand by an open window or doorway when in their respective headquarters. So many shots came from across the street that the saloon owners moved their bars about twenty feet back from the front doors to preserve what was left of the mahogany fittings and plate-glass mirrors.

4. The RUSS HOUSE, now the Nellie Cushman Hotel, is located at 5th and Toughnut Sts., an adobe building formerly operated as a boarding house by Nellie Cushman, a beloved early-day character. "Colonel Nellie" fed every hungry man and frequently turned her house into a hospital and nursed the sick regardless of race or creed. She worked faithfully for law and order and despised killers, yet, when a speculator erected an immense wooden stand with seats at $2.50 each, so that spectators might view and jeer the five Bisbee bandits who were to be hung en masse on a Tombstone street, she spoke to her friends and with them tore the stand apart before it could be used.

"Colonel Nellie," an Irish girl who came to Tombstone to make her fortune, wore overalls and could be emphatic when stirred. She was later well-known in the gold rush to the Klondike and to new fields in Mexico.

5. An immense hole indicates the MILLION DOLLAR STOPE, 5th and Toughnut Sts., from which a million dollars worth of silver was taken in Tombstone's initial boom. Stope mining is carried on in timber-supported passages. The labyrinthine passages beneath lead for miles under the surrounding country and connect with other mines. The large opening was made by a cave-in that engulfed a horse and delivery wagon. The driver jumped to safety and the horse was taken out two miles across town.

6. The LARGE ORE DUMPS, on the hillside directly opposite the entrance to the stope, are deposits from the Tough Nut Mine, one of the richest claims discovered by Ed Schieffelin. The name Tough Nut was possibly derived from difficulty in tracing float (stray pieces of rock-bearing ore) to its parent ledge.

The Schieffelin brothers had always been laborers, probably never earning more than three or four dollars daily. In 1879, when the Corbin brothers, Hamilton Disston of Philadelphia, and Simmons Squire of Boston, offered them $1,200,000 for their share, they sold. Richard Gird, their partner, argued with them for days and nights against accepting the offer, but it was more money than they had ever dreamed of owning.

Later Gird drew immense dividends and then sold his half for around two million dollars. On receipt of the money, Gird immediately shared it with the Schieffelins as though they were still co-owners.

7. The OFFICE OF THE TOMBSTONE EPITAPH, 5th St. between Fremont and Allen Sts., houses the town's only newspaper, the oldest weekly continuously published in Arizona. The first *Epitaph,* dating from May 1, 1880, was one of several dailies published in Tombstone; its office was on Fremont Street between 3rd and 4th Streets. Local wags say Tombstone is "the only city where one may sit down at the breakfast table and read his own *Epitaph.*"

John P. Clum, a crusading newspaper man who had worked briefly on the Tucson *Citizen,* came to the "rough and ready" boom town of Tombstone in 1880 with one thing in mind—to establish a newspaper which stood for law and order. What to name it? Clum argued with his associates that every Tombstone should have its epitaph and why shouldn't the City of Tombstone's newspaper have its Epitaph? His associates claimed the name would sound the death knell of the infant publication before it got started. How wrong they were is proved by the fact that the *Epitaph* has outlived nearly a dozen other newspapers, dailies and weeklies, to emerge the town's only paper. Its name and fame is known from coast to coast and in many foreign countries.

Clum crusaded for law and order and told of Tombstone's growth in glowing terms. The paper's early-day editors and owners were outspoken in editorial policy. Its readers did not invoke the aid of the courts for redress when they felt the paper maligned them, but called on the editor with hardware ready for action. The office witnessed many lively scraps and some shootings. Clum's successors for the most part followed in his footsteps.

8. The WYATT EARP MARKER, on Allen St. between 4th and 5th Sts., indicates the spot where Wyatt Earp, single handed, held off a mob of 300 would-be lynchers. Earp's version of the occurrence, which has never been verified, says that it took place after Johnny-Behind-the-Deuce, a gambler who gained the name because of his frequent winnings with that card, was arrested for killing the chief engineer of a Charleston smelter. The prisoner was turned over to Wyatt Earp, deputy United States Marshal, at Tombstone, and a mob, increased by 300 miners from the Tombstone hills, came to take Johnny-Behind-the-Deuce and hang him. Earp stood them off with a shotgun. Later, he took the prisoner to Tucson, where Johnny escaped before he was indicted.

9. The MORGAN EARP MARKER, across the street from the Wyatt Earp marker, another indication of Tombstone's gunpowder past, is the site of the saloon of Bob Hatch. In this saloon, while playing billiards, Morgan Earp was shot and killed; the assassin got him by firing through the rear glass door. Thus ended the career of one of the best-known of the tough Earp clan.

10. The CAN CAN RESTAURANT, NW. corner 4th and Allen Sts., now abandoned, was once famed for its delicacies. During the 1880's this restaurant employed hunters to provide it with bear, deer, and antelope, and imported lobsters and fish from Guaymas, Mexico by fast stage. The name can still be discerned on the galvanized-iron false front.

11. The ROSE TREE in the patio of an inn (*open daily, adm. 25¢*), 4th and Toughnut Sts., is locally known as the largest in the world, and sometimes, more specifically, as the largest rambler in the world. The tree is an extraordinarily interesting one, of the Lady Banksia variety, with extremely fragrant small white blossoms. It generally blooms in early April. The single trunk has a circumference of 54 inches at the base. The spreading arms are supported on some 60 posts and cover 4,000 square feet with a thick shade. The low adobe wall, cactus-banked, and the squat adobe buildings around the tree add charm to the spot.

12. The COURTHOUSE (*closed to public*), 3rd and Toughnut Sts., a two-story red-brick building, erected in 1882, was vacated in 1931 when the county seat was moved to Bisbee. The large court-room was the scene of many dramatic trials, and in the courtyard to the northwest there were several hangings.

It was from the jail of this courthouse that John Heath, accomplice of five masked men who killed five men and a woman while robbing a store in Bisbee, was taken and lynched on February 22, 1884. The policeman on duty at the City Hall heard a commotion in the direction of the courthouse early in the morning while he was raising the flag, and tying the flag where it was, only part way up the pole, he went to investigate. Thus it was that throughout the day John Heath was lynched the flag on Tombstone's City Hall, unnoticed in the excitement, hung at half-mast. The six-man coroner's jury that deliberated on the lynching of Heath rendered a whitewash verdict, declaring the deceased came to his untimely end "due to strangulation, self-inflicted or otherwise."

13. The SITE OF AN OLD BLACKSMITH SHOP, 3rd and Allen Sts., is now occupied by a service station. The iron scroll fence and adjoining gate, wrought by the blacksmith during off hours, are remnants of other days.

14. The WELLS-FARGO OFFICE, 3rd and Fremont Sts., a small adobe structure, indicated by a marker, was built in 1880. The building was a stage and express station and point of dispatch for large quantities of gold and silver bullion.

15. The EPISCOPAL CHURCH, 3rd and Safford Sts., an adobe structure built in 1881, is the oldest standing Protestant church in Arizona. The interior is simply decorated, having unadorned Gothic arches, high-pitched ceiling, and chandeliers. The old steeple, destroyed by lightning, was replaced by the present brick tower.

16. The O K CORRAL SITE, Fremont St. between 3rd and 4th Sts., indicated by a marker, was the scene of the Earp-Clanton clash in October, 1881. The Clanton cowboys had come into town for their usual amusement at the saloon and gambling halls. Ike Clanton was arrested by Virgil Earp, city marshal, on a charge of "disorderly conduct," and fined $50. The following morning when the cowboys were leaving the corral to ride back to their Babacomari Mountain ranch, they were attacked by the Earps and Doc Holliday. Ike Clanton and Tom McLowery were unarmed, Sheriff Behan having taken their guns away from them the preceding day, to assure peace. Billy Clanton and Tom and Frank McLowery were killed; Ike Clanton escaped. Virgil Earp was wounded in the leg. The Earps and Holliday gave themselves up and were tried behind closed doors by Justice of the Peace Spicer, who exonerated them on the grounds "of having acted as peace officers in performance of their duty."

17. The CITY HALL (*open 9-5 weekdays*), Fremont St. between 3rd and 4th Sts., is a large building of late French Renaissance design. It has been in continuous use since 1882 and houses the first fire department in Arizona.

18. SCHIEFFELIN HALL (museum), Fremont and 4th Sts. (*open 10-5; adm., adults 25¢; children 15¢*) was built in 1881 by Al Schieffelin, brother of Ed Schieffelin. Many illustrious dramatic actors of the day appeared with their companies on the Schieffelin Hall stage—Frederick Ward among them. John L. Sullivan and a company of boxers also gave performances at the hall.

19. BOOT HILL GRAVEYARD, at the NW. city limits adjoining

US 80, is the burial place, as its name implies, of men who died with their boots on. The first marker is over the three rock-covered Mc-Lowery-Clanton graves and bears the epitaph: "Tom McLowery, Frank McLowery, Billie Clanton, 'murdered on the streets of Tomb-stone.'" The uprights of the three large crosses once supported oil lamps on Tombstone's streets.

One marker is "Dedicated to the memory of all the unidentified," which includes practically all of the 276 buried here. Another gives this information: "John Heath, taken from County Jail and Lynched by Bisbee Mob in Tombstone, Feb. 22nd, 1884." The other five desperadoes involved in the same crime are also buried in Boot Hill cemetery.

"Dutch Annie," generous and much-admired lady of the night, the splendor of whose funeral ranked second only to that of Ed Schieffelin, lies in an unmarked grave.

HELLDORADO TOWN, the old town of Tombstone itself, in October of each year, is the stage for the re-enactment of the early history of the town. Men let their whiskers grow and the women wear old-fashioned clothes. The vigilantes re-enact the shootings and hangings and on the third day the annual Helldorado parade is held. Many hundreds of people from everywhere flock to Tombstone for this celebration when the clock is turned back to the town's turbulent history—the era of the Earps, the Clantons, the McLowerys, Doc Holliday and many other notorious characters.

POINTS OF INTEREST IN ENVIRONS

Schieffelin Monument, 2.6 *m.*; Charleston, 8 *m.* (*see TOUR 4b*).

Tucson

Railroad Station: E. Toole Ave. at N. 5th Ave., Southern Pacific Lines.
Bus Stations: Greyhound Terminal, S. Church at W. Broadway (also serves Arizona Bus Lines and Mt. Lemon Bus); American Trailways, 121 E. 10th St.; Citizens Auto Stage to Nogales at Greyhound.
Airport: Municipal, Nogales Highway (US 89) 6 *m.* S. of Tucson, for American Airlines, Frontier Airlines.
Taxis: 50¢ first ⅔ mile, 30¢ each mile thereafter. 50¢ extra beyond town zone. No charge for extra passengers or hand luggage.
City Busses: Tucson Rapid Transit Lines, 10¢ and 15¢.

Accommodations: 26 hotels; 60 tourist courts on principal highways; several guest ranches in area; rates usually higher winter.

Information Service: Sunshine Climate Club, Congress St. at 5th. Chamber of Commerce, 82 S. Stone Ave.

Radio Stations: KCNA (ABC); KVOA (NBC); KCTU (MBS); KOPO (CBS); KEVT; KTKT; KTKT-FM.
Television: KVOA-TV (channel 4); KOPO-TV (channel 13).
Motion Picture Houses: Seven (one specializes Mexican film); also six drive-ins.
Baseball: Tucson "Cowboys," Arizona-Mexico League at Hi Corbett Field; also spring training quarters Cleveland Indians.
Golf: Municipal Golf Course, E. Broadway, moderate fees; El Rio Golf and Country Club, W. Speedway; Tucson Country Club (private).
Gunnery Ranges: Trap and Skeet Club, E. 22nd St. at Pantano Wash; Tucson Rifle Club and Pima Pistol Club, Anklam Rd. W. of St. Mary Rd.
Museums: Arizona State Museum, University Campus; Kress art collection, University Library on Campus; Arizona Pioneers Historical Society, at the corner of Park Ave. and 2nd St.; Arizona-Sonora Desert Museum, Tucson Mountain Park.

Annual Events: Tucson Open Golf Tourney (usually in Jan.) Mid-winter Rodeo, La Fiesta de los Vaqueros (3rd week in Feb.) Festival of Arts (March or April); Tucson Livestock Show (March); Cinco de Mayo (May 5th); Feasts of St. Francis (Oct. 4 and Dec. 3) at San Xavier Mission; Pima County Fair (Usually in Oct.); Yaqui Indian Religious Festival at Easter.

TUCSON (pronounced too-sahn, 2,390 alt., 70,000 [1955] pop.), seat of Pima County and of the state university, is a health and winter resort that has grown up around one of the oldest Spanish towns in the United States. Dry desert air and bright winter sunshine are the chief commodities of this city, which is geared nine months of the year to the entertainment and accommodation of some 15 thousand winter residents and visitors. Even in summer Tucson's population, except for the Mexicans, consists principally of climate-conscious citizens who once lived in other parts of the country.

Sprawled beneath a persistent sun, the city covers about nine square miles in a broad desert valley. It is a place of unusual color and spaciousness, ringed by rolling foothills, with jagged peaks in the distance. The flat sand-gray desert, covered with green cacti, greasewood, and palo verde, contrasts with mountains of ever-changing deep blues and reds. The wide paved streets are pleasant with pepper and orange trees, Italian cypress and the feathery-leafed tamarisk. Stone Avenue divides the east-west streets; and Congress Street, much widened since early days, divides those running north and south. These two streets intersect near the center of the shopping district. Except for two box-like skyscrapers rising above their low-slung neighbors, the business buildings are mostly of one and two stories.

When the season is in full swing, traffic and business in Tucson's main section are remarkably brisk. On downtown streets limousines bearing out-of-state licenses and station wagons with brands of guest ranches painted on their doors are parked at the curbs in the company of old touring cars, new sedans, and roadsters conspicuous with rah-rah slogans and college stickers. Loaded with grub, sacks of cottonseed cake, and large blocks of salt, small trucks are seen on their way back to the range, saddles often lashed to their sideboards. Occasionally there is a spluttering Model A Ford driven by an old sourdough, his long mustaches whipping in the breeze. Coming in from El Paso and other points east are twenty-ton trailer trucks with their puffing exhausts, and tourist cars towing house trailers.

The Old Pueblo (Tucson's informal name) is a metropolitan city, but the mood and apparel of its main-street crowds combine those of a crossroads country store, a small college town, and rodeo week around New York's Madison Square Garden. Cowmen, big Stetsons pushed back from squinting eyes, squat on high-heeled boots, roll cigarettes, and discuss horses, grazing problems, and the price of beef. Mexicans stand against the warm buildings with their sombreros pulled down, their Spanish conversation punctuated with long silences. Railroad men in striped overalls or blue uniforms congregate on the lawn beside the Southern Pacific station. There they share tobacco, talk railroad, and watch the automobiles pop out of the underpass on their way downtown.

Strolling leisurely along the street—a fast walker in Tucson is stared at with wonder—are bare-headed college men in corduroys or cowboy levis (bibless overalls), and bare-legged college girls. Women in chic apparel stop to talk with equally smart friends in white sandals and summer suits. And Papago squaws extravagantly blanketed, giggle in front of shop windows or crowd around the counters of dime stores, where they shyly smell the perfumes and scented soaps. Occasionally visitors may observe, through an open billiard-parlor door, a Yaqui Indian in a fireman-red silk shirt shooting a masterly game of Chicago while his opponent chews his fingernails in desperation.

Smart as in San Francisco, the stores are of such number and variety as to provide adequately for all these contrasting types of people. There are numerous curio shops, most of them displaying Navajo rugs, sombreros, or ox-yokes over their doors. West on Congress Street near South Meyer are the barter stores, their windows cluttered with everything from saddles to guitars and miscellaneous trinkets.

Tucson is basically a residential community, but it now has 122 industries including many supplying the needs of the immediate vicinity. The most characteristic residential area surrounds the university campus, where every type of Southwestern architecture and landscaping is represented. The newest and most impressive homes are in the Catalina Foothills Estates, six and one-half miles northeast of the city center on Campbell Avenue, and the El Encanto Estates, two and one-half miles east in the Broadway area. In both of these sections the estates are complete with every possible convenience, usually including swimming pools, tennis courts, and stables. Few of the houses appear large, as they are in the Spanish-Pueblo style, which emphasizes ground-floor space rather than height. Though Paseo Redondo, the oldest of Tucson's fine residential sections, is only two blocks from Main Street, it seems to be the most secluded part of the city. Here in a gentle-sided hollow are English-style houses of the early 1900's, surrounded by lawns and brilliant flowers.

Residents of Mexican extraction comprise around 25 per cent of the Old Pueblo population. Most of them live in Old Town, called El Barrio Libre (Free Neighborhood) in Spanish. Old Town, centered around South Meyer Street near the city's main business area, is also peopled by Chinese and Negroes. The rather forbidding fronts of the flat-roofed, earth-colored adobes in Old Town often conceal patios or gardens, which are almost invariably grassless. The trees, flower beds, and arbors are surrounded by hard-tramped adobe, swept clean by women householders. Along Meyer Street are no signs reading *Se habla Español* (Spanish is spoken), such as decorate downtown store windows, for this is the exclusive Mexican shopping district. A visitor entering a Mexican store may hear the clerk praise his wares, saying "Esta muy hightone," and acknowledge pleasure over the sale with "Buena Okay." Though the present generation seems to have lost a good deal of its Mexican heritage, a few Mexican grandmothers still wear their *rebozos* (shawls) over their heads and have strict ideas about propriety for women. A good many of the men are employed as section hands by the Southern Pacific and the rest, except for a well-educated and successful minority, are clerks, domestics, and agricultural or day laborers.

Enlivening Tucson's tempo was the establishment, during World

War II, of Davis-Monthan Air Force Base, 8 miles east of the city via Broadway. This base maintains two B-47 jet bombardment wings, the 303rd Bomb Wing and the 43rd Bomb Wing. The 15th Fighter Squadron is also assigned to it, making it an all-jet base. Davis-Monthan was named after Lts. Oscar Monthan killed in 1924 crash and Samuel H. Davis, killed in 1921 crash, both natives of Tucson. Their families donated the land on which the base was activated, 1941.

In spite of its health-resort character, Tucson does not appear to be a city populated with invalids. The really sick people are in the thirty-odd hospitals and sanatoriums. The other health-seekers are for the most part afflicted with sinusitis, asthma, rheumatism, arthritis, and pulmonary infections in stages that yield to sunshine and dry air. These people, like their families and the winter residents who come merely for enjoyment, are out of doors most of the time. On Christmas Day they can sit without coats on their lawns or sundecks and patronize the passing ice cream peddler. In midsummer when the afternoon sun is merciless, it is still possible for Tucson residents to boast, with truth, that their cooling systems are adequate and their night air pleasant.

For amusement Tucson residents ride horses and hunt, play tennis and golf, attend performances of little theaters, the Tucson Symphony Orchestra, and the music-art programs of the University and the Saturday Morning Musical Club. Riding is the favorite pastime, on bridle paths that follow old Indian trails. On moonlight nights parties ride into the foothills, broil steaks over a campfire, and listen to a cowboy, dude or real, sing old-time western ballads.

At the professional wrestling and boxing matches held in the Sports Center, formally dressed men and women sit with the cowboys, Mexicans, and college students—and everybody cheers in his particular style and language. Starting late Saturday and far into Sunday morning there are swing shift dances at the Sports Center and at the Tucson Garden to western television bands. Later the crowds assemble at small night clubs and Mexican restaurants, where they dance and eat *tacos,* the Mexican equivalent of sandwiches.

An apex in Tucson's winter season is La Fiesta de los Vaqueros, one of the country's best rodeos. During this four-day celebration, late in February, the city is crowded and most people dress in pronounced western regalia. Top-notch riders compete for the large purses in bronc busting, bulldogging, steer riding, and roping. Papago Indians from the near-by reservation contribute to the excitement with their taki game.

Tucson's custom of Spanish nomenclature is its most obvious acknowledgment of a long Spanish past. Except for a few adobe bricks under glass on the courthouse lawn, there is little left, except in names and history books, to remind a modern city of its many years as a walled outpost of New Spain.

In prehistoric times, the Santa Cruz River, today a dry wash except during the brief rainy season, was a stream irrigating the rich valley land that now forms the environs of Tucson. These fertile bottoms attracted inhabitants for as long ago as 15,000 years, and an extensive culture existed in the Santa Cruz Valley then, and for a long time afterward. At the end of the seventeenth century, Padre Eusebio Kino, the Jesuit missionary, came into the valley to convert the Indians and establish missions. He was the first white man to record the existence of the Indian village then occupied by the brush shelters of the Pima and Sobaipuri Indians.

The Indian name for this settlement was *Stjukshon,* or Tucson, which has been variously translated to mean "dark spring" and "at the foot of a black hill." The springs were at the base of Sentinel Peak, in marshy ground along the west bank of the Santa Cruz River and were doubtless the chief reason for the location of the village. The term "dark" is explained by some authorities as the possible appearance of water standing on blackened cottonwood leaves.

In 1700 Padre Kino started to build the lovely mission San Xavier in the midst of an Indian village, which was called Bac by its settlers. Gradually he was followed into the valley by Spanish ranchers and mining men, who began to take the country away from the Indians. The Pima and Sobaipuri were for the most part docile and willing to adopt the religion and customs of the invaders; but the Apache, from the beginning and for two centuries thereafter, were the white man's shrewdest and most implacable enemies.

In 1751 the Pima themselves rebelled and plundered San Xavier Mission. The Spanish evacuated the region but returned the following year and garrisoned fifty men at near-by Tubac. During the next decade there were Apache attacks, and growing dissatisfaction among native tribes. The Jesuits were expelled from Spanish provinces in 1767 and mission work was taken over by the Franciscans.

In 1768 the Franciscan, Padre Francisco Tomas Garces, was placed in charge of the mission of San Xavier and the surrounding area. Apache raids did not deter Padre Garces from his work among the Indians. Captain Juan Bautista de Anza, commander of the Tubac Fort in 1775, noted the violence of the Apache, and ordered the garrison of Tubac removed to Tucson. Undocumented legends say that Padre Garces built a new mission nearby and named it San Jose del Tucson. The Royal Presidio of Tucson was built, 1776, near the settlement as a fortification against Indian attack. During Apache raids settlers from neighboring ranches congregated within. At least twice defenders withstood attacks of Apache war parties numbering more than a thousand. The largest *ranchos* in the valley flourished despite the raids; they raised grain, beans, chili, squash, watermelons, and pumpkins and grazed horses, sheep, goats, and cattle. Tucson was an isolated military fort populated by Spanish conquistadors and their families, a community as foreign to American ways as any village in Old Spain.

In 1822 with the termination of Spanish rule in Mexico, Tucson came under the jurisdiction of the province of Sonora. Mexican dominance did not greatly change its character, but as its population decreased the town became somewhat delapidated. The soldiers conducted intermittent campaigns against the Apache, and the well-irrigated river land continued to produce lavishly. In 1846 the American flag was first raised over Tucson by Lieutenant-Colonel Philip St. George Cooke, who led the Mormon Battalion through the settlement en route to the Pacific. Mexican troops evacuated before Cooke's arrival, but repossessed the town after the Mormons passed on.

In 1854 Tucson came within the territory acquired by the United States in the Gadsden Purchase, and later it was occupied by four companies of the First United States Dragoons. The town had by this time a sprinkling of adventurous American civilians—among them John B. "Pie" Allen, who sold pies to the American soldiers at a dollar apiece.

The overland stage service from San Antonio to San Diego began in 1857. At first trips were made every two weeks, but in 1858 a stage line was started from St. Louis to San Francisco, which brought passengers through Tucson twice a week. Accommodations in the Old Pueblo were so inadequate that the "Tucson bed," which the traveler made by lying on his stomach and covering himself with his back, became a byword in the public press. According to J. Ross Browne, an eyewitness of the period, Tucson ". . . was a place of resort for traders, speculators, gamblers, horse-thieves, murderers and vagrant politicians. Men who were no longer permitted to live in California found the climate of Tucson congenial to their health. If the world were searched over I suppose there could not be found so degraded a set of villains as then formed the principal society of Tucson. Every man went armed to the teeth, and street fights and bloody affrays were of daily occurrence. It was literally a paradise of devils."

One of the most popular Tucson characters of the time was Pete Kitchen, famed for Indian fighting, diligent drinking, and an infinite supply of profane language. Pete's ranch just south of town supplied the Tucson stores with hams, and the Indians in the vicinity furnished Pete with numerous escapades. One of Pete's favorite stories concerned the time in 1870 when three of the "varmints" stole some of his favorite horses. "I follared them nearly to the border," he said, "shot one, guess I got him; one got away; and I captured the third. I had him tied, but let him ride one of the hosses. On the way back we stopped to rest. I tied the Indian to a limb of a tree and left him sitting on the hoss, while I laid down and went to sleep. While I was asleep that damned hoss walked right out from under that Indian and left him hanging there."

Crime in Tucson was common, court proceedings were crude and often inadequate. Old Charles H. Meyer, a German by birth and a druggist by profession, served as justice of the peace. It is said that he had only two books in his library, *Materia Medica* and a treatise on fractured bones, and from these two volumes Meyer received his "inspiration" on points of law. Meyer replaced the old whipping post with the chain-gang system of punishment.

Early in December 1858 Father Joseph P. Machebeuf, Willa Cather's Joseph in *Death Comes for the Archbishop,* took up residence in Tucson. He described the town as "a village of about 800 souls, built around an ancient Mexican fortress."

The Civil War, which interrupted the stage service, added to the troubles of the Old Pueblo. Federal troops left the town, and Confederate soldiers from Texas marched in, only to retreat three months later before the California Volunteers. At each change of administration, sympathizers on the opposite side felt obliged to seek residence elsewhere. The Apache, uninformed about the Civil War, assumed that they were responsible for the frequent departures, and became bolder than ever.

Tucson was considered sympathetic to the Confederacy, and this prevented its selection as capital of the new territory of Arizona in 1864, when Governor John N. Goodwin came to Tucson and proclaimed it a district in the Arizona Territory. The territorial seat was moved to Tucson from Prescott in 1867, but was returned to Prescott ten years later.

After the Civil War the town outgrew its old adobe walls and began to tear them down and spread out over the valley. It became a distributing point for a string of forts in the Apache country, and the principal street was constantly jammed with army wagons. The population was still overwhelmingly Mexican, but the town became more Americanized every year. Quickly it had a newspaper, four restaurants, a good hotel, a brewery, thirteen wholesale and retail stores, two doctors, several saloons and gambling houses, and a bathtub in which citizens might refresh themselves after paying a small fee to the Negro barber.

Outside of saloon and dance hall, social life in the seventies revolved around the *bailes* and *fiestas* given by the Mexican and pioneer Americans. These were conducted according to the severest rules of Mexican etiquette, in which the *senoritas* were attended by stern-eyed *duennas*. The Sisters of St. Joseph started a girl's convent, and in 1870 a permanent public school for boys was established; a similar school for girls was opened the following year. The first Protestant church in the territory, Presbyterian, was organized in 1876. Other Protestant churches followed rapidly. A few years later the University of Arizona was given to the town by the territorial legislature to appease its anger over the loss of the capitol.

Business gained impetus with the discovery of silver and copper at Tombstone and Bisbee, and with the coming of the Southern Pacific Railroad in 1880. Exactly when Tucson first became famed for its climate is difficult to discover, but in the 1890's *Wayside Notes,* a Southern Pacific folder, announced that "Tucson receives the sick and sends them away every whit whole."

Unlike the Arizona boom towns, Tucson has had a continuous

existence. In 1900 its population was 7,531 and each subsequent census has shown an increase of more than 50 per cent. From its beginning, and until outnumbered by Phoenix in 1920, Tucson was the largest town in the territory or state—a distributing center for a mineral, livestock, and agricultural region. The 1954 estimated population of Greater Tucson is 180,000.

POINTS OF INTEREST

1. The TEMPLE OF MUSIC AND ART (*open 2-5 weekdays*), 330 S. Scott St., designed by Arthur W. Hawes and built by private subscription in 1927, is an excellent example of Spanish-Colonial architecture. The two-story white stucco building, constructed in three units around a large patio, houses an auditorium, several studios, lecture rooms, and the Milan School of Art, attracting students from all over the United States. The Saturday Morning Musical Club presents music and art programs here throughout the winter season.

2. SAN AUGUSTIN, S. Stone Ave. between W. Ochoa and W. Corral Sts., a Catholic cathedral of modified Spanish design with double towers and red-tile roof, was built in 1897 to replace old San Augustin. The stained-glass windows were brought from Mexico.

3. The CARNEGIE LIBRARY (*open 10-8 weekdays; 2-5 Sunday*) in LIBRARY PARK on S. 6th Ave. between E. 12th and E. 13th Sts., is a red-brick building with two wings, designed in the French Renaissance style and trimmed in terra cotta and cast stone. The main section was built in 1900 with H. C. Trost as architect. The wings, which conform in style with the original building, were designed by Richard Morse and completed in 1939. Each wing has a large patio used for outdoor reading, one reserved for children and the other for adults. The library contains 129,000 volumes, including the Solter collection of out-of-print and Southwest books, the Irene Labree Ackerman collection of Antiquaria, and a fine, steadily growing reference collection.

The PIONEER MEMORIAL, at the park's Sixth Ave. entrance, is a semicircular onyx seat with an Arizona marble back rest carved in relief. It was sculptured by Beniamino Bufano and dedicated in 1920 to Arizona's pioneers.

4. ARMORY PARK, or Plaza Militair, S. 5th Ave. between E. 12th and E. 13th Sts., used as a camp and parade ground by the California Volunteers in 1862, contains a WORLD WAR MEMORIAL. Sunday evening concerts of Spanish and Mexican music are frequently given in the armory bandstand.

5. The COURTHOUSE, on N. Court St. between W. Pennington and W. Alameda Sts., is a three-story building completed in 1928. Designed in the Spanish Colonial style, the structure has two wings forming a U-shaped composition around a forecourt. A graceful arcade with slender Renaissance columns forms a pleasing colonnade across the front of the court and along the sides of the flanking wings. A decorative green-tiled central dome rises above the elaborately encrusted west entrance pavilion. A deep archway leads through the pavilion to

the rear courtyard. The building was designed by Roy Place, architect.

On the south side of the courthouse are the only REMAINS OF TUCSON'S TOWN WALL. A granite boulder with a bronze marker indicates the southeast corner of the wall.

6. GOVERNOR'S CORNER, W. Alameda and N. Court Sts., is a stucco-covered adobe and is now used for an office building. The rear yard is a parking lot. The building, constructed in 1874, was the home of Territorial Governor L. C. Hughes, and occupies the site of the commandante's house in the old walled pueblo. Some of the adobe bricks in the Governor's Corner were taken from the commandante's house; others were made of clay that came from an old graveyard. Guides formerly undertook to point out bone-studded adobes made from the dirt of the burial grounds.

7. The KINO MEMORIAL, N. Main St. between W. Ott and W. Alameda Sts., is in a small park which also contains an Indian "picture" rock. The memorial, erected in 1936, honors Eusebio Francisco Kino (1645-1711), the Jesuit missionary. It consists of an oblong block of dark volcanic rock with a bronze plaque designed by Mahonri Young. Father Kino, led by an Indian boy, is shown in relief on the plaque.

8. The WISHING SHRINE, W. Simpson and S. Main Sts., is a parapet of weathered adobe bricks. According to one account it is the resting place of Juan Oliveras, Mexican youth murdered by his father-in-law for an illicit love affair with his mother-in-law. Following the Mexican custom in such cases, young Oliveras was buried where he fell, without rites of his church, in the year 1880. Mexican women afterwards burned candles over Juan's grave for the salvation of his soul. The shrine gradually came to be used by parents praying for wayward daughters. Finally the superstition arose that anyone who placed a lighted candle on the grave and made a wish would have the wish granted by dawn, providing the candle burned to its base. Variously shaped racks holding candles are within the adobe semicircle. The bricks are blackened and soaked with candle grease.

The appearance of the Wishing Shrine, viewed in the too-honest sunshine, is disappointing. It is after dark—when the tiny flame of a candle or two flickers over the adobes, softening hard lines and inviting the imagination—that the Wishing Shrine comes into its own.

9. The UNIVERSITY OF ARIZONA, N. Park Avenue between E. 2nd and E. 4th Sts., was authorized by a bill introduced in the legislative assembly of the territory in 1885. This bill, which also

---

TUCSON DOWNTOWN. Points of Interest

1. Temple of Music and Art
2. San Augustin
3. Library Park and Carnegie Library
4. Armory Park
5. Courthouse
6. Governor's Corner
7. Kino Memorial
8. Wishing Shrine

9. University of Arizona

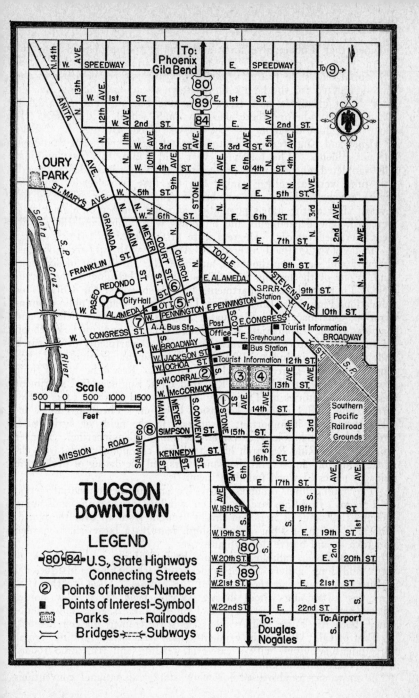

provided that Tucson give forty acres for a campus, passed; but for several years the citizens of Tucson, greatly annoyed over the loss of the capital and state prison, ignored it. Just before the lapse of the time designated for the land gift, the town's leading gamblers donated some desert ground a mile from town, and the university was established in 1890 before there was any high school in the state. It began with three departments—the College of Agriculture, the College of Mines and Engineering, and the Agricultural Experiment Station—but no students. The following year Old Main, the first building, was completed, and the eight professors had thirty-one students, though only nine were of college rank. For the first two decades the university advanced slowly, the number of graduates never exceeding ten a year. But as the state's population and the number of high schools increased, new departments and buildings were added and the enrollment increased rapidly. Degrees were first granted in 1917.

Today (1954) the University of Arizona, with fifty-six buildings, a faculty and staff of a thousand, and a regular enrollment of six thousand, is one of the leading institutions of higher learning in the Southwest. To the original departments have been added the Colleges of Education, Fine Arts, Liberal Arts, Law, Business and Public Administration, Pharmacy, and Graduate; Schools of Military Science and Tactics, Home Economics, with a model home and nursery school, Steward Observatory, and State Museum. Departments of Research and Extension include Agricultural Experiment Station and Extension Service, Bureau of Mines, Business Research, and Ethnic Research, Cooperative Wildlife Research Unit, Engineering Experiment Station, Laboratories of Tree Ring Research and Carbon 14 Age Determination, and University Extension Division. The University's location has given it important advantages in the fields of agriculture, anthropology, archaeology, astronomy, and mining engineering. Pioneer work in Tree Ring Research has established chronological data on climatic conditions for several thousand years and the dating of prehistoric ruins by pieces of wood found in them.

The main campus occupies eighty-five acres in the residential section of Tucson. Buildings are placed on winding drives and landscaping includes thousands of trees and shrubs brought from all over the world. One area, north of Men's Gymnasium, features a large cactus garden of Mexican and native desert plants.

OLD MAIN, a rambling one-story brick building with raised basement and long gallery porch, typical of early western institutional architecture, stands in the center of the campus. Used by the U.S. Navy as a training school during World War II, it now houses officers and classrooms of the School of Military Science and Tactics where both Air Force and Armor Cadets are trained for commissions.

East of Old Main is the Student Union Memorial Building, center for student activities, with a cafeteria, reading and recreation rooms, a large ballroom and offices for student publications and organizations. (The university is also used for many state and national conventions each year.) Adjacent is the new COOPERATIVE BOOK STORE operated by the Associated Students and selling textbooks and school supplies.

The UNIVERSITY LIBRARY (*open 8 a.m. to 10 p.m. weekdays; closes 6 p.m. Sat.*), a three-story red brick building trimmed in terra cotta, is near the main gate to the Campus at Park Avenue and Third St. In addition to the main reading room extending the length of the building on the second floor, enclosed outdoor patios with garden furniture are used for studies.

The library contains over a quarter-million volumes and large collections of Federal documents, periodicals, unbound bulletins and reports. The M. P. Freeman Collection contains more than a thousand volumes dealing with the history of New Mexico, Old Mexico, and Arizona. The Hanley Collection donated by T. E. Hanley now contains over thirty thousand volumes principally on the fine arts; and additional valuable works are added each year by the donor. Fifteen hundred volumes on drama and the theatre form The Thomas Wood Stevens Memorial Theatre Collection.

Temporarily housed in the library are the University of Arizona Art Collections (*open daily 11 a.m.-4 p.m.; Sun. 2-5.*) Twenty-five paintings from the Samuel H. Kress Foundation are excellent examples of the finest in Renaissance painting. The Pfeiffer Collection of Contemporary American Art includes over a hundred paintings by American artists from every section of the country. Other donations and loan exhibits include: Museum of Modern Art—two hundred prints; Edward J. Gallagher III Memorial—twenty-five contemporary French paintings; Smithsonian Institution—Woodcarvings; Kingan Memorial Collection—one hundred paintings from the turn of the century, and several hundred items from individual donors.

The ARIZONA STATE MUSEUM (*open 10 a.m.-5 p.m. Tues.-Sat.; 2-5 p.m. Sun.; closed Mon.*), facing the library, is a two-story building of Lombard Romanesque style. Featured in permanent display is a large collection of Tree Ring Research material, showing the use of cross sections in dating archaeological material. Other displays are maintained: archaeological, ethnological and natural history collections of the southwest and other areas of the world. Of special importance are several Navajo Indian sand paintings, probably the only ones preserved, because of the Indian belief that they must be destroyed on the day they were made. A large diorama shows a typical Arizona plateau as it was 10,000 years ago. Evidence that man lived in Arizona in prehistoric times is contained in the Ventana Cave and Naco Mammoth exhibits.

The AUDITORIUM, east of the Museum, is the largest in the Southwest, seating 2,500. It is used for productions of the University, including a series featuring international concert artists, and for conventions and community entertainment.

On the North Drive, west of Old Main, are the girls' dormitories, named for Arizona counties—Gila, Maricopa, Yuma and Coconino. Walled patios behind the dormitories are used for social occasions.

Sorority and fraternity houses, and student religious centers are located on streets adjacent to the campus.

The COLLEGE OF MINES AND METALLURGY, east of the girls' dormitories, is noted for its many graduates associated with mining properties throughout the world.

The COLLEGE OF BUSINESS AND PUBLIC ADMINISTRATION, northeast of Old Main, was completed in 1953. Located here is the Bureau of Business Research, whose monthly bulletins survey Arizona's economic conditions, including reports of the number of tourists.

The COLLEGE OF LIBERAL ARTS, southwest of Old Main, contains modern classrooms and offices, and an auditorium (capacity 600) where recitals and programs are held, many open to the public, free.

The COLLEGE OF AGRICULTURE faces the Liberal Arts Building. Experimental greenhouses are located on the east side, but major research is done at several large experimental farms owned by the University and located in various sections of the state.

On the south side of the parkway extending east from Old Main is the ADMINISTRATION BUILDING where maps of the campus and catalogs may be obtained from the Registrar. To the east is the CHEMISTRY-PHYSICS-PHARMACY BUILDING where the Carbon 14 Age Determination Laboratory, one of the few in the U.S. is located. Among the many uses of this massive but delicate equipment is that of determining age of organic materials found by archaeologists in ancient ruins.

East of the Student Union is the WOMEN'S GYMNASIUM, with an outdoor swimming pool. To the east is the STEWARD OBSERVATORY (*open to the public Tues. evenings when announced in newspapers*), world-famous through the research of Dr. A. E. Douglass, climatologist and originator of the tree-ring method of determining climatic cycles, Dr. E. F. Carpenter, with his studies of galaxies and Dr. W. J. Luyten of U. of Minn., for discovery of 80 per cent of all known White Dwarf Stars. Of five instruments, the largest is a 36-inch reflecting telescope with the first mirror ever cast in the United States.

Excellent facilities for men's athletics are located in the SE section of the campus: MEN'S GYMNASIUM, with adjacent outdoor swimming pool, BASEBALL FIELD and STADIUM (26,000 seats).

On South Drive is HERRING HALL, small theatre for student plays, open to the public, and offices of the COLLEGE OF FINE ARTS, and men's dormitory buildings—Cochise, Arizona, and Yavapai.

The ARIZONA PIONEERS HISTORICAL SOCIETY, temporarily housed in West Stadium, is now in its new building and museum west of the campus. Valuable manuscripts and relics of pioneer days are displayed.

POINTS OF INTEREST IN ENVIRONS

MISSION SAN XAVIER DEL BAC (no formal admission charge but voluntary contributions appreciated). Drive west on Congress St., turn left at Mission Rd.; continue on this road 9 *m*. The mission stands on a slight eminence, in accordance with the Spanish tradition, and faces south across the broad Santa Cruz Valley. In front of the church, which dominates the other buildings, lies the long narrow enclosed area, or "atrium," with the tiny mortuary chapel at the left end, and the low dormitories around a patio at the right. The entire mission forms a very pleasing asymmetrical composition.

Padre Kino, who founded the first mission here in 1700, had visited the Indian village of Bac on the Santa Cruz River seven years earlier and selected the site because of its beauty and fertility. Named in honor of the "Apostle to the Indies," the mission was to be one of a chain extending across Pimeria Alta to the Colorado River, such as was established a century later in California.

San Xavier had a duel purpose: to Christianize the Indians and to be the headquarters of a great ranch worked by them. A chapel and numerous service buildings had been constructed before the Pima revolted so successfully that the Mission was finally abandoned in 1751. It was again active from 1754 until 1767, when the Jesuits were driven from the Spanish colonial domain. Within a year, however, San Xavier was reopened by the Franciscans. The Apache sacked it almost immediately, but the Franciscans at once set to work rebuilding and started construction of the present church.

Reconstruction of the church required two decades, but it was at last dedicated in 1797 and the furnishings and ornaments originally brought to San Xavier by Father Kino were installed. The mission was again deserted when the mission lands were secularized during the Mexican regime, and it was not reoccupied until 1859, after the Gadsden Purchase and after Arizona had again become part of the Diocese of Santa Fe.

By 1906 when Bishop Granjon began the restoration of the mission with the aid of Indians, weather and mishaps had nearly destroyed the dormitories, and among other areas had seriously damaged the mortuary chapel and most of the service structures. Though he endeavored to follow the old plan in general, the bishop made several changes to meet modern needs. The atrium in front of the church is quite different from the original and the dormitories and their patio follow a new scheme.

The design of the church admirably exemplifies the late Spanish Renaissance, or Churrigueresque, style as interpreted by native craftsmen. Largely of burned adobe brick and lime plaster, its facade is divided into three parts, with the outer thirds relatively plain, each broken chiefly by one simple balconied door. These plain ends are part of the massive towers that support arcaded and buttressed belfries,

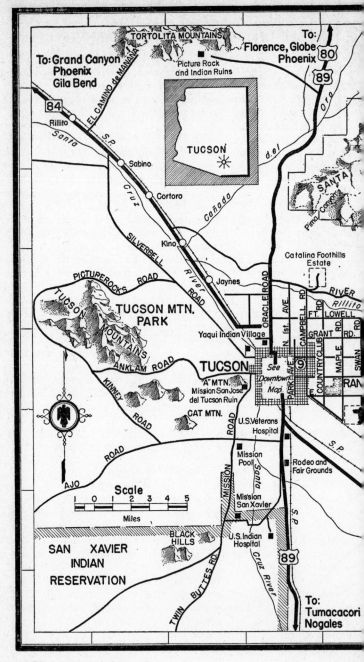

9. University of Arizona

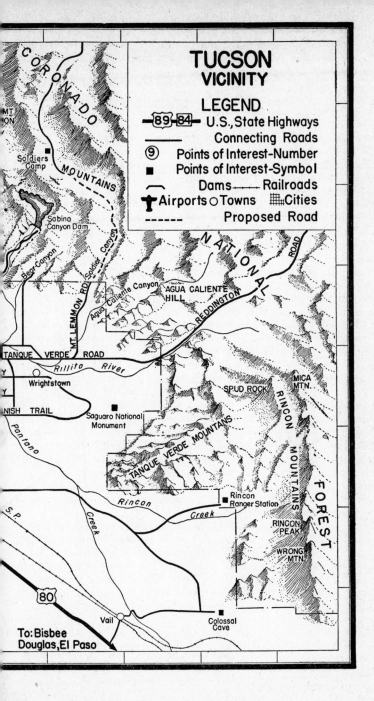

TUCSON
VICINITY

LEGEND

89 **84** U.S., State Highways

Connecting Roads

⑨ Points of Interest–Number

■ Points of Interest–Symbol

Dams——Railroads

✈ Airports ○ Towns ▦ Cities

------ Proposed Road

CORONADO

MT. ON

Soldiers Camp

MOUNTAINS

Sabino Canyon Dam

Bear Canyon

MT. LEMMON RD. Soldier Canyon

Agua Caliente Canyon

NATIONAL

AGUA CALIENTE HILL

REDDINGTON

ROAD

TANQUE VERDE ROAD

Rillito River

Y

Y

Wrightstown

SPUD ROCK

MICA MTN.

NISH TRAIL

Saguaro National Monument

RINCON

TANQUE VERDE MOUNTAINS

MOUNTAINS

Pantano

FOREST

Rincon

Creek

Rincon Ranger Station

S.P.

Creek

RINCON PEAK

WRONG MTN.

80

Vail

Colossal Cave

To: Bisbee Douglas, El Paso

one with a crowning dome, the other without. The central third of the facade is richly encrusted with naively executed Spanish baroque ornament—surface decorations of shells, arabesques, and swirling volutes that have weathered to soft reds in striking contrast with the smooth white plaster walls on either side. The entrance portal, framed by a low classic arch and flanked by niched figures of saints, is deeply recessed. Above it is a choirloft window with dark wooden balcony matching those on the tower. This rich central third of the wall is topped by a curved gable that rises above the cornice and roof parapet forming a false front. Perhaps the most impressive features of the exterior are heavy bracketed scrolls, part of the flying buttresses at the base of the belfries.

Within, an arcaded and vaulted apse leads to the sanctuary that holds the high altar. Framed by a wide and stilted sanctuary arch, the altar is adorned with images of the patron Saint Xavier and of the Virgin, and with cherubs and scrolls. It is richly painted in gilt and polychrome. On the corner piers of the domed crossing before the sanctuary are perched large carved wooden figures of angels bearing bright-colored banners. The plaster walls of the church have painted dadoes and a deeply modeled and painted cornice; the interior of the dome is also painted with figures of early saints. Other religious statues fill wall niches. At each side of the crossing are transept chapels, each containing two altars. Those in the Epistle Chapel on the right are dedicated to the Mother of Sorrows and to the Immaculate Conception; those in the Gospel Chapel on the left to the Passion of Our Lord and St. Joseph. Against the right pier is a wineglass canopied pulpit of carved wood.

The plaster molding and paintings, covering almost every inch of wall and ceiling, are of particular interest and deserve close study. They were undoubtedly conceived by a Spanish artist in the mode of the period but largely executed by the Indians. A series of panels gives the story of the life of Christ; between, below, and above them are scrolls, painted imitations of moldings, frames, bench-backs, and other architectural features. The colors have the vividness and lack of subtlety characteristic of work by very primitive painters and the faces of the pictured people have little expression.

The interior is best viewed from the choirloft, reached by a stair in the left tower. In the base of this tower is the old baptismal font; the walls around it and the stair well are covered with murals. Above the baptistry is the choir vestry, from which a stairway leads to the balustraded platform around the belfry. These towers were at one time used as lookouts for the Apaches. There are various legends to account for the absence of a dome on the second tower.

Arizona Desert Museum, 15 *m.;* Yaqui Indian Village, 4 *m.;* Ruins of Fort Lowell, 8.5 *m.;* Tumacacori Mission National Monument, 48.4 *m.* (*see TOUR 1c*). Saguaro National Monument and Colossal Cave, 30 *m.* (*see TOUR 4b*). Tucson County Mountain Park, 11.1 *m.;* Papago Indian Reservation, 30 *m.* (*see TOUR 4B*).

Yuma

Railroad Station: Southern Pacific Station, 281 Gila St., for Southern Pacific Lines.
Bus Station: Union Bus Terminal, 165 E. 3rd St., for Greyhound Bus Lines.
Airport: 4.5 m. S. on US 80; scheduled service, Bonanza Airlines.
Taxis: 50¢, and 75¢ zones, 20¢ a mile thereafter.
Traffic Regulations: One-hour parking limit in downtown area from 7 a.m. to 7 p.m. except Sun. and holidays.

Accommodations: Nine hotels; tourist lodges, auto camps; trailer courts.

Information Service: Chamber of Commerce, 200 First St.

Radio Station: KYUM (560 kc.); KOLD (250 kc.); KYMA (250 kc.).
Motion Picture Houses: Three; two drive-ins.
Swimming: Yuma Swimming Pool, 5th St. between 5th and 6th Aves.: adults 25¢, children 10¢.
Golf: Yuma Country Club, 4 m. S. on US 80, 9 holes, greens fee $2.50 weekdays, $3.50 Sun. and holidays.
Hunting: Deer, quail, duck in season.

Annual Events: Spring Rodeo; Hallowe'en Celebration for children.

YUMA (137 alt., 15,000 pop.), three miles west of the confluence of the Colorado and Gila rivers, is set on bluffs overlooking the Colorado and on sandy rocky hills back of the bluffs. One of the largest artificially irrigated areas in Arizona adjoins the city on three sides; its rich alluvial soil supports extensive citrus, date, and pecan orchards; fields of cotton, alfalfa, wheat, and barley; while miles of unreclaimed sandy wastes and desert lie beyond. In every direction jagged fantastic mountains show on the horizon—the Gila Mountains eastward; the Picacho and Chimney peaks of California to the northwest; and to the southwest the ranges of Mexico which border Arizona twenty-six miles south of Yuma.

Eight blocks of Yuma's Main Street constitute most of its main business district. Much of the flavor of Yuma is concentrated in the shadowed recesses of the covered sidewalks and the contrasting blaze of yellow sunlight on the wide street, designed to suit the pioneer need of room in which to turn the great lumbering transport wagons drawn by twenty-mule teams. If the day is warm or hot, as it almost invariably is in Yuma, Indians from the near-by Yuma and Cocopah Reservations, the men with scarfs around their hair, the women with gaudy shawls across their shoulders, congregate under the awnings over the sidewalks, along with swarthy Mexicans, engineers in stained khaki, businessmen in limp linens—all seeking relief from the intense sunlight. The upper stories of business houses jut out over the sidewalks, and most of the shops have signboards suspended from the sidewalk roofs.

J. Ross Browne, in Yuma during the 1860's, found the winter climate finer than that of Italy. But in *Adventures in the Apache Country, A Tour Through Arizona and Sonora,* he recorded the belief that "perhaps fastidious people might object to the temperature in summer, when rays of the sun attain their maximum force, and the hot winds sweep in from the desert. It is said that a wicked soldier died here, and was consigned to the fiery regions below for his manifold sins; but unable to stand the rigors of the climate, sent back for his blankets. I have even heard complaint made that the thermometer failed to show the true heat because the mercury dried up. Every thing dries; wagons dry; men dry; chickens dry; there is no juice left in any thing, living or dead, by the close of summer. Officers and soldiers are supposed to walk about creaking; mules, it is said, can only bray at midnight; and I have heard it hinted that the carcasses of cattle rattle inside their hides, and that snakes find a difficulty in bending their bodies, and horned frogs die of apoplexy."

Even though adjacent country to the confluence of the Gila and Colorado was a dry, harsh place for white men to live, it was destined to become a thriving community. In early days it was impossible for wagon trains to traverse the mountainous area north of the Gila River. They had to travel down the Gila and across the Colorado at the point where modern Yuma now stands.

Hernando de Alarcon, the Spanish navigator of the Colorado, cooperating with the land expedition of Coronado, passed Yuma's granite bluff in 1540. Padre Eusebio Francisco Kino made the first of several trips into this region in 1683, while searching for a route to California. A mission which he established here sometime prior to 1697 was destroyed that year by an Apache raid on the Yuma.

Padre Francisco Tomas Garces established two missions in 1779: the Mission de la Purisima Concepcion on the west bank of the river, opposite Yuma, and another, with the aid of Spanish colonists and soldiers, about eight miles down the river. In 1781 when the soldiers and 150 Spanish colonists were at mass, the Indians, angered because of the damage done to their crops by the soldiers' horses, attacked and killed Father Garces and nearly all the men, holding the women and children as captives. Thereafter little effort was made by Spaniards to occupy the region.

It was not until American troops marched through the Gila Valley in 1847, during the war with Mexico, that the country became generally known to Americans. The United States acquired this region by the Treaty of Guadalupe Hidalgo, ratified in 1848. The terms of the treaty stated that the California Line should follow the southern bank of the Colorado River and extend south one marine league from the confluence of the Colorado and Gila rivers. Consequently the 15e acres now partly occupied by Yuma legally belonged to California, though control of this area remained unsettled until 1873.

Many emigrants to the California gold fields came by way of southern Arizona, crossing the Colorado River at the present site of Yuma. In the fall of 1849 Lieutenant A. W. Whipple, while employed by the United States Government in making a boundary survey, came into this region and found it "populated only with Indians."

In the same year L. J. F. Jaeger established a ferry here to transport emigrants and their belongings across the Colorado River, and continued to operate it until 1877, when he sold it to the Southern Pacific Railroad.

Local tradition has it that the first ferry was a raft built in Michigan and drawn across the continent as a prairie schooner. In 1849 the schooner-raft is supposed to have been launched on the Gila River in central Arizona and floated down to the Colorado. The first white child born in Arizona is said to have been born on the raft during the trip—an anomaly for the driest state in the Union. Other ferries were established, one operated by Yuma Indians. In the fall and spring of 1850-51 one ferry was said to have carried 60,000 people en route to the gold fields of California, at two dollars a head.

In 1850 a United States military post was established on the west bank of the Colorado to protect the few white residents and the many emigrants to California. Unrest among the Indians grew into attacks upon the settlement and ferry service was suspended until six companies of troops marched across the Colorado desert in 1853 to help restore order.

The river steamer *Uncle Sam,* the first of its kind on the Colorado, reached the fort with supplies in 1852, and maintained regular service until it foundered two years later a few miles below Yuma.

In 1854 Colonel Charles D. Poston and a party of engineers, while making a tour of the area, reached the Colorado River where Yuma now stands. They were about to cross the Colorado when the ferryman, Jaeger, demanded twenty-five dollars as fare. The engineers couldn't or wouldn't pay so much, pitched camp for the night, and decided to lay out a town in the hope that Jaeger would make a trade. The next morning they surveyed the place, named it Colorado City, and drafted a map. The scheme worked—Jaeger exchanged their passage across the river for a corner lot, and the party proceeded on its way. Three years afterward Colorado City (later Arizona City, now Yuma) had a population of twelve, not counting soldiers and Indians.

In the middle 1850's occasional adventurers appeared with chunks of gold. They related Indian tales of places in the mountains covered with some kind of "heavy yellow stones." Felix Aubrey, the explorer, wrote in his journal of 1853 that gold was in such abundance along the banks of the Colorado River that it glistened in some places upon the ground. He said he sold some articles of old clothing to a group of Indians for more than $1,500 worth of gold, and saw one of the Indians put four gold bullets in his gun to shoot a rabbit. The enthusiasm following these reports was moderated, however, by gruesome stories of escape from the hostile Apache and by accounts of suffering, food shortage, and death from thirst in the far mountain and desert reaches.

Rich placer deposits, discovered in 1858 along the Colorado and Gila rivers near Yuma, precipitated a gold rush. Extensive shipping developed on the Colorado, though prohibitive freight rates limited shipments to supplies for military posts. Most of these cargoes were unloaded at Yuma, where a quartermaster's depot on the south side of the river facilitated handling, then hauled by twenty-mule teams across the desert to La Paz, Prescott, Tucson, and other points in the interior. Yuma's population increased rapidly, and the dance halls and gambling houses along Main Street were well patronized by Indians, miners, freighters, and outlaws. A vigilance committee organized in 1866 attempted to maintain law and order, but was only moderately successful.

In 1870 the county seat was transferred to Yuma from La Paz, now a ghost town, and in 1871 Yuma was incorporated by the territorial legislature. This action was taken in spite of California's claim to the area and even though that state was collecting taxes from Yuma citizens. During its first session in 1864, the Arizona legislature had sent a memorial to Congress, asking for annexation of the Yuma territory. No action was taken, however, until 1873, when the Public Land Commissioners decided in favor of Arizona. The city of Yuma then sued San Diego County for $40,000, claiming that it had illegally collected that sum in taxes; a compromise was reached and part of the claim was paid.

In this period a person traveling through the country and not possessing his own transportation was forced to go by one of the stage lines. These lines used Concord Stages which were stout, high-wheeled vehicles, usually pulled by six fast-stepping mustangs. These coaches had a passenger capacity of twelve or fourteen, with limited space for baggage.

The Southern Pacific, which entered Yuma from California in 1878, greatly reduced passenger service by way of the Gulf of California and the Colorado and Gila rivers. The railroad company built a bridge over the Colorado River at Yuma, but no provision was made for wagon transportation; the result was that ferries continued in operation until 1915, when the first highway bridge was built.

From 1860 Yuma County's gold output was estimated at from $20,000,000 to $42,000,000, the wide range resulting from the varying accounts of miners. The census of 1880 gave Yuma a population of 1,200, with only one Arizona town larger—Tucson. The placers began to play out in 1880; but improved mining methods and high prices for gold have again enabled mines in the surrounding hills to operate at a profit.

The first territorial prison was erected at Yuma in 1876. Though it had only seven prisoners at the time of its establishment, the penitentiary later received convicts from all over the United States, at one time confining 376. In 1909 Florence succeeded Yuma as site of the territorial prison.

Yuma's plan of government was reorganized in 1901. Since the city had 1,000 lots at its disposal, it was decided to pay city officials' salaries temporarily in land. Under this plan the village recorder received two lots a year, each councilman one lot every two years.

Irrigation of the surrounding desert was first attempted by Jose N. Redondo, an early settler, who dug a canal from the Colorado River to his ranch. The Reclamation Act of 1902, which provided for construction of Laguna Dam, fourteen miles north, introduced irrigation on a large scale and indirectly provided the greatest stimulus to Yuma's growth. The dam, which diverts water from the Colorado for irrigation of about 109,000 acres of desert wasteland, was completed in 1909. When the All-American Canal is finished in 1940, irrigation of the Yuma project will be conducted through the Imperial Dam and the All-American Canal system.

Construction of Laguna Dam stopped freighting on the river, and nearly all the boats then in service were purchased by the government. The *Searchlight* was used in work at the dam, and another of the last boats, the *Cochan,* was purchased by the *Searchlight's* skipper, Captain Smith. He dismantled it and used the materials in the construction of a country home—an act symbolic of Yuma's change from a river town to the commercial center for this extensive agricultural region.

POINTS OF INTEREST

1. The ALTHEE MODESTI STORE (*open*), S. side of 1st St. between Main St. and Madison Ave., was one of the first commercial houses in Yuma. This adobe structure, now abandoned, was operated by Althee Modesti, a prominent pioneer. The original signs, front and side, are still faintly legible.

2. The YUMA VALLEY MAIN CANAL AND INVERTED SYPHON OUTLET are at the N. end of N. 2nd Ave. The water, diverted on the California side at Laguna Dam, is carried under the Colorado River to the Arizona side through an inverted syphon. A network of irrigation canals then distributes the water throughout Yuma Valley.

3. On the GOVERNMENT GROUNDS (*open 9-5 daily*), N. end of N. 2nd Ave., are structures housing the Weather Bureau, Customs Bureau, Reclamation Service, and the Yuma Water Users' Association. A small park in the center of the grounds contains large eucalyptus trees and Burbank spineless cacti.

The OLD ADOBE housing the Weather and Customs Bureaus, a soft yellow in color, with a wide porch surrounding it and the windows reaching from floor to ceiling, was built in 1864 as a quartermaster's depot, barracks, and stables. Its walls are twenty-two inches thick.

Partly hidden by orange trees is an ADOBE RUIN built in 1864 as a supply depot.   Bars on the windows date from the Mexican Revolution of 1884.   Rebels chased by Nationals were seized by American authorities near Yuma.   For lack of a better place, they imprisoned them in the supply depot.   Here they enjoyed rest and good meals, a final indulgence before they were sent back across the line, where they were wiped out to a man.

4. The high adobe walls of the TERRITORIAL PRISON RUINS (*10-4 Mon.-Sat.*), on Prison Hill at Penitentiary Ave. and Prison Lane, are worn down and weathered.   Prison Hill, a granite bluff almost blocking the Colorado River, with hundreds of miles of desert in every direction was an ideal site.   Despite the prison's location and the co-operation of the Indians, who were paid fifty dollars for every escaped convict they returned, jail breaks occurred frequently.

The DUNGEON BLOCK, the first ruin encountered, contains twenty compartments, carved out of the rocky hill.   A door leads to the dungeon, a cave about fifteen feet square and ten feet high, locally known as the "Snake Den."   Rings on the floor were to separate fighting men in the same cell.

The twelve CELLS FOR INCORRIGIBLES, E. of the Dungeon Block, are also carved out of the solid rock hill.   On the walls of one of the cells *human "liberty"* is clearly inscribed, with the *"liberty"* in significant quotation marks.

Like all the Yuma prison habitations, the MAIN CELL BLOCK, N. of the Dungeon Block, was built by prisoners.   The stone and mortar building contains thirty-four cells, originally equipped with six bunks each, in tiers three to a side.   Only one cell still has the bunk frames. The ENTRANCE GATE, N. of the Main Cell Block, was the only means of access within the walls.   The MAIN GUARD TOWER, adjoining the Entrance Gate, housed a Gatling gun that was used to quell outbreaks. The GUARDS' QUARTERS, N. of the Main Tower, is remodeled and used as a clubhouse by the Veterans of Foreign Wars.

The PRISON CEMETERY, on a lower bluff directly above the Colorado River, contains a profusion of weathered redwood markers still showing the number, name, and date of death of each convict.   The paint used in inscribing the markers has preserved the wood beneath it, however deeply it is worn away around, giving the effect of overlaid letters and numbers.   The graves are dug in crumbling granite and the plot is barren save for an occasional pungent greasewood bush.   On the prison grounds is a museum and picnic area.

YUMA.   Points of Interest

1. First Store of Althee Modesti
2. Yuma Valley Main Canal and Inverted Syphon Outlet
3. Government Grounds
4. Territorial Prison Ruins

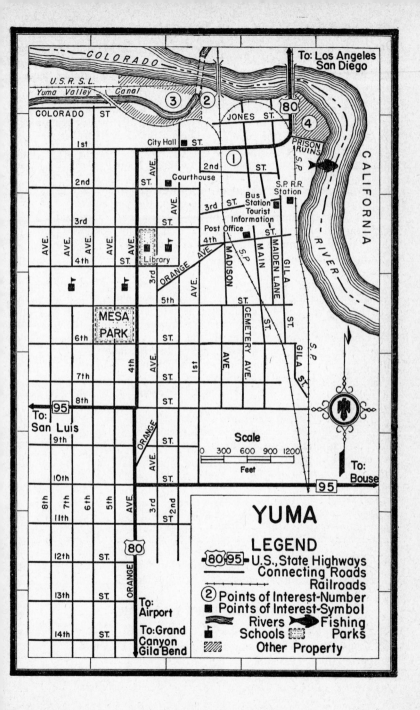

YUMA MESA

Stretching from Yuma on the Colorado River, south to the Mexican border and beyond to the Gulf of California, is a vast area of sandy loam soil, known as the Yuma Mesa, one of the most remarkably productive regions in the country. During the early 1920's it was discovered that it was practically a frost-free area. An Irrigation and Drainage District was formed and a pumping plant built in the Yuma Valley at the foot of the Mesa, and large acreages were planted to grapefruit and oranges. Most of the groves were planted to grapefruit which proved to be a very profitable crop, the per acre average production being the highest of any of the desert areas. The Yuma Mesa grapefruit is harvested and marketed over a long season, starting in October and continuing until May each year. This grapefruit has a very high sugar content. Many navel oranges are now grown on the Mesa also.

Date growing at the present time is a comparatively minor industry, but climatic conditions are the finest for dates, which are damaged by rainfall and high humidity at time of ripening. The Yuma Mesa has less rainfall and humidity at ripening time in the fall than any other date producing area in the country. Because of adequate water through irrigation a good crop is assured, and a variety of soil and temperature conditions permits production of many fine varieties. The Persian Gardens, located here, growing almost every variety, including the only true jet black date, "El Toby," is perhaps the finest date garden anywhere.

Since World War II Yuma Mesa has come into its own. The Yuma-Gila Project is completed and eventually 50,000 acres will be put into cultivation under the project. Much of this acreage was turned over to young ex-service men who are proving to be the progressive farmers of the day. Water for the new project is brought through a series of canals from the Colorado River to the fertile sands of the Mesa.

For several years alfalfa was the major crop but other crops are being grown at a profit. Grapes have proven profitable with some varieties ripening earlier than in most other grape-growing sections of the Southwest. Even though a variety of crops can be grown on the Yuma Mesa, many of the young farmers are setting out citrus groves as rapidly as the nursery stock can be secured.

TOUR IN NEAR-BY CALIFORNIA

Just west of Yuma, US 80 crosses the COLORADO RIVER BRIDGE, *0.4 m.,* and enters California. On a hill (R.) stands the YUMA INDIAN SCHOOL AND AGENCY, *0.5 m.,* which includes a mission and a playground. A STATUE OF FATHER GARCES in front of the mission was erected in 1929. Here in 1781 the Indians massacred the Franciscan, murdered soldiers and colonists, and destroyed the Mission de la Purisima Concepcion, which Father Garces had erected on these grounds in 1779. Fort Yuma was established on the site of the old mission in 1850.

A graveled road branching R. from US 80 at *0.7 m.* traverses the FORT YUMA INDIAN RESERVATION, 8,350 acres of irrigated land. Here live the impoverished remnants of the once-powerful Yuma tribe. When Father Kino came into this region he estimated the number of Yuma families at 6,000; there were about 3,000 Yumas here in 1853, and by 1932 the number had dwindled to 842. The small parched farms of the reservation indicate the poverty in which the Indians live. Scattered along the road are their thatched-roofed adobe huts with *ramadas* under which the Indians rest and upon which they hang their vegetables, animal skins, and tools. Those who do not farm, work as laborers or earn a little money by selling trinkets to tourists.

The graveled road continues to LAGUNA DAM, *12 m.* from the junction with US 80. Completed in 1909, this structure is of the Indian weir type; it raises the Colorado River surface about ten feet, forming a long narrow lake. The dam irrigates 64,000 acres of delta bottom-land around Yuma and 45,000 acres south and southeast of Yuma. After completion of the All-American Canal project in 1940, Laguna Dam no longer supplied water for the Yuma project. It serves only as the tail water control for the Imperial Dam, *17.5 m.,* which was completed in 1938 on schedule. Imperial Dam now diverts water into the All-American Canal on the California side of the Colorado River and into the Gravity Main Canal of the Gila project on the Arizona side of the river. Built by the United States Bureau of Reclamation, it has an overflow weir of the hollow concrete floating type, is 3,430 feet long and forty-five feet high. Immediately downstream is a mechanical desilting plant.

West of its junction with the graveled road US 80 crosses the ALL-AMERICAN CANAL, *6.3 m.,* begun in 1934 and then actually completed in 1940. The All-American Canal provides water for the Imperial and Coachella valleys in southern California. The main canal is eighty miles long, the branch to the Coachella Valley is 130 miles long.

POINTS OF INTEREST IN ENVIRONS

Cocopah Indian Reservation, 18.9 *m.;* San Luis, 26 *m.* (*see TOUR 4d*).

YUMA AIR BASE, located at Yuma County Airport, 6½ miles southeast of Yuma on US 80, is headquarters for the 4750th Training Wing (Air Defense). The Wing is a component of the nationwide Air Defense Command (ADC), which is charged with defense of the continental United States against aerial attack.

The mission of the Training Wing at Yuma is to provide an installation at which ADC fighter-interceptor squadrons may receive advanced training in the use of their weapons, including air-to-air rockets. The weapons are fired over a desert range extending approximately 70 miles east of Yuma.

The station was re-activated in June, 1951, having been inactive since shortly after the close of World War II. All jet units in the nation's Air Defense Command train in rocket gunnery at this installation.

YUMA TEST STATION, located 30 miles north of Yuma on State 95, one and one-half miles east of Imperial Dam, is unique in that it supports research and development for all technical services and field forces boards, whereas most research and development installations support only one technical service.

Established in 1943 by the Research and Development Laboratory of the Corps of Engineers, pontoon and bailey bridges were tested here on the Colorado River. In 1949 this branch was inactivated and the Corps of Engineers sought disposal of the area. Much of the present area was used by the Army for maneuvers in 1943-44 by General Patton; bringing units of division and larger units for desert training. The Station was reactivated in 1951 for the purpose of supporting hot weather desert research and development.

Many parts of the reservation are restricted because of various types of tests. The test area has a tank course, wheeled vehicle course, dynamometer course, vapor lock course, sand dune driving course, thirty-five mile artillery range, chemical and biological warfare range.

For other points of interest in California see CALIFORNIA: A GUIDE TO THE GOLDEN STATE.

PART III
Tours

Tour 1

(Kanab, Utah)—Cameron—Townsend—Flagstaff—Williams—Prescott—Phoenix—Florence—Tucson—Nogales (Nogales, Mexico); US 89.
Utah Line to Mexican Border, 604 *m.*

All-paved, all-year highway. Some curves south of Prescott over mountain ranges. Santa Fe Ry. roughly parallels US 89 between Flagstaff and Phoenix; the Southern Pacific between Phoenix and Nogales. All types of accommodations in and near larger towns; limited elsewhere.

Following a roundabout route between the Utah Line and the Mexican border, US 89, more than any other road, displays the great diversity of Arizona land and life. Though running through long arid stretches it is never monotonous; there is always a brilliance of color, constantly changing, that makes the wasteland memorable—yellows, browns, reds, dull greens, becoming purple in distant mountains, below a sky that is intense blue, pale-green, fiery red, according to the time of day.

The people along the route are as varied as the country, which ranges from plateau more than a mile above sea-level and snow patched even in summer to the subtropical Salt River Valley; along the northern end are lumberjacks living in camps, near the center are Arizona metropolitans in houses of extremely modern design, and along the lower end are the Mexicans—whose adobe houses can always be identified from afar in the fall by the strings of scarlet chili peppers. Wild animal life is abundant—deer and antelope graze within sight of motorists, Mexican quail dart from mesquite and sagebrush beside the road, and road runners streak across the road itself ahead of oncoming cars.

281

Section a. UTAH LINE to FLAGSTAFF; 201 m. US 89.

This section of the route runs through the snows and pines of the Kaibab Forest, crosses the Colorado's Marble Canyon, and runs through the western edge of the Navajo reservation, brilliant with the color in the Painted Desert.

Crossing the Utah Line, 0 *m.,* 2.5 miles south of Kanab, Utah, US 89 traverses Coconino County, second largest county in the United States; it covers 18,629 square miles. Coconino (pinon nut people) is what the Hopi called the Havasupai (*see Indians*).

The entire section of land between the Utah Line and the Grand Canyon is known as the Arizona Strip. Historically and culturally, it is linked with early Mormon Utah; the Saints wandered far south in their quest for more land to till and more pasture for their cattle. Thus in its background and traditions, the strip is a world apart from those areas occupied by the belligerent, gun-toting men of the early cow camps and mining towns of the Southwest.

FREDONIA, 3.5 *m.* (5,752 alt., 425 pop.), was settled in the 1880's by Mormons seeking freedom from religious persecution. A landmark to the west of Fredonia is a rock closely resembling a ship. (*Guides, horses, supplies for camping or hunting are available.*)

Right from Fredonia on an improved road into the KAIBAB (Paiute, on the mountain) INDIAN RESERVATION, 3 *m.* The Kaibab, a division of the Paiute, numbered 171 in 1873 but is now less than 100. The reservation borders the Utah Line for a distance of 18 miles and extends southward for 12 miles. Within the area are many horseback trails and much game.

The Paiute occupy parts of Arizona, Utah, Nevada, and California, but the main body lives near Walker River and Pyramid Lake in Nevada. Formerly they subsisted almost entirely on small game hunted by the men and on nuts, seeds, and roots gathered by the women; today their main support comes from herds of Hereford cattle, poultry, and the cereal crops they raise on small plots.

The Kaibab's name was applied to the northern plateau and subsequently to a limestone formation, to a national forest, and to a variety of deer and of squirrel found in that forest.

At 13.8 *m.* is a junction with a dirt road; R. on this road 4.7 *m.* to MOCCASIN the Paiute tribal offices. It consists of a dozen houses and a day school, and is the center of all social life on the reservation.

The Paiute story of the creation of their people displays originality in some of its details. For a long time the land had been under water but as the water receded Jurangwa (Mount Grant, SW. of Walker Lake in western Nevada) emerged. There was a fire at its top but the wind blew up waves that would have dashed it out if the sage hen had not fanned away the water with her wings. Her breast feathers were burned black by the fire she saved and have remained that color. After the great flood finally receded, leaving the earth as it is today, Numinaa (Our Father) stepped out of Mount Grant and went north to Carson Sink where he made his home. Ibidisii (Our Mother) followed him and became his wife. They had two sons and two daughters; the father made bows and arrows for the boys, and the mother made sticks for the girls with which to dig roots. One boy and a girl went south to Walker Lake and became raw-fish eaters, and the other two went to the north (Idaho) and became buffalo eaters. This separation accounts for the various branches of the tribe. After the departure of their children the parents went up to the eastern mountains and disappeared into the sky.

On the main side road, opposite the junction with the Moccasin road, is the entrance to PIPE SPRING NATIONAL MONUMENT, a forty acre tract set aside in 1923 as a memorial to pioneers. In 1858 Brigham Young, president of the Mormon church, sent a party to explore the Colorado River region and, if possible, to make a treaty of peace with the Navajo.

While some Mormons, under Jacob Hamblin, were camped at this spring a joke was played on William Hamblin, expert rifleman, who was challenged to puncture a silk handkerchief at 50 paces. He failed because the handkerchief, hung up by the upper edge, yielded to the bullet. Vexed, Hamblin declared and proved that he could shoot the bottom out of a pipe which was placed at some distance on a rock near the spring, with the bowl of the pipe facing toward him. The spring has since been called Pipe Spring.

Dr. James M. Whitmore and Robert McIntyre in 1863 built a dugout of earth and juniper logs as headquarters for their cattle ranch here. A few years later a band of Navajo and Paiute Indians stole some of their stock. In pursuing them, the two were killed. The Mormons later acquired this estate for a cattle ranch and in 1873 built a fort, consisting of two 2-storied red sandstone buildings. Sold in 1875 to private interests, the old fort and auxiliary buildings were finally acquired by the Federal Government and established as a national monument.

WINSOR CASTLE, now a museum in Pipe Spring National Monument, was constructed over the springs to prevent Indians from poisoning the settlement's water supply. This structure, which has loopholes in its walls, housed the first (1871) telegraph office in Arizona. The operator of the key was Mrs. David King Udall, a Mormon missionary.

From TOROWEAP POINT, 66 m., the inner gorge of the Colorado River is visible. The monument adjoins Grand Canyon National Park (see *Grand Canyon National Park*) on the west, and was created by presidential proclamation in 1932.

Within the bounds of the KAIBAB NATIONAL FOREST, 20.5 m., are ponderosa pine, Douglas fir, spruce, juniper, oak, and pinon. Because altitudes in the forest range from 5,000 to 9,200 feet it is delightfully cool in summer. The forest includes two mountain ranges, abounds with small game, and, although there are no running streams in the area, has excellent campsites. This reserve, set aside in 1893, has headquarters at Williams (see *TOUR 2b*).

From a curve in the highway at about 29 m., just north of a heavily wooded section is a sweeping view with the mountains of southern Utah, fifty miles away, forming a background of reds, greens, whites, and browns above the dull greens of the sagebrush and range grass.

JACOB LAKE, 33.3 m. (7,950 alt., 19 pop.), is a ranger station and campground at the junction with paved State 67 to the Grand Canyon (see *PARK TOUR 2*). In this vicinity are many Kaibab squirrels, distinguished by their bushy white tails.

From a point at about 44 m. descending from the Kaibab Plateau is the first glimpse of Vermilion Cliffs, ahead. Houserock Valley is in the foreground extending far R. and L.

US 89 crosses the eastern boundary of the Kaibab National Forest at 47 m.

HOUSEROCK, 47.9 m. (5,000 alt.), is headquarters for Arizona's annual wild buffalo (bison) hunt held (Jan.) in Houserock Valley. The herd when purchased by the Arizona Game and Fish Commission in 1927 numbered a hundred. In 1953 there were over 125 in the herd, despite the annual hunts, which are held to prevent the animals from becoming too numerous for their limited feeding range. The hunt is open to residents. All applications for drawing must be submitted to the office of the state game warden, who chooses a hunter by lot for each of several buffalo selected as victims. The privilege of participation is not transferable since alternates are also selected and the hunter must provide his own transportation. He is permitted to retain the head, hide, and one-quarter of the buffalo he kills. Several hundred applications for the hunting privilege are made yearly. An attendant who lives near the range accompanies the hunters and points out the animals to be killed. Each hunter, armed with a rifle, then stalks his animal in any way he desires. Although the buffalo run wild and their range is in a remote district, they are not dangerous and look upon men merely with curiosity.

East of Houserock for about 20 miles VERMILION CLIFFS are seen, rising steeply to a height of more than a thousand feet; the almost perpendicular face is a bright red, shading into orange and greens. Balanced rocks in the cliffs are oddly shaped, many resembling huge toadstools.

Near MARBLE CANYON, 73.9 *m.*, is Marble Canyon Lodge (*spring water, hotel and cottages*). Echo Cliffs and Kaibito Plateau, in the Navajo Reservation, are visible to the east.

Left from Marble Canyon filling station on a narrow side road, frequently little more than a creek bed, to LEE'S FERRY, 6 *m.*; from 1872 to the completion of Navajo Bridge this was the only possible crossing of the Colorado for many miles. It was established by John D. Lee, a Mormon pioneer who with his family, settled at the confluence of the Paria and Colorado rivers, built a log cabin, and acquired ferry rights at the point that had been held by the Mormon church. His first boat, the *Emma Dean,* had been abandoned on the bank of the Colorado by Major John Wesley Powell (*see Grand Canyon*). Later Lee built a boat of pine from the Kaibab Forest. Timbers were hauled sixty miles by ox team and hewn into planks two or three inches thick. The boat was sixteen feet wide and forty-five feet long, with two decks and could carry four wagons. It was operated by four men, two in the bow and two in the stern. The passage was always attended with peril since there are dangerous rapids both above and below the crossing. The ferry was so navigated that the river's current carried it across; it was also carried back by the current and then towed upstream to the starting point.

This ferry was used by the Mormons in their migration into the Little Colorado River Valley of northern Arizona. In 1873 a Mormon party established the first wagon road south of the Colorado River from the ferry.

In 1857 thirteen years before Lee settled on the Colorado, a massacre had taken place at Mountain Meadows, an isolated section of the Utah Territory. A group of men reputedly disguised as Indians had attacked a train of Arkansas and Missouri emigrants, killing 115. There was much uncertainty in placing the responsibility for the killings, but Lee was accused of leading the attackers and eventually was arrested and tried. A first trial resulted in a disagreement; a second in conviction and the death sentence which was executed in 1877.

The ferry was operated for several years by one of his widows and finally sold to the Mormon church. In 1909 the church sold the ferry to a cattle company that was then grazing stock on the ranges to the west. In 1916

Architecture

MORMON TEMPLE, MESA

(Two A.M. nine minute exposure. Star streaks show earth movement.)

LUHRS TOWER, PHOENIX

Joseph Miller

ARCADE

ENTRANCE

IMA COUNTY COURT HOUSE

Buehman Studio

BROPHY COLLEGE, PHOENIX

Jerry McLai

WOMEN'S BUILDING, UNIVERSITY OF ARIZONA, TUCSON

TATE CAPITOL, PHOENIX

MONTEZUM
CASTLE
NATIONAL
MONUMENT
NEAR
CAMP VERD
(12TH CENT

CASA GRANDE NATIONAL MONUMENT, NEAR COOLIDGE
(FOURTEENTH CENTURY)

Joseph Mill

SAN XAVIER DEL BAC MISSION, NEAR TUCSON

UMACACORI MISSION NATIONAL MONUMENT, NEAR NOGALES

HEARD SCOUT PUEBLO; PHOENIX SOUTH MOUNTAIN

William F. Fin

AIRVIEW, PHOENIX

Coconino County took over the property and operated it until the completion of Navajo Bridge. Lee's ranch is now a guest ranch.

NAVAJO BRIDGE, 75.4 *m.*, sometimes called Marble Canyon or Grand Canyon Bridge, is the only highway bridge crossing the turbulent Colorado for approximately a thousand miles—from Boulder Dam to Moab, Utah. An engineering accomplishment and an object of great beauty, it is 834 feet long, has a single arch with a span of 616 feet, and measures 467 feet between its floor and the surface of the river— about the height of a forty-story building. Since its completion in 1929 the bridge has superseded the old Lee's Ferry nearby.

The Colorado River is the western boundary of the Navajo Reservation, largest in the United States (*see TOUR 5*).

CEDAR RIDGE, 109.3 *m.*, is a small trading post named for a near-by grove of cedars. Good campsites are available. There are also tourist cabins built to resemble Navajo hogans.

At 137.2 *m.* is the junction with the Navajo-Hopi Indian Reservation Road (*see TOUR 5*).

South of this junction the road crosses a section of the PAINTED DESERT, which stretches along the northeast bank of the Little Colorado River from the Grand Canyon to the Petrified Forest (*see TOUR 2a*).

CAMERON, 146.8 *m.* (4,200 alt., 25 pop.), a combined Indian trading post and hotel on the edge of the Painted Desert, was named for Ralph Henry Cameron, last territorial delegate to Congress.

The Navajo girls in this area have not yet become addicted to rouge and lipstick, but they do like the perfume the traders sell at ten cents a bottle. The boys use highly perfumed hair oil which makes their black hair shine in the sunlight. Navajo men and boys have an odd way of showing their friendship. When two young men meet at the trading post, a "Sing", or a dance they greet each other, inquire about the health of their respective families, then stand silently some ten or fifteen minutes while one feels the other's arms, shoulders and chest.

At 147.8 *m.* is the junction with State 64 (*see Grand Canyon*).

GRAY MOUNTAIN, 157 *m.* is a trading post just outside the Navajo Indian Reservation, with Indian silversmiths at work manufacturing jewelry for the trade.

At 168.8 *m.* is the junction with an unimproved road.

Left on this road 5 *m.* to a group of ruins in the WUPATKI NATIONAL MONUMENT. The one that has been restored at the foot of the hill is NALAKIHU (Hopi, house alone) RUINS; it consists of several rooms, five of which have been excavated, two restored. The restoration was done in 1933 by the Museum of Northern Arizona employing Hopi workmen; the walls of coursed masonry now appear much as they did during the twelfth century when the dwelling was occupied.

On the mesa top overlooking a large depression are the RUINS OF TEU-WALANKI (Hopi, citadel) which has been partially excavated, but not restored.

Approximately 100 yards R. at 7.3 *m.* are EARTH CRACKS, fissures about one foot wide and a hundred feet deep, in the rock surface.

The most striking feature of the WUPATKI RUINS (Hopi, big house), 15 *m.*, is the manner in which the builders have utilized the natural walls of red sandstone, constructing above and around them, so that the buildings seem to grow right out of the earth. Occupied in the third or Great Pueblo Period, it contains many details characteristic of that culture in this area—the rectangular kiva at the southeast corner, the small ventilator in the outside wall of the first row of rooms, and the T-shaped doors. The most puzzling structure is the large circular pit, with high masonry walls and a bench of the same material running completely around. The entrance is on the northeast side. This at first led to the supposition that it was a kiva of the round type found in Chaco, New Mexico, but there are no other kiva features. Furthermore Wupatki has another kiva of the square type. From tree rings it is apparent that the site was occupied at the end of the eleventh century A.D., was rapidly expanded during the twelfth century, and declined by the beginning of the thirteenth. The ruins are strategically situated with a broad view of the Painted Desert.

The Wupatki National Monument was created in 1924, to include not only this site but also many others in the eight-hundred-acre tract. In 1937 the area of the monument was increased by more than thirty thousand acres that contain many more unexcavated ruins.

US 89 crosses the northern boundary, 184 m., of the COCONINO NATIONAL FOREST which contains American pine, the most valuable of the state's timber, and has many fine recreational sites. Although most of its area is comparatively flat, in the south it is cut by deep canyons and in the north rises abruptly to the San Francisco peaks. The fire hazard is greater here than in any other forest in the Southwest, largely owing to the frequent electrical storms of early summer which are accompanied by little or no rain. Man is not entirely guiltless, however, and the co-operation of visitors in fire prevention is earnestly sought.

At 189 m. is the junction with an unimproved road.

Left on this road to SUNSET CRATER NATIONAL MONUMENT, 2.5 m., a three-thousand-acre tract surrounding an extinct volcano.

BONITO LAVA FLOW, 3.5 m., poured in four directions from a disrupted cone in this area. The lava ejected into an intercone basin could not flow far and so piled up to a thickness of three hundred feet.

The ICE CAVES, 4.1 m., were caused by the mass cooling so unevenly that a crust formed on top while the material below was still molten. As this fluid lava drained away, caves were formed in the solid material that remained. Because lava is a poor conductor of heat, the cold air at the bottom of the intercone basin is protected. No matter how high the temperature is outside, within the Ice Caves there is snow on the floors and ice clinging to the ceilings.

A FURMAROLE, or spatter cone, is about 25 yards L. of the Ice Caves. When the lava had crusted over, vapors coming from the interior of the molten mass formed small cones. The brilliant colors in the formations were caused by gases.

SUNSET CRATER, 4.2 m., has a foot trail winding up the side (round trip takes about one hour). The crest of the crater rises 8,000 feet above sea level, 1,000 feet above the country at its base, and has a pit about 1300 feet in diameter and 400 feet deep. The name was suggested by its many colors, bright yellow at the crest, shading into orange, red, and finally a skirt of black volcanic ash. The crater spouted great quantities of black ash which completely engulfed Indian pueblos, very much as Vesuvius covered Pompeii.

The area abounds with fossils of various marine animals, evidence of the great sea that once covered this region.

FLAGSTAFF, 201 *m.,* is the junction with US 66 (*see TOUR 2*). Between this point and Ashfork Junction, a distance of 50 miles, US 89 and US 66 are one route (*see TOUR 2b*).

Section b. ASHFORK JUNCTION *to* WICKENBURG; 114.2 m. US 89.

Much of this section of the route is within the Prescott National Forest. It is sparsely inhabited except for Prescott, and contains Indian ruins, a prehistoric fort, a Joshua tree forest, and abandoned gold diggings.

South of Ashfork Junction, 0 *m.,* at 12.4 *m.* is a grove of juniper, cut regularly for lumber that is used in fine chests. Juniper is frequently but erroneously called cedar.

At 18 *m.* is HELL CANYON and the junction with an unimproved dirt road.

Left on this road to PERKINSVILLE, 11 *m.* (3,847 alt.), nearest approach to SYCAMORE CANYON, an undeveloped game-hunting section where dense brush, impassable even to horseback riders, shields lion, bear, deer, and smaller animals.

From a mesa south of Hell Canyon the Mingus Mountains are visible (L); at their base curls smoke from the copper smelter at Clarkdale, closed (*see TOUR 2a*).

The highway crosses VERDE (Sp., green) RIVER, 27.9 *m.,* almost at the river's source; this stream runs south and contributes its water to the Salt River Irrigation Project above Granite Reef Dam.

Between the highway and the Santa Fe Railway are ancient mounds called the DEL RIO RUINS (L), 30.5 *m.* When these remains of prehistoric dwellings were excavated brownish-red cooking bowls and black-gray pottery were found. The absence of arrowheads and the evidence of harvesting sites in the pinon forest several miles to the west indicate a people of peaceful and agricultural inclinations. Two small forts in the vicinity probably served them for defense.

In the CHINO VALLEY, 34.9 *m.* (4,610 alt., 500 pop.), are many small, prosperous ranches irrigated by water from Lake Watson in the hills (R), and from Willow Creek near the Granite Dells (*see below*). Several deep wells supplement the supply.

At 46.2 *m.* is the junction with Alt. US 89 (*see TOUR 2A*).

South of this junction the highway runs through GRANITE DELLS, 46.8 *m.,* a narrow gorge of rock. Centuries of erosion have topped the steep granite walls with grotesque figures resembling human and animal forms, and colored pink, gray, brown, and red. Scrubby growths of oak, small pools, shade trees, and Granite Creek, a clear mountain stream, make it a pleasant picnicking spot. Moving pictures taken on color-film in this gorge have been very successful.

At 47.1 *m.,* approximately the center of the dells, is the junction with a dirt road.

Right on this road to Arizona's GARDEN OF THE GODS, 0.2 *m.*, a grass-covered area (*swimming tank, swings, slides, dance pavilion, horseshoe-pitching courts*) completely walled in by varicolored rocks.

At 47.2 *m.* is the junction with a dirt road.

Left on this road 0.5 *m.* to GRANITE DELLS RECREATIONAL AREA (*cabins, campground, grocery store, dance pavilion*), much larger than the Garden of the Gods. A natural swimming pool in a rock depression (*boating, fishing*) is in the center of the area; winding in among the trees is a clear mountain brook.

WILLOW DAM (R), a P.W.A. project for the farmers of Chino Valley, is visible at 48 *m.*

At 50.6 *m.* is the junction with an improved dirt road (*see TOUR 1A*).

FORT WHIPPLE (R) is at 51.2 *m.* Just south of the fort is Fort Whipple Cemetery (L). The fort, now a Veterans Administration hospital on a seventeen hundred-acre reservation, was named for Brigadier General A. W. Whipple, who as a lieutenant served with the boundary survey of 1851 and was in charge of the railroad survey of 1853. The original Camp Whipple was in Little Chino Valley about 20 miles north of the present site of Prescott, and was occupied by two companies of California Volunteers, 1st Infantry, in 1863. The fort was established here the following year.

The 75-acre YAVAPAI INDIAN RESERVATION lies within the Fort Whipple military compound. The Yavapai, part of the Yuman family, have declined until there are only seventy members. They have neither traditions nor a culture of their own. All records of their early existence have been lost and they are glad to forget the past which, as they explain, consisted only of hardship. The men work at whatever employment they can find off the reservation; the women make baskets, beaded articles, and a little pottery. There are few tribal violations. When a member has broken a law of the reservation he must answer to both the civil authorities and the chief. Viola Jumulla, their tribal leader, is the only woman chief among North American Indians. Because she disapproves of all ritual dances there are no ceremonials among the Yavapai.

PRESCOTT, 52.2 *m.* (5,321 alt., 7,654 pop.), (*see Prescott*).

Points of Interest. The Old Governor's House, the Sharlot Hall Museum, the Grave of Pauline Weaver, Fort Misery, Arizona Pioneers' Home, Statue of Bucky O'Neill, Smoki Pueblo, and others.

Right from Prescott on an improved dirt road to IRON SPRINGS, 10 *m.* (6,400 alt., 400 pop.); formerly a stage station on the Phoenix-Wickenburg line, it is now a summer resort and residential district (*cottages, campgrounds*) named for the iron found in the sands about the springs.

Within the Prescott National Forest is the HASSAYAMPA MOUNTAIN CLUB (R), 55.2 *m.*, one of the state's foremost summer resorts. Most of the cabins are privately owned. (*For accommodations inquire at Prescott Chamber of Commerce.*)

Between a point at 57.2 *m.* and Kirkland Junction are a series of sharp mountain curves. (*Keep to the R.; drive with care.*)

At 77.1 *m.* is the junction with a paved road (Kirkland Junction).

Right on this road to KIRKLAND, 4 *m.* (4,000 alt., 50 pop.), a small trading center in a cattle and mining area. Its general merchandise store, garage, and service station are built with the false fronts typical of small western settlements. William H. Kirkland, for whom the town was named, arrived in Arizona in 1856 and was married in Tucson in May 1860. This is described as the first marriage in Arizona of a pioneer white couple. Kirkland was one of the earliest stage stations and according to an old record the meals served "for those times and circumstances were epicurean feasts."

On this road is SKULL VALLEY, 11 *m.* (4,112 alt., 75 pop.), a settlement serving a ranching and mining district. In 1864 soldiers under Lieutenant Monteith fought a party of Mojave and Tonto Apache here and left without burying the Indian dead. Many bones and skulls were found bleaching along the valley by emigrants traversing the route. Later Major Willis sent a scouting party to bury the bones and skulls "lying round everywhere," and named the site Skull Valley.

At 78.5 *m.* is Kirkland Creek.

Left on foot along the west bank of the creek, which is fringed with walnut trees, then over a boulder-strewn lava slope to the western base of a projecting plateau and the RUIN OF KIRKLAND CREEK FORTRESS, 0.1 *m.*, a prehistoric earth works in a surprisingly good state of preservation. It is on the plateau, approximately four thousand feet high, and affords a commanding view of Kirkland Valley to the north and Prescott National Forest to the east. On the east the cliffs are abrupt, forming a natural defense. The ruin consists largely of two walls: one—8 feet wide, 7 feet high, and 50 feet long—follows the contour lines of the promontory; the other, a meandering west and north wall, is 100 feet long. Although primitive farming was feasible along the creek and wild staples abundant the occupation of the spot was probably brief, perhaps owing to lack of a dependable water supply.

PEEPLES VALLEY, 82.7 *m.,* is a fertile farming valley (L) at the base of WEAVER MOUNTAINS. An elevation of thirty-five hundred feet and water from the mountains are responsible for abundant crops of hay and grain.

YARNELL, 88.9 *m.* (4,200 alt., 340 pop.), a fast-growing little community in a vacation area. The noted SHRINE OF ST. JOSEPH, magnificent sculpture in out-door setting.

Between the SUMMIT OF YARNELL HILL (4,877 alt.), 90.1 *m.* and Congress Junction the highway descends steeply (*keep cars to R.*).

LOOKOUT POINT, 91.5 *m.,* is a shoulder on ANTELOPE PEAK, important landmark in pioneer travel. The view includes a wide expanse of desert and mountains. South are the Vulture and Harqua Hala Mountains which hold rich mineral deposits (*see TOUR 3d*).

CONGRESS JUNCTION, 98.7 *m.* (3,028 alt., 80 pop.), is in part a ghost town. Remains of what was once an active cowboys' and miners' town are R. No longer described as "plenty tough," it is now a sheep- and cattle-shipping center. The place was named for the Congress Mine, three miles N.

Right from Congress Junction on State 71, 3 *m.* to junction with State 93. Right on State 93, 10 *m.* to JOSHUA TREE FOREST. These trees grow to height of 30-40 feet, and usually bloom in late May or early June.

From Congress Junction RICH HILL (L) is visible in the far distance. The long, light-colored streak reaching downward from the mountain's top was made by placer mining. Before the place was abandoned every foot of soil had been overturned and the gold seekers even emerged from the little swale to work on the almost perpendicular mountainside. The tumbled walls of the cabins built by these pioneers remain to this day on the hill's top. At the foot of the east side of Rich Hill on Weaver Creek was the little settlement of Weaver largely inhabited by Mexicans. With the exception of several houses the settlement has entirely disappeared. In the tiny graveyard few, if any, of the original headstones remain, but every one of the thirty-five or more that stood here in 1918 bore the legend, "Died with his boots on." In May 1863 shortly after the Walker Party (*see TOUR 1A*) had passed up the Hassayampa, an expedition organized by A. H. Peeples entered Arizona from California by way of Yuma, where they had found Pauline Weaver awaiting them in response to Peeples' request. Weaver (1800-67), who despite his given name was a rugged frontiersman of mixed Indian and white blood, led the party up the Colorado River to La Paz (*see TOUR 3d*), where the Mexicans had been placer mining for some time. They went east across the Plomosa range to the Cullen Valley. Near the mountains they found antelope. After Peeples had followed them and succeeded in killing five, he named the stream Antelope Creek and the mountain, which rose from its northern bank, Antelope Peak. The party camped near by and before sundown had panned some gold in a stream that they named Weaver Creek in honor of their guide. The next day four Mexicans who had joined the party at Yuma started off after their horses that had strayed during the night. In the evening they returned with their stock and taking Peeples aside showed him a large quantity of gold nuggets brought from the top of the mountain. After gathering a large amount of gold the Mexicans rode back to Mexico. The next morning the party went to the top of the hill where innumerable nuggets of gold were found in a sloping basin. Peeples picked up seven thousand dollars' worth before breakfast. In about a month all the surface gold had been gathered and the party disbanded, some remaining to work the gravel bars of Weaver Creek. It is estimated that during the first month gold valued at a quarter of a million dollars was gathered. Rich Hill has yielded many thousands of dollars in ore since that time.

There are greasewood, catclaw, and an occasional cactus or desert acacia along the highway between Congress Junction and Wickenburg. The desert acacia has a single fluffy bloom with a penetrating scent; it grows profusely in the washes of the Hieroglyphic Mountains to the southeast.

WICKENBURG, 114.2 *m.* (2,076 alt., 734 pop.) (*see TOUR 3b*), is at the junction with US 60-70 (*see TOUR 3*). Between this point and Phoenix, 168.3 *m.,* US 89 and US 60-70 are one route (*see TOUR 3c*).

Phoenix is at the junction with US 80 (*see TOUR 3*). Between Phoenix and Florence Junction, a distance of 49.2 miles, US 89-80 and US 60-70 are one route (*see TOUR 3b*).

Section c. FLORENCE JUNCTION to TUCSON, 83.9 m. US 89-80.

South of Florence Junction desert plants of various types are found on both sides of the road. The beauty of this region is much enhanced in the spring, when most of the plants blossom. There are more than a thousand species of cacti known to botanists and a majority of these are native to Arizona. They range in size from diminutive types, the size of a button, to those reaching a height of forty feet.

In Arizona is a reptile rarely found elsewhere—the Gila (pronounced HEE-la) monster; its most common habitat is in the desert land along the Gila River (*see ANIMAL LIFE*). Far from being a monster in size, it is a fat sluggish reptile about fourteen to sixteen inches long with an orange and black coat of bead scales. Though the Gila monster can snap only at near-by prey, it does not run swiftly and cannot jump or strike; hence it is seldom dangerous. Unlike the rattlesnake, which ejects poison from upper hypodermic fangs, this reptile has two lower teeth that are grooved for the flow of poison.

South of FLORENCE JUNCTION, 0 *m.* (1,883 alt., 45 pop.), which is a trading point for ranchers, the highway crosses the GILA (Yuma, flowing water that is salt) RIVER, 14.7 *m.* Prior to the Gadsden Purchase (1853) this river was the boundary between Arizona and Mexico. Onate, the Spanish explorer, called it El Rio Del Nombre de Jesus.

At 14.6 *m.* is the junction with a gravel road.

Right on this road to POSTON'S BUTTE, 2 *m.,* formerly called Parsee Hill, a lonely conical butte covered with malapai and spotted with abandoned mine shafts. It is named for Charles D. Poston, who began his adventures in Arizona in 1853 by sailing from San Francisco for the Port of Guaymas, Sonora with Herman Ehrenberg, an engineer (*see TOUR 3d*). The United States was negotiating the Gadsden Purchase at the time and the two adventurers set out to explore this region for minerals. The voyage ended in shipwreck on an island in the Gulf of California, but within a week they managed to make the mainland. Three months later Poston with fifteen men set out to explore the Gulf of California, following the coast to the mouth of the Colorado. Disappointed in not finding a place suitable for a port or town, they crossed the Papago country, visited the old Ajo copper mines (*see TOUR 4B*), and near Tubac (*see below*) discovered rich silver ore. In 1856 backed by the Texas Pacific Railroad company and a million dollar capital, Poston organized an exploring and mining company, and established his headquarters in the old Spanish presidio at Tubac. But in the spring of 1861 at the beginning of the Civil War, the United States troops were ordered out of the territory, leaving the pioneers at the mercy of Cochise and his Apache bands. Terror spread as one massacre after another occurred, and all of the surviving settlers either fled to the fortified city of Tucson or left the country entirely. After his brother John had been killed, Poston and Raphael Pumpelly made an overland journey to Fort Yuma and thence to the Pacific coast. Soon after Poston sailed for the Atlantic coast and spent most of the year 1862 in Washington working for, and finally securing, territorial government for Arizona. In 1863 Poston assumed his duties as Superintendent of Indian Affairs for Arizona, an office especially created for him; the following year he was elected delegate to Congress in the first territorial election. After completing his term in Congress, he traveled extensively in Europe and Asia and returned to Florence in 1878. While in India he became a sun worshiper and upon his return built a road, costing several thousand dollars, to the top of this butte, which he called "Parsee Hill," and where he erected a pyre of continuous fire as a temple to the sun. After burning for several months the fire died and the project became Poston's Folly. Poston served as consular agent at Nogales, military agent at El Paso, agent of the department of agriculture in Phoenix, and for a number of years was employed by departments in Washington studying and promoting government irrigation on desert lands. In 1899 the legislature voted him a small pension for public services rendered Arizona during its infancy. It was his wish that he be buried on Parsee Hill, but when he died in Phoenix in 1902, he was interred in a Phoenix cemetery. In 1925 Poston's body was reinterred here and the grave marked with a large pyramidal rock monument.

FLORENCE, 16.1 m. (1,493 alt., 1,318 pop.), is the seat of Pinal County and one of the oldest white settlements in the state. Except for the pavement and the overlaid modern fronts of Main Street, Florence looks much as it did in 1880, when 902 was the population. Unlike Tucson, where many of the old houses have been raised, or Yuma, where they have been carried away by flood, Florence has almost all its early adobes, including its first house, still standing.

In its desert setting surrounded by multicolored mountains the town appears as a part of the earth from which most of its buildings have been constructed. Some of the structures along its quiet streets are crumbling with age, and many of the adobe walls have been eroded at the base by rain, wind, and sand. Sheltering isolated houses are a few tamarisks, a palm, a mesquite, an olive, or a weeping willow. An occasional windmill, rising above the house roof, stands beside a corral enclosing a cow or two, a horse, and a few scratching chickens.

According to one account Florence was named for Governor McCormick's sister but a Florence pioneer insists it was so named because Florentines in the service of the U. S. Army were reminded of Italy by the hills and shadows of this mountain-rimmed valley.

From the town are visible Poston Butte in the northwest directly across the Gila River; the palisades of Superstition Mountain on the northern horizon; and chains of grotesque points and buttes in the east. Backed by cloud banks these peaks resemble nineteenth century Biblical drawings illustrating a rendezvous of displeased deity with mortal man.

Levi Ruggles, the first white settler, came in 1866 and the town developed so quickly that within four years it had a population estimated at six hundred. Soon after its founding Florence became a trading center for mines in this vicinity and an important stage stop, rousing predictions of a brilliant future that include "Fair Florence, wreathed in Gila green, a city yet to be, I ween." And it did come very close to being selected as the territorial capital; but after the railroad had been built to Maricopa, Florence's growth was stopped and it remains, in many ways, a living relic of pioneer Arizona.

Although farming in the vicinity has been carried on since 1868, it was not until the completion in 1921 of the Ashurst-Hayden Diversion Dam on the Gila River twelve miles east that Florence was definitely classified as an agricultural center. When the Coolidge storage dam on the upper Gila (*see TOUR 3a*) was completed in 1928 it further guaranteed the valley's agricultural future. In addition to alfalfa, cotton, corn, citrus fruits, figs, olives, pears, and strawberries, the valley produces an especially fine-flavored honey.

The COLLINGWOOD HOUSE, on Main St., a large one-story mud-colored adobe, occupies the entire block between 5th and 6th Streets. The second door from the 5th St. corner leads to the former stage and express office of Wells Fargo. Much of the lumber for this and other old buildings nearby was shipped up the Gulf of California to Yuma and hauled overland by mule team. A bullet mark on the door of this building at 6th St. facing Main St. was made during the Gabriel-Phy battle of 1888 when Joe Phy emptied his gun into Sheriff Pete Gabriel who was drinking at a bar. Before he collapsed Gabriel shot Phy through the stomach, wounding him fatally. Although several of Phy's bullets entered the sheriff's body—one just below the heart—the sheriff survived. A newcomer to Florence was standing in this doorway at the time of the shooting. According to the story some wag had solemnly warned him, just a minute or two before, that he couldn't be "too careful about stray bullets in this town." He escaped unhurt.

The PINAL COUNTY HOSPITAL, NW. corner of Main and 5th St., a rambling gray plastered adobe with a peaked roof and surrounded on the north and east sides by an enclosed screen porch, was built in 1879 as the courthouse and used by county officers until 1887. Hidden behind the hospital is the small stuccoed adobe house where Pete Gabriel lived.

The foundations southwest of the hospital are the remains of the first hotel and saloon.

The HOME OF PAULINE CUSHMAN, who served briefly as a Union spy during the Civil War, is a short block south of this foundation on W. 6th St. It is a stuccoed adobe with large tamarisks in front. Pauline Cushman was sentenced to death by the Confederates but was saved when they abandoned her during a retreat. She was commended by President Lincoln for her services. For many years she made a living by lecturing on her exploits and a press agent advertised her as "Major" Cushman. In 1879 she became the wife of Jere Fryer, Pinal County sheriff. Later she moved to San Francisco, where she lived in great poverty and committed suicide in 1893.

The MASON APARTMENTS, south side of 5th St. (L), have adobe walls built in the late 1860's. This building housed the first store and post office, which carried on a trade with the surrounding forts in the Indian country, giving Florence its original business impetus.

The last structure at the west end of 5th St., a boxlike adobe (R), is the LEVI RUGGLES HOUSE built in 1866. In 1873 the first land office in the Gadsden Purchase territory, south of the Gila River, occupied this adobe; Ruggles was the first registrar.

The CHURCH OF THE ASSUMPTION, three blocks west of Main St. on 8th St., was built in 1911. The eastern wing of the old adobe east of the church was built in 1870 and, excluding the missions, was the first Roman Catholic church in central Arizona. The former plaza in front was a gathering place for the soldiers of General Nelson A. Miles in his last campaign against the Apache.

The old green-shuttered adobe (R) nearly hidden in the olive trees on Main St. was built in 1884 by William Clark, a mining man, and served as the RESIDENCE OF RICHARD E. SLOAN, last territorial governor. To the rear are several large mesquites, one of them completely covered by a rambling red rose that blooms in April. The olive trees, planted in 1882, are unusually fine specimens.

Left from Florence on a paved road to the ARIZONA STATE PRISON (*open to visitors*), 1.2 *m.*, a walled-in-group of dun-colored buildings. The administration building, outside the prison walls, dominates the approach. Two steel gates guard the prison yard and a second pair of gates lead through the walls. Within the enclosure the long narrow buildings of the prison proper radiate from the powerhouse like the spokes of a wheel. The women's quarters, to the rear of the administration building, are separated from the rest of the penitentiary by a heavy wire enclosure. Inmates are housed in eight small rooms instead of the customary steel cells. The unit includes a bathroom, laundry, kitchen, dining room and an exhibit room for articles made by women prisoners. The male population is confined in three cell houses, heated in winter and air-cooled in summer. In Cell House No. 1 is the death chamber formerly used for hanging. Adjoining it is a row of cells for the condemned and a display of photographs of the men executed by the state since 1910 with the criminal record of each. Since Arizona instituted the use of lethal gas in 1929, a gas chamber has been constructed. In other buildings are the dining room and kitchen, laundry, combined ice plant and cannery, flour mill, recreation hall and library, tailor shop, barber shop, mattress factory, storage rooms, prison school, and hospital. Dungeons of dark cells, set off by themselves have a capacity of eighteen prisoners and are used for recalcitrants.

The prison farm has eight hundred acres irrigated by the San Carlos water system and is entirely cared for by prisoners. It furnishes occupation and quarters for about one-sixth of the inmates. Fruit, poultry, livestock, wheat, barley, cotton, dairy products, and vegetables are grown for prison use and sent to other state institutions. The prison is under the control of the State Board of Institutions, which consists of the governor, the state treasurer, and an appointed executive secretary.

Administration is handicapped by inadequate housing, insufficient work for the prisoners, and lack of facilities for separating youthful and first offenders from habitual criminals; however, officials strive for a well-regulated schedule of work, training, and recreation. Inmates operate the prison industries and, whenever feasible, trusties are placed in supervisory positions. A prison school gives instruction in secondary school subjects, and courses in various trades. A library, recreation hall equipped with a stage and scenery, and a baseball field for outdoor sports provide diversion. The only disciplinary measures used are withdrawal of privileges, and solitary confinement. The first prison in Arizona was the Territorial Prison at Yuma built in 1876 (*see Yuma*). Acting on the recommendations of Governor Joseph H. Kibbey, the legislature in 1907 authorized the removal of the prison to Florence and the construction of a modern plant.

The new prison, built almost entirely by convict labor, was completed in 1909 and maintains its own electric-light plant, water works, sewage system, laundry, hospital, cold storage and ice plant. Since 1918 a strict regime has followed the former policy of laxity in prison discipline. For many years the State Board of Pardons and Paroles was under fire for alleged looseness in granting paroles. The criticism reached a climax when 443 pardons were said to have been issued during an eighteen-month period.

South of Florence is an area that contains almost every species of Arizona's desert plant life. The most spectacular of the group is the giant saguaro (pronounced sa-WAH-ro), a member of the cereus family; its bloom is the state flower of Arizona (*see TOUR 4b*).

Storied association has given a glamour to the night-blooming cactus, also called *La Reina de la Noche* (Sp., *queen of the night*). The plant usually is only two feet tall, has slender stems that look much like crooked sticks, and grows under other shrubbery so that it is difficult to find. Its large white flowers have a spicy fragrance and open but once a year—from sunset till early morning—usually in the latter part of June.

The cholla (pronounced CHO-yah) is conspicuous because of its stout trunk and short branches covered so thickly with glistening white or yellow spines that they appear fuzzy. The loosely attached joints readily fasten themselves to passing objects, hence its nickname, jumping cactus.

Prickly pear, another cactus common to this section, has flat paddle-like joints, many needles, a yellow flower, and a purple pear-shaped fruit that is eaten not only by man but by coyotes, foxes, and other desert wild life.

The barrel cactus resembles a young saguaro but is wider at the base, a darker green in color, has deeper ridges, and longer and more elaborate spines. The latter, which grow in evenly spaced rosettes, are brilliantly colored with red and purple and have hooks on their clear amber tips. The roots of this desert water tank descend only a few inches below the surface but often extend more than ten feet away from the plant and after every rain absorb an amazing amount of moisture, which causes the cactus to expand and its ridges to flatten. As the sun evaporates the water, the plant contracts and the flutings are pulled together. They are so much deeper and closer on the southwestern side, which receives the most intense heat, that they cause the whole plant to lean toward the southwest and thus become a dependable compass. The barrel cactus furnishes a refreshing drink to anyone venturing to cut off the top and loosen and squeeze the pulp within. The Indians make an exceedingly intoxicating liquor from this juice, prepare a candy from the pulp, and consider its sugary dried fruit a delicacy. Pioneers reported that the Indians cooked their food in this plant by removing the pulp and dropping hot stones into the juice that remained in the cavity. In the blooming season (*July-Sept.*) the barrel cactus wears a wreath of funnel-shaped yellow flowers whose many petals are delicately curled and fluted.

At 57.3 *m.* is the junction with State 77.

Left on State 77 to ORACLE, 12 *m.* (4,154 alt., 500 pop.), a health resort area, mining and ranching community. There are a number of guest ranches in the surrounding hills, which are covered with oak, yucca, mesquite, cholla, prickly pear, and desert grass.

Right from Oracle to SAN MANUEL, 9 *m.* (4,500 alt., 7,000 pop.) the new copper mining camp. The mine will tap what experts say is one of the largest known bodies of low-grade copper ore in the U.S. This $111 million development of mine, mill, and smelter, is under construction by the San Manuel Copper Corporation, wholly-owned subsidiary of the Magma Copper Company of Superior, and is eight miles from the corporation's mine in the Tiger-Mammoth district. A complete modern town of 2,000 homes, parks, theater, shopping centers, schools, churches, bank, etc., has literally sprung up overnight from a cactus-studded desert to a model community.

State 77 passes through country of giant cactus, cholla forests, and pastel-tinted hills to MAMMOTH, 24 *m.* (2,399 alt., 500 pop.), named for an early mine in this rich mining district. The one-street town extends half a mile along a road bordered by sloping hills that descend on the north to the San Pedro River and then rise, topping mesas and buttes, to the high Galiuro Mountains. Many of Mammoth's homes and stores, some of which have fallen into ruin, are built entirely of adobe. In the early 1880's it was one of the busiest and most lusty mining camps in the county.

The SANTA CATALINA MOUNTAINS (L) are in the CORONADO NATIONAL FOREST. Mount Lemmon (9,180 alt.) is the highest peak in the range.

The low rolling country at 72.7 *m.* is covered with chollas and greasewood. Occasionally there is a white adobe sanatorium half-hidden against a hillside. As the highway rounds the western side of the Catalinas, the Santa Rita Mountains loom far to the south. The Santa Ritas have been mined extensively and still yield large amounts of gold.

Among the several highly romantic tales of lost Arizona mines is the often credited tale of the Escalante—the Mine with the Iron Door —believed to be somewhere in the Santa Catalina Mountains south of Oracle. The usual story is that it was discovered by Indians hunting deer in the Santa Catalinas in 1698, and that Father Escalante (a Jesuit assistant to Father Kino at the Mission San Xavier del Bac) was the first to work it. He employed Indians to pack the gold to the foot of the mountain. There it was ground into *arrastras* and smelted into gold bars, which were hidden in a secret strong room dug in the mountainside and closed with an iron door. The vein of gold grew richer as the tunnel penetrated farther into the mountain. Apaches are said to have attacked and completely obliterated the little colony of

Indian miners and their families. Then, since the Apaches cared nothing for gold, the place was deserted and no trace of the shaft or iron door could be discovered until recently, when it was reported that bits of wood had been found. However the only living person who has received any treasure from the Mine With the Iron Door is Harold Bell Wright, who used that name for the title of one of his books.

Rillito (pronounced ree-YEE-toh) Creek is at 77.9 *m.* Rillito is a Spanish word meaning *little river.*

At 79.4 *m.* is the junction with State 84 (*see TOUR 4c*) and with the Fort Lowell Road.

Left on the Fort Lowell Road to the RUINS OF FORT LOWELL, 4 *m.*, one of the key outposts in the long and deadly war carried on by settlers against the Apache. The city of Tucson has acquired a part of the former military preserve and intends (1939) to create a park here. At least one of the old adobe buildings, now in an advanced state of decay, will be restored.

A military camp was established in the southeast section of Tucson (in the vicinity of Armory Park) by an advance column of California Volunteers who marched into Arizona in 1862 in pursuit of the Confederate Captain Hunter and his Texas Rifles. After the Civil War the camp, which had been named Lowell in 1866, became a supply depot for military posts in southern Arizona and the scene of much of Tucson's social life.

In 1873 Camp Lowell was moved here and these adobes were built. A country site was selected with the intention of separating the military personnel from the temptation of Tucson's many and entertaining diversions. The drives were once tree-lined and the large-roomed, high-ceiled adobes had wide porches and were covered with vines. Visitors were extravagantly entertained. The fort was abandoned in 1891 soon after the Apache warfare had ended. The adobes are now halfweathered away, all trace of the trees has vanished, and greasewood and other desert verdure have grown over the ruins, some even on the floors of the rooms. The view from the site is especially pleasing, with the high Santa Catalinas to the north beyond Rillito Creek and the Rincons to the east.

The city owns only the eastern part of the fort grounds. About 200 yards west of the new adobe wall, on Fort Lowell Road, is the Post Trader's Building (L), with large palo verde, mesquite, and mulberry trees in front. In the days of fort occupation it was a saloon and recreation center but is now a private dwelling.

Immediately east of the Post Trader's Building is the adobe ruin of the commissary. Across the road is the stone and adobe ruin of the guard house where captured Apaches were imprisoned.

The entrance to the city park is in the middle of the new adobe wall, which encloses several ruins. The large adobe with fragile arches still holding up against rain and wind was the Post Hospital. Remains of two barracks for infantry are north of the hospital and immediately west of the second infantry barracks are the ruins of the cavalry barracks. The row of adobes running from east to west south of the hospital were officers' quarters. They are little more than outlines at present, with the exception of the one farthest west which was the Commanding Officer's Quarters.

At approximately 80.4 *m.* is the junction with an unmarked dirt road.

Right on this road to the Yaqui village of PASCUA, 0.5 *m.*, a hamlet of sixty-five Indian huts constructed of mud-chinked cactus sticks, rusty sheet iron, and other materials salvaged from junk heaps.

Pascua, the largest Yaqui village in Arizona, is not on a reservation and the Yaqui are not wards of the United States. Two thousand are estimated to have migrated to this country in the last thirty years, exiles from their ancestral home near the Yaqui River, four hundred miles south of Nogales. Because they have been the most warlike and incorrigible of the Indians south of the border the Mexican Government has practically outlawed the tribe. Only eight villages remain in Mexico, all effectively hidden in the mountains.

Yaqui arts are extremely primitive although ornaments for religious rites are made with considerable skill. These are considered sacred and money cannot buy them.

The Roman Catholic ritual pleased the Yaqui and they appropriated its form but retained many tribal details. Yaqui ceremonials are largely concentrated in the period of Lent and come to a climax on Good Friday. All attending flaunt highly colored and fantastic costumes, some wear grotesque masks and wide belts of animal claws or bells. The triumph of life over death seems to be the theme of the ceremonials.

There are two churches in the village, the Yaqui church and the recognized Catholic church. The native church is headed by a *maestro,* who reads both Spanish and Latin and who conducts the complicated and lengthy pseudo-Catholic services. The building is constructed of oddly assembled pieces of scrap sheet iron nailed over a wooden frame.

TUCSON, 83.9 *m.* (2,374 alt., 70,000 pop., 1955) (*see Tucson*).

Points of Interest: University of Arizona, Courthouse, Father Kino Monument, Wishing Shrine, and others.

Tucson is at junction of US 80 (*see TOUR 4b*) and State 86 the AJO ROAD (*see TOUR 4B*).

Section d.   TUCSON to NOGALES; 65 m.   US 89-80, US 89.

The region between Tucson and Nogales was crossed and recrossed by the trails of the early Spaniards who introduced cattle as well as horses to the New World. Here in southern Arizona the United States cattle industry had its beginning from the descendants of the Spaniards' cattle, a wild breed called Mexican blackhorns. Later English-speaking settlers rounded them up, branded, and sold them just as they did wild range horses. In 1883 fifty thousand Texas longhorns were driven in. An old Spanish-American cattleman, Senor Benarbe Robles, thus compared the two breeds: "They [the blackhorns] were a shiny black creeter weeth horns like fine polished ebon—very slim and very very sharp points were these horns. And very ferocious were these bull with theese so beautiful horn. Theese horn measure from 2 feet to maybe—so three feet long, but—*Santa Maria!* Wheen we see these horn on theese Texas longhorn, *Holy Madre!* We think theese blackhorn no have any horn at all."

Most of the ranches were soon stocked with this new cattle, distinguished by their horns that often had a six-foot spread. Although they were ill-adapted to timbered country they were superior beef and the blackhorns soon disappeared. In the late eighties a ranch in the Tonto Basin was stocked with a shipment of white-faced Herefords with blunt horns only five or six inches long. This new breed, one of the finest for beef in America, soon displaced the longhorns.

US 89, ascending the Santa Cruz Valley, follows the locally famous route of the pioneer Pete Kitchen—"Tucson, Tubac, Tumacacori, and Tohell"; the last destination being that threatened by frequent Apache raids.

South of Tucson at 2.5 *m.* is the junction with US 80 (*see TOUR 4*); L. is a VETERAN'S ADMINISTRATION HOSPITAL, a group of Mexican colonial buildings with red tile roofs.

At 3.2 *m.* is the junction with State 86, Indian School Rd.

Right on this road through a farm to the INDIAN TRAINING SCHOOL of the Presbyterian Church, 0.8 *m.*, established in 1888. Instruction is given from 7th through 12th grades in household arts for girls and in manual arts and agriculture for boys. The present enrollment of one hundred includes Pimas, Papagos, Maricopas, Mojaves, Yaquis, Apaches, and Monos. The plant consists of an administration building, dormitories, practice cottage, teachers' home, laundry, employees' cottages, shops, and farm buildings. In the home maintained by this school in Tucson for its graduates who are attending high school or the state university are housed some girl students.

In the PIMA COUNTY FAIRGROUNDS (L), 6.1 *m.*, a fair is held annually. The SAN XAVIER INDIAN RESERVATION (R), set aside in 1874 for the Papago (*see TOUR 4B*), now contains more than seventy thousand acres. A few rustic dwellings are near the highway or hidden in a far off mesquite thicket. The two thousand acres of fertile farmland are irrigated partly by primitive methods and partly by a modern system being developed by the Indian Irrigation Service. All farming is directed from the Sells Agency, west of Tucson (*see TOUR 4B*).

At 6.7 *m.* is the junction with a dirt road.

Right here 2.3 *m.* to MISSION SAN XAVIER DEL BAC (*see Tucson*).

The main highway now passes through a typical mesquite thicket. From the fragrant creamy flowers, which bloom from April to June, the bees make a delicious honey. The pods mature in September and October and are pounded into meal by Indians and Mexicans. Many animals also seek these pods. Mesquite wood is used for fuel and fence posts.

SAHUARITA (Sp., little saguaro), 17.9 *m.* (2,540 alt., 200 pop.), was an early stagecoach station. The name is pronounced sah-wah-REE-tah. The country is now irrigated for farming, but was once thick with saguaros. Cotton is the principal crop in this area. Eagle Picher Mining and Smelting Company mine is seen on R.

CONTINENTAL (Left *1 m.*), 26 *m.*, by-passed by the highway, is a cotton farm. Some water stands erected by the Continental Rubber Company in 1914, to experiment in producing rubber from guayule are still standing.

Here the highway crosses the Santa Cruz (Sp., Holy Cross) River which rises in the Sierra Marquilla of Mexico and flows north to its confluence with the Pantano River near Tucson.

At 36.5 *m.* is the junction with a dirt road.

Right on this road is ARIVACA, 22 m. (3,640 alt., 100 pop.), established by early Spanish missionaries and now the center of a stock-raising and mining section. The Ora Blanca mountains are south of the community.

East of AMADO, 39.3 m. (2,885 alt., 50 pop.), a trading center of an agricultural, stock-raising, and mining district, is Mount Hopkins (8,072 alt.). The town was named for a wealthy Mexican settler.

SARDINA PEAK is visible (R) from 41 m. and at 45.6 m. is (L) OLD BALDY (9,432 alt.), sometimes called Mount Wrightson. Baldy is the highest peak in Santa Cruz County.

At 45.2 m. is the junction with a dirt road.

Left on this road to TUBAC (Pima, burned place), 0.5 m. (3,600 alt., 515 pop.), a cluster of mud-colored adobe houses and stores built around a white-plastered adobe Roman Catholic church. Guarded on the west by the Diablito Mountains and on the east by the Santa Ritas, Tubac drowses over its past and ignores the promotion and commotion of the twentieth century. This quiet, off-the-road, farming, stock-raising, and mining community in 1776 was the assembly point of Anzas' colonizing party before his epochal journey to San Francisco. The oldest town founded by white men in the state, it was garrisoned by the Spanish in 1752 and became the first Mormon settlement in Arizona just a hundred years later. With Hermann Ehrenberg, a mining engineer, Charles D. Poston spent the winter of 1854 prospecting in the hills above Tubac. In 1856 he led an expedition sent out by the Sonora Exploring and Mining Company which developed the Heintzelman mine, thirty miles from Tubac.

In 1858 Tubac was described as having a population of eight hundred—five-sixth being Mexican—and having peach orchards and pomegranates. *Boletas,* paper money issued in Tubac and redeemable in silver, were the medium of exchange. As few of the Mexicans could read, *boletas* had pictures on them denoting their respective denominations. That bearing a pig was worth a bit, a calf, two-bits or twenty-five cents; a rooster, half a dollar; a horse, a dollar; and a bull, five dollars.

When the *Weekly Arizonian,* first newspaper published in the territory, was started here in 1859 Tubac was the area's most important settlement. But by 1861 it was virtually abandoned owing to continual bandit and Apache raids; when Poston returned in 1864, after an absence of eight years, he found the place in an advanced state of decay.

TUMACACORI (tu-mah-CAH-coh-ry) NATIONAL MONU-MENT (L), 48.4 m., under the jurisdiction of the National Park Service, was created in 1908 to protect the RUINS OF TUMACACORI (Pima, caliche rock) MISSION. At the entrance to the monument is a museum designed to conform to the Spanish style of the Sonora-Arizona missions. Within the museum are a lobby (*information*); a series of rooms containing exhibits pertaining to the early life of the mission and models showing its early appearance and the activities of its inhabitants; a room with a statue of Father Kino and a view room with a model of the mission establishment as it was about 1800.

The church, more than fifty feet wide and a hundred feet long, was built of sundried adobe bricks and burned bricks laid in clay mortar; the walls are five to six feet thick at the base and nearly 10 feet thick under the tower. The massive two-story corner tower is topped with an arcaded belfry. The first story was used as a baptistry, the second probably as a robing room for the choir. The outside walls are finished with plaster made with lime produced by burning the local limestone. Black and red brick fragments were imbedded in the plaster on the outside walls.

The principal facade with its false gable end is boldly accented by a classic molding that outlines the corners of the wall and by the graceful curve of the arched gable. The deeply recessed entrance portal is framed in the traditional Spanish Renaissance manner by a superimposed ordinance of coupled columns, and is topped with a restored pediment. Between the columns at each level are semi-circular niches, which formerly contained the figures of saints.

It is believed this mission—built by Franciscans—is near the site of a mission or *visitas* founded by Father Kino in 1696; in 1701 a priest was in charge of the Sobaipuris Indian village at Guevavi. In his diary Kino speaks of three missions—Guevavi, Tumacacori, and San Luys—part of the chain he planned from Sonora to California: "In all places buildings were constructed and very good beginnings were made in spiritual and temporal matters." The present building probably was dedicated in 1822 but was abandoned a few years later when the Franciscans were expelled from their churches shortly after Mexico had won her independence from Spain. A small chapel, it is said, existed here until 1730, which is believed to have been replaced by a later one which apparently was damaged by an Apache raid.

In 1860 Professor W. Wrightson gave the following report on Tumacacori Mission to the mining company by which he was employed and it is in all probability the best description of the mission as it was at that time, which has come down in official record: "The church is an adobe building, plastered with cement and coped with burnt brick. The front is of the Moorish style and had on the southwest corner a tower, the top of which was of burnt brick. The roof of the church was flat and covered with cement and tiles. (The timbers have now fallen and decayed.) The chancel was surrounded with a dome which is still well preserved. Adjacent to the church in the form of a hollow square were the priests' residences containing spacious and airy rooms with every evidence of comfort and refinement, while surrounding those in the interior was an arched colonnade, forming a shady walk around the whole enclosure. Here are still the remains of furnaces and quantities of slag, attesting the purpose for which this was formerly used; and further still to the west was the five-acre garden surrounded by a wall. Fruit trees and vines are still growing; while in the rear of the church is the Campus Sancti, a burial ground surrounded by a strong adobe wall, well covered with cement and even now the best inclosure in Arizona. On the south and front of the mission building, there was a large plaza which was surrounded by peon houses, thus forming a respectable village."

The mission garden, once had an elaborate irrigation system to water its orchards and vineyards. The museum patio has been planted in a manner resembling a Spanish garden of the early 1800's. In the cemetery inclosure is a mortuary chapel.

At 56.3 *m.* is a junction with an unimproved dirt road.

Left on this road to a sign at about 3.7 *m.* indicating the RUINS OF GUEVAVI (gweh-VAH-vy) MISSION across the river (*difficult to find without a guide*). Once a splendid example of Spanish colonial architecture, it is now crumbling walls and trash-filled yards that have been ransacked by pot hunters. Guevavi, founded in 1692 by Father Kino, was the first church erected by Europeans in what is now southern Arizona.

South of the Tumacacori National Monument the Patagonia Mountains appear on the horizon (L). The high mountain (R) is Dick's Peak.

At 56.4 *m.* is the junction with a a dirt road.

Left on this road to CALABASAS, 2 *m.,* one of Arizona's numerous ghost towns. In the early eighteenth century it was a Papago village visited by Jesuit missionaries. As early as 1777 mines in the vicinity were worked by the Spaniards. For a period it was a Mexican military post, then headquarters of a large rancho. In 1856 the United States Dragoons (cavalry) occupied it as a military base, and in 1865 an American settlement was established and named by the Calabasas Land and Mining Company. In 1882 a turbulent boom town, it is now marked by a few scattered ruins.

A cottonwood grove (L) lines an old river bottom south of Calabasas.

On a rocky hill (R) is the old adobe PETE KITCHEN RANCH HOUSE, 58.5 *m.* The roof is surrounded by a parapet three or four feet high on which a lookout was stationed in the days of the Apache wars. Although the Indians killed or drove away all his neighbors, they never succeeded in ousting Pete Kitchen. A contemporary account describes his defense: "There is a sentinel posted on the roof, there is another out in the cienega with the stock, and the men ploughing in the bottoms are obliged to carry rifles, cocked and loaded, swung to the plough handle. Every man and boy, and indeed, the women too, go armed. There are revolvers and rifles and shotguns along the walls and in every corner. Everything speaks of a land of warfare and bloodshed."

Pete Kitchen came to Arizona in 1854. Frank C. Lockwood in *Arizona Characters* says that he was a rough charcoal sketch of a civilized man, the connecting link between savagery and civilization. He "farmed the rich, broad acres on Potrero Creek near its junction with the Santa Cruz. During the bloodiest days of Indian warfare his name was a household word among the white settlers, and to the wild Apache he was 'more terrible than an army with banners.' His hacienda, on the summit of a rocky hill overlooking the valleys in every direction, was as much a fort as a ranch-house. On their raids through the valleys the Apaches passed it both coming and going. Kitchen was almost the last settler to hang on after the withdrawal of troops in 1861. His ranch was the safest point between Tucson and Magdalena,

Sonora and during the darkest days of Apache warfare miners, settlers, and travelers made it a sort of rallying point. Thomas Casanega, who lived on a near-by ranch in the early days and who married a niece of Pete Kitchen's, told me that there were more men killed between Potrero and Magdalena than in all the rest of the Apache territory. He said that so many men lost their lives between these two points that if their bodies were laid side by side like railroad ties, they would make a track from Nogales to Potrero. . . .

"Pete Kitchen was the only settler whom the Apaches could not dislodge. They made raid after raid, and shot his pigs so full of arrows that they looked like 'walking pin cushions.' They killed or drove out his bravest neighbors; they killed his herder; and they slaughtered his stepson; but Pete Kitchen fought on undaunted. His name struck terror to every Apache heart; and at last, finding that he was too tough a nut to crack, they passed him by."

In front of his ranch house is KITCHEN'S BOOT-HILL CEMETERY, where the outlaws and desperadoes whom he killed were buried. Dona Rosa, his wife, was a good Catholic and she faithfully burned candles on the graves of her husband's fallen adversaries.

NOGALES (Sp., walnuts), 65.5 *m.* (3,869 alt., 6,500 pop.) (*see Nogales*).

Points of Interest. Santa Cruz County Courthouse, Immigration Inspection Station, and others.

In Nogales is the junction with State 82 (*see TOUR 4A*).

NOGALES, SONORA, MEXICO, 66.8 *m.* (3,869 alt., 25,000 pop.) (*see Nogales, also General Information for Tours*).

Points of Interest. The Cavern, Twenty-eighth of August Monument, Municipal Market, and others.

Tour 1A

Prescott—Humboldt—Mayer—Cordes—Rock Springs—Phoenix Junction; 94 *m.,* State 69 (Black Canyon Highway).

New paved highway with few curves and no steep grades. Limited accommodations; garages in most points. Santa Fe branch line roughly parallels route between Prescott and Cordes.

This route through the Bradshaw Mountains runs beside pine, oak and cedar forests, grass-covered hills, and cool bubbling springs. These mountains are rich in gold, copper, silver, lead, and many other minerals. Only after summer rains are there streams in the deep narrow canyons and washes. Between Phoenix and the confluence of the Agua Fria and New Rivers, State 69 traverses the desert-floor and the arable Salt River Valley.

The story of this country includes prehistoric inhabitants, mine discoveries, Indian wars, outlawry, and the expeditions of pioneers. First known as the Woolsey Trail, for King S. Woolsey (*see below*), this road, used by an early stage-coach line, provided the only access to northern Arizona. The huge Concord stage that rolled daily out of Prescott at about six in the morning arrived in Phoenix the following day at noon.

State 69 branches east from US 89, 0 *m.,* on the northern outskirts of Prescott (*see TOUR 1b*).

At 3.2 *m.* is the junction with a dirt road.

Right on this road to WALKER, 7 *m.* (6,300 alt., 39 pop.), a noted mining town on Lynx Creek, which was Arizona's richest placer gold-mining stream during the early days. The town's name honors Captain Joseph R. Walker who in 1853 had led a trapping and exploring expedition sent by Captain Bonneville from Great Salt Lake to California. Walker was prospecting in what is now Yavapai County, Arizona, in 1861 and made an important gold discovery, but he had already returned to California before the rocks and washings his men had taken with them were proven to contain gold. After joining Kit Carson in New Mexico in an Indian campaign, Walker returned to Yavapai County with thirty-five men to continue prospecting. In May 1863 a member of the party named Miller washed a pan of sand from Lynx Creek and obtained more than four dollars' worth of gold. News of the rich sand was sent to Walker who moved the main camp from the Hassayampa River to Lynx Creek, organized his party into a company, staked and filed claims, and began actual mining. In addition to the placer workings pieces of pure metal worth hundreds of dollars were found in the bedrock; only butcher knives were needed to dig "pay" from rock seams; and gold worth $5,000 was found under a single boulder.

Almost as soon as this discovery was known the gulches and ravines paralleling the Woolsey Trail were crowded with adventurers; camps grew, mills flourished, and claims were hastily staked throughout the area. Menacing excitement was added by the Apache who effectively fought white settlements here until they were subdued by General Crook.

Southwest of Walker is Mount Union (7,974 alt.).

East of the Walker Road junction the country changes from short gullies and winding roads to long valleys.

From a point at 9 *m.* the Mingus Mountains (7,720 alt.) form a background to a long sweep of typical cattle range.

DEWEY, 13 *m.* (4,500 alt., 26 pop.), named for a pioneer settler, is a former mining town that has become the trading center of a farming and stock-raising district.

At 14.5 *m.* is the junction with a dirt road.

Left on this road 0.5 *m.* to the site of KING WOOLSEY'S YAVAPAI COUNTY RANCH, a midway station on the road between Prescott and the Upper Verde River. King S. Woolsey (1832-79) arrived in Yuma in 1860 with a horse, a rifle, a pistol, and five dollars. In the next few years he made a fortune in cattle ranching, mining, and flour milling. He was appointed a lieutenant colonel of the territorial military and was five times elected a member of Arizona's upper house, but he is best known for his prowess as an Indian fighter. He was familiar with the ways of the red man and more than a match for him in courage, strength, cunning, and ruthlessness. He took a conspicuous part in the Harquahala Springs encounter in 1869 and led the settlers against the Tonto Apache at Bloody Tanks (*see TOUR 3a*). He chose this site for his ranch in 1863 when, as a member of the Walker party (*see above*), he was prospecting around Prescott. At that time the Apache were causing considerable trouble in this section. Woolsey fortified his house and corrals and was successful not only in repelling several Indian raids here but also in his expeditions to punish marauders who had stolen horses or cattle.

Later the Woolsey property was purchased by the Bowers brothers, northern Arizona cattlemen. In June 1871 after 137 cattle had been stolen from the ranch, John Townsend, noted scout, organized an expedition to recover the stock. Twelve civilians from Prescott, all good riflemen, and a small detachment of soldiers from Fort Verde under Townsend's command killed fifty-six Apaches in a gorge where they were feasting on horse flesh, and returned most of the cattle without suffering any casualties themselves.

Townsend was a relentless foe of Indians, especially the Apache. It is said that in his youth in Texas, members of his family had been killed and scalped in an Indian raid. He made most of his reprisals while traveling alone at night, aided by his uncanny ability to follow Indians. Before being ambushed and killed, not far from the Woolsey Trail, he had taken fifty scalps. The Indians respected Townsend and as a tribute to his bravery left his body unmutilated and covered with a fine blanket held down at the corners with heavy stones.

HUMBOLDT, 15 *m.* (4,600 alt., 175 pop.), named for the German scientist and explorer Baron Alexander von Humboldt (1769-1859), was a boom town smelting gold and silver from surrounding mines in 1928. But placer mining declined, the smelter closed, and the machinery was sold, leaving the town only half alive.

In the large goat ranges, 20.4 *m.,* the goats often stand on their hind legs to reach leaves on the brush, which they nibble from the ground upward. The enclosures (L) are shipping pens.

MAYER, 24 *m.* (4,371 alt., 400 pop.), is named for Joe Mayer who established a store and saloon in the town. From a stage station it became a trading center for a sheep, cattle, and mining area. COPPER MOUNTAIN is directly east. On the southern outskirts of town are many prospect holes and an abandoned smelter in the hills (L).

Right from Mayer on an unimproved road to BLUEBELL, 4.1 *m.* (4,620 alt., 10 pop.) in the foothills of the Bradshaw Mountains. In this settlement, now almost abandoned, was the Blue Bell Mine, one of the most important copper mines in Yavapai County. It was the property of the Southwest Metals Corporation which also owned the Humboldt Smelter to which the ore was shipped for treatment. An aerial tram transported the ore from the mine to Blue Bell Siding, a distance of several miles. At this siding, a short distance south of Mayer, the big buckets dumped the ore into a great ore house from which it was loaded, through gravity chutes, into freight cars and shipped to the Humboldt Smelter.

This district received considerable attention in 1884 when Billy Gavin, a prospector, discovered deposits of almost pure silver by tracing dark metallic pieces of float to their source. Although he had no fortune at the time he refused $150,000 for the property, which was known as the Pine Spring and became one of the steadily worked mines of territorial days.

The stacks of copper ore, 29.5 *m.*, have been abandoned since boom days.

CORDES, 33 *m.* (3,773 alt., 15 pop.), is named for Hank Cordes, an early settler.

Left from Cordes on the graded dirt Bloody Basin Road to the Horseshoe Ranch, and a second graded dirt road, 8 *m.;* R. on this to the Brooklyn Mine Road, 14.1 *m.;* L. to another dirt road, 16.4 *m.;* L. on this road to 17 *m.* R. 0.5 *m.* on foot over malapai rock to the BABY CANYON INDIAN RUINS, on the south bank of the Agua Fria River in Baby Canyon. The major site containing approximately 100 rooms is below the escarpment of the canyon rim and overlooks eight lesser sites consisting of 12 to 40 rooms. This ancient city is crumbling to dust, and aside from the bands of sheep and herds of wild burros that roam Perry Mesa, the prevailing silence is broken only by the chirp of a bird, or the screech of a hawk. Archeologists believe that these ruins were occupied for a short time during the late Pueblo III and the early Pueblo IV periods. While the majority of rooms were of one story, partial excavation has disclosed evidences of a number of two-story buildings.

The pottery types found are Gila redware, black-on-white sherds, Gila polychrome, and a yellow ware with black or brown decorations. Pictographs in this region are similar to those occurring in the Hohokam Culture.

Bordering the ruins, numerous terraced gardens were arranged so that their patches of corn, beans, and squash could be irrigated. Many awls were found in one of the rooms and the debris indicated that these people hunted game.

From the top of the cliff forming the left side of BLACK CANYON, 37.8 *m.,* is a sweeping panorama of colors and intricate rock formations. The Bradshaw Mountains are south.

Black Canyon Hill, scene of many holdups, was a dangerous one-way grade where drivers awaited each other at turnouts.

Stage drivers carried long tin horns like those used in fogs on New England fishing smacks. A long blast sounded an approach, two blasts an acknowledgment. At night the candle-power head-lighting systems cast only dim beams from the coaches. When thunder or other noises drowned the sound of the horns so that two stages met at impassable places, the "up" team was unhitched, two men grasped the tongue of the vehicle and rolled it down hill until reaching a place where it could be passed.

It was on this hill, two miles from Gillette station, early in 1880, that I. E. Solomon, a merchant of Solomonsville, Captain Gordon of the U. S. Cavalry, and a doctor were ordered from their conveyance by two masked men who robbed them of $300 and two gold watches. About this time was heard the approach of a stage. The highwaymen ordered Solomon's party to stand by, commanded all passengers to leave the coach, and relieved them of their valuables. Later, at Solomon's request, the bandits returned two watches and a few dollars to allow the victims to reach Phoenix and buy drinks and breakfast.

South of this point the road is exceedingly narrow and winding (*drive slowly*), following much the same route as the old stagecoach line. The shallow streams are forded as they have no bridges.

At 39.6 *m.* is the junction with a graded dirt road.

Right on this road through the Bradshaw Mountains to an improved dirt road beside the CROWN KING MINE (R), 19.8 m., which has yielded fortunes in gold. In 1876 an army officer stationed at Fort Whipple hired a prospector to do assessment work (required by law to keep valid a mining claim on the public domain) on his claim here. The prospector met jovial friends at old Tiger camp and deputized two bullwhackers to do the work, leaving them at the claim with drills and other tools. The bullwhackers were husky and made dirt fly as long as it was only dirt. Then came harder ground which needed "shooting." One bullwhacker remarked to the other, "Guess you'll have to drill a hole or two." The reply was "Hell, I thought you could drill. I couldn't even load a hole." Finally concluding that for assessment purposes two holes were better than one, they found a place free from brush which looked easy to dig and started the second open cut. A vein about four inches wide opened up something that looked like ore. After working a couple of days they visited a near-by camp; when asked whether they had struck anything, one replied, "Naw, nothing but a streak o' this here sort o' brass or iron 'pirates,' or whatever you call it," and he tossed a piece to the nearest man. "Iron pyrites—hell. Why, man, it's gold—all gold!" This fabulously rich strike was the first made in the Crown King section, but not the last. Bradshaw City grew just under Mount Wasson in the highest point of the mountains amid pine, quaking aspen, fir, and spruce. Once a rollicking camp of 5,000 people it is now almost depopulated.

Left from the junction at Crown King Mine to HORSE THIEF BASIN, 25.9 m. (6,000 alt., 15 pop.), leased in 1936 from the Forest Service by the city of Phoenix for a resort area. The city constructed a dam on the site to provide pure mountain water, built a dance pavilion and a number of cabins and larger houses, provided recreation sites, and equipment for children's play, and installed a sewer system. The region is delightfully cool in summer and there is excellent fishing and game in season.

The first white man to build a cabin in the basin was a rustler called Horse Thief Davis; in those days the Horse Thief Trail from Utah to Mexico ran near here and stolen horses were held on Horse Mesa Ranch just east of Lane Mountain and south of the basin. Davis was later joined by Horse Thief Thompson, with whom he shared his cabin till the rapid development of the country destroyed their isolation and forced them both to leave. Before Horse Thief Cabin, in which the thieves had lived, was removed in 1938, a persistent rumor of a cache beneath its floor had lured many treasure seekers to diligent but vain excavating. The corrals in which the stolen horses were kept still stands.

About a mile north of Bumble Bee the country changes from low mountains to desert. The higher climatic zone of the northern half of the state merges with the semitropical south where the ocotillo, saguaro, and prickly pear indicate moderate temperature in the winters and hot summer days.

At 45 m. is a junction with a dirt and gravel road.

Right on this road to BUMBLE BEE, 5 m. (2,509 alt. 50 pop.), an early day stage station in a rich placer and lode mining area. It was named by a group of prospectors who were badly stung when they found a bumble-bees' nest in the cliffs above Turkey Creek.

ROCK SPRINGS, 54 m. (2,025 alt., 300 pop.), was named for a fine spring of cold water that comes up through the rocks here. The principal industry aside from the tourist trade, is ranching and mining in the area.

A story of an eventful stage trip over this route in 1892 behind a drunken driver is told by Will C. Barnes, Arizona rancher-author.

On one of the rocky shelved declines, the drunken driver released the brake and as he wielded his whip he emitted a wild Apache war whoop. The mules grew more wild with each lash, the stage rocked like a storm-tossed schooner, plunged, skidded around altitudinous curves, and bounced in and out of chuckholes. Bucky O'Neil and Price Behan, two of the passengers, decided it was time for action. Emerging from within the coach they grasped the iron top railing, and climbed to the top of the coach. Behan's left arm soon held the driver's neck while O'Neil pulled him to the roof beside them, giving him a clout on the head with his gun. They handcuffed him and placed him in a big leather boot on the back of the stage where he slept for the remainder of the journey while Behan and O'Neil took turns driving.

It was midnight when the stage circled out of the hills to the bank of the turbulent Agua Fria River. Stiff with cold from the raw pelting rain, Behan and O'Neil made plans to ford the stream. Across it the bedraggled passengers saw lights of the next station bidding shelter; beyond was a warm desert and the end of the hazardous road.

Filling a bucket with small stones to pelt the team, Behan and O'Neil loosed the brakes, yelled at the mules and, ignorant of the water's depth, drove the coach into the current. Two men, each with a woman by his side, clung to the top railing, leaning far back on the upstream side of the coach in order to balance it against the tremendous pressure of the water. In the event of an overturn, each man was to try to rescue a woman. When the water reached the mules' bellies they lost their footing and swam with the coach floating free. While Behan struggled to keep the harness untangled, the wheels on the stage's lower side struck a submerged rock. For a tormenting moment it rose and tipped. But finally the lead mules touched bottom with their front feet, and slowly and steadily the coach regained its balance and forged ahead.

BUTTE PEAK (L) is a landmark at 64 m.

NEW RIVER, 65 m., was an early stage station owned by Darrel Duppa, who came to Phoenix in the 1860's. Duppa, reputed to be a scion of English nobility, spoke several languages, had been educated in European universities, and had traveled extensively. Although he could afford to live in fashionable society he made his home in a ramada in New River. Much of the time he lived as a hobo but at intervals he would shave and appear as a charming well-groomed man with courtly manners.

His New River station was a curious place in the flaming desert. The roof was of willows, the thin unplastered walls of ironwood interlaced with rawhide. Unpainted furniture stood on the dirt floor upon which guests slept on blankets taken from the piles stacked against the walls. Guns, ammunition, saddles, whips, and spurs were suspended from the joists and cross-beams.   Many dogs and mules were a part of the establishment and a guttural-voiced gnome appeared only to prepare delicious and unusual meals in a corner of the room equipped as a kitchen.   Rattling pots, pans, and Dutch ovens, Duppa commanded, "Hash pile!   Come a runnin'!"

A gorgeous desert vista (L) opens at 76.7 *m*.   Near the highway is a hill of volcanic rock and lava.

The road crosses the Arizona Canal, 90 *m*.   At 94 *m*. is a junction with US 89 and 60-70 (*see TOUR 3c*) just northwest of Phoenix, 3 *m*.

Tour 2

(Gallup, N. M.)—Holbrook—Winslow—Flagstaff—Williams—Ash Fork—Kingman (Needles, Calif.); US 66.
New Mexico Line to California Line, 379.5 *m*.

All-paved, all-year highway; slow down for cattle on the open ranges.
Santa Fe Ry. and Trans. & Western Air lines roughly parallel entire route.
All types of accommodations at Holbrook, Winslow, Flagstaff, and Kingman; limited elsewhere.

This route crosses the high plateau of Northern Arizona, a land of wide horizons and small towns, castellated mesas and deep gorges cut by the Colorado, Little Colorado, and their tributary streams and washes.   Wind as well as water has gashed canyons in the soft sand and clay and revealed their many shades of red and yellow that pale and deepen as the light is filtered through passing clouds.

The vegetation consists mostly of juniper, pinon, greasewood, and sage, except for the tall pines of the national forests in the central section and the chollas, prickly pear, Joshua trees, and Spanish bayonets near the Colorado River.   The invigorating climate of the area makes this route a favorite with summer travelers.

Section a.   NEW MEXICO LINE to FLAGSTAFF; 165 m. US 66.

Along this section of US 66, which crosses the Navajo country, are the painted Desert, the Petrified Forest, an agricultural community settled by Mormons, a meteor crater, two national forests, and several ruins of early Indian villages.   From the highway are many glimpses of Navajo men riding their scrubby ponies, of Navajo women weaving beside their igloo-shaped hogans, and of their children guarding the sheep. Though many of the tribesmen, with a newly acquired business sense, have built brush ramadas near the highway and hung them with blankets and rugs for sale to tourists, they do all their purchasing at the trading post. There the men, women and children gather in groups with their exquisite handiwork. The men usually wear gaudy shirts, blue denim trousers, earrings, belts studded with huge silver conchos, and either worn Stetsons or bright bands tied around their long hair; the women, clad in velvet tunics and flowered or brightly colored voluminous skirts, often carry their black-eyed babies strapped in cradleboards.

Twenty-four miles west of Gallup, N. M., US 6 crosses the New Mexico Line, 0 *m.*, and traverses a small corner of the NAVAJO RESERVATION (75,000 pop.). This reserve, the largest in the United States, comprises twenty-five thousand square miles in northeastern Arizona, Utah, Colorado, and New Mexico.

The vermilion cliffs on both sides of the highway are a fitting introduction to a land where sun, dryness, and mineral content of the rocks combine to produce a highly colored landscape.

LUPTON, 1.1 *m.* (6,300 alt., 125 pop.), is a western cow town, named for a pioneer, G. W. Lupton, trainmaster at Winslow, 1905.

LUPTON WASH, 1.9 *m.,* like many southwestern waterways, is dry except after sudden rains.

HOUCK, 11 *m.* (c. 50 pop.), trading point and post office in the Navajo country, serving half dozen trading posts in the area, whose businesses depend almost entirely on trade of the tribesmen. Tegakwitha Indian Mission and School located here.

SANDERS, 20.8 *m.* (5,800 alt., 56 pop.), named for an early trader, and CHAMBERS, 26.9 *m.* (5,754 alt., 25 pop.), are also trading posts.

Right from Chambers on an improved dirt road to KIN TIEL (Navajo, wide) RUIN, 18.6 *m.,* which covers thirty acres and is among the largest pueblo sites in the Southwest. Most of the walls have recently been razed. When a few rooms were excavated in 1929 by Haury and Hargrave for the National Geographic Society, primarily to obtain datable beams, the outer walls were unbroken and terraced dwellings looked down on open courts. This is one of the earliest of the sites possessing kivas of the square Hopi type instead of the round Pueblo Bonito type. From the beams in the kiva roofs archeologists estimate these rooms were built between 1264 and 1285 A.D., indicating Pueblo III and early Pueblo IV periods of occupation. The finding here of several new pottery types associated with dated beams has assisted in clarifying the relationship of prehistoric Hopi cultures.

At 37.2 *m.* on this road is GANADO (*see TOUR 5*).

NAVAJO, 34.9 *m.* (5,700 alt., c. 50 pop.), is another trading post, with cabins, general store, service station and post office.

Left from Navajo on an unimproved road to NAVAJO SPRINGS, 3.5 *m.,* where the territorial government of Arizona was set up by Governor J. B. Goodwin on December 29, 1863. The territory had been created ten months earlier by order of President Lincoln. When the governor, with a small retinue of officials, entered this region, it was a dangerous wilderness. A little later the capital was established at Prescott with headquarters in a log structure that still stands.

From a point at 47.2 *m.* is the most extensive view along this highway of the PAINTED DESERT (R). The yellow, red, magenta, and mauve sands appear in terrace, mesa, and hill formations.

At 47.4 *m.* is the junction with a paved road.

Right on this loop drive, which skirts the most brilliant section of the Painted Desert, an addition made to the Petrified Forest National Monument in 1932.

The Painted Desert extends for 300 miles along the north bank of the Little Colorado—a stretch of vividly banded earth beneath a brilliant sky; at times even the air above this lonely land glows with a pink mist or a purple haze. Eons of rain and wind have exposed the highly-colored shales, marls, and sandstones. Warm, almost unreal tints waver across the sands, dance along the mesa tops, stain the lomas and ledges, and splash scarlet hues from horizon to horizon. The caprices of heat, light, and desert dust frequently change the colors from blue, amethyst, and saffron to russet, lilac, and blood red. In the early morning and evening the mesas seem to broaden; the miniature escarpments break open; mountains a hundred miles away rise in clear profile. The oblique light deepens the shadows and causes the terraced wall faces and tiny chasms to glow with crimson. Geologically this stratum belongs to the Chinle formation, which is softer than the strata above and below it. The predominant reds and yellows result from the presence of limonite and hematite; some seams and small veins contain gypsum; and certain levels of the Chinle contain petrified wood, fossil plants, and the bones of extinct reptiles and amphibians.

The PAINTED DESERT INN, 1.9 *m.*, a pueblo-type structure with varying floor levels, is surrounded by walled-in landscaped terraces. This building, completed in 1939 by the National Park Service, contains a trading post for Indian-made products, lunch counter, information office, and museum, which is open summer only.

At 4.5 *m.* is the junction with US 66.

At 50.1 *m.* is junction with Petrified Forest Highway.

Left on latter to northern checking station of PETRIFIED FOREST NATIONAL MONUMENT (*15-day permit for cars and motorcycles, 50¢; visitors forbidden to take wood*), 5.2 *m.*, a ninety-two-thousand-acre tract containing five separate forests of petrified wood, and many points of archeological and geological interest. Early records show that the region was visited by Lieutenant A. W. Whipple in 1853 and described as a place "Where trees have been converted into jasper." The wood is extremely hard and capable of taking a high polish. At one time the forest was threatened with depletion by pilferers; whole carloads were shipped away to jewelers and curio merchants. In 1906 a section of about forty square miles was made a national monument, and in 1931 enlarged to include Black Forest, which is in the Painted Desert and inaccessible by automobile.

An Indian legend tells of a goddess, hungry, cold, and exhausted, who was pleased when she found hundreds of logs lying on the ground here. She killed a rabbit with a club, expecting to prepare a meal. But the logs were too wet to burn. Enraged, she cursed the spot, turning the logs to stone so they could never burn. Geologists estimate that approximately a hundred and fifty million years ago this area formed part of a valley which covered western Texas. New Mexico, eastern Utah, and northeastern Arizona. Araucaria-like trees (similar to Norfolk Island pine) covered the land and perched along banks of streams that slowly wound across the valley. (Fossilized ferns and bones of giant amphibians and reptiles have been found.)

To the east the ancestral Rocky Mountains formed a boundary as did another ancient range to the southwest. As there were no Sierra Nevada, a long plain sloped west to the Pacific. The network of streams occasionally rose to flood stage and from the surrounding uplands carried sediments that slowly filled the entire valley with sand and silt and covered the forest to a depth of nearly three thousand feet. Before the trees had time to decay minerals dissolved in the ground water seeped into the trunks until the wood cells were filled with stone. (Some of the minerals found in the different stages of petrifaction are silica, iron, manganese, aluminum, copper, lithium, and carbon.) A shallow ocean spread over this region during the Cretaceous period, which ended about sixty million years ago when the mountain-making period began. The present range of Rocky Mountains uplifted and the interior basin of the Petrified Forest region consequently rose from three thousand feet below sea level to five thousand feet above, buried under a blanket of sand, silt, and limestone 3,000 feet deep. The petrified logs were uncovered as water carried the silty substance into the Puerco and Little Colorado rivers. The forest is still being exposed by this erosion. In the deep washes logs have been found 250 feet below the surrounding land surface.

RIO PUERCO RANGER STATION, 5.4 m. on this drive is a checking station of National Park Service to inspect cars leaving the monument and furnish information to those entering. Directly behind the building is a rock marked with petroglyphs believed to have been inscribed by an ancient people. Left 0.2 m. on a foot path to the PUERCO RIVER INDIAN RUIN, 3 rooms of which have been partly excavated.

At 6.2 m. the road makes a junction with side road; R. 0.3 m. on this to a parking area (guides); R. 100 yds. on a foot trail down steep rock steps to NEWSPAPER ROCK, a massive boulder with figures representing hands, spirals, frogs, unidentified four-legged animals, and numerous unintelligible designs scratched on two sides, presumably a prehistoric record.

THE TEEPEES (R), 8.2 m., are eroded mounds of clay banded with blue, purple, and white.

The side road now comes to some of the most interesting natural phenomena in the state of Arizona.

At 10 m. is a junction with a side road; L. here is a side drive six miles round trip through BLUE FOREST, a badland region with many petrified logs; chips; and several pedestal logs balanced on narrow ridges. Colorfully banded beds of red, blue, and white clay. Foot path into badlands from loop drive.

At 12.3 m. is a junction with a paved road. Left on this 0.2 m. to AGATE BRIDGE, a partly buried petrified log, 111 feet long. Either the tall old tree fell across a small stream or erosion has washed away the soil underneath till the log forms a natural bridge over a forty-foot-wide arroyo. To prevent this large log of petrified wood from falling down, a concrete support was constructed in 1917. A cowboy, who bet $10 he could ride across its treacherous surface, removed the shoes from his pony for surer footing and collected the bet. Right 0.1 m. from Agate Bridge on a footpath to PEDESTAL LOG, a petrified tree supported on a rocky base.

In the FIRST FOREST, 12.7 m. (R), is a surfaced road that winds through fields of petrified logs. Although most of them are chipping away, hundreds are practically intact; many have a deep rich coloring and are filled with crystals. In the northern section of the Petrified Forest where silica is the only mineral found in the trees they are mostly white and gray. Toward the south the amounts of manganese and iron in the logs increase and their colors are more brilliant. In the early days considerable damage was done in this section by man and much wood was removed. Many smaller pieces are now scattered over the ground.

The SECOND FOREST (L), 14.7 m., contains some exceptionally well-preserved logs having a dull yellow tinge and encrusted with coral-like formations.

Many of the latter bear impressions of sea shells and deep in the hollow of a petrified log a mussel fossil was found.

At 20.3 *m.* is a junction with a paved road. Left 0.5 *m.* on this to the parking area at the entrance to THIRD FOREST which has intensely colored wood. Right from the parking area 0.5 *m.* on a footpath to AGATE HOUSE, the ruin of an Indian house estimated to have been built about 1100 A.D. The walls are pieces of petrified wood set in an adobe plaster.

The PETRIFIED FOREST ADMINISTRATION BUILDING, 20.5 *m.,* constructed of local sandstone, has a central hall containing the finest stone specimens from all parts of the reserve, many polished to display their brilliant hues.

It also contains an exhibit of early animal life that inhabited this region, and a collection of exceptionally well-preserved ferns imbedded in rocks. A naturalist is on duty here; publications and colored slides on sale.

RAINBOW LODGE (there are no overnight accommodations available) is on the administration grounds. A footpath leads back of the administration building into RAINBOW FOREST; innumerable petrified trees—unequaled in intricacy of pattern and brilliance of color—are still lying here as they fell millions of years ago.

The US 260 RANGER STATION, 20.9 *m.,* is another Park Service checking station.

This is at the junction with US 260; R. 20 *m.* to HOLBROOK (*see below*), and a junction with US 66.

Near TWIN WASH, 63.5 *m.,* are many tumble weeds, or Russian thistles which grow in the shape of a ball, become very dry in the late summer, and are uprooted by the wind that rolls them across prairies and mesas, scattering their seeds. From a distance these rolling weeds resemble running animals. They often stack against fences or barns and completely bury them.

HOLBROOK, 75.9 *m.* (5,080 alt., 1,115 pop.), was named for H. R. Holbrook, first engineer of the Atlantic & Pacific R.R., which later became the Santa Fe. It is the seat of Navajo County and until 1914 was said to be the only county seat in the United States without a church. Shortly after the advent of the railroad in 1881 a company was formed to utilize the right-of-way land grants for grazing. Forty thousand head of cattle were turned loose on the plains to the west and within a year Holbrook became a tough little cow town. The Aztec Land and Cattle Company, called the Hash Knife outfit for the shape of its brand, frequently drove cattle here from Texas. The Aztec, organized in the 1880's and one of the largest outfits in the Southwest, had its ranch headquarters on the Little Colorado across from Joseph City (*see below*). The attending cowboys would gallop through Holbrook with blazing guns, yelling, "Hide out, kids, the cowboys are in town," shoot out the lights at dances, and otherwise justify wildest western traditions. Several Hash Knife men were known to be killers.

Holbrook's first settler was said to have been Juan Padilla who came with an ox team in 1879. He set up a saloon and put Berado, a Spaniard, in charge. Berado and his wife, who added a store and an eating house to the saloon, were so well noted for their hospitality, that a self-appointed busybody put up a sign on the front: "No Money, No Eat"; but Senora Berado wrote underneath: "No money, eatie anyhow." This generous woman was later kidnapped by Henry

Huning's partner who, on Huning's instructions, got Berado drunk on his own whisky and then carried the senora to Huning's home at Show Low. On his next sober day Berado started in pursuit, a hopeless one, he soon discovered, because of Huning's power and influence. Soon thereafter Berado abandoned his home and store, and left the country.

The old BLEVINS HOUSE on Central St., a white frame structure, was the scene of a gun battle between Sheriff Commodore Owens and four members of the Graham faction, who had taken a leading part in the Pleasant Valley War (see TOUR 10A). Owens held a warrant for the arrest of Andy Cooper as a cattle rustler. (Cooper, one of the Blevins brothers, had changed his name when he came to Arizona because he was wanted for murder in Texas.) On September 4, 1887 the sheriff went alone to the Blevins' house and demanded Cooper's surrender. In the fight that followed Andy Cooper was mortally wounded, his 16-year-old brother, Sam Houston Blevins, was killed, John Blevins was wounded, and Mose Roberts, a member of the Blevins' household, was killed.

The highway crosses the boundary of a farming district, 82.5 m., and parallels an irrigation ditch (L). The green of the cultivated crops forms a contrast with the wild plant life to the east. On the western skyline are the usually snow-capped San Francisco Peaks, the highest mountains in Arizona.

JOSEPH CITY, 96.8 m. (5,083 alt., 400 pop.), founded in 1876 as Allen's Camp, is the lone survivor of five early Mormon settlements on the Little Colorado River, and the oldest town in Navajo County. The Mormons made heroic attempts to dam the Little Colorado, one of the most capricious rivers in the nation, in order to provide water for irrigation. Before 1925 when the present (1939) dam was built, they had themselves financed and wholly or partly constructed fourteen dams here. (These many thwarted efforts caused the abandonment of the other four settlements.) The first dam, built three miles east of the present site in 1876, required 960 days of work and an expenditure of $5,000, but was washed out by the first flood. Five hundred workdays had been expended on the ditch to convey the water to the farms, and seed, hauled 400 miles by wagon, had just been planted. The total value of that year's crop was about twenty dollars. The successive attempts to put effective dams in the quicksand bed of the river led Andrew Jensen, Mormon church historian, to call the settlement "the leading community in pain, determination and unflinching courage in dealing with the elements around them." Agriculture is still the principal industry.

At 104.2 m. is the junction with a graded dirt road.

Right on this to another section of the PAINTED DESERT, 14 m., a source of colored sands for the dry-sand paintings of the Hopi and Navajo.

The road enters the Navajo Indian Reservation (see above), 18.4 m., and the Hopi Indian Reservation, 43.6 m., as it winds through the Hopi Buttes, which are the eagle-trapping grounds of certain clans. Formerly the men hid in traps baited with rabbits and seized the eagles that pounced on the prey. Now, every June several men of each clan climb the steep rough mountains to the eyries, take the young birds from their nests (but leave a few so they will not be exterminated), and carry them to the village where they are tied on the housetops. Their heads are washed with yucca suds, as are those of new born babies, and their feathers are made into prayer sticks. Then the eaglets are killed and buried with a solemn ritual in a special crevice in the rocks. At the last appearance of the Kachinas in mid-July (see TOUR 5), the prayer sticks are offered to the gods and the eagles' graves are sprinkled with sacred meal and decorated with Kachina dolls and small bows and arrows. The Hopi speak of the eagles as "our animals," regarding them as the best carriers of prayers to the rain-bringing gods. At an eagle shrine near Walpi (see TOUR 5) is a collection of wooden ovals—some very old while others still show traces of white paint and feathers. These are representations of eggs and are made during the Winter Solstice Ceremony as prayers for the increase of eagles.

WINSLOW, 108.9 m. (3,730 alt., 3,917 pop.), was first settled in 1882 as a division terminal of the Santa Fe Ry. As the stock-raising industry developed, it became one of the largest towns in northern Arizona. Hotel LA POSADA, of the Fred Harvey system, is a copy of a Spanish hacienda and holds many pieces of furniture in use long before the territory was organized.

At 109.1 m. is a junction with a graveled road leading to the Winslow Airport.

Left on this to the WINSLOW AIRPORT, 1.5 m., a stop on the Transcontinental and Western Air Lines.

At 119.6 m. is the junction with an unimproved road running to the Navajo subagency.

Right on this to another dirt road, 16 m.; R. 1 m. on this to LEUPP, a Navajo subagency (meals available; no sleeping accommodations), near the Little Colorado. Half dozen red sandstone buildings, formerly housing 500 children, are now unoccupied except for a small elementary boarding school of about 60 children. An experimental wool-washing and carding plant is in one building, and an experimental tannery in another.

The waters of RED LAKE (R) are visible from 27 m. on the main side road. This lake surrounded by trees and tall reeds provides a refuge for wild ducks.

RED BUTTES (L), 40 m., are eroded into the likeness of medieval castles. Here the road crosses the HOPI INDIAN RESERVATION boundary.

ORAIBI, 67 m., a very old Hopi village, is at the junction with a dirt road (see TOUR 5).

At 129 m. is the junction with a surfaced road which takes the tourist to Meteor Crater.

Left on this to the METEOR CRATER, 7 m. At the edge of Meteor Crater is a MUSEUM AND OBSERVATORY (adm. 35¢). Here is a great pockmark about one mile in diameter and 600 feet deep in the face of the desert. Although some geologists estimate that the meteor which caused the crater struck this continent about 50,000 years ago, promoters like to quote a date nearer 2,000 years ago, thereby lending support to those who call it the Star of Bethlehem. Scientists estimate that the meteor displaced between five and six million tons of rock and soil. Efforts to find the meteorite under the crater were begun in 1905. The first test holes, sent down in the center, failed but subsequent drilling at the south edge revealed at a depth of 1,376 feet a hard mass that may be a meteor. Meteor fragments that are scattered about this area are principally iron, with some nickel and platinum; some of them contain diamonds. Several tons of these fragments—ranging from small pieces of iron to some weighing over 1,000 pounds—have been picked up. The meteor is thought to have struck at an angle from the north, leaving a surrounding ridge higher on the south edge. Though this crater has aroused much scientific speculation, the site has been purchased by a Pittsburg company with the evident intention of future mining operations.

CANYON DIABLO (5,429 alt.), 132.8 m., a typical gorge in the Kaibab sandstone (shading from a yellow to a salmon color), 225 feet deep and 500 feet wide and so named because travelers experienced great difficulty in crossing it. In 1857 when Edward F. Beale was surveying for a wagon road from Ft. Defiance, New Mexico to the Colorado, he passed here with his camels (see TOUR 3d) and noted "It is appropriately named being a deep chasm with perpendicular walls. . . ."

On March 21, 1889 an Atlantic & Pacific train was stopped at the Canyon Diablo station by four bandits who robbed the express strongbox and fled northward. A posse consisting of Sheriff William "Bucky" O'Neill and three deputies chased the robbers 300 miles in two weeks before finally sighting them in southeastern Utah, 40 miles east of Canyonville. The citizens of Canyonville had already attempted to arrest the desperadoes, but were themselves held up, forced to stack their arms and retreat. Shortly thereafter the sheriff's men closed in; during the pitched battle that followed the fifty shots fired succeeded only in wounding a robber's mount. The fugitives abandoned their horses and plunged into the mountains on foot but were soon captured by the posse, and the money they were carrying—about $1000—was recovered. Smith, one of the robbers, escaped through a car window on the return trip but was later recaptured.

The route crosses the boundary of the COCONINO NATIONAL FOREST, 148.8 m., which contains western yellow pine, the most valuable of the state's timber.

WINONA, 156.8 m. (6,000 alt.), has a general store, service station, garage, and tourist camp.

At 157 m. is the junction with an unimproved road.

Right on this 0.5 m. to the RUINS OF A GAME COURT. Although carefully excavated in 1936 by the Museum of Northern Arizona and the State Teachers College at Flagstaff, the site has been partly filled with soil. It is one of several similar prehistoric ruins in Arizona, and since it is the same type described by the early Spanish writers in Mexico and Yucatan, it links the culture of the Mayas and Aztecs with that of the Pueblo area.

On the same road are the excellently preserved REMAINS OF A PIT HOUSE, 0.7 m., of the early Pueblo period. About 20 feet square and 10 feet deep, it was roofed over with perishable materials at the time of occupation. The walls are of coursed masonry and the fireplace is in the approximate center of the floor. This is one of the largest of the many pit houses found in the Southwest. It was also excavated in 1936.

At 158.8 *m.* on US 66 is the junction with an unimproved road.

Right on this road to another unimproved dirt road, 16 *m.;* L. on this to the GRAND FALLS OF THE LITTLE COLORADO, 27.2 *m.*, which drop 185 feet. Except during the rainy season of late summer the falls are practically non-existent and in the spring the Indians water their stock in the pool below. After a storm in the upper basin the usually dry bed of the river roars with a turbulent muddy flood, and the falls become a chocolate-colored Niagara. They were formed when a stream of molten basalt from Rodin's crater, between this point and the San Francisco Peaks, blocked a canyon that the Little Colorado had cut through the limestone and sandstone of the plateau and forced the river out of its channel. The diverted waters wore a second gorge nearly 60 miles long around the tongue of lava, then dropped over the high rim of its former canyon into its old course. This volcanic interruption accounts for the basalt western bank and the limestone baked to a reddish color by the intense heat of the lava. There are many ruins of cliff dwellings in the hills to the west and south of the falls.

At 160.6 *m.* on US 66 is the junction with a dirt road.

Left on this to the Park Service's WALNUT CANYON NATIONAL MONUMENT, 5 *m.* On the sides of this gorge which is cut in a limestone plateau are the remains of about 300 cliff dwellings, believed to have been built and occupied from about 900 to 1100 A.D. and abandoned because of prolonged drought. Matting, stone implements (including hoes), and other relics have been uncovered. The northern wall of the canyon served as a windbreak and shelter. Water was carried up to the cliffs on a well-built trail. Large shells are often found in the vicinity and fossils abound.

At 161 *m.* on US 66 is the junction with an unimproved road.

Left on this to TURKEY HILL RUINS, 0.1 *m.* By the tree-ring method of dating, it has been estimated that the pueblo-type structures on this site were built between 1203 and 1278 A.D. This was one of the largest pueblos in the region and also one of the last to be abandoned. A large mound covers what is believed to be the remains of a three-story building with perhaps fifteen basal rooms, and a one-story extension of eleven rooms to the northeast. Three small extensions of four-room houses lie a few yards to the southeast. Between the largest of these is a depression that archeologists believe might show a kiva if excavated. An outcrop of lava north of the ruin was used as permanent metates. Although not as large as Elden Pueblo (*see below*), potsherds indicate this site was occupied at a later date. Well preserved painted arm bands made of basketry were found on arm bones in the burial grounds.

TOWNSEND, 163 *m.* (6,938 alt.), called Doney for a Civil War veteran who lived here till his death in 1932, and renamed in 1936 for John Townsend, the Indian fighter. Here is the junction with a road leading to the Elden Pueblo ruins.

Right from Townsend on an unimproved dirt road to ELDEN PUEBLO, 0.1 *m.*, a moundlike ruin in a clearing of pines at the foot of Elden Mountain (9,000 alt.). The pueblo is a rectangular structure, 145 feet long and 125 feet wide, with the remaining walls only two to seven feet in height. Originally it had two stories; the lower one was used as a granary and contained a large communal or ceremonial room with a low seat extending completely around the inner wall. Near by are many smaller ruins and two burial grounds that have yielded ollas, ladles, jugs, necklaces, turquoise ear pendants, rings, clay images of quadrupeds, a small clay effigy of a bird with spread wings, and miniature vessels painted black-on-white. It was the custom to bury the dead near by so that their spirits might remain close to friends and relatives. They were always fully ornamented and any articles they valued in life were buried with them. Offerings were presumably placed before the small shrine at the south-west corner of the pueblo facing the sunset point of the winter solstice.

Flagstaff, 165 *m*. (6,907 alt., 7,663 pop.) (*see Flagstaff*).
Section *b*. *FLAGSTAFF to ASHFORK JUNCTION 50 m., US 66, US 66-89.*

West of Flagstaff, 0 *m.*, the road continues through two national forests whose pines give the route much beauty as their dark forms are silhouetted against the drifting clouds of a summer sky or assume a Christmas-card prettiness under a winter snow. Because of the high altitude the air is always dry; summers are cool and winters sometimes have sub-zero temperatures. There are many Indian ruins and two hundred extinct volcanoes in this vicinity. In the forests are bear, lion, deer, and smaller game but they are seldom seen; occasionally a bear will lumber across the road or a motorist glimpse one or more deer bounding away through the pine and juniper.

Before the advent of barbed wire and domestic stock, every mesa and valley of any size from sea level to seven thousand feet supported thousands of these animals. On the grassy plateaus and open pine tablelands of the north the American pronghorn ranged, and in the desert and southern grassland mesas, the duller-coated Mexican pronghorn.

The American pronghorn is the only antelope that annually sheds the hard covering of its horns, and the only one with horns that are branched. Both sexes are horned, the females having much the smaller growth. Shortly after the breeding season in the fall, these black varnished shells peel off, exposing a dark skin covering on the bony core beneath. The coarse hair that protects this skin drops off as the new shell hardens. Although they are primarily grazing animals, weeds and shrubs make up much of their diet, and the desert pronghorns have become almost entirely browsers.

In late April and May the does quietly drift away from the herd to drop two, or occasionally three fawns, or kids, which they hide separately near shrubs or rocks or in the long grass and weeds. Every winter these antelopes, most gregarious of all the large game animals except the bison, band together in herds which include all of their number for miles around.

The largest herds in Arizona are usually southeast and north of Flagstaff and north of Kingman, Seligman, and Ashfork. Many smaller herds are scattered from the Grand Canyon to Prescott. In southern Arizona there are remnants of herds in Pima and Cochise Counties and a few good-sized groups in southern Yuma County. The Mexican variety ranges far into Sonora but the northern species moves within a comparatively small area.

Flagstaff is at the junction with US Alt. 89 (*see TOUR 2A*).

Points of Interest. Arizona State Teachers College, Public Library, City Park, and others (see *Flagstaff.*)

1. Right from Flagstaff two blocks on Beaver Street to Birch Avenue; L. on Birch Avenue to an improved dirt road; L. here to LOWELL OBSERVATORY (*open daily 1:30 to 2:30*), 1.4 *m.*, on top of Mars Hill on the edge of a volcanic mesa 350 feet higher than the city. Dr. Percival Lowell (1855-1916) founded the observatory at Flagstaff in 1894 and endowed it permanently. Lowell advanced the theory that Mars was inhabited by intelligent beings who constructed its canals. In a theoretical treatise he predicted the course of a then unknown planet. In 1930 Clyde W. Tombaugh of the observatory discovered a planet in exactly the position that Dr. Lowell had calculated. It was subsequently named Pluto. The staff (1940) consists of three astronomers and four assistants.

2. Right from Flagstaff on Beaver Street nine blocks to Columbus Ave.; L. on Columbus to the graded dirt Country Club road; R. on Country Club road to the MUSEUM OF NORTHERN ARIZONA, 3 *m.*, constructed in 1934 to promote archeological research and preserve one of the largest collections of mammals, birds, reptiles, and invertebrates in the state. The museum contains research rooms, laboratories, a library room, and an art gallery. Each year during July Hopi Indian handiwork is exhibited to several thousand visitors.

Straight ahead on Country Club road (open *May-Oct.*) to the three SAN FRANCISCO PEAKS, 12.5 *m.*, Humphreys (12,670 alt.), Agassiz (12,340 alt.), and Fremont (11,940 alt.). Their names honor Andrew Atkinson Humphreys (1810-83), who surveyed for a railroad to the Pacific, was an authority on river hydraulics, a corps commander of the Army of the Potomac, and became chief engineer of the army; Jean Louis Rodolphe Agassiz (1807-73), the geologist and zoologist noted for his classification of marine fossils and theory of the glacial epoch; and John Charles Fremont (1813-90), governor of Arizona territory (1878-82), whose appellation the pathfinder has been changed by recent biographers to pathmaker. Early in the seventeenth century the Franciscans who established a mission at Oraibi (*see TOUR 5*) gave the name San Francisco to these peaks to honor St. Francis of Assisi, the founder of their order. These mountains are so high and the air in the surrounding valleys and plains usually so clear that points in Utah, California, and Nevada are often visible from their crests. When seen from a distance in the early morning the lower slopes are hidden by haze and the peaks seem to hang from the sky. They are amazingly symmetrical and their snowy summits are constantly changing in color. At sunrise they appear gold; at noon they are Carrara marble against a turquoise sky; at sunset they are polished copper, ruby, coral, and finally amethyst.

The Hopi call these peaks the Nuvat-i-kyan-bi (place of the snow peaks).

US 66 and US 89 are one route between Flagstaff and the junction with US 89, 0.3 *m.* east of Ashfork.

US 66 crosses the eastern boundary of the KAIBAB NATIONAL FOREST (*see TOUR 1a*) at 10 *m.*

BELLEMONT, 11 *m.* (7,132 alt., 35 pop.), is a trading point in a stock-raising and lumbering region. KENDRICK PEAK (10,418 alt.), visible to the north, was named for Major H. L. Kendrick, who brought a military party through here in the gold rush days of forty-nine.

NAVAJO ORDNANCE DEPOT, 12 *m.* (7,130 alt.), operated by the U. S. Army Ordnance Corps for receipt, issue, and storage of ammunition. It was activated in 1942 and occupies 45 square miles. The main source of labor consists of Navajo and Hopi Indians, most of whom reside on the depot reservation.

The light bark of a grove of aspens (L), 15 *m.*, contrasts with the dark green pines.

The highest point (7,040 alt.) on US 66 is at 16 *m.*

Near PARKS, 20 *m.*, which consists of a post office, store, and tourist cabins, is a series of natural clearings in the forest (R) which have been intensively cultivated.

Grand Canyon Junction, 30 *m.*, is the junction with State 64 (*see Grand Canyon*).

Though WILLIAMS, 32 *m.* (6,762 alt., 3,000 pop.), is a lumber town most of its buildings are of brick. The main street straggles down the west shoulder of Bill Williams Mountain between a series of one- and two-story business houses. Above, spreading gradually across the slope of the mountain, is a residential section with an occasional modern hotel indicating the lively tourist trade Williams owes to the Grand Canyon. Livestock, shipping, and railroad repair shops are additional sources of revenue.

Charles T. Rodgers, cattleman who ran the 111 brand, homesteaded this site in 1878. In 1881 when the area had become more settled he was appointed postmaster. The lumber industry developed after the Atlantic & Pacific Railroad was built in 1882.

Both the town and mountain are named for Old Bill Williams (1787-1849), the trapper and guide. He had been a Baptist circuit rider in Missouri when he was seventeen, and had lived for more than ten years with the Osage as one of them before he plunged into the wilderness and emerged as a mountaineer described thus by Will H. Robinson: "Long, sinewy and bony, with a chin and nose almost meeting, he was the typical plainsman of the dime novel. He always rode an Indian pony, and his Mexican stirrups were big as coal scuttles. His buckskin suit was bedaubed with grease until it had the appearance of polished leather; his feet were never encased in anything but moccasins, and his buckskin trousers had the traditional fringe on the outer seam. Naturally, Indian signs were an open book to him, and he was even readier to take a scalp than an Apache, who preferred to crush the heads of his victims and let their hair stay." As paradoxical as he was incredible, Williams was acknowledged one of the most skillful guides in the West, yet was blamed by Fremont for the failure of Fremont's fourth expedition and was accused of incompetence, treachery, and cannibalism—charges which have since been disproved. He was finally killed by the Utes with whom he had once lived and by whom he had been treated as a tribesman until he went on a spree with their money, then led soldiers against them and took an active part in the attack.

Left from Williams on the Williams-Perkinsville road to BILL WILLIAMS SKI AREA, 4 *m.*, and WHITE HORSE LAKE, J. D. LAKE; also to SYCAMORE CANYON WILDERNESS AREA. (Inquire at Williams for information.)

Left from Williams on Williams-Perkinsville road to the junction with Lookout Trail (open May-Nov.) 4 *m.* (*horses and guides available at Timber Mt. Ranch*); R. 4.5 *m.* on this to fire lookout on the rounded summit of BILL WILLIAMS MOUNTAIN (9,264 alt.) called by the Havauspai Hue-ga-woo-la (Bear Mountain) and by the Apache-Mojave, Jack-ha-weha (covered with cedar). In 1851 R. H. Kern placed it on the map that accompanied the report of the Sitgreaves Survey—of which he was a member—as Bill Williams Mountain.

From a point at 42 *m.* a broad view of open country covered with juniper and sagebrush stretches for miles to the west.

At 50 *m.* is a junction (L) with US 89 (*see TOUR 1b*). The highway crosses the western boundary of the Kaibab National Forest near this point. West of the junction Picacho Butte dominates the horizon.

Section c. ASHFORK JUNCTION *to* CALIFORNIA LINE;
164.5 *m.* US 66

Between the junction with US 89, 0 *m.,* and the California Line are the high mesas of the Hualapi Reservation, the Mojave country, several mining communities, and the border of the Mojave Desert.

ASHFORK, 0.3 *m.* (5,144 alt., 894 pop.), is a stock-raising center (*information here concerning trip to Cathedral Cave*) and has developed considerable business in quarrying a tinted sandstone, found about ten miles away. This stone was used in many of the town's buildings and a large amount is being shipped to California.

Left from Ashfork on a road (*almost impassable for cars*) to CATHEDRAL CAVE, 14 *m.* Through a narrow crevice between two huge boulders, visitors descend by ladders to the floor of the cave where many stalactites and stalagmites create a fantastic effect (difficult to locate without guide).

SELIGMAN, 25.3 *m.* (5,242 alt., 1,000 pop.), a shipping and trading point for miners and cattle ranchers, is headquarters for Diamond A Cattle Company which controls extensive ranges (R) from State 64 to the Colorado River.

On the western horizon (L) are Twin Buttes.

US 66 crosses the eastern boundary of the HUALPAI (sometimes spelled Walapai) INDIAN RESERVATION, 58.1 *m.* (600 pop.), which comprises almost a million acres bounded on the north by Lake Mead and the Colorado River, and forms the lower part of an irregular octagon. In this southern part of the reservation are wide mesas; in the north, giant buttes form a series of steps to the rim of the Grand Canyon; while to the south and west are jagged barren mountains characteristic of the desert. On this reservation, which is under the supervision of the Truxton Canyon Agency, is only one settlement,

Peach Springs (*see below*), from which roads radiate to the farthest points.

The present census shows more than 600 surviving members of the Hualpai tribe. (Some of these live in towns off the reservation.) Their health is comparatively good perhaps because of the clear dry climate—days of brilliant sun and invigorating cold. They were never a large tribe even when they roamed from the Bill Williams River to the Grand Canyon. Unlike most Indians of the Southwest they developed little agriculture and lived on deer, antelope, mountain sheep, badgers, rabbits, porcupines, birds, many varieties of cacti, both fresh and dried, century plants, yuccas, pine nuts, mesquite beans, acorns, and walnuts. The pine nut is still important in their diet. They had also wild berries, grapes, and wild tobacco. In their tiny gardens in the depths of canyons corn, beans, squash, melons, and a few peaches were grown.

The Hualpai built a small dome-shaped house on a four-post foundation, filled out with framework of small poles and branches, and covered with a thatch of juniper bark. Few of these houses survive; the present-day Hualpai prefer frame houses from the sawmill erected by the government.

Their arts were never highly developed; among them skill in the dressing of hides and a distinctive basketry were alone noteworthy. They wove blankets of strips of rabbit skin and made basketry bottles waterproofed with red paint and pitch. The clothing of the men consisted of a buckskin shirt, breech clout, and moccasins; that of the women two aprons, a long one in front that covered the breasts, and a short one in back that extended from the waist down; all were ornamented with simple geometric designs.

They developed no group ceremonials, but instead considered each daily individual act or duty a rite to be fulfilled according to the instructions in their elaborate creation legend.

The Hualpai stubbornly resisted the white man's invasion but in 1874 were subdued and transported from their desert-mountain home here to La Paz, in the Colorado Valley south of Parker, where they died by scores. In 1883 the government established this reservation for them. The remnant that returned from exile in 1875 soon drifted into railroad-construction camps and mines, and subsisted meagerly for half a century. In 1915 the government began to make amends and issued ten head of cattle to each fifteen families, a plan that has been continued to the present. The depression wiped out their always slight subsistence, and a new government program was therefore developed to give them good homes, augment their herds, and teach them to become self-supporting on their own lands.

In PEACH SPRINGS, 62.4 *m.* (4,800 alt., 129 pop.), is the trading post of the Hualpai Indian Reservation.

Litigation between the Indians and the railroad over rights to the springs has extended over a long period. Father Garces, Franciscan missionary, camped at Peach Springs in 1776 on his way to the Hopi villages. His route from the Colorado River to the springs closely approximated that now followed by the Santa Fe Ry.

The following reservation roads radiating from Peach Springs are unpaved and generally unmapped; guides essential.

1. Right from Peach Springs on the western road to MERIWITICA CANYON, 35 *m.*, a thousand foot gash in the mesa, at the bottom of which are a few acres of garden land cultivated from time immemorial by the Hualpai. It was here that they took final refuge from the invading white man, but even here he eventually starved them out. The canyon is similar to but smaller than the one occupied by the Havasupai, their cousins in the Grand Canyon. In the wooded land above the canyon graze several thousand fine Herefords, common property of the tribe.

Meriwitica Canyon and Diamond Canyon (*see below*) are both within the Boulder Dam Recreation Area (*see TOUR 2B*).

2. Right from Peach Springs on the eastern road across a wide stretch of desert and into a thirty-nine-thousand-acre FOREST OF YELLOW PINE. The government is beginning to make the resources of the section available to the Indians, improving the road, erecting a sawmill, and conducting experiments in dry farming. There are twenty-thousand acres along the stream beds suitable for such development.

3. Right from Peach Springs on the northern road (*almost impassable for cars*) along Peach Springs Draw into DIAMOND CANYON, 21 *m.*, where the old Diamond Creek Hotel was operated until the railroad between Williams and Grand Canyon was built in 1907. Before that time Diamond Canyon had been the most popular place from which to view the Grand Canyon, though the walls in this western section of the Colorado's gorge are only 2000 feet high which is less than half their height in the national park area. The trip was made by horse-drawn stages and took ten hours because of a three thousand foot drop in elevation on the last eighteen miles of the journey. Diamond Creek Hotel was a frame structure with nine bedrooms, a dining room, and a lobby. After its abandonment the hotel was carried off in pieces by Indians and ranchers until only the foundation forms remain. John Nelson, the stage driver who still lives in Peach Springs and escorts parties to the canyon, can remember when the Diamond Creek Hotel entertained guests from practically every state in the Union, and from Europe.

In VALENTINE, 79 *m.* (3,800 alt., 110 pop.), formerly called Truxton but renamed for Robert G. Valentine, Commissioner of Indian Affairs (1908-10), is the Truxton Canyon Indian Subagency on a tract of 640 acres bisected by the Santa Fe Ry. The agency building, erected in 1900, housed a boarding school for two hundred Indian boys and girls, but was discontinued in 1936.

On the desert southwest of Valentine changes of weather effect sudden and complete transformations. Under a clear blue heaven this is a land of tawny yellows and reds; when there are clouds they throw dark purple shadows on the ground and intensify the golden glow of the sunlight; but as columns of rain advance over the mesas it is a world of blue and gray-green shadows. Desert rains are usually so definitely demarked that the story of the man who washed his hands in the edge of an Arizona thunder shower without wetting his cuffs seems almost credible.

Many are repelled by the desert's vast stretches of mesas and buttes with their sagebrush and yucca; by its gigantic masses of sharp, broken rock; and by its wind-beaten wastes, so still at times beneath the blazing sun that the wavering heat vibrations are the only movement. Under the withering summer heat, the cacti droop, the desert fauna seek the shade of the mesquite; only the lizard, skirting swiftly over the parched floor, braves the sun's glare. The plant life bears visible evidence of its struggle to exist in these extremely arid conditions. Branches are reduced to stubs and thorns, leaves are varnished or dispensed with, flowering and fruiting processes are withheld through rainless periods sometimes for years. Yet the desert has a compensatory beauty. The cacti bear brilliant flowers. The yellow, red, and orange of the bisagna, the white of the saguaro, the red, pink, and gold of the ocotillo and cholla, and the yellow of the palo verde are spread across the desert to the horizon where sky, mountains, and cacti dissolve in a Tyrian haze. Under clouds and oppressive heat the sky often glows with carmines, chrome-yellows, magentas, pinks, grays, and browns and at times these are reflected on the desert floor till it becomes a symphony of color. On rare occasions even the moon that silvers the mountain spires, turrets, and peaks bridges them with a faint arc in all the colors of the spectrum—a rainbow of moonlight.

KINGMAN, 114.5 m. (3,336 alt., 4,000 pop.), since 1882 has been the shopping and shipping center for a large and sparsely populated western area. It is the seat of Mohave County, which contains over three hundred thousand acres of grazing land but derives its principal income from the tourist trade. The lode mines in this region have yielded many millions of dollars' worth of gold in bygone years.

The town is built on gently sloping land between the Hualpai, Cerbat, and Black Mountains. US 66 follows the main thoroughfare, Front Street, which has business buildings on one side, with warehouses, storage depots, and the station of the Santa Fe Ry. On the other side, a modern retail shopping center covers five city blocks. Its two Federal highways and its proximity to Boulder Dam have brought many tourists to Kingman and fringed the town with auto courts.

The gold miners, cowboys, and Hualpai Indians (who depend on Kingman for shopping and recreation) and an occasional old-fashioned prospector who passes through, driving burros packed with bedroll, Dutch oven, picks, and drills, gives the town a realistic western atmosphere.

Mohave County Fair is held for three days in September, where agricultural, mineral, domestic, arts and crafts, floral and commercial exhibits of the county are displayed.

Kingman is at the junction with US 93-466, to Boulder Dam and Lake Mead National Recreational Area (see TOUR 2B).

Right on US 93-466, 5 m. to the junction with State 68. Right on State 68, now the route, to DAVIS DAM, 25 m.

Construction of Davis Dam was started in March, 1946, and the first power was generated in January, 1951. The power plant has been in full production since June, 1951, and has an installed capacity of 225,000 kilowatts. The dam, its power plant and related features, and over a thousand miles of transmission lines and sub-stations cost almost 120 million dollars.

The Davis Dam site, originally called "Bullshead" after a nearby rock formation said to resemble the head of a bull, was renamed in 1941 in honor of Arthur P. Davis, pioneer reclamation engineer. The dam, 138 feet high above the level of Colorado R., is an earth and rock-fill embankment with concrete spillway, intake structure, and power plant. Its crest length is 1,600 feet. Its reservoir, Lake Mohave, has a capacity of almost two million acre feet and extends for 67 miles upstream, and is not more than four miles across at its widest point.

The government has constructed a permanent camp, known as Davis Dam, about a mile downstream from the dam for housing the building and maintenance employees of the Bureau of Reclamation. The town's population in 1953 was about 600.

Left from Bullhead City Junction with State 68, near the Dam, is BULLHEAD CITY, 2 *m.* (540 alt., 400 pop.), the boom town which failed to become a ghost town after completion of Davis Dam as predicted. Located in a farming, mining, cattle raising area, is a resort headquarters for excellent trout and bass fishing. With nearby Havasu Lake and Lake Mohave, created by reclamation dams on Colorado River, is center of great activity among sportsmen and tourists.

At 118.5 *m.* is a junction with US 66, new super-highway through Yucca to Topock and the California Line for tourists not wishing to continue over the old road, now the route. Mileage is about the same although new US 66 avoids mountainous route.

Left on this road to YUCCA, 20 *m.* (2,000 alt., 75 pop.), a small settlement that caters to employees of the near-by Yucca-Tungsten, Borrianna, and Signal mines (*open on application*). The Borrianna in which was discovered Arizona's first tungsten in commercial quantities, is still (1939) the state's largest tungsten producer. Small amounts of tungsten are used in electric lamp filaments though its chief value is for hardening steel.

GOLDROAD, 140.9 *m.* (5,225 alt., 52 pop.), is a typical small mining community.

OATMAN, 143.3 *m.* (2,600 alt., 500 pop.), an old-time mining camp with modern touches, strings up and down blue-shadowed foothills of the Black Mountains. Flanking the town are gray tiers of cyanide-mill tailings, smooth and graceful as frozen waterfalls; some of the mine shafts and workings are visible in the surrounding hills.

US 66 follows the only street, built on a long hillside with stores and offices in an unbroken row up one side of it. In front of the stores is a wide plank boardwalk raised on stilts at the lower end to make it level and reached by flights of worn wooden steps. Old wooden awnings on the store fronts shadow the shop windows and make the walk resemble an old-fashioned front porch. Among the several bars in this block is one called the Health Center, a combination saloon, ice-cream parlor and drug store. Because of several bad fires the opposite side of the street has fewer and somewhat newer buildings. One of these, a neat frame fire station, contains a red fire engine that leads all town parades. Next to the fire house is a vacant lot where mine-drilling contests are held.

The houses of the community are small and cheaply-constructed; some are gay with paint, and others, weather-beaten gray. Many are perched on hilltops that give an excellent view of the mountains and are reached by narrow winding dirt roads or trails. Although water is very expensive in this semiarid country each house has some shrubbery or a few flowers which are kept alive by carefully conserved waste water.

In spite of its high food prices and isolation the miners like to work in Oatman. Its spirit and morale are unusually high. The nearest movie is in Kingman, 29 miles over the mountains, so the citizens depend on their community gatherings for recreation. In good weather dances, boxing matches, and other entertainments are held in the pavilion on the main street. Wrestling contests between young men of the town, who sometimes perform barefooted, are well attended. The male spectators squat around the mats that are placed in the center of the pavilion and the women and their small children sit on wooden benches in the back. A great to-do is made over choosing a referee, who seldom lasts more than one match. While a contest is in progress the miners shout and urge their favorites to bite, kick, and gouge but when it is ended they cheer the loser as well as the winner.

Families from miles around come to Oatman on Labor Day; an Indian band plays all day long, and the streets are jammed with good-natured crowds. The competitive events of the day, which consist of girls' tug-o'-war and a women's nail-driving competition, are climaxed by mucking and drilling contests for the miners (*see above*).

Oatman was named for a pioneer family that was attacked by Apaches near Gila Bend in 1851; the parents were killed, two girls taken into captivity, and a boy beaten into unconsciousness. The girls were hidden at a spring a half mile north of the present townsite (locally known as Ollie Oatman Spring), and were overlooked by soldiers who had been detailed to their rescue. The boy recovered. The younger sister, Mary Ann, died a captive, but Olive, the older, was released in 1856 through efforts of a rancher and joined her brother at Fort Yuma.

Throughout its history Oatman has prospered and languished by turn after the manner of mining towns. In the early days a narrow-gauge railway extended from the near-by mines to Fort Mojave on the Colorado River; to that point a ferry brought supplies from Needles, California. From 1904-7 three million dollars' worth of gold was taken from this vicinity and the town boasted two banks, ten stores, and a chamber of commerce.

West of Oatman is the traditional territory of the Mojave Indians who now live on the Mojave Indian Reservation to the north and on the Colorado River Indian Reservation at Parker to the south (*see TOUR 3B.*)

When Father Garces, Spanish missionary and explorer, went up the Colorado River in 1775 he estimated the Mojave at three thousand although they now have less than nine hundred members. The Mojave language is still very much alive; the older folk use it almost entirely and many of the children do not know English when they enter school.

Formerly one of the fiercest tribes of the Southwest, the Mojave are now farmers who raise fruits, vegetables, and cotton on the rich lowlands of the Colorado Valley. On the Colorado River Reservation ten acres of land have been allotted each family (*see TOUR 3B*).

The Colorado River is glimpsed (L) from a point at 160 *m.* The black rocks along the roadside here are of volcanic origin.

TOPOCK, 164 *m.* (505 alt., 65 pop.), lowest point in elevation on the Arizona section of US 66, is located at the east end of Colorado River bridge. Topock is Mohave for "bridge."

The halfway point on the bridge over the Colorado River is the Arizona-California boundary, 164.5 *m.*

※※※

Tour 2A

Flagstaff—Cottonwood—Clarkdale—Junction with US 89; 87.1 *m.,* US Alt. 89 (Oak Creek Canyon Highway).

Asphalt-paved.
Heavy snows in the northern part sometimes block travel temporarily.
Excellent accommodations.

Most of this route is within the boundaries of either the Coconino or the Prescott National Forests. It traverses the edge of the Coconino Plateau and winds down the gorge of Oak Creek Canyon, dropping from an altitude of 7,000 feet to 2,500 feet in lower Oak Creek. Before the days of the automobile this area had an atmosphere quite different from that of the lumbering, mining, and stock-raising sections. In the late 1920's the state appropriated funds for the highway, and Flagstaff and Prescott civic organizations boosted the enterprise. But old-timers, who knew Oak Creek as a retreat from work, worry, and the ever-increasing roar of civilization, fought bitterly against promoting this wilderness, loved for its long trout, brilliantly colored scenery, and deep canyons. With the highway came lodges, tourist camps, filling stations, swimming pools, and other marks of progress.

South of Oak Creek Canyon what is known as Lower Oak Creek

suddenly overlaps into the Verde. Verde (Sp., green) in the nineteenth century meant any place south of the Mogollon Rim and along the Verde River. It was the center for probably the most active cattle raising and ranging in northern Arizona, though not notorious for gunplay, feuds, or wild towns. Its cowboys, in the old days, heated many a branding iron over juniper fires between Ashfork and Payson.

From the bottom lands of the Verde the road climbs abruptly up the sides of the Mingus Mountains where the town of Jerome appears at night to be hitched to the stars. By day travelers are amazed to see how five thousand people trust the man made braces, beams, and other supports that alone keep their homes and buildings from rolling into the valley below. Southwest of the town the highway again reaches a seven-thousand-foot elevation, then gradually slopes down toward Prescott and the west.

US Alt. 89 branches south from US 66, 0 m. (see TOUR 2b), in FLAGSTAFF, near the northern entrance to the Arizona State College campus. To the right is the mill of the Arizona Lumber and Timber Company, 0.2 m. Left, side by side, are two large log mansions owned by the Riordan brothers, former lumber barons of northern Arizona.

This section of the COCONINO NATIONAL FOREST was logged late in the nineteenth century. Stumps on both sides of the road are mute evidence of the industry that once supplied the principal employment in the vicinity. Instead of the iced runways and rivers utilized in the northern states, big two-wheeled carts were used to drag logs from the Arizona forests. Parts of a narrow-gauge lumber railroad are along the road. The one-room shanty homes of the loggers were built on runners and moved from one camp to another.

At 1.7 m. is the junction with a dirt road (see TOUR 10).

FORT TUTHILL, 4 m., was named for Brigadier General Alexander Tuthill, commander of the Arizona National Guard, who make this their headquarters. Summer encampment, during the latter part of August, provides drills, target practice, and sham battles (inactive).

The road continues through a section heavily wooded with birch, pine, fir, and scrub oak; the evergreens give off delightfully pungent odors, especially after rains. In summer at the sound of approaching danger, tiny chipmunks, brown squirrels, and rabbits scurry to hiding places over the forest's leaves and needles.

South of LOOKOUT POINT, 13.4 m., which is at the head of OAK CREEK CANYON, and approximately two thousand feet above the stream bed, the highway descends to the canyon floor where it twists through broad red-walled gorges and miles of green pine, maple, sycamore, cedar, oak, aspen, and fern. The few cabins and farms in secluded glens only emphasize the solitude. The dark green of the occasional patches of pine growing in the ledges of the carmine walls is intensified by the deep blue of the sky. Deep in the canyon the trees appear larger and more dense and partly conceal the outlines of the rock; but the size of this ragged rent in the earth seems even greater—

an immense space filled with bronze masses of stone formed into symmetrical buttes or upheavals of purple and red. The grandeur of these massive canyon walls is enhanced by their orange-yellow ledges, saffron seams and fissures, and towering russet buttes. From the floor the canyon's sides appear so high it is difficult to see their tops and their colors are constantly changing. In the sunlight the rock glistens with a scarlet luster; after sunset the colors darken and deepen till the whole canyon fills with Tyrian shadows. In places the canyon floor is a soft mat of fragrant pine needles, elsewhere the green of its ferns and grass is splashed with magenta Indian paintbrushes, purple asters, blue-bells, lavender-pink primroses, yellow columbines, and golden mescal. Between the highway and the great red walls, Oak Creek cuts its way through deep ravines and narrow gorges, plunging its transparent waters in white cascades over scores of tiny falls. The sound of its churning and rushing merges with that of the wind in the trees. In the fall the foliage matches the rich reds, magenta, carmine, and scarlet of the sculptured walls and buttes. This region is said to have been the setting for Zane Grey's *Call of the Canyon*.

Oak Creek Canyon was formed by the faulting of the rock formation in the basic Coconino sandstone. Subsequent centuries of washing by the waters of the creek, and of winds blowing sand against its relatively soft walls have completed its architecture. This fault, which is apparent—the wall on the right being higher than that on the left—extended for many miles and formed an opening for great volcanic activity. Today a cap of basalt, a smooth black layer, is visible along both rims at the upper end of the canyon. On either side are basalt dikes or upthrusts marking the openings through which the lava reached the surface.

Between 13.4 *m*. and 15.4 *m*. the road follows mountain curves that are dangerous but wide enough for passing (*keep to the right; watch for sliding rocks*).

The STATE FISH FARM, 15 *m.,* is one of many maintained by the state game department to stock lakes and streams. In 1935 seventy thousand fish from this hatchery, including rainbow trout and bony-tail, were placed in Oak Creek (inactive).

Between the fish farm and 40 *m.* the road drops approximately five thousand feet and the mountain trees and flowers are replaced by desert cactus and brush.

US Alt. 89 crosses to the eastern side of Oak Creek on a curved concrete bridge at PUMP HOUSE WASH, 15.7 *m.* There are numerous well-marked public campgrounds between this point and Sedona. As the road runs along the canyon floor, the towering walls obscure the sky.

The color of the sandstone changes from white to red at approximately 22 *m.* Scrub oak and buck brush replace mountain pines. Clinging to sharp cliffs' walls (R) an odd irrigation system of wooden troughs carries water to orchards of the lower canyon. Here the road crosses Oak Creek to the western side and a short trail leads (L) to a natural swimming hole (*boating and picnicking*). To the right at Indian Gardens, above the ranch, is a natural bridge.

A panorama at approximately 23 *m.* includes the trout stream, steep red cliffs, and small patches of orchard on the widening bottom lands to the south.

Where Oak Creek enters a box canyon formed of deep red limestone, 28.3 *m.*, the road leaves the bottom of the canyon, and climbs over red Supai sandstone. Among the trees in this region is the Arizona wild blue cypress. As the canyon bottom widens several small orchards appear, lying along the old creek bed. Plums, apples, grapes, peaches, and pears are grown here for sale in near-by towns. The cathedral-like rocks to the south are splendid landmarks.

SEDONA, 29 *m.* (4,500 alt., 1,350 pop.), a Mormon settlement, has long been a community center for the stock and fruit ranchers. In the last several years Sedona has grown to ten times its former size, and aside from becoming the home of many semi-retired and retired residents who have erected beautiful homes in eight subdivisions, Sedona has been the site of a great many motion pictures.

1. Right from Sedona over good road to RUINS OF RED ROCKS, 25 *m.*, on upper Verde River. Dwellings were built in man-made caves.

2. Left from Sedona on an improved dirt road to SCHNEBLEY HILL, 11 *m.* From its summit is a view of Verde Valley and a vast panorama of rock cliffs where contrasting reds, pinks, orange, purple, and golden colors form one of the most brilliant scenes in Arizona. Because of its beauty it is often used as a motion picture location.

Southwest of Sedona on high mesas (R) is BARNEY PASTURE, home of many black-tailed (mule) deer and a favorite hunting ground of northern Arizona sportsmen.

From a point at 44.7 *m.* a particularly imposing view of the country to the southwest reveals Mingus Mountain (7,720 alt.), majestic against the sky; at its base are the smokestacks of Cottonwood (R) and Clemenceau (L); between the stacks and against the mountainside is Jerome.

At 47.5 *m.* is a junction with a paved road.

Left on this, through the low rolling foothills and green fields of the Verde Valley, to CORNVILLE, 3.5 *m.* (3,400 alt., 200 pop.). In the settlement are a gas station and a general store where cowboys from the outlying range country gather to talk and drink beer. At 12.8 *m.* on this paved road is the junction with the improved dirt Beaver Creek Road.

Left 2.1 *m.* on Beaver Creek Road to MONTEZUMA'S WELL (*adm. free*). The well, which is 470 feet in diameter and has been sounded to a depth of 55 feet before finding bottom, looks very much like a small volcanic crater. There is a flow of one million nine hundred thousand gallons from the well every twenty-four hours. This water supply was probably the essential factor in the settlement of the region; surrounding the rocky wall of the well are twelve cliff dwellings, all in a remarkable state of preservation. Leading from the well are remains of ditches and a prehistoric irrigation system constructed with no little engineering skill. A calcareous substance deposited by the water in these ditches had accumulated during their long usage till it formed a stone lining. Although it is estimated that both dwellings and ditches were built about 1200 or 1300 A.D., parts of the ditch linings are practically intact. It is believed that the well was discovered by the army of Cortez, since it was shown on a deerskin map that belonged to the explorer.

On the main side route is a junction with a paved road, 15.6 m.; L. on this 1.1 m. to MONTEZUMA CASTLE NATIONAL MONUMENT (adm. .25), a five-hundred-acre tract surrounding one of the best preserved prehistoric cliff dwellings. The castle is in a recess halfway up the face of a perpendicular rock cliff 145 feet high. Early white visitors erroneously associated the place with Montezuma. It is thought the inhabitants of the castle were absorbed by other pueblo-building tribes; at any rate they completely vanished.

The ash-pink adobe castle was reached by a series of ladders placed against the face of the cliff. Its first floor is a horizontal row of eight rooms—some of the adobe bricks set in cement show the fingerprints of the original mason. Roofs were constructed in the usual pueblo manner—sycamore beams with successive toppings of small sticks, reeds, and a thick layer of adobe that formed the floor of the story above. As the community grew, each new family constructed its own addition to the castle. The structure is forty feet high and the fifth story reaches the very top of the natural cave. The number of rooms decreases in each ascending story till the fifth has but two rooms and a plaza.

At 20.4 m. on the main side route is CAMP VERDE (3,100 alt., 765 pop.), a cattle and farming center settled as Camp Lincoln in 1866 by Arizona volunteers dispatched from Whipple Barracks, near Prescott, to protect immigrants from marauding Indians. In 1868 the encampment's name was changed to Camp Verde by the U.S. army. By 1890 the district had become comparatively peaceable and the fort reservation was sold. At present many Yavapai and Apaches, now friendly cattlemen and farmers, live in their native wickiups a stone's throw from town. Right from Camp Verde on an improved dirt road to the junction wtih US Alt. 89, 39.1 m.

US Alt. 89 crosses the VERDE RIVER, 48.6 m., the eastern boundary of a section of the PRESCOTT NATIONAL FOREST which has headquarters in Prescott. There is a wealth of timber in this reserve and good forage for about seventy-three thousand head of cattle and sheep. West of the Verde River is a farming district known as BRIDGEPORT.

At 49.5 m. is the junction with the dirt road to Camp Verde (see above).

COTTONWOOD, 50.7 m. (3,310 alt., 2,500 pop.), at the entrance to lower Oak Creek Canyon in the upper Verde Valley is bordered on the south, east, and west by high mountains, and on the north by mesas, buttes, and lomas. It is a pleasant, quiet little community serving a rich agricultural, livestock, and mining district. Typical of Arizona's small towns, it is one street wide with several off-shoots leading to various residential areas. Familiar figures in the town are the cowboys from the range and the prospector or "desert rat" who wanders in from his camp in the mountains to break the monotony of his lonely life. The first permanent settler, James Oliver Bristow, arrived with his family in 1875 and sheltered them in a dug-out until he could build a more comfortable house.

Left on a graveled road from the eastern edge of Cottonwood to CLEMENCEAU, 0.5 m. (3,300 alt., 800 pop.), named for the French World War I statesman. The United Verde Extension Mining Company smelter was opened here in 1918 and closed permanently in January 1937. (Good airport at Clemenceau.)

CLARKDALE, 54.6 *m.* (2,568 alt., 2,800 pop.), on a sloping desert mesa at the foot of the Black Hills was a smelter town built in 1911 by the United Verde Copper Company (later owned by the Phelps Dodge Corporation) because the United Verde mines had outgrown their smelter in Jerome on Woodchuck Mountain and cave-ins and lack of space prevented building a larger one there. The new town was named for William A. Clark, Senator from Montana (1901-07) and former owner of the United Verde mines, who purchased this site then known as the Jordan Ranch. From a green square with a bandstand, surrounded by company-owned brick bungalows, the main street runs through a shopping and business block. On the north are the treeless streets and squat frame or brick houses of the company's Lower Town. Mexican- or Patiotown, which is outside the planned area, trails along the smelter yards into sandy fields. It is made up of several dozen cottages in the middle of green lawns, and parallel alleys of long two-family barracks.

In 1950 the smelter, which was completed in 1915 and had treated most of the Jerome production, was closed permanently after the closing of the Jerome mine due to exhaustion of ore reserves. It had a monthly capacity of four million five hundred thousand pounds of ore, and had furnished employment to thousands. The smoke from the smelter had been the cause of much controversy in this area, as farmers and ranchers in the Verde Valley asserted that the heavy smoke had damaged their crops and grazing lands.

Today the smelter smoke is gone, the miners have gone, but the future of the model town is bright. The town, smelter, and appendages has been sold by Phelps Dodge to a company which will operate a giant cement plant here. This new industry includes a 120-mile, five-inch pipeline, which will carry the crushed stone by gravity to Phoenix for finishing, at the rate of 1,200 tons a day. This is said to be the first time anyone will have attempted to move raw cement over such a great distance by pipe.

1. Left from Clarkdale to PECK'S LAKE, 1 *m.*, in the center of Verde Valley golf course (*greens fee $1, week days, $1.50 Sat., Sun.*).

2. Right from Clarkdale on a dirt road crossing Verde River to TUZI-GOOT NATIONAL MONUMENT, 2.4 *m.*, an ancient pueblo originally built of stone mortared with mud and now partially restored. The pueblo was occupied about the year 1200. When it was abandoned has not been definitely established, but it is supposed that the inhabitants were among the antecedents of the modern Hopi. The pueblo housed several hundred persons. Articles found in the ruin indicate a high degree of culture. Many have been left exactly as they were revealed in the excavation of the rooms. TUZIGOOT MUSEUM, patterned after the ruin itself, displays beadwork, shell and turquoise mosaics, several varieties of pottery, storage ollas 24 to 27 inches in height and diameter, and stone and bone implements more symmetrical than the average specimens found in Arizona pueblos. The numerous grinding stones indicate that corn was the staple food.

Before JEROME, 60.7 *m.* (5,435 alt., 800 pop.), former copper-mining town, is reached it is in view, hanging precariously on the side of Mingus Mountain in the Black Hills; its frame houses a jumble on stilts. With a fifteen-hundred-foot difference in elevation between the highest and lowest perches, the town has some houses with basements reached by a climb up three flights of steps, others with roofs below the level of the streets on which they face, and yet others with garages on their roofs. Many householders can lean out of their kitchen windows and scratch matches on their neighbors' chimneys.

Since 1925 when two hundred and fifty pounds of dynamite was used for blasting in the Black Pit, the entire town has moved three-eighths of an inch a month; neither banks nor the Federal government will accept the average Jerome house as collateral for a loan. Everywhere are braces, beams, and concrete blocks to keep buildings from tumbling into the valley, a quarter of a mile below. These give the town architectural peculiarities so distinctive that the inhabitants have reached a certain boastfulness about them and have even added to them when talking with outsiders—thus contributing an authentic page to Arizona folk lore.

Because of the terrain Jerome has no street cars or busses and the inhabitants must climb trails and flights of steps in going about town. The single unifying factor is the curving highway. In spite of disadvantages Jerome is able to boast that no town in Arizona has so many dwellings with magnificent views. A man need only walk to the window to behold a panorama of the Verde Valley, where the towns of Clarkdale and Clemenceau appear as clusters of white and green against the red-streaked cliffs of Oak Creek Canyon.

Lodged on red splintered rocks of Yeager Canyon was the English-speaking district, crowding down to Hogback and Lower Hogback, on flatter land and formerly inhabited chiefly by Slavs. Beyond the little business district is Bitter Creek where Mexicans lived. A few Italians and Cornishmen scattered through the various districts completed the town's racial mixture.

Copper determined Jerome's settlement and position and for nearly sixty years the price of copper has determined the size of its population and its degree of prosperity. The Indians had worked copper here long before white men arrived. In the period after the Civil War John Ruffner and August McKinnon, ranchers from the vicinity of Prescott, came into the valley. Ruffner later established his claim to what became the United Verde property though claim for the rediscovery of the copper may have belonged to McKinnon or to the Indian scout Al Sieber (*see TOUR 10*). Ruffner who was busy with his ranch, decided to lease his claim to Governor Tritle. Tritle in time got financial support for developing the property from Eugene Jerome of New York, who insisted that the camp be named for him. It was not, however, until the Atlantic & Pacific Railroad arrived at Ashfork in 1882 that the chances for profitable exploitation appeared. Even at that the difficulties were great. Tritle had to break the road from Ashfork to the mine to bring in his smelter—the one now exhibited at Clarkdale (*see above*). Coke for the smelter had also to be freighted in from Ashfork after a very roundabout and expensive trip from Wales and through San Francisco. Even with these difficulties enormous amounts of copper were produced at a cost of seven cents a pound. Later, coke from New Mexico was used but it was not until a freight branch of the Santa Fe railroad was built in 1894 that mining became highly profitable here.

W. A. Clark of Montana had purchased the mining properties in 1886 and it was he who was able to bring the railroad south to what is now Jerome Junction, though he himself had to build a narrow-gauge road from the branch into Jerome. He installed a new smelter that could handle a half a million pounds of ore a month and improved the mining and smelting methods.

Until Clark bought the property the camp had been a cluster of shacks with the unmarried men living at the Mulligan boardinghouse. To attract a more stable population—men with families—Clark built some frame houses and in 1888 promoted the construction of the Montana House, in its early days the largest stone structure in Arizona and capable of holding a thousand men. Its high-columned porch overlooking the empty Verde Valley was the pride of the community, which began to see itself as a metropolis. In spite of the new elegance Jerome lacked water, and in three instances its population was forced to camp on the hills after fire had destroyed most of its frame houses and its fourteen frame saloons. (Among those who profited from Jerome's water needs was Pancho Villa, the Mexican revolutionist, who in 1900 had two hundred burros bringing water to the town.)

As Jerome expanded, its chances for the title, "the toughest little town in the West," increased and when it was incorporated in 1899 the citizens were able to support the claim by pointing to the number of thick stone shutters on the fronts of all saloons, gambling halls, and other places of business for protection against gunfire.

Jerome became even more important in 1900 when J. J. Fisher discovered and laid claim to the Little Daisy in Bitter Creek. This became the United Verde Extension Mine in 1910. The town had a setback in 1915 when the United moved its smelter to Clarkdale, but prospered because of the World War demand for copper. Prosperity boomed in 1917 with the opening of the Verde Central Mine—nicknamed the Chivas (Sp. goat) for the goatee worn by one of the foremen.

A town with Jerome's hardy spirit could not escape labor troubles. In 1907 the miners staged their first strike and succeeded in reducing their ten-hour workday to eight and in obtaining a daily wage of $2.75. In 1917 before the United Verde had come under control of the Phelps Dodge Corporation, the Industrial Workers of the World—the I.W.W. —led a strike so lively that several hundred miners and outside agitators were ousted from their company-owned houses, loaded on boxcars with the aid of guns and pickaxes, and shipped to a remote point on the southeastern desert country of Arizona, where they were dumped without ceremony. This drive precipitated the similar deportation of the Bisbee miners.

In the post-war years Jerome began to adopt a more sedate civic attitude and even developed a town "square"—stone bleachers banked on the south side of the almost level half-block in the business district. From these bleachers on the Fourth of July and Labor Day the towns-people witnessed the games, parades, and the mucking and drilling con-tests of miners—held in the street below.

In happy 1929 Jerome had a population of fifteen thousand but this dropped steadily thereafter as the price of copper declined. Due to the exhaustion of ore reserves, the Phelps Dodge Corp. permanently closed the mine at Jerome in 1953.

The BIG PIT which is W. on Three-Hundred-Foot Level, is an ore hole more than a thousand feet deep in Woodchuck Mountain. The Ore Bin Cut, a slice of the north slope of the mountain that was cut through to the three hundred-foot level, leads to a shelf of the funnel-shaped pit whose terraced walls are colored red, black, and brown by the different ores. A safety shed and set of searchlights stand at the top of a wide truck road that is built on a ledge of the pit walls, and coils down to the narrow flat floor. This floor is visible 560 feet below the collar of the original shaft of the United Verde mines, which had been sunk on the surface or the zero-level of the mountain. Excavation of this surface began in 1920. Since that year eighteen million cubic yards of material and ten million tons of ore have been scooped out of the mountain. In the pit floor miners dig holes with long-handled electric and steam drills; pack the holes with powder and sand; and blast them. The blown-up ore is steam-shoveled into trucks, and dumped from the trucks through shaft-holes that lead from the pit floor to the one thousand-foot level where the ore drops into bins. Electric trains carry it from the Hopewell Tunnel at the foot of the bins to the smelter at Clarkdale. Probably the richest ores in the Verde district have been taken from this pit.

The THREE HUNDRED-FOOT LEVEL, W. on Main St., is a flat plateau of rock materials scooped out of the Big Pit. It bridges the town of Jerome and the properties of the Phelps Dodge Corporation. West on the plateau are the swimming pool and a street of frame and corrugated iron houses for employees.

SUNSHINE HILL, W. on Three Hundred-Foot Level, overlooks Bitter Creek and slopes down into Verde Valley. The churches of Jerome participate in joint Easter sunrise services around the two crosses on its summit. At the foot of the hill are the general offices of the Phelps Dodge Corporation.

UNITED VERDE EXTENSION MINE (Little Daisy), N. on State 79 (closed in 1938), is on a spur of flat land in Bitter Creek. The long hotel and hospital building of the company are on a hill overlooking the offices, the headframe of the single shaft, and the hoisting room. During the thirty-six years this mine was operated, four million tons of ore were removed. On the one-thousand-five-hundred-foot level of the shaft the Josephine Train Tunnel carried ores to the company smelter at Clemenceau. Just east of the properties is the large, yellow pueblo-type home of the president of the company.

On SECOND SUMMIT, 68.4 *m.* (7,029 alt.), the saddle of Mingus Mountain, is the junction with a dirt road.

Left on this road to a Forest Service recreational area (*swings, slides for children; picnic tables*) 2 *m.*

Southwest of Second Summit is flat grazing land. Though the rocks show copper stains only one mine in the area, the Yeager, has attained commercial production. The tableland, a grass country, was once called Jackass Flats by the cowboys.

From a point at 86.2 *m.* is a view of GRANITE DELLS (*see TOUR 1b*).

At 87.1 *m.* US Alt. 89 joins US 89 (*see TOUR 1b*) 6 miles north of Prescott.

<<<<<<<<<<<<<<<<<<<<<<<<<<<<<<<<<<<<<<<<<<<<<<<>>>>>>>>>>>>>>>>>>>>>>>>>>>>>>>>>>>>>>>

Tour 2B

Kingman—Boulder Dam—(Las Vegas, Nev.) ; *81 m.,* US 93-466.

All-paved, all-year highway.
Service stations but no other accommodations between Kingman and Boulder City, Nev.; all types of accommodations in Boulder City.

This route to tremendous Boulder Dam and the recreation area rapidly developing around its reservoir, Lake Mead, crosses an almost uninhabited desert flanked by jagged ranges where colors change with the light from red to purple or blue. At intervals the highway traverses forests of yucca that stretch for many miles, at others it is shut in by cliffs formed like pillars.

US 93-466 branches north from US 66 (*see TOUR 2c*) in KINGMAN, 0 *m.*

CASTLE ROCKS, 3 *m.,* resemble a gigantic edifice.

From the summit of COYOTE HILL, 5 *m.,* is an excellent view of Kingman, the Walapai Mountains (R), the sawtooth peaks bordering the Colorado River (L), and the California ranges to the west. North of Coyote Hill the highway is bordered by mountains that have yielded fortunes in gold, silver, and lead.

At 18 *m.* is a junction with paved road.

Right to CHLORIDE, 4 *m.* settled as silver-mining center, distributing point for several mines. These have very old workings; a few—Tiffany of N.Y. owns the largest—produce turquoise.

Along the Sacramento Wash is a large FOREST OF JOSHUA TREES (*see TOUR 1b*), 23 *m.,* sometimes called yucca palms; they are 25 to 30 feet high, have dagger-shaped olive-green leaves and, in the spring, clusters of white flowers. From this point are visible the Cerbat (Coco-Maricopa, big horn sheep) Mountains (R) and the Black Mountains (L). The road builders' many cuts in the hills here reveal the same pinks, yellows, and blues found in the Grand Canyon near by.

The rich red, purple, and tan slopes of the BLACK MOUNTAINS, 61 *m.,* belie their name. In this deep gorge called BLACK CANYON (L) the Colorado River has been replaced by new LAKE MOHAVE, creating placid waters where formerly rapids were to be found. In the rough hills are deep slashes exposing colors that change continually with every variation in the light. At 75 *m.* FORTIFICATION HILL on the Arizona side, bursts into view (R). From the brilliant red at its base this fortlike mountain rises in a mass of colors—reds, blues, and yellows, streaked with long fingers of black—and is reflected in Lake Mead.

BOULDER DAM, 81 *m.* (640 alt. at river bed), was completed in 1936 at a cost of seventy-six million, or one hundred and twenty-five million including the power plant. It shares with Grand Coulee Dam in Washington the distinction of being the greatest water and power projects ever undertaken; but Boulder is quite alone in its spectacular situation. Only through comparison is it possible to realize the dam's immensity; it is 727 feet high—only 65 feet less than New York's Woolworth Building—660 feet thick at the base and 1,282 feet long at the crest. By recent federal law it was renamed Hoover Dam.

The dam was planned and constructed by the U. S. Bureau of Reclamation with the fourfold purpose of checking floods and erosion, and of providing a dependable water supply and electric power. For countless centuries the Colorado River had cut its way into the surface of the earth forming the Grand Canyon. Silt carried downstream had filled in the upper end of the Gulf of California and formed the Imperial Valley. This silt came from a watershed that includes large areas belonging to Arizona, California, Colorado, Nevada, New Mexico, Wyoming, and Utah. Though beautiful to behold, the changes wrought by the Colorado in its rush to the sea are examples of destruction and waste—water erosion at its worst. By harnessing the river's energy the dam has transformed its power from a destroyer of land to a servant of man.

Beside providing abundant power the dam regulates the river to an even flow, thus preventing the floods, formerly so disastrous to the rich agricultural lands to the south. It has made it possible to build the Parker Diversion Dam, take-off of the great aqueduct of the Metropolitan Water District of Southern California; the Gila irrigation project, comprising five hundred and twenty-five thousand fertile acres in southwestern Arizona; and the All-American Canal in the Imperial and Coachella valleys of California.

Perhaps its most desirable recreational feature is LAKE MEAD (scenic lake tours from Boulder Beach), one of the world's largest artificial lakes. It has a shore line 550 miles long and extends 115 miles into little-known, rugged, highly colored canyons of the Colorado and its tributaries. Just back of the dam the reservoir's depth is more than 550 feet. This lake, one of the finest in the West for boating, sailing, and water skiing, under supervision of the National Park Service, is well stocked with game fish, and resorts and other facilities are developing along its shores. Boulder Yacht Harbor offers services for all types of boats as well as moorage. Nearby is Boulder Beach, excellent for bathing and swimming. An excellent campground is available for public use.

Lake Mead National Recreation Area offers outstanding opportunities to enjoy Nature at her best. Such highly scenic spots as the Paint Pots (located near Dam), and Valley of Fire (on N. arm of Lake), and Pierce's Ferry (at lower end of the Grand Canyon) are key features. There is a wide assortment of animal life, more than 250 different species of birds and 57 varieties of mammals. In springtime the slopes and canyons display myriads of flowers. The area is rich in history and archaeology; a number of Indian sites have been located.

Both litigation and militia were used by Arizona to fight the building of Boulder Dam and its subsidiary projects because of the state's dissatisfaction with the Santa Fe Compact which allocated to seven states their share of the Colorado's flow. California, able to make immediate use of the water and power from the projected works, claimed a prior right, while Arizona struggled to reserve rights that would provide for its future development. In 1928 construction of Boulder Dam was authorized by Congress (Swing-Johnson Bill) and a hundred and sixty-five million dollars were appropriated for the purpose construction was begun in 1930 and the dam was completed in 1936.

Although the dam is in Black Canyon, the original plan was to place it in Boulder Canyon—hence the name. An immense amount of preliminary work was necessary before the actual construction: the Union Pacific R.R. laid a branch line 20 miles long from near Las Vegas to Boulder City, the Bureau of Reclamation extended it to the bottom of Black Canyon and to the various plants. An electric transmission line, 222 miles long, was constructed from San Bernardino, California, and Boulder City was created to provide homes for workers, who at one time numbered 5,250. Before a start could be made on the dam itself, four tunnels, fifty feet in diameter, had to be bored through the canyon walls to divert the river's flow from its bed at the proposed site. Coffer dams were constructed, one above to force the flow into the tunnels, and one below to prevent backflow. One of the most hazardous phases of the early work was the scaling of the canyon walls and the drilling and blasting of loose or nearly loose masses of rock that hung precariously over the site. Except for 13 deaths caused by heat, this work was responsible for almost all of the 110 deaths that occurred during the dam's construction. A total of 9,000,000 cubic yards of rock was excavated on the project. An interesting construction problem was that of cooling the concrete, 400,000 cubic yards of which were used—an amount sufficient to build a pavement 20 feet wide from Florida to California. It was estimated that 150 years would be required to cool the mass to the temperature of the surrounding canyon walls, and that stresses thus set up would result in continual cracking. The remedy was an artificial cooling system consisting of one-inch pipes set five feet apart, through which refrigerated water was run. As the concrete contracted the pipes were withdrawn and the holes filled.

There are two spillways for surplus water, four intake towers 375 feet in height, and a U-shaped powerhouse one-quarter mile in length at the base of the dam. This power plant was the largest in the world in 1939, but will be exceeded in size by the proposed plant at Grand Coulee. Energy generated is carried as far as Los Angeles. Elevators entered from the highway take visitors to the POWERHOUSE (*adm. 25¢; guides*), which contains fifteen 115,000-horsepower and two 55,000-horsepower vertical turbines, eleven 60-cycle and four 50-cycle main generating units of 82,500 kilovolt-ampere capacity each.

The outlets are watched in operation from one of the walks along the base of the plant. These openings are called needle valves. Six on each side are 72 inches in diameter. Behind these valves are outlet works consisting of a concrete plug 142 feet in length, 85 feet high, and 105 feet wide. Water spilling from these needle valves is sent either through the generator turbines or directly to the outlets—which answers what guides call the most surprising of all questions: "What do you do with the water after you've taken the power out of it?"

Pipe sections 30 feet in diameter connect the intake towers and the needle valves directly. Because of the size required, the pipe for the dam was manufactured at a factory erected for the purpose near the site.

The road crosses the dam to Boulder City, Nevada, which is 23 miles southwest of Las Vegas.

Tour 3

(Lordsburg, N.M.)—Safford—Globe—Phoenix—Wickenburg—Ehrenberg—(Blythe, Calif.) ; US 70.
New Mexico Line to California Line, 390.5 *m.*

All-paved, all-year highway throughout; few sharp curves between Safford and Globe; avoid cattle.
A branch of the Southern Pacific parallels route between Safford and Miami; Southern Pacific main line between Mesa and Phoenix; a Santa Fe branch between Phoenix and Salome.
All types of accommodations along route.

This route traverses desert, mountains, and irrigated farm lands. Near the New Mexico Line it sweeps through low hills and fertile valleys. Just east of Coolidge Dam US 70 climbs steadily and winds beside the clear blue waters of San Carlos Lake. Between Miami and Superior it twists through brilliantly colored rock formations that rise abruptly like the walls and turrets of castles. West of Superior the desert with its giant saguaros is patched with the green of farm lands.

Section a. **NEW MEXICO LINE to FLORENCE JUNCTION;**
182.4 m., US 70, US 70-60.

This eastern section of US 70 passes mining towns, Indian ruins, and irrigated farm lands developed by the Mormons. For almost half the distance the highway borders the Gila River and approximates the route followed during the Mexican War by General Stephen W. Kearny, commander of the Army of the West. Ordered to seize California and govern it, Kearny left Santa Fe in September 1846 with three hundred dragoons and two howitzers. Near the Rio Grande he met Kit Carson going east with the news that Commodore Robert F. Stockton was in control of California. Carson's papers were sent on by another man so Carson could guide Kearny across Arizona and the California desert. In Arizona they followed the Gila most of the way but were forced by the high mountains and deep canyons to make frequent detours. Even after they had abandoned the heavy wagons at Carson's suggestion and substituted pack mules, the journey was very difficult and both men and animals suffered from hunger, thirst, and fatigue. When Kearny reached California in December he was joined by a detachment sent by Stockton and was attacked by Mexicans who were repulsed with great difficulty.

US 70 crosses the New Mexico Line, 0 *m.,* at a point 30 miles west of Lordsburg, N.M.

FRANKLIN, 2.9 *m.* (3,676 alt., 350 pop.), was settled in 1897 by Mormons, who dug irrigation ditches and brought a strip of desolate land under cultivation. Water from the GILA (HEE-la) RIVER is used for irrigation in the Coolidge Dam reclamation project.

In DUNCAN, 5.8 *m.* (3,642 alt., 1,050 pop.), is the State Highway Checking Station (*see Gen. Information*). Duncan, now a marketing center for a farming district irrigated by the Gila River and a shipping point for cattle and ore, was a "tough town" in territorial days. Its citizens were obliged to contend not only with Apache, but also with notorious bad men including "Black Jack" Ketchum, stagecoach and express robber, and his gang. The area's chief crop now is cotton.

In the hills west of Duncan a heavy rain transforms the tufts of yellow bunch grass into a carpet of green, completely changing the landscape's color. Terraces and check dams by the thousands indicate the battle waged by the Civilian Conservation Corps against soil erosion.

The GILA MOUNTAINS (R) dominate the horizon. On hazy days and especially at dawn and sunset, this sky line appears so unreal that it suggests the painted backdrop of a stage setting. On both sides of the highway the ground is covered with greasewood and covillea interspersed with an occasional Spanish dagger, or yucca. Greasewood is an evergreen bush, usually four or five feet high, that grows very thickly and is extremely pungent immediately after a rain, when its perfume is carried far over the countryside. In spring the mesas are yellow with the tiny greasewood blossoms and yucca stalks burst into white masses of bell-shaped flowers. Yuccas in this vicinity seldom exceed ten feet in height.

Mt. Graham (10,750 alt.), is visible from 21.8 *m.,* straight west on the horizon. Mt. Turnbull rises in the distance to the northwest.

Near a filling station and store (L), 23.7 *m.,* is a comparatively low formation shaped like a Mexican hat and named SOMBRERO HILL. At the base of this hill Seth and Lorenzo Wright, two young brothers, were killed in 1885 by Apaches who had stolen a number of horses and were being pursued by the boys.

At 36 *m.* is the junction with US 666 (*see TOUR 7b*), which unites with US 70 between this point and Safford. Cholla (CHO-yah), a branching cactus so thickly covered with spines that it appears fuzzy, and prickly pear, a flat jointed cactus, grow densely on both sides of the highway.

"GRIPE," 38.8 *m.* (3,211 alt.), is merely an inspection point (*baggage may be searched*), maintained to prevent the spread of insect pests and plant diseases in Arizona. All plants and fruits, especially citrus fruits, cotton bolls and seeds, pecans, sweet potatoes, and honey, are usually inspected. Its name, posted on the main building, was bestowed by officers of the Arizona Commission of Agriculture and Horticulture assigned to duty here.

Motorists usually spend their enforced stop admiring a cactus garden that contains most of the local varieties.

SOLOMON, 41 *m.* (3,000 alt., 600 pop.), was named for Isador E. Solomon, who settled here in 1873, established a store, and for many years was a leading citizen. On several occasions members of the Solomon family narrowly escaped attacks by Indians. Once when sickness caused a delay, the stage on which the family had intended to travel was captured and all of the occupants were killed.

Excluding the Indians and several Mexicans, who were in the upper Gila Valley as early as 1871, the first settlement here was made in 1872 by ranchers from Gila Bend on the lower Gila River. The seat of Graham County was here from 1883 to 1915, when it was moved to Safford.

In the summer of 1879 the first Mormon settlers arrived. Their history is one of sacrifice, hardship, and struggle. In the beginning the chief crops planted were wheat, oats, barley, corn, and vegetables— later alfalfa, yielding six and seven crops a year and still later cotton, of which ten to fourteen thousand bales are produced here annually. Today there are approximately thirty-five thousand acres of farming land in the upper Gila Valley; the soil is a rich sandy loam, its fertility continually replenished by the silt carried in the irrigation water.

Left from Solomon on a graveled road to a prehistoric ruin, 3 *m.*, believed to be Chichilticalli (the red house), mentioned by several Spanish explorers including Coronado. Only a reddish mound remains. Solomon first bore the name of Pueblo Viejo (Sp., old town) from its proximity to the ruin.

The SAN SIMON RIVER (or wash), 44.1 *m.*, is a narrow gulch lined with willow, mesquite, and covillea. Throughout most of the year it is dry but in flood times it empties into the Gila River one mile west of Solomon.

SAFFORD, 46 *m.* (2,920 alt., 4,000 pop.), seat of Graham County, on the south bank of the Gila River. In the center of the upper Gila Valley agricultural district, cotton is the main crop; also grain, fruit, and other crops; also cattle and sheep raising, and being in the center of a scenic area, the tourist trade is an economic factor. Safford was founded in 1872 when a group of farmers migrated from Gila Bend, settled in the vicinity, and constructed the Montezuma Canal. A township was established and named in honor of A.P.K. Safford, third territorial governor of Arizona. The early settlers were later joined by Mormons from the northern part of the territory and a fort was erected as a protection against Indians.

At Safford is the junction with US 666 (*see TOUR 7c*).

THATCHER, 49 *m.* (2,929 alt., 1,300 pop.), was named for Apostle Moses Thatcher of the Mormon Church by the first settlers who arrived in 1881. The community soon became headquarters of a stage line and contained a number of stores.

Eastern Arizona JUNIOR COLLEGE, in a gray sandstone building, was founded in Central in 1891 as St. Joseph Stake Academy, most of the patrons and students being Mormons. (A stake is a subdivision of the Mormon Church somewhat like a diocese.) In 1892 the school was moved to Thatcher. A principal and two assistants constituted the faculty, with salaries paid mostly in produce—flour, beans, honey, milk, butter, and sometimes meat. In 1917 the school was recognized by the North Central Association of Secondary Schools and Colleges. In 1921 first-year college courses were introduced and a little later second-year courses. In 1926 it was accredited by the University of Arizona for two years of college work and in 1930 by the American Association of Junior Colleges. In 1933, after forty-three years under the Latter-day Saints, the school became a county junior college and all courses of a religious nature were eliminated. Professional, business and vocational courses; outstanding sports participation, and community service are emphasized at this community college.

Northwest of Thatcher, Mt. Turnbull appears as two adjoining peaks. Mountains to the right are part of the Gila range.

CENTRAL, 53.9 *m.* (2,900 alt., 290 pop.), trading center for Mormon farmers, was named for the canal that flows through the center of the valley. At one time farms near by appeared to be doomed because of alkaline underground water that rose to the surface; but a drainage system brought the land back to productivity.

PIMA, 55 *m.* (2,848 alt., 850 pop.), another trading point for farmers, was named for the Pima Indians.

At 62 *m.* is a junction with a dirt road.

1. Right on this road to INDIAN HOT SPRINGS, 5 *m.*, once a camping spot of Apache and other Indians who believed the waters had curative powers. Today the area is a modern health resort. Four large springs and many smaller ones within 100 yards of the hotel have a combined daily flow that exceeds one-and-a-half million gallons. Beauty Springs has a temperature of 119°; Iron Springs and Mud Springs 116°; Rock Springs 118° and Magnesium Springs 81°.

2. Left on this road to RED KNOLLS, 1 *m.*, beautifully eroded and rising like a giant tabernacle from the flat valley. Nature has carved a theater among the knolls, with stages, off-stage recesses, and a crescent-shaped auditorium having almost perfect acoustics. A rock-capped sandstone formation rises like a pipe organ two hundred feet above the floor of the auditorium. The off-stage rooms accommodate several hundred persons and provide a place for properties when pageants are presented by Gila College. Evidences of an early occupation are numerous on both levels of the knolls. Foundations of common pit houses, bits of broken pottery that represent at least two different early cultures, arrowheads, and manos and metates are still in evidence. These heights, undoubtedly prized as a fortress and as an observation and signaling point, command a view to the northwest of two old military posts, Camp Goodwin and Camp Thomas (*see below*). In the days of rustlers the coves and bays of the knolls served as excellent corrals for holding and branding cattle.

ASHURST, 64 *m.* (2,739 alt., 100 pop.), is a farm village named for Henry Ashurst, Senator from Arizona, serving his fifth term in 1939. It was originally called Redlands because of the color of the soil.

FT. THOMAS, 68 *m.* (2,705 alt., 250 pop.), mining, cattle-raising and farming community, was an important scouting point for soldiers in Indian warfare. In 1878 Camp Thomas was moved here from its first site now occupied by the town of Geronimo (*see below*).

In the 1920's this village was the home of three cowboys acclaimed world's champions in rodeo competition: Breezy Cox, Everet Bowman (winner in 1936), and Hugh Bennet.

GERONIMO (Je RON imō), 74 *m.* (2,700 alt., 75 pop.), the original Camp Thomas, was named for Geronimo, the Apache troublemaker of the eighties (*see TOUR 4a*). Cattle raising as well as farming have been the principal industries of the community for many years. The town was by the river and later moved to its present site.

Early-day Geronimo citizens fraternized with the outlaws who frequently visited the town. On hot nights it was the custom to sleep on the flat-roofed housetops; places where outlaws slept were easily identified because their ladders were hauled up.

Northwest of Geronimo the highway drops to a straight course across a sunbaked flat beside the Gila River (R).

The highway crosses the boundary of the SAN CARLOS INDIAN RESERVATION (pop. 4,019) for the Apache at 77.7 *m.* On the northwestern horizon are the Triplets, peaks known as landmarks.

Native wickiups (*see TOUR 8*) are a few hundred feet (R) from the highway at 80.6 *m.* Stout flexible sticks set in a circle and lashed together at the top give the structure a round igloo effect. The covering depends upon the materials at hand. Sometimes grass and discarded pieces of sheet-iron roofing are used; but more often the frame is sheathed—except for a small opening left at the top for a smoke vent —with sundry materials such as pieces of old canvas and corrugated iron that are removed in hot weather. Often the wickiup has an adjoining ramada, a shelter built of poles and brush.

The Apache were, at one time, the most warlike tribe in the Southwest. This was especially evident in the period 1870-1900, when the encroachments of white settlers roused them to fierce resentment.

In BYLAS (Apache, one who does all the talking), 80 *m.* (3,000 alt., 1,500 pop.), a trading point for farmers and Indians, is the headquarters of a subsistence gardening project managed by the Indians belonging to San Carlos Reservation. The EVANGELICAL LUTHERAN MISSION FOR APACHES, which has about ninety pupils, is housed in a gray rock structure (*church services Wed. and Sun.*).

CALVA, 86 *m.,* is a shortening of Calvario (Sp., Calvary). This railroad point, from which the old Chiricahua Cattle Company and the Double Circle outfit have shipped many thousand head of cattle, is still a shipping point for Apache cattle.

An old Chiricahua puncher tells of an incident here in the fall of 1927: "The cattle were penned for the night, and since the pens were plumb full we built a rope corral long side for the saddle horses. We turned in early and every thing went fine until a freight train came along about midnight. To make matters worse the engineer blowed his whistle when he was directly opposite the pens. The cattle was penned so tight they couldn't get a run at the fence, but the saddle horses went through that rope corral as if it was made of twine.

"We were camped at the lower end of the pens and when the ponies passed us they were goin' like a bat out of hell. Fact is some of the boys took to the brush for fear they'd get run over. But Otho Cox (brother of the noted Breezy) managed to get a mane holt and swing aboard one as they went by. When he did the pony went to buckin'. At that you can't blame the pony none. He probably thought a ghost had crawled him, for Otho didn't have nothin' on except his underwear. When they hit the river the pony was 'still abuckin' but Otho stuck. Riding with nothin' but a mane holt he finally got the ponies headed and drove them back to the pens. Breezy has won plenty of money in big-time rodeos but Breezy never made a better ride than his brother made that night."

It was at Calva that Kearny's expedition, unable to drag their two heavy howitzers through Box Canyon, began one of their arduous detours. To cover 23 miles—that now require only half an hour by automobile—took Kearny two days and left his men and mules so exhausted they were forced to rest for two days before they could continue.

The SAN CARLOS RESERVOIR (R), 100.8 *m.,* formed by the Coolidge Dam across the Gila River, is 23 miles long and has a capacity of 1,200,000 acre-feet. The annual run off of the Gila River is 385,000 acre-feet. Other glimpses of the water, sparkling bits of blue in the red-and-tan landscape, are visible to the west.

US 70 crosses the COOLIDGE DAM, 108 *m.,* the first and largest multiple-dome (egg-shaped) dam ever built. It was named for former President Calvin Coolidge and dedicated by him in 1930. After the dedication Will Rogers spoke—at that time the lake had just begun to fill and there was more grass to be seen than water. "If this was my lake," said Rogers, "I'd mow it." The project has wrought a tremendous change in the valley, an increase from about twenty thousand to almost one hundred twenty thousand cultivated acres, and has provided abundant electric power.

The top of the dam is 259 feet above bedrock; its domes are twenty-one feet thick at the base and four feet thick at the top. The dam itself cost five million five hundred thousand dollars and the entire project ten million dollars. Completion of the dam marked the end of a fifty-year struggle by valley settlers. Its construction was delayed by public apathy, especially in the East, and by strong opposition from the Apache, who claimed that the creation of San Carlos Reservoir would violate their treaty rights. A compromise was finally made with the Indians, and the tribal burying grounds and the old camp from which Geronimo started his bloody raids now lie deep under the waters of the reservoir. It was proposed to disinter the bodies but the Apache vehemently objected to what they considered desecration of the dead, so a concrete slab was laid over the principal burying ground at a cost of $11,000.

COOLIDGE DAM POST OFFICE, 110 *m.,* is a trading post for workers at the dam, and tourists on US 70.

At 119.7 *m.* is the junction with an unimproved dirt road.

Right on this road to PERIDOT, 8 *m.,* an Indian community. In this vicinity many rough peridots and smoky topaz stones are found. Peridots, which resemble emeralds when cut and mounted, make beautiful necklaces and rings.

SAN CARLOS, 13 *m.,* is at the junction with State 73 (*see TOUR 8*).

On the western horizon visible from about 124 *m.* are the Pinal Mountains (L), and Four Peaks (R), a landmark near Roosevelt Dam.

CUTTER, 127 *m.,* the junction with State 73 (*see TOUR 8*), on the Apache Reservation, at one time was a cattle-shipping point. In years past the flats in this vicinity were often filled with bawling, milling stock awaiting shipment from the Bar F Bar, Cross S, Five L, and other ranches.

At 132 *m.* is the junction with State 77.

Left on this road to CHRISTMAS, 30 *m.* (2,990 alt.), no longer a post office but once known as a point "where Santa Claus lived," because of the heavy mail routed here by stamp collectors and children. In the 1880's three prospectors, including Dr. James Douglas, were forced to abandon their copper claims here when this land was found to be within the San Carlos Reservation. In December 1902 news that reservation lines had been changed was wired to George Crittenden and N. H. Mellor, who hurried here to take up claims and named the site for the day of their arrival—Christmas.

WINKLEMAN, 36 *m.* (1,947 alt., 729 pop.), on the same road, is a commercial center for mines. Fruit, cattle, and Angora goats are raised in the vicinity.

Right from Winkleman to HAYDEN, 37 *m.* (2,051 alt., 1,800 pop.), site of two smelter and reduction plants. The town was named for Charles Hayden, a mining company official.

A cattle guard across US 70 marks the western boundary of the SAN CARLOS INDIAN RESERVATION, 130 *m.* and the eastern boundary of the TONTO NATIONAL FOREST in which are several thousand cattle, sheep, goats, and deer, as well as many lions, lynxes, foxes, raccoons, bears, and javalinas or wild pigs. (*For campsites apply at headquarters in Phoenix.*) It was made a reserve in 1908 and named for General George Crook, who was in command of the Military Department of Arizona during the campaign against the Apache in 1872-73 and again in 1882-86.

From 136.7 *m.* the SLEEPING BEAUTY, the figure of a woman formed by rugged mountains, is outlined on the western skyline. This figure is most clearly apparent near sunset.

At 138 *m.* is the junction with US 60 (*see TOUR 12*), which unites with US 70 between this point and the California Line.

GLOBE, 134 *m.* (3,504 alt., 6,419 pop.) (*see GLOBE*).

Points of Interest: Old Dominion Mine and Smelter, Old Dominion Library, Globe Cemetery, Gila County Courthouse, Former Residence of George W. P. Hunt, Gila County Museum, and others.

Left from Globe on improved paved road to the BESH-BA-GOWAH (Besh-ba-gow-AH) PUEBLO (R), 1 *m.*, which has been restored and now resembles the modern Hopi villages. Besh-Ba-Gowah (Apache, camp for metal) is on a high mesa overlooking Pinal Creek, and was inhabited from about 1225 to 1375. There are more than 115 rooms, hallways, and patios. The walls are of rock and adobe and some parts of the ruin are two stories high. In the burials found beneath the floors, pottery and jewelry were lying beside the skeletons. A living room can be entered by a ladder extending to the floor through an opening in the roof. The fire pits, the plaster on the walls, the grinding stones on the floor, and large storage jars against the wall remain as they were more than 550 years ago.

Relics from Besh-Ba-Gowah, on display in Dominion Hotel, include ollas, bowls, ladles, effigy forms, stone tools, dried grains, animal bones, awls, daggers, baskets, cloth, and examples of shell jewelry. The last named evi-

Mining : Lumbering

MINERS' MEMORIAL, BISBEE

SMELTER IN THE COPPER COUNTRY, CLARKDALE

"ROASTING" COPPER ORE, CLARKDALE SMELTER

ORE TRAIN FROM JEROME MINES TO CLARKDALE SMELTER

POLAND TUNNEL, IN GOLD MINE NEAR PRESCOTT (3,000 FT. LONG)

E. E. Hartzell

PROSPECTOR AT ORE GRINDING MACHINE

SACRAMENTO PIT, BISBEE

Higrade Studio

JEROME

ORE TRAINS, EARLY MINING DAYS

OLD SILVER KING MINE

TOPPING TREES

Max Kegley

FELLING TREES,
NORTHERN ARIZONA

EARLY PLACER WORKINGS, NEAR PRESCOTT

LUMBER MILL, NORTHERN ARIZONA

dently were brought by primitive traders from the Gulf of California. Of exceptional interest is a piece of painted basket of a type rarely found. Mineral paints used in prehistoric times are displayed; green made from copper ore, red from iron ore, and other pigments. In one room in the Pueblo was a large jar almost filled with copper ore. Copper bells were found but these are believed to have been obtained from peoples to the south.

In the Pinal Mountains is the FERNDALE RECREATIONAL AREA (*cabins for rent, inquire locally; no hunting*), 17 *m.*, a region of spruce, fir, quaking aspen, pine, maple, and oak, abounding with wild life, especially deer. Signal Peak (7,875 alt.) was once a main relay station in the army's heliograph system; the supporting posts of the heliographer's canopy are still upright on its rocky top. From the mountain's crest is a view of Apacheland for 100 miles in all directions; visible in the recesses of deep canyons and on the ridges are the threads of old Indian trails. On clear days mountain and desert cities may be seen far to the northeast; while high above the deep basins and precipitous ranges is Mogollon Rim, the southeastern edge of the plateau.

The OLD DOMINION MINE (R), 140 *m.,* produced copper worth several million dollars. It was closed early in the 1930's because underground water prevented profitable operation. The man-made hills nearest the road are slag dumps.

CLAYPOOL, 139 *m.,* is the junction (R) with State 88 (*see TOUR 3A*).

In the tailings (R)—waste from the mill after the ore has been extracted—streaks of blue-green indicate the presence of copper.

At 140 *m.* is the junction with asphalt-paved Smelter Road.

Right on Smelter Road to the INTERNATIONAL SMELTING COMPANY PROPERTIES, 2.1 *m.,* on a hill whose sides are black with slag. It is owned by a subsidiary of the Anaconda Copper Mining Company. Most conspicuous of the buildings is an electric power converter plant, where high-tension electricity carried from Apache Lake and Horse Mesa dam below Roosevelt is transformed into commercial cycles for use in local mining operations. The smelter itself is of the modern reverberatory furnace type.

INSPIRATION, 3.6 *m.* (3,570 alt., c. 400 pop.), is a well-kept companyowned village for the officials, supervisors, and skilled employees; it has a post office, a school, and a profit-sharing company store. The houses are attractive gray stucco cottages with copper roofs. Those in the two main sections—the Upper Circle and the Lower Circle—are built along streets that wind around the high hilltop. Moonshine Hill, the other section, is across the road. Below the Upper Circle drive are the cavings, and the remains of the Mexican village, Los Adobes, abandoned when the ground around it began to sink.

On Smelter Road at 4.5 *m.* is the INSPIRATION CONSOLIDATED COPPER COMPANY PROPERTY, equipped to handle ten thousand tons of ore daily. The huge vats of the leaching plant can be seen in the gulch below.

At 141 *m.* on US 70 is the junction with the Miami Hill Road.

Right here to the MIAMI COPPER COMPANY PLANT, 0.9 *m.,* towering above the town on the hills north of the business section. Surrounding the No. 5 Shaft are a large concentrating mill—into which ore is raised out of the mines from a depth of 1,120 feet—and other buildings, including a modern leaching plant. The road passes abandoned underground workings—marked by a vast crater area of sunken earth known as the cabins—the red-shingled, copper-roofed buildings of the general offices and employees' club, then follows the top of the tailing dumps to a section of pleasant frame and stucco homes, usually white or gray with red roofs. Their yards are very green, and across the road is a swimming pool built on top of the tailings dump.

MIAMI, 142 *m.* (3,408 alt., 5,000 pop.) (*see* MIAMI).

Points of Interest: A tortilla factory, post office, and Silver Belt Building.

The bridge at 144 *m.* approximately marks BLOODY TANKS, the site of an engagement in 1864 between a party of whites and their Maricopa Indian allies on one side, and Apaches, who greatly outnumbered them, on the other. The allies were under the command of Colonel King S. Woolsey (*see TOUR 1A*), a veteran of Indian wars. Because of their superior arms and the use of typical Indian stratagems, such as building campfires and immediately abandoning them, the party escaped with the loss of a single life. It is said that nineteen Apaches were fatally shot, and that when they crawled through brush and rock to reach water, blood from their wounds colored the holes red. The fighting began at a peace parley to which both sides took weapons in violation of their agreement. Because of the rumor that many of the Apaches died from strychnine in the pinole given them for gifts at the parley, this engagement is often called the Pinole treaty.

On the western horizon at 149.3 *m.* is a view of Weaver's Needle, appearing like the end of a thumb above the sky line. It was named for Pauline Weaver (*see TOUR 1b*).

An old wagon road (L), 149 *m.,* is the trail of "old man" Irions who, persuaded by a traveler's description of this area, came here from Colorado in 1878.

Old furnishings in the IRIONS RANCH HOUSE (L), 153 *m.,* now known as Pinal Ranch, still show the marks of bullets and arrows. For half a century this house, now remodeled, was a haven for all manner of travelers.

In early times this site was inhabited by a band of Apaches. It is an almost impregnable fastness surrounded by lookout peaks and acccessible only by obscure trails. Its abundant fuel, wild fruits and nuts, pasturage, and game attracted friendly neighboring tribes seeking provisions. Chief of one of these was Eskiminzin, who owned a corn and melon patch here. Though he had once been a relentless fighter, during his later years Eskiminzin bore without bitterness a series of injustices —the massacre of his family, imprisonment, recurring destructive raids on the small plots the government allowed him to farm—and the loss of his land to white people. Yet he consistently maintained a friendly and understanding attitude toward his white and Indian persecutors.

In 1870 Camp Pinal, garrisoned with 400 cavalrymen, was here.

The road chiseled in sheer rock walls winds down through a narrow gorge, 156 *m.,* bordered with spires, balanced rocks, and formations that appear fantastic even in the light of day. In the half-light they resemble gigantic men and monsters, turrets, towers, and massive forts differing only in extent from the Wonderland of Rocks in the Chiricahua National Monument (*see TOUR 4a*).

QUEEN CREEK TUNNEL AND BRIDGE, 157 *m.,* cut through solid rock, is 1,217 feet long, 22 feet high and 42 feet, wall to wall. It has has electronically controlled lighting. This new tunnel and bridge supplant the old narrow, winding and hazardous mountain trail and old narrow Claypool Tunnel.

APACHE LEAP (R), 159.9 *m.,* is a high red-streaked cliff visible from the highway. In the seventies after a signal operator had watched the retreat of an Apache raiding party and discovered the long-sought base from which the Indians operated, cavalry from Camp Pinal was sent after them. About seventy-five of the Apaches, driven to the cliff by the troops and unwilling to surrender, plunged over the edge to death on the rocks below.

SUPERIOR, 160 *m.* (2,750 alt., 5,000 pop.), is the scene of many Apache raids; however, the Indian depredations ended earlier than in other districts of Arizona because of the development of mining—for a mine with a number of men capable of fighting was more formidable than an isolated ranch. The discovery of the rich Silver King mine in 1875 first attracted attention to the district. Subsequent opening of the Silver Queen increased the influx of fortune seekers. As the silver capping of the Silver Queen played out, large underlying deposits of copper were uncovered. In 1910 the Magma Copper Company was formed to take over the Silver Queen properties and fourteen years later it constructed a large smelter here to handle all its ore as well as hundreds of carloads from smaller mines. So rich is the ore taken from the Magma shafts that their mines and smelter were kept in operation even during the period from 1929 to 1933, when many mines throughout the country were being shut down.

Southwest of Superior massive PICKET POST MOUNTAIN (L) dominates the country-side. On its flat top was a heliograph station in Indian-war days.

The THOMPSON SOUTHWEST ARBORETUM (*open*), 165 *m.,* was founded by William Boyce Thompson on a tract of 120 acres. It contains a great variety of rare and beautiful plants and flowers, special attention being given to the southwestern flora.

In this area near the highway are thick growths of saguaro, cholla, and ocotillo (oh-ko-TEE-yo), a spray of graceful prickly stalks usually five to ten feet in height and topped with scarlet blossoms in the spring.

At FLORENCE JUNCTION, 175 *m.,* is the junction (L) with US 80-89 (*see TOUR 1c*); west of this point US 80-89 and US 70-60 are one route. This junction, a trading center for ranchers, has limited accommodations for tourists.

Section b. FLORENCE JUNCTION to PHOENIX; 49.3 m. *US 70-60-89-80.*

Along US 70 between Florence Junction and Phoenix are irrigated farm lands, a Mormon Temple, a Yaqui village, and a large Pueblo ruin.

West of the junction there are impressive views (R) of SUPER-
STITION MOUNTAIN (5,057 alt.). The eroded forms resembling human figures on top of the mountain are responsible for its
name. A Pima legend describes them as Indians who sought refuge
on the mountain from a great flood and were warned not to make any
sound until all the waters had receded; they disobeyed and were turned
to stone.

The light streak running under them is said to mark the height
of the flood. The Spanish called this Sierra de Espuma (foam mountain). Somewhere in its recesses, reputedly near Weaver's Needle, is
the Lost Dutchman Mine, the subject of many legends (*see Folklore
and Folkways*). Thousands have sought the mine and at least a dozen
have been killed in the search. Each February, the Dons' Superstition
Mountain Lost Gold Trek, a mock search for the Lost Dutchman
Mine, is conducted by a young men's organization of Phoenix. This
event, arranged for the entertainment of winter visitors, has grown to
such proportions that all reservations are usually taken weeks in advance.
This noncommercial venture is an all-day hike and exploration enlivened
with Western lore, food, and entertainment. A campfire fiesta at night
concludes the outing.

APACHE JUNCTION, 19 *m.,* is the western junction with State
88 (*see TOUR 3A*). The privately owned APACHE JUNCTION ZOO
(*open*) contains many Arizona wild animals including bear, deer, bobcats, pumas, badgers, quails, desert turtles, porcupines, timber squirrels,
coyotes, hawks, horned and monkey-faced owls, rattlesnakes, a golden
eagle, and Gila monsters.

At 27 *m.* is the junction with a graveled road; from the junction is
visible far to the north a slanting red rock butte, marking the position
of Granite Reef Dam.

Right on this road, which affords a noteworthy view at 15.9 *m.,* to STEWART
MOUNTAIN DAM (1,535 alt.), 16 *m.,* creating the ten-mile-long SAGUARO
LAKE. This unit in the Salt River irrigation and power development was
completed in 1930 at a cost of $2,515,000. It is 212 feet high and has a power
plant capable of generating 17,300-horsepower.
GRANITE REEF DAM, 18 *m.,* just below the confluence of the Salt and
Verde rivers, was completed in 1907 to divert water into the valley's irrigation
canals.

West of the junction, the eastern entrance to the Salt River Valley,
are cultivated fields and groves that contrast with the desert to the east.
Some 20,000 families farm this two hundred seventy-eight thousand-
acre stretch which yields alfalfa, lettuce, cantaloupes, cotton (*see
TOUR 11*), grain, sorghum, citrus fruit, dates (*see TOUR 4d*), and
grapes. Although agriculture was practiced in the valley in antiquity,
it was not until 1868 that white settlers began to cultivate the region.
Until 1908 its history was one of alternate prosperity and failure; flood
after flood boiled down the Salt River and carried away the farmers'
crude brush dams. By the time the dams could be repaired the flow
was often insufficient for irrigation purposes. Realizing that water

storage would solve the problem, Arizona worked for the Federal Reclamation Act, that was passed in 1902. The Salt River Project was the first undertaken under the act. Since the construction of Roosevelt Dam at the junction of Salt River and Tonto Creek, water shortage and crop failure have been unknown in the valley. In 1936 the Salt River Project comprised Roosevelt, Horse Mesa, Mormon Flat, and Stewart Mountain Dams—forming a chain of beautiful mountain lakes fifty-nine miles long, and providing a total generating power of more than ninety-eight thousand horsepower (*see TOUR 3A*).

MESA (Sp., tableland), 33.1 *m.* (1,161 alt., 20,000 pop.) with power and water from Roosevelt Dam, has several cotton gins, a cotton-oil mill, citrus fruit-packing houses, lettuce-packing sheds, and a flour and feed mill, in a vast agricultural area.

Mesa was founded in 1878 on a square mile tract by a group of Mormons; in each block were four homesites—a dwelling surrounded by a garden and an orchard—a plan soon afterward abandoned for smaller units. The Mormons were the only American settlers to design their city streets for the then unpredictable future; Mesa, like other Mormon towns, has thoroughfares broad enough for all modern traffic and parking needs. In 1931 the original square mile was enlarged by the annexation of several suburbs.

The ARIZONA MORMON TEMPLE, on a landscaped twenty-acre tract at the eastern edge of the city, can be approached on Fifth Ave. and visitors to the grounds are admitted at the west gate. Entrance to the temple itself is reserved to members of the church who are in good standing. There are only seven Mormon temples—five of them in the United States. This one was completed in 1927 at a cost of eight hundred thousand dollars. It is designed, like other Mormon temples, after the Temple of Solomon although it is twice the size. The walls have friezes depicting the gathering of Israel, and the baptismal font rests upon the backs of twelve life-size terra-cotta oxen representing the twelve tribes of Israel. A flower-bordered reflecting pool stretching from the gate to the main temple entrance, mirrors the white building and slender Italian cypresses. The dark blue-green foliage of an orange grove on the grounds forms a pleasing contrast with the whiteness of the temple.

Mesa is the junction with State 87 (*see TOUR 4C*).

On the UNIVERSITY OF ARIZONA EXPERIMENT FARM (L), 37 *m.*, conducted by the College of Agriculture, rows of feathery green date palms are near the highway (*see TOUR 4d*).

TEMPE, 39.7 *m.* (1,150 alt., 9,000 pop.), is on the south bank of the Salt River at the foot of Tempe Butte. Tall cottonwood, tamarisk, eucalyptus, and palm trees border its broad paved streets, and its modern brick business buildings are interspersed with low flat-roofed adobes. It was so named by an early settler and English expatriate, Darrell Duppa (*see TOUR 1A*), because of its likeness in contour to the Vale of Tempe between Mounts Olympus and Ossa in Thessaly. It is on the Salt River in the midst of a general crop-growing, dairying, and stock-raising region.   In 1872 Tempe was but a trading post, called Hayden's Ferry for Charles Trumbull Hayden, who in 1849 had brought an ox-cart load of goods to Santa Fe and had remained there as a merchant till 1858 when he moved to Tucson.   During these years Hayden's trading expeditions had taken him as far south as Sonora where he had many Indian fights.   In 1872 he moved to this site, built a ferry and a flour mill, and opened a store that became the trading center for all the southern Salt River Valley.   His son, Carl Hayden, is (1954) a United States Senator, who has had a long term in office, serving in Congress since statehood, 1912.

ARIZONA STATE COLLEGE, near the town's center, the state's oldest institution of higher education, occupies 42 buildings on an 85-acre campus, with adjoining 360-acre farm.   Established by the territorial legislature, 1885, was known as Tempe Normal; later Arizona State Teachers College; since 1945 Arizona State College at Tempe.   The institution offers a complete college curriculum, giving degrees in Bachelor of Arts, Bachelor of Science, Bachelor of Arts in Education, Master of Arts in Education, and Doctorate in Education.   Arizona State College is the southwest's largest teacher training institution.   Enrollment, 1952-53 was 4,700, including students from Arizona, six U.S. foreign possessions, and 14 foreign countries.   Summer session classes in 1952 totalled 2,000.   Extension centers are maintained in many towns in Arizona with more than 700 students enrolled.

OLD MAIN, erected in 1894, oldest of the buildings, is devoted chiefly to classrooms.   Of the 42 buildings on the campus, a few of the newer and more outstanding are the AGRICULTURE, BUSINESS ADMINISTRATION AND ADMINISTRATION BUILDING, largest on the campus; ARTHUR J. MATHEWS LIBRARY, a modern, fire-proof, air-conditioned building, houses, besides its fine collection of books, the famous Collection of American Art, valued at more than $350,000, and contributed by an anonymous donor.   The new million-dollar MEN'S GYMNASIUM is one of the finest in the Southwest.   The SCIENCE BUILDING was recently completed.   The ARTS BUILDING houses the departments of Art, Music and Social Studies.

The highway crosses the Salt River over TEMPE BRIDGE, 42.8 m., a concrete structure with a span supported on ten arches.   Sidewalks have cupola-covered benches at intervals.

PAPAGO STATE PARK (R), 41.5 m., is a vast area with cactus plants, fish hatcheries, red rocks, rifle ranges, picnic grounds, a large outdoor natural stadium for mass meetings, a botanical garden and other points of interest.   The white pyramid on a prominent hill marks the GRAVE OF GEORGE W. P. HUNT (1859-1934) and that of his wife. Hunt, first governor of the state, held office for seven terms.

At this point is the junction with Washington Boulevard, an alternate route to Phoenix.

Left on Washington Boulevard to a dirt road, 2.1 *m.;* L. 0.1 *m.* on this to PUEBLO GRANDE RUIN and laboratory (*open 9 to 5 except Mon.*).

Pueblo Grande (Sp., big town) is unusual because of the great amount of stone contained in its walls. The partly excavated mound is approximately 300 feet long, 150 feet wide, and 30 feet high measuring from the original ground level. A protective wall still stands on three sides. The 125 miles of prehistoric irrigation canals remaining in the Salt River Valley were dug by people similar in culture to those who built Pueblo Grande. Remains of three canals are on an adjoining ten-acre tract. It is evident that the dwelling was deserted because of poor drainage and floods. The aged and infirm were probably left to shift for themselves while the young and strong went on. There are indications that those left behind lived on the upper story. A village of one-room adobe houses was spread around the pueblo, which served as a storehouse or place of protection.

Washington Boulevard continues to Phoenix and a junction with US 70 at 7.2 *m.* (*see below*).

PHOENIX, 49.3 *m.* (1,080 alt., 150,000 pop.) (*see Phoenix*).

Points of Interest: State Capitol, Indian School, Heard Museum, Arizona Museum, La Ciudad (ruins).

In Phoenix is the junction with US 80 (*see TOUR 11*), and with State 69 (*see TOUR 1A*).

1. Left from Phoenix on South Central Ave. to a paved road, 4.1 *m.;* R. to another paved road, 6.6 *m.;* L. to a paved road, 7.7 *m.;* R. to a paved road, 8.7 *m.;* L. to a paved road, 9.8 *m.;* R. to a gravel road, 10.7 *m.;* L. here to KOMATKE, 17.1 *m.,* a Pima village in the Gila River Indian Reservation. Its many scattered houses are one-room structures built of ocotillo or saguaro ribs plastered with mud.

In the center of the settlement is the Franciscan ST. JOHN'S MISSION of about twenty buildings. The chapel and adjoining dormitory are designed in the Spanish-Mission style with Indian motifs on their interior walls and ceilings. Children of five tribes, Apache, Yuma, Maricopa, Pima, and Papago, attend the mission. In the fall when new children enter the school the enmity that once existed between various tribes sometimes is expressed in resentment that Pimas and Apaches, Yumas and Papagos, are to be housed under the same roof. But before long children work and play together without regard for the quarrels of their forefathers.

On St. John the Baptist Day (June 24) Indians from various parts of the reservation gather at the mission to celebrate the saint's day.

At 7 *m.* on South Central Avenue is the PHOENIX SOUTH MOUNTAIN PARK (*picnic grounds, rest rooms*), covering fifteen thousand acres in the Salt River Mountains. It is traversed by roads and trails with innumerable good views of the Salt River Valley; from the summit road (so called because it reaches the summit of the South Mountains) is a view into the Gila River Valley to the southwest.

Within the park is HIEROGLYPH CANYON containing ancient Indian pictographs; the representations include wolves, horned sheep, lizards, snakes, men, and geometrical designs, and are similar to those found on pottery excavated in near-by ruins.

2. Right from Phoenix on North Central Avenue to the GRAND CANAL, 4.6 *m.,* fed from Roosevelt and its auxiliary lakes (*see TOUR 3A*). This canal irrigates the desert around Phoenix and makes possible the tropical flowers and shrubs, citrus groves, and extensive farms that now flourish in this once arid country.

ST. FRANCIS SCHOOL (R) and CHURCH OF ST. FRANCIS XAVIER, 4.7 *m.,* were founded in 1928 by Mrs. Ellen M. Brophy. The cream-colored building, a structure of the modified Spanish Colonial type with a high belfry, was built in memory of her husband, William H. Brophy. The "college" was opened as a Roman Catholic preparatory school but later became a day school for children.

Between 6.1 *m.* and 8.9 *m.* large ash trees arch above Central Avenue; the brightness of their foliage is enhanced by the dusty green of the olive trees beyond them. Both ash and olive trees were planted by W. J. Murphy, an early settler.

At 8.9 *m.* is a junction with a dirt road (R), which becomes the main side route; it runs along the south bank of the ARIZONA CANAL, main carrier of irrigation water in the Salt River Valley. Throughout much of its forty-one miles the canal is bordered with cottonwood and eucalyptus trees. It winds through citrus orchards, date gardens, and farm lands. Doves in great numbers make their homes along its banks, especially in summer. This canal was built in 1885 by W. J. Murphy and his Arizona Canal Company. After the U. S. Bureau of Reclamation was established in 1902, it bought all canals in the valley and in 1908 replaced the old brush dam of the reservoir that fed the Arizona Canal with the present Granite Reef Dam (*see below*). The Roosevelt Dam built in 1910 (*see TOUR 3A*) provides additional water for this canal, which can cover four thousand acres with one foot of water in twenty-four hours.

SUNNYSLOPE (L), at 9.1 *m.,* has some hundreds of modern dwellings scattered over approximately three square miles of desert. People suffering from tuberculosis have come to this area from many parts of the United States in order to be benefited by the abundant sunshine.

Beyond Sunnyslope are the PHOENIX MOUNTAINS, serrated pastel-shaded hills. Their highest point is SQUAW PEAK.

A large headgate for diverting water to the fields below is at 9.6 *m.*

In early May the dense growth of palo verde trees, 10.4 *m.,* is golden with bloom, and the few ironwood trees become huge lavender bouquets.

Adjoining the adobe-plastered Arizona Biltmore's stables (L), 13 *m.,* is a small ground where rodeos are held for guests (*each Sun. in winter; free to public*).

On the top of a high landscaped hill (R) is the rambling two-story HOME OF WILLIAM WRIGLEY JR. (1861-1932). This Mediterranean-type house of cream-colored stucco with a red tile roof is built on different levels and contains more than fifty rooms.

The ARIZONA BILTMORE, 13.5 *m.,* is an impressive structure designed in the modern manner by Frank Lloyd Wright. Its outer walls are of moulded concrete blocks and ornamented with geometric designs. The rambling building is from one to four stories high with numerous roof terraces, loggias and towering pavilions. On the grounds are cottages, a swimming pool, and cabanas. The gray concrete walls form a striking contrast with the deep purple of Squaw Peak immediately beyond, with the vivid tropical flowers in the hotel garden, and with the green fairways of its cactus-studded golf course. Twenty-five miles of bridle trails lead from the hotel to Squaw Peak and its summit.

At 15.5 *m.* is the junction with Camelback Road which is lined with spacious winter homes and their gardens. Left on this, now the main side route. Purplish red cliffs (L) enclose Echo Canyon (see below) in the head of the "camel" formed by CAMELBACK MOUNTAIN.

The modified Spanish type HOME OF W. E. TRAVIS, president of Pacific Greyhound Lines, is set far back (L) in extensive walled grounds, 17 *m.* It stands at the end of a long straight driveway bordered with tall palms. Along the front walls, lining the road, are extraordinary specimens of greasewood and creosote bush that show the decorative possibilities of cultivated native plants.

In ARCADIA, 18 *m.,* a section of palatial homes on the lower slopes of

Camelback, all roads follow natural contours and the native cacti, bushes, and shrubs have been preserved and enhanced by judicious landscaping.

The grounds of JOKAKE INN (L), 18.4 *m.*, a winter resort of modified Spanish-Pueblo type buildings tinted to match the cliffs of Echo Canyon, are ornamented with indigenous plants.

Below the large red mountain ahead (L), MCDOWELL BUTTE, is Granite Reef Dam where irrigation waters are diverted from the Salt River. Far beyond are the Mazatzal Mountains, surmounted by FOUR PEAKS (*see TOUR 10*), a quartet of evenly shaped mountain tops. Below these (R) is Superstition Mountain (*see above*) flat-topped and massive. In the clear atmosphere the more distant mountains have an ethereal appearance with their many shades of translucent blue and purple. Almost every day in summer "dust devils"—dust caught in a whirling wind—dance in the valley. Sometimes large, sometimes small, they appear suddenly, swirl furiously over the landscape and then mysteriously vanish.

At 18.9 *m.* is the junction with unpaved Invergordon Road. Left on this to a view at 20.5 *m.* of the PRAYING WOMAN (L) on the side of Camelback Mountain. It is especially effective at dusk when the mountains and the figure are in silhouette; the huge rock resembles a woman kneeling with bowed head.

At 21 *m.* is the junction with Lincoln Drive (L), now the route.

The group of cream-colored buildings designed in a modified Spanish-Pueblo style and arranged in a circle with a central court or plaza at 22.6 *m.* is CAMELBACK INN (R), a winter resort patronized by wealthy visitors.

At 23.3 *m.* the road turns L. to MacDonald Drive, 23.8 *m.;* R. here to a dirt road, 24 *m.*

Left 0.3 *m.* on this road to ECHO CANYON. If three or four syllables are shouted across the canyon at a certain point, the clearly enunciated echo will be heard immediately.

At 26.3 *m.* on MacDonald Drive is the junction with Camelback Road. Right on this road to North Central Avenue, 30.1 *m.*, and L. on North Central Avenue to the junction with US 70, 35.2 *m.* in PHOENIX.

Section c. PHOENIX to WICKENBURG; 54.1 m. US 70-60-89.

Part of the desert between PHOENIX, 0 *m.*, and Wickenburg is irrigated with water from Carl Pleasant Lake, accessible from this section of US 70.

GLENDALE, 9.1 *m.* (1,100 alt., 10,000 pop.), in the center of a highly productive agricultural area, has cotton gins, a cotton-oil mill, flour and feed mills, and grape, lettuce, and cantaloupe packing sheds. Glendale was settled in the 1890's but made little progress until the completion of Roosevelt Dam which assured a dependable water supply.

AMERICAN INSTITUTE FOR FOREIGN TRADE, N. 5 *m.*, school for employees of firms having foreign branches or foreign trade.

PEORIA, 13.2 *m.* (1,400 alt., 1,500 pop.), is the trading center of an area in which grapefruit, oranges, cotton, lettuce, and cantaloupes are the principal products. The town was founded in 1897 by settlers from Peoria, Illinois.

MARINETTE, 16.4 *m.* (1,080 alt., 576 pop.), with a cotton gin, a store, a post office, and labor camps, is the center of an eight thousand acre tract of cotton fields that is irrigated by deep-well pumps. The tract is owned and operated by the J. G. Boswell Company, cotton growers and oil millers.

At 17 *m.* is a junction with an improved earth road.

Right on this road to CARL PLEASANT DAM, 20 *m.*, on the Agua Fria River, an unusually long and high multiple-arch dam, completed in 1927 at a cost of $4,500,000. It forms a lake eight miles long. The Agua Fria River has a history of treachery and violence. Records show that its flow can leap from virtually nothing to 100,000 cubic feet a second; before the dam was built, floods were almost a yearly occurrence. The Agua Fria Water and Land Company, formed in the early nineties to develop lands on the west shore of the river, acquired title to water rights and bought 40,000 acres from the Santa Fe Ry. The construction program was eventually undertaken, with the aid of Carl Pleasant, engineer and contractor-builder. The dam goes down 80 feet to bedrock, is 250 feet high, and 253 feet thick at the bottom of the longest buttress.

Two miles below the dam is a low masonry diversion dam, which creates a second lake backing against the higher dam to a depth of ten feet. The main irrigation canal opens out of this lake on the east side.

EL MIRAGE, 21 *m.* (1,200 pop.), is a pretty new community in a vast farming area. BEARDSLEY, 24 *m.*, is named for a pioneer who started an irrigation project here in 1888.

Just northwest of WITTMAN, 35.6 *m.* (1,697 alt., 80 pop.)—a farming and stock-raising community—Barney Martin, his wife, and three children were killed in a holdup and robbery in 1886; the charred remains of their bodies were found partly buried. Although horse tracks were followed into the foothills from the scene of the crime the perpetrators escaped. They were believed to have been members of the Valenzuela gang (*see TOUR 11*), one of whom was later killed near Gila Bend by a posse seeking him for another murder. The other two fled into Mexico.

MORRISTOWN, 43.1 *m.* (1,791 alt., 100 pop.), was originally called Hot Springs Junction, but is now named for its first inhabitant, George Morris, who discovered the Mack Morris Mine, one of the well-known early workings.

Right from Morristown on an improved earth road to CASTLE HOT SPRINGS, 30 *m.* (2,300 alt., 120 pop.), in a beautiful valley between foothills of the Bradshaw Mountains. Mineral water flows from crevices in the rocks at the rate of four hundred thousand gallons every twenty-four hours, and ranges in temperature from 115° to 122°. There are bathing pools of various temperatures, and services of a masseur and masseuse at nominal fees. This is a winter resort.

The highway crosses the HASSAYAMPA RIVER, 54 *m.*, on a steel and concrete bridge. The effect of drinking the Hassayampa's water is the subject of many legends variously attributed to the Indians, the cowboys, and the pioneers. One of them is: "He who drinks above the trail is ever truthful, while he who drinks below is lost to truth." To call a man a "Hassayamp" in Arizona is a polite way of calling him a liar.

WICKENBURG, 54.1 *m.* (2,076 alt., 1,750 pop.), was trading point for mining, cattle raising, and more recently became a dude-ranching and winter resort area. Henry Wickenburg came to Arizona in 1862 seeking gold and the next year discovered the Vulture Mine. The town, which grew as a result of the mine's operation, was built here so that the water of the Hassayampa could be used for milling. By 1866 it was one of the largest cities in the state and missed being chosen as the capital by only two votes.

Dude ranches, open here the year round, combine the rudeness of corrals and stables with modern hotel luxury; Indian designs influence the decoration, and the atmosphere suggests that of the Spanish haciendas.

In the eastern edge of the town, left of the Hassayampa River Bridge, is OLD WICKENBURG. Weathered and worn adobe buildings stand flush with the street in the Mexican fashion.

The JAIL TREE, at Tegner and Center St., is an old mesquite standing before an adobe building which was in former days a saloon. There was no jail in the town's early days so prisoners, chained to this tree, served their sentences beneath its branches. George Sayers later known as the King of Gunsight, a small desert town, was a frequent offender. On one occasion he was chained to a giant log instead of the mesquite. He spent the night in drunken slumber but in the morning awakened and wanted a drink. The King—who had a blaring voice even when sober—bellowed like a range bull, rousing the whole town and half the countryside as well; then he took matters into his own hands. Shouldering his log, which would have been a good load for a pack mule, he carried it into the nearest saloon and demanded a drink. He got it.

The OLD STAGE STATION, at the NW. corner of Tegner and 1st St., is surrounded by a hotel, a saloon, and a boardinghouse, all built in the seventies.

South on Tegner St., 0.4 m., is WICKENBURG'S RANCH HOUSE. The ranch originally included all the land south of the town to the base of the hills bounding the valley.

About eighteen miles northeast of Wickenburg on the Hassayampa River was Walnut Grove Dam, long since washed away. Known to be of weak construction, the dam was being strengthened and an additional spillway to carry off flood water was being built in 1890, when a terrific rainstorm caused fear for the safety of the people in the lower valley. A rider mounted a swift horse and set out to warn those in danger, but stopped at the first saloon for a drink and lingered. The flood broke the dam and washed away the saloon with those inside. A heavy steel safe containing five thousand dollars in gold dust was never found, nor was the rider who had delayed. Approximately eighty lives were lost in the flood—one of Arizona's worst disasters. Wickenburg's ranch was ruined by a deposit of sand and rocks that rendered cultivation impossible. He retired to his house, a broken old man, often saying that he was tired of living. In 1905 on his eighty-eighth birthday he walked into the Walnut Grove near his house at sunset and shot himself.

Wickenburg is the junction with US 89 (*see TOUR 1b*).

Right from Wickenburg on an improved earth road to CONSTELLATION, 12 *m.* (3,300 alt., 23 pop.), named for an old mine near by. In its environs are goat ranges, and are also mines that yield a high grade silver ore and abundant copper ore.

Section d. WICKENBURG to CALIFORNIA LINE, 112.1 m.
US 70-60.

West of Wickenburg, 0 *m.,* US 60-70 crosses an area of rolling hills and dude ranches. The pioneer road between Wickenburg and Ehrenberg on the Colorado River was called the Trail of Graves because of the many travelers who perished—some from lack of water in the desert, others at the hands of Mojave Indians.

At 2.1 *m.* is the junction with the Vulture Mine Road.

Left on this road to VULTURE GOLD MINE, 12.2 *m.* (*caretaker on premises*), discovered by Henry Wickenburg (*see above*) in 1863, and who realized only a small portion of the millions it produced. One of the stories of the finding of this gold is that Wickenburg shot a vulture and when he went to pick it up, noticed gold nuggets lying on the ground. Another version is that while throwing rocks at his runaway burro, he found the rocks contained gold. The only old building left is the Old Rock House, a long oblong structure with a peaked roof and walls three feet thick. Once an assay office, it was built by Wickenburg in 1865 as a bullion room. The gold ore contained in the waste rocks of which it is constructed is valued at $3,000. When the first buildings, erected to house the miners, were torn down, the rock used in their construction was run through a stamp mill and yielded twenty dollars a ton in gold. The mine now stands deserted.

During the Civil War and in the following reconstruction period, when the national government was sorely in need of gold, the Vulture produced heavily. By 1865 forty arrastras (mills) were running on Vulture ore, sold by Wickenburg at fifteen dollars a ton, with the mining and sorting performed by the buyers. During 1865 and 1866 four mills were built along the Hassayampa; one had twenty stamps and later twenty more were added.

Gold filled the pockets of miners and pioneers, weight-stamped bullion passed as coin on the stages, in stores and saloons, and purchased the necessities of life in town and on the ranches.

The discovery of the Vulture increased both population and crime in the territory. During the first fifteen years of Wickenburg's existence, more than 400 white men were killed by Apaches in the surrounding territory and there were many murders committed by the town's lawless citizenry. Wells-Fargo boxes, carrying gold on the stages, were so often seized by bandits that the lives of bullion carriers from the Vulture were always in jeopardy.

Many of the misfortunes during the early days of active production were due to the mine's distance from its water supply, and to dismanagement and theft. Though large quantities of gold were removed between 1866 and 1876, high-grading and fraudulent manipulation of the company's affairs by its officers forced the sale of the property to satisfy creditors.

The first sale of the Vulture was to a New Yorker, named Phillips, for eighty-five thousand dollars, of which Henry Wickenburg received one-fifth in cash. So much litigation followed that the balance of the purchase price was never paid.

A bronze REPRODUCTION OF A STAGECOACH on a conical base constructed of chunks of ore, at 4.5 *m.,* marks the spot where in 1871

Indians ambushed the Wickenburg-Ehrenburg stage and killed six of the passengers. Two of the party escaped on foot, but one of them, a woman, died later from her wounds. The Monument bears this inscription: WICKENBURG MASSACRE—In this vicinity, Nov. 5, 1871, Wickenburg-Ehrenberg stage ambushed by Apache-Mojave Indians.

Although the rattlesnake, the best known and most feared of desert life, is not always encountered by the visitor—many people have lived in the state ten years without seeing one—leather boots and a supply of antivenom are advisable for those walking in the desert.

About 6 *m.* west of Wickenburg is CULLING'S WELL (R), three miles from the highway over unbroken desert. The well was named for Tom Culling, an Englishman, who kept a station on the old stage road. After Culling's death the station was operated by Joe Drew. In the 1860's as Drew sat reading late one night a man staggered out of the desert and fell at Drew's door, weak and nearly dead from thirst. He had seen the light in the station window. The next night Drew erected a tall pole and each night for several years he hoisted a lighted lantern to its top for the guidance of travelers on the desert. He was later called the Keeper of the Desert Lighthouse.

From 21.8 *m.* the BIG HORN MOUNTAINS are visible (L). The range was named for the bighorn sheep, stocky animals that weigh as much as three hundred pounds and have a shaggy growth of wool. The male has two massive curled horns, measuring three and a half feet on the outside curve. The bighorn is not common and is protected by state game laws. During winter and early spring these sheep occupy the sand flats of the lowlands rather than the higher parts of the desert mountains—unusual behavior for Rocky Mountain sheep. In southern Yuma County the native species is the short-haired Gaillard bighorn, large amber-eyed animals with hair instead of wool, and horns on both sexes.

From 23 *m.* the HARQUAHALA (Mojave, running water) MOUNTAINS (3,200 alt.) are visible (L); on their slopes are several noted mines. The Harqua Hala Mine was sold for one million three hundred thirty-five thousand dollars.

EAGLE'S EYE MOUNTAIN (c. 2,000 alt.), in the Harqua Hala foothills, is visible (L) at 25.3 *m.* The hole eroded through the mountain top guided many stagecoach drivers carrying precious cargoes of bullion.

AGUILA, 26.8 *m.* (2,180 alt., 150 pop.), is in McMullen Valley which was named for an early stagecoach driver. Mining and stock raising.

WENDEN, 49.1 *m.* (1,780 alt., 200 pop.), in the center of McMullen Valley, was an important early-day freighting point for mines in the vicinity. Manganese depot, receiving point for western area.

SALOME, 54.4 *m.* (1,980 alt., 450 pop.), was the home of Dick Wick Hall (1877-1926), Arizona's first widely-known humorist, who credited the town with an annual growth of 100 per cent a year: "19 people in 19 years."

Across the highway going through town is a white sign with letters a foot high that reads: "Salome, Arizona—Where She danced." Anyone who has tried to go barefoot on the Arizona desert will appreciate Hall's disclaimer: "Everybody seems to think I'm the man that made Salome dance, but it wasn't my fault at all. I told her to keep her shoes on or the sand would burn her feet." The town was named for Mrs. Grace Salome Pratt. Hall's seven-year-old pet frog, which was desert-bred and had never learned to swim, became almost as well-known as its owner. His mimeographed newspaper, *The Salome Sun,* was devoted to tall tales and gibes at Salome, the desert heat, and the desert roads.

He describes one road thus:

"Sixty years ago the Indians chased an old prospector
From the Colorado River to where Phoenix now is—
He hit some of the high places and
Dodged around through the brush something like
A spring chicken after a grasshopper—like a
Cricket on a hot stove—or the lady on the back seat
This old prospector made the trail you are now hitting—
The natural and shortest route to the coast—
The scenic highway—scenery high and in the way—
But don't blame the old prospector—he was in a hurry—
He knew the Indians were following him but
He never expected you to— . . ."

He was particularly eloquent concerning the fertility of the land: "Melons don't do very well here becuz the vines grow so fast they wear the melons out dragging them around the ground—and in dry years we sometimes have to plant onions in between the rows of potatoes and then scratch the onions to make the potatoes eyes water enough to irrigate the rest of the garden—and the kids sure do hate to scratch the onions on moonlight nights."

Another yarn of Hall's is the story of Mac, the Yale sprinter who took a job herding sheep in Arizona several weeks before the lambing season, and was warned by Reed, his boss, not to lose any of the lambs:

"The sheep and Mac soon disappeared in the brush and nothing more was thought of them until supper time came and no sign of Mac or the sheep. Reed commenced to worry, about the sheep, and about seven o'clock was about to start out looking for them when Mac at last came driving them up through the brush into the corral and, after shutting them in, came up to the chuck tent, streaked with dust and perspiration and from all appearances, tired out. Before Reed could say anything, Mac burst out:

" 'Boss,' he said, 'I'm through. They thought back east that I was a foot racer, but I'm not. Almost any sheep herder that can herd that band for a week and not lose those lambs can beat all the world's records. I didn't lose any today and I ran every one of those damn lambs back into the band every time they tried to get away, but one day is enough for me. I'm all in, but they are all there. Go and count them up and then give me my time. I'm done.'

"Reed, knowing that there were no lambs in the band and that none of the ewes could have lambed yet, went down to the coral to investigate and, off in one corner, huddled up by themselves, he counted 47 jackrabbits and 16 cottontails."

Left from Salome on a dirt road to the HARRISBURG CEMETERY, 3 *m.*, on top of a knoll. Here a miniature covered wagon, the body of copper and the cover of silver, stands on a base of white quartz flaked with gold. It marks the place where Indians killed the members of a covered wagon party on its way to California in 1849. Months later another party of gold seekers found the bleaching bones, carted them to the top of this knoll, and buried them.

At 54.5 *m.* on US 70 is a junction with a dirt road.

Right on this road, 0.1 *m.* to HALL'S "LAUGHIN' GAS SERVIS STATION AND GARAGE," abandoned since his death in 1926. The signs "Tickle lizzie's car-bureter with our laughing gas," "Smile, you don't have to stay here but we do," and others remain as Hall painted them. Across the tracks (R), 0.2 *m.*, is DICK WICK HALL'S GRAVE. After his death miners, cowboys, writers, and others who knew him piled choice ore specimens into a small monument.

West of Salome the long sweep of desert gives way to rocky hills covered with cactus and other desert growth. Here close to the high-way are rock formations and vegetation that motorists usually have to go some distance from the road to inspect.

HOPE, 61.3 *m.* (560 alt., 50 pop.), is the junction with State 72 (*see TOUR 3B*).

QUARTZSITE, 92 *m.* (879 alt., 200 pop.), was formerly called Tyson's Well and was an important stage station. It is said that the name was intended to be Quartzite, but the "s" was added by the Post Office Department. Quartzsite stores still have scales for weighing gold.

Quartzsite is the junction with State 95 (*see TOUR 13*).

FORT TYSON (L), 92.3 *m.*, built in 1856, and named for Charles Tyson, a settler, is now only a reminder of the days when Indians were feared. Never a regular army post, the fort was a sturdy structure built by settlers as a protection against the Mojave.

In the Quartzsite cemetery about 200 yards (R) from the highway, is the GRAVE OF HADJI ALI (c. 1845-1902), 94.2 *m.*, a Syrian camel driver locally called Hi Jolly. Monument of native rock with copper camel.

Arizona's camels were an experiment in desert transportation urged by Edward Fitzgerald Beale and authorized by the War Department. Beale (1822-93) who later (1876-77) served as minister to Austria-Hungary, had joined the navy when he was fourteen and in 1846 was serving under Commodore Stockton when the latter seized California. He was one of the naval officers sent by Stockton to meet General Kearny, and after Kearny's forces were attacked by Mexicans, Beale and Kit Carson succeeded in creeping through the enemy's lines and making their way on foot by separate routes to inform Stockton of Kearny's plight. The following year Beale accompanied Carson east to Washington with official dispatches. At this period Beale conceived the idea of using camels for transportation. Jefferson Davis, Secretary of War, became a convert to Beale's idea and sent agents to Tunis, Egypt, and Smyrna who obtained thirty-three camels and several drivers. The camels, including those born during the voyage, were landed at Indianola, Texas in 1856. The next year forty-seven more were brought over and were used to open a road from Fort Defiance across Arizona to the Colorado River over an unexplored wilderness of forest, plain, and desert. Confronted with danger on the long trip most of the Arab drivers rebelled. Hadji Ali alone remained.

Traveling twenty-five or thirty miles a day, the camels carried water for mules accompanying the wagon train on the long trek, in addition to their six hundred pounds of other supplies. They climbed with packs through snow-covered mountains where the unloaded mules could scarcely be forced to go. They plunged into streams and swam with ease; but horses, mules, and cattle stampeded in all directions at sight of the strange beasts, and the soldiers who acted as drivers could not adjust themselves as did Hi Jolly to the "sea swell" motion. The Civil War cut short this bizarre experiment. Uncared for, many of the camels were sold, others slipped away and became nomadic outcasts of the desert.

Hi Jolly, erstwhile camel driver, bought a mule and started prospecting. Many times thereafter the camels were encountered, appearing like ghosts on moonlight nights, haunting the superstitious, and stampeding domestic animals. Mule skinners shot some of them on sight. In addition they were hunted but were not easily killed off. Time and again they appeared, singly or in bands. Some were caught and used to pack ore from the mines. Many legends grew up around them.

One of these concerned a great rusty-red beast who for years was seen at intervals carrying a dead rider strapped to his back. Occasionally a piece of the ghost rider would be torn off. The burden grew less and less until only a pair of legs remained. Finally when the animal was shot it bore only the rawhide straps, with which the rider had been tied.

Indians were not slow in including the camels in their legends. One of them defied the gods of thunder and lightning and was turned to rock on the desert sands where he remains near Phoenix in the form of Camelback Mountain (*see above*).

A low range of hills at about 99.5 m. is colored by the setting sun till it resembles Indian sand paintings. Beyond, perhaps 100 miles away, is the blue of the far-off California Mountains. Here also is a view of the Colorado River.

West of this point the highway winds and twists through river-bottom country, the habitat of the burro deer, a smaller variety than the Mexican mule deer found in other desert sections.

At 101.4 m. is the junction with an unimproved dirt road.

Right on this road to the ghost town of LA PAZ, about 8 m., which until 1870 was the seat of Yuma County. Gold was discovered in the vicinity by

Pauline Weaver (*see TOUR 1b*) and a party of trappers in 1862. The town that sprang into existence was set two miles back from the river in order to avoid inundation by floods; it soon housed about six thousand people and was perhaps the most important settlement in Arizona at that time. In a period of seven years millions in gold were taken from the placers. To avoid danger of Indian raids in overland transportation, the bullion was generally shipped from Ehrenberg (*see below*) down the river and the Gulf of California to Mexico, to be refined and minted. Ehrenberg's gold helped to replenish the depleted treasury in Civil War days.

La Paz had the heterogeneous population characteristic of western mushroom towns. Few men brought their families with them. Mojave squaws, comely and vigorous women, did the housework and, as one writer put it, "met the domestic needs of the camp."

The placers soon played out and La Paz' inhabitants vanished. It is now possible to pass over and around it and hardly suspect that it ever existed.

BOOTHILL CEMETERY (L), 111.6 *m.*, established in 1856, is a fitting end to the Trail of Graves. Countless unmarked graves contain bones of pioneers who died with their boots on. Employees of the Arizona Highway Department have erected a monument here with a base that is a veritable museum of miner and cowboy accoutrements. Embedded in the cement are guns, burro shoes, branding irons, spurs, kettles, dutch ovens, miners' candles, picks, and numerous other articles. In this cemetery is buried a stranger from the East who had plenty of money and a good horse; there was gunplay in the streets and the stranger lost. When he was buried his grave was marked "J.C.1867," the brand on his horse and the year he died—no one knew his name or whence he came.

Motorists must slow down at the ARIZONA CHECKING STATION, 111.8 *m.*, until motioned on by the officer in charge.

By the highway at this point is (R) the ghost town of EHRENBERG, named for Hermann Ehrenberg, German mining engineer who came to Arizona in 1854 (*see TOUR 1d*). When the lower Colorado River was used for transportation this town was a shipping point for Prescott and other mining districts. In 1871 it had a population of about five hundred. Old adobe walls are all that remain and these are fast becoming one with the ground on which they stand.

US 70-60 crosses the Rio Colorado bridge over the Colorado which forms the California Line, 112.1 *m.*, at a point 4.5 miles east of Blythe, California.

Tour 3A

Claypool—Roosevelt—Apache Junction; 79 *m.,* State 88 (Apache Trail).

Paved roadbed about 20 miles at each end; elsewhere graveled.
Limited accom., Roosevelt, Apache Junction, and Tortilla Flat.

This entire route runs through mountains and, though the road is well maintained and not dangerous to drive, it contains many hairpin curves and has several points where the depth of the canyons below and the sheerness of their walls are terrifying. The road winds along the many gorges and caves formed by the streams that flow into the Salt River and for 60 miles follows a chain of man-made lakes whose blue surfaces on still, clear days reflect the surrounding mountains, flowers, and trees. In the typical desert growth along the route are many flowering trees. The ironwoods are covered with lavender flowers in May and June, and the palo verdes with their bright green trunks and branches, become huge golden bouquets. The mesquite trees have dark foliage and small scented blossoms that develop long bean pods in the summer. Both palo verde and mesquite pods are used as food by the Indians.

Trails of the Apache, who once roamed the region, crisscross the highway. Although members of the tribe worked on the construction of the road itself, there are none now living anywhere along the route.

State 88 branches north from US 70-60, at a junction called Claypool, 0 *m.,* which is 4 miles west of Globe (*see TOUR 3a*).

The golf course (L) of the CORBRE VALLEY COUNTRY CLUB (*greens fee $1*) is at 0.2 *m.*

BURCH, 2 *m.,* was once a small trading post on the banks of Pinal Creek, is the site of a mining camp. At the height of the silver stampede that began in 1876 numerous small silver and gold mines were opened on the Sleeping Beauty Mountain and in the hills to the west— now covered with tailings dumps. Most of these mines yielded rich ores near the surface but quickly played out. At the present time there is new open pit mining here by the Copper Cities Mining Co.

State 88 crosses a boundary of the TONTO NATIONAL FOREST (*see TOUR 3a*) at 3 *m.*

In WHEATFIELDS, 7 *m.,* was an agricultural area once cultivated by the Apache, and was the site of a silver mill. King Woolsey (*see TOUR 1A*), the Indian fighter, raided this spot in 1864 and destroyed the Indians' crops. Before the Globe bonanza was discovered, Wheatfields was visited by many prospectors seeking the rich mines that were reported to exist in some rugged mountains inhabited by Apaches who fired silver bullets at intruders. Most exciting of these accounts was the story of Doc Thorne who, having cured an Indian of an eye ailment, was persuaded to treat some similarly afflicted Arizona Apaches. He returned from their country with stories of huge gold and silver nuggets lying in a mountainous area near a hat-shaped butte. In July 1869 A. F. Banta, chief guide and scout at Fort Whipple (1865-71), accompanied by C. E. Cooley, founder of Show Low, H. W. Dodd, and a few friendly Apaches, set out to find the Doc Thorne mines and managed to reach the vicinity of what is now known as Sombrero Butte, but they were frightened by local Indians and hastened on to Camp Reno. In 1871 after a prospector named Miner had reported finding a treasure field in the general direction of a "butte that looks like a hat," the greatest treasure hunt in the Southwest since the days of the Spanish conquistadors and the search for the Seven Cities of Cibola was organized. Territorial Governor A. P. K. Safford, a pioneer of Nevada's Comstock Lode days, set aside his official duties to lead the expedition; the Safford party entered the Apache reservation from the Gila River, crossed Salt River to Sombrero Butte, explored the Cherry Creek section and the Sierra Ancha, and reached Wheatfields, after having passed completely around the spot at which five years later a rich silver vein was discovered. The Safford party dispersed at Wheatfields and the prospector, who had failed to find his way back, was discredited.

Northwest of Wheatfields the road ascends a summit that overlooks the Salt River and Tonto Basins.

SMOKE SIGNAL PEAK, 13 m., thrusts up its sharp irregular head R. This was one of several peaks in the vicinity used by Indians for communicating by smoke signals. It was also used by Federal troops for heliograph and wigwag signals and played a part in a Globe gambling frame-up. About 1910 the election of a sheriff had been close and could not be decided without returns from Pleasant Valley, at that time three days' travel away. Gamblers arranged to intercept the messenger, learn the result, secretly relay news of the election results by fires from Smoke Signal Peak and profit from their advance information. The gamblers' observers, however, misread the signals and the would-be framers were themselves fleeced for their trouble.

On the horizon (L) Four Peaks (7,645 alt.), are visible for many miles in every direction. In winter they usually are topped with snow. Here, also, is a glimpse of Roosevelt Lake. Northwest of this point is a long hill called the Hog Back.

At 17.5 m. is the junction with Feud Turnoff, an improved earth road (see TOUR 10A), now known as the Young Road.

High cliffs on the horizon (R) are in the Sierra Ancha (Sp., wide mountains) whose spots of white below the rims are not snow but the tailings of abandoned asbestos mines. Asbestos is still being mined in other parts of the range. In the rugged Sierra Ancha (6,505 alt.) are virgin stands of western yellow pine, Douglas fir and white fir, an abundance of wild game, and many prehistoric dwellings, several of which are known only to cowboys who have discovered them in precipitous canyons, far from beaten paths. Other remnants of the early civilization include picture writings, bits of colored pottery, sandals, arrowheads, and the remains of reservoirs and irrigation ditches.

From 21.2 *m.* the massive block of Cathedral Rock (L) looms on the horizon like a huge church.

At 28.4 *m.* is a junction with an oiled road.

Left here to TONTO NATIONAL MONUMENT (2,800 alt.), 1 *m.*, 1,120-acre tract with two prehistoric cliff dwellings built in the 14th century by Pueblo Indians. The lower house has two stories and twenty-nine rooms. Its front wall was possibly originally blank, except for portholes, and it is not certain where the entrance was. These buildings, as in other pueblos, were graneries, fortresses, and living quarters—all combined. The situation is admirable for defense; in addition to being sheltered in a cave in the cliff, the dwellings have a single approach on a cactus-covered hillside that offers no cover to an enemy. The upper house is larger and much more irregular in plan, because of periodic additions. Originally it was two stories high and contained 30 to 40 rooms. The outer walls have deteriorated to such an extent that original entrances are not discernible.

The road skirts the shore of ROOSEVELT LAKE, 28 *m.*, which, on calm days, reflects the opposite sky line. Flocks of wild ducks of several species, hundreds of pelicans, and occasionally gulls winter here.

ROOSEVELT, 31.6 *m.* (2,225 alt., 25 pop.), is on the flats overlooking the lake and the low mesas to the north. Homes of most of the employees at the dam are about a mile from Roosevelt. There is a general store, auto court and service station at Roosevelt and two boat docks, operated from here, are nearby.

This site at the junction of Tonto Creek and the Salt River was called The Crossing by the early settlers whose farms and cattle ranches bordered these waters. A settlement that developed at The Crossing has been quite submerged by Roosevelt Lake, though at one time the tops of some of its old structures as well as a vast archeological field where pottery and other artifacts of a bygone people have frequently been exposed.

At 32.2 *m.* is the junction with the graveled Tonto Basin Road (*see TOUR 10*).

ROOSEVELT DAM (2,146 alt.), 32.4 *m.,* is in a narrow gorge just below the confluence of Tonto Creek and Salt River. This dam, impounding the water used to irrigate the Salt River Valley (and now supplemented by four other dams on the Salt River that form a sixty-mile chain of lakes) was begun in 1906, and was the government's first large undertaking of this kind. Prior to its construction, which was supervised by the Reclamation Bureau, 60 miles of wagon road had to be cut through precipitous mountains for the transportation of materials by mule teams. This road, now improved for automobile travel, forms the western section of State 88. Much of the road was built by Apache workmen who were so reliable that they were sent out in squads without white overseers or timekeepers. Another road was built into the Sierra Ancha and a mill established there to provide lumber. A specially constructed thirteen-mile canal provided temporary power for placing the giant rocks and concrete in the dam, and a cement mill was operated near by.

The dam is 284 feet high, 184 feet thick at the base, and 16 feet thick at the top. The power plant at the base has a 24,000-horse-power capacity. The reservoir is 23 miles long, covers 17,800 acres, and has a drainage area of 5,760 square miles.

The road circles high above the dam and descends into Salt River Canyon passing grotesque rock formations—the Pyramids, Flatiron Mountain, Eagle Rock, and Old Woman's Shoe.

On the mountainside across the river are hundreds of saguaros (*see TOUR 4b*) and along the Salt River grows wild tobacco (*Nicotina rustica*), a branching shrub six to fifteen feet high with smooth thick leaves and dull yellow flowers that hang in clusters from the ends.

Southwest of Roosevelt Dam are several good views of Apache Lake (R) formed by Horse Mesa Dam which is not visible from the highway. Apache Lake is a vivid color that changes with the intensity of the sunlight and is surrounded by delicately colored but boldly outlined mountains, buttes, and terraced mesas.

At 45.8 *m.* is the junction with a dirt road.

Right on this road to APACHE LAKE, 1.6 *m.* (*boating, fishing*).

In FISH CREEK CANYON, 50 *m.*, sycamore, Arizona ash, cottonwood, and willow trees grow along the creek. The vertical rock walls of the gorge, known as WALLS OF BRONZE, are a dark red-brown with great spots of a dull moss green, which give the effect of aging bronze. In the depths of this almost perfect box canyon the road is completely hemmed in by towering walls which conceal the way out—a narrow cut in the cliff (R). The road climbs the cliff in a long ascent.

From 51.4 *m.* a view of the PAINTED CLIFFS (R) below reveals great surfaces of rock in varying shades of green tinted with gold.

At 55.2 *m.*, southwest of Fish Creek Canyon, is the junction with a dirt road.

Right on this road to HORSE MESA DAM, 6 *m.* (1,920 alt.), a reservoir and power unit of the Salt River Project completed in 1927 at a cost of $4,237,000. The dam is named for a natural rock formation used as a horse corral by both Indians and cowboys. The structure is a variable-radius arch type, 305 feet high and 784 feet long. The power plant has a 43,000 horsepower capacity, and the reservoir, Apache Lake, covers 2,600 acres and is 17 miles long.

The gorge near the dam is so extremely narrow that it almost excludes the rays of the sun. Two-thirds of the distance up the face of the rocky wall on the road side of the river is a ledge or bench with a natural cave behind. Access to the cave is gained by climbing a steep mountainside, crossing a lava bed, and descending from the rim of the gorge by a trail on the face of the cliff (*guides essential*).

This cave, considered by the Apache one of their safest and strongest retreats, is the SCENE OF THE BATTLE OF THE CAVES, a sanguinary and fantastic encounter that was won for the whites by ricocheting bullets. The battle was the climax of General Crook's campaign of 1872-73 against the bands of Apaches who had been conducting surprise raids from their mountain hide-outs. On a December night in 1872 the United States soldiers determined to use the Indians' own strategy and, led by friendly Indian scouts, stealthily climbed the mountain and sent an advance party to within fifty feet of the cave without being detected by the Indians within. All night they lay in wait. As the unsuspecting Apaches emerged at dawn a murderous volley felled six of them. The others called upon to surrender, replied with whoops and the chanting of war songs. After failing in several attempts to dislodge the soldiers by charges, the surviving Indians retreated and fought from behind the natural bulwarks within the cave. The troopers, unable to see their foes, directed their bullets against the rocky ceiling and sides of the cave, whence they glanced downward like hail. Seventy-six Apaches were killed and eighteen taken prisoner. Among these was a Mojave-Apache lad of seven. The boy was adopted and named Mike Burns by one of the leaders of the United States cavalry, Captain James Burns. (Mike died in 1934.)

TORTILLA FLAT, 60.1 m. (1,750 alt., 102 pop.), so called for giant masses of rocks resembling a platter of tortillas (Sp., pancakes), is a cluster of frame and adobe houses whose occupants cater to tourists. Surrounding the settlement are the Tortilla, Superstition, and Mazatzal Mountains; to the west are forests of saguaros.

From 63 m. is a view of Canyon Lake (R) with many houseboats of valley residents on its waters and numerous vacation cabins on its shores. Mormon Flat Dam (R) is visible at the far end of the lake.

At 65.1 m. is the junction with a dirt road.

Right on this road to MORMON FLAT DAM, 3 m. (1,671 alt.), com-pleted in 1925 at a cost of $1,559,000. A power plant with a 10,000 horse-power capacity adjoins. The dam, 229 feet high and 623 feet long, creates CANYON LAKE (*swimming, fishing, boating*), which covers (R) a thousand acres and is ten miles long.

The soft sandstone surface of WHIRLPOOL ROCK, 65.5 m., was cut by erosion into patterns resembling swirling water.

On the low horizon (L) at 72 m. is a view of Weaver's Needle (4,535 alt.), a conspicuous formation on Superstition Mountain (*see TOUR 3b*).

In GOLDFIELD, 74 m., is a mine that was once very productive, and from which some gold is still taken.

APACHE JUNCTION, 79 m., is the junction with US 70-60 (*see TOUR 3b*).

Tour 3B

Hope—Parker—Earp, Calif.—Parker Dam; 68.1 m.

State 72 and Water District Rd.
Santa Fe Ry. roughly parallels route throughout. Asphalt—paved roadbed.
Washes and dips in the road are dangerous after rains in the mountains.
Accommodations at Parker.

This route connects Hope with Parker Dam on the Colorado River just below its confluence with the Williams River. For the most part the country is flat and—except for greasewood, palo verde, and iron-wood—barren. At intervals, however, the road approaches rocky mountains that rise abruptly from the level plain. Some of these have sharp jagged peaks while others have flat mesalike tops. Gold worth many millions of dollars has been taken from this area. The northern part of the route is in the Colorado River Indian Reservation.

State 72 branches northwest from US 70-60 (see TOUR 3d) at HOPE, 0 m. The Harcuvar Mountains (R), visible across Mineral Valley, are known to contain gold. At one time "Shorty" Alger—who had been grubstaked by Dick Wick Hall (see TOUR 3d) to do some prospecting in this district—was climbing up a little hill to the north of Tank Pass. He slipped and to save himself from falling struck his prospector's pick into the ground. When he pulled it out he found impaled on the point a gold nugget that weighed more than half a pound. It was the top of a small glory hole that yielded over $100,000 worth of ore besides what was stolen by the hordes of "boomers" who rushed to the spot. Claims were filed on land extending for miles on either side of the discovery and hundreds of thousands of dollars changed hands before the excitement subsided. Dick Wick Hall carried as a pocket piece a nugget worth more than $100 which was taken out of the hole. Efforts to discover the downward continuation of this freak deposit have been both expensive and fruitless.

VICKSBURG, 4 m. (1,382 alt., 180 pop.), named for Vic Satter-dahl, who started a store here in the late nineties, is in a mining and stock-raising area and is on the Phoenix-Los Angeles branch of the Santa Fe Ry.

Northwest of Vicksburg the country is more level, and reveals a sweeping view of the desert floor.

BOUSE, 23.8 m., named for Tom Bouse, a trader and storekeeper here in early days. Tom was first called Brayton when it was the store for the famous Harqua Hala Mine, owned by Brayton Commercial Company. The old timers wanted the name changed to Bouse, in honor of the old timer.

The highway crosses the eastern boundary of the COLORADO RIVER INDIAN RESERVATION, 44.1 *m.,* the home of two tribes: the Mojave which has 1,175 members, and the Chemehuevi with 309 members. The agency headquarters is at Parker (*see below*). The Mojave, the darkest skinned of the Southwest tribes, are good farmers and breeders of horses.

The Mojave, unlike most Indians, liked to fight in hand-to-hand combat and was usually the victor against a single opponent; when outnumbered he would fight until he was killed. Immigrants following southwestern trails were frequently warned that the most perilous part of the journey was through the Mojave country. A mining explorer who visited Arizona in 1864 told of finding the bodies of men, women, children, and horses and the remains of wagons and baggage strewn for several miles along the trail, one day's journey east of the Colorado River. More than seventy persons moving from Texas and Arkansas had been killed and scalped. In 1859 fifty cavalrymen, on their way down the Colorado to Fort Yuma, were attacked by 1,500 Mojaves, but carried on a running fight and were able to escape, because of their superior arms. Fort Mohave on the Colorado River west of Oatman, in what is now the Mojave Indian Reservation—also under the jurisdiction of the agency at Parker—was established in 1858, abandoned in 1861 at the outbreak of the Civil War, and regarrisoned in 1869. No formal treaty of peace was ever made between the Mojave and the United States, but in 1867 at La Paz (*see TOUR 3d*) a treaty was signed by the Mojave and Chemehuevi tribes, in which each agreed to respect the persons and property of the other and to commit no depredations on the white settlers. By an act of Congress in 1886 the Mojave were assigned the Colorado River reservation, the land they had long claimed.

Mojave arts are few. Pottery making, practised in the early days, has been discontinued; making beaded bags, belts, and necklaces, in which the women are skilled, is the only present handicraft. The Mojave still follow tribal marriage customs that do not include a ceremony. The man and the woman live together at will, and separate when either party desires. All powers are ascribed to the mythological deity, Mastamho, who created the Colorado River, produced light, shaped the land, taught agriculture, saved the people from floods, and instituted the clans. The most interesting Mojave ceremony is that held for the dead during cremation. The tribe assemble in what is known as the "Cry House" and sing over the body; then take it to the "Cremation Ground," where it is placed on a pile of logs, and burned at sunrise, to the accompaniment of singing, dancing, and wailing. Attendance at the "Cries" and the following ceremonies is considered a duty.

Chemehuevi, the smaller tribe on this reservation, are a branch of the Paiute of northern Arizona (*see TOUR 1a*). When Father Francisco Garces made a trip up the Colorado in 1775-6, they were living

Formerly the Chemehuevi raised cattle, did subsistence farming and grew some grain and cotton for the market, on their Reservation farms. But the bottom lands of their old allotments have now been completely inundated under the waters of Lake Havasu, created by Parker Dam. What is left of the old allotments is virtually valueless except for possible manganese deposits and recreational sites on the lake. Many Chemehuevi have moved further along on Colorado River Reservation where they have received farm land. Their women are excellent basket weavers.

Though not of the same stock, the Chemehuevi rituals are largely those of the Mojave. They do not cremate their dead, but join in an all-night ceremony of dancing and singing after a death; their funeral music is of Mojave origin.

PARKER, 50.9 *m.* (413 alt., 1,200 pop.), is the trading center for a mining and grazing area. On its streets are many dark-skinned Chemehuevi and Mojave squaws—some having tribal designs tattooed on their foreheads—who sit in the shade of its cloistered walks or parade the streets with several small children clinging to the folds of the mothers' voluminous cotton skirts. The men, who are usually large and are dressed in dungarees, blue cotton shirts, and Stetson hats—a few wear bands around their heads—in their leisurely manner stroll through the streets, and lean stolidly against parked cars as they talk.

Because Arizona claimed water rights that California denied, Governor Moeur sent the Arizona National Guard here in 1934 to prevent construction on Arizona territory of Parker Dam, which diverts water from the Colorado River for California. The guardsmen were intended only to make the protest more formal and after a few weeks were withdrawn. Later the U. S. Supreme Court rendered a decision against Arizona.

State 72 crosses the California Line on the PARKER COLORADO RIVER BRIDGE, 51.8 *m.,* a graceful steel and concrete structure spanning the Colorado River. Its waters, formerly a muddy brown at this point, are now clear and green because Parker Davis and Boulder dams cause the river to deposit most of its silt.

At 52.5 *m.,* is the junction with a road built by the Metropolitan Water District of Southern California.

Left on this road to EARP, Calif., 0.1 *m.* (400 alt., 40 pop.), a general store, post office, and tourist camp on the west bank of the Colorado.

Right on the water district road, which is now the main route, to HEAD ROCK DAM (R), 54.5 *m.,* built to supply water to the Indian reservation (*see above*). The Parker-Gila Project, which includes this dam, has reclaimed some of the richest alluvial land in the state.

At 67.5 *m.* is the junction with the paved Gene Pump Plant Road. Left here to the junction with the paved Intake Pump Plant Road, 1.5 *m.,* R. 1.9 *m.*

on this to the INTAKE PUMP PLANT, where water is diverted through a giant aqueduct from the Colorado River to Southern California cities.

At 1.9 *m.* on the Gene Pump Plant Road is the junction with a dirt road. Right 0.1 *m.*, on this to the GENE WASH DAM, 0.1 *m.*

At 2.5 *m.* on the Gene Pump Plant Road is the GENE PUMP PLANT.

PARKER DAM, 68.1 *m.*, just below the confluence of the Bill Williams River (*see TOUR 2b*) and the Colorado River, is a concrete arch-type structure with a maximum height of 383 feet. The roadway crosses the top of the dam, which is 800 feet long, and 50 feet wide at the spillway crest. One of the deepest holes ever made for a dam foundation was excavated for this structure when the builders had to go down 235 feet to reach bedrock. Approximately 1,702,000 cubic yards were removed in excavating. The reservoir created by the dam covers 25,000 acres and extends 45 miles up the river to a point near Needles, California. This dam, built by the U.S. Bureau of Reclamation with funds supplied by The Metropolitan Water District of Southern California, is the diversion dam for the 392-mile Colorado River Aqueduct, which supplements the water supply of Los Angeles and twelve neighboring cities. The main aqueduct, built by the water district and financed through the sale of district bonds to the Reconstruction Finance Corporation is the longest yet (1939) built; it has twenty-nine tunnels that total 92 miles. One of these, the East Coachella, is 18 miles long and 16 feet in diameter. The dam cost $13,000,000, the main aqueduct approximately $140,000,000 and the distribution system about $45,000,000.

Tour 4

(Lordsburg, N.M.)—Douglas—Tucson—Gila Bend—Yuma—(El Centro, Calif.) ; US 80, State 84, and US 80.
New Mexico Line to California Line 417.2 *m.*

All-paved, all-year highway throughout. Cattle may stray on highway, especially at night.
Southern Pacific R.R. parallels route throughout.
All types of accommodations at Douglas, Bisbee, Tucson, and Yuma; limited elsewhere.

This route between New Mexico and California traverses the southern desert and reveals varieties of vegetation typical of its elevations, which vary from five thousand feet to virtual sea level. Between the high areas west of Bisbee and the Colorado River at Yuma is a general descent. Although the highway is continually surrounded by mountains—some of these rise abruptly from the desert while others, massed against each other, appear like dark storm clouds on the distant horizon—it never crosses them but makes its way through surprisingly wide valleys. These desert ranges are unlike the peaks of the high plateaus of northern and eastern Arizona; in the distance they are a hazy blue or purple and seem to belong more to the sky than to the earth; close at hand, they are dull brown, red, and gray, clearly etched, and reveal their upthrust formation in diagonal bands of rock.

Distances are so deceptive that a range or peak twenty or more miles away may appear to be very near. This high degree of visibility is the subject of many stories including that of the cowboy who swore he saw a woman wink at him when she was a mile away.

Parts of this route retrace the California Column's eastward course as well as that taken by the Mormon Battalion and by prospectors and settlers migrating westward. Northwest of Tucson it coincides with the trail used in the beginning of the eighteenth century by Father Kino and near the end of the century by Juan Bautista de Anza.

Section a. NEW MEXICO LINE to DOUGLAS; 48.2 m. US 80.

In the rough mountainous country east of Douglas are acres of lava rocks, caves, canyons, and the Chiricahua National Monument with its Wonderland of Rocks that once served the Apache as a hide-out.

US 80 crosses the New Mexico Line, 0 m., at the junction with an improved paved road, 50.2 miles west of Lordsburg, N.M.

Right on this road 6.9 m. to the CORONADO NATIONAL FOREST, through which the road runs for 25 miles. The forest abounds with large and small game and its streams with trout. The latter attract many sports-men who camp by the clear mountain streams during the fishing season (April to July). At 7.4 m. PORTAL PEAK (6,520 alt.) to the northwest forms a splash of red in the background. At 8.3 m. the dirt road turns L. and runs through a narrow gorge with rock walls that shade from yellow into orange and red. Juniper, Chihuahua pine, cottonwood, and scrub oak increase in size as the road climbs to higher altitudes.

PORTAL (ranger station, supplies, guides for Crystal Cave), 10.6 m. (5,000 alt., 55 pop.), entirely surrounded by mountains, is the center of a fruit- and alfalfa-growing, stock raising, and recreational area. Hundreds of visitors each year come here to escape the heat in the lower altitudes, enjoy the recreational facilities, and, in season, to hunt and fish. Portal, founded by a prospector named Duffener who discovered the Crystal Cave, was given its name because it is at the entrance to Cave Creek Canyon (see below).

At 11.5 m. on the dirt road is the junction with a second improved dirt road. Left on this 2 m. to CAVE CREEK CANYON which is boxed by cliffs that tower one and two thousand feet and are eroded into pinnacles, turrets, and castle-like forms. At intervals the clear waters of Cave Creek reflect the pastel pinks, greens, yellows, and tans of these masses of latite rock.

In Cave Creek Canyon at 5.2 m. is the junction with a marked, fairly steep foot trail; R. 0.7 m. on this to CRYSTAL CAVE (guide essential). A few hundred feet from the entrance is Devil's Elbow, a treacherous and difficult passage. Beyond King Solomon's Temple has a dome-like ceiling, walls that sparkle with crystal deposits, and in its center a throne formed of carbonated lime deposited by constantly dropping water. Icicle-like stalactites are directly overhead; THE PINNACLE (R) is a stalagmite resembling a beehive. The temple, the only one of the rooms that has been fully explored, has countless unexplored passages branching from it.

At 16.7 m. on the first dirt road is PARADISE (5,500 alt., 10 pop.), a score of weatherworn frame buildings scattered along the narrow, winding mountain road. Almost all the buildings of this former boom camp have false fronts that are now sagging remnants; all but two or three are abandoned and those lived in are scarcely distinguishable from the others. The remaining residents carry on a limited trade with near-by miners and ranchers.

Right 3 m. from Paradise to the ghost town of GALEYVILLE (5,700 alt., 12 pop.), in a small well watered canyon in the Chiricahuas. A few miners and cattlemen reside in the district. Though miners attracted by the gold and other minerals in the area had lived here since 1870, a few dim trails were Galeyville's only transportation routes, and high production costs eventually made further extraction of gold unprofitable. With the passing of mining activities, however, Galeyville began a new era. Far from the sheriff's office and almost inaccessible from the Tombstone side, it became a resort for American and Mexican smugglers and rustlers.

Among the outlaws who found refuge in its isolation and recreation in its many saloons and dives were Curly Bill Brocius and his handsome lieutenant, John Ringo. Curly Bill, a bronzed blue-eyed giant with dark kinky hair, always wore high-heeled fancy-stitched boots, a wide-brimmed white sombrero, and two criss-crossed gun belts that held his twin forty-fours. He was a discriminating bandit, robbing only the prosperous. Caravans of Mexican smugglers were his special delight; and he showed such a preference in his rustling for Mexican cattle that his name was mentioned prominently in a number of warm-worded diplomatic notes passed between the two governments. Nevertheless he was popular and enjoyed the friendship of many men, including the deputy sheriff, Billie Breckenridge, who used the bandit to help him collect taxes.

In lawless Cochise County this was one of the sheriff's most difficult and hazardous tasks. But whenever Breckenridge and Curly Bill called the ranchers were eager to pay up, and the deputy completed his rounds in record time, returning with his saddle pouches bulging with tax dollars.

Curly Bill's end is uncertain. Though Wyatt Earp (see Tombstone) reported that he had shot Curly Bill Brocius in an engagement at Mescal Springs in the Whetstone mountains, William Sparks, an Arizona territorial ranger, said that a short time after his supposed death Curly Bill dined at Spark's ranch on the Blue River, and old timers who knew Curly Bill say he visited in Tombstone in the 1920's.

John Ringo was an adventurer, gambler, and gunman who had come to Arizona in 1881 from Wichita, Dodge City, and other lively Kansas towns. His family name was Ringgold and he is described as tall, lean, blond, and usually amiable, though at times sullen and vicious. It was in Evilizer's Saloon in Galeyville that Ringo was annoyed by the dealing in a poker game. When a pat hand—four aces—sheared him of his cash, he protested, but was advised to go and "grow more wool." He left but in a short time returned to the game and remarked: "Two guns 'll beat four aces any time."

Later Deputy Billie Breckenridge served him with a warrant charging armed robbery.

"Listen, Billie," Ringo said, "I've got some business to attend to first. You go back to Tombstone and I'll come tomorrow."

The next day he showed up in Tombstone, paid his fine and rode away. Though for years Ringo had been an outlaw, he later about-faced and rode with the Law and Order League in an attempted cleanup. He gave no reason for his change of heart, and none was asked. Gradually he dropped into obscurity; and one day, his body was found in Turkey Creek Canyon with a bullet hole through his skull. Some thought he had shot himself; but others pointed to Johnny-Behind-the-Deuce—a gambler who had held a special grudge against Ringo—as the killer. Though killings were frequent Galeyville was seldom disturbed by the law until the rustlers stole cattle belonging to John Slaughter, Sheriff of Chochise County. The cleanup with which Slaughter retaliated ended the town.

At 19.9 *m.* is the junction with another dirt road. Left on this 3 *m.* to RUSTLER CANYON an early-day hide-out for outlaws.

The main dirt road leaves the mountains at 31 *m.* and the landscape changes to rolling hills dotted with scrub oak and juniper.

The CHIRICAHUA NATIONAL MONUMENT (*guides available*), 34.2 *m.*, contains some 10,530 acres of varicolored monoliths carved by erosion into grotesque figures that seem to march along the mountainside like invaders from some fantastic region. It was made a national monument in 1924. Although some of the formations for which the area is famous are visible from the motor road, the best are reached only by hiking or riding along the 15 miles of graded trails. Chiricahua is the result of a billion years of geologic changes. At one time the ancient landscape consisted of granite, gneiss, and schist. There was at least one epoch of inundation by the sea, followed by violent volcanic activity in which rock formations were thrown up in almost every conceivable form. The pillars, cliffs, balanced masses and solitary figures were composed of varied rock layers of different hardness. Gradually water, frost, and wind eroded the softer deposits, and sculptured the columns, spires, and balanced rocks. Seeping waters dissolved minerals in higher layers to redeposit them at lower levels.

THE PRAYING PADRE (R) is visible from 36.2 *m.*, THE CHINAMAN'S HEAD (R) from 37.5 *m.*, THE BISHOP or Bandmaster (R) from 37.9 *m.*, and from 38.4 *m.* the UGLY DUCKLING (L), CATHEDRAL ROCK (L), and THE BOXING GLOVE (R).

MASSAI POINT, 41.4 *m.* (6,871 alt.), was named for a "bronco" Apache who has become a legend. He was one of those deported in 1886 after Geronimo's surrender. Somewhere east of St. Louis, Massai escaped from the prison train that was taking him to Florida and found his way back to his homeland. For three years he fought singlehanded against the United States, Mexico, and the "tame" reservation Apaches, whom he despised. Massai stole women from the reservations, took them to his mountain hide-outs, and, when he was through with them, killed them. He was so wild and furtive that no one ever heard his full story—what little is known of him he told to a White Mountain squaw whom he loved and allowed to return to the reservation.

From the lookout tower on Massai Point are visible (R to L) the TOTEM POLE, 137 feet high, the CHINESE WALL, the MUSHROOM, and the BALANCED ROCK. Two hundred yards below the point is another huge rock balanced on a base that is only one-tenth of its size. COCHISE HEAD is a massive formation resembling the features of the Apache chief who waged bitter warfare in this part of Arizona between 1861-71 (*see TOUR 7c.*). The Apache called this area Say Yahdesut (point of rocks) and believed they could hear the voices of their dead, whose spirits lingered here.

This wonderland of rocks was accidentally discovered late in 1886 by Colonel Hughes Stafford and Sergeant Neil Erickson, who had homesteads near by. After a favorite horse of Colonel Stafford's was stolen by Massai and his squaw, the two soldiers took up the pursuit and followed the trail through the rocks to the formation later called Massai Point, where they recovered the horse though the Indians escaped. Night had come and in the moonlight the scene seemed even more fantastic to the two pursuers. Erickson afterwards spent many days in the region and expended much time and effort in bringing it to the attention of the government and the general public.

From 5.7 *m.* is a good view of SENTINEL PEAK (R), sometimes called Square Peak.

The GERONIMO MONUMENT, 9.3 *m.*, commemorates the Apache leader's capitulation on September 5, 1886 in Skeleton Canyon (*see below*). Geronimo (1829-1909), classified in army reports as a Chiricahua Apache, called himself a member of the Bedonkohe Apaches, who lived just north of their allies, the Chiricahua. He described his early life as a series of raids into Mexico undertaken in revenge for the killing by Mexicans of his wife and children. Because of the prowess he displayed in leading these expeditions he was made a war chief of the Apache. Though he several times made peace with the United States and brought his followers to the Apache reservation, then called the White Mountain (*see TOUR 8*), he was always dissatisfied with the Indians' meager rations and the army's prohibitions against tizwin (a corn brew), drinking and wife beating. Between 1881 and 1886 he led several outbreaks, killing and plundering as he made his way into the mountains of Mexico, where he maintained himself and his followers by means of raids on ranches in Mexico, Arizona, and New Mexico. When hard pressed by the army he would offer to return to the reservation and keep the peace. Following an outbreak in 1885 Geronimo's band took about one hundred lives before they were finally subdued. In January 1886 they were cornered by General Crook in the almost impenetrable Sierra Madre of Mexico, and Geronimo promised to meet Crook on the border in March to discuss terms of capitulation. In the parley Geronimo agreed to surrender at Fort Bowie and started north. But at San Bernardino the Indians got drunk on whiskey sold them by a white man and Geronimo, Natches, son of Cochise (*see TOUR 7c*), and about thirty of their followers fled; Chief Chihuahua and sixty or more Indians continued to Bowie and surrendered. Crook, severely criticized for his handling of this affair, asked to be relieved and General Nelson A. Miles was put in command. The following September Lieutenant Charles B. Gatewood, alone and unarmed, entered Geronimo's camp and persuaded him to surrender. Geronimo and his followers were imprisoned for two years in Fort Pickens, Florida— though they had been assured that they would be sent to join their relatives at Fort Marion. In 1888 they were united with their families in Alabama and in 1894 Geronimo was moved to Fort Sill, Oklahoma where he remained until his death.

APACHE, 9.8 *m.,* is a checking station (*all cars inspected for diseased fruit; proof of car ownership may be asked*).

Left from Apache on a dirt road to SKELETON CANYON, 6 *m.,* which winds through the wildest part of the Peloncilla Mountains from the Animas Valley in New Mexico to the San Bernardino Valley in Arizona.

At 6 *m.* the canyon opens out into the San Bernardino Valley; on the west stands ROSS SLOAN'S RANCH HOUSE (R). Near by is the SITE OF GERONIMO'S SURRENDER. Two brutal encounters between outlaws and smugglers took place in this canyon within a mile of Sloan's house, one almost in his front yard. The last serious encounter occurred in 1882 when Curly Bill, with other bad men, waylaid a band of Mexican smugglers who were raiding the country. About fifteen were killed and their bodies were left where they fell. Coyotes and buzzards picked their bones, some were washed away by storm waters in the creek, others were taken as curiosities by travelers, and some of the skulls picked up by cowboys became soap dishes in San Bernardino ranch houses. But fragments of the skeletons remain scattered throughout the canyon. Once echoing to the cries of battle and death, Skeleton Canyon is now a place of peace and solitude—its stillness broken only by the occasional bawl of cattle and the night cry of a prowling coyote.

The long flat-topped mountain (R) at 17 *m.* is MONTE VISTA PEAK.

The highway passes through a field of cinder cones, evidence of volcanic activity, at approximately 25 *m.*

In BERNARDINO, 26.9 *m.,* are cattle-shipping pens (R).

Left from Bernardino on a dirt road to another dirt road, 9 *m.;* R. on this to an improved road, 18 *m.;* R. on this to SAN BERNARDINO, 19 *m.* on the Mexican Border, once the headquarters of the San Bernardino ranch, an early Spanish hacienda and army post. In 1846 it was visited by the Mormon Battalion (*see History*) and was mentioned by its commander, Lieutenant Colonel Cooke, who also described the thousands of wild cattle grazing in the territory. At that time the ranch covered more than seventy-three thousand acres, two thousand in Arizona and the remainder in Sonora. The Sonora section was sold by the Mexican government for ninety dollars. In 1884 John H. Slaughter drove cattle into the San Pedro Valley and purchased the ranch. Slaughter served as sheriff of Cochise County, fought the Apache for fifteen years, and was present at the surrender of Geronimo in Skeleton Canyon.

The many acres of black lava rocks (L), 27.2 *m.,* reveal the volcanic nature of the near-by mountains. Southwest of this point is a bed of prickly pear cactus. The mountains visible far to the south are the Sierra de San Bernardo in Mexico.

Southwest of CAZADOR, 35.7 *m.,* a railroad station named for an Apache chief, the road runs between the Pedrogosa Mountains (R) and the Perilla Mountains (L), which mark the eastern edge of Sulphur Springs Valley, an area dotted with farms and cattle ranches and now noted for its guest ranches, hotels, and winter resorts. These mountains as well as the Mule Mountains, forming the western boundary of the valley, have yielded gold, silver, and copper ore. College Peaks (L), 36 *m.,* are said to have been named for a college student who fell to his death from one of the cliffs.

In the trough of Sulphur Springs Valley, surrounded by miles of short yellow bunch grass and distant purple peaks, is DOUGLAS, 48.2 *m.* (3,980 alt., 9,828 pop.) (*see Douglas*).

Points of Interest: Company of Mary Novitiate; Church Park; Agua Prieta, Mexico; and others.

Section b. DOUGLAS to TUCSON; 121.8 m. US 80.

The Mule Mountains northwest of DOUGLAS, 0 *m.,* with their rich copper mines and their smooth, round orange and brown foot hills, were the scene of Apache raids and train robberies. Along the route are several of Arizona's toughest frontier mining towns, a noted cave, and some of the state's finest saguaros.

The DOUGLAS SMELTERS, 1 *m.,* are identified by revolving columns of white smoke climbing high into the sky.

At 2.1 *m.* is the junction with US 666 (*see TOUR 7c*).
At 22.7 *m.* is the junction with a paved road.

Right on latter 0.2 *m.* is the Denn shaft, once owned by Shattuck-Denn Mining Corporation, now operated by Phelps Dodge Corporation. Above the shaft is the gallows frame, about 100 feet high supporting the sheave wheels and cables that raise and lower the cages in the 2,900-foot shaft.

Development of this mine was begun in 1905 by L. C. Shattuck, former saloon keeper in Bisbee, and Maurice Denn, prospector and miner. The first large ore body, with a grade of six to ten per cent copper, was found on the 1,700-foot level.

In the EVERGREEN CEMETERY (R), 22.8 *m.*, about 100 yards north of the main entrance, is GEORGE WARREN'S GRAVE, marked by a stone monument with a copper plaque showing Warren as a prospector. After his death in 1892 the burial place of the man who found the Copper Queen (*see Bisbee*) was forgotten till 1914, when it was identified by a rotted wooden headboard marked "G. W." in an out-of-the-way section of the cemetery. The body was transferred to its present prominent place in 1917.

At 22.9 *m.* is the junction with the Traffic Circle. The town of Warren is reached from here.

Left here to the paved Warren Road, 0.1 *m.* Left on this to CAMPBELL SHAFT (R), 0.3 *m.*, one of several shafts into the Copper Queen mines. The fenced surface yards contain the usual hoist room, change and locker rooms, and gallows frame above the shaft.

Most of the ore taken from the Copper Queen mines has been from rich deposits occurring as replacements of limestone, though they also contain large quantities of leaner ore, which have been left in the ground as reserves. The ore from these mines is smelted at Douglas.

The Warren Road continues to WARREN, 1 *m.* (5,000 alt., 3,500 pop.), developed by a real estate promoter early in the twentieth century and named for George Warren. In the center is the long, rectangular Vista Park, from which the town spreads out across gently-rolling terrain. Behind Warren on the southeast rises Black Knob Hill and beyond it is Geronimo Peak, a finger of hooked rock named for the Apache chief (*see above*). The more prosperous people of Bisbee have deserted their old homes on the precipitous hillside in favor of pleasant conventional houses here, with trim lawns and gardens; several mine officials and business men have built expensive houses surrounded by landscaped grounds. Warren is a well-developed town with a motion picture theater, schools, churches, and a large shopping district.

On the Naco Road at 2 *m.* is TINTOWN, a Mexican village with a tradition of independence and gaiety. Tintown has two unpaved streets, a paved plaza with a band stand, about thirty adobe and wooden houses. Although the inhabitants of this picturesquely named hamlet are quite poor, they indulge their love of music and dancing. About 1904 the first houses in this community were made of flattened tin cans, oil containers, and scraps of discarded lumber by Mexicans from East Bisbee, where the other residents had objected to the Mexicans' loud laughter and song late at night. Several of the first families of Tintown were *pajareros* (bird-catchers) who trapped wild birds, put them into roughly-made cages, and sold them as pets to the housewives of Bisbee. Tintown grew slowly during its first decade and rapidly during the second, when most of the Mexicans were able to find employment around the mine yards. In the 1920's the town was filled to overflowing, with the houses "about three inches apart" and two or three families living in each. The place was very gay and rowdy during this period, with many cantinas and dance halls, and a certain amount of disorder.

Among Tintown's many legends is one of a drunkard about forty years old who claimed to be the father of everybody. *"Yo soy el padre de todos!"* he would shout on approaching Tintown. To each individual, young or old, he would say *"Yo soy tu padre"* (Sp., I am your father), and would look so fierce that no one dared contradict him. One day, however, a very old man replied, "you certainly can't be my father, since I am older than you are." This so enraged the self-styled parent that he brutally attacked the old man who whipped out his pistol and shot the braggart.

The road continues to NACO, 9 *m.* (5,200 alt., 2,100 pop.), on the International Boundary separating Naco, Arizona, from Naco, Sonora. Surrounding both Nacos is desert country, but in the distance to the south are the white-tipped, blue mountains of Mexico.

The United States section of the town, a quarter-mile of highway lined with small houses and stores, has few noteworthy buildings except the Mexican Consulate (R) and the U. S. Custom Building (L) near the boundary. Naco, Arizona, was extremely popular during Mexican revolutions as a comparatively safe observation point from which to watch the wars waged for possession of the Mexican custom offices.

One-story adobes border both the wide dusty streets of Naco, Sonora. In the business section, which consists of ten or twelve of these buildings—some covered with a grey-white stucco—are bars that sell fine Mexican beers, fiery mescal, tequila, and other native liquors; curio shops filled with glassware, pottery, hand-woven textile, baskets, metal work—most of it beautiful and inexpensive—and food stores that carry Mexican condiments, sweet cakes, cigarettes and staple groceries. All will accept United States currency.

LOWELL, 23.3 *m.* (5,100 alt., 2,500 pop.), is surrounded by Lavender Pit and mine shafts built above deep mine workings at the lower end of steep Mule Pass Gulch. Lavender Pit is the name of the huge new open-pit operation in the Bisbee District, and will cover an area approximately four times that of old Sacramento Pit. This development is named for the late H. M. Lavender, who was Vice-President and General Manager of Phelps Dodge Corporation. The pit operation is a 25-million dollar project, where an estimated 41 million tons of concentrating ore is hidden. About 60,000 tons waste rock are removed daily. A portion of old Sacramento Pit is being filled with waste. The mine is so extensive that entire businesses and residential areas in Bisbee District have had to be relocated to make way for the project. Lavender Pit will be more than 2/3 mile long and about ½ mile wide at its greatest dimensions, and from the highest point to the bottom of the finished excavation the depth will be about 1,000 feet. It will take until the end of 1954 before the pit is fully developed and new plant facilities completed for treatment of low grade ore.

Lowell's business section surrounds Lowell Plaza, now used as a parking lot. For three or four blocks US 80, the main street, is lined with modern and old-fashioned one- and two-story business buildings. Lowell's trade is an extension of Bisbee's and for the most part serves the entire district. Some Bisbee lumber, feed, and fuel concerns, needing more room than they could find in a bigger town, moved here.

They receive much of the farm and ranch trade from the near-by valleys.

Lowell, formerly considered a pleasant residential town, was settled by large colonies of miners including Finns, Montenegrins, Serbians and people of other nationalities.   Former Jiggerville, now within the Lavender Pit area, was inhabited principally by jigger bosses (underground sub-bosses), and East Lowell, also in the present pit area, was the stronghold of the Scandinavians and Finns with their *saunas* (steam baths).

Left from Lowell to JUNCTION SHAFT, 0.1 *m.*, which was sunk in 1905, is 2,700 feet deep and opens into the largest operating mine in the Warrent District.   A very large mine-water pumping plant on the 2,200 foot level, operating 24 hours a day throughout the year, keeps the mine clear of surface seepage and underground waters.

BISBEE, 25.5 *m.* (5,265 alt., 6,000 pop.) (*see Bisbee*).

Points of Interest: Copper Queen Mine Glory Hole, Brewery Gulch Gazette Building, Cochise County Courthouse, and other structures.

DIVIDE MONUMENT, 28.7 *m.* on US 80, was erected on the summit (6,030 alt.) of a divide in the Mule Mountains as a memorial to the life-termers from the Arizona State Prison who built the divide highway in 1913-14.   From this point there is a good view of Bisbee, clinging to the sides of Tombstone Canyon.

Along the highway as it descends from the divide to a rolling plain, are buck brush and scrub oak, typical of the elevation.   Far to the west are visible the Patagonia Mountains and, in the distance to the north, the long blue range of the Dragoon Mountains, stronghold of Cochise (*see TOUR 7c*).   The MULE MOUNTAINS, named for two peaks resembling mule's ears, are immediately to the west.   Few mountains in Arizona are more beautiful; under a brilliant sun the intensity of their color is softened, but on a cloudy day their grays, rich earthen reds, and browns are vivid against the green-desert foreground.

TOMBSTONE, 49.1 *m.* (4,539 alt., 1,200 pop.) (*see Tombstone*).

Points of Interest: Bird Cage Theater, Can Can Restaurant, O.K. Corral Site, Crystal Palace Saloon, Rose Tree Inn, Episcopal Church, and others.

1.   Left from Tombstone on an unimproved dirt road to the ghost town of CHARLESTON, 8 *m.*, on the banks of the San Pedro River.   Owing to lack of water in Tombstone, the stamp mill of the Tombstone Mining and Milling Company was built here.   In 1880 when the town was very lively, Alfred Henry Lewis, an eastern newspaper man, spent a short time here gathering material for stories.   Charleston was fictionized as "Red Dog" and Tombstone as "Wolfville."

Periodically, the Law and Order League—fifty heavily armed men—rode forth from Tombstone to kill or to tame the outlaws in Charleston and Galeyville.   On one such trip the posse halted before crossing the bridge that spanned the San Pedro and led into Charleston.   For on the opposite bank stood a lone man, John Ringo.   "Come on," Ringo invited; "I'm a-waitin'."

"Let's not be hasty, boys," the league leader advised. "Ringo hits what he shoots at."

The townsite is now marked by a clump of tall cottonwoods shading scattered, crumbling adobe walls.

2. Left from Tombstone on Allen Street to the marked GRAVE OF ED SCHIEFFELIN (R), 2.6 *m.*, on a granite point at the place where he was camping when he filed the Tombstone claim (*see Tombstone*). After he had sold his share in the Tombstone mines he left Arizona. Later he resumed prospecting, this time in the Yukon Valley in Alaska. Though he died in Alaska, he was buried here near his "first find" in compliance with a request in his will.

At 52.3 *m.* is a junction (L) with State 82 (*see TOUR 4A*).

ST. DAVID, 66.1 *m.* (3,850 alt., 800 pop.), settled by Mormons in 1877, is dependent on farming. After the earthquake of 1887 had opened up new sources of water, the settlers dug artesian wells that were the first of this type developed in Arizona.

The highway crosses the San Pedro River at 67.5 *m.* Along its valley are some irrigated areas that produce alfalfa, small grains, truck vegetables, cattle, hogs, and poultry. Two canals lead from the river on the east side, one to the St. David area, and the other to the Pomerene area, north of Benson. Coronado followed the San Pedro in his journey northward from Mexico. It was in the San Pedro Valley that Colonel Cooke and his Mormon Battalion were attacked (1846) by wild bulls. A member of the Battalion, Sergeant Daniel Tyler, in his *History of the Mormon Battalion,* related the story of this, the only engagement on their long march. "The animals, congregated on the line of our route, on hearing the rumblings of our approaching wagons, were startled, and some ran off in afright. Others, however, to gratify their curiosity, perhaps, marched toward us. . . . Their terribly beautiful forms and majestic appearance were quite impressive.

"Contrary to the orders of the Colonel, as previously noticed, every man had his musket loaded, and a battle followed. In the open ground, where the cattle could see us from a distance, they would run away, but when near us, whether wounded or not, they were the assaulting party. Hence, the roar of musketry was heard from one end of the line to the other. One small lead mule in a team was thrown on the horns of a bull over its mate on the near side, and the near mule, now on the off side and next to the bull, was gored until he had to be left with entrails hanging a foot below his body. One or two pack-mules were also killed. The endgates of one or two wagons were stove in, and the sick, who were riding in them, were of course, frightened. Some of the men climbed upon the wheels of the wagons and poured a deadly fire into the enemy's ranks. Some of them threw themselves down and allowed the beasts to run over them; others fired and dodged behind mesquite brush to re-load their guns, while the beasts kept them dodging to keep out of the way. Others, still, climbed up in small trees, there being now and then one available."

During this battle, which started early in the morning and continued until noon, a dozen or more men were wounded, some seriously. The number of bulls killed is not known, but is estimated at sixty. One writer says that eighty-one were killed outright, before they suddenly retreated.

At 71.6 *m.,* in a heavy mesquite thicket, is the junction with a dirt road.

Left on this road to the APACHE POWDER COMPANY PLANT, 3 *m.* (*no visitors*), established in 1919 to furnish high explosives for the Arizona mining industry. The forty acres of ground covered by the plant are divided into safety and danger areas. In the danger section are the buildings where nitroglycerine and powder are manufactured and packed.

BENSON, 73.2 *m.* (3,581 alt., 1,400 pop.), is on the bank of the San Pedro River and close to mountains. In all directions are rolling lomas, mesas, and escarpments cut and broken by erosion. The town, built along the highway, consists mostly of arched and flat-topped adobes, and frame false-fronted structures, some of which are gray with age and badly in need of paint. Cowboys, miners, and Mexicans still frequent this town that for many years was filled with saloons, tinhorns, rustlers, hustlers, cribs, and crap games. It was here that Jack the Ripper was killed in Fisher's saloon (*see Blood and Thunder Days*).

The area around Benson has been inhabited for centuries. A Spanish officer wrote in 1697 of houses along the San Pedro between Quiburi and the Gila River, and mentioned the extreme fertility and prosperity of these ranches although they were continually raided by savages. Benson was founded in 1880 as the railroad town for Tombstone; as early as 1860, however, its site was famous as the spot where the old Butterfield stages crossed the San Pedro. For years it was the American end of the old Sonora Railroad, built by the Santa Fe in 1882 to reach the harbor of Guaymas, Sonora, Mexico. This road also served the Tombstone mines' large mills at Contention City (*see TOUR 4A*), and was the nearest railroad connection to Fort Huachuca.

The mesa northwest of Benson is a vast garden of yucca with great white flowers opening in May and June; dull gray patches of grama grass, green mesquite trees, and light gray salt brush cover the flats. The brown, symmetrical Whetstones (L) ascend from the mesa floor. The foothill ranges (R) form a bare rocky barrier to the higher and distant Rincons which glow with purple and pink lights in the rays of the setting sun; pine growths on the highest slopes merge with the shadows of the peaks and summits. East, from any position on the mesa, the broken ranges of the Dragoon Mountains appear to move in and out of the dark shadows cast by overhanging clouds. MOUNT GLEN (7,512 alt.) is a prominent peak at the northern end of the Dragoons and RINCON PEAK (8,465 alt.) the highest point in the Rincon Mountains. The whistles of freight trains slowly ascending to the rim of the mesa have a strange and lonely sound in this weird, uninhabitated region.

PANTANO, 90.8 *m.* (3,547 alt., 25 pop.), was for a time called La Cienega (Sp., marsh or swamp), also Tulleyville for a pioneer freighter. This little town that drowses in the midday sun was once a noteḍ ranch and stage station. The old PANTANO CEMETERY near the station is filled with graves of pioneers who were killed by Apaches.

Mrs. Granville H. Oury, wife of Arizona's delegate to the Confederate Congress of 1861, described this section in her diary: "We are traveling through country which has always been infested by Indians, and very recently they have committed depredations and horrible atrocities on this very road. Our party is very small and there would be no escape for us if a party of Apaches were to attack us. We all realize this and are trusting to some good fortune or fate to get us through safely."

In 1867 W. A. Smith, later known as Shotgun Smith, and three companions were attacked by Apaches here at daybreak. His comrades were killed early in the encounter, but Smith, single-handed, fought with such ferocity and dealt such destruction with his shotgun that the Apaches withdrew at noon.

The LAMAR COBB MONUMENT (L), 98 *m.*, a five-foot shaft with a bronze plaque, honors the first state highway engineer of Arizona.

At 100.8 is the junction with a dirt road.

Right on this road to VAIL, 1 *m.* (3,345 alt., 40 pop.), named for an early cattleman, Walter Vail.

COLOSSAL CAVE (*adm. $1, children 50¢*), 8 *m.*, though dry and dusty now, was carved by underground waters into formations resembling animals, buildings, and people—all in countless connecting rooms. In the eighty's a Southern Pacific train in this vicinity was robbed of $62,000 by masked bandits, who eluded a sheriff's posse somewhere in the recesses of Colossal Cave. For three weeks the officers waited at the mouth of the cave and built fires within, hoping to smoke the robbers out. The fugitives escaped through another exit, but later were cornered in Willcox where three of them were killed in a gun battle. The fourth man was captured and sentenced to serve twenty-eight years. Released in 1912 he returned to Tucson for two weeks, then disappeared. An agent of the Wells-Fargo Express Company trailed the man to this cave, and found several empty money sacks; the man was never found again.

SAGUARO NATIONAL MONUMENT, just north of the cave in the Tanque Verde Mountains, is a tract of more than sixty-three thousand acres set aside in 1933 to preserve Arizona's finest saguaros. These corrugated giants with their perpendicular trunks and equally perpendicular branches, which often grow from opposite sides like the arms of a candelabrum, resemble in their stark rigidity the newest of modern designs. Many here are more than a hundred years old and have attained a height of fifty feet. Their ability to store water is second only to that of the barrel cactus; full grown saguaros have a root system that spreads fifty feet in all directions, mainly near the surface. Water absorbed during a rainy season is sucked into the trunk, which expands its spine-covered accordion pleats to serve as a reservoir. There are no leaves to give off moisture and even the saguaro's branches are controlled by the climate so that in very dry areas the saguaro may consist of only a fluted column; but in more favorable places its branches range from a small knob to a limb twenty feet long. Waxy white blossoms appear on the rounded ends of the branches in May and develop into purple fruit that ripens about the end of June. The saguaro fruit is a favorite food of the Papago who celebrate their New Year at the time of its ripening with an elaborate festival (*see TOUR 4B*). They eat the juicy crimson pulp both fresh and sun dried; boil the juice into syrup that becomes very intoxicating if allowed to ferment; and grind the black seeds into chicken feed. The Papago use the fiber of the saguaro for a building material and make drinking vessels of the strong knots formed where woodpeckers have bored into the cactus. In addition to the saguaro and other cacti this tract has heavy growths of palo verde—their trunks and branches a bright green—and of mesquite and catclaw trees (*see TOUR 4B*).

There is a dense growth of ocotillo at 106.3 *m.* When this plant, which has long prickly branches radiating from the root, blooms in the spring, its long spiked rods sway in the desert breeze like wands tipped with scarlet.

The Santa Catalina Mountains (R) and the Santa Rita range (L) frame a desert picture of greasewood, cholla, prickly pear, and barrel cactus.

UNITED STATES VETERANS HOSPITAL is (L) at 118.7 *m.* (*see TOUR 1d*).

At 118.8 *m.* is the junction with US 89 (*see TOUR 1d*), which unites with US 80 for several miles north of Tucson.

TUCSON, 121.8 *m.* (2,374 alt., 70,000 pop., 1955) (*see Tucson*).

Points of Interest: University of Arizona, Courthouse, Father Kino Memorial, Wishing Shrine, and others.

Tucson is at the junction with a road into the Papago Indian country (*see TOUR 4B*). (Ajo Way)

Section c.   TUCSON to GILA BEND; 125 m.   US 80-89, State 84, US 80.

State 84, the southern route between TUCSON, 0 *m.,* and Gila Bend, runs through a thinly populated desert region, much of which has been made productive by irrigation. It is shorter than the US highway and avoids the heavy traffic in and around Phoenix.

At 3.5 *m.* on US 80-89 is the junction with State 84, now the route.

CORTARO (Sp., cut-off), 12.9 *m.* (2,156 alt., 250 pop.), is in a farming and stock-raising district once covered with mesquite and ironwood.

RILLITO (Sp., small stream), 18.2 *m.* (2,069 alt., 50 pop.), named for the near-by creek that flows into the Santa Cruz River, is in an agricultural district.

MARANA (Sp., jungle), 22 *m.* (1,990 alt., 1,500 pop.), founded in 1890 as a station on the Southern Pacific R.R., was probably named for the dense growth of catclaw and mesquite that then covered this region; cotton is now the principal crop of the area.

REDROCK, 32.8 *m.* (1,864 alt., 50 pop.), settled in 1881, was named for a prominent red butte near by.

PICACHO PASS, 38 *m.,* is below PICACHO PEAK. In February 1862 Confederate Captain Sherod Hunter had led a troop of Texas cavalry to Tucson. On April fifteenth, sixteen of these men under Lieutenant Jack Swilling—while returning from the Pima country where they had confiscated provisions intended for the Union troops at Fort Yuma—

were attacked here by twelve Union men commanded by Lieutenant James Barrett. Barrett and two of his men were killed and three men were captured. This was the only Civil War encounter on Arizona soil.

PICACHO, 46.2 *m.* (1,621 alt., 500 pop.), an early stagecoach stop, is surrounded by a grazing and agricultural area, mostly cotton.

At 48 *m.* is a junction with State 87 (*see TOUR 4C*).

Between this point and Eloy cotton and alfalfa fields border the road. The desert ground squirrels that abound in southern Arizona frequently race across the highway.

ELOY, 50.5 *m.* (1,400 alt., 5,500 pop.), is in the fertile Santa Cruz Valley where lettuce, asparagus, carrots, broccoli, and cotton are grown. Two vegetable-packing sheds and ten cotton gins employ transients in the picking and packing seasons.

TOLTEC, 55.1 *m.* (1,504 alt., 10 pop.), named for the Toltecs who preceded the Aztecs in Mexico, is in the Pantano Valley farming district.

From 61.6 *m.* the Sacaton Mountains (R) and the Casa Grande Mountains (L) are visible.

ARIZOLA, 63.2 *m.* (1,480 alt., 10 pop.), a small desert station, was established in 1892 on the Southern Pacific R.R. It was once the headquarters of an adventurer, who called himself the Baron of the Colorados, but who was known as the Baron of Arizona.

James Addison Reavis invaded Arizona in 1880 as a subscription solicitor for the San Francisco *Examiner* and at the same time gained information for the scheme he had devised while driving a horsecar in St. Joseph, Missouri. Relying upon the terms of the Treaty of Guadalupe Hidalgo in 1848 and the Gadsden Purchase in 1853, in which the United States agreed to recognize all former land titles, Reavis in 1885 formally filed application for the survey and confirmation of the Willing grant. He alleged, with all required documents and proofs, that on December 20, 1748, Ferdinand VI, King of Spain, had made Senor Don Miguel del Peralta de Cordoba Baron of the Colorados, and had granted to him three hundred square leagues of land in New Spain; this area included most of the Salt and Gila River valleys, together with all their waters and mining rights, a tract 236 miles long and 78 miles wide. According to papers, Father Pauver and Father Garces had agreed the area did not encroach on mission lands. The claim was traced to Miguel Peralta, who was said to have deeded the land to Willing in 1864. Reavis was able to show a deed to himself, from Willing's attorney-in-fact, dated 1867.

At this point Reavis cemented his case by marrying a beautiful girl, "the only blood descendant of Don Miguel de Peralta de Cordoba" and displayed documents proving her birth, christening, and parentage. The overwheling coincidence of their romantic meeting was explained by Reavis as an "accidental encounter in a Mexican hamlet while investigating the Willing title."

This claim which threatened to make vassals or tenants of former property owners spread consternation throughout the "barony." Tom Weedin, editor of the *Florence Citizen,* gave vigorous editorial expression to doubts of the legitimacy of both the claim and of the baron himself, and was only partly subdued when it was reported that Robert G. Ingersoll and other prominent lawyers had pronounced the claim flawless and authentic.

The baron meanwhile had established his headquarters here and was living in state. It was said that the Southern Pacific railroad paid him $50,000 for its right-of-way across Peralta properties; the Silver King mine contributed lavishly to his funds, and the larger property owners were forced to pay tribute. Two children were born, and Reavis had them clad in garments of purple velvet. Other luxurious homes were set up in Washington, St. Louis, and Chihuahua. The family traveled extensively, living in the most expensive hotels; in Madrid they maintained a permanent establishment and a large staff of servants. From 1887 until 1893 the story of the Reavis family had all the glamour of a tale from the *Arabian Nights.*

Then suddenly the baron's world was shattered by a stammering printer named Bill, who worked for Tom Weedin, the editor. While looking over old documents filed at the Capitol in Phoenix Bill had discovered that one of the "ancient" papers of the Peralta claim had been printed in a type invented only a few years before the claim was filed; and that another paper bore the water mark of a Wisconsin paper mill that had been running only ten or twelve years (*see Newspapers and Radio*).

Investigation revealed that cleverly written pages had been interpolated into old record books. A microscope proved the document appointing Don Miguel Peralta "Baron of the Colorados" to be a manuscript of another sort entirely. Reavis' wife testified he had convinced her that she really was the last of the Peralta line. Actually she was a half-breed Indian girl who had been living on a reservation in northern California. Reavis had taken her to Mexico to establish local color and train her for the part she was to play.

In January 1895 Reavis was convicted and sentenced to six years in the Santa Fe penitentiary. His wife left him, taking the two children —who were said to look more royally Spanish than the Hapsburgs and Bourbons themselves. When last heard of, she was living in poverty in an obscure Mexican village; Reavis' friends, however, succeeded in effecting his release in less than two years. He was sometimes seen on the streets of Phoenix looking worn and ill, but always about to recoup his lost fortune and position with some wonderful legitimate promotion.

The Papago Indian huts (R), 63.4 *m.,* made of mud and sticks, are little different from the Papago dwellings of a century ago.

CASA GRANDE (Sp., big house), 65.1 *m.* (1,395 alt., 6,000 pop.), was named for the Casa Grande ruins to the northeast (*see TOUR 4C*). The Casa Grande Valley, in the San Carlos Irrigation Project, utilizes water stored by Coolidge Dam and produces cotton, citrus, and seven crops of alfalfa each season. Remains of a prehistoric canal system can still be traced in the valley. This is an interesting example of ancient irrigation engineering.

A cottonseed oil processing plant is at the west edge of the town.

The flat-topped formation (L) at 71 m. is TABLE TOP MOUN-TAIN. Here long stretches of desert brush parallel the highway. The graceful outlines of ANTELOPE PEAK (5,786 alt.) appear R. of Table Top Mountain from 79 m.

Quite as interesting as the desert plant life of this section is its insect and animal life. There are many tarantulas, black or brown hairy spiders sometimes five or six inches across, but normally about three. Although there is a popular belief that they can jump 20 feet or more and that their bite will cause almost instant death, actually they can not jump 20 inches and their bite causes nothing more serious than a slight temporary swelling, comparable with a bee sting. The tarantula is one of the best bluffers in nature; his formidable appearance as he rears back on his hairy legs and opens his jaws is his natural protection. Despite his eight eyes he is practically blind, the eyes distinguishing only light and darkness. He lives almost entirely by his sense of touch, waiting near his den until some small insect brushes him and then springing for the kill.

STANFIELD, 78 m. (1,470 alt., 300 pop.), is in the center of a farming area with cotton raising and cotton ginning the major indus-tries. Stanfield is one of Arizona's newest towns, due to the cotton boom. For six months each year the town's population is greatly aug-mented when hundreds of transients arrive and seek employment here as cotton pickers.

Far to the west at 101.4 m. are TWIN BUTTES, two round knobs on a mountain top. From this point each mountain in the horizon ap-pears to be matched by an adjacent mountain with a similar outline.

At 123.5 m. is the junction with US 80 (see TOUR 11).

GILA BEND, 125 m. (777 alt., 1,216 pop.), is in the wide Gila River Valley but the river, owing to dam construction, now carries little water. Padre Kino in 1699 found a flourishing Opa (Maricopa) Indian rancheria in this vicinity, raising two crops of grain annually by irrigation. Anza and Garces, visiting the same rancheria in 1774, called it the Pueblo de los Santos Apostales San Simon y Judas. Other pros-perous rancherias of that time were along the Gila and used its waters in irrigating large tracts of land. Today it is the center of a stock-raising and cotton-growing district; lands are irrigated with water stored by Gillespie Dam.

In the desert surrounding Gila Bend are many pack rats, sometimes called trade rats from their habit of carrying off articles which they replace with a stick, a rock, or a piece of cactus. Pack rats have prob-ably been responsible for many unsolved mysteries in Arizona. Three prospectors all but dissolved partnership because of strangely missing articles; the success of a surveying project was threatened when a pack rat absconded with the surveyor's only ruler; and a miner just missed landing on six purloined sticks of his own dynamite when he jumped a stream near his claim. Pack rats are indefatigable collectors. Slipping into camp they will take scissors, combs, socks, can openers, or any other articles that they are able to carry. These the rats invariably pay for in their own coin, and seem to think a pine cone for a razor is a fair exchange. They also hide things they do not take, putting thumb tacks in shoes, and socks in coat pockets. For their nests they work out individual architectural schemes, often developing formidable affairs. When cholla joints are plentiful, they fortify their nests with these spiney pieces of cactus till they are impregnable. In northern Arizona the Navajo rob the nests of the pack rats, use their store of nuts or sell them to the traders, and then eat the rats.

Section d. *GILA BEND to YUMA; 122.2 m. US 80.*

From GILA BEND, 0 *m.,* to Yuma the highway runs beside the old stagecoach trail along the Gila River. The route was also followed by Kino, Garces, Anza, Kearny, the Mormon Battalion, and the California Volunteers (*see History*). (*After heavy rains pavement dips are flooded and at times temporarily impassable.*)

TARTRON, 21.4 *m.,* is a station on the Southern Pacific R.R. At 22.4 *m.* is the junction with a dirt road.

Right on this to the PAINTED ROCK MOUNTAINS, 11 *m.,* an acre of rocks 40 to 50 feet high that are covered with crude pictures of men, insects, snakes, turtles, birds, and checkered figures. It is believed they marked the boundary between the Maricopa and the Yuma and indicated a permanent treaty of peace between these two tribes. Father Kino, Father Garces, and Kit Carson mentioned these hieroglyphics.

Near 25 *m.* is Sentinel Peak (R), once an important landmark for travelers.

SENTINEL, 29.9 *m.* (675 alt., 78 pop.), is a trading post, in the approximate center of four hundred square miles of lava beds of a recent geologic age. A knob of moderate height to the northeast is the remains of a crater; the long ridge to the southeast is believed to mark another. The Gila River has cut a trench 100 feet deep across the northern part of the lava crust; several wells near the Sentinel railroad siding have been drilled through 60 to 100 feet of the lava to provide a good water supply from the underlying sands.

From Sentinel Plain are visible the lofty Growler Mountains far to the south; the Aguila Mountain, closer and to the southwest, culminating in a high northward-sloping plateau of lava; and the Aztec Hills to the west. To the southeast, Hat Mountain is conspicuous.

The wide desert plains are often densely covered with the yellow-flowering greasewood. Rainfall is so scant here that even the reservoirs of rainwater created by damming washes in the hills are not dependable as water holes for cattle and depletion by evaporation averages more than six feet a year. The Gila River is the only stream that flows continuously, and the few springs are widely scattered.

AZTEC, 43.9 m. (494 alt., 65 pop.), a railroad stop, is a trading point for ranchers and tourists.

DATELAND, 50 m. (434 alt.), in a district that produces dates, alfalfa, and some wheat; cattle feeding; guest ranching.

MOHAWK, 63.4 m. (540 alt., 125 pop.), was a station for Butterfield's stages. Though desert mountains are usually far from the highway, at Mohawk the rocky, barren, pastel-pink mountains are close.

TACNA, 79.6 m. (340 alt., 7 pop.), began as a stage station called Antelope Hill. In the seventeenth century a Greek priest named Tachnapolis came to this region from California and spent his last days with the Indians, who called him Tacna, the name later given to the station. Center of farming, cattle raising and mining.

Right from Tacna on an improved road to ROLL, 5 m., in a section that produces more alfalfa seed to the acre than any other area in the state. An eighteen-acre plot in 1936 averaged 1,204 pounds to the acre for one cutting.

Left from Roll on a dirt road to RADIUM HOT SPRINGS, 9 m., where the water is said to be radioactive.

This area abounds with foxes, coyotes, reptiles, and other animals characteristic of Arizona's arid regions. The nocturnal and mournful howls of coyotes were at one time a characteristic of Arizona, but they are becoming less frequent, and are almost never heard near the cities. This particular region is the home of the desert species. The Mearns coyote inhabits the southern areas, and the Great Basin coyote, a large and beautiful animal, the northern. Though ranchers hate the coyote because he preys on chickens, calves, and lambs, he is not entirely carnivorous, and will eat fruits, melons, and berries. Coyote puppies look like diminutive collies and play about in a carefully hidden den, eating the game that the father brings them until they learn to sniff game trails. The parents, ever wary of man, usually have three or four dens and move quickly and furtively when their home is discovered. The coyote runs away instinctively, but is a good fighter. A dog may corner a coyote but is likely to regret it—if he lives. Westerners insist that the coyote has a sense of humor, and his recognition of guns is startling. If he is approached by a person carrying a stick he is not much impressed; at the sight of a real gun he becomes a flash in the distance.

WELLTON, 86.3 m. (254 alt., 400 pop.), named for several deep wells that were sunk at the time of the railroad construction, is principally dependent on farming in an irrigation farming area.

Left from Wellton on a graveled road known as the Smugglers' Trail because of the narcotic and liquor smugglers who sometimes use this route from Mexico. Near TINAJAS ALTAS (Sp., high tanks), 30 m., are eight natural cavities in the granite rocks of the mountains. These retain rain water for most of the year—the only water found in this area. In Tinajas Altas are wheel ruts marking the fearful Camino del Diablo (Sp., devil's road), the trail followed by Father Kino on his missionary trip from his headquarters in Sonora to the Colorado River. This old trail crossed the present Mexican border at Quitovaquita, south of Ajo; thence it led north then west to Las Playas and northwest through Tinajas Altas to Yuma, keeping on the south side of the Gila Range. It was so named for the toll it took among travelers; according to one historian three thousand to four thousand have died on it from hunger, thirst, and fatigue.

Near TELEGRAPH PASS, 104.3 *m.,* in the Gila Mountains the many greasewood bushes begin in March to burst into yellow blossom; the plants flower earlier in these low elevations than in any other part of the state. Between TELEGRAPH PASS SUMMIT (1,980 alt.), 107 *m.,* and the Colorado River the road makes a gradual descent.

FLY FIELD, 115.6 *m.,* is an airport named for Benjamin F. Fly, early resident of Yuma.

At 117 *m.* is the junction with a paved road (State 95).

Left on State 95 to SOMERTON, 15 *m.* (141 alt., 2,000 pop.), in the heart of a great irrigated empire, where main crops are cotton, alfalfa, lettuce, melons, citrus and other fruits, vegetables and grains. In the vicinity are cotton gins, lettuce, cantaloupe and citrus packing sheds.

To the west of Somerton is the Cocopah Indian Reservation, which contains only a remnant of this once extensive tribe, which Padre Garces numbered at about three thousand in 1775, and which today numbers a few hundred, many of whom are farming in this vicinity.

SAN LUIS, 25 *m.* (36 alt., 23 pop.), a port of entry to Sonora, Mexico, is a typical little Mexican border town with rambling, low adobes and a leisurely, passive atmosphere. It has several general stores, a curio shop and a few bars.

SAN LUIS, SONORA 26 *m.,* is a town with a population of over 10,000, and has beautiful residences and many business establishments, and its population is growing at a rapid rate. Most of the present day visitors are tourists and those attracted by the excellent fishing at Santa Clara, Sonora, on the Gulf of California, 70 miles south of San Luis.

YUMA, 122.2 *m.* (137 alt., 15,000 pop.) (*see Yuma*).

Points of Interest: First Store of Althee Modesti, The Government Grounds, Territorial Prison Ruins, Yuma Mesa, Fort Yuma Indian Reservation, Laguna Dam on the Colorado River, the All-American Canal, and others.

Left from Yuma on 8th Street to CAPTAIN SMITH'S HOME (R), 2 *m.,* built with materials taken from the steamboat *Cochan,* one of the last river boats on the Colorado. The pilot house tops the structure.

In the DATE GARDENS, 2 *m.,* at the corner of 8th and Avenue B, are many varieties of palms. One of the most successful is the Deglet Noor imported from North Africa. The white blooms that appear in the spring below the feathery green fronds are carefully pollinated by hand with anthers from selected male palms. Tests have proved that not only the size, texture, and sugar content of the fruit are affected by pollination but that its time of ripening can be altered twenty to thirty days by the use of different pollens. Glassine bags are often placed over the inflorescence to prevent their receiving pollen from the wrong tree. Many of the taller palms have platforms resembling painters' scaffolds attached to their trunks to facilitate pollinating and picking. The clusters of dates that ripen in the early fall are often protected from insects and dust by burlap or glassine bags. Dates thrive in an alkaline soil but require intense heat and so much water that they are often irrigated two or three times a month. A date processing plant (*open to visitors*) is on the grounds.

US 80 crosses a bridge over the Colorado River, 122.2 *m.*, into California, 59 miles east of El Centro, California.

$$\text{\scriptsize «««««««««««««««««««««««««««««‹‹‹›››»»»»»»»»»»»»»»»»»»»»»»»»»»»»»}$$

Tour 4A

Tombstone Junction—Fairbank—Patagonia—Nogales; 65 *m.* State 82.

Paved highway entire route.
All types of accommodations at Nogales; limited elsewhere.

State 82 traverses a grassy region that more nearly resembles the prairies of Kansas or the Dakotas than it does the cactus studded desert or precipitous peaks elsewhere in Arizona. Varicolored mountain ranges line the horizon in all directions; isolated, almost desolate, ranch houses rise above slope, plain, or mesa; herds of Hereford cattle graze over the excellent grasslands; occasionally cowboys appear in the distance—roping, branding, or performing other range duties.

Father Kino, the Jesuit missionary, probably used a trail that approximates this route on his trips to Quiburi Mission (*see below*) and over these same hills Curly Bill, John Ringo (*see TOUR 4a*), the Clantons, Earps, McLowerys, Johnny-Behind-the-Deuce, Ed Schieffelin, and a host of other colorful figures rode, fought, robbed, gambled, or sought gold (*see Tombstone*).

The adobe structures that composed the camps and towns along the way and housed the gambling resorts and saloons have already begun to crumble. The rolling hills alone, remain the same—relatively bare except for yucca or Spanish bayonet, lofty mescal, yellow grass, scrub oak, and mesquite.

State 82 branches west from US 80, 0 *m.* (*see TOUR 4b*), at a point 3 miles north of TOMBSTONE.

FAIRBANK, 5.2 *m.* (3,800 alt., 50 pop.), on the San Pedro river, is a small cluster of arched adobes and a couple of sagging frame structures, having the usual architectural appendages—false fronts. With its buildings half empty and its one dusty street only occasionally accommodating a wagon, an automobile, or pedestrian, Fairbank is today a far cry from the turbulent 1880's when it was a supply point for Tombstone and served the many freighters hauling ore from the Tombstone mines to the mills at Contention. It was an important point on the railroad running between Guaymas, Mexico and Benson, and a stage terminal for mail and express. Although some authorities believe the town's name is a corruption of "faro bank" it was probably named for N. K. Fairbank, a Chicago merchant who had mining interests in this area. There was an Indian village called Santa Cruz on this site in 1700 and nearly every heavy rain still exposes bones, ollas, arrowheads, and broken pottery. Today Fairbank is a trading center for a cattle and mining district; much of the surrounding country is owned by the Boquillas Cattle Company.

At 8 *m.* is the junction with an unimproved dirt road.

Right on this road to a RAILROAD SECTION HOUSE, 0.2 *m.*, on the west bank of the San Pedro River. Across the river is the ghost town of CONTENTION CITY. Only a few fallen adobes here mark the site of the Contention Mine Mills. William Henry Bishop in *Old Mexico and Her Lost Provinces* mentions a visit to the town in 1882: "We changed horses and lunched at Contention City. One naturally expected a certain belligerency in such a place, but none appeared on the surface during our stay. There were plenty of saloons—the 'Dew-drop'; the 'Head-light,' and others—and at the door of one of them a Spanish senorita smoked a cigarette and showed her white teeth.

"Contention City is the seat of stamp-mills for crushing ore, which is brought to it from Tombstone. The latter place is without an efficient water-power. The stamps are rows of heavy beams, which drop upon the mineral, on the mortar and pestle plan, with a continuous dull roar, by night as well as day.

" 'That's the music I like to hear,' said our driver, gathering up his reins, 'poundin' out the gold and silver. There ain't no brass bands ekils it.' "

Today the only sounds Contention City hears are the slow crumbling of its own heavy adobe brick walls and the whispering of the desert winds.

Left from the section house 0.6 *m.* on foot along the railroad tracks to the RUINS OF QUIBURI (L), a mission founded by Father Kino some time before the year 1700. It was on a direct line between San Xavier and the Apache stronghold in the Dragoon Mountains and saw a great deal of fighting. The structure was in the nature of a fort with four walls, each about three hundred feet in length. The church proper stood at the center of the south wall. The only entrance is on the east wall facing the San Pedro River. Considering the 240 years that have elapsed since the walls were built, they are remarkably preserved.

At 16 *m.* is the junction with paved State 92.

Left on this road to FORT HUACHUCA, 10 *m.*, established as a camp in 1877 to protect settlers and travelers from the Apache. They, however, carefully watched the maneuvers of the troops and planned their raids accordingly. In 1882 the camp was made permanent, but saw little activity after Geronimo's surrender in 1886 until the Madero revolt in Mexico in 1911. It then became a base for border patrols. The fort, garrisoned by Negro troops during World War II, is now U. S. Electronics Proving Ground.

Visible from 19 *m.* is (R) GRANITE PEAK (7,387 alt.) in the Whetstone Mountains, scene of a skirmish in 1871 between Apaches and troopers who were pursuing Chief Cochise (*see TOUR 7*), and in which the American officer in command, Lieutenant Howard B. Cushing, was killed.

At 25 *m.* is the junction with a dirt road.

Left on this road to ELGIN, 4 *m.* (4,710 alt., 140 pop.), five or six adobe houses and a combined filling station, general store, and post office that serves as a limited shopping center for residents and guests of a number of large dude ranches in this district, including working cattle ranches.

Most of these ranches include several thousand acres of rolling grassland on which herds of registered cattle graze. Noted for their ability to restore health, the ranches afford a varied program. Some guests rise early; breakfast on steak, fried potatoes, and coffee; sling their gear on a bronc and are out in the hills by sunrise. Although the true cowboy seldom bothers with a noon meal when he is far from camp, dudes usually carry lunches in their saddlebags. Less strenuous visitors sleep until noon; enjoy their breakfast, morning mail, and newspaper in bed before taking a hot shower in a bathroom that resembles a DeMille movie set; play bridge or poker with other guests, while acquiring their sun tan; charter a streamlined plane for an afternoon view of the surrounding hills and return in time to don formal clothes for an evening dance. Some dude ranches have their own swimming pools, polo fields and target ranges; many give elaborate rodeos on holidays; and others maintain cabin stations in the hills for guests who prefer solitude.

Each guest dresses to suit his activities. A pair of dollar dungarees are as popular as fifty-dollar leather chaparejos; imported shorts are enlivened with a gaudy ten-cent bandana; Indian jewelry of hammered silver and turquoise is worn with costumes designed in Hollywood or Paris.

To satisfy the guests' demand for novelty, the managers of these "spreads" stress the local customs and traditions, dramatize all the pioneer history they can unearth, and fabricate whatever they feel will add interest or romance to the setting.

The name of SONOITA, 35 *m.* (4,865 alt., 150 pop.), a village in a cattle raising district, is derived from Sonot (Papago, place where the corn grows). Father Kino built a mission here but it has been completely destroyed. In early days there was a thriving sawmill.

West of Sonoita the road runs through the CORONADO NATIONAL FOREST, which includes several mountain ranges, has good grazing and recreational areas, and is important as the watershed of the surrounding valleys. The country is rough, with the only good saw-timber—principally pine—high up and inaccessible; at lower elevations are heavy stands of oak, with some pinon and juniper. The headquarters of this forest are in Tucson.

The marked SITE OF FORT CRITTENDEN is at 38 *m.* Large quantities of military supplies, stored during President Buchanan's administration at this fort, which was then called Fort Buchanan, were destroyed at the outbreak of the Civil War by the officer in command, to prevent their seizure by a column of Confederates advancing into Arizona. Many settlers at Fort Crittenden and on ranches along Sonoita Creek were tortured and killed by Apaches who boldly stole tents from the rear of the officers' quarters of the fort, drove off cattle and horses from the ranges, and plundered homes. In 1872 Apaches captured two men from a small contingent escorting army wagons from the camp to Tucson. One was slain outright; the other—who had made four hundred trips through the canyon during his three years of carrying mail between Fort Crittenden and Tucson—was tied to a tree and tortured in full view of his companions. His body, later recovered, showed at least one hundred wounds from the firebrands that had been thrust into his flesh.

When Apaches surrounded the Hughes' ranch near Fort Crittenden while most of the men were away, the wife of Hughes' partner ran from the cornfield, barricaded the house, and forced a sick farm hand (who wanted to attempt an escape) to help her repel the attack. Her husband returning from Camp Crittenden, looked down on the ranch house and, horrified by the sight of so many Apaches, dashed for help to the camp of Lieutenant Hall where some soldiers were stationed. For more than two hours the woman and the sick man held at bay more than a hundred warriors, while her husband and Lieutenant Hall with twenty-five soldiers were galloping toward them. The Indians fled at sight of the troops, and the rescuers found the wife and children safe within the adobe house, though three farm hands who had been weeding corn were dead.

In his book, *Arizona's Yesterday,* John Cady, a pioneer, tells of the time when he and three others from Camp Crittenden, cultivating gardens maintained by the company of the old Sanford Rancho nearby, were attacked by a large body of Indians. One man was immediately killed, and there was a lively fight before the Indians withdrew. The frontiersmen, however, knew they would make another charge, so the soldiers drew lots to see which one would attempt to ride to the fort for help. Cady drew the short straw. "I look back on that desperate ride now with feelings akin to horror. Surrounded with murderous savages, with only a decrepit mule to ride and fourteen miles to go, it seemed impossible that I could get through safely. My companions said good-bye to me as though I were a scaffold victim about to be executed. But get through I did—how I do not know—and the chillingly weird war-calls of the Indians howling at me from the hills as I rode return to my ears even now with extraordinary vividness."

The old Paige Ranch in this vicinity was the scene of an Indian raid in 1858 during which Mrs. Paige, the daughter of a noted pioneer family named Pennington, was captured, speared through the back, and thrown over a cliff. At one time a searching party came within a few feet of her, but because of her wounds the woman was unable to cry out, and the searchers passed on. After dragging herself through rocks and brush for two days and a night, she found shelter and eventually recovered. Eleven years later her father and brother Green, were plowing in their fields when Indians ambushed them, killing Mr. Pennington outright. Green, not knowing his father was dead, made no attempt to escape but stayed and fought off the Apaches alone. He was mortally wounded and died a few days later. Both were buried in the cemetery near the site of old Fort Buchanan.

PATAGONIA, 47 *m.* (4,050 alt., 700 pop.), with its low one-story buildings that line the road for a quarter of a mile is the center of a mining, agricultural, and cattle-raising district. The region was known to the Indians as the Enchanted Land, possibly because of the abundance of water and game. The present name is derived from patagon (Sp., a large foot) used by the Spaniards to describe the Indians of this region. On the eastern outskirts of Patagonia was HEADQUARTERS OF THE

CHIRICAHUA CATTLE CO., once one of the largest ranches in Arizona (*small hotel; tourist camp*), now cut up into small ranches.

Left from Patagonia on a dirt road to HARSHAW, 8 *m.*, a town of a few Mexican and American miners and their families. The Mexican name for the town is Durazno.

MOWRY MINE, 14 *m.*, is now a ghost town. Many sturdy adobe buildings mark the site of one of the earliest mines in Arizona. It was known to the Jesuits, worked by Mexicans in the 1850's and purchased in 1859 by Lieutenant Sylvester Mowry, an army officer at Fort Crittenden. About $1,500,- 000 worth of silver and lead ore was taken out. During the Civil War, Mowry was interned at Fort Yuma under the accusation that he made bullets for the Confederates of lead from the mine.

Of the seventeen white men buried in the MOWRY MINE CEMETERY, fifteen were victims of violence. The cemetery is on a little knoll overlooking the deserted mine. Neither the buildings nor cemetery can be seen from the highway, but are only a few yards back in the hills. Two of the victims, J. B. Mills and Edwin Stevens, were ambushed by Indians when returning to Mowry from the San Antonio mines just across the border. They were hung head downward from a tree limb, as the Indians kindled a slow fire under them. Their remains were carried to Mowry for burial. Later Dr. Titus and a Delaware Indian were attacked in nearly the same place. The Delaware Indian was immediately killed. Dr. Titus dismounted from his horse and fought his way on foot 200 yards up the canyon before he was wounded in the hip. Preferring death to capture, he killed himself. He was buried at Mowry.

At 17 *m.* on this road is Duquesne (*see below*) and at 22 *m.* Lochiel (*see below*).

Southwest of Patagonia State 82 borders the Sonoita River, and curves through the foothills of the Patagonia Mountains (*no steep grades but many curves*). On both sides of the highway is a long strip of rich land, once an old Spanish grant called the San Jose de Sonoita.

The entrance to the Circle Z, an all-year guest ranch is (R) at 52.6 *m.* On the landscaped grounds of the ranch are a large swimming pool and polo grounds.

Planes entering or leaving Mexico are inspected at the NOGALES INTERNATIONAL AIRPORT (L) 61 *m.*

At 65 *m.* is the junction with an unimproved road.

Left on this road to WASHINGTON CAMP, 16 *m.*, the old smelting center of the Westinghouse group of mines. The ore was carried by means of an aerial tram from the old Bonanza shaft a mile away. Some of the stations of the aerial tramway can still be seen from the road.

On the same road is DUQUESNE, 17 *m.*, formerly the mining center of the Washington Camp smelters. Though deserted now it was a thriving camp of a thousand people. The ruins of fine homes of the mining officials still stand. There are several million tons of ore in the stopes and in the dumps but its removal is not profitable. Lead, silver, zinc, and copper predominate.

Bordering the road (L) at 19 *m.*, are the AMERICAN HEADQUARTERS OF THE GREEN CATTLE COMPANY. This is the breeding ranch for the registered Hereford bulls used on the company's two-million-acre ranch across the border in Mexico. Known as the San Rafael Ranch, formerly an old Spanish land grant, it is today the largest exclusive bull-breeding ranch in Arizona.

LOCHIEL, 22 *m.*, on the Mexican border, is a small port of entry at which much petty smuggling is said to occur. There was an old smelter in Lochiel before Mowry smelted his own ore. There have been many fights in this vicinity between Mexicans and Indians. In 1858 a little Mexican girl, Inez Gonzales, was abducted and her uncle and the larger part of a military escort were killed in the fight to regain her. Later the girl was retaken by Boundary Commissioner John R. Bartlett and returned to her people at Santa Cruz, Mexico.

At 63 *m.* (R) is a YUCCA FOREST. Yucca is called by the Mexicans "the candle of our Lord." The species here is said to be slightly different from those found elsewhere in Arizona.

Though the road that winds through the hills approaching Nogales has a predominantly Mexican atmosphere created by sombreros and sun-baked adobe houses, with an occasional string of bright red chili peppers hanging from the rafters; it is also given a cosmopolitan touch by the many winter tourists and the border officials from Nogales, the largest port of entry on the Arizona-Mexico border.

NOGALES, 65 *m.* (3,896 alt., 6,500 pop.) (*see Nogales*) is at the junction with US 89 (*see TOUR 1d*).

Points of Interest: Santa Cruz County Courthouse, Immigration Inspection Station, and others.

《《》》》》》》》》》》》》》》》》》》》》》》》》》》》》》》》》》》》》》》

Tour 4B

Tucson—Sells—Ajo—Gila Bend; 174 *m.* (Ajo Road, Papago Indian Reservation Road) State 86, State 85.

Asphalt-paved roadbed throughout. Limited accommodations at Ajo and Gila Bend; elsewhere few filling stations or lunchrooms.

In this dry rocky country west of Tucson, giant saguaros and rare organ pipe cacti stand stiff and green against the jagged bronze hills. Along the highway are the site of the Indian village of Tucson, Mission San Xavier del Bac—probably the finest example of Spanish-mission architecture in this country, the Papago Indian Reservation, and the little copper-mining town of Ajo.

The route branches west on Congress Street from junction with US 80 in Tucson, crosses Tucson Freeway, and Santa Cruz River. On west bank (R) is GARDEN OF GETHSEMANE, statues of Holy Family, Crucifixion, and Last Supper, by Felix Lucero.

At 1.1 *m.* is the junction with Mission Road (Grande Ave.).

Left on latter to site of SAN JOSE DEL TUCSON MISSION (L), 0.2 *m.*, built by Father Garces, 1775. The adobe remains are no longer visible and there are few signs of the original building.

The stone foundation of an old mill (R) is at 1.5 *m.* on Mission Road, and the stone ditch that diverted water from the river is still visible along the side of the hill, which is called Sentinel Peak. At its base is the original SITE OF STJUKSHON (Indian, dark spring), the Indian village that became Tucson (*see Tucson*).

At 9 *m.* on Mission Road is Mission San Xavier Del Bac (*see Tucson.*)

At 4.3 *m.,* turn R. on paved Ajo Road.

Left on this road to Mission San Xavier Del Bac, 5 *m.* (*see Tucson.*)

From 5.4 *m.* Tucson, with its two or three tall buildings towering above its many one- and two-story structures, seems very white and small against the somber desert and bright blue sky.

At 8.4 *m.* is the junction with Kinney Road, a paved country road.

Right on Kinney Road to TUCSON MT. PARK, and Old Tucson Movie Set, replica of Tucson in Civil War days. (*Square dancing Sundays; Curio shops open daily*), a 28,000 acre recreational area covered with a SAGUARO FOREST.

At 5.5 *m.* on Kinney Road is the junction with an improved dirt road; R. on this road 2.5 *m.* to GATES PASS, through which the road leaves the Tucson Mountains.

Left at same point, paved road leads to ARIZONA-SONORA DESERT MUSEUM, 3 *m.* (*open 10-6*), where insects, reptiles, animals and plant life, native to the Southwest desert are exhibited. There is also a geology and mineral room.

At 11 *m.* on Kinney Road is the junction with King Canyon Road; R. on this road 1.4 *m.* to the MAM-A-GAH PICNIC GROUNDS (*shelters, fireplaces, restrooms*). Marked roads lead from this area to similar grounds elsewhere in the park.

1. Right on a marked foot trail 2 *m.* to the top of WASSON TRIANGULATION STATION (approx. 5,000 alt.), highest point in the TUCSON MOUNTAINS, which encircle the park.

2. Left on a foot trail 1 *m.,* to the MAM-A-GAH PICTURE ROCKS which have been covered by the Indians with pictures of men and animals as well as strange designs.

From 14 *m.,* on the Ajo Road, the Sierritas (Sp., little mountains) are visible to the south and the Coyote Mountains, named for the numerous coyotes that inhabit the district, to the west.

ROBLES' RANCH (R), 23.9 *m.,* is one of the pioneer ranches of the Southwest. The founder was the grandfather of little June Robles, whose kidnapping in 1934, when she was six years old, attracted wide notice. The child, seized by two men as she was returning from school in Tucson, was taken into the desert and confined nineteen days in a box sunk into the ground. She was rescued after a mysterious note, mailed in Chicago, was received in Phoenix by Benjamin B. Moeur, who was then governor of Arizona. Although in misery from insects and the desert heat the girl suffered no permanent injury.

The road crosses the eastern boundary of the PAPAGO INDIAN RESERVATION, 29.6 *m.* West of this point the road is graveled. This two million eight hundred thousand acre reservation extending 100 miles north from the Mexican border, is typical Arizona desert. It is covered with cactus, mesquite, ironwood and palo verde; has no permanent streams and few year-round springs; and its sharp, bare mountain ranges are separated by wide, gently sloping valleys. The population of the reservation in 1953 was 7,600 Papago Indians and 300 white people in Government service, mission work, trading, and mining.

The name Papago is a corruption of the Papago words *pavi* (beans), *koa* (to eat), and *awotam* (people), the nickname of one of the seven dialect groups forming the tribe. Today the principal livelihood is from livestock, supplemented by seasonal wage work off the reservation.

The five Government schools on the reservation had an enrollment in 1950 of 650, the five Roman Catholic schools had 350 students, and some 450 older children were in off-reservation boarding schools. The chief native crafts are basket and pottery-making. The best examples of baskets are treasured in the family and seldom sold to visitors. The traditional type of ceremonial basket is a large flat bowl, white, with a black design. Papago baskets are sewed, not woven. The colors, white, red, green, and black, are inherent in the materials. The black strands, from the pod of the devil's claw, are one of the few true blacks in nature.

The characteristic Papago dwelling is a one-room hut of saguaro or ocotillo ribs plastered with mud, but this is fast being replaced by homes of more permanent adobe. Every house, or family cluster of houses, has a ramada, a rectangular shelter made of four upright mesquite posts roofed with brush and earth. This open-air kitchen contains the fireplace, grinding stones, water ollas, and storage baskets, tightly woven and waterproof.

Food purchased at the trading posts is supplemented by corn, beans, squash, and melons, when sufficient rain falls at the right time to mature a crop, and by gathered wild foods. The early Papago man wore a buckskin breech cloth and the Papago woman a buckskin or cotton skirt. Today, the man is usually dressed in blue jeans, the older women in a long full skirt and blouse, and the younger women in a modern store-bought dress.

The tribe has a large measure of self-government, with its own police, courts, and law and order code. The reservation is divided politically into nine districts; the smaller San Xavier and Gila Bend Reservations each forms an additional district. Each district is governed by a council composed of delegates from the component villages; each district council elects two delegates to the tribal council. The tribe operates trading posts, a breeding herd, a loan board, and a fair and rodeo association, and advises the Indian Service regarding the wishes of its members.

The Papago reservation is the only one in which the mineral rights are not owned by the Indians, but are open to prospecting under the mining code of the United States. The area has been mined since early Spanish times; in the great silver boom of the 1880's many millions in ore were extracted; and today small mines and prospect holes dot the mountain sides.

Though the visitas instituted in the Papago country by Father Kino in 1692 were not maintained continuously, most of the native rituals have been greatly influenced by those of the Roman Catholic Church or have been dropped entirely. The New Year begins with the ripening of the saguaro fruit in June. Every four years there is a harvest festival, in which elaborate effigies are carried in processions. Another ceremony is the taking of salt from the Gulf of California. In the spring of 1936 the agency superintendent was called upon to bail out a salt party that had been detained at the Mexican border charged with illegal entry. Music occupies an important place in Papago life. The native songs are both lyrical expressions and long narrative cycles. The right to sing or dance the songs belongs to the composer or his family or to whomever they favor with the honor.

In SELLS, 61.9 m. (2,300 alt.) the trading center for the Papagos, are the Indian Service and Tribal headquarters, a consolidated Indian Service-Public School, trading posts, cafes, service stations, garage, and post office. A rodeo is held annually in late October or early November.

It will be noted that in the Papago country the highway across the reservation intentionally misses the Papago villages, both to eliminate the traffic hazard and to provide a measure of privacy.

Mount Divine in the north Comobabi Mountains (R) is visible from 80 m. and the Alvarez Mountains (L) from 83 m.

Graves in the Papago cemetery (L), 83.6 m., are marked with roughly hewn crosses and decorated with colored crepe paper.

At 82 m. is the junction with a dirt road.

Left on this road to the ruins of QUIJOTOA, 3 m., on the slope of the basket-shaped Ben Nevis Mountain. Though it is said that an old Spanish manuscript found in a mission in Lower California mentioned ore being carried out of the Quijotoa region as early as 1774, the American city started with the discovery of copper beneath an iron capping in 1879 and was given impetus by the finding of even richer croppings in 1883. A town that covered half a square mile and boasted several stores, a post office, a telegraph station, daily stage service, and a newspaper mushroomed on the mountain. But the ore proved shallow and Quijotoa was practically abandoned in 1885. It became a complete ghost though its buildings are now reduced to crumbled walls and it has no human inhabitants, bells have been heard ringing and doors creaking on their hinges.

At 84 m. on the Ajo road is the junction with an improved dirt road.

Right on this road to SANTA ROSA, 13 m. (2,180 alt.), at the base of the Santa Rosa mountains. It is the largest summer rancheria of the Papago. The native name is Kuat-shi (Ind., big peak).

Left 1 m. from Santa Rosa on an improved dirt road to the WELL OF SACRIFICE, a sacred shrine, and the scene of rites religiously adhered to by the native inhabitants. Its origin is attributed by legend to prehistoric times when a hunter watched a badger dig into the earth and attempted to follow it. Suddenly a spout of water came from the hole, covered the ground and increased in volume until four villages were under water. The terrified inhabitants called a council of chiefs, two from each village. (The eight stone seats on which they sat are still at the site of the council.) After a solemn all-night discussion the chiefs decreed that human sacrifices were necessary to appease the angry gods. From each village a beautiful child was taken—two boys and two girls. The children were dressed in tribal garments and told that they were not to die but to go to a more beautiful land where all their wishes would be fulfilled; then they were thrown into the well and earth and heavy stones piled upon them. When the Owl Woman, who had refused to sacrifice her child and had hidden her in a mat behind the mountain till the ceremony was over, went to rescue her daughter, she found only sea foam on the mat. The name of the shrine is Alihihiani (Ind., child cemetery). A mound of heavy stones three feet high and surrounded by an ocotillo fence now marks the site of the well. Openings on the four sides allow the exit of the soul of each child when it wishes to escape. The custom is to renew the ocotillo branches each year, piling the old ones on the side, but never destroying them. It is said that hunters wishing good luck, sacrifice valuable trinkets on this mound, and that on stormy nights before a rain the children's voices can be heard issuing from the grave.

COVERED WELLS, 86 *m.*, is named for a well, protected by a wooden cover and once owned by an Indian. Later the well was improved by Pima County for the benefit of travelers.

West of Covered Wells the road enters the QUIJOTOA MOUNTAINS.

A fine natural garden of saguaros, 91.4 *m.*, includes some baby saguaros only four inches high.

Another desert garden, 115.4 *m.*, includes saguaros, chollas, yucca, and prickly pear.

From 117 *m.* Nine Mile Peak is (R) visible far from the highway.

At 121 *m.* is the junction with a paved road.

Left on this to the ORGAN PIPE CACTUS NATIONAL MONUMENT (*no supplies, or gasoline between Ajo and Sonoyta, Mexico, except water at Monument Headquarters, 17.5 m. S. of Monument entrance*), 5 *m.*, a 300,000 acre tract set aside to preserve one of the most outstanding unspoiled deserts in the United States. One of the rare plants, found in the United States only in this vicinity, is the Organ Pipe Cactus for which the monument is named. Its dozens of tubular arms branch from the main stem at the ground and grow straight up for twenty or more feet forming a cluster of perpendicular branches that resemble organ pipes. It may be found on the southern exposed hillsides and one must leave the highway to see the larger stands. A forty mile loop road leaves from the headquarters traversing some of the most spectacular sections of the desert.

LUKEVILLE, 28 *m.*, named for Charles Luke, Phoenician, who owns 67 acres on which the village is located. The town has grown up around the entry port. A 30-ton ice plant here services fish trucks and fishermen on the Rocky Point route.

The Mexican Customs House (*see General Information*) is at 28.5 *m.*

SONOYTA, SONORA, MEXICO, 30.7 *m.* (1,900 alt., 500 pop.), is a delightful border town of mud-colored huts and white plastered adobes surrounded by green plots of corn, grains, and vegetables.

Right 62 *m.* from Sonoyta on an unimproved dirt road (*4 hour drive*) to Rocky Point, a port on the Gulf of California that is becoming increasingly popular with sportsmen (*boat, with crew, license, and tackle, $10 to $20 a day; best season, fall, winter and spring*). Among the game fish caught here are marlin (weighing 130 to 300 lbs.), giant white sea bass (160 lbs.), giant ray (1500 lbs.), shark (300 lbs.), broadbill swordfish and sailfish (175 to 300 lbs.) and jew fish (250 lbs.).

On the Ajo Road the Growler Mountains are visible ahead and L. at 130 *m.* The gray line on the desert horizon is the Ajo slag dump.

In ROWOOD, 135.7 *m.,* the Mexican section of Ajo (*see below*), is a large slag dump (R).

The CORNELIA MINE AND SMELTER, 130.5 *m.,* is the New Cornelia Branch of the Phelps Dodge Corporation.

AJO (ah-ho), 132 *m.* (1,859 alt., 7,000 pop.), is in the center of one of the most important mining districts in the Southwest. The place was formerly called Muy Vavi (Papago, warm water), but was changed to Ajo (Sp., garlic) for the wild garlic that is plentiful in the surrounding hills in good seasons.

Spaniards worked mines in this vicinity as early as 1750 and one of their old mines, called the Old Bat Hole, still contains the "chicken ladders" that they used to bring the ore to the surface. The shaft was on a sixty degree angle and about every ten feet a layer of mesquite logs 4 feet long and 3 feet wide were placed at ten foot intervals to serve as rest stations for the men who carried the ore in rawhide buckets strapped to their backs. The Ajo Copper Company, organized in 1854, sent ore by pack mules to Yuma, 100 miles away, whence it was shipped down the Colorado River and around Cape Horn to Swansea, Wales, for smelting. After 1916 when John C. Greenway took control of the mines and organized the New Cornelia Copper Company, Ajo's prosperity began and the town grew rapidly. In 1931 this company was absorbed by the Phelps Dodge Corporation. Ajo's population fluctuates with the price of copper; in 1939 its mine employed about 1,300 men and its population was estimated at 5,000.

The town has several stores, a hospital, a theater, three small hotels, two auto courts, and a golf course (*greens fee $1.00*). The business structures, built in a modified Spanish style with cloistered walks, outline a large plaza whose tall green palms form a pleasing contrast with the light-colored buildings and cast lacy shadows on the plaza lawn. Its public buildings consist of the Curley School and the City Jail, the latter used only spasmodically. Ajo's transportation facilities are one train daily to Gila Bend; bus service twice daily to and from Phoenix; one flight daily Bonanza Airlines; and its entire water supply—for town, mine, mill and crusher—is a well 7 miles to the north. This well is seven hundred feet deep and cost a million dollars. Many sportsmen stop at Ajo on their way to the Gulf of California for game fishing.

The Mexican national holidays, *Cinco de Mayo* and *Diez y Seis de Septiembre,* are gaily celebrated in Ajo by the large Mexican population.

In Ajo is the junction with State 85, now the route.

For a few miles south of Gila Bend the road parallels the Tucson,

Cornelia, and Gila Bend R.R. On both sides are desert and jagged purple mountains as far as the eye can see.

GILA BEND, 180.2 *m.,* is at junction with US 80 (*see TOUR 4*).

≪≪≪≪≪≪≪≪≪≪≪≪≪≪≪≪≪≪≪≪≪≪≪≪≪◇≫≫≫≫≫≫≫≫≫≫≫≫≫≫≫≫≫≫≫≫≫≫≫

Tour 4C

Picacho Junction—Coolidge—Chandler—Mesa; 59 *m.* State 87.

Paved roadbed throughout.
All types of accommodations.

This route past Casa Grande National Monument runs through a section of the Gila River Indian Reservation, and the fertile agricultural areas of the Gila and Salt River Valleys. Visible from all points on State 87 is the symmetrical peak of Walker Butte which rises like a pyramid a few miles north of Coolidge.

State 87 branches north from State 84, 0 *m.,* at a point 2 miles west of PICACHO (*see TOUR 4c*).

At 12.5 *m.* (L) is the ARIZONA CHILDREN'S COLONY (*visitors are welcome*), the state resident school for mentally deficient children opened March 19, 1952. Any mentally deficient child under 21 years of age, whose parents or guardian have been residents of the state for three years is eligible for admission. The Colony is a cottage type institution, built on a community plan, located on an 80 acre campus. The capacity of the institution is 384, with an ultimate plan for 1,000 children.

The Colony is a training institution. The theme is to train each boy and girl in those things he or she can make use of when they become a man or woman in years. The training program is broad, ranging from simple habit formation at the infant level through classroom, shop, and vocational training.

RANDOLPH, 13 *m.* (1,560 alt., 250 pop.), named for Colonel E. Randolph, former vice-president and general manager of Southern Pacific lines, is a farming and livestock center.

COOLIDGE, 17 *m.* (1,400 alt., 4,500 pop.) is in the heart of a vast agricultural area opened to irrigation by Coolidge Dam (*see TOUR 3a*). Cotton and cattle raising are important.

A bronze monument (L), 19 *m.,* with a miniature of the Casa Grande marks the entrance to the CASA GRANDE NATIONAL MONUMENT (*adm. 25¢; guides 8-5; picnic grounds*), an area of more than four hundred acres that was designated a national monument in 1918.

Left through the gates to the Casa Grande Ruins, 0.8 *m.*, considered by many archeologists the best preserved and most interesting prehistoric structure in southern Arizona. The remains of the ancient city lie in what was formerly a desert plain, now widely cultivated, with a horizon of low jagged mountains. Remnants of prehistoric canals are close by.

The first white man known to have visited the ruins was the Jesuit missionary, Father Eusebio Francisco Kino (1644-1711). In his *Memoirs of Pimeria Alta* (1694) he tells of "The Casa Grande—a four-story building as large as a castle and equal to the finest church in these lands of Sonora." In 1697 Lieutenant Juan Mateo Mange visited the ruins with Father Kino and left a more detailed description: "One of these houses is a large edifice whose principal room in the middle is of four stories, those adjoining being of three. Its walls are two veras [roughly five feet] thick, made of strong cement and clay and are so smooth on the inside that they resemble planed boards and so polished that they shine like pueblo pottery. The angles of the windows, which are square, are very true and without jambs or crown pieces of wood, and they must have made them without frame or mold." These and other early accounts indicate that the main structure was virtually intact seven hundred years after it had been built. Yet the report of Father Francisco Garces in 1775, less than a century later, tells of the ruins being in an advanced state of deterioration.

With the waning of the Spanish mission period authentic reports of Casa Grande became fragmentary. In 1825 two trappers, James and his father Sylvester Pattie stumbled on the ruins, and in 1832 Pauline Weaver (*see TOUR 1b*), trapper and prospector, visited them and carved his name on one of the walls. Other reports of the ruin were made during the nineteenth century by Colonel W. H. Emory, who accompanied Kearny in 1846 and in 1856 was appointed commissioner to complete the survey of the Gadsen purchase; by Charles Poston (*see TOUR 1c*) and by A. F. Bandelier (1840-1914) the noted archeologist. The first scientific investigation of the Casa Grande ruins was made by Dr. J. Walter Fewkes of the Smithsonian Institution, who conducted excavations in 1892, 1906, and 1908. These and other studies indicate that the builders developed an increasingly complex culture over a period of several hundred years and then abandoned their laboriously constructed pueblos.

The exodus is attributed to attacking tribes and the increasing alkalization of the soil, caused by centuries of continual irrigation. The Pima who occupied this district at the coming of the Spaniards professed little knowledge of the builders of the pueblos, alluding to them as *Hohokam* (the ancient ones or those who have departed). The name has been retained by modern archeologists.

W. H. Emory includes in his *Notes of a Military Reconnoissance* the legend of the Hohokam told to him by a Pima: " . . . in bygone days, a woman of surpassing beauty resided in a green spot in the mountains near the place where we [Kearny's expedition] were encamped. All the men admired, and paid court to her. She received the tributes of their devotion, grain, skins, etc., but gave no love or other favor in return. Her virtue, and her determination to remain unmarried were equally firm. There came a drought which threatened the world with famine. In their distress, people applied to her, and she gave corn from her stock, and the supply seemed to be endless. Her goodness was unbounded. One day, as she was lying asleep with her body exposed, a drop of rain fell on her stomach, which produced conception. A son was the issue, who was the founder of a new race which built all these houses."

The first known dwellings in the valley were of the pithouse type—light mud-plastered superstructures over pits some eighteen inches deep. Whether these were the first dwellings of the Hohokam after their arrival in the early Christian era or whether they were built by aborigines whom the Hohokam displaced has not been definitely determined. The original village gradually extended westward as new and more complex houses were constructed. Reinforced walls, built by lashing horizontal poles to upright posts, were replaced with solid walls. Gradually the Hohokam learned to erect buildings two or three stories in height and with an increasing number of rooms. Just as the white pioneers built stockades for protection against hostile Indians, the Hohokam erected defensive walls about ten feet high around their compounds. They also raised watchtowers so that raiding parties could be seen at a distance. The walls had no openings; entrance to the village was by means of ladders. Marauding hill tribes learned that there was plenty of food to be pillaged in the pueblos after a harvest and allowed the villagers to plant, cultivate, and gather their crops in peace. After the grain had been stored sporadic raiding began.

The CASA GRANDE TOWER, called America's first skyscraper, in the village designated by archeologists as COMPOUND A, is the tallest of the watchposts and the dominating feature of the ruins. In this structure pueblo architecture reached a climax. Built more than eight hundred years ago, the tower stands four stories in its center room and three stories in its four outside rooms, the walls rising about forty feet above the desert level. In construction it is typical of later Hohokam buildings. The walls, made of adobe containing caliche (kah-LEE-chay), taper on the ouside from a thickness of four feet at the bottom to eighteen inches at the apex. Caliche is the local Arizona name for a lime-earth of cement-like hardness which occurs throughout the southwestern United States and at Casa Grande is quite close to the surface. The builders laid the walls horizontally, two vertical feet at a time to allow a gradual hardening as more height and weight were added.

The building is 40 feet wide, 60 feet long, and contains eleven rooms, five each on two floors and one on the top floor. The five rooms on the ground floor were filled in to form an artificial terrace. At various floor levels wooden poles were laid crosswise and covered with layers of light sticks, arrow weed, and mud to form the finished floors. The floor poles were of mesquite, ironwood, and juniper; some of them must have been transported from mountains at least 50 miles distant. The poles were probably floated down the Gila to within a mile of the village, then carried overland to the building site. The original finish was deftly applied with a rotary motion to obliterate handprints, and contrasts sharply with later patches which were obviously patted on. Much of the original plaster still adheres to the walls. Rooms on the first floor were partly filled with dirt to enable the walls to support the weight of the upper stories.

The waist-high doorways are typical of pueblo architecture. Holes were cut in the north and south rooms, possibly for shooting arrows against invaders. Other holes in the west and north rooms may have been for drainage or ventilation. The purpose of nine small holes in the walls of the center room is still a mystery to archeologists.

Of particular interest are the so-called CALENDAR HOLES, two small apertures in the east and center rooms, so placed that the rising sun shoots a shaft of light through the outer hole and strikes within a quarter inch of the inner hole on the seventh day of March and again on the seventh day of October but on no other days. Unquestionably, the sun shone through both holes when the building was occupied, and the walls have since settled enough out of plumb to cause the discrepancy. The calendar holes may have enabled the Hohokam to reckon time and determine the proper seasons for planting and storing ceremonies.

Names and dates have been carved on the walls by modern visitors, but there are only two decorations attributed to the builders. One is a spiral design common to southwestern tribes for the past two thousand years. The other, on the north wall of the center room, is a peculiar labyrinthine design found on Cretan coins about two thousand years old. No satisfactory explanation for this coincidence is known.

Compound A, the largest of the villages, contains twelve or fifteen houses as well as the Casa Grande, and covers about two acres of land. It was surrounded by a wall ten feet high. The wall and most of the buildings had worn to near ground level and have recently been covered with cement to preserve them. At the southwestern corner of the compound is a large three-story building with five rooms on the ground floor, four on the second and one on the third.

COMPOUND B, 165 feet wide and 300 feet long is 300 yards north of Compound A. It contains two terraces surrounded by rooms. The other compounds within the limits of the monument are more disintegrated and of interest only to archeologists. All contained more primitive structures than Compound A, and are older. The only other ruin near by is the so-called CLAN HOUSE, which contains remains of what appears to have been a throne. There are five distinct series of ditches between the adjacent fields and the Gila River to the north. One of these ancient canals was so well preserved at the time of Father Kino's visit in 1694 that he thought it could be readily restored for use.

The Hohokam possessed well-developed artistic ability. Their pottery, the red-on-buff type, survived through the various stages of their culture. Finely engraved necklaces, rings, bracelets, and bangles were made from shells—probably brought from the Gulf of California two hundred miles away, where the Hohokam may have gone to obtain salt. Their religion incorporated a belief in life after death; they cremated their dead and buried the ashes with a supply of food and tools to be used by the departed spirits.

CASA GRANDE MUSEUM on the reservation contains most of the artifacts. It is a modern adaptation of the prehistoric architectural style of the ruins. In addition to excellent collections of stone axes, spades, metates, and pottery there are several unusual exhibits, among which a square-and-compass emblem carved from a sea shell has caused much speculation. A group of turquoise inlay and mosaic work, consisting of a necklace, bangles and bracelet, has been called one of the most beautiful examples of its type found in American ruins. Two or three pieces of surprisingly fine hand-woven cloth show a treatment now termed punch-work embroidery.

At *30.8 m.*, is the junction with a graveled road.

Left on this road to SACATON, 3.6 m. (1,049 alt., 350 pop.), the headquarters for the Pima reservation. Today there is little other than their language, physical appearance, and basketry to distinguish the Pimas from other alfalfa growers and stock raisers of the irrigated valleys. Though they are now so completely absorbed in their crops and herds that the life of songs and ceremonies exists only in the memories of the old people, they once possessed a culture almost identical to that of the Papago (*see TOUR 4B*), and broke the monotony of their existence with a cycle of ceremonies—with salt expeditions to the Gulf of California, wars with the Apache, and the singing of songs that were individually owned and used for specific purposes. Most of these were revealed in dreams. One of their medicine songs is translated thus by Frank Russell in *The Pima Indians:*

"See the destructive lightning
Going to kill the distant tree.
It is going, my youngest brother,
To split the distant tree.

The lightning like reddish snakes
Tries to lash and shiver the trees.
The lightning tries to strike them,
But it fails and they yet stand."

Early in the nineteenth century the Pima were living beside the Gila in villages surrounded with fields of corn, beans, and squash and supplementing their diet with wild fruits and game. Although not good farmers according to present day standards, they raised enough for their needs and were very generous in supplying food to travelers. In 1846 General Kearny (*see TOUR 3a*) and his men were grateful for their hospitality. In Kearny's report of his march to California he says: ". . . These Indians [the Pima] we found living comfortably, having made a good crop this year, and we remained with them two days to rest our men, recruit our animals, and obtain provisions. . . . The Penios (Pima) Indians, who make crops of wheat, corn, vegetables, etc., irrigate the land by water from the Gila as did the Aztecs (the former inhabitants of the country), the remains of whose sequias or little canals were seen by us, as well as the position of many of their dwellings, and a large quantity of broken pottery and earthenware used by them." Kearny was apparently referring to the builders of the Casa Grande whom he erroneously believed to be Aztecs. W. H. Emory (*see above*), who served in Kearny's expedition as chief engineering officer, had only praise for the Pima: "To us it was a rare sight to be thrown into the midst of a large nation of what is termed wild Indians, surpassing many of the Christian nations in agriculture, little behind them in the useful arts, and immeasurably before them in honesty and virtue."

The Pima houses (L), 34 *m.,* are built of stakes plastered with mud, have roofs of grass and brush and a shade consisting of four uprights supporting a thatched grass roof. The desert vegetation of saguaro, cholla, and mesquite contrasts with the feed crops in the irrigated sections.

From 35 *m.* the irregular outline of the SANTAN MOUNTAINS is close to the road and the SACATON MOUNTAINS (L) are visible in the distance.

At 47 *m.* is the junction with a paved road.

Right on this to CHANDLER HEIGHTS, 9 *m.* (1,400 alt., 400 pop.), center of a vast irrigation farming area, whose principal industries are cotton, citrus and dairy farming. QUEEN CREEK and HIGLEY are other highly productive centers in this area.

CHANDLER, 51 *m.* (1,225 alt., 4,000 pop.), in the irrigated area of the Salt River Valley, was founded in 1915 by Dr. A. J. Chandler, Arizona pioneer. Although agriculture and its associated pursuits are the town's principal sources of income, it has a resort hotel catering to winter visitors and providing golf, riding, and desert outings. The Spanish-type buildings of Chandler's small business section enclose a large tree-shaded plaza that is surrounded with colonnaded walks to resemble the cloisters of the southwestern missions.

At Chandler is the junction with a paved road.

Right on this to WILLIAMS AIR FORCE BASE, 8 *m.,* nation's first jet air school, established, 1941, and named for Lt. Chas. L. Williams, Arizonan, who died in a plane accident in 1927.
During World War II the base trained bomber pilots and pilots of conventional fighters. Now (1954) the base is training center for jet fighters.

MESA, 59 *m.,* is at the junction with US 70 (*see TOUR 3b*).

Tour 5

(Gallup, N.M.)—St. Michaels—Ganado—Keams Canyon—Oraibi—
Tuba City—Junction with US 89; Moenkopi—St. Michaels Rd.
New Mexico Line to junction with US 89; 185.4 *m*.

Roadbed paved first 45 *m*. Balance of road good. (Entire route scheduled
for hard-surfacing by 1955); Supplies, water, and gasoline available.
Accommodations at trading posts, motels, and government employees' clubs.

This road, entirely within the Navajo and Hopi Indian reservations,
traverses land that still belongs to the Indian—where the only white
people encountered are those who depend on him for their livelihood—
traders, missionaries, and government employees. Consequently the
landscape has been little changed by civilization, and an occasional
hogan, sheep corral, or Hopi village on a rocky mesa are the only evidences of this area's long and continued habitation.

The Navajo country in Arizona—the tribe occupies an equally large
area in New Mexico—is characterized by elevations that range for the
most part between 5,500 and 9,000 feet above sea level and by a broad
plateau modified by mesas, buttes, volcanic necks, gorges, and washes.
On the sculptured ledges of its canyons are the remains of cliff dwellings
a thousand years old. Wind-blown brown sand covers the area in an
uneven layer. Its sagebrush, greasewood, yucca, and grasses are varied
by pine forests and zones of pinon and juniper. In the region are many
rabbits, prairie dogs, coyotes, trade rats, lizards, snakes, and a few porcupines, wolves, foxes, and bears.

Of all the Indian tribes in the United States today, the Navajo is
not only the largest—approximately some fifty thousand live on the
reservations in Arizona—but is one of the greatest cultural borrowers.
The many Navajo hogans along this route are built of logs and covered
with mud and sod; each has a doorway facing the east and a smoke hole
in the center of the roof, but there the uniformity ends. In some the
logs are laid horizontally, with six or eight sides and a dome-shaped
roof; in others the logs are vertical and the hut has a roughly conical
form. Generally there is a sheep corral and a summer arbor near by.
Although the hogan is but a mud hut, its mythical prototype is thus
described by the Navajo: "Built of poles of white shell, turquoise,
obsidian, jet, and red sandstone" at the entrance is "a fourfold curtain
of dawn, skyblue, evening twilight, and darkness."

Some of the Navajos farm to a slight extent, particularly those who
hold lands in suitable places like Canyon de Chelly (*see TOUR 5A*),
but their chief support comes from sheep and goats. A few raise cattle,
and all possess a number of horses. Some have off-reservation jobs.

The beauty and richness of Navajo culture is not readily appreciated as their myths, songs, and long chants can be heard only at certain times and after many years of living among them. Because the knowledge necessary to hold a chant often takes twelve years to acquire, the medicine men have become the most learned in tribal lore, and frequently the richest and most powerful of the people. A chant consists of a long series of ritualistic acts carried out in a prescribed order and manner, the change of any one of which would destroy the efficacy of the whole. It involves preparation, purification, knowledge of songs and prayers, the making of prayer sticks, the use of herbal medicines, and the making and using of sand paintings. The best known of their twenty or more major chants are the Night Chant and the Mountain Chant. Though chants are used primarily as cures, the Navajo considers his life incomplete if he has not had one sung for him; hence an individual sometimes has a sing as preventive medicine.

Each chant is believed to be a cure for or protection against a specific disease—caused by elements, animals, or persons who create discord. The theory behind the nine-day chant is to appease the trouble making forces by honoring them, and thus persuade them to be helpful and harmonious rather than harmful.

Although visitors rarely have an opportunity of witnessing the entire nine-day performance, since it generally occurs in the fall and winter, certain parts such as the Fire Dance are given at the Flagstaff Powwow. In these songs and prayers is much of the poetry and imagery that have made the Navajos' oral literature so widely quoted. Among the translations by Washington Matthews in his *Navaho Legends* is:

> The voice that beautifies the land
> The voice above
> The voice of the thunder
> Within the dark cloud
> Again and again it sounds
> The voice that beautifies the land.

A long prayer to the thunder-bird begins:

> In Tsegihi,
> In the house made of dawn,
> In the house made of the evening twilight,
> In the house made of the dark cloud,
> In the house made of the he-rain,
> In the house made of the dark mist,
> In the house made of the she-rain,
> In the house made of pollen,
> In the house made of grasshoppers,
> Where the dark mist curtains the doorway,
> The patch to which is on the rainbow,
> Where the zigzag lightning stands on top,
> Where the he-rain stands on top,
> Oh, male divinity!
> With your moccasins of dark cloud, come to us.

The St. Michaels-Moenkopi Road, a continuation of State 68 in New Mexico, crosses the NEW MEXICO LINE, 0 *m.*, 17 miles west

Agriculture

TURNING WATER FROM LATERAL INTO FARM DITCH.
SALT RIVER VALLEY IRRIGATION PROJECT

AIRVIEW, SOUTHERN ARIZONA RANCH

DATE GROVES, YUMA IRRIGATION PROJECT

McCulloch Bros.

ROOSEVELT DAM, WORLD'S HIGHEST MASONRY DAM
SALT RIVER PROJECT

CITRUS GROVES, SALT RIVER VALLEY IRRIGATION PROJECT

Don Keller

LETTUCE FIELD NEAR PHOENIX

PACKING CANTALOUPES

CHILDREN OF MIGRATORY WORKERS

Jerry McLain

SHEPHERD AND FLOCK

CORRALLING HORSES

Forman Hanna

ON THE RANGE, NEAR BISBEE

SHEEP RANGE ABOVE TIMBERLINE, NORTHERN ARIZONA

Max Kegley

CORRALLING CATTLE, ROUNDUP TIME, NEAR PRESCOTT

BRANDING CALVES

Max Kegley

of its junction with US 666 at a point 8 miles north of Gallup, N.M.
At 0.6 *m.* is the junction with a paved road.

Right on this road to WINDOW ROCK, 1.4 *m.*, a sandstone cliff with a wind
eroded opening that reveals a broad expanse of country and looks as if it had
been made by the poke of a giant's finger. This is the site of the $1,500,000
NAVAJO CENTRAL AGENCY BUILDINGS, constructed with PWA funds to take the
place of the many different agencies scattered through the reservation. These
new flat-roofed rubble structures, designed in an adaptation of the Indian
style of architecture, are among sandstone hills that have been worn to great
smooth mounds and are called THE HAYSTACKS. In a central position is the
NAVAJO COUNCIL HOUSE, an octagonal structure with a rubble buttress at each
angle, and a recessed second floor. Round beams project from the angles of
the upper floor, pierce the square buttresses, and extend beyond them like
cannon from a turret.

FORT DEFIANCE, 5.2 *m.*, for many years was a military post used in warfare
with the then unsubdued tribes. Later it served as an administrative headquarters for the army and the Indian Bureau in their dealings with the
Navajo.

ST. MICHAELS, 4 *m.* (6,800 alt., 135 pop.), the center of Roman
Catholic church work on the reservation, is named for its mission.

GANADO, 33.9 *m.* (6,400 alt., 200 pop.), is a large trading post
(*limited accommodations*) and a Presbyterian hospital and mission.
Originally it was named Pueblo Colorado, but this was changed to
Ganado (Sp. herds) by J. Lorenzo Hubbell to avoid confusion with the
city of Pueblo, Colorado. The first post, established about 1870 by
Crary, was sold to "old man" Leonard in 1875 and to Hubbell the
following year. It has become one of the most noted posts in the
Navajo country, and houses a collection of paintings given to Hubbell
by various artists who have enjoyed its hospitality. These include many
Navajo and Hopi scenes. Among the better known artists represented
are Louis Aitken, Albert Croll, and Maynard Dixon.

Hubbell was one of the first to see the commercial possibilities of
the Indian arts and did much to encourage the Navajo weavers and
silversmiths to trade their products. Money is rarely used at trading
posts. The Indian brings in his rug, bracelet, or wool, and is credited
with the value of his product; from this credit he purchases coffee, flour,
sugar, velvet, or other goods—both men and women wear velvet jackets.
These materials are often purchased on credit and paid for when the
sheep are sheared, as the wool crop is the chief means by which the
trader balances his accounts. When a Navajo is paid in cash, he usually
points out what he wants, leaves his change on the counter, and continues to point until his money is all spent. If his purchases have not
exhausted his funds he generally buys silver and turquoise, which he
can always trade and which seems to him to have more intrinsic value
than money; all business is conducted in the Navajo language.

At 40.2 *m.* is the junction with a dirt road (*see TOUR 5A*).

The Navajo place names, often descriptive, are sometimes reminiscent
of incidents in the past. A dry wash where the eight-mule teams of
the early traders bogged down is known as Where the Mexican Wept.
Canyon de Chelly (*see TOUR 5A*) is In The Rocks, Keams Canyon

(*see below*) is known as Black Reed, and a small wash that flows into Steamboat Canyon is called Water Without Ambition.

The road follows the floor of STEAMBOAT CANYON, 52.8 *m.*, for about five miles. In places the sandstone walls are close together; toward the west they gradually separate until they disappear. The canyon was named for a large rock formation (R), 54.9 *m.*, whose striking resemblance to a vessel is more apparent when viewed from the west.

The road crosses the eastern boundary of the HOPI INDIAN RESERVATION (approx. 3,000 Hopi and 3,000 Navajos), 59.8 *m.*, which is completely surrounded by the territory of the Navajo, their traditional enemies. The Hopi are agriculturists and the only Pueblo (Sp. village) Indians in Arizona. In most respects they contrast with the Navajo, although they have acquired a few similarities from contact.

All but one of the Hopis' twelve villages are on mesa tops. Undoubtedly the practice of building their houses in such inaccessible places is a carry-over from the past when it afforded protection from marauding enemies. Each village is autonomous, possessing its own lands, its own social and ceremonial organization, and displaying as much tribal solidarity as the Greek city-states. Although they all speak the same language and have similar customs there is no feeling of unity among the villages. Along the road are their fields of corn, beans, and squash —crops that have formed their chief sustenance for untold centuries. Close to the villages are the peach orchards, and the small irrigated gardens of chili, onions, and other delicacies, terraced so that no drop of water from the spring above is lost. They grow most of their crops without other moisture than the rain, an agricultural achievement.

The Hopi are a matrilineal people—that is, relationship and inheritance are on the mother's side of the family. The houses are owned by the women, the land by the clans, and a man after marriage lives in his wife's house and cultivates fields in the lands of her clan. In the old days the only goods owned by a man were his ceremonial paraphernalia. Today, however, many goods are owned by the men—sheep, horses, wagons, cars, and trucks. Hopi men hold all the important offices, but the succession passes from a chief to his younger brother and then to his sister's son. Frequently the men marry girls from different villages. If one of them is asked where he lives he will reply, "I live in Mishongnovi, but I stay with my wife in Sipaulavi." His home is always the house in which he was born, and to it he returns for all important ceremonies; to it also he will be brought if his family thinks he is dying.

Marriage involves a long series of exchanges—the bride and her family making plaques and grinding large amounts of white and blue corn meal, the groom weaving a white wedding robe with a wide belt, making buckskin moccasins and a ceremonial robe for the girl. On the day before the marriage is consummated, the women of the groom's father's clan have a mud fight with the bride, because she is taking their sweetheart away from them.

The Hopi have many arts, making pottery, two types of basketry, and weaving cotton garments and woolen blankets. They are the only tribe in North America in which the men do the weaving. They supply the Pueblo Indians of the Rio Grande with ceremonial kilts and sashes in exchange for turquoises.

But the great preoccupation of the Hopi is with their religious ceremonies, centering around various magical devices to produce rain, ward off illness, and promote their welfare. The head of each village is known as the House Chief and is always a member of the Bear Clan, which, according to their legends, was the first to arrive at the village. Assisting him is an Announcer, who calls from the roof top the time of each ceremony. Every other officer is the head of a society that performs a ceremony at a fixed time (but not necessarily the date announced except for Pa-mu-ya on Jan. 23) and belongs to the clan that traditionally owns the rights to the ceremony and its various sacred objects. Some of these dances occur in the Hopi villages almost every month in the year. Probably the best known is the Snake Dance, actually a nine-day performance by the Snake and Antelope Societies, most of which is secret and held in the kivas. Visitors are permitted to see only the culminating rite on the last day. To one who has attended all the dances throughout the year, and noted the regularity with which they recur, and the repetition of phrases in song and prayer, this dance becomes but one of many, with several features common to the others. The fact that the dancers actually hold snakes including rattlers, in their mouths, induces many visitors erroneously to believe that they work themselves into a frenzy. To the contrary, everything about the dance is measured, prescribed, and orderly. A more beautiful, if less spectacular, dance is Home Dance, the final appearance of the Kachinas (masked gods bringing rain and other blessings), which occurs at every village in July. The Kachinas come to the village to dance several times between the Bean Planting Ceremony in February and this farewell. Masked and painted figures file into the plaza, line up, sing, and dance, then distribute presents to the children. This is repeated all day long as the Kachinas are led about the village and sprinkled with corn meal by a man who answers the words of their songs. At the end of the day this spokesman thanks them and gives the Kachinas the Hopi's wish to carry to the cloud chiefs of the different directions. Each Kachina is then given sacred corn meal and a prayer stick, is smoked upon, and sprinkled with water. The dancers finally leave the plaza, their feathers waving and rattles clicking to the measured tread.

From 78.3 *m.* is a glimpse of KEAMS CANYON, site of the Hopi agency, a half mile below. It is named for Thomas Keam, a trader in this region in the 1880's and 1890's.

From POLACCA, *93.1* m. (6,000 alt., 200 pop.), a settlement that has developed around the Mesa, the three villages on the First Mesa are visible.

Right from Polacca on a dirt road to the summit of the First Mesa, (6,233 alt.), 1 *m.*, which affords a view of the fields and gardens on both sides of the mesa. HANO, 1.1 *m.* (6,200 alt., 250 pop.), is composed of Tewa-speaking Indians from the Rio Grande section who came to assist Walpi in the seventeenth century and settled here. SHITCHUMOVI, 1.2 *m.* (6,218 alt., 110 pop.), is little more than a suburb of Walpi. WALPI (*Snake Dance, Aug., odd years*), 2 *m.* (6,225 alt., 80 pop.), is perched so precariously on the narrow tip of the steep rock cliff, and the stone of its angular houses merges so imperceptibly with the stone of the mesa, that it suggests a castle in the sky. This village is a favorite subject of photographers and artists who are attracted by its eerie appearance at night. Walpi's houses, built two and three stories high, are crowded together on its narrow site, not wasting an inch.

On its winding ascent of the Second Mesa (6,233 alt.) the road passes the villages of MISHONGNOVI (*Snake Dance, Aug., odd years*), 96.1 *m.* (6,230 alt., 125 pop.), and SIPAULAVI (*Snake Dance, Aug., even years*), 96.3 *m.* (6,230 alt., 85 pop.). Just below the two promontories on which the villages are built three stores run by Hopis sell native handwork in basketry, weaving, and silver.

At 106.7 *m.* on the Moenkopi—St. Michaels Road, is a junction with a dirt road.

1. Left on this road to another of the Second Mesa villages, SHUNGOPAVI (*Snake Dance, Aug., even years*), 6 *m.* (6,562 alt., 250 pop.), which claims to be the mother village. It is the largest of the three and is quite conservative. The beautiful Butterfly Dance is often held here in August before the children return to boarding school. This is not a religious dance but a social affair.

2. Right from the junction with the main route on a dirt road to PINON, 30 *m.* (6,497 alt., 10 pop.), a trading post and government school for Navajos. From Pinon roads lead to KAYENTA, 79.9 *m.* (*see TOUR 6*), and CANYON DE CHELLY, 72.9 *m.* (*see TOUR 5A*).

Lower ORAIBI (*trading posts*), 117.3 *m.* (6,070 alt., 250 pop.), is a collection of Hopi houses and peach orchards at the foot of the third or westernmost Hopi mesa. It is called Kyakatsmovi by the Hopi, for the spring from which the people of Oraibi draw their water. Although there are two kivas in this lower village, no ceremonies are ever held here.

On the top of the mesa, 118.4 *m.,* is the OLD PUEBLO OF ORAIBI (6,497 alt., 100 pop.), visited by Father Garces in 1776. Though it was once the largest of the Hopi towns, numbering more than eight hundred at the beginning of the twentieth century, today barely a hundred people remain with an old chief. In 1907 the conservative half of the populace moved seven miles west to found the village of Hotevilla (*see below*). Another group settled the small village of Bakabi the following year.

At 124.5 *m.* is a junction with a dirt road.

Right on this road to the small village of BAKABI, 2 *m.,* named for the reed that grows beside the near-by spring.

HOTEVILLA (*Snake Dance, Aug., even years*), 125.5 *m.* (5,905 alt., 200 pop.), is the most conservative of all the Hopi towns. Yukeoma, its old chief, was frequently in jail and in trouble with the authorities for opposing the ways of white men. His followers refused to let their children attend the government school and resisted all innovations. In 1912 he was sent to Washington to meet the chief of all the *pahanas* (white men), President Taft. It was hoped the meeting would awe him into submission but neither Washington's officials nor its buildings made the desired impression and he remained as adamant as ever.

West of Hotevilla the road winds down from the mesa and reveals a panorama of fields laid out in squares with little patches of terraced gardens watered by the women.

From 143.4 *m.* is a view of COAL CANYON, a deep gash in the earth, with many varicolored and odd formations projecting from its walls and floors.

The LARGE SAND DUNES, 167.1 *m.,* are piled in ever-changing forms by the shifting winds.

At 168.2 *m.* is the junction with a graded dirt cut off.

Left on this 14 *m.* to the junction with US 89 (*see TOUR 1a*).

MOENKOPI, 170.1 *m.* (4,550 alt., 388 pop.), is another Hopi town. It was started by a few people from Old Oraibi who came here to plant where they could irrigate their fields with the waters of the wash. The people all return to Old Oraibi for all important ceremonies, and the chief of the old pueblo is their chief. West of Moenkopi is a valley with orchards and fields of corn and beans, that suggests a land of milk and honey when contrasted with the sand dunes and desert vegetation to the east. The houses of the village rise in serried ranks along the west wall of the wash.

TUBA CITY, 172.4 *m.* (4,550 alt., 124 pop.), is an important Navajo trading point. It was established in 1877 by Jacob Hamblin, Mormon missionary, and is now headquarters for the western Navajo jurisdiction, with a school and hospital. At Tuba City is the junction with the dirt Klethla Valley road (*see TOUR 6*).

DINOSAUR TRACKS (R), 182.6 *m.,* great three-toed imprints in white calcareous sandstone, are estimated to have been made more than a hundred million years ago. Directly across the road and over a little knoll is DEVIL'S PUMPKIN PATCH (L), a striking conglomeration of rocks of fantastic form, many of which resemble petrified pumpkins.

At 185.4 *m.* is the junction with US 89 (*see TOUR 1a*) at a point 9.6 miles north of Cameron.

Tour 5A

Junction with Moenkopi—St. Michaels Rd.—Chinle—Canyon de Chelly National Monument; 36.1 *m.*, Chinle Rd.

Limited accommodations at Chinle.

The Canyon de Chelly National Monument includes Canyon de Chelly and its tributaries Canyon del Muerto (Sp., canyon of death) and Monument Canyon. The three form a series of long, deep gorges cut in the red sandstone of the Defiance Plateau by streams that carry the largest part of the runoff from the Chuska and Tunitcha mountains. The sheer, smooth walls of the canyon parallel each other for miles and in some places are more than a thousand feet high. In niches in their sides the remains of prehistoric dwellings cling precariously. Along the canyon bottoms, where the water can be utilized for irrigation, are the fields and summer hogans of the Navajo.

The basic formation underlying all of the Defiance Uplift is a granite ridge, probably an old land mass of the Pre-Cambrian age. In the Permian it was buried by the red beds of the Supai, upon which have been deposited the de Chelly red sandstone—the actual material exposed in the canyons. It was probably deposited at about the same time as the Coconino sandstone of the west and south, found in the Grand Canyon (*see GRAND CANYON NATIONAL PARK*) and Oak Creek Canyon (*see TOUR 2A*).

In this one region is a resume of the development of ancient southwestern civilizations, with but few periods lacking. Remains of the Basketmaker and Post-Basketmaker periods have been unearthed in some of the caverns; the later relics indicate the beginning of agriculture, pottery making, and the storage of food in slab-lined pits. Remains of the Pueblo period were discovered in Mummy Cave and in the White House, which is the most spectacular of all the ruins.

Canyon de Chelly was created a national monument in 1931 and is administered by the National Park Service, through a resident custodian, who is assisted in summer by two rangers. It was officially discovered by the exploring expedition of 1849 under Lieutenant James H. Simpson, who, in addition to leaving a voluminous report of his journey, revealed that it was not the unassailable Navajo stronghold it had been regarded. Actually, Spanish settlers had entered the canyon and fought with the Navajo of the region in the early nineteenth century, as the evidence of Massacre Cave (*see below*) attests.

Later, in 1863-4 Kit Carson's men marched the entire length of the canyon as part of the campaign that resulted in the rounding up of seven thousand Navajos and their removal to the Bosque Redondo in New

Mexico—the Navajo "Long Walk." This, called by Carson's biog-raphers, his greatest feat, was accomplished by destroying the Indians' crops and then carrying on the campaign against them with such "vigor and energy" as to "fully convince them of the folly of further re-sistence." The Navajo chiefs had already been informed that all who desired peace should come to Wingate for transportation to the Bosque Redondo; and that all others would be destroyed. Some had come, but many had taken refuge in Canyon de Chelly when Carson sent a detach-ment of men under Captain Albert Pfeiffer, who traversed Canyon del Muerto from east to west, then guarded the western entrance while Captain A. B. Carey led his men from west to east through the main gorge of Canyon de Chelly.

Excerpts of the military reports of this phase of the campaign give some idea of the soldiers' difficulties and of the canyon itself.

Carson's letter to Carleton written in July 1863 raises a question concerning the Utes employed as spies and guides: ". . . It is expected by the Utes, and has, I believe, been customary, to allow them to keep the women and children and the property captured by them for their own use and benefit, and as there is no other way to sufficiently recom-pense these Indians for their invaluable services, and as a means of insuring their continued zeal and activity, I ask it as a favor that they may be permitted to retain all that they may capture. I make this request the more readily as I am satisfied that the future of the captives disposed of in this manner would be much better than if sent even to the Bosque Redondo. As a general thing, the Utes dispose of their captives to Mexican families, where they are fed and taken care of, and thus cease to require any further attention on the part of the Govern-ment. Besides this, their being distributed as servants through the Territory causes them to lose that collectiveness of interest as a tribe which they will retain if kept together at any one place. Will you please let me know your views on this matter as soon as possible, that I may govern my conduct accordingly? . . ." Carleton replied that *all* prisoners should be sent to Santa Fe.

Pfeiffer makes the following report of his progress through Canyon del Muerto: ". . . my travel through the canon, for the first 12 miles, was accomplished on the ice of the bed of the stream which courses through it. . . . Lieut. C. M. Hubbell, who was in charge of the rear, had a great deal of trouble in proceeding with the pack trains, as the mules frequently broke through the ice and tumbled down with their loads. All the Indian prisoners taken thus far were half starved and naked. The canyon has no road except the bottom of the creek. We traveled mostly on the ice, our animals breaking through every few minutes, and one mule split completely open under the exhausting fatigue of the march. On the 12th instant traveled 8 miles; had several skirmishes with the enemy. Indians on both sides of the canon whooping, yelling and cursing, firing shots and throwing rocks down upon my command. Killed two buck Indians in the encounter and one squaw, who obstinately persisted in hurling rocks and pieces of wood at the soldiers. Six prisoners were captured on this occasion. Lieutenant Hubbell followed up some Indians in a tributary canon, but could not overtake them on account of the steepness of the hillsides, where nothing save an Indian or a mountain goat could make their way. . . . From this point westward the canon widens, the rocky precipice being about 1,200 or 1,500 feet high. At some places it spreads out like a beautiful savanna, where the corn-fields of the savages are laid out with farmer-like taste, and supplied with acequias for irrigation. At other places the cañon is confined to a narrow compass in a zigzag, meandering course, with high projecting rocks and houses built thereon, perforated with caverns and mountain fastnesses 300 or 400 feet above the ground as hiding places. Here the Navajos sought refuge when pursued by the invading force, whether of neighboring tribes or the arms of the Government, and here they were enabled to jump about on the ledges of the rocks like mountain cats, halloing at me, swearing and cursing and threatening vengeance on my command in every variety of Spanish they were capable of mastering. A couple of shots from my soldiers with their trusty rifles caused the red-skins to disperse instantly and gave me a safe passage through this celebrated Gibraltar of Navajodom.

"On the 13th, traveled about 10 miles, making 30 miles in all—the whole length of the canyon, more or less-according to my estimate of distances. As I proceeded west the cañon became more gently sloping and spreading out wider, and mostly overflowed by the river, which runs in a westerly direction and rises and sinks every few alternate miles until it disappears in the bosom of the earth. At the mouth of the west opening I met Maj. Jose D. Sena, in command of the forces under Colonel Carson as an advance scout, to whom I reported."

Carey also related difficulties: ". . . The Indians in the meantime had followed my line of march and soon came into camp in large numbers, and were disposed of in such manner as to prevent injury to my command should they prove treacherous. That night I counted 150 full-grown Indians in my camp, besides many children. I informed them of the humane intentions of the department commander concerning them, and that a full and complete submission to his wishes were required, and that under no other circumstances would they be treated with, except as enemies to be fought. They then said they surrendered themselves to me, and would accompany me wherever I desired, but many wished to return to their homes in the mountains to collect and bring in their families. . . . On the morning of the 17th instant I resumed my march and marched about 2 miles in the cañon, when I commenced the ascent to gain the table-land on the south side of the cañon by the only practicable trail leading out of this branch. The trail was very difficult, and I found it necessary to unpack my mules in order to enable them to go up the trail, the men carrying the loads. . . ."

In a report written to Carleton in April 1864, Carson urged that the Indians be fed: ". . . I have unofficially learned that Captain McCabe lost while en route by desertion one hundred Indians, headed by a son of the late Chief Juanico; cause, want of sufficient to eat. I would respectfully suggest to you the propriety and good feeling of giving to the Indians, while at Fort Canby and Wingate, and while en route to the Bosque Redondo, a sufficiency to eat. It is here and when en route that we must convince them by our treatment of them the kind intentions of the Government towards them, otherwise I fear that they will lose confidence in our promises, and desert also. . . ."

Carleton, who shared Carson's views on this matter, included in his own report: ". . . This is the first time any troops, whether when the country belonged to Mexico or since we acquired it, have been able to pass through the Canyon de Chelly, which, for its great depth, its length, its perpendicular walls, and its labyrinthine character, has been regarded by eminent geologists as the most remarkable of any "fissure" (for such it is held to be) upon the face of the globe. It has been the great fortress of the tribe since time out of mind. To this point they fled when pressed by our troops. Colonel Washington, Colonel Sumner, and many other commanders have made an attempt to go through it, but had to retrace their steps. It was reserved for Colonel Carson to be the first to succeed. . . .

". . . I beg respectfully to call the serious attention of the government to the destitute condition of the captives, and beg for authority to provide clothing for the women and children. Every preparation will be made to plant large crops for their subsistence at the Bosque Redondo the coming spring. Whether the Indian department will do anything for these Indians or not you will know. But whatever is to be done should be done at once. At all events, as I before wrote you, 'we can feed them cheaper than we can fight them.' "

The route branches north from its junction with the Moenkopi-St. Michaels Road, 0 m. (see TOUR 5), at a point 6.3 miles west of Ganado and follows the rim of a high mesa (L), called by the Navajo, BLACK MOUNTAINS (8,000 alt.); it is dotted with scrub growths of juniper and piñon trees.

From 17 m. is a view of BEAUTIFUL VALLEY, its varied strata shaped into hills and terraces, and cut by gullies that reveal vermilion, gray, blue, green, and magenta layers.

Stone buildings in CHINLE, 31.5 m., house the administrative headquarters and a boarding school for more than a hundred Navajo children in the lower grades.

Here the route turns R., 1 m. to the NATIONAL PARK SERVICE HEADQUARTERS (3 camp sites with tables, fireplaces, in area) and THUNDERBIRD RANCH ($10.75 per day Am. plan. Meals served only to resident guests. Half day trips into the canyons in special car $20 for 1 to 3 persons, or $5 each for 4 or more persons. Horseback trips into the canyon $6.50 per day per person).

Self-guiding trail into CANYON DE CHELLY NATIONAL MONUMENT, and the WHITE HOUSE RUIN. The Rim Tour can be taken in a personally owned car at any time of the year.

RIM TOUR

The road branches southeast from the National Park Service Headquarters, 0 *m.* and passes a group of yellowish brown SAND DUNES (R), 1.4 *m.,* heaped up in rolling hills, and devoid of vegetation. Except for those southwest of Yuma (*see TOUR 4d*) bare hills of sand waved by the wind are rarely found in the Arizona desert.

Left from the FIRST LOOKOUT, 2.4 *m.,* is a glimpse of the towering walls of the canyon. In a fault on the near side is a black rock formation (R). The hogans and cornfields of the Navajo, 350 feet below, appear in miniature.

At 4.3 *m.* is the junction with a dirt road.

Left on this road; from 0.8 *m.* is a view of the apparently impregnable WHITE HOUSE (*see CANYON DE CHELLY TOUR*) set in a cranny of the opposite wall. When occupied it was reached by ladders, which could be drawn up at the approach of enemies. From the flat white sands of the canyon floor the red sandstone cliff rises in a smooth straight line as if some giant mason had first leveled off the floor, then squared the soft wall with one firm sure stroke. After every heavy rain, water pours from the slight indentations at the top of the cliff, falls in thin white veils of spray, and streaks the rose-pink face of the rock with dark brown, iron stains. The series of tiny depressions winding up the face of the cliff to the left of the ruin is a hand and toe trail used by the Indians for countless years.

About 800 feet to the R. is an easy horse trail leading down to the floor of the canyon more than 500 feet below.

At 6.5 *m.* is the junction with a dirt road.

Left on this road to the junction with a foot trail, 0.5 *m.* L. on this 0.5 *m.* to the END OF TRAIL LOOKOUT. At this point the bottom of the canyon is between 600 to 700 feet below the rim. The zigzag course of the stream, and the tendency of the walls to parallel each other are clearly evident.

An old peach orchard (R), 7.5 *m.,* is believed by some to have been planted by the Spanish in the early years of their colonization of the Southwest.

At 13 *m.* is the junction with a foot trail.

Left on this trail to the brink of MONUMENT CANYON (*may be explored on foot or horseback*), 3 *m.,* which was so named for the many slender obelisks and spires of rocks that have been separated from the canyon walls by erosion and rise like monster stalagmites from the canyon floor. Two of these known as THE MONUMENTS are more than eight hundred feet high, great towers of red sandstone taller than the Woolworth Building and half again as tall as the Washington Monument.

CANYON DE CHELLY TOUR

Canyon de Chelly and its branches contain more than 300 prehistoric sites and 138 major ruins; most of them because of their position high on the north wall are not accessible.

The route branches northeast from the Park Service Headquarters, 0 *m.,* and enters the canyon mouth, 1 *m.* Here the walls, only 20 to

30 feet high, descend vertically to the soft loose sand of the floor. Farther up the canyon, the sides become increasingly higher.

At 4 *m.* Canyon del Muerto branches L. (*see CANYON DEL MUERTO TOUR*).

The FIRST RUIN (L), 4.1 *m.,* is high in the cliff, and so perfectly protected that its walls have suffered little since it was abandoned. How its occupants descended to the bottom to cultivate their fields and returned is not obvious today.

A peach orchard (L), 4.7 *m.,* is cultivated by the Navajo; these lands can be easily irrigated, and water can be obtained anywhere by digging a shallow well in the floor of the canyon.

From 6.1 *m.* is a view (L) of the hand and toe trail up the north wall of the canyon (*see RIM TOUR*).

The WHITE HOUSE (*visitors not allowed to enter ruins*), 6.5 *m.,* is one of the largest and best preserved of the ruins in the monument. (*The lower part resting on the floor is accessible, but the upper section, set in the cave above cannot be reached*). It was occupied between 1050 and 1300 A.D., according to the tree-ring dates, in the Great Pueblo period. The abandoning of this site marked the end of the pueblo peoples in Canyon de Chelly, and may have been contemporaneous with the arrival of the Navajo, who regarded it as their stronghold for many years. Formerly, the lower ruin was four or five stories high and ladders extended from the roof to the upper building. The walls are of carefully laid stones, in courses, and even today seem as straight as if they had been built with the aid of a plumb line. There are four kivas in the lower site, all of the circular type, with a masonry bench running completely around the wall.

The depth of the canyon increases toward the east till at 7 *m.* the smooth sides towering five hundred to six hundred feet, are completely vertical, and are barely five hundred feet apart.

SLIDING ROCK RUIN (L), 7.5 *m.,* is so called because the walls of the old houses are gradually falling down into the canyon. The approach is over a relatively gentle slope of sandstone, but is a difficult climb. So much of the village has fallen away that the exact number of rooms that once perched on the ledge is not known.

Near the very top of the left cliff are the BEEHIVE RUINS, 10 *m.,* which must have been approached from the rim rather than from the bottom. They appear to be set in very narrow circular caves, but it is impossible to gage their size from below.

A cave is visible through THE WINDOW, 11 *m.,* which is a natural aperture about a hundred feet wide and more than a hundred feet high, worn through a thin wall of rock that projects into the canyon at one of its many sharp, angular turns. Although the canyon's general direction is east and west, its actual course is so tortuous that it travels north and south for a great part of the distance. Here the height of the wall exceeds seven hundred feet.

Another ruin visible (L) at 14.2 *m.* is high in the cliff.

MONUMENT CANYON (R), 14.3 *m.,* is guarded by SPIDER

Rock and Face Rock, two large sandstone obelisks commonly called The Monuments (*see above*). The one at the R. of the entrance towers almost eight hundred feet and when viewed from its base appears higher than the walls of the canyon, though they are more than one thousand feet at this point. The tall column of stone to the L. is not yet completely detached from the wall. Although Monument Canyon is 15 miles long and de Chelly extends another 15 miles from here, the bed of canyons is not passable by cars beyond this point.

CANYON DEL MUERTO TOUR

This route branches northeast from its junction with the Canyon de Chelly Tour, 0 *m.,* at a point 4 miles east of the Park Service Headquarters (*see above*). CANYON DEL MUERTO has the same geological formation and appearance as Canyon de Chelly, but is more impressive because its walls are even closer together, and at intervals are so undercut that from its floor the sky resembles a narrow ribbon of blue.

Antelope House (L), 3 *m.* from the junction with Canyon de-Chelly, is a large ruin built close to the wall, in a corner where the cliff has been undercut, and is thus protected against the weather. It is named for pictographs painted in brown and white by an early Navajo artist on the wall to the L. of the buildings. A wall still standing indicates that the house was formerly four stories high.

The Standing Cow Ruins, 5 *m.,* named for a pictograph (R), also contains round kivas. Left of the buildings is a pictograph showing mounted Spanish soldiers and priests carrying crosses. Since the pueblo sites had all been abondoned before the discovery of America, it is probable that the pictographs were made by the Navajo who subsequently occupied this area. Navajo hogans and sheep corrals, L. of the ruin, are protected by the same overhanging cliff that shelters the old pueblo.

At 10 *m.* are side canyons branching L. and R. with Navajo trails in each. The height of the rim here exceeds seven hundred feet, but seems greater, because of the short distance between the walls. In places the walls are so undercut that large sections have fallen down and buried themselves in the sandy floor, or piled up on the talus.

Mummy Cave Ruin (R), 14 *m.,* is in a cavern 80 feet above a slope of loose earth and rock, and about 300 feet above the bottom of the canyon. The buildings were three stories high; the western section is 100 feet long and 75 feet deep; the eastern is 200 feet long and 100 feet deep. On the ledge that connects the two sections are low buildings and a tower. The western section must have had about twenty rooms, although only ten are clearly visible now. Forty-four rooms and four circular kivas, are still distinguishable in the eastern section. A piece of charcoal, bearing tree-rings indicating that it dates from 348 A.D., was found in the debris on the slope and one of 1284 A.D. was found in the square tower, which is a feature characteristic of pueblos in the

San Juan drainage area but lacking in those of the Navajo National Monument (*see TOUR 6 and TOUR 6A*).

Upstream on foot 1 *m.* from Mummy Cave to MASSACRE CAVE, in which are the marks made by bullets that ricocheted when fired into the interior. These marks were made about 1805, when Spanish raiders trapped a number of Navajos including women and children in this shallow cave and shot them from a near-by point.

Tour 6

Tuba City—Tonalea—Kayenta—Monument Valley—(Mexican Hat, Utah); Klethla Valley Rd.
Tuba City to Utah Line 113.4 *m.*

Graded shale roadbed in Arizona; graded dirt in Utah. Passable except after heavy snows or rains.
Limited accommodations at Tonalea and Kayenta. Water, gasoline, and other emergency supplies should be carried.

This route traverses the northwestern section of the vast Navajo Indian Reservation, the most inaccessible portion of their whole territory. Except for the occasional Navajo hogans, the only signs of human habitation are at the trading posts of Tonalea and Kayenta. The road mounts the Shonto (Navajo, mirror) Plateau, which forms the divide for water flowing north to the San Juan, west to the Colorado, southwest to the Little Colorado, and eastward by way of Tyende and Chinle creeks into the San Juan. The land is marked with broad valleys and poorly defined mesas, which change in the northern section to deep canyons and high cliffs.

The Klethla Valley Road branches northeast from the St. Michaels-Moenkopi Road at TUBA CITY, 0 *m.* (*see TOUR 5*), and turns L. at the junction with another unnumbered dirt road, 1.1 *m.*

At 10 *m.* is the junction with an unimproved dirt road.

Right on this road to BLUE CANYON, 16 *m.*, a large gash cut in the soft sands by a tributary of the Moenkopi Wash. The Indians call this Dot Klish (Navajo, blue clay) because of the color of the oddly-shaped rocks and hard clays that have resisted erosion.

Minor Navajo ceremonies are held at many points in this country. (A dance called *When the Thunder Sleeps* is given after the first frost.) Many horsemen and wagons all going in the same direction are a certain sign that some Navajo function is to take place (*see TOUR 5*). One of them, the Squaw Dance, which now serves the older people as a general gathering and the younger as a mating ceremony, occurs in the summer and fall. In this dance, which often begins at midnight and continues until dawn, a girl chooses a man by tugging at his coat; if he likes her he continues to dance with her, but if he prefers another maiden he must pay his partner (usually a dime or quarter) to get rid of her. Frequently some older man will harangue the younger tribesmen, urging them to come out and dance and not be stingy about paying.

At 22.5 m. are seen (L) the two most distinctive landmarks of the Kaibito Plateau, Wildcat Peak (6,648 alt.) and White Mesa. The former is a needlelike igneous formation visible for more than 50 miles. White Mesa is a high flat-topped mass of sandstone, carved into many box canyons; its white rimmed top distinguishes it from other mesas.

TONALEA (Navajo, big lake), 25.2 m. (6,457 alt., 15 pop.), a trading post (*dining room, cabin bedrooms*), displays the Paiute's fine coiled baskets, which the Navajo purchase for their wedding ceremonies as well as for use in their hogans. Below the post is a small body of water called RED LAKE because of the color of the surrounding soil.

ELEPHANT LEGS, 26 m., are gigantic columns of eroded tan sandstone resembling the feet and legs of an elephant.

At 32.1 m. is the junction (L) with a dirt road (*see TOUR 6A*).

At 35.5 m. is the junction with a graded dirt road.

Left on this road to a foot trail, 31 m.; L. 1 m. on this trail to the BETATAKIN RUIN (Navajo, hillside house), one of the three major cliff dwellings in the NAVAJO NATIONAL MONUMENT. This ruin, in the Segi branch of Laguna Canyon, was built in a long cave well guarded against approach from below. The major part of the ruin stands on the abruptly sloping floor of the cave; the walls are supported by steps pecked in the sandstone. On the face of the cliff (R) are paintings of a horned animal and of a mythical being, called by the Navajo, the Bat Woman. The rooms in this cliff house are rectangular and few sections are more than two stories high though the different levels of their foundations give the whole a terraced effect. In this village the kivas are rectangular and above the ground and the walls are of two types—stones set in adobe plaster and interwoven willows covered with adobe plaster. There were about 130 ground-floor rooms that extended approximately 450 feet along the cliff's ledge; thirteen roofing beams found here were cut between 1242 and 1286 A.D. This is one of the three large cliff villages of the Great Pueblo period in northern Arizona.

Right (north) 8 m. from Betatakin Ruin in the Laguna (Segi) Canyon is KEET SEEL (*reached only on foot or horseback*), the best preserved of the ruins of the Navajo National Monument; it is on the opposite side of the canyon from Betatakin. Keet Seel formerly contained about 150 rooms besides the kivas. As at Betatakin, the masonry of the buildings is comparable to the stonework of Mesa Verde, but this site has the circular subterranean kivas usually found in the larger ruins of the San Juan drainage area.

In addition to the circular kivas, there are also square ceremonial chambers, large rectangular rooms, others with a fireplace in the center of the floor, and rooms containing grinding stones in bins. The cave that it occupies is very deep and the houses are arranged to form a village with several courts and streets. Pottery from both of these sites is of three types, corrugated, black-on-white, and polychrome. Some of the Hopi clans are thought to have come from Keet Seel and its neighboring ruins. The rings of five ceiling beams indicate dates between 1274 and 1286 A.D.

In MARSH PASS, 61.1 *m.*, on the Klethla Valley Road, between Black Mesa (R) and the Navajo Plateau, are great outcroppings of red and brown sandstones. From Boiling Springs, its source deep in the Segi Canyon, Laguna Creek flows through Laguna Canyon (L). As recently as 1918 this region contained a chain of lakes, which have since been drained as the canyon has been eroded to greater depth.

The walls of the pass open at 67.6 *m.* into a gradually widening valley and reveal gently sloping tan sandstones against a background of sheer, deep red and brown cliffs.

The unusual shapes in stone that appear at 70 *m.* are forerunners of the Monument Valley formations.

In KAYENTA, 81.3 *m.* (5,700 alt., 20 pop.), are a trading post (*limited accommodations, filling station*), a tuberculosis hospital for the Indians, and a day school.

In the southern end of MONUMENT VALLEY is AGATHLA PEAK (6,825 alt.), 88.6 *m.*, a volcanic neck (R) with a spire that rises 1,255 feet above its sloping base. Scattered about the valley, which extends north to the San Juan River and west to the Segi Mesas, are outcrops of red sandstone several hundred feet high. These have been eroded into pillars and spires, or into huge rectangular blocks with grooved sides that suggest columns; and talus slopes outward at their bases in terraces, resembling steps. From a distance these rose-colored blue-shadowed "monuments" looming above the desert appear to be the ruins of immense Greek temples. The beauty of this long-isolated area has become better known to the public since the motion picture *Stagecoach* was photographed here in 1938.

In 1863-4, when Kit Carson rounded up the Navajo in Canyon de Chelly (*see TOUR 5A*), Chief Hoskinini led his people and their flocks to this valley, where he lived in complete independence till his death in 1909 and where his son, Hoskinini-begay, still makes his home. There were rumors that Hoskinini had a valuable silver mine and in 1880, though it was known that no prospectors were tolerated in this area, two men, named Merrick and Mitchell, made their way into the valley and returned with quantities of almost pure silver. From their second trip neither returned. Beside a butte, now named for Mitchell, both had been shot—according to Hoskinini-begay's story—by some Paiutes who had accused the prospectors of using water belonging to the Indians. Mitchell was killed immediately, but Merrick lived to reach another butte about 3 miles away, where he died. The coveted mine has not since been found by white men though some of the samples taken from it in 1880 are said to be in Utah and Colorado.

From 112 *m.* two large square monuments (R) are visible a little south of the Utah Line. MITCHELL BUTTE is the one nearer the road and MERRICK BUTTE, where the second prospector died, is the one farther east.

The Valley's dome-shaped floor reaches an elevation of more than 5,000 feet at the Utah Line, which the road crosses at 113.4 *m.* This point offers a good view of the MITTENS (L), one in Arizona and the other in Utah. Though the larger part of the valley is in Arizona some of its most spectacular features are in Utah.

At 114 *m.* is a junction with a dirt road.

Left on this to GOULDING'S POST, 1.9 *m.* (*limited accommodations; service station; saddle horses*), at Red Gate. From this post trips can be arranged to Rainbow Bridge (*see TOUR 6A*) and to such outstanding monuments as Train Rock, Organ Rock, and Mointer Mesa.

MONUMENT PASS, 114.5 *m.,* is so called because here the road is closely bordered on both sides by monuments. On the west side about a hundred yards (L) from the road are CASTLE ROCK and SETTING HEN. The buttes and spires (R) that extend from a hundred yards to half a mile to the east include the EMPEROR, distinguished by two prongs; the STAGE COACH; the BEAR and the RABBIT, facing each other; the BIG CHIEF; and BRIGHAM'S TOMB. Mitten Butte, Merrick Butte, and Mitchell Butte are visible from this point also.

The view from the north side of the pass, across windswept sand dunes with their few twisted cedars, includes the BEAR'S EARS, 50 miles to the north; Navajo Mountain (*see TOUR 6A*), to the west; and, to the northwest, DOUGLAS MESA, named for a prospector who, weary of "waiting for the San Juan River to dry up so he could find gold" threw himself from the San Juan bridge in 1929.

In the barren desert valleys a few Navajos are seen, grazing their flocks of goats on the desert shrubs or leading a string of horses to a water hole.

A sign at 117.8 *m.* indicates a point slightly west of the road where there is good water.

The ALHAMBRA (L), visible from 126.5 *m.,* is a dyke, several hundred feet in diameter, of black igneous rock that has been eroded into so many slender columns that its outline suggests a group of sky-scrapers rather than the Moorish fort for which it was named.

Through narrow slashes in the precipitous canyon walls the road approaches the bridge over the San Juan River, 133.6 *m.,* leading to MEXICAN HAT, Utah 134 *m.,* which was named for the sombrero-shaped boulder balanced on a tremendous rock near by. Before the bridge was erected here in 1909 this river had been a barrier to Indians and settlers alike. It formed the southern boundary of the Utes' terri-tory and though they sometimes raided south of the river they were often checked by its high waters. Beyond it the soldiers were unable to follow Hoskinini when he fled from Canyon de Chelly, and the few explorers, settlers, and prospectors who dared to enter the region found it a constant menace. In the diminutive settlement here are MEXICAN HAT LODGE (*limited accommodations*), an oil well, a government sta-tion measuring the silt in the river, and a kerosene-motored refrigerator that usually contains iced beer.

Tour 6A

Junction with Klethla Valley Road—Inscription House Lodge—Rainbow Lodge—Rainbow Bridge National Monument, Utah; 76.3 *m.*, Rainbow Bridge Rd.

Graded dirt roadbed to Inscription House Lodge; between Inscription House Lodge and Rainbow Lodge only a pair of wheel tracks crossing rock ledges, sand, and washes,—hazardous for modern cars, but passable; closed only December 1 to March 20, if there is a heavy snow.
Limited accom. Inscription House and Rainbow Lodge (*Pack trip from Rainbow Lodge to Rainbow Bridge $20. per person per day, everything incl.*)
2-day trip to Rainbow Bridge; 3-day return trip to Colorado River.

The route, wholly within the Navajo Indian Reservation, crosses a rough rocky section cut by numerous canyons that have been formed by tributaries of the Colorado River and vary in depth from two hundred to two thousand feet.

The Rainbow Bridge Road branches north from its junction with the Klethla Valley Road, 0 *m.*, at a point 6.5 miles east of TONALEA (*see TOUR 6*).

INSCRIPTION HOUSE LODGE (*horses available for trips*) is at 21.9 *m.*

Left on a dirt road from Inscription House Lodge to a point at 2.5 *m.* where the road becomes a trail leading 3.5 *m.* through NAVAJO CANYON to INSCRIPTION HOUSE, in a cave high in the east wall of the canyon. This prehistoric ruin, one of three in the Navajo National Monument (*see TOUR 6*), contains about forty-eight rooms, and was occupied during the Great Pueblo period. A Spanish inscription carved on the walls is no longer legible though the date 1661 is distinguishable.

The Rainbow Trail from Inscription House Lodge to Rainbow Lodge was constructed in 1925 by Hubert Richardson, Indian trader of Cameron with the assistance of Navajo.

Through an opening at 27.8 *m.* in the thick growth of juniper is a view of NAVAJO CANYON (L). Its vivid red and tan sandstone walls are alternately smooth, rounded, or intricately carved and in some places are as steep as those of Canyon de Chelly (*see TOUR 5A*); to the right is a broad valley dotted with junipers amid broad outcroppings of sandstone.

The trail winds along a narrow neck of land, 33 *m.*, between Navajo Canyon (L), and Paiute Canyon (R). Distant Navajo Mountain (R) presents the same profile from any approach. This striking landmark is constantly in view between this point and the end of the route.

PAIUTE CANYON (R), 42.2 *m.*, with its seemingly endless variety of formations, has been greatly eroded in recent years. The overtowering plateau is so carved with canyons that the mesas normally found between two streams are but slightly developed, and buttes, mesas, and domes crowd upon one another so closely that they are difficult to distinguish.

The road parallels the southern base of NAVAJO MOUNTAIN (10,416 alt.) at 50 m. This, the most commanding feature of the Rainbow Plateau, stands alone without even a rolling foothill for company. Its rocky lower slopes are cut by numerous canyons and deep gorges; its upper slopes and rounded summit are covered with vegetation that contrasts with that of the surrounding country. There are stands of pinon and juniper and yellow pine 50 to 60 feet high; there are occasional patches of red fir, Rocky Mountain fir, and aspen. In spring the yellow-green of the willows forms a background for pale pink roses, deeper pink manzanita blossoms, red splashes of Indian paintbrush, blue, lavender, and yellow clematis, and deep purple sage.

A peculiarly formed rock (L) at 55.9 m. resembles a straw pile.

From the summit of Navajo Mountain (*reached by a steep, hazardous trail· 24 m. horseback trip from Rainbow Lodge*), 4,000 feet above the surrounding country, on the edge of Glen Canyon of the Colorado, is the widest view offered anywhere on the whole northern plateau. The landmarks clearly visible from LOOKOUT RIDGE, which runs westward from the summit, are: Abajo Peaks about 95 miles to the northeast; the Henry Mountains to the north; in the background slightly west, the flat Aquarius Plateau edged by cliffs; in the foreground the Kaiparowits Plateau and the canyons of both the San Juan and the Colorado rivers. Vermilion Cliffs (*see TOUR 1a*), in the west, mark the junction of the gorge of the Little Colorado with the Grand Canyon. To the southwest are the San Francisco Peaks, justifying their description in Navajo mythology as the supports of the sky. Black Mesa is far to the southeast and the intervening land is gashed by countless gorges whose spires, domes, and tables were carved from their multicolored rocks by streams that empty into a gulch tributary of Paiute and Navajo Canyons. RAINBOW LODGE (6,450 alt.), 59 m. (*all expense pack trip to Rainbow Bridge $20 per day, to summit of Navajo Mountain $15*), comprising a dining room, trading post, and furnished cottages among the pines on the south side of Navajo Mountain, is the terminus of the motor trail.

North of the lodge the pack-horse trail climbs 6 m. to the top of a divide. From this point the view suggests the Grand Canyon. The trail that zigzags to the bottom and follows the creek beds of various gorges.

From about 13 m. is a view of Rainbow Bridge, forming an extraordinary frame for Navajo Mountain.

RAINBOW BRIDGE, 14 m., in Rainbow Bridge National Monument, is a natural arch of salmon-pink sandstone spanning the red, buff, brown, and gray walls of Bridge Canyon, which was carved by a tributary of the Colorado River. Unlike most natural bridges, which are flat on top, both its arch line and crest line are curved and symmetrical. From a distance the arch, seen between the towering sides of the canyon, seems small though it is 309 feet high—more than twice the height of bridges that clear ocean-going vessels—40 feet thick at the top, and has a span of 278 feet. It would curve over New York's Flatiron Building with 40 feet to spare.

Despite many published descriptions, Rainbow Bridge is little known and seldom visited. An account appearing in the *National Geographic* of September, 1925, described it as "one of the most marvelous and awe-inspiring works of nature to be found in North America."

Called Nonnezosheboko (Navajo, great arch) or Barahoini (Paiute, the rainbow), the bridge was well known and revered by the Indians of this vicinity though the first known visit by white men was not made till 1909, when a party headed by Prof. Byron Cummings, then of the University of Utah, and by W. B. Douglas of the U. S. General Land Office was guided here by a Paiute Indian, Nashja-begay.

Oren Arnold's *Wonders of the West* includes a Navajo legend accounting for the creation of Rainbow Bridge:

"Many, many years ago a certain handsome young god, who ruled over the hunting activities of the Navajo Indians and was much admired by them, took his own bow and arrows and himself went hunting. He decided to look for game where few men dared go— into that strange but beautiful canyon of reds and purples, known as Nonnezosheboko.

"The canyon was in an extremely rugged country. At places it was so narrow that a man could span it with his legs, yet so deep that from the bottom the sky appeared like a mere thread of light far above. Only the most difficult trail led down into its wider portions because towering cliffs walled it in. Almost nothing grew there and usually it was absolutely dry.

"However, on this particular morning a sudden rainstorm in the nearby mountains sent waters flooding and roaring down the deep valley. The young god found himself trapped. There in the beautiful canyon, with a literal wall of water rushing toward him, he seemed doomed to die of drowning.

"At that moment the great Sky Father came to his rescue. A rainbow suddenly appeared in front of the threatening torrent. The water was halted and the young god climbed up the rainbow to safety and all was well. Then the rainbow was turned to stone, so that it might be seen as proof that the great Sky Father watches over his beloved earth children."

Tour 7

Sanders—Springerville—Clifton—Safford—Bowie Junction—Cochise—Douglas; 399.2 *m.*, US 666 (Coronado Trail).

Concrete-paved roadbed between St. Johns and Springerville; elsewhere graveled; occasionally blocked by snow in winter and dangerous during rains; cautious driving and local inquiry concerning condition of road advisable.

This route crosses a thinly populated region used primarily for cattle grazing though it contains several producing mines and two national forests that abound with game and attract an increasing number of sportsmen each year.

Section a.   SANDERS to SPRINGERVILLE; 83 m., US 666

Between Sanders and Springerville is a country of broad horizons and varicolored mesas.   The strange peaks that rise along the way are so dwarfed by the vast sweep of the earth and the immensity of the sky that they resemble the tiny mountains of a miniature garden.

US 666 branches south from its junction with US 66 in the trading post of SANDERS, 0 *m.* (*see TOUR 2a*).

ST. JOHNS, 51.1 *m.* (5,630 alt., 1,300 pop.), was founded in 1874 by Sol Barth who had just won several thousand head of sheep and a few thousand dollars from some Mexicans in a card game.   He named his town in honor of the first woman resident, Senora Maria San Juan de Padilla de Baca.   In 1880 its population was augmented by Mormons brought here by Jesse N. Smith and D. K. Udall.

A reservoir formed by Lymans Dam supplies the district with water and makes possible the tall poplars that line St. John's streets and the green fields that give a pleasing freshness to its outskirts.   St. Johns is the seat of Apache County, and center of a cattle raising, farming and lumbering district.

At St. Johns is the junction with US 260, which unites with US 666 to Alpine (*see below*).

Right on paved US 260 to CONCHO, 14 *m.* (5,000 alt., 200 pop.), center of a grazing and agricultural district.   Its little red adobe houses contrast sharply with the green of the fertile valley and the Lombardy poplars.   This town, founded in the 1870's, is inhabited almost entirely by Mexicans.   Among the earliest settlers was Juan Candaleria, who controlled some forty square miles of surrounding grazing land including the town.   He left the town, land, and stock to his three sons who carried on for years.

At 66.1 *m.* is the junction with a graveled road.

Left on this road to LYMANS DAM, 2 *m.*, on the Little Colorado River.   The reservoir formed here supplies water for a large irrigation district.   The first dam, constructed by Mormon settlers, was leveled by a flood in 1903; after the Mormons had rebuilt it at a cost of $200,000, it was again destroyed by flood in April, 1915. The present dam, costing $800,000 was built by the state.

At 78.2 *m.* is the junction with US 60 (*see TOUR 12*), which unites with US 666 between this point and Springerville.

From 82.1 *m.* is a view of the Little Colorado River flowing from the mountains in a narrow, sparkling stream, very different from the swirling, muddy river it becomes a few miles to the north.

SPRINGERVILLE, 83 *m.* (6,856 alt., 700 pop.), is surrounded by the extensive forests of the White Mountains, 300 miles of trout streams, and game lands on which are bear, mountain lion, wild turkey, and several species of deer. The climate is cold in winter and bracing in summer, owing to the elevation. Springerville's principal source of income are livestock, poultry, grains, and vegetables; catering to sportsmen, however, is becoming increasingly profitable. An experimental grain station has been established here by the University of Arizona.

It was from Springerville that Joe Pearce and Clay Hunter rode into New Mexico in 1912 and captured the notorious Maris and two of his men, who had stolen some Zuni and Navajo horses—a capture that helped to end rustling in northern Arizona and in New Mexico. Pearce, a former Arizona ranger, was at that time a line rider patroling the Arizona-New Mexico Line from Utah to Springerville. He answered the call for aid, and though the trail was two days old and led him beyond his jurisdiction he followed the bandits 160 miles into New Mexico. A few days later, to the astonishment of citizens who were familiar with Maris, Pearce and Hunter brought the culprits in alive and returned all the stolen horses except one that had been ridden to death in the chase.

In the center of town is the MADONNA OF THE TRAILS, a granite statue eighteen feet high of a pioneer mother with a baby in her arms. It is by August Lienback, and was placed here to commemorate the covered wagon trail that passed through Springerville in early days.

Springerville is at the junction with US 60 (*see TOUR 12*).

Section b.   SPRINGERVILLE to JUNCTION with US 70;
164 m., US 666

Between SPRINGERVILLE, 0 *m.,* and the desert valleys south of Clifton US 666 touches the route believed to have been taken by Coronado in 1540 when he was searching for the Seven Cities of Cibola. Crossing two national forests, the highway is hemmed in by dense growth of quaking aspen, Douglas fir, and mountain fern. For 135 miles, as it winds and twists over mountains abounding with game, the road is wide enough for only one car (*car going down backs to a turn-out if another car approaches from below*). Through occasional clearings are vistas of cabins and lodges surrounded by green valleys and distant mountains that shade from lapis lazuli to purple.

The road crosses the northern boundary of the APACHE NATIONAL FOREST at 3.9 *m*. Though the reserve abounds with big game, many thousand head of cattle, horses, and sheep graze here. Timber in this area is chiefly western yellow pine, Douglas fir, white fir, and spruce. Sportsmen are attracted by the trout-filled streams and the wild turkeys. The variety of turkey found here is the Merriam, which closely resembles the domesticated bird. Formerly hunted with a shotgun and slaughtered on its roost at night, it is now protected to a degree by game laws and may be hunted only with a rifle.

ALPINE, 28 *m*. (8,005 alt., 300 pop.), in a mountain valley (*good hunting and fishing*) with surrounding pine-covered ranges, has an excellent summer climate because of its elevation. The place was first called Bush Valley for its first settler, Anderson Bush, who arrived in 1876; three years later it was colonized by Mormons who renamed it Frisco because of its proximity to the San Francisco River, then changed the name to Alpine because of a fancied resemblance between these mountains and the Alps. Near-by are several hunting lodges and two sawmills that turn out a considerable amount of lumber, principally Arizona yellow pine.

Left from Alpine on a dirt road into a hunting country that contains many large predators. The black or brown bear inhabits most of the forested areas of northern Arizona. Bears formerly ranged over the entire state, but have been exterminated in many areas. At present bear hunting is allowed north of the Gila River only. The black or brown bear is usually omnivorous, eating fruit, berries, grass, roots, insects, honey, fish, frogs, carrion, and anything else available; occasionally it kills young domestic stock and has to be removed by state or federal hunters. There is considerable evidence to indicate that the bear, a hibernating animal, does not hibernate in southern Arizona, where the winters are mild even in the mountains. When the single or twin cubs are born in the spring they are very small and helpless. Growth is rapid, however, and at maturity the animal weighs 450 to 475 pounds. At one time grizzly bears, better known as silver tips were common in this part of the state, but except in a few isolated places they are now extinct. In Arizona the grizzly when mature weighs as much as eight hundred pounds. Stewart Edward White called the grizzly, when roused, the most dangerous animal on the North American Continent, and old-timers expressed their admiration for hunters who killed a silver tip with the old single-shot muzzle-loading rifle by calling him "muches hombre" (Sp., much of a man).

"Timberline" Bill Sparks, Arizona Ranger, peace officer, and professional game hunter for the mining camps of Metcalf and Clifton, once trapped a big grizzly in this area. The trail was easy to follow as the bear had been caught by a forepaw and in his pain and rage was striking so furiously at everything in sight that he left a wide swath in his wake, at one point slashing through a grove of saplings. Being an experienced hunter Bill took every precaution; but the bear, evidently scenting him, doubled back and overtook him from behind, rushing him from the top of a steep hillside. Knocked down by the bear's attack and bitten through the thigh, Bill managed to hold onto his rifle, while the bear shook him violently. At times they rolled down the steep hillside together, the bear holding Bill and Bill clinging to his rifle. Finally Bill, half fainting and dizzy, managed to get the muzzle of his rifle against the bear's ear and pulled the trigger; the grizzly went limp. Then Bill applied tourniquets to his wounds, while sitting in an icy trout stream to staunch the flow of blood, and worked his way back towards camp using his rifle as a crutch; his partner found him hours later and packed him in to a doctor in Clifton, where he recovered.

A puncher from the old Wine Glass outfit tells of the time a grizzly took over their camp at Pigeon Springs: "The cook was alone an he didn't see the bear until he was almost in camp an it scairt the cook so he ran an jumped onto a horse that was picketed near. They was makin' a race for it too until the pony hit the end of the picket rope and turned plumb over with him. The cook in his excitement had fergot to pull the picket pin. Any way he finished the race on foot."

HANNAGAN MEADOW, 51 *m.* (5,000 alt.), is a resort (*cabins and dining room*) in a mountain valley. Close to the lodge is a field of blue gentians, and in July and August on sunny days the field looks as if bits of blue sky had been dropped to earth.

In the meadow (R), 52.1 *m.,* is a marker pointing out the route that some historians say Coronado followed in 1540; most authorities believe, however, that he followed the San Francisco River and consequently entered New Mexico several miles south of this point.

The road descends at 71 *m.* from MOGOLLON RIM, a natural barrier stretching across 200 miles in the eastern half of the state. The rim is the northern boundary of GILA NATIONAL FOREST, a reserve containing extensive timber, forage, and wild life (*camping sites through headquarters at Silver City, N.M., see TOUR 3a*).

South of the Mogollon Rim the highway crosses the Blue Range. When this area was first used for grazing in the latter part of the nineteenth century, the Apache were so real a menace that many old-time Arizona cowmen still say "the only good Indians are dead Indians." The Triple X, one of the first cow ranches on the southern part of the Blue Range was established in 1885 by Fred Fritz who was soon joined by Nat Widdom, as a partner. Within a short time Toles Cospor, Benton Rasberry, and the Luther Brothers also had ranches on the lower Blue. While Fritz was in Clifton getting supplies he heard that Apaches were raiding and, heedless of his own safety, headed back to rescue his partner, who was alone on the ranch. But at Blue river he came upon signs of a large band of Apaches who had crossed ahead of him, and were already heading south with some stolen cattle. At his ranch Fritz found the mutilated body of his partner. The Cospor place had been raided, but the Cospors had escaped. Benton Rasberry and the Luther brothers had also been killed and their property looted.

STRAY HORSE CANYON, 64 *m.,* contains a PUBLIC CAMP-GROUND (L).

From 81 *m.* ROSE PEAK (9,525 alt.) is visible (R). For many years the Government has hired hunters to protect livestock and deer from mountain lions, which once took a heavy toll among the ranches in this vicinity. Though they are no longer very numerous there are still enough lions in this and other sections of the state to keep federal and state hunters busy. Their range coincides with that of the large mammals, especially deer, upon which they depended almost entirely for food before the presence of cattle, sheep, and other livestock augmented their diet. It is estimated that a lion kills an average of one mule deer a week or seventy-five whitetails a year. Few animals are known by as many different names. He has been called catamount, American lion, cougar, puma, painter, and panther; but in Arizona he is simply lion. There are two varieties here, the Mexican cougar, which ranges throughout the state but avoids the open treeless valleys and mesas, and the Yuma lion, a somewhat smaller and paler animal found in Yuma County and western Pima County. A fully grown lion weighs from 175 to 200 pounds and measures seven or eight feet in length. One to five cubs are born in almost any month in the year. Dogs trained to hunt lion ignore all other scents, but the average dog requires years of schooling before he is dependable; Cleve Miller, a former Government hunter in this area, once said that a man's lifetime was just long enough to break one mule and train one pack of lion dogs. During the month of February, 1923, Cleve killed fifteen lions with the aid of his hounds. A cowboy near Willcox once roped and tied a lion. "The country was fairly open when I jumped him," said the puncher, "and I caught him first throw, but the lion run through the loop and instead of ketchin' him round the neck the loop drawed up around his belly. Naturally the pony didn't think much of it an' I was in a hell of a fix with the horse and lion both buckin' on the end of a thirty-five-foot rope. But I managed to get enough slack to pitch my rope over a big bush an pull the lion off the ground; then I anchored my pony and killed the lion with rocks."

Bull Moore and another puncher from the Double Circle once ran a lion to his cave. Bull crawled into the entrance and built a fire, hoping to smoke the big cat out. "I was watchin' the entrance," said his partner, "when I heard a riot inside. For a minute I thought Bull had gone crazy an had tried to ride the lion out as they shot out of the cave together with Bull a holdin' the lion around the belly with both hands. When they hit the ground together Bull was knocked out by the fall, but otherwise wasn't hurt. When he came to, Bull said he didn't remember takin' holt of any lion, but he was so scairt when the cat ran over him he guessed that's what he done."

At 96 *m.* is the junction with a dirt road.

Right on this road to the DOUBLE CIRCLE RANCH (*visited by permission*), 12 *m.*, established in 1880, when all supplies, including farm machinery and household furnishings, had to be packed in over several miles of rough, mountainous country. Even a piano was carried over the trail by Mexicans, who were able to lug it only a few steps at a time without putting it down.

THE TRAIN ROBBERS GRAVES hold four of a band of Texas bandits, who took jobs at the Double Circle. When finally trailed to the ranch by a posse and two Texas rangers, the outlaw punchers fought a desperate battle. These four were buried where they fell.

On this ranch in 1881 White Mountain Apaches ambushed and killed Captain Pinkard and all but one of his sixty men.

The narrow road twists along the bottom of a deep and unusually beautiful canyon whose brilliantly colored and precipitous walls are known as the VERMILION CLIFFS, 126 *m.* Where these red canyon walls have been cut in building the road, they are flecked with azure copper markings.

METCALF, 113 *m.* (now obliterated), settled in 1872, when gold was discovered—copper discoveries came later—once boasted two thousand people. Its beginnings were marked by frequent outlaw and Indian raids. Some of the richest mineral deposits were found in GOLD GULCH, one mile north of town.

The Coronado railroad, a 9-mile narrow gauge road was opened between Metcalf and Clifton in 1878, the first railroad in the Territory. Its mule power was later replaced by locomotive, so light that when it jumped the track—which happened quite often—four men could lift it back. This locomotive is now in the Arizona Museum at Phoenix.

When the gold played out and the price of copper fell, Metcalf's prosperity ended and today nothing is left to be seen here.

South of Metcalf the road winds down through the canyon where there are hundreds of abandoned tunnels in the once ore-laden mountain sides. Most of the buildings of the camp are gone and the few that remain are disintegrating and merging into the terraced hills on which they stand. Many miles of railroad track rust in tunnels blasted through solid rock; these tunnels divert Chase Creek from its course when, after heavy rains in the mountains, it roars down in a muddy flood. During dry seasons its waters trickle quietly past the deserted workings, forming placid, cobalt blue pools.

CLIFTON, 120 *m.* (3,460 alt., 3,451 pop.), the center of a copper mining district, was settled by eastern prospectors in the spring of 1872, although a little group of Mexican placer miners had been busy here since 1867. Chase Creek, the main business thoroughfare of early days, was a narrow crooked street with board sidewalks and buildings jammed together on both sides. Many of these were saloons, and gun play was frequent. Though mining in this area was begun with little equipment and less knowledge of methods of treating ore, Clifton's present copper smelter, controlled by the Phelps Dodge Corporation, is one of the most modern and efficient in the country. At one time it handled ore from the mines of both Clifton and Morenci. The town's population and prosperity fluctuate with the copper market. Often only three-quarters of the buildings are occupied, but an increase in mining operations changes the picture entirely.

CLIFTON HOT SPRINGS whose waters bubble up from the San Francisco River almost in the center of the city, have been privately developed. The Spanish-mission type bathhouse and swimming pool are open the year round. The water, which has a large salt content, comes from the ground at 130°. It is now a Phelps Dodge hospital.

CLIFTON CLIFF JAIL was blasted from the side of a mountain on the edge of town. Though bad men in the old days were often as ingenious as ruthless, it is claimed that none ever left Clifton Cliff except under escort. The jail was built in 1881 by the Lezinsky brothers, owners of the copper mines, who let the contract for the blasting to a Mexican. Immediately on completion of the work he invested his pay in mescal (a drink made from a plant bearing the same name and containing a narcotic stimulant) and participated in a "shooting up" at Hovey's Dance Hall: the creator of Clifton Cliff jail was installed as its first guest.

In the days when good character was considered security for a loan, Clifton's banker, who owned a saloon, a gambling house, and a brothel, was asked to lend $500 to a newcomer. "I think you had better give it to him," the banker told his cashier. "I believe he is a good man because I have never seen him anywhere around my places of business."

Beyond Clifton 6 *m.* on US 666 and State 75 is MORENCI (4,836 alt., 6,500 pop.), site of one of the largest open pit copper mines in the U.S. The Clifton-Morenci mining district is one of the oldest copper producers in Arizona. First indication of copper ore was discovered in 1865 by members of Colonel Carleton's Regiment of California Volunteers. The town of Morenci was founded in 1871 and the first crude copper produced in 1872. The early years of exploration were fraught with hardship, disappointments and failures. All ore was mined underground by hand and hauled away by pack burros or in wagons.

Mining at Morenci is now conducted with maximum mechanization. The open pit is a bowl 1½ miles across, east to west, and a mile, north to south. The benches which line the inside of this great bowl are 50 feet high and about 100 feet wide. Highest level is 5,600 and lowest 4,400 feet above sea level.

About 150,000 tons of rock per day is moved, of which 50,000 is ore and is processed in reduction works comprising concentrating mills, smelting furnaces, power generators and huge shops. The site can be spotted from great distances by the smelter chimney, a structure taller than the Washington Monument.

At 153 *m.* is the junction with US 70 (*see TOUR 3a*) which unites with US 666 between this point and Safford, 164 *m.* (*see TOUR 3a*).

Section c. SAFFORD to DOUGLAS; 124 m. US 666

South of Safford are grazing lands and a mountainous desert. The Sulphur Spring Valley, between Pearce and Douglas, was a prized hunting ground of the Apache and a favorite haunt of both Cochise and Geronimo. Its copper, gold, and silver lured miners; its thick grass that grew stirrup-high attracted cattlemen; and its inaccessibility made it a haven for rustlers and smugglers. In the early settlements saloons and honky-tonks flourished and, though gunplay was frequent, the residents preferred to settle their quarrels without the aid of peace officers. Only the cattle remain. The grass is no longer waist-high and the hell-roaring camps have become quiet villages or have vanished entirely.

US 666 south of SAFFORD, 0 *m.,* is lined with cotton fields, truck gardens, and dairy farms.

The new and old Arizona are dramatically contrasted at 1.8 *m.* where the green fields of the Gila Valley's irrigated farms are bounded by an area covered with greasewood.

At 5 *m.* Lebanon Hot Springs (R) (bath facilities).

MOUNT GRAHAM (10,750 alt.) rises majestically on the east above the valley, where cottonwood trees mark the creek beds; small mesas outline the skyline on the south and west; and the WHITLOCK MOUNTAINS are distinguishable in the distance on the southeast.

SWIFT TRAIL JUNCTION, 7.3 *m.* (3,321 alt., 30 pop.).

Right from the junction on Swift Trail (*open May-Oct.*), paved for 3 miles then graveled, to the GRAHAM MOUNTAIN RECREATION AREA, 3.5 *m.,* within the boundaries of the CORONADO NATIONAL FOREST.

Though Mount Graham rises from the desert floor, in winter it is capped with snow that frequently reaches an average depth of ten feet and drifts much higher in the canyons. During summer the area offers relief from the sweltering heat in the desert towns below. Many who live in Gila Valley, move to the mountains in the summer and drive to work each morning. Scores of cabins and summer homes have been built among the ponderosa pine, Douglas fir, white fir and aspen. Trout streams, bear, mountain lion (*see above*), deer and an occasional lobo wolf make this area attractive to sportsmen. Clyde Miller, a government hunter, in 1935 killed twenty-six lions in this area. It is not unusual for hunters to leave the valley in the morning, kill their deer, and be back in the valley for lunch.

At 3.8 *m.* is a junction with an improved dirt road; R. on this 3 *m.* to MARIJILDA CANYON (*picnic facilities; shelters*). Trout is abundant in the upper reaches of Marijilda Creek, named for Marijilda Orijalva, a Mexican, noted scout and interpreter. When a boy, he was captured (c. 1852), by Indians and held captive seven and a half years; he escaped in 1859.

TURKEY FLAT (7,500 alt.), 14.4 *m.* on Swift Trail, is a summer colony patronized by Gila Valley residents; has a store, service station (*cabins*).

At 25 *m.* on Swift Trail is a junction with an improved gravel road; R. 1 *m.* on this to the HELIOGRAPH FIRE LOOKOUT TOWER (*open to visitors May-July*), used by the army as a heliograph station during the Indian troubles. On clear days the view from this point (10,030 alt.) extends into Mexico and New Mexico.

The highway crosses an old creek bottom, 10.1 *m.,* that is overgrown with mesquite and catclaw brush. As late as 1900 there was no San Simon River or dry wash and the SAN SIMON VALLEY (L) was fertile and beautiful. But overgrazing and the cutting of moisture- and soil-holding brush and timber so hastened erosion that some of the present residents have watched the wash develop from a single wagon track to a gorge 100 feet wide and tributary gullies 20 feet across and 30 feet deep. The federal government is struggling to check the rapid runoff that causes the erosion by restoring the vegetation and constructing diversion ditches, terraces, dikes, spillways, spreading works, and dams. Thousands of these are visible from this and other Arizona highways.

At 18.8 *m.* there is a junction with an improved dirt road.

Right here through a section of the CORONADO NATIONAL FOREST to BONITA (Sp., beautiful), 15 *m.* (4,500 alt., 248 pop.). Here is the SIERRA BONITA RANCH, once owned by Henry Hooker, who drove in herds of cattle from Texas and New Mexico. Later he acquired blooded stock; built elaborate corrals, a blacksmith shop, paddock, and a windmill with a twenty-thousand-gallon tank; grew fruit trees and vegetables; raised poultry and hogs; lavishly entertained many prominent people; and lived in the manner of a feudal baron of the Middle Ages. Augustus Thomas who had been a guest used it as the setting of his play *Arizona,* but did not attempt to represent its luxuriousness. In an article printed in the *Saturday Evening Post,* Thomas quoted Hooker as saying: "We take a man here and ask no questions. We know when he throws his saddle on his horse whether he understands his business or not. He may be a minister backslidin', or a banker savin' his last lung, or a train robber on his vacation—we don't care. A good many of our most useful men have made their mistakes. All we care about now is, will they stand the gaff? Will they sit sixty hours in the saddle, holdin' a herd that's tryin' to stampede all the time?"

The STATE INDUSTRIAL SCHOOL, 18 *m.* (5,000 alt.), occupies the building of old FORT GRANT, which was established by the government in 1859 to protect settlers from the Indians. Its contingent was withdrawn in 1898 to participate in the Spanish-American War, and the fort was abandoned in 1905. Seven years later the government gave the buildings to the state and the reform school for boys was moved from Benson to this site.

South of BOWIE JUNCTION, 34 *m.* (3,900 alt.) loom the DOS CABEZAS (Sp., two heads) MOUNTAINS. Yucca and grazing grass as far as the eye can see indicate a good cattle country.

Left from Bowie Junction on State 86 to BOWIE, 9 *m.* (3,690 alt., 800 pop.), named for old Fort Bowie. Curly Bill (*see TOUR 4a*), the outlaw, occasionally dropped into Bowie for fun or deviltry, depending on his mood. On one occasion four riders, who had sauntered over to the station as the westbound passenger train came in, were watching the engineer at work with his oil can. Their curly-haired leader asked, "Do you want to sell this thing?" The engineer, thinking they were cowpunchers having their little joke, did not answer. Again the leader spoke, shoving his six-shooter into the engineer's middle, "I asked ya a civil question an' that's the kind of answer I want." The engineer reached for the sky with both hands. "I can't sell it," he stuttered, "I can't, honest." "In that case," said the leader, "we'll borrow the thing for a spell." The four cut off the locomotive, piled into the cab and roared down the track. The engineer had just rushed into the station to report the theft when back came the locomotive, only to disappear down the track once more before the eyes of the astounded train crew. For half an hour, while the trainmen ran in circles, Curly Bill and his outlaws raced the engine up and down the track, blowing the whistle; then they backed into the station, walked leisurely to their ponies, mounted, and rode at a walk out of town. When the revivalists, Moody and Sankey, passed through Arizona on their way to the coast, their train stopped at many of the little desert stations. Curly Bill and some of his men happened to be at one of their stops and, carrying a gunny sack full of bottled beer, climbed aboard. "Mr. Moody," said the outlaw, "we know you ain't got time to preach me an' the boys here a sermon as much as we'd like to hear you. But we would like to hear Mr. Sankey sing 'Pull for the Shore.'" Mr. Sankey declined till Curly Bill produced his six shooter. Then Mr. Sankey sang. It is reported that the revivalists refused the bottled beer, but, after the outlaws had drunk to their health, shook hands all around.

Right from Bowie 12 *m.* on Apache Pass Road (improved dirt-gravel). L. here (ruins can be reached on foot only). 1.1 *m.* to the ruins of FORT BOWIE, established in 1862 at the eastern entrance to Apache Pass, probably the most dangerous point on the immigrant road to California. This rough defile that twists between the foothills of the Dos Cabezas Mountains on the north and the Chiricahua Mountains on the south, was possibly reached by Cabeza de Vaca in 1536. In July, 1862, eleven companies of Union infantry, on their way from Tucson to New Mexico, were attacked here by Apaches under Cochise and Mangas Coloradas. The Indians, hidden behind trees and rocks on the steep side of the canyon, surprised the troops with a musket volley but fled in confusion when the soldiers returned the fire with howitzers. Robinson, the historian, quoted one of the braves as having remarked later, "We would have done well if you hadn't fired wagon wheels at us." The pass had become the grave of so many soldiers, prospectors, and immigrants that triple pay was offered to men who would make the stagecoach run through it in the years from 1861 to 1874, when Cochise was rampant, but few drivers lived to collect it.

From Fort Bowie is a view of the San Simon Valley to the northeast and, far to the west in the pass, the old Butterfield stage road was once visible, twisting along the wash at the canyon bottom. HELEN'S DOME (6,363 alt.), a high conical mountain south of the fort, was an early landmark; immediately southeast, on BOWIE PEAK (6,110 alt.), was Arizona's busiest heliograph station. Thick adobe walls mark the sight of the fort itself, on the summit of a flat-tapped hill. Remnants of about thirty other structures are scattered over a five-acre area among the mesquite, greasewood, and scrub oak. In redoubts of rock and mortar that still stand in strategic positions on the brush covered hillsides, soldiers were stationed to guard the stages and immigrant trains.

A visitor to Bowie Camp in 1867, described one of the tragic blunders that made the place notorious: "A few days before our arrival at Fort Bowie happened a sad incident that impressed me very much . . . An alarm was given by some of the herders that had been attacked by Indians. The captain indiscreetly mounted his horse, with only one assistant, and galloped off to where the Indians were last seen. The wily Apaches concealed themselves, and when the captain approached near enough, instead of shooting him as they generally did, they roped him, jerked him off his horse, and dragged him to death."

In 1872 a large area west of Fort Bowie was set aside for the Chiricahua Apache; but in 1876 the order creating the reservation was revoked, the territory was restored to the public domain, and, in spite of the protests of General Crook and others familiar with these Indians, the Chiricahua Apache—who were deeply attached to this area—were moved to the San Carlos reservation (see TOURS 3a and 8). In 1896 the old fort, whose name honored Colonel George W. Bowie of the California Volunteers, was abandoned and in 1911 the lands of the former reservation were sold at public auction to local farmers.

Right from Fort Bowie, following the wash, on the route traversed by the old Butterfield stages, to the FORT BOWIE CEMETERY (reached only on foot), 0.7 m. When the fort was abandoned the remains of the soldiers buried here and those of most of the immigrants were removed; later the weathered crosses, inscribed "Killed by Apaches," or "Tortured to Death by Apaches," that marked the remaining graves were stolen by souvenir hunters; only the faint outlines of a few burials are still visible.

RASO, 38 m. (4,120 alt.), is at the west end of Dragoon Pass on the Southern Pacific R.R.

South of the yucca-covered land is a sandy greasewood-covered flat on which are a few farmhouses, and ranches stocked with cattle.

WILLCOX, 46 m. (4,163 alt., 1300 pop.), is a cow town named for General Orlando B. Willcox (1823-1907), who served with distinction at the Battle of Bull Run, 1861, and was made Commander of the Department of Arizona (1878-82). On the southern edge of the village are stock yards (L) from which some 400,000 cattle are shipped annually. The large cattle ranches in the hills and valleys around Willcox are no longer refuges for outlaws. In the old days most outfits had more than one puncher who carefully avoided peace officers.

"I'd hired out to a man in Willcox," said an old timer, "an' was looking fer the camp his outfit was workin' from when I happened onto a puncher huntin' horses. From the brand on his horse I knowed he was workin' for the spread I was huntin'. When I asked where the camp was located an' didn't mention I was goin' to work I could see he had me pegged for an officer. Finally he pointed out the camp an' rode on.

"When I rode into camp there was saddles an' bed rolls layin' all about the place. Supper was just ready an' there was bread in the Dutch ovens for at least twenty men, but there wasn't a man in sight except the cook.

"He laughed when I rode up; it happened I knowed him. When he yelled they all come sneakin' in a looking kind of foolish. For it seems this puncher I had met had rode ahead and spread the word that an officer was on his way to camp. Not knowin' which man was wanted the whole doggone outfit had took to the brush."

Left from Willcox on a dirt road to DOS CABEZAS, 16 *m.* (5,100 alt., 50 pop.), named for the near-by mountain peaks. Like many little villages in southern Arizona this town with its sun-baked adobes seems to belong to Old Mexico. Its early inhabitants were prospectors who relied upon Fort Bowie for protection from the Apache. Dos Cabezas now is just a rapidly crumbling ghost town. Aside from the grammar school there are no public buildings, churches, or theaters. Visiting priests and ministers occasionally hold services in private homes or in the schoolhouse. In the surrounding hills and mountains are gold and silver mines.

On this road is the CHIRICAHUA NATIONAL MONUMENT, 40 *m.* (*see TOUR 4a*).

The scene of an unusual train hold-up of many years ago is at about 47 *m.* Two cowpunchers, embarking on careers in crime, placed dynamite on the messenger's strongbox and weighted it down with sacks of 'dobe dollars (Mexican pesos) which they found in the express car. The first charge blew the roof off the express car, scattering 'dobe dollars all over the flat. It took their last charge of powder to blow open the safe. While they were telling about the holdup later in cowcamp, a puncher asked what they intended to do if that last charge had not opened the safe.

"We talked that over at the time," said one of the robbers, "and I was to hold the train while my pardner went back to Willcox for more powder."

DRY LAKE BED, 50 *m.,* which is covered with an extensive layer of alkali, frequently creates mirages. The scene varies according to the atmospheric conditions. Sometimes the reflections of trees appear to be mirrored in clear blue water. At other times the water is rippled as though stirred by the wind. Alkali dust raised by the feet of a cow or horse often makes the animal look as if it were splashing at the water's edge. Occasionally a mirage blocks out the lower part of a mountain, leaving the peaks, which assume strange forms and seem to float in the air. Many men lost in the desert and crazed from thirst have exhausted their remaining strength in trying to reach a mirage only to have the supposed lake vanish entirely or move still farther away.

COCHISE, 59 m. (4,250 alt., 175 pop.), an adobe hotel, a school-house, a few filling stations and small stores, and a scattering of houses, was established in 1887 as a station on the Southern Pacific Railway serving near-by cattle ranches and mines. Though stage and train robberies were formerly so frequent in this area that they provoked little comment, the theft here on September 9, 1899, of more than $10,000 from a Southern Pacific train attracted particular attention because two officers of the law participated in the crime. Five months later when Jess Dunlap, a cowboy horse thief known as Three-Fingered Jack, was dying from a wound received at Fairbank while he was robbing the express car of a Benson-Nogales train, he gave the authorities information on the Cochise holdup. It had been planned by Burt Alvord, constable of Willcox (*see above*) and by William Downing, a prosperous cattleman, but was executed by Matt Burts, a cowboy, and by W. N. Stiles, deputy-constable of Pearce. Both officers had used their authority to lead pursuers and investigators away from the real criminals. Stiles confessed and promised to be a witness for the prosecution, but before the trial he entered the Tombstone jail, shot and wounded the jailor, and freed Alvord. Later in the same year Stiles surrendered and served a term at Yuma, as did Burts. In 1902 Alvord, who had been followed to Sonora, Mexico, agreed to surrender when he was promised clemency. In Tombstone he was discharged, partly because he had assisted in capturing Chacon, the Mexican desperado, and partly because death, the penalty for convicted train robbers, was considered too severe. A year later Alvord and Stiles were again in the Tombstone jail but this time dug their way to freedom. Alvord was subsequently seen in Panama and in 1908 Stiles was killed in Nevada, where he was known as Larkin. Downing served two terms in Arizona and was killed by an Arizona ranger in 1908. After his death it was learned that he had been a member of the notorious Sam Bass gang in Texas.

Right from Cochise on a graveled road to DRAGOON, 13 m. (4,613 alt., 275 pop.), a copper mining and cattle raising community; many Mexicans idling before the stores and drowsing in the shade give the town a Mexican atmosphere though most of the population is white and white men run most of the shops. On the same road is BENSON, 27 m. (*see TOUR 4b*).

South of Cochise is a good view of APACHE PASS (L) and the rock points (R) of the Dragoon Mountains (*see below*).

The old emigrant trail that crosses the present highway at 70.8 m. was used by the Butterfield stage line, which encountered many difficulties in this part of its route. Lack of water was as much a menace as were the attacks by Indians, Mexicans, and outlaw Americans. For many years the old trail was marked with the wrecks of wagons half covered by drifting sands, skeletons of horses and mules, and the bones of cattle that had died of thirst.

At 73.7 *m.* is a junction with a dirt road.

Left on this road to SULPHUR SPRINGS, 6 *m.*, the only water available to emigrant trains between Apache Pass and Dragoon Springs. It is now a watering place for livestock.

At 75.3 *m.*, just south of the point where the range opens into grassland, is the junction with a dirt road.

Right on this road to STRONGHOLD CANYON, now COCHISE MEMORIAL PARK (*shaded picnic grounds*), 8 *m.*, in the Dragoon Mountains (7,512 alt.). The canyon was the stronghold of the Apache chief Cochise, who for twelve years led his warriors in sanguinary raids on emigrant trains, coaches, ranches, and settlements,—a stronghold from which the white men never succeeded in routing him. Unlike many other Apaches, Cochise had not molested Americans until 1860, when he was accused of leading a raid on a ranch near his domain. This he denied, but he was taken into custody by a tactless army officer and told he was lying. Cochise escaped almost immediately. Until 1872, when he practically dictated the terms of his peace, he carried on a warfare of the bloodiest sort throughout the whole of southeastern Arizona. For more than ten years he kept the U. S. Army at bay, and yielded at last only through the mediation of the one white man he admired and trusted—Tom Jeffords, who operated a stage line over the old Butterfield route upon which the Apaches preyed. After twenty-two of his men had been killed in sixteen months, Jeffords rode alone to Cochise's hide-out. The Apache so respected Jeffords that a friendship developed, culminating with a ceremony making him a blood-brother. Jeffords' stages were never molested after that. When President Grant assigned General O. O. Howard to make peace with Cochise, Tom Jeffords persuaded the Indians to attend the parley.

During his conversation with General Howard, Cochise turned to his white blood-brother.

"Can this man's word be depended upon?" he asked.

"I don't know," Jeffords replied, "but I believe it can."

Cochise agreed to the terms of the treaty only upon the condition that Jeffords be made Indian Agent. Jeffords accepted the post though it meant great financial loss to him.

When Cochise died he was buried in his stronghold. On the night of his death his followers ran their horses up and down the canyon from dusk to dawn beating out every possible trace of the grave. Only one white man knew the exact burial place—Tom Jeffords—and he never revealed the secret during the forty years that he survived Cochise. Every year the Apache go into these mountains to gather beyotas (Sp., acorns), one of their favorite foods; but in Stronghold Canyon, though the acorns are plentiful, they remain unharvested. It is the spiritland of Cochise.

Across Sulphur Spring Valley from the stronghold is the old RANCH OF THE CHIRICAHUA CATTLE COMPANY (L). The fortress-like walls, parapets above the roof, and rack that once held old army 45-70 rifles, are eloquent evidence of the obstacles to cattle raising in the early days.

PEARCE, 75 *m.* (4,255 alt., 98 pop.), is almost a ghost town. Its rambling adobes whisper of old John Pearce, a rancher, who made a gold strike in 1894. During the next eight years the town grew into a fair-sized city and shipped out thirty million dollars in gold ore. When Pearce sold out for a quarter of a million he received only a fraction of his property's value, yet he is one of the few Arizona prospectors who realized a substantial sum from his find. After the peak of production had been reached in 1896, the mine was operated till 1904, when cave-ins necessitated a temporary shutdown. The following year a cyanide plant was erected and another fortune extracted from the tailings.

In the late nineties, while Pearce was still a rip-roaring cowboy-and mining-town, it became headquarters for the Alvord-Stiles gang (*see above*) and witnessed several killings. To frustrate the outlaws, bullion in the form of bars, which were too heavy to be carried away on horseback, was transported to the Cochise station in ordinary farm wagons.

Right from Pearce on a graveled road to COURTLAND, 9 *m.* (4,640 alt., 144 pop.), founded in 1909 and named for Courtland Young, a mine owner. This is a trading center in an area where copper and some gold are mined. Though low grade copper is found near GLEESON, 13 *m.*, also named for a miner, cattle raising is its main support.

SULPHUR SPRING VALLEY, 86.7 *m.*, once a rich game country, is now heavily stocked with cattle. Farming is made possible by pumping the water found a few feet below the surface and by utilizing floodlands.

ELFRIDA, 98 *m.* (200 pop.), is a fast growing community. During the past ten years the Valley has developed thousands of acres of raw land into rich productive soil, with cotton, chili, alfalfa, beans, and cattle the principal crops.

West of McNEAL, 104 *m.* (4,150 alt., 150 pop.), named for a judge who was one of its first settlers, are the Mule Mountains (*see TOUR 4b*).

South of McNeal is a mountain-lined horizon with the Pedregosa Mountains (L) rising in strange and fantastic outlines.

From the road at 117 *m.*, on clear days, the smoke from the Douglas smelters is seen pouring from the giant stacks in straight gray-green columns against the sky of blue. Again it hangs over the earth in great stormy-looking clouds that blot out the valley.

At 124 *m.* is the junction with US 80 (*see TOUR 4b*) on the western edge of DOUGLAS (*see Douglas*).

Tour 8

Springerville—Eagar—McNary Junction—Fort Apache—San Carlos—Coolidge Dam Junction; 139.3 *m.;* State 73 and San Carlos Indian Reservation Rd.

Graveled roadbed with many mountain curves; sometimes blocked by snows in winter or washes during heavy rains (July-Sept.) ; inquire locally.

Accommodations at McNary, Springerville; limited accommodations at White River, Fort Apache and San Carlos.

This route crosses the two Arizona Apache reservations. At some points it winds through juniper, manzanita, and pine; again, it crosses low hills covered by yucca, prickly pear, and creosote bush. Between Black River and San Carlos it approximates the trail followed by Father Marcos de Niza in 1539.

State 73 branches south from its junction in SPRINGERVILLE, 0 *m.,* with US 60 (*see TOUR 12*) and US 666 (*see TOUR 7*).

Between Springerville and the summit of the White Mountains (8,000 alt.), 10 *m.,* is a steady climb. In this region of natural parks where large numbers of sheep and cattle grow fat on lush green grass, the wooded peaks rising more than ten thousand feet above sea level seem little more than rolling hills.

State 73 crosses the boundary of APACHE NATIONAL FOREST at 12 *m.,* and the western boundary of the FORT APACHE INDIAN RESERVATION (2,781 pop.) at 35 *m.* The Apache in Arizona live on this and on the San Carlos Reservation, which adjoins it on the south. These two reservations (formerly called the White Mountain Reservation), covering more than five thousand square miles, contain forests, arable land, grazing land, and extensive mineral resources. This is one instance in which the Indians did not receive poor land. Three and a half million acres of the fine cattle land is at the service of the Indians to develop as one of the largest cattle ranches in the world.

The Apache were the bitterest enemies of the settlers who moved into the Southwest. But their treachery was a war measure to meet treachery, their theft of movable property the answer to the usurpation of their lands, and murder their reply to murder. It took the white man's utmost guile to subdue and confine them to a limited area. This reservation, in spite of its size, was unable to support so many people entirely dependent on hunting, and for more than a generation the tribe declined. After they began stocking their lands with cattle, the growth of their herds brought independence and an improvel morale; the bitterness of their suffering and defeat is being forgotten.

The Western Apache, those who were living in what is now Arizona when white men first entered the territory, had five divisions—White Mountain, Cibecue, San Carlos, Southern Tonto, and Northern Tonto —each of which regarded itself as a distinct social unit, possessing similar linguistic dialects and customs, but no specific political unity. These divisions were separated into bands living in a definite territory, and bands were composed of a number of local groups, the basic unit in Apache social organization. Each local group possessed its own chief —chosen from among the head men—who led it in war, and served as executive in relation with other groups. The head woman was a complementary office. Each local group consisted of from nine to thirty households, most of them members of one clan or related by marriage. Children were considered as belonging to the mother and a man always lived with his wife's family, and group. Unlike the large divisions and groups the clans were not based on geographical position and overlapped the other bases of organization. Since the government has intervened in the affairs of the Western Apache and established reservations (1871-73), the old distinction between groups has broken down, and power of the chief now resides in the Tribal Councils. But within the groups many of the old forms and functions are maintained and the head man is still a vital factor in local affairs.

In former times the Western Apache had four sources of food—wild animals, hunted by the men; wild plants, gathered by the women; small agricultural plots; and livestock and food plants obtained by raiding the settlements of the Mexicans to the south and the Navajo to the north. Families were kept moving during the hunting season, during the fruiting season of the saguaro, mescal, prickly pear and other important plants, and during the acorn harvest. Some of the old ways of living persist in the gathering of wild plants, the type of house built, and the organization and life of the family; but cattle raising has replaced hunting. Apache arts, limited by the mobility of their life, were confined mostly to making baskets and dressing buckskin. The Apache woven basket is outstanding; usually it has the shape and size of a generous wastebasket and is made of split willow or squawbrush, decorated with black dye from the martynia or devil's claw, and finished with fringe and thongs of buckskin. The *tus* or water jar is less finely woven; it has a narrow neck, a wide mouth, and is covered with pinon pitch until it is watertight.

Many years ago the Apache woman adopted a style of white woman's dress from which the appeals of social workers cannot budge her. Of eighteen yards of the brightest calico the trader has in stock, she makes a full skirt, probably with a flounce and several rows of ornamental braid. Her blouse is invariably a truncated Mother Hubbard hanging to the hips from a smooth yoke. Men wear blue jeans and bright cotton shirts; on special occasions they don boldly printed satin ones. The cowboy hat is standard headgear. Some Apaches still prefer a tepee or wickiup but live in houses more and more.

One of the most colorful of the Apache rituals is an all-night ceremony staged when a girl reaches puberty. The girl herself begins the rite with a dance. She is followed by devil dancers, four black-masked men in towering painted headdresses whose purpose is to discourage the power of evil. Their naked bodies above the short kilts of buckskin or plaid wool are elaborately painted; they wear high fringed moccasins and carry fantastic swords and eagle plumes. In their dance the devils employ every antic and contortion of which their bodies are capable, waving swords and uttering weird cries. The rite ends with the girl on her knees facing the morning sun, her body swaying with the beating of drums.

There have been missionaries, both Roman Catholic and Evangelical Lutheran, on the reservation since very early days, but the number of converts has been small, and the number of practicing Christians still smaller.

Logging operations are marked by great piles of cut timber along the roadside and by occasional camps. Timber is hauled by truck to the sawmill at McNary.

McNARY, 39 *m.* (7,200 alt., 2,000 pop.), is a company town completely dependent for its existence upon the large sawmill (*pass to inspect mill procured at employment office*). The town was founded in 1919 and named Cooley for Corydon E. Cooley, who won the ranch, now the town of Show Low, in a card game (*see TOUR 9*). The mill was purchased by James G. McNary, in August, 1935. At the same time he acquired the subsidiaries of the former owners, the Cady Lumber Company, including the Apache Railway Company, Standard Lumber Mills Incorporated and the Southwest Lumber Sales Corporation for a little more than eight hundred thousand dollars.

Except for one filling station, everything in town is owned by the company—commissary, pool hall, motion picture theater, and dwellings. Many Negroes have been imported from Louisiana to supplement the supply of unskilled labor, formerly Mexican.

In INDIAN PINE, 41.2 *m.*, the junction with state 173 (*see TOUR 9*), is a restaurant and garage.

WHITERIVER, 61 *m.* (5,000 alt., 1,500 pop.), is the agency and main trading center for the Fort Apache reservation.

At 65.1 *m.* is Fort Apache. Dirt road from here to San Carlos.

Left at this point to FORT APACHE, 1 *m.* (5,200 alt., 700 pop.), established in 1870 and once important in warfare against the Indians. In it is now a trading post, a government school, and a sanitarium for the treatment of trachoma among the Indians.

Right on the reservation road, now the main route, through rugged country where the rich red color of the mountains contrasts with the dark green junipers and bright blue sky. The highest point on the northwestern horizon is Kelly Butte. It is said to have been named for a white soldier who incurred the especial enmity of several Apaches; they pursued him to the top of the butte and killed him.

At 69.4 *m.* is the junction with a dirt road.

Right on this road across an undulating flat to KINISHBA RUIN, 2 *m.*, once called Fort Apache Ruin. It covers a great area and is made up of two large buildings separated by an arroyo, and six smaller structures scattered to the north. Part of the structures were apparently in two and possibly three stories. Some of the walls are eight feet high. It is estimated that the village was built in the period 1232-1320 A.D. It reveals three main cultures, those of the Salt River, the Central Gila, and the Little Colorado people. More than fourteen kinds of pottery have been found, including polished bowls and specimens with a glaze seldom found in prehistoric ruins. The larger part of the immense ruin is still untouched, although some of its more than seven hundred rooms have been reconstructed and two burial grounds uncovered.

Kinishba has become a training ground for students of archeology in the University of Arizona, which has done much of the excavation. The principal find in 1935 was an underground ceremonial chamber, one of the richest in artifacts ever opened; fine tools and ornaments, a cache of more than one thousand gypsum pendants, an abundance of shell jewelry, finely inlaid shell pendants, turquoise and coral are indications of Kinishba's wealth. An outstanding find in 1936 was an ancient lip plug of green soapstone; it is perforated, and apparently was worn in the lower lip as earrings are worn in ears. The walls of the ruins were made of stone plastered with adobe, irregular stone masonry, and coursed masonry of selected sandstone blocks carefully chinked with stone slivers.

Evidence of hasty abandonment hints at some long-ago tragedy. An Apache legend tells of an earthquake that destroyed the pueblo, and the drying up of an ancient spring in the arroyo between the two large unit houses possibly contributed to the abandonment. The best of the specimens from Kinishba Ruin are housed in the State Museum at the University of Arizona in Tucson.

At 74.5 *m.* is a junction with a dirt road.

Right on this road to CIBEQUE, 31 *m.* (*see TOUR 12*).

Beside the bridge over the BLACK RIVER, 90 *m.,* is a filling station. This river, which is the boundary between Fort Apache and the San Carlos reservations, contains more beaver than any other stream in Arizona. Conservationists place a higher value on the beaver's engineering ability than on their coveted fur. The Soil Conservation Service is enlisting the beavers' aid in flood and erosion control by moving them from the downstream areas—where they destroy fruit trees, flood crop lands, and block irrigation systems—and taking them to the headwaters. Here their dams check the force of the flow in flood times, catch silt, and store water that drains slowly into the larger rivers and is available for irrigation during dry seasons. In less than two years ten beavers transferred to a mountain stream built a dam storing five acre feet of water, which would have cost the government $2,500 to duplicate. The beavers will stay in the selected area providing it has an adequate supply of aspen, cottonwood, or willow trees—when there are too many beavers for the available food the entire colony migrates—and providing they are all from the same colony. Beavers from different ponds will not work together, neither will they fight—they just move.

Between Black River and San Carlos the road follows the trail made by Friar Marcos de Niza in 1539 in search of the mythical Seven Cities of Cibola.

BRONCO CANYON (L), 90.4 *m.,* is a wild region rich in game; because it is part of the Indian reservation it is not open to white hunters. Mountain lion, America's largest predator (*see TOUR 7b*), bear, deer, turkey, and smaller game abound.

Carl Larsen, called the Swede, often hunted in this area. While employed as a government hunter, he broke all existing state records by killing sixty-three mountain lions in sixteen months. Larsen occasionally took a lion alive. Two O. G. Rail cowpunchers who once went hunting with him told the following story:

"When we rode up the dogs had the lion treed in a juniper. Swede said it was a yearlin', it looked bigger than that to us but not bein' varmint hunters we took Swede's word for it—what's more we give him all the room he wanted when he decided to take it alive. But he roped and tied this fightin' thing without any more fuss than we'd make in tyin' a calf, an' to top it off he put the cat in a big gunny sack and tied it behind the saddle. Even the mule he was ridin' took it all as a matter of course.

"When we got to the ranch we went into the corn crib to watch Swede put a collar and chain on the varmint. But the lion had chawed the piggin string in two and he was plumb loose when Swede shook him out of the sack. That was when me and my pardner stampeded an' in our excitement we locked Swede in with the lion—even after Swede got a collar and chain on the varmint we was afraid to unlock the door. We knowed the lion was harmless enough but we wasn't so sure of the Swede."

The corrals of the Cross S Horse Camp (L) are at 103.8 m. The Cross S once ran thousands of head of cattle in this region. The horse pasture alone was said to be 25 miles around.

In 1910 Fred Kibbe and A. F. Hillpot were murdered there. After a chase that led into the northern part of the state, James Steel and William Stewart, two ex-cavalrymen, were captured by Sheriff Henry Thompson, famous old-time Arizona peace officer. Steel and Stewart were tried for the murders, convicted, and hanged in Globe.

The high point (6,000 alt.) on the road, at 104.4 m., called locally the Summit, offers a memorable view of the valley ahead where the road drops abruptly at the edge of the Natanes Plateau and winds down to Cassadore Mesa below. On the far horizon (L) are the Graham Mountains (10,750 alt.), Mt. Turnbull (7,970 alt.), straight ahead, and (R) Stanley Butte (6,520 alt.) ; all are landmarks of this region. On clear days yellow mesas, broken only by deep canyons that appear as blue and purple gashes, stretch away to the distant tumbled ranges. Under a summer sky, with thunderheads boiling up from the horizons and shadowing the yellow mesas with dark purple splotches, the distant peaks appear to hang from the sky. It is possible to see two or more rain storms 20 miles apart, and to sit in the bright sunlight and watch storm clouds blot out the valley and the lightning flash far below.

CASSADORE MESA, 112.3 m., is in the Cassadore Range, a particularly colorful mountain area that has excellent campgrounds with a year-round water supply. Cassadore Spring is near the highway. The area was named for a sub-chief of the San Carlos Apache tribe who lived with a small band in the Gila Valley. In 1873 citizens were so incensed by the murder of several white people near Cassadora's Camp that troops were sent for Cassadora and told to "take no prisoners."

"Cassadora and all his band, fearing death, immediately took to the hills. A troop of cavalry under Captain J. M. Hamilton found their trail" and as the Indians were all on foot quickly reached them. In the evening an Apache squaw came from Cassadora's camp and announced that the Indians would surrender. Though she had been told the troop's orders were to take no prisoners, the "next morning the entire band, holding their hands in the air as a token of peace, appeared outside Hamilton's camp. With Cassadora at their head the Indians asked for mercy. He told Hamilton 'We were afraid because some bad Indians had killed white men, so we ran away. That was wrong. We cannot fight for we have no arms or ammunition. Our food is gone; we are suffering from hunger; our moccasins are worn out, you can see our tracks on the rocks where our feet left blood. We do not want to die but if we must, we prefer to die by bullets from your soldiers' guns than from hunger. So we have come to your camp asking for peace.' Hamilton fed them and sent word to headquarters where the order to take no prisoners was promptly rescinded. Cassadora and his band surrendered to Hamilton on February 18, 1874, and were escorted by the troopers back to the homes they had left so suddenly."

Near the highway are the CORRALS (L), 116.8 m., a rock formation used by Indians and cowboys since early days.

The road crosses Seven Mile Wash, 124 m., which is likely to be suddenly flooded (*dangerous in rainy weather*).

The old Cross S Headquarters Ranch was about 12 miles up the wash. Fuel was never any problem at the ranch for it was simple to go out in a wagon after Seven Mile Wash "had come down" and get all that was needed.

Like many Arizona names, Seven Mile Wash is a misnomer. Old-timers and cowpunchers who have ridden to its head say that the distance is closer to 30 miles.

Both above and below Seven Mile Crossing and where the road skirts San Carlos River are farms and Apache houses and a few wickiups.

SAN CARLOS, 126.6 m. (2,635 alt., 2,800 pop.), founded as Rice, is the agency and main trading center for the San Carlos Indian Reservation (*Devil Dance, July Fourth*). When the old settlement of San Carlos was in danger of inundation from the San Carlos Reservoir, it was moved here, to the site of the Indian School. The new agency and school are handsome structures of a native tufa stone, and are surrounded by many acres of lawn and shaded roadways.

Gilson Wash, which the highway skirts at 133.4 m., was named for the old Gilson Ranch, a landmark of early days; today only a corral and a water tank mark the site.

At 139.3 m. is a junction with US 70 (*see TOUR 3α*) just north of Coolidge Dam.

Tour 9

Holbrook—Snowflake—Show Low—McNary Junction; 63 *m.,* State 77, State 173.

All paved, all-year highway throughout.
Good accommodations in towns.

The northern part of this route crosses a level plateau covered with sage, yucca, pinon, and juniper; in the White Mountains it traverses a dense forest of pine, fir, and aspen at an elevation of seventy-five hundred feet—a region of small lakes and mountain streams. The few towns along the route are typical Mormon settlements, surrounding a man-made body of water used to irrigate the fields.

State 77 branches south from its junction with US 66 in HOLBROOK, 0 *m.* (*see TOUR 2a*).

At 1 *m.* is the junction with US 260.

Left on US 260 to the PETRIFIED FOREST NATIONAL MONUMENT, 19 *m.* (*see TOUR 2a*).

Though the San Francisco Peaks (*see TOUR 2b*) are a hundred miles away, on clear days they are visible on the western horizon.

At 3.3 *m.* is the junction (R) with the Young-Heber Road (*see TOUR 10A*).

The barren stretches of country south of Holbrook change in color every hour of the day. Near Snowflake are many gnarled and twisted junipers.

SNOWFLAKE, 27 *m.* (5,600 alt., 1,200 pop.), with its scattered brick or false fronted business buildings and its two-story gabled houses of brick or frame, is a farming community, named for its founder, William J. Flake (who later bought the Show Low Ranch) and his friend, Erastus Snow. In the autumn of 1878 twelve families from the southern states arrived at Snowflake destitute after thirteen months on the road. They were housed in adobe stables on the place now known as Stinson's ranch (*see TOUR 10A*), and Flake cut up his wagon covers and tarpaulins as well as his grain bags to make clothing for them. Within a few years most of them moved to the warmer areas around the Gila.

Left from Snowflake on an unimproved dirt road to the SINKS, about 10 *m.,* a series of earth depressions in which rustlers formerly hid stolen cattle.

The Sinks vary in size from one 25 feet deep with a circumference no larger than an old-fashioned well, to others 900 feet in diameter and more than 200 feet deep. Water from the heaviest rains disappears in them almost immediately. Immense beds of rock salt lie beneath the depressions and water in most of the wells in towns near the Sinks is salty or brackish. One of the largest sinks contains a cave partly filled with ice that never melts. Another has excellent acoustic properties and is used as an amphitheater. A person speaking in an ordinary tone from the bottom can be distinctly heard anywhere on the rim. Trails have been built down its steep sides, and terraces cut for seats. The floor has a dense growth of grass. The Snowflake Union High School has held commencement exercises here for several years.

Through the section south of Snowflake are many sparkling little lakes used for watering stock and, in some instances, for irrigating. In autumn they usually are spotted with ducks (*hunting permitted during limited season; state license required; information at local store*).

TAYLOR, 31 *m.* (5,700 alt., 500 pop.), is a Mormon farming community established in 1881 on the site of a stage station and named for John Taylor, the English-born Mormon who was wounded in 1844 by the mob that killed Joseph Smith. Taylor translated the *Book of Mormon* into French, edited *The Mormon,* a church magazine, became president of the church in 1877, and for two years before his death was in hiding to avoid arrest for polygamy.

SHUMWAY, 36 *m.* (5,700 alt., 100 pop.), named for Charles Shumway, Mormon pioneer who settled here at an early date. A farming, dairying community.

Here State 77 crosses the northern boundary of SITGREAVES NATIONAL FOREST (for permission to hunt inquire Game and Fish Dept., Phoenix), that extends into Apache, Navajo, and Coconino Counties. The wild life includes elk, deer, turkey, bear, mountain lion, and many pronghorn antelope; all of which are protected by closed season.

Because of cultivated plots bordering each store and residence, SHOW LOW, 47 *m.* (6,500 alt., 1,000 pop.), in a clearing among the pines, looks more like a farming community than a town. It was at first, about 1875, C. E. Cooley's home where he lived with his wife, "Mollie," daughter of old Chief Pedro of the White Mountain Apache tribe. Cooley and Marion Clark made the settlement together. They decided later there was room for but one location, so they agreed to play a game of Seven-Up to decide which of them should move. When the last hand was dealt Cooley needed but one point to win. Clark ran his cards over and said: "If you can show low you win." Cooley threw down his hand and said, "Show low it is." The place has been called Show Low ever since. Clark later moved up the creek near the present town of Pinetop (*see below*) and located a ranch where he lived for many years. Later the ranch was sold to the Mormon Church and opened for settlement.

Of the many Indian ruins in this vicinity, the largest yet (1939) excavated is on the ranch of Edson Whipple in the center of town. Though there are no longer any artifacts here and a modern house has been built on the site, this ruin is important archeologically because a beam taken from one of its rooms was the basis of the first tree-ring dating of a prehistoric village. Apparently the village had been destroyed by fire, for charred willow corn cribs and ollas and bowls containing charred pinon nuts, beans, and squash seeds were found. The objects removed include turquoise beads, carved bear claws, and pottery of three distinct types—black-on-white (the oldest), a buff ware, and a red decorated in black and white (the most recent). This pueblo was built and occupied between 1174 and 1382 A.D., the late Pueblo III or early Pueblo IV period.

In Show Low is the junction with US 60 (*see TOUR 12*), and State 173, now the route.

LAKESIDE, 55 *m*. (7,000 alt., 550 pop.), named for three near-by lakes (*excellent rainbow-trout fishing*), is a Mormon settlement of sturdy houses and a few business buildings. It serves an agricultural area devoted chiefly to stock raising, though some vegetables, barley, and alfalfa are grown. One of the sources of the lakes, Adair Spring, has a flow of approximately a million gallons a day.

PINETOP, 59 *m*. (7,000 alt., 37 pop.), is another Mormon community surrounded by a sheep and cattle raising area. It was first settled in 1886. Like Lakeside it is a summer resort.

At 60 *m*. is a junction with a dirt road.

Left on this road 0.2 *m*. to the State's PINETOP FISH HATCHERY, supplying trout for the state fish farms at Williams Creek, Tonto Basin and Page Springs. The eggs are imported and then hatched, the fish being kept in the inside troughs until they are two inches long, then in outside troughs until they are about five inches. They are then moved to the pond before being planted in the streams and lakes. The water is kept moving in all the troughs, and from the time the fish are hatched, they always tend to swim upstream. The most important factor in controlling their growth is the temperature of the water, which is maintained at 53 degrees. Only three species of trout are raised here in this hatchery: eastern brook trout, the German brown, and rainbow trout which sometimes is more than 30 inches long. Though all of these species of trout are cannibals, the hatchery minimizes the loss from fish eating their neighbors by feeding them a diet of processed beef liver, horse meat, salmon eggs, and oatmeal.

State 173 crosses the northern boundary of the Apache reservation (*see TOUR 8*) at 62 *m*.

McNARY JUNCTION, 63 *m*., is the junction with State 73 (*see TOUR 8*).

Tour 10

Flagstaff Junction—Mormon Lake—Long Valley—Pine—Payson—Roosevelt Junction; 144 *m.*, Tonto Basin Rd.

Roadbed paved to Mormon Lake; rest graveled.   At times blocked by snow.
Limited accommodations at Lake Mary, Mormon Lake, Pine, and Payson.

This road through the cow-country settings of many western yarns passes sites of Indian battles, and a number of lakes that offer excellent fishing and duck hunting; the entire route is within national forests whose pine and brush shelter much wild life.   In addition to the pine, their timber includes oak and juniper, or madrono-mountain mahogany. In winter the hills are snowclad; in summer they are covered with succulent grasses, ferns, sumachs, and gorgeously colored flowers, including phlox, marguerite, chrysanthemum, verbena, goldenrod, columbine, and forget-me-not.

The Tonto Basin Road branches southeast from its junction with Alt. US 89, 0 *m.* (*see TOUR 2A*), at a point 2.4 miles south of Flagstaff.

Herds of pronghorn antelope roam about taking little notice of motorists and frequently approach the roadside (*see TOUR 2b*).

LAKE MARY, 7 *m.* (*camps, supplies, boating, fishing*), is an artificial lake formed in a ravine of the Mogollon highlands.   Originally the adjunct of a large sawmill, it was presented by its owners to Coconino County for a public recreational area.

MORMON LAKE, 26 *m.* (*limited accommodations; lake is sometimes dry; hunting; also guides and horses available*), is one of Arizona's most popular summer playgrounds.   Inns, lodges, and cabins line the forest edge along the shore for 10 miles.   There are numerous motor drives and sightseeing trails in the vicinity.

The lake bed was formerly grazing land for the cattle of a Mormon community, drained through underground channels.   By 1900 the drainage channels had become so filled with sediment that a lake began to form.   Though not deep, it has an area of twelve square miles and is apparently permanent.

At 33 *m.* is the junction with a graveled side road.

Right on this road to STONEMAN LAKE (*boating facilities, camps*), 5 *m.*, in the midst of a pine forest.   Formed in a two-hundred-foot depression between precipitous rock walls, this lake is half a mile in diameter and has no visible outlet.   The site, which is popular with summer vacationers, is named for General George Stoneman (1822-94) who, as a lieutenant, commanded the escort for Lieutenant John G. Parke's survey from San Diego, California, along the Gila to the San Pedro River in 1854.   At the outbreak of the Civil War, Stoneman, commanding Fort Brown, Texas, disobeyed orders to surrender to the Confederates and escaped with his troops by steamer to New

York. He served with distinction throughout the war, retired from the army in 1871, and was elected governor of California in 1883.

CLINT'S WELL, 54 m. is at a junction (L) with State 65.

LONG VALLEY, 58 m. is a narrow glen noted for its annual (Aug.) rodeos.

At 72 m. is a junction (L) with Mogollon Rim Road (see TOUR 10A).

A steep ascent leads to Mogollon Rim (9,998 alt.) at about 74 m., the northern boundary of TONTO NATIONAL FOREST, which has headquarters in Phoenix and includes the Sierra Ancha, Superstition and Mazatzal Mountains, the Tonto Basin and four reservoirs that control the flow of water into the Salt River Valley (see TOUR 3A).

STRAWBERRY, 74 m. is a junction with the Jerome Highway (R) a graveled road, which continues to the junction with Alt. US 89 (see TOUR 2A) at 54 m.

PINE (inns, free campgrounds), 78 m. (5,448 alt., 75 pop.), an isolated Mormon settlement on Pine Creek, was established in the 1870's by pioneers from Salt Lake City. Church authorities control all social, commercial, and industrial activities. Only five or six of the village's gable-roofed, frame houses are built near the general store, postoffice, and service station. The others are widely scattered and partly concealed by tall pine trees. Between the summer season when the cool climate attracts vacationers and the fall hunting season, the enterprising residents carefully irrigate their small but productive orchards and gardens and tend their herds that roam the woodlands. The town is surrounded by one of the state's favorite hunting grounds at the foot of the Mogollon Rim and October and November bring an army of sportsmen to the lowlands and hills near Pine to shoot bear, elk, deer, wild turkey, and quail. This is a cattle raising area.

At 83 m. is the junction with an unimproved dirt road.

Right on this road to TONTO NATURAL BRIDGE (adm. $1.00; hotel accommodations), 3 m. (4,660 alt.). This arch of travertine, rearing itself 183 feet above the stream and its tree-shaded canyon, is so vast that an orchard, a corn field, and vegetable and flower gardens grow on its five-acre top. Visitors seeking the bridge are often astonished to find they are on it. It contains about six billion cubic yards of travertine, so hard that no commercially practicable way of quarrying and shipping it has been devised. It spans, and at this point fills, Pine Creek Canyon—a vast stalactitic formation built up of lime deposited by springs that for countless years have been washing over the sides of the canyon. Hats, shoes, or other articles left in the creek become encrusted with travertine and appear to be made of stone. Beneath the arch a series of galleries, chambers, grottoes, and aisles that lead far into the mountains are reached by tall ladders. In this labyrinth of caves, which has never been entirely explored, evidences of aboriginal habitation are scattered among the myriads of glistening stalactites and stalagmites. A precipitous but safe trail leads from the top to the bed of Pine Creek below. Here the spring-fed waters sparkle over boulders and form little pools whose bright surfaces reflect the blue sky and green leaves of the trees that tower above them. About 1877 Dave Gowan, while seeking a refuge from pursuing Apaches, discovered this site and later homesteaded the property; it is still privately owned.

PAYSON, 95 *m.* (5,000 alt., 750 pop.), as real a cow town as when it was founded in 1886, preserves the true appearance of a frontier settlement. It has a few frame store buildings and a modern log hotel that caters to the needs of residents and visitors. But it has neither dude ranches nor dude cowboys.

Louis Edwin Payson, Representative from Illinois, never visited this town which bears his name. When John H. Hise, Surveyor-General of Arizona, platted the place he named it for the political patron responsible for his appointment. During Indian wars a fort was built for protection, and the village grew despite Apache depredations. For many troublesome years Payson served as a retreat for participants in the ranchmen's feuds.

Until a few years ago, annual rodeos which are now given in a rodeo ground (last wk. in Aug.), were held in the main street. Horse racing down this street has always been a favorite pastime. Dances, following true western traditions, last all night during the three-day rodeo celebration and, like the rodeo, are conducted with zest and spontaneity.

Payson has appeared in several motion pictures of cowboy life.

In RYE, 105 *m.,* and in the Rye Creek region is a scattered population that formerly constituted an important Gila County election precinct known as "Wild Rye." Everything below the Mogollon Rim was erroneously called Tonto Basin in the old days, though Tonto Basin proper includes only Tonto and Rye Creek.

This was a crossing point for expeditions of every sort—soldiers, bandits, feudists, and Indians. It was neutral territory and a refuge for belligerents of the Graham-Tewksbury feud (*see TOUR 10A*). John Gilleland, one of the first men wounded, rode 30 miles to Rye Creek, where a resident squeezed out the bullet after making an incision with a razor; Gilleland recovered.

Though this country and its quarrels between cattle and sheep men have furnished material for many writers, an eighty-four-year-old woman who had lived near Rye and whose husband had been a Tonto feudist found little glamour in the memory of those days. When, in 1937, he wished to buy a ranch and return here she remonstrated: "So help me!—you buy that place and I'll quit you! I'll go to Los Angeles after I law you out of my share of all the property I've helped you get. You, a great grand daddy, wantin' to go back to that pesticated country, even if the fight is over. I'm sick of such goings on and I can't forget how I used to get up at night and cook for them outlaws and go back to bed before you let 'em in, because you didn't want me to see who they were. . . ."

The feudists were not the only ones fighting in this area in the 1870's. The basin was made the objective of the campaign against the Apache (1872-73) by General Crook, who had the commanders of the various forts, camps, and posts near here lead their forces into

Tonto Basin and radiate from it in a thorough search for hostile Indians hiding in the surrounding canyons or mountains.

Between Rye and Roosevelt Lake the western horizon is formed by the MAZATZAL MOUNTAINS (8,065 alt)., which were the scene of several skirmishes during Crook's campaign. After having left Camp McDowell in December, 1872, Captain James Burns's command had scoured these mountains, killing several Apaches before joining Major William H. Brown's forces for their concerted attack on the Salt River Canyon cave (*see TOUR 3A*).

FOUR PEAKS, a group of rocky heights in the southern part of the Mazatzals, appear almost due south of Rye. These peaks are said to have ended the migration from Mexico of an Indian tribe that considered "four" a sacred number, meaning finality, completeness, and the end of life. When the Indians reached the Salt River Valley, they gazed in awe on these four equally high peaks, which, they decided, must mark the edge of the world.

TONTO BASIN, 127 *m.* (2,750 alt., 80 pop.), often called Pumpkin Center, is also known as Packard's in honor of a pioneer family whose members maintained a store here for several years. The post office, schoolhouse, and ranger station of the Tonto National Forest form the nucleus of the present settlement. It is in the center of the Tonto Creek area, a triangle of wild and striking beauty, three thousand feet below the Mogollon Rim, the Mazatzal Mountains, and the Sierra Ancha. Small fields of strawberries, potatoes, and peaches in the basin are irrigated from Tonto Creek, which flows down rugged ravines into Roosevelt Lake. In these farm lands are pine, walnut, and oak trees, mescal, and Spanish bayonet.

Tonto Basin is excellent grazing country for both cattle and sheep; the latter thrive on pine grass and the alfilaria, a European weed sometimes called wild clover. Agriculturists believe alfilaria was introduced to the southwestern United States from the Mediterranean by seeds that clung to the wool of the merino sheep brought over by the Spaniards.

Deer, bear, and mountain lion are hunted in the surrounding mountains.

From the floor of the basin south of town the upper reaches of ROOSEVELT LAKE (*see TOUR 3A*) are visible with the thousands of pelicans that make these waters their feeding grounds. During dry seasons the exposed parts of the lake bottom provide excellent grazing.

The SIEBER MONUMENT (L), 143 *m.,* of local stone, on Sieber Mountain, honors Al Sieber, one of Arizona's greatest scouts. He was powerfully built, more than six feet tall, and weighed about 190 pounds; he was resolute, courageous, and clever, as well as capable of enduring greater privations than the strongest Indians; they called him "Man of Iron." Born in Germany, Sieber spent his boyhood in Pennsylvania, and was wounded in the Battle of Gettysburg. After the Civil War he came to Arizona (1868), and for twenty years (1871-1891) served as chief of scouts at San Carlos under Generals Crook, Howard, and

Miles. He commanded the Apache Kid, Tom Horn, and Talkalai; several times he trailed Geronimo into Mexico, and invariably he was called upon when some difficult work had to be done. Using both firmness and justice, he controlled bands of Apaches planning mutiny when no one else could do so. Nevertheless both Sieber and Talkalai, for a long period in their old age, had no thanks, no pay, and little recognition. But when the Roosevelt Dam was begun Apaches, employed to do much of the road work, were directed by Al Sieber. In 1907, during this construction a rocky point was blasted leaving a huge boulder precariously balanced on a small stone. The old scout, who during the frontier warfare had not hesitated to shoot Indians, realized the danger and saved his Apache helpers by himself knocking out the supporting stone. But his lame leg, twice cracked by rifle balls, hindered his retreat and he was killed by the plunging rock. The monument, erected with contributions from Sieber's Apache laborers, marks the exact spot where the boulder crushed him.

From this point Roosevelt Lake and Dam are visible (*see TOUR 3A*).

At 144 *m.* is the junction with State 88 (*see TOUR 3A*) at a point 0.6 miles west of Roosevelt.

Tour 10A

Junction with Tonto Basin Rd.—Young—Junction with State 88; 136.1 *m.*, Mogollon Rim Rd., Young-Holbrook Rd., and Salt River Pleasant Valley Rd.

Graveled and improved-dirt roadbed; dangerous after rains; occasionally blocked by snow in winter; sharp curves.
Limited accommodations at Young and at hunting lodges from April to November.

This route crosses rugged and heavily wooded mountains that abound with wild life, and range in altitude from 3,500 to 8,000 feet. For many years they were inhabited by the Apache who sought refuge here when pursued by U. S. troops. In its course along the Mogollon Rim and through Pleasant Valley, the road passes many scenes described by Zane Grey, Dane Coolidge, and Earl Forrest, for this is the setting of the Graham-Tewksbury feud, known as the Pleasant Valley War and often dramatized in western fiction. Many of the streams, peaks, and canyons are named for people whose exploits are recorded in tales of the range country. Some of them still live in this area and may greet the traveler who pauses for information at a wayside ranch house.

All details of this war are controversial. A popularly accepted but unproved version is that the Tewksburys and Grahams had already quarreled over cattle stolen from James Stinson, their employer, when the Tewksburys gave protection to a band of sheep driven over the Mogollon Rim in 1887 by the Daggs brothers. The arrival of sheep caused settlers who had previously taken no part in the Tewksbury-Graham quarrel to unite in defending their range against the "woolies." Defiant cattlemen killed a Navajo sheepherder and drove out or destroyed the sheep. The Tewksburys retaliated, and the struggle became a five-year bushwhacking feud that was responsible for nineteen known deaths and was credited with many more. Attempts by representatives of law and order to end hostilities were futile. Every man who remained in the valley was eventually drawn into this conflict in which no quarter was asked or given. An enemy was hunted like a wild animal and death was the penalty for an unguarded moment. The feud ended in 1892 when Tom, last of the Grahams, was killed in Tempe, where he had moved from the valley. Although Tom Graham swore before he died that the men who ambushed him were Ed Tewksbury and John Rhodes, and witnesses later identified the two men in court when they were tried for murder, Rhodes and Tewksbury finally went free.

The men who took part in the feud are almost as much of a mystery as the cause of the trouble. During pioneer days in the cattle country no one asked who a man was or whence he came and the few people yet living who knew the feudists are still reluctant to talk. Earl Forrest, who has written a book on this affair, says that John Tewksbury, Sr., was born in Boston and sailed around the Horn to California about 1850. He appeared in Globe about 1880 with three grown, half-breed sons, John, James, and Edwin, all expert marksmen. Jim is even described as being able to shoot backwards; it is said that when warned of danger he put his gun over his shoulder and killed his enemy without turning around. In Globe the elder Tewksbury married a widow and moved to Pleasant Valley.

The Grahams, who came to Pleasant Valley in 1882, were from Iowa. Tom, the oldest of three brothers, all of whom were killed in the feud, was the leader of their faction though he is said to have had a restraining influence on his followers until his youngest brother, Billy, was killed. Andy Cooper, the alias used by one of the five Blevins boys, who was said to be wanted in Texas for murder, is credited by some authors with responsibility for most of the ruthlessness among the Graham faction in the early part of the feud. Andy, described as the leader of the Pleasant Valley cattle rustlers, and his brother, Sam Houston Blevins, were both killed in Holbrook in a gun fight with Sheriff Owens, who had attempted to arrest Andy for stealing horses (*see TOUR 2a*).

During the feud, the father of the Blevins boys disappeared, Charles and Hampton Blevins were killed in the valley, and John, wounded by Sheriff Owens, served a penitentiary sentence for his part in the Holbrook battle.

Within the Tonto National Forest the Mogollon Rim Road branches east from its junction with the Tonto Basin Road, 0 *m.* (*see TOUR 10*), at a point 7.2 miles south of Long Valley.

At 2.5 *m.* is a junction with a dirt road.

Right on this road 0.3 *m.* to BAKER'S BUTTE (8,282 alt.). The view from this point includes part of the Painted Desert beyond an immense expanse of yellow pine.

At 14.1 *m.* on the Mogollon Rim Road is a junction with a dirt road marked by a stone monument with a bronze plate.

Left on this to General Spring and the PINCHOT RANGER STATION, 0.1 *m.* The road continues through a parklike forest, with trees so evenly spaced as to resemble an artificial landscape, to a cattle corral, 6 *m.;* L. here to the SITE OF THE BATTLE OF THE BIG DRY WASH, 7 *m.* On July 17, 1882 more than fifty Indians on the San Carlos reservation killed Captain J. L. "Cibicue Charlie" Colvig, the chief of scouts, and escaped, murdering settlers, burning, ranches, stealing livestock, and loading themselves with plunder on their flight. Troops from both the Sixth Cavalry under Captain Adna Romanza Chaffee and from the Third Cavalry started in pursuit. A shrewd campaigner, Chaffee brought extra mounts, but soon the trail through Tonto Basin and over the rough mountainous country along the Mogollon Rim was lined with worn-out horses. The fugitives, warned of the soldiers' approach by Indian smoke-signals, gathered boulders at the crest of a thousand-foot precipice above a tributary of East Clear Creek (known as Chevalon's Fork but described in army reports as Big Dry Wash) where the troops were expected to pass. But scouts under Al Sieber discovered the trap and the troops were halted on the edge of the canyon. Chaffee, given command by his senior officer, Major Andrew Wallace Evans, detailed troops to cross the ravine to the east and the west and surround the Indians while those stationed opposite them kept up a fire to hold their attention. After several hours of fighting in which most of the Indians had been shot from their cliff nests and their bodies hurled into the canyon, the daylight faded and the darkness permitted a few of the Indians to escape.

The tunnel (L), 21.5 *m.,* 20 feet long, was begun about 1890 by the Arizona Mineral Belt Railroad to connect the mining district of Globe with the vast timber reserves of northern Arizona. The project collapsed after seven years of struggle by its promoters.

At 54.2 *m.* is the junction with the Young-Holbrook Rd. Right on this, now the main route. The gradual descent from the Mogollon Rim into Pleasant Valley affords many views of serried purple ranges glimpsed through pines and aspens. Herds of fifteen or twenty elk and five or ten deer often browse in these forests within sight of the road. The valley itself is a peaceful place. In the early morning and evening, when a purple haze softens the wild beauty of this secluded glen and of the rugged mountains that enclose it, its turbulent history seems incredible. Today the old ranges are fenced, but cattle still graze on the hillsides, as they did when this was the scene of the Graham-Tewksbury feud.

At 57.7 *m.* on the Young-Holbrook Road, is the junction with the dirt O W ranch road.

Left on this to the O W RANCH, 5 m., the former home of the Blevins family of Pleasant Valley War fame. It was on the Blevins range at a point about 5 miles northeast of the ranch house that the triple lynching of James W. Stott, Billy Wilson, and Jim Scott occurred. During the summer of 1888 horse stealing became so flagrant that livestock owners formed a vigilance committee and rode onto the Rim, bent on stern measures. Stott, a youth of 26, was possessed of ample means and had come west to settle. It is said that he was a hospitable youth and a poor judge of character. He ignored the warning that his associates were known criminals. That the hanging was a mistake was generally believed at the time by a shocked public, and members of the lynching party reluctantly admitted the mistake in later years. One story that has endured through the years is that the party first executed Wilson and Scott, forcing Stott to witness the proceeding as an object lesson. Then it dawned upon them that Stott, as a witness, might endanger their own lives. On the theory that "dead men tell no tales," he was hanged to the same tree.

BOTTLE SPRING, 67.6 m., on the Young-Holbrook Road, is a camp patronized by sportsmen during hunting season.

Left from Bottle Spring on the Q-Ranch Road to the Q-RANCH gate, 7.1 m. From 20.1 m. are visible the headquarters of this ranch, once the home of Helen Duett Ellison, who married George W. P. Hunt, Arizona's first state governor.

On the former WILSON RANCH (R), 23.1 m., on the Q-Ranch road, Hampton Blevins and John Paine were killed, in August, 1887, during one of the earliest battles of the feud. The site of the house is marked by a rock chimney and fireplace; the house was mysteriously burned a few hours after the shooting. Behind the chimney are two piles of stones, marking the shallow graves of Blevins and Paine.

Details of this killing are as disputed as those surrounding other feud fatalities. One version is that Old Man Blevins, father of the five sons, had been missing more than a week when Hampton Blevins set out to look for him. Hampton was accompanied by several Hashknife (see TOUR 2a) cowboys, including John Paine, who was noted as a fighter and had been brought here from Texas to keep out the sheep. The cowboys stopped at Wilson's ranch and asked for supper. Contrary to the usual hospitality of the cow country they were refused by Jim Tewksbury, who answered their inquiry; as they turned to leave, they were stopped by a volley of shots that killed two of them and wounded three others.

The Tewksburys claimed that the cattlemen had served notice on several settlers to leave the valley and that the men had gathered in Wilson's house to resist eviction. When the cowboys rode up and ordered them to depart, Hampton Blevins started the shooting that resulted in the two deaths.

At 73.5 m. on the Young-Holbrook Road is a junction with a dirt road.

Right 1.1 m. on this to a circle of stones that marks the GRAVE OF THE SHEEPHERDER (L), killed while guarding the Daggs sheep, after they had crossed the Mogollon Rim (see above).

At 77 m. on the Young-Holbrook Road is the junction with the Cherry Creek Road.

Left on this road to the YOUNG COMMUNITY DANCE HALL (L), 0.1 m., built on the site of the old Stinson corral, where John Gilleland, Stinson's ranch foreman, was shot by Ed Tewksbury after Gilleland had accused him of stealing some of Stinson's saddlehorses. At the community hall is a junction with another graded dirt road.

Right 0.2 m. on this to the old AL ROSE CABIN, on the ZT Ranch. The cabin, built of large adz-hewn logs with grooved corner settings, contains two large rooms separated by a court and fronted with an ample porch having log railings. Though the roof and floor are in a state of disrepair, the walls are still very substantial. A huge fireplace and well-constructed rock chimney are in the north end of the structure. The Rose ranch harbored many members of the Graham faction during the feud and much of their strategy was planned here. Rose's acknowledged leadership rendered him second only to Tom Graham as an object of hatred by the Tewksburys.

The site of the ELDER TEWKSBURY RANCH is (L) at 2.2 m. on the Cherry Creek Road (*impassable in bad weather*). The only remnant of the buildings is a rock chimney. Left across a field, about 0.2 m. from this chimney, on a little knoll, marked by a wild walnut tree and a piece of white timber, is the GRAVE OF THE ELDER TEWKSBURY, who survived the feud and died on his ranch in the 1890's.

At 2.4 m. on the Cherry Creek Road is a junction with the McKinney Ranch Road; R. 1 m. on this over sloping grass-covered hills to the TEWKSBURY CABIN on the McKinney Ranch. This cabin, built by the father of the Tewksbury boys, was moved by Mr. McKinney to its present site. Near loopholes, the massive log walls are bespattered with bullet holes and on the flooring boards, now a part of the ceiling, is a large black splotch where the wood was soaked with blood.

At 5.8 m. on the Cherry Creek Road is the site of the LOWER TEWKSBURY RANCH where John Tewksbury and Bill Jacobs were killed in a fight with the Grahams. During the battle Mrs. John Tewksbury, ignoring enemy guns, walked from the house and covered the bodies of the slain men to protect them from rooting hogs. The Grahams ceased firing temporarily as a gesture to the bravery of the slain man's wife.

On the Young-Holbrook Road at 77.1 m. is the site of the STINSON RANCH, for years a noted landmark but now gone. James Stinson, one of the first Pleasant Valley settlers, is said to have offered a reward for the head of any man caught driving sheep over the Mogollon Rim. Before 1877 he hired the Grahams and Tewksburys to work for him. After he had left the valley, Stinson gave his explanation of the feud, "My cattle began disappearing and pretty soon the Grahams and the Tewksburys were fighting over them."

The YOUNG CEMETERY (R), 77.2 m., on the Young-Holbrook Road, is a barren plot that contains the marked graves of five members of the Graham faction killed in the feud. Harry Middleton, ambushed by the Tewksbury forces, was buried in a coffin built from old packing boxes found at the Perkins Store, a more pretentious interment than that given most of the vendetta victims. When Al Rose, one of the principal Graham fighters, was killed from ambush near the Houdon ranch, members of the Graham faction lashed his body across his saddlehorse with his lariat and rode toward the cemetery. In this same row are the graves of Charles Blevins and William and John Graham.

Far from heavily traveled highways and miles from a railroad, in the quiet of Pleasant Valley, is YOUNG, 77.6 m. (5,070 alt., 367 pop.), a few frame buildings scattered along a country road and up sloping grass-covered hills. It is named for William Young, who acquired the Graham ranch and herd under a business arrangement with Tom Graham when the latter moved to Salt River Valley. The steadying influence of the Youngs developed a new atmosphere.

Right from Young on a dirt road to the old GRAHAM CABIN, 0.4 *m.*, on the Young Ranch. This one-room structure pierced with loopholes was built like a fort for protection from Indian assaults. During feud days it was a stronghold for the Graham faction. William Graham died here on a pallet to which he was brought by Joe Ellenwood, who had found him wounded on the trail. Shortly afterward Ellenwood himself lay in the same corner with a leg shattered in a fight with the Tewksburys. Later this cabin, which is now sagging and in need of repair, was used as Young's first schoolhouse.

South of Young the route is the Salt River-Pleasant Valley Road.

It was from the old PERKINS STORE and ROCK HOUSE, 79.2 *m.*, that Sheriff Mulvenon together with his men killed John Graham and Charles Blevins. The rocks of this long, one-story, flat-roofed structure are set in adobe and its sides are pierced with loopholes—openings cut with gun-swing angles so that they are about five inches square on the outside but much larger inside to permit a wider range in shooting. When the sheriff and his Yavapai County posse entered the valley to establish order, he was joined by an Apache County posse under Joe McKinney, the Winslow constable, who had been trailing train bandits. They held warrants for most of the belligerents, and together worked out a plan to lure some of the feudists into a trap. They went to Perkins' store before dawn and part of the posse boldly rode through the valley in broad day on a circling expedition intended to attract attention, while Mulvenon, McKinney, and others remained hidden behind the then partly constructed walls of the Rock House. After the decoys had disappeared in the hills, Graham and Blevins warily rode from the Graham ranch to investigate; they circled the store at a distance, and finally approached. Mulvenon stepped out and commanded them to throw up their hands. Both men reached for their guns and were killed.

Between Pleasant Valley and the summit at McFadden Hill, 81.2 *m.* (5,000 alt.), the road winds through scrub oak and pines up the northeastern slope of the Sierra Ancha, which extends for 75 miles across the northeastern part of Gila County, sweeping upward from the mountainous desert floor to the south. In these mountains are many summer cottages and resorts that cater to summer visitors and offer accommodations to sportsmen who come here to hunt elk, bear, lion, deer, turkey, and smaller game in season.

AZTEC LODGE, 86.9 *m.*, situated among pines by Workman Creek, is a group of log cabins around a dining hall.

The U.S. Forest Service's PARKER CREEK EXPERIMENTAL STATION, 92.4 *m.*, in a setting of white oak and juniper, conducts experiments in forestry and watershed management; the many separate studies made in the Sierra Ancha include observations of stream-flow and silt movement.

South of INDIAN SPRINGS, 92.5 *m.*, which consists of a general store and gas station, the road drops to Black Mesa in the Salt River basin, which has a profusion of desert flora—palo verde, jojobas, saguaro, creosote, and cholla.

At 106 *m*. is a junction with an unimproved road.

Left on this road to the head of Cherry Creek and some INDIAN CLIFF DWELLINGS, 8 *m*., built between 1348 and 1385 by the Salado (Salt River) branch of the modern Zuni. They migrated south from the Mogollon plateau in the fourteenth century and built, in addition to these houses, the Tonto Cliff Dwellings (*see TOUR 3A*) and the Casa Grande (*see TOUR 4C*). Because of their inaccessibility these cliff dwellings have not suffered from vandalism.

At 136.1 *m*. is a junction with State 88 (*see TOUR 3A*) at a point 15 miles west of Claypool.

<hr>

Tour 11

Phoenix—Cashion—Buckeye—Gila Bend Junction; 74.8 *m*., US 80.

All-paved, all-year highway; heavy trucks, vans, auto traffic.
Good accommodations all along route.

US 80 between Phoenix and the junction with State 84, crosses the lower Salt River Valley agricultural area, and part of the Gila Valley. Along this route irrigation is pushing the desert farther back each year, and in its place small farmhouses arise, surrounded by deep, brown furrows or the green of alfalfa, melons, lettuce, cotton, and grains.

US 80 follows Van Buren Street west from its junction with US 70, 0 *m*. (*see TOUR 3b*), in PHOENIX (*see Phoenix*).

The steam-electric plant (R), 3.9 *m*., supplies auxiliary power to the city of Phoenix whenever the electricity generated at Roosevelt Dam is insufficient.

In winter the fields of alfalfa, vegetables, and cotton that line the highway are used as pastures for great numbers of sheep brought down from higher elevations.

CASHION, 12.7 *m*. (991 alt., 500 pop.), consists of a store, garage, service station, and cabins, in a farming and cattle raising area.

The usually dry bed of the AGUA FRIA (Sp., cold water) RIVER, 14.6 *m*., marks the eastern boundary of the Roosevelt Irrigation District, a strip 3 miles wide that extends west to the Hassayampa River. The Agua Fria's water is diverted by the Carl Pleasant dam into Lake Pleasant, leaving this a dry crossing, except during the rainy seasons. Forests of cottonwoods cover the Agua Fria's flood plain.

At 16.5 *m*. is a junction with a paved road.

Right on this road to LITCHFIELD PARK, 5 *m.* (975 alt., 1,100 pop.), a company town built by the Southwest Cotton Company, a subsidiary of the Goodyear Tire and Rubber Company. The little village has pretty homes on paved streets lined with palm and pepper trees, a shopping center, schools, a nine-hole golf course, tennis courts and a swimming pool. The HOME OF PAUL W. LITCHFIELD, president of the Goodyear Company, is a ranch house of Spanish design built with three large guest houses on La Loma hill. Litchfield spent twenty-five thousand dollars trucking soil to the top of a bald, rocky knob in order to transform it into a garden of native and exotic plants. The WIGWAM INN, a group of about fifteen pueblo-type yellow plastered adobes, is noted as a winter resort. The company plantation at Litchfield includes two hundred acres of citrus fruit trees, two thousand acres of alfalfa, and five thousand acres of long-fibered American-Egyptian cotton used in the manufacture of automobile tires. The plantation serves as a proving ground for tires and other products of the Goodyear company as a well as for plows, tractors, and other farm machines made by the International Harvester Company. American-Egyptian cotton has been developed by the U.S. Department of Agriculture through years of research and selection. After the boll weevil had destroyed the soft bolls of the long-fibered sea island cotton, and with them the prosperity of Georgia's and South Carolina's coastal plantations, American growers turned to the more resistant short-fibered types, and American manufacturers depended for fine texture and long fibers on cotton imported from Egypt. In 1903 the Department of Agriculture planted several varieties of Egyptian cotton in the Salt River Valley of Arizona where conditions are similar to those of the Nile Valley. In five years descendants of the Mit Affi produced a desirable type called Yuma, which in turn produced the Pima, a plant with finer, lighter colored, and longer fibers. By 1918 ninety-two thousand bales of Pima were grown in Arizona. The latest type developed by the department (SXP30) is a cross between Pima and Sakellaridis, seems to have as much silkiness as any cotton native to the Nile, and thrives in Arizona.

LUKE AIR FORCE BASE, 7 *m.,* advanced fighter training base, where pilots are thoroughly trained in gunnery, skip-bombing and rocket firing. Constructed in 1941, it became the largest advanced training center for fighter pilots. Named for Frank Luke Jr., of Phoenix, famous World War I pilot and "balloon buster," who was killed in France in 1918. Luke Air Base is one of the great air bases in the Phoenix area. The other is Williams Air Force Base; and there is in this area, also the Naval Air Force Facility.

In Buckeye Valley, one of the state's richest agricultural belts, is BUCKEYE, 32 *m.* (960 alt., 2,000 pop.), noted for its lettuce, its lint cotton, and its annual celebration of "Helzapoppin" (Nov. 3rd week), a name borrowed by the 1938 Broadway show. "Helzapoppin," which drew thirty thousand visitors in its fourth year, was originated in 1935 to raise money for stranded families of migratory lettuce packers and cotton pickers. This celebration was abandoned during the war. Buckeye is in a farming and cattle-raising area and in the winter season, thousands of sheep are brought down from the high country to graze.

PALO VERDE (Sp. green wood), 38 *m.* (900 alt., 500 pop.), consists of a store, school, and service station.

The waters of the HASSAYAMPA RIVER, 40.7 *m.,* are said to affect the truthfulness of those who drink them.

Just west of the river is a junction with a dirt road.

Right on this road to TONOPAH HOT WELLS, 22 *m.* (1,200 alt., 50 pop.), in a mountainous desert valley. This embryonic health resort has two small hotels for guests attracted by the hot mineral baths. It serves also as the post office and trading point for a large desert area that has been home-steaded since 1929.

WOOLSEY PEAK (3,199 alt.) in the Gila Bend Mountains to the southwest was named for King S. Woolsey, Indian fighter, miner, rancher, and legislator.

POWERS BUTTE, 42 *m.,* a short distance (L) from the highway, is the site of a prehistoric fortress, of a type uncommon in the Gila River basin. Several of the levels are protected by walls and boulders; the crest of the butte, which is 150 feet long, is enclosed by a masonry wall except for a gap on the south side where the cliff is so abrupt that it is inaccessible.

ARLINGTON, 43.6 *m.* (800 alt., 300 pop.), surrounded by green fields of cotton, alfalfa, and barley, has a service station, garage, general store, and pool hall. The black rocks along the roadside in this area are of volcanic origin.

Left 2 *m.* from Arlington on a dirt road along the river to some of the best preserved INDIAN PICTOGLYPHS in the state. These undeciphered designs and representations of men and animals are believed to have been scratched on the rocks by the Hohokam (*see TOUR 4C*) between 1100 and 1400 A.D.

At 49.1 *m.* on US 80 is the junction with an improved dirt road.

Right on this road to AGUA CALIENTE (Sp., hot water) SPRINGS, 41 *m.,* visited by Father Kino, the Jesuit missionary, in 1699, and owned for several years by King Woolsey (*see TOUR 1A*). The spot is now a health resort equipped with tubs for those who wish to bathe in the water.

South of the junction typical Arizona mesquite thickets, palo verde trees, ironwoods, and cacti are on both sides of the highway. The cliff (R) is the remains of an ancient lava flow. Desert mountains in this section have caused the Gila River to swing southward in what is known as the Big Bend. Near the river the view is restricted by jagged purple hills.

US 80 crosses a bridge over the GILA RIVER, 52 *m.,* at the old ford where early stagecoaches made their dangerous crossing, threatened by both Indians and flood waters. On one occasion two nuns, a gambler, and a soldier hung on the outside and upstream side of the coach in order to counterbalance the flood current. As the story goes, this stratagem, plus the driver's goading of his struggling horses, the nuns' praying, the gambler's cursing, and the soldier's shouted encouragement, brought the coach safely to the opposite shore.

GILLESPIE DAM (L), 52 *m.,* was built to replace the old wood and rock dam that was washed away by a flood in 1900. Ranchers down the river built barns and houses of timbers salvaged from the old dam. Like many of the hills in this area the one (L) near the dam is dotted with picture rocks. Just north of the dam a bandit was killed. Gribble, the superintendent of the Vulture Mine (*see TOUR*

3), accompanied by a mounted guard and a driver, had left the assay office at the mine 55 miles north of here with forty pounds of gold bullion. He was half way to Phoenix when three Mexicans waylaid him, killed him and his two men, shot one horse, and stole the other two horses and the gold. A posse followed the trail to the site of the present bridge and dam, where they overtook the Mexicans, and killed one of them who was identified as Innocente Valenzuela and was wearing Gribble's watch. The other two bandits escaped into Mexico and were never captured but the bullion was found wrapped in a blanket near this site.

At 70 *m.* is the junction with an unimproved road.

Right on this road in the Gila Bend Mountains, to an early INDIAN FORTRESS, 3 *m.* Old trails lead throughout the village. Its forty houses range in size from one 9 feet wide and 19 feet long to one 12 feet wide and 20 feet long; the walls are thick, some measuring 30 inches, and the outer walls are chinked with spalls. When the defense wall, which is in two sections each more than a hundred feet long, was built there were no houses on the downhill side. But as the population increased, either by birth or the admission of other clans, houses were constructed beyond the enclosure. The almost total lack of arrow heads indicates that these people were chiefly agriculturists, and their potsherds place them in the late prehistoric period. On one of the boulders an ancient artist with a sharp stone has drawn a lizard, a scroll, and other designs now almost obliterated.

At 74.8 *m.* is the junction with State 84 (*see TOUR 4d*) at the eastern edge of Gila Bend.

Tour 12

(Quemado, N. M.)—Springerville—Show Low—Carrizo—Globe Junction; US 60. New Mexico Line to Junction with US 70, 137.9 *m.*

All-paved, all-year highway; many mountain curves. Good accommodations in larger towns.

The northeastern part of this route, which cuts through both Apache reservations and keeps almost entirely within the Apache, Sitgreaves, and Tonto national forests, is in an area dense with pine and juniper. South of Black River Canyon, where it winds to the bottom of the gorge, the highway crosses high juniper mesas and rolling hills covered with prickly pear, yucca and greasewood.

US 60 crosses the New Mexico Line, 0 *m.*, at a point 36 miles west of Quemado, N. M., and traverses a rolling country covered with grama, on which thousands of range cattle and sheep forage. The rounded foothills of the White Mountains (L) are covered with heavy stands of pine, aspen, juniper, manzanita and oak; the plateau (R) extends northward to the horizon and landmarks 50 miles away are often visible; only an occasional crimson, purple, or yellow mesa rising above the flat surface shortens the view.

In SPRINGERVILLE, 15.1 *m.* (6,856 alt., 700 pop.) (*see TOUR 7a*), is the junction with north-south highways, US 666, and US 260 (*see TOUR 7a*). West of this junction is rolling country with many volcanic hills whose rough malapai surfaces are covered with yellow wire grass. Between this point and Show Low are occasional ranch houses half-hidden among the hills; cattle bunched under the shade of juniper trees or grazing on the slopes; a few isolated windmills; and thin wisps of smoke climbing above the pine from small lumber mills.

At 19.9 *m.* is the northwestern junction with US 666 (*see TOUR 7a*).

South of SHOW LOW, 61.6 *m.* (6,500 alt., 450 pop.) (*see TOUR 9*), which is at the junction with State 77 (*see TOUR 9*), towering pines border the road in dense stands to CARRIZO CREEK, 65.8 *m.* The highway parallels the creek in its zigzag course through a narrow red-walled gorge to CARRIZO, 84 *m.* (5,222 alt., 10 pop.), which consists of a general store and tourist camp amid pine- and juniper-covered hills. In the APACHE FARMING COMMUNITY (R) are several wickiups in which the Indians live while tending their fields of corn, squash and grass.

At 88 *m.* is the junction with an unimproved dirt road.

1. Right on this road to CIBECUE, 13.9 *m.* (5,200 alt., 1,000 pop.), a very old Apache settlement with a general store and an Indian school surrounded by vegetable gardens and fruit orchards. The Indians graze their cattle in the rough mountains that extend in all directions from the town; Brush Mountain rises more than a thousand feet above the village to the west. On August 30, 1881, a detachment of eighty-five cavalrymen was sent here from Fort Apache to arrest a medicine man, who had been causing trouble for several months by predicting the expulsion of the white men and the return of the land to the Indians. Twenty-three supposedly friendly Indian scouts joined many hostile Apaches in an attack on the detachment, killing Captain Hentig as well as six other soldiers, and pursuing the survivors the entire 40 miles back to the fort, which they attacked two days later, killing several of the garrison. A volunteer started for help to Fort Thomas, 90 miles to the south, following the usual wagon route; his mutilated body was found a week later. A second volunteer, Will C. Barnes (1858-1936)—who later served many years with the U. S. Forest Service and wrote several books on Arizona—took to a hill trail, slipped through the besieging Indians and reached a rope ferry over the Black River. There he found another Indian camp but by wrapping his horse's hoofs in blankets, was able to pass the camp and reach a ford. The rushing current loosened the blanket wrappings and the Indians, hearing the clatter of iron shoes on rocks, fired in the direction of the sounds just as Barnes climbed the opposite bank. He escaped and as soon as a relief party arrived from Fort Thomas the Indians here quickly dispersed.

2. Left on this road to FORT APACHE, 27.9 *m.* (*see TOUR 8.*)

The road winds through mountain passes to BLACK RIVER CANYON, 100 *m*. A few years ago this magnificent area was accessible only to pack outfits. Old cow-punchers, remembering the difficulties once encountered here even with sure-footed mule trains, are amazed at the paved road that now twists along the canyon walls to the bottom of the gorge. The grandeur of the immense peaks and caverns and the carving of the spires remains the same, but the beautiful hues of the rose and crimson walls continually change with the shifting light as blue and purple shadows drift across them and deepen in the twilight.

On the canyon floor, within sound of the tumbling waters of Black River, is a general store, restaurant, and tourist camp, 105 *m.,* called JIMANA INN (3,600 alt.).

The white tailings (R) from asbestos mines are visible along the canyon walls at 108 *m*. One group of claims along the river belonged to George England, who took in two other old cowpunchers as partners, and talked in such extravagant figures that this place was called Millionaire Camp by the Cross-S cowboys. Eventually the claims were sold for $80,000 and as soon as the three old cowpunchers received the first payment of $7,000, they headed for town, "high tailed it," as one of the Cross-S hands said, "an' got drunker than seven thousand dollars." Only one payment was ever made so the claims reverted to their original owners. Old George was philosophical about the deal. "Mebbe it was just as well," he said, "for if we'd drunk that $80,000 up it might have killed all three of us."

For years George trapped "loafer" (lobo) wolves and hunted mountain lion and bear on the Cross-S range with two old spotted hounds called Rattler and Rusty. Unlike most lion hunters he let his dogs do as they pleased and Rattler and Rusty would run anything from a lizard to a cow. When George was staying with Bill Teal at the Cross-S Horse Camp the dogs followed Bill who was hunting a horse. Presently the dogs discovered a fresh trail and were soon out of hearing. As soon as Bill found the horse he returned to camp. Old George asked for the dogs and was told they were running something but Bill didn't know what it was. "How was they runnin'?" asked George. "They was runnin' neck and neck when they passed me," said Bill.

"That's a lion," said George, and without another word he saddled up a horse and went to find his dogs. Bill wondered at his friend's assurance but in an hour George came riding in, with Rattler and Rusty at his heels and a huge lion skin tied behind him on the saddle.

George's dogs were always his first consideration. On one roundup when the Cross-S outfit camped at Tanks Canyon and had no night hawk (night wrangler), each puncher stood two hours horse guard during the night. George had walked into camp at sundown and his dogs had immediately taken the place over; they barked each time the guard went out; they bawled when the guard came in; occasionally they were quiet for a spell but none of the punchers really slept. Next morning George cussed the whole irate outfit for keeping Rattler and Rusty awake.

George trapped and hunted on the Cross-S range for years and was paid fifty dollars by the outfit for each lion and wolf he brought in. When the U. S. Biological Survey began to hire hunters on a straight salary and sent Carl Larsen into this area George expressed his resentment, "You tell that Swede to leave my lions alone." Though George never became entirely reconciled to the intrusion he and Larsen often hunted together. The outfit kept the old trapper in chuck, but when Larsen stopped at his camp on the way to town, his requests seldom varied: "Just bring me a gallon of whiskey an' some readin'."

SENECA, 112 *m.* (3,800 alt., 10 pop.), surrounded by mountains, is on a flat formerly used as a roundup ground. The old Cross-S Ranch headquarters built by Shanleys, the original owners of the brand, was a short distance down the canyon.

Most cow outfits of any size have a special rider whose string is made up of broncs (young horses he is breaking) and old outlaws that the average cowboy either can't or won't ride. Pride is his chief incentive for he receives only about ten dollars extra a month to ride these wild devils and do the work of a regular hand besides.

Pebbles, a bucking horse at the Cross-S outfit, spent his whole life in the rough string. Unlike others of his kind, he would often go for a month without as much as a hump in his back; but the instant he felt his rider off balance he would begin bucking violently and seldom failed to throw his man.

One autumn in the early twenties when Robinson and Young owned the outfit, Pebbles was in the rough string ridden by a kid from Texas. For two weeks Pebbles behaved and the kid grew careless. He was trying to head a steer on a steep hillside when it happened. None of the punchers saw the ride but all of them heard it. Some of the horse's jumps were thirty feet, straight off the hill, and each time he hit the ground it started a small avalanche. One of the punchers roped Pebbles as he came in sight of the holdup. He had bucked off both saddle and bridle. At the foot of the hill they found the kid, unconscious and up-side-down but still in the saddle with both feet planted firmly in the stirrups. In a little while he came to and was able to ride a gentle horse to camp where the wrangler held him while the cook painted his face, hands, and arms with iodine. For three days the cook fed him soup from a spoon. By the fourth morning when the outfit was preparing to move, one of the kid's eyes had opened a little and he was able to use one hand. Every man offered to lend him a gentle horse but the kid declined. "I can't lace up a tree," he said, "but if you boys will saddle him for me I'll try Pebbles again." And it was Pebbles he rode.

Bronc riders have always been a breed unto themselves. An old Cross-S cowpuncher once remarked: "A bronc rider may be long and thin and then again he may be short but no matter how he's built, one thing is certain. He's made of whalebone and rawhide."

At 115 *m.* is the junction with an unimproved dirt road.

1. Right on this road to CHRYSOTILE, 4 *m.* (4,600 alt., 15 pop.), an asbestos mining camp (*no supplies or gas*) at the bottom of Ash Creek Canyon,

which is more than a thousand feet deep and four thousand feet wide at this point. The first asbestos claims in this vicinity were filed in 1913 by the West Brothers and Fred Patee. Trains of a hundred burros carried the shipments to the railroad at Globe. The inaccessibility of the mines has prevented the utilization of the lower grade deposits, though Arizona chrysotile asbestos has a relatively low iron content and is especially suitable for electric-insulation. It is also extensively used in roofing, and in plaster and paint. The General Electric Company used great quantities of asbestos from this district in installing the hydro-electric plant at Boulder Dam (*see TOUR 2B*). In addition to the holdings of Johns-Manville Products Corporation, Emsco Asbestos Company, and the Roger Kyle Asbestos Company there are about a score of small operators who mine here and sell to brokers.

2. Left on this road to SAW MILL, 15.6 *m.* (*see TOUR 8*).

At 132 *m.* on US 60 is the junction with an unimproved dirt road.

Right on this road to McMILLENVILLE, 0.1 *m.* (3,900 alt., 5 pop.), the ghost of a noted mining town. Only a few adobe ruins, a broken stamp mill, and the great Stonewall Jackson Shaft (L) mark the site, though small claims in the vicinity are still worked.

Silver ore was accidentally discovered here in February 1874, by Charles McMillen and his tenderfoot partner, Theodore ("Dory") Harris. While they were on a prospecting trip McMillen had spent an indulgent night in town and the next day had to stop for a nap along the route. Harris, who didn't drink, sat impatiently beside a mossy ledge into which he idly dug his prospector's pick. When the pick broke off a chunk of quartz webbed with some metal Dory was not particularly interested, but later asked McMillen what the stuff was.

McMillen, still in a bad temper, glanced at the rock, then jumped to his feet shouting: "It's native silver." This was the discovery of the Stonewall Jackson Mine, which brought great riches to the two prospectors.

The Washington, the Robert E. Lee, and the Hannibal, also heavy producers, were later opened near here. The camp, named McMillenville in honor of Charles McMillen, almost overnight had a population of about 1,700.

The Stonewall Jackson ledge of silver was traceable for ten miles. Though it extended within the San Carlos reservation, the mines were worked frantically regardless of legal rights, and most of the silver was cleaned up before Congress got around to severing the Twelve Mile Strip, a piece that runs about on a straight line from Chrome Butte to Sombrero Butte and is on the Indian reservation land.

After Harris and McMillen had taken out ore worth about $60,000 they sold their mine for $160,000 to a Californian who mined about $2,000,000 worth of silver. McMillen drank himself to death within a few months; Harris went to California, bought a seat on the San Francisco Mining Exchange, and lost his entire fortune in less than ninety days. He washed dishes in a restaurant in Globe for awhile, joined the Salvation Army, married one of the lassies, and eventually dropped from sight.

Production in McMillenville had slowed by 1884; in 1885 there were about seven claims being worked, and by 1886 the last legal claims were filed. From about 1890 the sole occupant of the town was "Uncle Charlie" Newton, who sat on his rickety porch beneath a gnarled apple tree puffing his pipe and waiting for McMillenville to "come back." The walls of his hut were papered with yellowed editions of the *Arizona Silver Belt,* the Globe newspaper published when McMillenville made the news.

The road descends gently toward Globe and reveals at 146 *m.* an extensive view of serried ranges that graduate from dark purple masses to faint blue outlines.

At 150 *m.* is the junction with US 70 (*see TOUR 3a*), 1.6 miles east of Globe.

‹‹‹›››

Tour 13

Quartzsite—Yuma; 84 *m.*   State 95.

Paved roadbed; washes impassable during heavy rains; inquire locally. No accommodations, no service stations on route; water must be carried for all purposes.

This route runs through Arizona's yesterday; for 72 miles no occupied habitations are visible. The mountains shut out all movement except the "dust devils" that whirl across the desert, the buzzards that circle in lazy flight, or the coyotes that pause on hillsides to watch passing automobiles. Vegetation is scarce throughout. The road has practically no grades; it follows the desert floor along a route formerly used by 20-mule-team wagons hauling ore. Many of them, worn, broken, or crushed, lie beside the road among the greasewood and ocotillo where freighters abandoned them after the last haul. The distant mountains that rise along the way appear as grotesquely shaped masses of blue, red, purple, or chocolate brown. The scene lacks only a lone prospector with his burro outlined against the hills, or a train of covered wagons rumbling over the desert to be the Arizona of pioneer days. Though there are many mines near the route, both operating and abandoned, the difficulty of reaching them outweighs their interest to visitors.

State 95 branches south from US 60 (*see TOUR 3d*) in QUARTZSITE.

At 19 *m.* is a junction with an unimproved poorly defined road.

Left on this road (*bearing* R.) to a CAMPGROUND (*no water*), 6.8 *m.*, in the Kofa Mountains (1,800 alt.), where the road ends. East of here is a cliff about five hundred feet high. Straight ahead about 1.5 *m.* on foot to a wide canyon (*R. of the cliff, no signs or trail*) to a side gorge (L) called PALM CANYON (2,500 alt.), containing the only native palms in Arizona. The trees, growing on the steep sides of the gorge, are extremely green and beautiful against the red granite and are not visible until the canyon mouth is reached. The canyon, with a maximum width of 30 feet, gets only a few hours of sunlight a day. The palms, fifty or sixty in number, are a species of fan palm known as *Washingtonia Arizonica,* and are closely related to the variety in Palm Springs, California. They are extraordinarily healthy, growing in a canyon of southern exposure and so narrow that its granite sides act as a fireless cooker, reflecting and storing heat. It is assumed that these trees are the remnant of growths that once extended over a vast area.

From a high point east of the palms is a wide view including the Colorado River. Southwest are the Castle Dome Mountains, and beyond is a great stretch of arroyo-veined desert. In a canyon northwest of the palms are REDROCK TANKS, three natural cavities in the rocks about ten feet wide and three feet deep that are generally full of rainwater. The Kofa mine—the word is a contraction of King of Arizona—is on the southern slope of the prominent S. H. Mountains, so called by prospectors because from a distance the range resembles a privy. The town of Kofa, which arose near the mine, is now practically abandoned.

STONE CABIN, 30.5 m., is the ruins of a halfway house on the old mining road between Yuma and Quartzsite.

From the road at 45 m., CASTLE DOME (5,316 alt.), a landmark conspicuous throughout much of Yuma County is seen (L). The dome tops a mass whose sheer walls rise symmetrically. To the right are the Chocolate Mountains.

The windmill (R) at 64 m. is maintained by Yuma County and provides the only water between Quartzsite and Dome. Around the windmill are several ore wagons that in the old mining days were drawn by 20-mule teams.

At 67 m. is a junction with a dirt road.

Right on this road about 5 m. to a PETRIFIED FOREST (see TOUR 2) that is rapidly being depleted by souvenir takers. The wood is not highly colored.

At 72 m. is a junction with a dirt road.

Right on this road to the ruins of HACIENDA DE SAN YSIDRO, 3 m., known as Redondo Ruins; this was one of the greatest Spanish ranches in what is now Arizona. Jose Maria Redondo developed an intricate irrigation system on his extensive acreage, utilizing waters of the Colorado River by means of 27 miles of canals and ditches. The diversion dams from the river were of brush and had to be constantly replaced. From 200 to 300 men were steadily employed. Redondo served as a supply point for La Paz and the gold camps along the Colorado. One of the largest of these was at the Arroyo de la Tenaja, 7 miles east of the Colorado, where Pauline Weaver (see TOUR 1b) discovered a rich gold placer mine in 1862. When United States land laws were applied to territorial possessions, Redondo's extensive estate was broken up. Rumors that Redondo had left gold buried beneath the floors of the hacienda caused an influx of fortune hunters who dug so many holes that the walls crumbled from lack of support.

The GILA RIVER SUSPENSION BRIDGE, 72.5 m., is a graceful structure with a span of 970 feet over the generally dry Gila. It was completed in 1929.

Immediately south of the bridge is a junction with a graveled road.

Left on this road to the SITE OF GILA CITY, 3 m. (168 alt.), on the Gila River 24 miles east of Yuma. In 1858 rich gold placers were discovered here and the site mushroomed into a turbulent city of 1,200 persons, but was deserted by 1864. In that year, according to one historian, it consisted of "three chimneys and a coyote."

The road continues to DOME, 4 m. (188 alt.), a mining and farming district in the Gila Valley. It was named for Castle Dome Mountains and was formerly called Castle Dome. The Muggins Mountains are to the north.

YUMA, 84 m. (see Yuma), is the junction with US 80 (see TOUR 4d).

Recreation

Max Kealey
"HIGH, WIDE, AND HANDSOME"—PHOENIX WORLD CHAMPIONSHIP RODEO

STEER BULLDOGGING, PRESCOTT FRONTIER DAYS RODEO

DUDE RANCH RODEO DAY

DUDE STRING

ARIZONA BILTMORE HOTEL, NEAR PHOENIX

A DUDE RANCH HOUSE LOUNGE

Don Keller

EL CONQUISTADOR HOTEL, TUCSON

SAN MARCOS HOTEL, CHANDLER

GOLF

McCulloch Bros.

AQUAPLANING ON LAKE MEAD

SIGHTSEEING LAUNCH, LAKE MEAD, AT BASE OF BOULDER DAM

FISHING IN TROUT STREAM, NORTHERN ARIZONA

PICNIC PARTY, PHOENIX SOUTH MOUNTAIN PARK

McCulloch Bros.

Grand Canyon National Park

Season: South Rim, open all year; North Rim, May 15-Sept. 30, or later if roads are clear.

Administrative Offices: South Rim, Grand Canyon Village; North Rim 11 miles south of entrance gate, address North Rim, Arizona.

Permit Fee: $1 entrance fee for automobile, motorcycle, or trailer.

Transportation: (South Rim) Santa Fé Ry., train, Fred Harvey bus from Williams, Navahopi bus from Flagstaff; (North Rim) busses of Utah Parks Co., subsidiary of Union Pacific R.R. from Cedar City. Independent busses connect with Utah Parks busses at Jacob Lake.

South Rim Sightseeing Trips: West Rim Drive, $3. East Rim Drive, $6, combined $7. All-expense overnight mule trip to Phantom Ranch, $32.75. All-expense 3-day mule trip to Phantom Ranch and Ribbon Falls, $66. Cross-canyon, 2-day, all-expense mule trip, $62.50. Supai Motor-pony trip: private cars may be driven to Hilltop; Indian pony, Hilltop to Supai, round trip $12.50. Accommodations at Supai limited, telephone for reservations; bed, $3, no meals but there is a kitchen, ponies with guide trip $3.50. Tuba City and Moenkopi 1-day all-expense automobile trip $60 a trip for 1-2-3 persons. Also chartered automobiles.

North Rim Sightseeing Trips: From Grand Canyon Lodge to Cape Royal and Point Imperial, $3 a person; from Grand Canyon Lodge to Point Sublime, 3 persons minimum, $5 a person.

North Rim Trail Trips: 1-day all-expense mule trip to Roaring Springs, $12.25 a person; 2-day all-expense mule trip to Phantom Ranch, $35.75 a person; 2-day cross canyon mule trip (*see South Rim*). Saddle horses without guide ½ day, $5. Guide, half day, $4, full day, $7.50. Also camping trips.

Airplane Service: Grand Canyon Airlines, Inc. (summer only) landing strip near each rim, 125-mile flights, including 60 miles of Grand Canyon, 3 persons maximum, $10 each; cross-canyon flight, 1 person maximum, 1 way, $15 each; round trip, indefinite stopover, $22.50 each. Also charter flights.

Accommodations: South Rim: El Tovar Hotel, European Plan, from $3.50 a day. Bright Angel Lodge, E. plan, from $2 a day; breakfast, $1 up, luncheon, 90¢ up, dinners, $1.60 up. Auto camp, $1.50 and $3 a day; housekeeping cabins, $3.50 a day, no dishes-cooking utensils. Phantom Ranch, bottom of canyon, hikers, Am. plan $10 a day. Free National Park Service camp site with wood and water at auto camp and Desert View. North Rim: Grand Canyon Lodge, E. plan. rooms from $2.50. Breakfast, $1.50 and luncheon, $1.75, dinner, $3. Free National Park Service sites with water and fuel. Cafeteria at auto camp; breakfast, 70¢, luncheon, $1, dinner, $1.50.

Climate: South Rim: Air dry, evenings cool, summers warm with occasional thunder showers. Some snow in winter. Inner canyon usually 20° warmer than plateaus. North Rim: June and Sept. evenings chilly, July and August warm, with frequent thunder showers. Deep snow during winter.

Clothing and Equipment: Warm clothing in winter; warm wraps for evening in summer; long sleeved shirt, sun hat, and boots for trails. Riding clothes and shade hats rentable.

Medical Service: South Rim: hospital, doctor and trained nurses; North Rim: nurse at Grand Canyon Lodge.

Naturalist Service: South Rim: Ranger-naturalist lecturing, daily, at 1:45 p.m. also at 8:30 a.m. in summer. Campfire talks during summer 8:30 p.m. nightly. Evening talk by Naturalist, at Bright Angel Lodge during summer. North Rim: ranger-naturalist lecturing daily at 3 p.m. at Cape Royal. Nature walk daily at 9 a.m. to tip of Bright Angel Point, with Ranger-naturalist lecturing. Campfire talks: 8:30 p.m. nightly. Lodge talk 8:30 p.m. at Lodge.

Warnings and Regulations: Protection of plant and animal life and of natural features strictly enforced. Camps: Use designated areas. Fires: Only in designated areas, extinguish fire before leaving. Dogs and cats must be kept on leash or penned. Trail Travel: Hikers and riders must keep to trails; pedestrians must stand quietly on side of trail until saddle animals have passed. Hunting prohibited. Fishing: in certain park streams. Arizona license required.

The dark pines of the Kaibab National Forest conceal the Grand Canyon of the Colorado till its very rim is reached. There, spread out for seemingly endless miles, is an ocean of color. From misty blue depths rise gigantic islands of crimson sandstone. Their undulating bands of reds and purples grow softer in color and outline toward the horizon, where a single firm stroke seems to separate the rosy depths from the sky above. Its immensity is awful; the boldness of its contours overwhelming; its immobility terrifying.

Its colors, however, continually change in an endless pageant as the shifting light reveals a different spectacle each hour of the day. In the early morning, ruddy buttes and walls emerge from fast-moving blue and purple shadows; at noon under the full glare of the sun the carving of the walls is reduced and their colors show less contrast; sunset brings a blaze of glory as promontories gleam with red, gold and purple against the opaque blues of the side-canyons. In the western canyon, clearly defined against a rising mist, are the sharp blue silhouettes of eroded spurs. Under the white light of the moon the canyon appears cold and mysterious.

Even greater are the changes created by the different seasons. In late summer, thunder storms shut out the blue sky and veil the red buttes in a gray scarf of rain. In winter the evergreens on the plateau are sprinkled with snow that piles in deep drifts below the north rim. Fleecy white clouds drift through the canyon, and cling to the red buttes, sometimes filling the entire abyss with their milky mass.

Except for brief glimpses, the muddy Colorado, surging in the narrow confines of its dark Granite Gorge beneath the red buttes, is hidden from the rims by the sharp angles of the inner wall. But occasionally, when the wind that blows so steadily in the canyon is stilled, the sound of the water roaring over boulders and falls can be heard on the plateau a mile above.

A comprehensive picture of the canyon is quickly gained from the air. To east, to north, and to west, the Kaibab Plateau, covered with a dense growth of trees, drops off to wide mesas that are themselves thousands of feet high. The walls on each side of the river appear to be half of a mountain range. Huge basins, studded with buttes, make wide scallops in the rims, and the contrasting colors of the eighteen-mile-wide gorge are vividly displayed. From this height the Colorado is diminished to a quiet brook and its rapids seem like windblown ripples.

The story of the canyon, beginning more than a billion, five hundred million years ago, is as fascinating as its colors. The dark Archean rocks in the inner gorge are a part of the oldest rock system in the world. During millions of years they were laid down as sediment, solidified into rock, and then pushed by movements of the earth's crust into high mountains. Through another indefinably long period of time, the Archean mountains were worn down to a flat plain that sank below the ocean. If any life existed during the first chapter of time it was destroyed by the tremendous pressure and heat to which the Archean rocks were subjected. The miles of sediment that again covered the rock plain and hardened into the vermilion Algonkian rocks bear traces of a one-celled plant known as algae. The history of the Archean rocks was repeated and a second range of high mountains arose and was eroded till only remnants remain in the Grand Canyon area.

Lying above these are rock strata deposited during the Paleozoic era. The lavender-brown beds—known as the Tapeats sandstone—that make a cliff just above the Granite Gorge and were probably the deposit of an ancient beach were formed in Cambrian time, as was the broad green central portion of the canyon, called the Tonto Platform, which is more than 3,000 feet below the plateau. This Cambrian series bears traces of trilobites (crustacea), seaweeds, and shells.

The Devonian, represented only by small lavender deposits in hollows of the Cambrian Tonto and Algonkian rocks, contains fossil remains of freshwater fish.

Above the Tonto Platform is the 550-foot-thick Redwall, which forms the massive base of the buttes and extends beyond them in graceful cirques and long slender arms. Many fossils of seashells, corals, and other forms of marine life have been found in this limestone that was formed in a calm sea where animals and plants sank quietly to the bottom. Its color is really blue-gray, but it has been dyed red by iron oxides washed down over its face from the shales and sandstones.

Above the Redwall, the Supai formation, about eight hundred feet of glowing red sandstone and shales, bears fern prints and tracks of primitive four-footed animals. Its alternate hard and soft layers form the terraces of the buttes.

Hermit Shale, the top layer of the red strata, contains fossils of plants, amphibians, and reptiles, as well as rain-drop dimples—ripples where the water in pools was blown against the shore—and cracks that formed when the pools dried up under a hot sun.

The buff-colored Coconino sandstone, the pale band 350 feet below the rim, once lay here as shifting sand dunes and holds the fossil footprints of four-footed creatures and tracks left by insects and worms.

Creamy and gray Kaibab limestone forms the surface layer of the

NAVAJO BRIDGE

RAINBOW NATURAL BRIDGE

89

MARBLE CANYON PT. IMPERIAL

THE PAINTED DESERT

NAVAJO INDIAN RESERVATION

TUBA

FOREST

WALHALLA PLATEAU

MOENKOPI PUEBLO

SUSPENSION BRIDGE

CAPE ROYAL

CAPE SOLITUDE

CANYON OF THE LITTLE COLORADO

CAMERON

BRAHMA TEMPLE

ZOROASTER TEMPLE

DESERT VIEW AND WATCH TOWER

GALERAS HILL

MELGOSA PETRIFIED FOREST

COCONINO RIM

RIVER

LIPAN PT. WAYSIDE MUSEUM OF ARCHAEOLOGY

COLORADO

89

MORAN PT.

NSION GE

THE TIP OFF

GRANDVIEW PT.

To: Flagstaff

KAIBAB TRAIL

TRAIL

TONTO

YAKI POINT

64

OAD

FOREST

GRAND CANYON NATIONAL PARK

ARIZONA

Kaibab Plateau. Embedded in the rock are quantities of shells, corals, sponges, and the teeth of an early form of shark. The several thousand feet of red shales and sandstones that lay above it in the Mesozoic era were stripped from the Grand Canyon region in a long period of erosion, called the Great Denudation. The only remnants here of these rocks, which still spread over the Painted Desert and form great cliffs in Utah, are Cedar Mountain and Red Butte (*see below*).

After the Great Denudation, crustal pressure again elevated the area, and the river, which had followed a winding course across the plain, began digging a deeper channel to the sea. The Colorado, second longest river in the United States, flowing from the mountains of Wyoming, Colorado, and Utah, drains 250,000 square miles. From its junction with the Green River in Utah it drops more than six thousand feet to the Gulf of California. Through the Grand Canyon the Colorado flows at a speed that varies from 2.5 to 20 miles an hour. From the deep, narrow channel made by the river, water, wind, and rapid changes in temperature have worn back the walls and carved the buttes.

Compared to the age of its rocks, man's advent in the canyon is very recent, though the ruins here are believed to have been built about 1200 A.D. by Pueblo Indians. There is evidence that they moved away (probably east) during the thirteenth century. More than seven hundred sites of their habitations have been identified within the park. Food caches, in rock cavities sealed with mud, and small ears of corn indicate that these Indians were agriculturalists; that they also hunted, wove baskets and textiles, and made pottery, is known from artifacts found in the ruins and now displayed at the Wayside Museum of Archaeology (*see PARK TOUR 1b*).

The Spaniards are believed to have been the first white men to see the canyon. In 1540 when Francisco Vasquez Coronado was seeking the Seven Cities of Cibola, he was told by the Indians of a great river to the north, and sent twelve men under Garcia Lopez de Cardenas to investigate. After twenty days travel, during which Cardenas and his men climbed a high mesa (the Kaibab Plateau), they came to a chasm where they could see a thread of river far below. Against the advice of their Indian guides several of the Spaniards tried to descend to the water. But finding the buttes and towers that "appeared from above to be the height of a man were higher than the tower of the Cathedral of Seville," they abandoned their attempt and returned to the plateau. Cardenas reported to Coronado that the river was of no use to them.

In 1776 Father Garcés saw a great river red with mud and called it the Colorado (Sp., red). He climbed down into the canyon, and visited the Havasupai in the same village where they now live.

Among the mountain men and trappers who saw the Grand Canyon region was James O. Pattie. His description of the Colorado in 1826 is not attractive: ". . : the horrid mountains, which cage it up, as to deprive all human beings of the ability to descend its banks and make use of its waters."

The government, seeking a good route to the Pacific, sent several expeditions to explore the Colorado. In 1851 Captain Lorenzo Sitgreaves was instructed to "pursue the Zuni to its junction with the Colorado . . ." and "the Colorado to the Gulf of California," but turned southwest at the Grand Falls of the Little Colorado because the proposed route was "too hazardous." A. W. Whipple, surveying in 1854 for a railroad route along the thirty-fifth parallel, reported that the Colorado was navigable for several miles above the Williams River. Lieutenant Joseph Ives in 1857 ascended the Colorado in the steamboat *Explorer* as far as Boulder Canyon, then returned to the Mojave Valley and went east by land, exploring the Grand Canyon area near Diamond Creek. The chief obstacle on this hazardous trip was lack of water. Ives reported that "—the mules, ignorant of what was before them, refused, as mules often do, to drink on the morning before leaving camp." The mules had reason to regret their improvidence. They were three days without water, became "too thirsty to graze," and filled "the air with their distressing cries." Though at the first sight of the "Big Canon," Ives "paused in wondering delight" and reported that "fissures so profound that the eye cannot penetrate their depths are separated by walls whose thickness one can almost span, and slender spires that seem tottering on their bases shoot up thousands of feet from the vaults below" he appraised the region as "altogether valueless . . . It can be approached only from the south and after entering it there is nothing to do but leave. Ours has been the first and will doubtless be the last party of whites to visit this profitless locality."

Only twelve years later it was not only visited, but the river was navigated by John Wesley Powell (1834-1902), a one-armed veteran of the Civil War who was influential in organizing the U. S. Geological Survey in 1879 and served as its director from 1881 to 1894. His expedition of ten men started from Green River City, Wyoming, on May 24, 1869, in four small rowboats, three of them twenty-one feet long, the other, five feet shorter. At Disaster Falls one of the boats was wrecked. After passing through Marble Canyon, whose walls Powell described as more than half a mile high with many buttresslike projections and domed recesses, the expedition reached the mouth of the Little Colorado where it stayed from the tenth to the thirteenth of August, mapping, drying the rations, and repairing the boats.

The trip through the Granite Gorge of the Grand Canyon was marked by ceaseless toil and a series of narrow escapes. At times, Powell said, their excitement was so great that they "forgot the danger till they heard the roar of a great fall below." Three days after leaving the Little Colorado they reached a stream of clear water which was named Bright Angel, in contrast to Dirty Devil, a muddy stream at the foot of Narrow Canyon. For several days they worked their way down the river, portaging, lining, or running the rapids. Their food was nearly gone and the men, exhausted by the violence of the river, were relieved when they emerged from the Granite Gorge. But below Diamond Creek was a succession of falls and rapids that appeared more dangerous than any above. Three of the men, who refused to risk it and started on foot for civilization, were killed by Indians. Those remaining climbed into the two large boats and plunged over the fall, successfully avoiding a large rock below, and running several rapids. But while attempting to lower a boat over another fall by a line from the top of a cliff they found their rope was too short and were unable either to draw the boat back or let it down. The current battered it against a rock till the stem post broke and the boat was free. Bradley, its lone passenger, pulled on the scull oar so the bow would go over first. Powell, watching from the bank, was horrified, "One, two strokes he makes, and a third just as she goes over, and the boat is fairly turned, and she goes down almost beyond our sight . . . then she comes up again on a great wave, and down and up, then around behind some great rocks and is lost in the mad white foam below. We stand frozen with fear, for we see no boat." But Bradley and his craft survived and the watchers jumped in the remaining boat and followed him over the fall. The next day they were out of the canyon and on August thirtieth, ninety-eight days after they had started, were greeted by Mormons at the mouth of the Virgin River.

Powell made a second trip down the Colorado and explored many of its side canyons. His laudatory descriptions of the region caused several expeditions to follow him.

In 1909 Julius Stone made a complete photographic record of Grand Canyon. Accompanied by Galloway, who had made the trip in 1896, Stone's expedition went from Green River to Needles in the record time of thirty-eight days. Ellsworth and Emory Kolb took the first motion pictures of the Grand Canyon in 1911, and accompanied a Geological Survey party that mapped the area in 1923. In 1937 Buzz Holstrom built his own boat and made the trip alone. The next year two women botanists joined a party from Northwestern University and were the first women to run the rapids of the Colorado.

Reports of the explorers so interested the public that during the 1890's tourists traveled by stage from the railroad that was more than 60 miles south in order to view the canyon from the rim. To accommodate their increasing numbers a hotel was built in 1897 and in 1901 the Santa Fe purchased a mining road and continued it to the South Rim of the canyon. In 1902 the canyon was made a national monument and eleven years later an area of more than a thousand square miles around it was set aside as a national park.

Within the park boundaries the Grand Canyon is 4 to 18 miles wide and about a mile deep. The area includes both rims (the north is more than a mile above the river, and the south is a thousand feet lower), as well as the lower part of Marble Canyon on the east and Havasu Canyon on the west. In the fifty miles between them the Colorado churns through more than a hundred miles of tortuous inner gorge.

Because of the great depth of the canyon there is a variety of climates within the park and a correspondingly wide range of plant and animal life. From the river level, where desert cacti flourish, to the North Rim with its blue spruce and Douglas fir are four of the seven zones into which all plant life is divided. In spite of the dry air there are many flowers. Delphinium is followed by the white sego lily, white thistle poppy, scarlet bugle, blue locoweed (which turns lavender as it ripens and causes a nervous disorder in cattle that eat it), many penstemons, several varieties of lupin, scarlet gilia, and Solomon's seal. Prickly pear, with yellow blossoms, and pincushion cactus, with vivid pink flowers, bloom along the rims and in the forest during summer. Yucca sends up a stalk of creamy white flowers, southwestern locust bears lovely panicles of lavender, and redbud flames with magenta blossoms in the spring.

The diversification of wild life in the park—naturalists have recorded 187 birds, more than 60 mammals, 29 reptiles, and 5 amphibians —is due not only to the differences in elevation, but also to the barrier created by the river and the canyon itself. The habitat of the Kaibab squirrel, a dark animal with a plumy white tail and tufted ears, is limited to the North Rim. The only other squirrel with tufted ears found in the United States is the Abert squirrel of the South Rim; it is smaller than the Kaibab, has a red-brown body, and a gray tail. There are also beavers, deer, mountain sheep, porcupines, a few mountain lions, some beautifully colored lizards and snakes, meadow larks, mocking birds, long-tailed chats, spurred towhees, water ouzels, and road runners.

PARK TOUR 1

Williams Junction—Grand Canyon village—Desert View—Cameron; 113.7 *m.* State 64.

Oil-surfaced roadbed; *watch out for cattle.*

Section a. *WILLIAMS JUNCTION to GRAND CANYON VILLAGE. 57.3 m.*

State 64 branches north from US 66-89, 0 *m.,* at a point 2 miles east of Williams (*see TOUR 2b*), and passes through country dotted with lava flows and growths of brush, small junipers, and pinons. The rolling surface precludes any wide view to the north.

RED LAKE (R), 8 *m.* (*service stations; cabins*), is a shallow pool of rain water held in a basin of red rocks.

RED BUTTE (R), 36 *m.,* rising nine hundred feet above the plateau, is one of the few remnants in the Grand Canyon area of the Mesozoic rocks that once spread over this entire region.

State 64 crosses the southern boundary of the KAIBAB NATIONAL FOREST, 38 *m.,* which extends 50 miles north of this point and has an exceedingly fine large stand of ponderosa pine; it also contains white and Douglas fir, Engelmann and Colorado blue spruce, and quaking aspen.

At 42 *m.* is a junction with a dirt road.

Right on this to the GRAND CANYON AIRPORT, 2.5 *m.* (*hangars, servicing day and night*), from which closed cabin planes make daylight flights over the Grand Canyon (summer only).

A service station and lunch counter is at 50 *m.* (Tusayan Camp). MOQUI CAMP (*cabins, meals, motor supplies*), 52.1 *m.*, is also merely a service point. A rustic gate, 52.2 *m.*, marks the southern boundary of Grand Canyon National Park.

North of the CHECKING STATION, 56.8 *m.*, is another service station.

In GRAND CANYON VILLAGE, 57.3 *m.* (6,866 alt., 1,100 pop.), are the park administration building, a general store and post office, a community recreation building (*movies two nights a week*), a public campground with cottages, a campfire area where lectures are given (*8:30 P.M. nightly in summer*), a hospital, a railroad station, and a garage. Along the rim are Verkamp's souvenir shop, housing Louis Aiken's painting of the canyon; a reproduction of a Hopi house, and several Navajo hogans, where the Indians demonstrate their crafts and perform the Buffalo, Eagle, or Hoop Dance (*5:30 P.M. daily*); the luxurious El Tovar Hotel; the Kolb brothers' studio (*movies of boat trip down Colorado; 11:30 A.M. daily, 40¢*); and Bright Angel Lodge (*Sun. church services*).

The parking area near Bright Angel Lodge overlooks a wide canyon formed by erosion along the Bright Angel Fault; this fault continues north across the river where it has formed Bright Angel Canyon. Parts of Bright Angel Trail descending this canyon are visible, and on the Tonto Platform several thousand feet below trail parties, tiny as ants, are sometimes seen. The patch of green in the center of the valley is Indian Gardens. The red butte below Maricopa Point (L) is the Battleship. The rim is parapeted along the village and footpaths lead to the Powell memorial and to Yavapai Point.

In the village are junctions with West Rim Drive (*see Park TOUR 2*), *Topocoba Road* (*see PARK TOUR 3*), Bright Angel Trail (*see TRAIL TOUR 1*).

Section b. GRAND CANYON VILLAGE *to* CAMERON
JUNCTION; 56.4 m. State 64.

Between the village and Desert View the highway, known as East Rim Drive, runs along the edge of the canyon and has several turnouts that afford excellent views. East of East Entrance Station the road descends from the Kaibab Plateau with its tall trees to the Coconino Plateau and the Painted Desert.

The route turns R. at the garage in GRAND CANYON VILLAGE, 0 *m.*, and runs through a forest of ponderosa pine abounding with deer and Abert squirrels.

At 0.7 *m.* is a junction with a paved road which leads to Yapai Point and a magnificent view.

Left here to YAVAPAI POINT, 1 *m.* (7,050 alt.). On the promontory are an observation station (*open 8:30-5*), with eighteen telescopes and exhibits of the canyon's geology, flora and fauna; a garden (L), containing plants of the different life zones found in the park.

The view from Yavapai Point includes the North Rim, 12 miles away, with the broad fluted gash of Bright Angel Canyon reaching from the North Rim to the Colorado. At night twinkling lights mark the site of Phantom Ranch near the river. Just R. of Bright Angel Canyon the suspension bridge and its shadow across the muddy Colorado are visible. On the east side of Bright Angel Canyon are three beautiful buttes, with Zoroaster Temple (7,130 alt.) in the foreground. The next deeply cut canyon to the east is Clear Creek. In the spring when the snows on the North Rim melt, Cheyava Fall can be seen plunging 800 feet down its Redwall limestone. The eastern point of the North Rim is Cape Royal, and below it are the solid terraced mass of Wotan's Throne (7,700 alt.), and the graceful red and white Vishnu Temple rising on the tongue of land running out from the cape. At sunset the sheer east wall of the canyon beyond Vishnu Temple is golden-rose and lavender. West of Bright Angel Canyon, near the river, is Cheops Pyramid. Northwest of Cheops Pyramid, Isis Temple, a large, evenly terraced red mass, topped by a dumpling of buff sandstone, rises above symmetrical out-lying buttes. The formation (L) with the flat forested top is Shiva Temple (7,650 alt.), explored by Dr. Harold E. Anthony of the American Museum of Natural History in September, 1937. The scientific results of the expedition were somewhat disappointing. (Because of its sheer walls this plateau was expected to yield specimens of animal life that had been isolated for twenty thousand years. Instead there was proof that deer and other large animals ascend and descend Shiva every year.) But the scientists did add three hun-dred acres to the canyon's studied areas and proved the usefulness of aero-planes in mountain exploring. Among their supplies dropped by parachute was a carton of eggs and not a shell was cracked! Below on the Tonto Platform is a network of tiny trails worn by game. The bright green curve on the platform (L) are trees growing along Indian Garden Creek. Bright Angel Trail follows this creek and descends to the Colorado through a break in the Granite Gorge.

At 2.8 *m.* is a junction with an oiled road.

Left to YAKI POINT (7,268 alt.), 0.6 *m.,* where a short footpath leads to the viewpoint. West is the white dot of Yavapai Point's observation station; east on the South Rim is the tiny finger of the Desert Watch Tower. The Kaibab Trail (*see TRAIL TOUR 2*) starts from Yaki Point and is visible below (L), winding along the top of O'Neill Butte; it descends to the Tonto Platform at the eastern end of the butte. Only a glimpse of the Colorado is visible to the east. Left from the viewpoint on an easy trail to an observation platform surrounded by pinons and junipers a few hundred feet below the rim.

East of Yaki Point along the rim drive the rather open stand of pinon, ragged-bark juniper, cliffrose and sage brush merges into a forest of tall ponderosa pine, interspersed with low green Gambel's oak.

At 10.8 *m.* is a junction with an oiled road.

Left to GRAND VIEW POINT, 0.5 *m.* (7,496 alt.); R. on a footpath across privately owned land to a viewpoint. The canyon here is a maze of forma-tions that glow in deep reds shot with purple and violet, and are crowned with creamy rocks. Beyond the rose and gold eastern wall of the canyon stretches the delicately toned Painted Desert; the Vermilion Cliffs form a low line against the northeastern horizon, and more than a hundred miles away rises the soft blue dome of Navajo Mountain. The Sinking Ship (R), extending from the South Rim, is an eroded part of the fold that joins the Kaibab Plateau to a lower plateau on the east.

The first building on Grand View Point was a log structure erected in 1892 by Pete Berry who had helped to build Bright Angel Trail. Berry made a 4-mile trail (*now unsafe*) to his copper mine, which was 2,500 feet below the rim, on the east side of Horse Shoe Mesa and packed the ore out on mules. In some places along the cliff the trail consisted only of logs anchored to the wall by chains. A three-story log hotel was built here in 1897 to accommodate tourists who came in horse-drawn stages from Flagstaff. In 1913 William Randolph Hearst acquired the Grand View property. Captain John Hance, who had served as an Indian scout with Kit Carson, built the Hance Trail down Red Canyon (R) to the river. Mrs. Edward Ayres who descended this trail in 1882, is said to have been the first white woman to reach the bottom of Grand Canyon. The cabin Hance erected at the head of his trail in 1892 was the first house built on the canyon rim.

The East Rim Drive continues through rolling and wooded country where vistas of the brilliant North Rim are framed by dark trees.

At 17 *m.* is a junction with a paved road.

Left on this road to MORAN POINT, 0.2 *m.* (7,187 alt.), named for Thomas Moran, whose painting made from this point hangs in the Capitol in Washington. On a semi-detached butte at the end of Moran Point are remnants of a wall probably built by Indians during the twelfth century. The Colorado River can be seen from this point.

East of Moran Point the forest through which the road is cut changes to piñons and junipers.

At 20.7 *m.* is a junction with a road.

Right here to the WAYSIDE MUSEUM OF ARCHEOLOGY, 0.1 *m.* (*open 8:30-5; archaeologist in attendance during summer*), which contains exhibits and charts relating to prehistoric man in the southwest. Back of the museum is the TUSAYAN RUIN, a small, U-shaped pueblo built by Indians about 1200 A.D. and probably abandoned near the end of the thirteenth century. It was partly excavated in 1930, and many of the artifacts found are displayed in the Wayside Museum.

At 22.2 *m.* is a junction with an oiled road.

Left on this along the backbone of LIPAN POINT, 0.3 *m.* (7,400 alt.), from which the southward slope of the Kaibab Plateau is clearly evident and the long, banded wall of the North Rim is visible for 30 miles.

South of the East Rim Drive, which follows the rolling contour of the plateau, the forest is very dense.

From NAVAJO POINT (*campground*), 24.4 *m.* (7,050 alt.), the observation point farthest east on the South Rim, the views of the canyon are magnificent and varied. In the depths, almost a mile below, the Colorado River appears broad and quiet; across the river, in Unkar and Chuar Basins, are white-crowned ruddy buttes; and to the west the Grand Canyon bristles with massive buttes and temples between its banded walls. To the east is the confluence of the Colorado and Little Colorado rivers at the beginning of the Grand and the end of Marble Canyon; Cedar Mountain (R) is a flat-topped remnant of the Mesozoic rocks that once covered the entire region; the dark shadow on the

Painted Desert is really a low hill of dark lava, called Shadow Mountain.

Under the bright blue desert sky the plateaus and desert seem flat, and the level line of the horizon is but little disturbed by the Vermilion and White Cliffs of Utah in the northeast, and the white triangular summits of the San Francisco Mountains to the south.

The old Tanner Trail, built in 1889 by a group of men including Seth Tanner, a descendant of John D. Lee (*see TOUR 1a*), starts below Navajo Point and descends to the Colorado River. From the Tanner Trail a route led across the Colorado and connected with the Nankoweap Trail, built under Major Powell's direction in 1882 for a geological party. Horsethieves took advantage of these two trails to drive horses between Arizona and Utah.

The DESERT VIEW WATCHTOWER (*open 8:30-5; adm. 25¢*), resembles an Indian tower, and is decorated with copies of Indian pictures. From its lower roof excellent views of the canyon and Painted Desert are reflected in black mirrors that eliminate sun glare. The first floor of the tower contains a reconstruction of a HOPI KIVA. The telescopes on the top floor reveal Tuba City, Moenkopi, and the bright green farms in Moenkopi Wash (*see TOUR 5*) as well as the white dump of Grand View Mine on Horseshoe Mesa, the three houses built by Pete Berry in 1892, and Hance Rapids, a raging, boiling stretch of water considered one of the worst in the Colorado.

East of Entrance Gate (6,850 alt.), 24.6 *m.*, State 64, called the Navahopi Road, descends the dip of the Kaibab Plateau. South, across the Coconino Basin the cliffs have dense growths of tall trees, but at the Kaibab Forest boundary, 25.3 *m.*, the trees are small and far apart.

The Painted Desert to the east is broken by many mesas, and the gorges of the Colorado and the Little Colorado are visible (L) winding through the desert.

At 40.6 *m.* is a junction with an unpaved road.

Left on this road to a parking area, 0.4 *m.*, where a path leads 200 feet to a viewpoint above the Little Colorado River's canyon of tan and ocher walls. In the summer, except after a heavy rain, the sandy bed holds only a few pools of water.

DEAD INDIAN CANYON BRIDGE, 45.6 *m.*, crosses a sandy watercourse, but the strength of the bridge indicates the torrents that sometimes rage down this canyon. Hogans and corrals appear along the road and Navajo children on horses sit watching while sheep and goats browse.

At 56.4 *m.* is the junction with US 89 (*see TOUR 1a*) at the southern edge of Cameron.

PARK TOUR 2

Grand Canyon Village—Hermit's Rest; 7.2 *m.* West Rim Drive.

Oil surfaced road.

West Rim Drive branches west from Bright Angel Lodge in GRAND CANYON VILLAGE, 0 *m.* (*see PARK TOUR 1a*), and follows the extreme edge of the canyon rim.

At 2.5 *m.* is a junction with an oiled road.

Right 0.1 *m.* to a parking place. A footpath, through pinon, cliffrose, and Utah juniper, leads to POWELL MEMORIAL (7,050 alt.), a stone monument with a brass bas-relief of John Wesley Powell and the names of the men who finished the two trips down the Colorado with him. From this point two small sections of the river are visible, and the North Rim appears massive and powerful above red buttes and steep canyons. In the full midday sun its colors are softened with a blue haze, and shadows define the horizontal strata so that the rocks resemble evenly laid courses of masonry. The niches in the redwall, outlined by arches of blue shadow, seem small, though some could hold the Washington Monument.

HOPI POINT, 2.6 *m.* (7,071 alt.), reveals several stretches of the Colorado. Toward the west are the flat line of Powell's Plateau, and the extinct volcanic cones of Mount Trumbull and Mount Logan on the horizon. In the east the long length of the North Rim is visible as far as Cape Royal. At one time, SHIVA TEMPLE (*see PARK TOUR 1b*), the flat-topped, wooded butte across the river, was part of the North Rim.

From MOHAVE POINT, 3.9 *m.* (7,000 alt.), several long stretches of the rushing Colorado are visible. The recumbent mass of vivid red shales and sandstone just below the point is known as the Alligator. At the mouth of the gorge cut by Hermit Creek (L) are the dangerous HERMIT RAPIDS. Left of the point, surrounding a deep bay, is the sheer, three-thousand-foot-high MOHAVE WALL.

At 6.5 *m.* is a junction with an oiled road.

Right 0.2 *m.* to PIMA POINT (6,750 alt.). To the west is a view of the Colorado with both sides of the dark Granite Gorge visible; at sunset the muddy yellow surface of the river turns to silver and the walls of the gorge are a deep violet. Farther west Grand Canyon curves around Powell Plateau. A sheer-walled canyon (R) between Mohave and Pima Points is drained by Monument Creek, which has dumped a barrier of boulders into the Colorado to form Monument Rapids. They can be identified by an arrow-head of white foam on the river, and their roar can be heard on Pima Point. The canyon floor—green, gray, brown and tan, lightly covered with desert brush and scored by game trails—looks smooth, but is really very rugged and difficult to travel. Just on the other side of the river is symmetrical Cheops Pyramid whose four almost even sides rise to a sharp point.

At HERMIT'S REST, 7.2 *m.* (6,300 alt.), are a parking place and a rustic stone building (*open 8:30-5:30*) with a wide porch and large fireplace. Mesa Ermita blocks the view of the South Rim to the west but visible across the canyon is Point Sublime and east of it, in the

Hindu Amphitheater, the deep gorge cut through the Archean Rock by Crystal Creek. Spread before Shiva Temple, directly opposite, are Osiris Temple, with a pale sandstone top, Tower of Ra, Horus Temple and Isis Temple. The Redwall base of these buttes is scalloped into great amphitheaters and cirques, divided by long graceful, buff-colored arms. When the late afternoon sun shines behind these buttes it reveals the many gorges and canyons that separate them from each other and from the rims.

Right from Hermit's Rest parking place, the road continues a few hundred feet to the head of Hermit Trail (*see TRAIL TOUR 3*).

PARK TOUR 3

Grand Canyon Village—Rowe's Well—Hilltop—Supai—Mooney Falls; 53 *m.* Havasupai Rd., Topocoba Trail.

Rough automobile road between Grand Canyon Village and Topocoba Hilltop (3 hours drive); 14-mile pony trail between Hilltop and Supai Village.

This is a seldom traveled route through the Kaibab Forest south of the rim. With the exception of the side route to Havasupai Point, it offers few views of the canyon between Grand Canyon Village and Hilltop, where the descent by pony trail begins. The road is difficult, the accommodations meager, and the heat at Supai intense in the summer; yet the remoteness of the Havasupai reservation makes the trip outstanding to those surfeited with civilization.

West from Bright Angel Lodge, 0 *m.,* in GRAND CANYON VILLAGE (*see PARK TOUR 1a*), to a fork, 0.3 *m.*

Left here through a forest of ponderosa and piñon. ROWE'S WELL (*cabins, store, bar*), 2.8 *m.,* in the tall pines, was patented when copper was mined here. The mine was closed because of seepage, but the well, which is valuable in so arid a country, was preserved.

At the end of the graded road, 11.3 *m.,* the route turns R. (west) following the rocky Topocoba Trail (*drive slowly*) of the Havasupai. Scrubby pinons, sage, and other desert growths sparsely cover the irregular surface of the plateau.

In PASTURE WASH, 22 *m.,* a shallow valley that runs north to the edge of Grand Canyon, is the junction with the Havasupai Point road, a rough fire trail.

Right here, past PASTURE WASH RANGER STATION (L), 3.4 *m.,* and through a gate at 3.7 *m.* (*close after driving through*). At 5.5 *m.* is a junction. Left is an alternate route to Bass Camp (*see below*). The Havasupai Point road continues R. At 7 *m.* is a Fire Signal Tower; L. to Signal Hill Fork, 7.2 *m.* and the junction with the deeply rutted Signal Fork Road.

Left here 1.6 *m.* to the unmarked site of BASS CAMP. Several stone heaps are remnants of Indian shelters. At the base of Mount Huethawali (6,280 alt.), the cone-shaped butte (L) about a mile and a half distant, is a spring revered by the Havasupai. In 1883, William Bass, who had a ranch near Williams, visited the Havasupai Village; later he built a hunting camp here at the head of the Havasupai's trail to Mount Huethawali, and continued the trail to the Colorado. He began driving tourists here from the railroad at Ash-fork in stages drawn by four horses; as his venture prospered, he built a small tram across the Colorado and planted orchards and vegetables on the fertile land along the Shinumo Creek.

The Havasupai Point road turns sharply R. at Signal Hill Fork.

The view is magnificent from HAVASUPAI POINT (6,700 alt.), 8.9 *m.*, which projects far into the canyon, where the Colorado makes a wide bend.

The DRIFT FENCE, 24.1 m., marks the eastern boundary of the Havasupai grazing land.

HILLTOP, 35.5 *m.* (5,415 alt.), is the end of the automobile road (*park cars off road; telephone at E. end of 2nd building, pull switch to make contact*), and the head of the Topocoba (Ind., curve flanked by two arms) Trail, now the route, which skirts a sheer-walled gorge to a blunt-ended arm of Lee Canyon and zigzags down a steep slope. The walls of Lee Canyon are pale gray limestone and buff sandstone. On the east side of the canyon are traces of an old wagon road started by an early mining company. At the foot of the slope is TOPOCOBA SPRING (L).

The trail continues down the sandy floor of Lee Canyon for several miles and at the junction of Rattlesnake Canyon (R), 2 *m.*, enters Havasu Canyon, a fantastically eroded cut in the redwall limestone.

In Hualpai Canyon, which joins Havasu Canyon at about 47.5 *m.*, is the junction with Hualpai Trail.

Left here to the plateau, 4 *m.*, and a rough automobile road to SELIGMAN (*see TOUR 2c*) 65 *m.*, or a better road to Peach Springs via Frazer Wells.

On the Topocoba Trail just north of the junction with Hualpai Canyon, a number of springs gush from the floor of Havasu Canyon, and add their waters to sparkling HAVASU CREEK (Ind., green-blue), tumbling over the red-brown rocks. The water is clear here but becomes translucent blue-green below Navajo Falls (*see below*). Jays, wrens, desert sparrows, flycatchers and water ousels dart among the shrubbery.

The canyon widens and the Redwall curves to form a rough circle about half a mile in diameter at 49 *m.* The pale coloring of the upper strata forms a pleasing contrast to the red of the lower walls, the green of the grass and trees, and the blue of the desert sky.

Two pillars on a projection of the redwall (L) are known to the Indians as the Prince and Princess; legend says their fall means the doom of the Havasupai.

SUPAI, 49.5 *m.* (3,201 alt., 200 pop.) (*accom. limited, no meals, post office and telephone*), is the village and government center of the Havasupai Indian Reservation. In the white schoolhouse at the north end of the cottonwood-lined road, the children receive instruction through the sixth grade. The building also serves as a meeting place for the 4-H farm club, and for the domestic science club, of which the Havasupai women are exceedingly proud. Father Garcés visited the

Havasupai here in 1776 and described them as a happy and industrious people. Leslie Spier, author of *Havasupai Ethnology,* considers this the only spot in the United States where native culture has remained in anything like its pristine condition. According to Spier, the Havasupai live in close contact with the earth and have little speculative life. Their only desires seem to be to have enough to eat and to live in their canyon undisturbed. Their ceremonials are few and simple. To their biggest festival, the Peach Dance (*Aug.*), they invite the Hopi and Hualpai.

They still treat illness with sings at night (*see TOUR 5*) and by placing the patient in the sweathouse. The men tan beautiful white deer-skins; the women weave rather coarse, shallow food trays and conical seed baskets for their own use, and other baskets in more conventional shapes for sale. They are of Yuman stock, heavy set and quite dark. The men cut their hair short, and wear blue jeans and black felt hats. The women's hair is shoulder length with bangs down to their eyebrows; their voluminous dresses are usually of small-patterned prints. Several generations of a family live together and their hogans and summer brush shelters are grouped around a community fire. They treat their children with great gentleness, believing that harsh words or cruel punishments shrivel a child's soul.

When John D. Lee (*see TOUR 1a*) was in hiding after the Mountain Meadow Massacre, he spent three years with the Havasupai here. He taught them better farming methods and started peach orchards that produced excellent fruit. Most of the trees, however, were washed out in a big flood a few years ago.

The main trail continues through the village, and runs along the river, through fields of corn, beans, melons and squash, to NAVAJO FALLS, 51.5 *m.,* which drop about fifty feet in a broad curtain, veiled with white spray. Above this point the stream flows through a series of shallow cascades shaded by green trees and bushes. Soluble lime, carried by Havasu Creek, forms a travertine coating around all solid objects. On the brown-green travertine fans deposited on both sides of the fall are maidenhair ferns and other bright green plants flourishing in the spray. In the pool below the fall the water has a milky blue-green tint.

HAVASU FALLS (R), 52 *m.,* are about a hundred feet high and have a large pool at their base.

A silver mine in Carbonate Canyon (R) was worked some years ago. A little beyond Havasu Falls, in a tangle of grapevines and trees, are a forge and a little house where the men lived. They lifted the ore by a hoist (L) to the canyon rim.

MOONEY FALLS, 53 *m.,* fill the air with thunder as the water rushes over the bluff and drops nine hundred feet into a wide pool. Almost the entire face of the bluff, which extends across the canyon, is covered with a travertine deposit. The horse trail ends here, but a foot path leads down the face of the bluff for several hundred feet, and descends through a tunnel in the travertine. The lower entrance, opposite the center of the fall, affords an excellent view of the pool and the clouds of white foam. Below this opening rude steps cut in the cliff (*dangerous when wet*) and an equally rude hand rail lead to the verdant canyon below. The falls were named for a prospector who attempted to work below the falls here in the 1890's. He made a loop in the end of a rope, and sat in it while the Indians let him down over the cliff. But the rope caught in a crack and Mooney hung here for two days while the men tried to reach him by tunneling through the soft travertine which is honeycombed with small caves. On the third day he fell and was killed on the rocks below. Seven iron ladders that later prospectors spiked to the cliff are on the canyon wall (L). A second mine in a hole R. of the cave is reached by a path along the cliff.

PARK TOUR 4

Jacob Lake—Entrance Station—Bright Angel Point; 44.4 *m.*   State 67.

Oil-surfaced roadbed. Season May-Oct.
Wild life protected; drive carefully.

This route, connecting US 89 with the North Rim of the Grand Canyon, traverses the northern section of the Kaibab National Forest, which abounds with wild life, and offers what are considered by some the finest views of the canyon.

State 67 branches south from US 89 (*see TOUR 1a*) at a village called JACOB LAKE, 0 *m.,* and traverses the Kaibab Plateau, which is covered with swales, ridges, narrow valleys, meadows, and sink holes. This part of the Kaibab National Forest has dense stands of spruce and fir, as well as open meadows, bordered by groves of light-trunked aspens. The first frost turns their shining green leaves to glittering masses of yellow, gold and orange. The Kaibab limestone is so porous that surface water usually seeps through it, but in places where it has become clogged with silt melted snow and rain form ponds that hold water all the year round.

At 1 *m.* is a junction with a dirt road.

Right to JACOB LAKE (5,260 alt.), 0.5 *m.,* a shallow pond named for Jacob Hamblin, who explored the Grand Canyon country in the sixties and seventies looking for possible farm and town sites for the Mormons.

High on the plateau the air is brisk and even during July, when the sun is warm on the road, there are patches of snow in the shade of the trees.

At 26.2 *m.* is a junction with a dirt road.

Right here to KAIBAB LODGE (8,900 alt.), 0.1 *m. (cabins, service station, meals, May 15-Nov. 15).* Deer feed on the meadows here at sunset. When cougars were killing off the deer, Uncle Jimmy Owens, noted Arizona lion hunter, shot an enormous number and brought Theodore Roosevelt here on a lion hunting trip.

The boundary of the Grand Canyon National Park is at 31.9 *m.* and the ENTRANCE STATION (9,100 alt.) at 32 *m.*

At 32.3 *m.* is a junction with a graded dirt road (*sometimes blocked by snow till June*).

Right on this across a wide meadow and into a thick forest of spruce and fir, then down into the shallow, grassy valley of Kanabownits Canyon. Meadows spangled with lady's slipper, wild geranium, yarrow, Indian paintbrush and lupin, are bordered by groves of aspen, their pale trunks and delicate green foilage outlined against the darker evergreens.

A watering trough, (R), 6.5 *m.*, that catches the water from a spring above and is placed here for the deer, is surrounded with a thicket of juniper. The soft notes of mourning doves and the harsh cry of jays occasionally break the silence, and deer browse on the slopes among bracken and shrubs.

KANABOWNITS SPRING (L), 7.6 *m.*, flows into a green bordered basin and continues as a little stream, crossing the road at 7.8 *m.* (*Last water between here and Point Sublime.*)

The trees are no longer typical of the Canadian forest but of the Transition Zone. Stately ponderosa pines grow far apart and are the home of many Kaibab squirrels.

A short steep climb ends at VIEWPOINT, 10.8 *m.* on the canyon rim just above the Hindu Amphitheater, which has been cut far back in the soft red strata. The Dragon's Head, a long red butte (L) is outlined against Shiva Temple, and 60 miles south of Grand Canyon are the San Francisco Mountains.

The route continues on the headland and pines give way to piñons and juniper. The road crosses to the west side of the headland at about 15 *m.* Here are magnificent views into the huge Shinumo Amphitheater that separates Point Sublime and Powell Plateau.

A picnic ground is at 16.2 *m.* (*tables, fireplace; no water*).

The view from POINT SUBLIME, 16.5 *m.* (7,464 alt.), includes, from east to west, more than 150 miles, and was described in 1881 by Captain Clarence E. Dutton, noted geologist, as "by far the most sublime of all earthly spectacles." The promontory extends almost 10 miles out into the canyon between huge basins that lie more than 3,000 feet below. Although Boucher Rapids (E), is the only section of the Colorado visible, the course of the river can be followed as it approaches in slow curves from the east to make a deep northward curve into Shinumo Amphitheater (W), and then bend sharply south to skirt Powell Plateau. Below the point is the ruddy Sagittarius Ridge, parallel to the river, and sharply R are massive red walls and red shales. The South Rim is cut by many canyons, each one showing the sandy line of a creek bed. The long point on the South Rim, almost due west, is Havasupai. The western view is tremendous: from each rim the great outlying spurs, topped by imposing buttes, run down to the Granite Gorge; at sunset they are blue silhouettes bathed in a blue mist. Eastward on both sides of the huge bulk of Shiva Temple the wide, eroded basin of Grand Canyon is filled with a multitude of red buttes, rising above the green Tonto Platform and backed by the banded walls of the canyon. In the clear air details and color show plainly for more than 20 miles, and the water tank at Grand Canyon Village appears as a little black stub an inch high. The color effects are richer early in the morning and late in the afternoon, and sunset here is something never to be forgotten. In summer the smooth blue sky often contains high-piled white clouds and sometimes six or seven small rainstorms fall at once, forming a semi-transparent gray mist through which the red, buff, and green canyon walls and formations are dimly seen. When the sun penetrates the mist to form a rainbow, spectators realize what Powell meant when he wrote that at the Grand Canyon "a concept of sublimity can be obtained never again to be equalled on the hither side of Paradise."

On both sides of State 67 are low hills covered with blue and green conifers, and groups of white-trunked aspens. Sego lilies, lupines, penstemon, phlox, and gilias bloom beside the road and in the grassy meadows. Deer browse beneath the trees and frequently cross the road.

At 41.3 *m.* is the junction with the oil-surfaced Cape Royal Road (*see PARK TOUR 5*).

At 42.4 *m.* is the junction (L) with the Kaibab Trail (*see TRAIL TOUR 4*).

From the route, as it continues along Bright Angel Point, are occasional glimpses (L) into Manzanita and Bright Angel Canyons.

At 43 *m.* is a junction with a dirt road.

Right to NATIONAL PARK SERVICE HEADQUARTERS, 0.1 *m.* (*information, specimens of plants and animals*).

At 43.2 *m.* is a junction with an oiled road.

Right to PUBLIC CAMPGROUND (*cabins, store, cafeteria; free campsites with fuel and water; campfire talks, 8:30 P.M.*).

From GRAND CANYON LODGE, 44.4 *m.* (8,153 alt.) (*cabins, lounge, diningroom, cocktail room*), a path leads L. to the tip of Bright Angel Point, and roughly follows the rim of the canyon to the public campground (R).

PARK TOUR 5

Junction with State 67—Point Imperial—Cape Royal; 17.4 *m.* Cape Royal Rd.

Oil surfaced roadbed.

This route, through beautiful meadows and woods, reveals some of the most majestic views of the canyon and touches both the highest and the southernmost points on the North Rim.

The Cape Royal Road branches northeast from State 67 (*see PARK TOUR 4*), 0 *m.*, 3.5 miles north of Bright Angel Point, and crosses grassy meadows between hills with dense stands of conifers. Aspens grow in groups below the spruce and fir; southwestern locust, elderberry and wild rose grow beside the road.

At 3.5 *m.* is the junction with the oiled Point Imperial Road.

Left to POINT IMPERIAL, 4 *m.* (8,801 alt.). Visible from this, the highest point along the rims of Grand Canyon, are the line of the Vermillion Cliffs running into the northeast and the solitary cone of Navajo Mountain (*see TOUR 6A*), 100 miles away. East are Echo Cliffs and the Painted Desert. The gorge of the Colorado twisting across the desert, and the walls of Marble Canyon are distinguishable from this height. Below in the glowing cherry-red basin is Nankoweap (Paiute, singing or echo) Creek, so named by Powell because the sheer-walled gorge threw back an echo. The upper slopes of Nankoweap Basin are green with vegetation but its lower walls are bare.

The main route continues R. from Imperial Junction to FAIRVIEW POINT, 4.4 *m.* (8,300 alt.) ; here a wide view of the Painted Desert extends north into Utah. The column of smoke on the desert is from the powerhouse at Tuba City.

In the dense forest here a spotted fawn can sometimes be seen standing quietly beside its mother.

Formerly there was a fence across the entrance to Walhalla Plateau, 5.3 *m.,* to keep the cattle that grazed on the plateau in summer from straying. Only half a mile of fence was needed to protect the stock on 25,000 acres of land. Greenland Lake, a sink hole just a little past the entrance to the Plateau, is a favorite drinking place for deer. Its water is usually covered by green growth.

At 16.3 *m.* is a view of the Colorado running through the red Algonkian rocks. Straight below is Unkar Creek, and what appears from above to be faint ripples at the junction of the creek and the Colorado, are Unkar Rapids. South of this point views of the canyon are frequent. On the edges of the plateau, surrounded by the hot depths of the canyon, the forest changes from pines to piñons. Many prehistoric Indian sites are on this plateau.

CAPE ROYAL (*parking area; picnic grounds*), 17.4 *m.* (7,876 alt.), was so named in 1861 by Dutton who said that from this point "to the south and west the vista of the Grand Canyon stretches away to its fullest measure of sublimity."

1. Left from Cape Royal on a footpath to ANGEL'S WINDOW POINT (*do not walk out on point if subject to dizziness or if there is a strong wind*) where a large hole has been eroded, several hundred feet below the rim, through a spur of Kaibab limestone that projects into the canyon.

2. Right to the TIP OF CAPE ROYAL in the widest part of the Grand Canyon; the South Rim is 18 miles distant and the Colorado, glimpsed curving between sandbars, is more than a mile below. WOTAN'S THRONE (7,700 alt.), is (R) separated from the North Rim by a deep gorge, and on its western side is Clear Creek Canyon. The graceful white-topped butte just below Cape Royal, is Visnu Temple (7,537 alt.), described by Dutton as seeming "to surpass in beauty anything we have yet seen." It is surrounded by many smaller buttes, and below them are long graceful arms of red limestone reaching toward the river. The cream, buff, red, and green strata of the South Rim extend west for nearly 30 miles. Beyond the dusky east wall of the canyon, Cedar Mountain looks like a gigantic ant-heap with its top sheared off. On the South Rim is the tiny finger of the Desert Watchtower, and along the south horizon are the San Francisco Peaks and Hendricks, Sitgreaves, and Bill Williams Mountains.

TRAIL TOUR 1

Grand Canyon Village—Indian Garden—Colorado River; 7 *m.* Bright Angel Trail.

Bright Angel Trail descending in easy switchbacks across the back of the canyon, affords spectacular views. The steep cliffs were dissected by Bright Angel fault then eroded to shallow slopes. The displacement of this fault can be clearly distinguished when the trail reaches the red shale. The earliest path here was made by the Havasupai, to reach their primitive farms below. Scars of the first Bright Angel trail built in 1890-91 by Ralph Cameron and Pete Berry are visible from the present route.

Bright Angel Trail branches west from the trail corral (6,870 alt.), 0 *m.,* in GRAND CANYON VILLAGE (*see PARK TOUR 1a*).

JACOB'S LADDER, 1.5 *m.,* a series of short, quite steep switchbacks through the redwall, ends at the rugged bush-covered TONTO PLATFORM (4,250 alt.), 2 *m.*

INDIAN GARDEN, 4 *m.* (3,876 alt.), was named by prospectors who found here patches of beans and squash that had been planted by the Havasupai, and irrigated from a near-by spring. Long Jim, who still wears the plug hat and frock coat given him by President Theodore Roosevelt and the medals presented to him by Albert of Belgium when the latter visited Grand Canyon, was born here. He remembers when his mother and father made the long trip to Prescott to verify rumors that there were men with white faces. The big cottonwood trees were planted in 1903 when Dick Gilliland and Niles Cameron brought the saplings from a creek just east of Pipe Creek.

The trail follows the course of Indian Garden Creek—which is densely bordered with willow, grape, arrowweed, and redbud—to the gorge cut by Pipe Creek, and descends along a rugged shoulder known as the DEVIL'S CORKSCREW. The last section of the trail follows Pipe Creek through the dark walls of the oldest rock known to man. Though this is called the Granite Gorge, these Archean rocks are mainly gneiss and schist but include large masses of pink or white granite.

The COLORADO RIVER, 7 *m.* (2,500 alt.), broad and muddy, flows swiftly past the sandbar at the foot of the canyon; its depth here varies from 12 to 40 feet. The Havasupai call the Colorado the Place of the Roaring Sound.

TRAIL TOUR 2

Yaki Point—Colorado River—Phantom Ranch; 7.5 *m.* Kaibab Trail.

Bus from hotels to Yaki Point.
Telephone for reservations at Phantom Ranch.

This route, which offers the tourist some even more spectacular scenery than the Bright Angel, is the only trail in Grand Canyon that crosses the river.   Part of the way it descends a spur that projects far out from the rim and so allows unlimited views both up and down the canyon.

From the YAKI POINT corrals, 0 *m.* (*see PARK TOUR 1b*), Kaibab Trail leads through the forest for a short distance to the canyon rim, follows a series of switchbacks across the head of a canyon, and then descends an easy grade on the west side of Yaki Point.   By a second series of sharp switchbacks, the trail reaches the top of O'NEILL BUTTE (6,050 alt.), 2 *m.*   The small noises and movements of the trail party make the vastness and quiet of the canyon more striking.   Above are pale cliffs of limestone and sandstone that circle the canyon rims and below are the massive red buttes.

Near O'Neill Butte, fossil ferns and footprints are arranged as trail-side exhibits.   At the end of the butte the trail descends by the white switchbacks, to the Tonto Platform, and winds over the brush dotted desert to the edge of the Granite Gorge to the Tipoff (*see TRAIL TOUR 1*).   Here the steady roar of the Colorado is heard.

A tunnel more than a hundred feet long leads to the KAIBAB SUSPENSION BRIDGE, 6.5 *m.,* completed in 1928.   Its steel sections packed down from the rim on mules, but the ten cables which support the bridge were unrolled and carried down the trail on the shoulders of Indians.

Under the bridge, the Colorado is about four hundred feet wide, and each day carries an average of 500,000 tons of suspended silt. (On September 13, 1927, 27,600,000 tons were carried down in twenty-four hours.)   Prospectors used to say that the Colorado was too thick to drink, but too thin to plow.

PHANTOM RANCH (*cabins, dining-room, swimming pool and recreation hall*), 7.5 *m.* (2,500 alt.), built in 1921, is the only resort in the bottom of Grand Canyon.   The first settlement was made here in 1903, and in 1907 a tram carrying a cage large enough to hold one mule was put across the river.   For several years after Theodore Roosevelt came to the Grand Canyon in 1913 on a hunting trip and stayed here, the ranch was known as Roosevelt Camp.

At Phantom Ranch is a junction with the Kaibab Trail from the North Rim (*see TRAIL TOUR 4*).

TRAIL TOUR 3

Hermit Rest—Hermit Basin—Dripping Springs; 47 *m.* via unmaintained Hermit Trail.

From Hermit Rest a four-hundred foot descent is accomplished by switchbacks, and then the trail turns away from Grand Canyon toward the wide deep amphitheater of Hermit Basin, whose steep walls are green with grass and trees.

Large sandstone slabs, marked with fossil footprints, lie above the switchbacks in the red sandstone.

At 1.2 m. (5,280 alt.), on the floor of the amphitheater, is a junction with the Waldron Trail.

1. Right on this 250 feet to a water trough filled by a small spring (*water usually dirty*).

2. Left on the abandoned Waldron Trail, which climbs the back of the steep amphitheater.

The Hermit Trail crosses a small rise of red shale, and circles around the head of Hermit Gorge, a deep, smooth cut through the redwall limestone. The narrow walls frame a view of the North Rim.

DRIPPING SPRINGS, 4.7 m., drops from clumps of maidenhair in the roof of a wide sandstone ledge into a pool below (left 2 m. on Dripping Springs Trail).

TRAIL TOUR 4

Junction with State 67—Roaring Springs—Ribbon Falls—Phantom Ranch; 13.1 m., Kaibab Trail.

To Roaring Springs and return is a one-day trip. Section between Roaring Springs and Phantom Ranch open all year.

This northern section of the Kaibab Trail descends precipitous red walls in easy grades, passes the spectacular Roaring Springs Fall and follows the clear waters of Bright Angel Creek for 8 miles. The Kaibab Trail branches east from State 67 (*see Park Tour 4*), 0 m., 2 miles north of Bright Angel Point and descends slopes, covered with trees and brush, in long easy switchbacks. There are frequent views of Manzanita Canyon and of the eastern wall of Bright Angel Canyon about 4 miles away. The water pipe visible at intervals along the trail carries water pumped from Bright Angel Creek to the North Rim. The steep walls of Manzanita Canyon are descended in switchbacks. Along the redwall, which is nearly perpendicular, a three-quarter tunnel has been blasted from the solid limestone. The open side affords views of the canyon and of a pretty little creek.

ROARING SPRINGS (L) are visible at 4 m., gushing from the canyon wall and plunging 400 feet down a steep, fern-covered slope. The roar of these springs can be heard on the tip of Bright Angel Point.

At 4.5 m. is the junction with a trail.

Left on this 0.5 m. to the creek below Roaring Springs. The one-day trip ends here, with lunch in a pretty grove (*trout fishing above and below dam.*) Half a mile below, the stream flows into Bright Angel Creek.

The POWER HOUSE, 5.2 *m.,* on the Kaibab Trail, supplies electricity and water to the North Rim. All equipment is carried down on muleback.

Just below the power house the trail crosses Bright Angel Creek, and descends Bright Angel Canyon. The original trail crossed the stream ninety-four times; now only seven crossings are necessary.

At 7.5 *m.* is a junction with a trail.

Right to RIBBON FALLS, 0.5 *m.,* plunging 148 feet from a crevice in the rock. At the base of the falls is a moss covered deposit of travertine 42 feet high. The sun shinning on the spray of this waterfall forms a rainbow.

BOX CANYON, 12 *m.* has narrow, perpendicular walls, through which the trail twists to emerge in the wider, lower section of Bright Angel Canyon.

PHANTOM RANCH, 13.1 *m.* (*see TRAIL TOUR 2*) is at the junction with the Kaibab Trail from the South Rim (*see TRAIL TOUR 2*).

PART IV
Appendices

Chronology

797 (circa) Caves along Rio Puerco are occupied by aborigines.

1100 (circa) Cliff dwellers, who are pottery makers, are at Walnut Canyon.

1200 (circa) Oraibi, oldest continuously inhabited town in United States, is established.

1274–97 Great drought.

1300 (circa) Irrigation canals (approximately 185 miles in extent) serve Indian farmers in Gila and Salt River Valleys. Pueblo culture at its height at Casa Grande and Pueblo Grande.

1526 Don Jose de Basconales (according to some accounts) reaches Zuni from Mexico—the first European to cross Arizona.

1539 Friar Marcos de Niza, seeking Seven Cities of Cibola, sights native place of "stone houses"; claims new land for Spain.

1540 Francisco Vasquez de Coronado extends boundaries of New Spain over Southwest. Pedro de Tovar discovers Hopi country. Garcia Lopez de Cardenas discovers Grand Canyon.

1582 Antonio de Espejo leads expedition into Arizona region and finds silver ore west of Prescott.

1600 Franciscans build missions and convert Hopi.

1680 Pueblo dwellers kill priests and destroy missions.

1692 Mission work begun in Santa Cruz and San Pedro Valleys by Father Eusebio Francisco Kino. Guevavi Mission founded.

1694 Pima Indians revolt.

1696 Tumacacori Mission built.

1700 San Xavier del Bac Mission founded. (Rebuilt 1784–97.)

1751 Pima and Papago Indians unite in revolt.

1752 First white settlers establish Tubac *presidio* in Santa Cruz Valley.

1767 Jesuits are expelled from New Spain.

1768 Franciscans under Father Francisco Tomas Garces take over missionary work.

1776 Garces travels 2500 miles preaching Christianity to northern Arizona Indians. Tubac *presidio* moved to Tucson.

1781 Garces and Spanish soldiers massacred by Yumas.

1782 General Teodoro de Croix and Spanish soldiers punish Yuma tribe.

1810–11 Mexican Insurrection.

1821–22 Mexico wins independence from Spain.

1824 Trappers from United States explore along Gila, Salt, Colorado rivers.
Mexico, now a republic, creates Territory of Nuevo Mexico which includes Arizona region.

1827　Mexico expels Franciscans; Arizona mission era ends.

1830　Trappers report rich resources in furs, land, minerals; trade and settlement increase.

1846　United States declares war on Mexico. Colonel Stephen W. Kearny, commanding the Army of the West, takes Santa Fe; crosses Arizona en route to California.

1846–47　Mormon Battalion, unit of Army of the West, crosses Arizona marking first wagon road from Santa Fe to the Pacific.

1848　Mexican War ends. Land north of Gila River, including most of Arizona, ceded to United States.

1850　Arizona made part of New Mexico Territory by Act of Congress.

1852　Survey party under Captain Lorenzo Sitgreaves follows Little Colorado in quest of outlet to sea; sees Grand Falls, Wupatki pueblo, San Francisco mountains; follows Colorado River to Yuma. Fort Yuma established.

1853　Captain James Gadsden, representing United States in Mexico, negotiates purchase by United States of 20,000,000-acre Mesilla Valley. Gadsden Treaty, ratified in 1854, extends Arizona's southern border to present line; secures valuable pass through Rockies for railroad right of way.

1853–54　Government surveying party, headed by Lieutenant A. W. Whipple, makes survey across Arizona along the 35th parallel.

1854　Prospectors discover rich copper vein one hundred miles southeast of Fort Yuma; name town Ajo. First copper mine opened at Ajo.

1856　Citizens of Arizona petition Congress to set up separate territory named Arizona.

1857　First stagecoach line established. Edward F. Beale marks wagon road from Fort Defiance to Colorado, using camels as pack animals.

1858　Gold placers discovered on Gila River above Fort Yuma.

1859　First newspaper is published, *The Weekly Arizonian*, at Tubac.

1861　Conventions at Tucson and Mesilla declare area Confederate territory.

1862　Retreating Confederate troops skirmish with California Volunteer Column in Picacho Pass, only engagement fought in Arizona during Civil War. Apaches under Mangas Coloradas and Cochise defeated at Apache Pass.

1863　Congress separates Arizona from New Mexico, creating the Territory of Arizona (February 24). Captain Joseph Walker pans Hassayampa River searching for gold for Confederate cause. First Anglo-American settlement at Beaver Dams (now Littlefield). Prescott is located.

1864　Henry Wickenburg discovers Vulture mine.
First Territorial Delegate, Charles D. Poston, leaves for Washington, D.C.
First Territorial Legislature begins sessions September 26, adjourns November 10.

1867　Tucson, by majority of one vote, is made territorial capital.

1868　Settlement is made near present site of Phoenix.

1869　John Wesley Powell explores Grand Canyon by boat.

1870   General George Stoneman takes command of forces fighting Indians. Population (U. S. Census), 9,658.

1871   General George Crook forces surrender of Hualpai, Tonto, and Yavapai Indians.

1873   Mormon immigrants trek through Painted Desert; settle along the Little Colorado.

1877   George Warren locates the Copper Queen mine in Bisbee. Prescott again chosen as capital.

1878   Southern Pacific Railway connects Yuma with West Coast.

1880   Population, 40,440.
City of Phoenix incorporated. Southern Pacific Railway extended to Tucson.

1883   M. H. Sherman elected superintendent of schools and drafts code of school laws.

1885   University and normal schools provided for.

1886   Geronimo and outlaw Apaches transported to Florida and imprisoned.

1887   James Reavis collects rent on 12,500,000 acres, under fraudulent land grant from Philip V. of Spain. Reavis lives as feudal baron until hoax is exposed and he is sentenced to six years in prison.

1889   Capital removed from Prescott to Phoenix.

1890   Population, 88,243.

1898   Arizona cowboys rally behind Bucky O'Neill, join Rough Riders, for war service in Cuba.

1900   Population, 122,931.

1901   New Capitol dedicated at Phoenix.

1902   Arizona opposes union with New Mexico as a state.

1910   Population, 204,354.

1911   Theodore Roosevelt dedicates Roosevelt Dam, world's highest masonry dam, making possible the irrigation of 220,000 acres.

1912   February 14, Arizona admitted into Union as the forty-eighth state. George W. P. Hunt elected first governor.

1914   Mines work at capacity producing metals for warring Europe.

1917   Vigilantes and Home Guard crush miners' unions by wholesale deportations.

1920   Population, 334,162. Legislature passes Workmen's Compensation Act.

1930   Population, 435,573. Calvin Coolidge dedicates Coolidge Dam, world's highest multiple-dome dam.

1932   Mines, stores, saw mills, packing plants closed by business depression. State finances in precarious position.

1933   Legislature levies tax on retail sales.

1934   Governor Moeur, fearing California exploitation, orders Arizona National Guard to prevent erection of Parker Dam.

1935   Work begun on Yuma-Gila reclamation project.

1936   President Franklin D. Roosevelt officially opens giant spillways of Boulder Dam, world's highest dam (727 ft.); it starts potential irrigation for 500,000 acres in southwestern Arizona.

1939   Bartlett Dam, world's highest multiple-arch dam, is completed.

1940　Population, 499,261

1941　Battleship Arizona sunk in Japanese attack on Pearl Harbor.
Davis-Monthan Air Force bomber base established near Tucson.
Williams Air Force bomber base established—largest jet air school;
Luke Air Force Base, largest advanced training center for fighter
pilots.

1942　Generation of power at Parker Dam on Colorado River, world's
"deepest" dam (completed in 1938), begins. Goodyear Aircraft
Corporation plant at Litchfield Park starts production of plane assemblies for Navy. $35 million Aluminum Company of America war
industry plant started at Phoenix. AiResearch Manufacturing Company, high altitude plane equipment plant at Phoenix begins operations. Navajo Ordnance Depot near Flagstaff activated.

1946　Constitutional amendment outlawing "closed shop" adopted. American Institute For Foreign Trade established near Glendale. Rey-
nolds Metals Company reactivated aluminum plant for extrusion of
aluminum shapes and tubing.

1948　Oil drilling wave sweeps state. Several major oil companies and
many private concerns granted drilling permits. Indians meeting
state educational requirements granted vote.

1949　Navajo Reservation in Northern Arizona revealed as number two
source of nation's uranium.

1950　Population, 749,587. Phoenix, capital, and largest city, has population gain from 65,414 to 106,818 in decade. Arizona surpasses Oklahoma for first time with largest Indian population in U. S. with
65,761 (U. S. Census).

1951　Luke Air Force Base reactivated; trains fighter bomber pilots.

1952　Law passed prohibiting secondary boycott in strikes. Davis Dam,
last of four major barriers harnessing the lower Colorado River,
dedicated. Arizona Children's Colony for mentally deficient children,
established near Coolidge. Hughes Aircraft Company, manufacturing electronic devices, established near Tucson.

1953　Population estimate, 900,000. Extensive annexations and influx of
new residents raises Phoenix population to 150,000, and Tucson to
55,000; Greater Phoenix, 300,000, Greater Tucson, 170,000. Arizona produces record crop of over a million bales of cotton on
680,000 irrigated acres. Yuma Mesa well strikes oil-indicating
sand. Development of Lavender Pit, huge open pit copper mine, at
Bisbee, underway. $111 million development begins at San Manuel,
new copper camp on desert northeast of Tucson, complete with mine,
mill, and smelter, town of 2,000 model homes. Desegregation in
Phoenix high schools ordered.

1954　Fort Huachuca reactivated as secret U.S. Electronics proving ground.
First natural gas flow begins commercially on Navajo Reservation.

1955　Estimated population, 1,000,000.

Selective Bibliography

Books have been selected from the point of view of availability and appeal to the general reader for supplementary reading. The bibliography has been augmented in some cases by references to United States Government documents when there was nothing else authoritative on the subject.

GENERAL REFERENCE

Arizona Year Book, 1930–31. Phoenix, Arizona, Year Book, Inc., 1930.

Barnes, Will Croft. *Arizona Place Names*. University of Arizona. General Bulletin. Vol. VI, No. 1. Tucson, University of Arizona, Jan. 1935.

Goddard, Pliny Earle. *Indians of the Southwest*. Handbook series No. 2. New York, Museum of Natural History, 1921.

Hodge, Frederick W. *Handbook of American Indians*. U. S. Bureau of American Ethnology. Bulletin 30. 2 Pts. Washington, D. C., (Pt. 1, 1907), (Pt. 2, 1910).

University of Arizona. *Arizona and Its Heritage*. General Bulletin No. 3, Tucson, University of Arizona, 1936.

GEOGRAPHY, TOPOGRAPHY, CLIMATE

James, George Wharton. *Arizona, the Wonderland*. Boston, The Page Company, 1917.

Robinson, William Henry. *Under Turquoise Skies*. New York, Macmillan Company, 1928.

U. S. Department of Commerce. *Commercial survey of the Pacific southwest*. Domestic Commerce Series, No. 37, by C. R. Niklason. Washington, D. C., Government Printing Office, 1930.

Van Dyke, John Charles. *The Desert*. New York, Charles Scribner's Sons, 1930.

GEOLOGY, RESOURCES, AND CONSERVATION

Eddy, Clyde. *Down the World's Most Dangerous River*. New York, Frederick A. Stokes Company, 1929.

Guild, F. N. *The Mineralogy of Arizona*. Easton, Pa., Chemical Publishing Company, 1910.

Simmons, Ralph B. *Boulder Dam and the Great Southwest*. Los Angeles, Pacific Publishers, 1936.

Stanton, Robert Brewster. *Colorado River Controversies.* New York, Dodd, Mead and Company, 1932.

University of Arizona. State Bureau of Mines. *Directory of Arizona Minerals.* Bulletin No. 3, Mineral Technology Series No. 1, by Charles F. Willis. Tucson, University of Arizona, 1915.

—— State Bureau of Mines. *Resumé of Arizona Geology* by Nelson Horatio Darton. Bulletin 119. Tucson, University of Arizona, 1925.

U. S. Congress 57th, 2nd session. Senate Doc. 142. *Letter from Secretary of the Interior (Albert B. Fall) transmitting report of the Director of the Reclamation Service (A. P. Davis) on Problems of the Imperial Valley and Vicinity with respect to irrigation from the Colorado River.* Washington, D. C., Government Printing Office, 1928.

U. S. Congress 65th, 3rd session. Senate Doc. 436. *Gila River Flood Control* by F. H. Olmsted. Washington, D. C., Government Printing Office, 1919.

U. S. Geological Survey. Water supply paper 395. *Colorado River and Its Utilization* by E. C. La Rue. Washington, D. C., Government Printing Office, 1916.

—— Bulletin 613, Pt. C. *Guidebook of the Western United States, Santa Fe Route* by Nelson Horatio Darton. Washington, D. C., Government Printing Office, 1915.

—— Bulletin 845, Pt. F. *Guidebook of the Western United States, Southern Pacific Lines* by Nelson Horatio Darton. Washington, D. C., Government Printing Office, 1933.

PLANT AND ANIMAL LIFE

Armstrong, Margaret N., and Thornber, John James. *Field Book of Western Wild Flowers.* New York, G. P. Putnam's Sons, 1915.

Ganson, Mrs. Eve. *Desert Mavericks, Caught and Branded or Who's Who on the Desert.* Santa Barbara, Cal., W. Hebbard, 1928.

Hamilton, Frances L. *The Desert Garden;* native plants of Phoenix and vicinity. Phoenix, Author, 1933.

Jaeger, Edmund Carroll. *Denizens of the Desert;* book of southwestern mammals, birds, and reptiles. Boston, Houghton Mifflin, 1922.

O'Connor, Jack. *Game in the Desert.* New York, Derrydale Press, 1939.

Thornber, John James, and Bonker, Frances. *The Fantastic Clan.* New York, Macmillan, 1932.

University of Arizona. Agricultural Station Bulletin 83. *Poisonous Animals of the Desert* by C. T. Vorhies. Tucson, University of Arizona, 1925.

ARCHEOLOGY AND INDIANS

Note: Publications of the U. S. Bureau of American Ethnology, annual reports and bulletins, bulletins of the Museum of Northern Arizona at Flagstaff, and publications of the Gila Pueblo Archeological Foundation at Globe, Arizona contain much reliable and informative material.

Douglass, Andrew Ellicott. *Dating Pueblo Bonito and other ruins of The Southwest.* National Geographic Society. Technical papers. Pueblo Bonito series No. 1. Washington, D. C., National Geographic Society, 1935.

Hewett, Edgar Lee. *Ancient Life in the American Southwest.* Indianapolis, Bobbs-Merrill, 1930.

Kidder, Alfred Vincent. *Introduction to the study of Southwestern Archeology.* New Haven, Yale University Press, 1924. Bibliography on archeology.

Morris, Ann Axtell. *Digging in the Southwest.* Garden City, New York, Doubleday, Doran, 1933.

Apache

Arizona, Works Progress Administration. Federal Writers' Project. *The Apache.* Bulletin No. 1. Aug. 1939. Flagstaff, Arizona State Teachers College, 1939.

Bourke, John Gregory. *On the Border with Crook.* New York, Charles Scribner's Sons, 1892.

Clum, Woodworth. *Apache Agent.* New York, Houghton Mifflin, 1936.

Davis, Britton. *The Truth About Geronimo.* New Haven, Yale University Press, 1929.

Lockwood, Francis C. *The Apache Indians.* New York, Macmillan, 1938.

Yuman Stock

(Cocopa, Mojave, Yuma, Maricopa, Havasupai, Hualapai, and Chemehuevi)

Coues, Elliott, trans. and ed. *On the Trail of a Spanish Pioneer.* The diary and itinerary of Francisco Garcés, 1775–76. 2 vols. New York, Francis P. Harper, 1900.

Densmore, Frances. *Yuman and Yaqui Music.* Bureau of American Ethnology. Bulletin 110. Washington, D. C., Government Printing Office, 1932.

Kroeber, A. L., ed. *Walapai Ethnography.* Memoirs of the American Anthropological Assn. No. 42. Menasha, Wisc., American Anthropological Assn., 1935.

Spier, Leslie. *Yuman Tribes of the Gila River.* Chicago, University of Chicago Press, 1933.

Hopi (Moqui)

Arizona, Works Progress Administration. *The Hopi.* Bulletin No. 2. Sept. 1937, Flagstaff, Arizona State Teachers College, 1937.

Coolidge, Mary R. *The Rain-makers.* Boston, Houghton Mifflin, 1929.

Crane, Leo. *Indians of the Enchanted Desert.* Boston, Little, Brown, 1925.

Earle, Edwin. Text by Kennard, Edward A. *Hopi Kachinas.* New York, J. J. Augustin, 1938.

Gilman, Benjamin I. "Hopi Songs." *Journal of American Ethnology, and Archeology,* Vol. 5, 1908.

Nelson, John L. *Rhythm for Rain.* Boston, Houghton Mifflin, 1937.

Parsons, Elsie Clewes, ed. *Hopi Journal of Alexander M. Stephen.* 2 vols. New York, Columbia University Press, 1936.

Smith, Dama Margaret. *Hopi Girl.* Stanford University, Cal., Stanford University Press, 1931.

Underhill, Ruth M. *First Penthouse Dwellers of America.* New York, J. J. Augustin, 1938.

University of Arizona. Bulletin No. 4, Vol. 4. *The Unwritten Literature of the Hopi,* by Hattie Green Lockett. Tucson, University of Arizona, 1933.

Navajo (Navaho)

Amsden, Charles Avery. *Navaho Weaving, its Technic and History.* Santa Ana, Cal. Fine Arts Press, 1934.

Arizona, Works Progress Administration. *The Navaho,* Bulletin No. 4, November 1937. Arizona State Teachers College, 1937.

Coolidge, Dane and Mary R. *Navajo Indians.* Boston, Houghton Mifflin, 1930.

Gillmor, Frances and Wetherill, Louisa Wade. *Traders to the Navajos;* the story of the Wetherills of Kayenta. Boston, Houghton Mifflin, 1934.

Newcomb, F. J. Text by Reichard, Gladys A. *Sandpaintings of the Navajo Shooting Chant.* New York, J. J. Augustin, 1937.

Reichard, Gladys A. *Spider Woman;* a story of Navaho Weavers and Chanters. New York, Macmillan, 1934.

Reichard, Gladys A. *Dezba, Woman of the Desert.* New York, J. J. Augustin, 1939.

Sullivan, Belle Shafer. *The Unvanishing Navajos.* Philadelphia, Dorrance & Co., 1938.

Whitman, William. *Navajo Tales, Retold.* Boston, Houghton Mifflin, 1925.

Papago

Arizona, Works Progress Administration. *The Papago.* Bulletin No. 3, October 1939. Flagstaff, Arizona State Teachers College, 1939.

Densmore, Frances. *Papago Music.* Bureau of American Ethnology Bulletin 90. Washington, D. C., Government Printing Office, 1929.

Kissell, Mary L. *Basketry of the Papago and Pima.* Anthropological papers, vol. 17, part 4. New York, American Museum of Natural History, 1916.

Lumholtz, Karl S. *New Trails in Mexico.* New York, Charles Scribner's Sons, 1912.

Underhill, Ruth. *The Autobiography of a Papago Woman.* Memoirs No. 46, Menasha, Wisc. American Anthropological Assn., 1936.

Underhill, Ruth M. *Singing for Power.* Berkeley, University of California Press, 1938.
Wright, Harold Bell. *Long Ago Told;* Legends of The Papago Indians. New York, Appleton, 1929.

Pima

Lloyd, J. William. *Aw-Aw-Tam Indian Nights;* being the myths and legends of the Pimas of Arizona. Westfield, N. J., Lloyd group, 1911.
Russell, Frank. *Pima Indians;* extract from the 26th Annual Report of the Bureau of American Ethnology. Washington, D. C., Government Printing Office, 1908.

HISTORY

General

Bancroft, Hubert Howe. Works, Vol. XVII. *History of Arizona and New Mexico.* San Francisco, History Co., 1889.
Dodge, Ida Flood. *Our Arizona.* New York, Charles Scribner's Sons, 1929.
Farish, Thomas Edwin. *History of Arizona.* 8 vols. San Francisco, Filmer Bros., 1915.
Kelly, George H. *Legislative History Arizona.* 1864–1912. Phoenix, Manufacturing Stationers, 1926.
Lockwood, Francis Cummins. *Pioneer Days in Arizona.* New York, Macmillan, 1932.
McClintock, James Harvey. *Arizona, prehistoric, aboriginal, pioneer, modern.* 3 vols. Chicago, S. J. Clarke, 1916.

SPANISH EXPLORERS

Bandelier, Fanny, trans. Bandelier, Adolph F. A., ed. *Journey of Alvar Nunez Cabeza de Vaca . . . together with the report of Father Marcos of Nizza and a letter from The viceroy Mendoza.* New York, Allerton Book Co., 1922.
Bolton, Herbert Eugene. *The Padre on Horseback.* San Francisco, Sonora Press, 1932.
—————— *Rim of Christendom;* biography of Eusebio Francisco Kino. New York, Macmillan, 1936.
Bolton, Herbert Eugene, ed. and trans. *Kino's Historical Memoir of Pimeriá Alta.* 2 vols. Cleveland, Arthur H. Clark, 1919.
Bolton, Herbert Eugene, ed. *Anza's California Expeditions 1774–76.* 5 vols. Berkeley, Cal., University of California, 1930.
Coues, Elliott, ed. and trans. *On the Trail of A Spanish Pioneer;* the diary and itinerary of Francisco Garcés. 2 vols. New York, Francis P. Harper, 1900.

Forrest, Earle Robert. *Missions and Pueblos of the Old Southwest.* Cleveland, A. H. Clarke, 1929.

Winship, George P., ed. and trans. *The Journey of Coronado . . .* as told by himself and his followers. New York, A. S. Barnes, 1904. (Also to be found in the 26th report of the Bureau of American Ethnology, 1908.

AMERICAN PERIOD

Bechdolt, Frederick R. *When the West Was Young.* New York, Century, 1922.

Bourke, J. G. *On the Border With Crook.* New York, Charles Scribner's Sons, 1892.

Breakenridge, William M. *Helldorado,* bringing the law to the mesquite. Boston, Houghton Mifflin, 1928.

Browne, J. Ross. *Adventures in the Apache Country.* New York, Harper and Bros., 1869.

Burns, Walter Noble. *Tombstone;* an Iliad of the Southwest. Garden City, N. Y., Doubleday, Doran, 1927.

Coolidge, Dane. *Fighting Men of the West.* New York, E. P. Dutton, 1932.

Favour, Alpheus H. *Old Bill Williams, Mountain Man.* Chapel Hill, University of North Carolina Press, 1936.

Forrest, Earle R. *Arizona's Dark and Bloody Ground.* Caldwell, Idaho, Caxton Printers, Ltd., 1936. (Graham-Tewksbury feud.)

Freeman, M. P. *City of Tucson.* Tucson, Acme Printing Co., 1939.

Golder, Frank Alfred, ed. *The March of the Mormon Battalion.* New York, Century, 1928.

Hafen, Leroy R. *The Overland Mail 1849-69.* Cleveland, Arthur H. Clark, 1926.

Lake, Stuart N. *Wyatt Earp, Frontier Marshal.* Boston, Houghton Mifflin, 1931.

Lockwood, Francis Cummins. *Arizona Characters.* Los Angeles, Times-Mirror, 1928.

Lockwood, Francis C., and Page, Capt. D. W. *Tucson, the Old Pueblo.* Phoenix, Manufacturing Stationers, 1930.

McClintock, James Harvey. *Mormon Settlement in Arizona.* Phoenix, Arizona, Manufacturing Stationers, 1921.

Mitchell, John D. *Lost Mines of the Great Southwest.* Phoenix, Journal Co., 1933.

Pattie, James O. *Personal Narrative of James O. Pattie;* ed. by Timothy Flint. Chicago, Donnelley and Sons, 1930.

Rak, Mary Kidder. *Border Patrol.* Boston, Houghton Mifflin, 1938.

Rockfellow, John A. *Log of an Arizona Trail Blazer.* Tucson, Acme Printing Co., 1933.

Sloan, Richard E. *Memories of an Arizona Judge.* Stanford Univ., Cal., Stanford University Press, 1932.

Stacey, May Humphreys, Lesley, B. L., ed. *Uncle Sam's Camels.* Journal
supplemented by the Report of Edward Fitzerald Beale, 1857–1858.
Cambridge, Harvard University Press, 1929.

Summerhayes, Martha. *Vanished Arizona.* Salem, Mass., Salem Press,
1911.

EDUCATION

U. S. Bureau of Education. Bulletin 17, 1918. *History of Public School
Education in Arizona,* by S. B. Weeks. Washington, D. C., Government Printing Office, 1918.

INDUSTRY, LUMBER, MINING, AGRICULTURE

Rak, Mary Kidder. *Mountain Cattle.* Boston, Houghton Mifflin, 1936.

University of Arizona. State Bureau of Mines. Bulletin 129. *Second
Report of Mineral Industries,* by J. B. Tenney. Tucson, University
of Arizona, 1931.

University of Arizona. Agricultural Experiment Station. Bulletins on
date growing, alfalfa, cotton, etc. Tucson, University of Arizona.

U. S. Forest Service. *The National Forests of Arizona.* Washington,
D. C., Government Printing Office, 1924.

U. S. Dept. of Interior. Bureau of Mines. *Minerals Year Book,* 1939.
Washington, D. C., Government Printing Office.

COWBOYS

Coolidge, Dane. *Arizona Cowboys.* New York, Dutton, 1938.

King, Frank M. *Wranglin' the Past.* Los Angeles, Cal., Author, 1935.
(Tonto Basin.)

Lomax, John Avery, ed. *Cowboy Songs and other Frontier Ballads.* New
York, Sturgis and Walton, 1916.

Lomax, John Avery, ed. *Songs of the Cattle Trail and Cow Camp.* New
York, The Macmillan Co., 1919.

Rollins, Philip Ashton. *The Cowboy.* New York, Charles Scribner's
Sons, 1936.

Santee, Ross. *Cowboy.* New York, Farrar and Rinehart, 1928.

ART AND ARCHITECTURE

Arizona, Works Progress Administration. *Mission San Xavier del Bac.*
New York, Hastings House, 1940.

Borg, Carl Oscar. *The Great Southwest.* Etchings. Compiled and edited
by Everett C. Maxwell. Los Angeles, Fine Arts Press, 1936.

Duell, Prent. *Mission Architecture exemplified in San Xavier del Bac.*
Tucson, Arizona Archaeological and Historical Society, 1919.

Lutrell, Estelle. *Mission San Xavier del Bac.* Tucson, Acme Press, 1923.

Mason, Otis Tufton. *Indian Basketry.* 2 vols. New York, Doubleday, Page, 1904.

Sides, Dorothy Smith. *Decorative Art of the Southwestern Indians.* Santa Ana, Fine Arts Press, 1936.

LITERATURE

Applegate, Frank Guy. *Indian Stories from the Pueblos.* Philadelphia, J. P. Lippincott, 1929.

Armer, Laura. *Waterless Mountain.* New York, Longmans, Green, 1931. (Newberry Prize book for 1931. Story of Navajo boy.)

Bandelier, Adolph F. A. *The Delight Makers.* New York, Dodd, Mead & Co., 1916. (Story of prehistoric Arizona.)

Barnes, Will Croft. *Tales from the X-Bar Horse Camp.* Chicago, Breeders' Gazette, 1920.

Boyer, Mary G. *Arizona in Literature.* Glendale, Cal., Arthur H. Clark, 1934.

Clarke, Charles Badger. *Sun and Saddle Leather.* Boston, R. G. Badger, 1922. (Poetry)

Cronyn, George, editor. *The Path on the Rainbow;* an anthology of songs and chants from the Indians of North America. New York, Boni-Liveright, 1918.

Dobie, J. Frank. *Apache Gold and Yaqui Silver.* Boston, Little, Brown & Co., 1939.

Gillmor, Frances. *Windsinger.* New York, Minton, Balch, 1930. (Story of Navajo Medicine Man.)

Grey, Zane. *The Call of the Canyon.* New York, Harper and Bros., 1924. (Scene laid in Oak Creek Canyon.)

Hall, Sharlot M. *Cactus and Pine.* Phoenix, Arizona Republican Print Shop, 1924. (Poetry)

Hooker, Forrestine Cooper. *When Geronimo Rode.* Garden City, N. Y., Doubleday, Page, 1924.

King, Captain Charles. *The Colonel's Daughter.* Philadelphia, J. B. Lippincott, 1910. (Story of Army life at Camp Verde.)

Knibbs, Henry Herbert. *Saddle Songs and Other Verse.* Boston and New York, Houghton Mifflin, 1916.

La Farge, Oliver. *Laughing Boy.* Boston, Houghton Mifflin, 1929. (Pulitzer Prize novel, 1929.)

La Farge, Oliver. *The Enemy Gods.* Boston, Houghton Mifflin, 1937.

Lewis, Alfred Henry. *Wolfville.* New York, F. A. Stokes, 1897. (Early Arizona.)

O'Connor, Jack. *Boom Town.* New York, Alfred A. Knopf, 1938.

Robinson, Will H. *Thirsty Earth.* New York, Julian Messner, Inc., 1937. (Settlers' struggle for water.)

Santee, Ross. *Men and Horses.* New York, Century, 1926. (Twenty stories of life on the range.)

Weadock, Jack. *Dust of the Desert;* plain tales of the Desert and Border. New York, Appleton-Century, 1936.

White, Stewart Edward. *Arizona Nights.* New York, McClure, 1907.

Wister, Owen. *Red Men and White.* New York, Harper Bros., 1896. (Contains story of Wham payroll robbery.)

Wright, Harold Bell. *Mine with the Iron Door.* New York, D. Appleton, 1923.

Wright, Harold Bell. *When a Man's a Man.* New York, A. L. Burt, 1918. (Scene laid near Prescott.)

SOME BOOKS ABOUT ARIZONA PUBLISHED SINCE 1940

Adair, John. *The Navajo and Pueblo Silversmiths.* Norman, University of Oklahoma Press, 1944, $4.00.

Adams, Ramon. *Western Words.* Norman, University of Oklahoma Press, 1945, $3.00. (Dictionary of range, cow camp and trail.)

Arnold, Elliott. *Blood Brother.* New York, Duell, Sloan and Pearce, 1947, $3.00. (Story of Cochise, Apache Chief.)

Arnold, Oren. *Savage Son.* Albuquerque, University of New Mexico Press, 1951, $4.50. (Story of Carlos Montezuma, Apache.)

Bolton, Herbert E. *Coronado, Knight of Pueblos and Plains.* New York, McGraw-Hill, 1949, $6.00.

Brandt, Herbert. *Arizona and its Bird Life.* Cleveland, Bird Research Foundation, 1951, $15.00.

Brooks, Juanita. *Mountain Meadows Massacre.* Stanford, Stanford University Press, 1950, $5.00.

Browne, J. Ross. *A Tour Through Arizona, 1864.* Tucson, Arizona Silhouettes, 1951, $7.50. (Republished.) (Adventures in the Apache Country.)

Clark, Ann (Nolan). *Little Navajo Bluebird.* New York, Viking Press, 1943, $2.50. (Children's book on Navajo Indians.)

Cleland, Robert Glass. *History of Phelps Dodge, 1834-1950.* New York, Alfred A. Knopf, 1952, $4.00.

Conkling, Roscoe P. and Margaret B. *The Butterfield Overland Mail, 1857-1869.* (3 vol.) Glendale, Arthur H. Clark Company, 1947, $25.00.

Corbett, Pearson H. *Jacob Hamblin, the Peacemaker.* Salt Lake City, Deseret Book Company, 1952, $5.00.

Corle, Edwin. *Desert Country.* New York, Duell, Sloan and Pearce, 1941, $3.00.

—— *The Gila, River of the Southwest.* New York, Rinehart and Company, 1951, $4.50.

Cosulich, Bernice. *Tucson.* Tucson, Arizona Silhouettes, 1953, $5.00.

Dale, Edward Everett. *Indians of the Southwest.* Norman, University of Oklahoma Press, 1949, $4.00.

Darrah, William Culp. *Powell of the Colorado.* Princeton, Princeton University Press, 1951, $6.00.

Dobie, J. Frank. *Life and Literature of the Southwest.* Dallas, Southern Methodist University Press, 1952, $3.50.

———— *The Longhorns.* Boston, Little, Brown and Co., 1941, $3.50.

———— *The Mustangs.* Boston, Little, Brown and Co., 1952, $7.50.

DuPuy, William Atherton. *The Baron of the Colorados.* San Antonio, Naylor Company, 1940, $2.00 (Peralta-Reavis Land Grant.)

Fergusson, Erna. *Our Southwest.* New York, Alfred A. Knopf, 1940, $3.50.

Forbes, Robert H. *Crabbe's Filibustering Expedition in Sonora, 1857.* Tucson, Arizona Silhouettes, 1952, $5.00.

Forrest, Earle R. *Arizona's Dark and Bloody Ground.* Caldwell, Idaho, Caxton Printers, Ltd., 1950, $4.00. Revised and enlarged edition.) (Graham-Tewksbury Feud.)

Gillmor, Frances. *Fruit Out of Rock.* New York, Duell, Sloan and Pearce, 1940, $2.50.

Haley, J. Evetts. *Jeff Milton, a Good Man With a Gun.* Norman, University of Oklahoma Press, 1948, $5.00.

Hannum, Alberta. *Spin a Silver Dollar.* New York, Viking Press, 1945, $3.75. (Trading Post life in Navajo Country.)

Hunt, Frazier. *Cap Mossman, Last of the Great Cowmen.* New York, Hastings House, 1951, $3.75.

———— *Horses and Heroes.* New York, Charles Scribner's Sons, 1949, $6.00.

Jaeger, Edmund C. *Our Desert Neighbors.* Stanford, Stanford University Press, 1950, $5.00. (Arizona fauna.)

Joseph, Alice. *Desert People, a study of the Papago Indians.* Chicago, University of Chicago Press, 1949, $6.00.

Kearney, Thomas H. and Peebles, Robert H. *Arizona Flora.* Berkeley, University of California Press, 1951, $7.50

Keithley, Ralph. *Buckey O'Neill.* Caldwell, Idaho, Caxton Printers, Ltd., 1949, $3.50.

King, Frank M. *Mavericks.* Pasadena, Trails End Publishing Co., 1947, $3.75. (Salty comments of an old Cowpuncher.)

Kluckholm, Clyde, and Leighton, Dorothea. *The Navaho.* Cambridge, Harvard University Press, 1947, $4.50.

Krutch, Joseph Wood. *The Desert Year.* New York, William Sloane Associates, 1952, $3.75. (A visitor's year at Tucson.)

Lauritzen, Jonreed. *Arrows Into the Sun.* New York, Alfred A. Knopf, 1943, $3.00.

———— *Song Before Sunrise.* Garden City, Doubleday and Co., 1948, $3.00.

Lockwood, Frank C. *Apaches and Longhorns.* Los Angeles, Ward Ritchie Press, 1941, $2.50. (Reminiscences of Will C. Barnes.)

Long, Haniel. *Pinon Country.* New York, Duell, Sloan and Pearce, 1941, $3.00.

Marshall, James. *Santa Fe, the Railroad That Built an Empire.* New York, Random House, 1945, $3.75.

Martin, Douglas D. *Tombstone's Epitaph.* Albuquerque, University of New Mexico Press, 1951, $4.50.

Miller, Joseph. *The Arizona Story*. New York, Hastings House, 1952, $5.00.

Myers, John Myers. *The Last Chance, Tombstone's Early Years*. New York, E. P. Dutton, 1950, $3.50.

Phelps, Margaret. *Antelope Boy, and other stories*. Philadelphia, Macrae-Smith Co., 1946, $2.50. (Indian stories for children.)

Sanford, Trent Elwood. *Architecture of the Southwest*. New York, W. W. Norton and Company, 1950, $5.00.

Santee, Ross. *The Bubbling Spring*. New York, Charles Scribner's Sons, 1949, $3.75.

———— *Hardrock and Silver Sage*. New York, Charles Scribner's Sons, 1951, $3.00.

———— *Lost Pony Tracks*. New York, Charles Scribner's Sons, 1953, $3.95.

Schmitt, Martin F. *General George Crook, his Autobiography*. Norman, University of Oklahoma Press, 1946, $3.00.

Sonnichsen, C. L. *Billy King's Tombstone*. Caldwell, Idaho, Caxton Printers, 1942, $3.00.

Stegner, Wallace. *Mormon Country*. New York, Duell, Sloan and Pearce, 1942, $3.75.

Taylor, Rosemary. *Chicken Every Sunday*. New York, Whittlesey House, 1943, $2.75. (Life with mother's boarders in Tucson.)

Underhill, Ruth M. *Hawk Over Whirlpools*. New York, J. J. Augustin, 1940, $2.75.

Waters, Frank. *The Colorado*. New York, Rinehart and Co., 1946, $3.00. (Rivers of America Series.)

Westermeier, Clifford P. *Man, Beast, Dust*. Denver, World Press, 1948, $5.00. (Story of the Rodeo.)

Wilson, Neill C. and Taylor, Frank J. *Southern Pacific*. New York, McGraw-Hill, 1952, $4.50. (Story of a Railroad.)

Wyllys, Rufus Kay. *Arizona, History of a Frontier State*. Phoenix, Hobson and Herr, 1950, $6.00.

Index to Cities and Towns

MAP OF
ARIZONA
IN SIX SECTIONS

LEGEND FOR STATE MAP

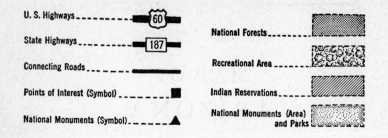

U. S. Highways _ _ _ _ _ _ _ _ _ _ **60**

State Highways _ _ _ _ _ _ _ _ _ _ **187**

Connecting Roads _ _ _ _ _ _ _ _

Points of Interest (Symbol) _ _ _ _ _ ■

National Monuments (Symbol) _ _ _ _ _ ▲

National Forests _ _ _ _ _ _ _ _ _

Recreational Area _ _ _ _ _ _ _

Indian Reservations _ _ _ _ _ _

National Monuments (Area) and Parks

MAP SHOWING SECTIONAL DIVISION OF STATE MAP

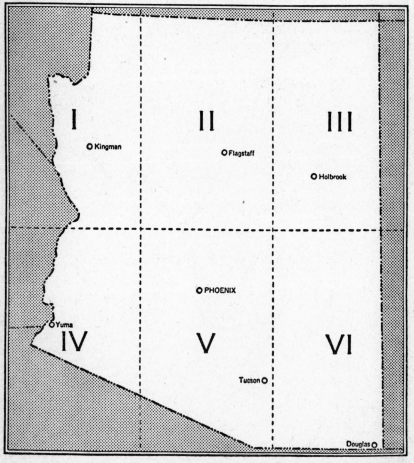

I   O Kingman

II   O Flagstaff

III   O Holbrook

O PHOENIX

IV   O Yuma

V   Tucson O

VI   Douglas O

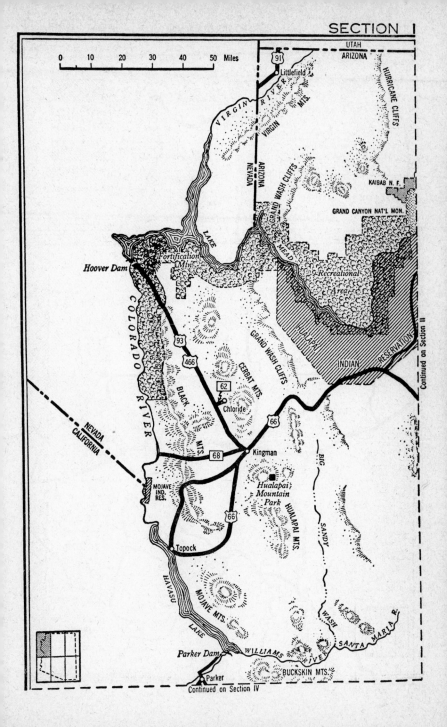

Continued on Section II

Continued on Section IV

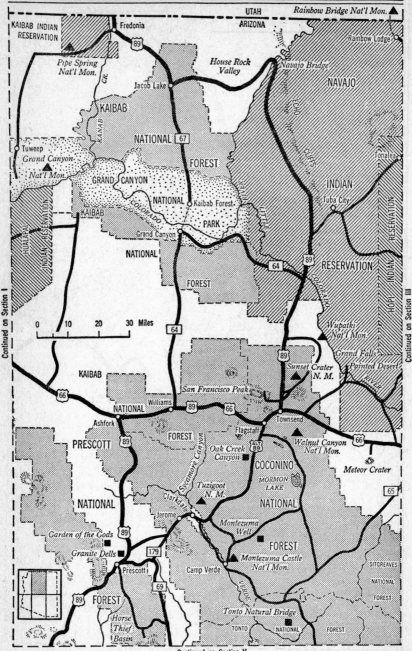

Continued on Section I

Continued on Section III

Continued on Section V

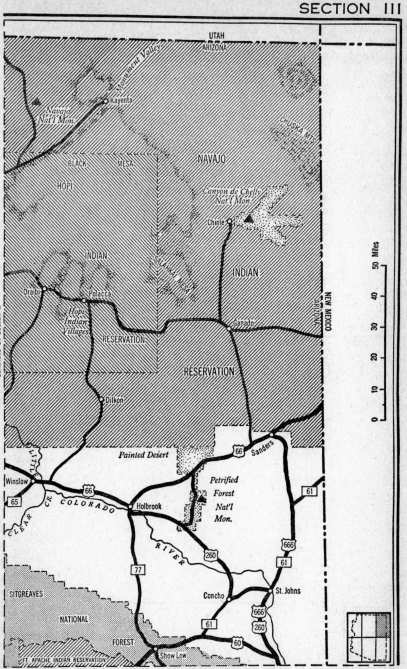

Continued on Section II

Continued on Section VI

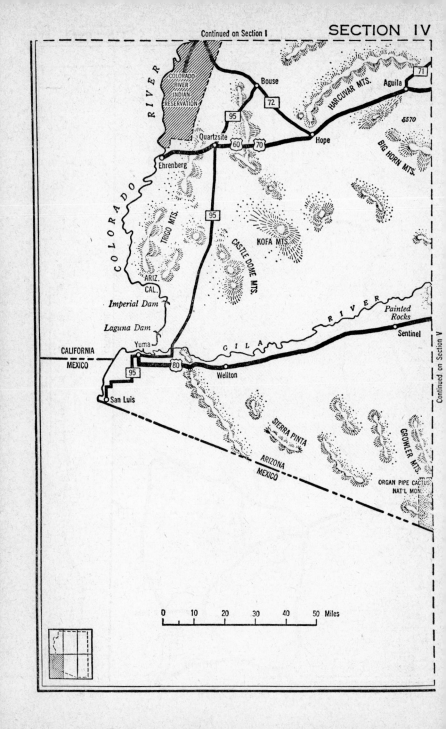

Continued on Section V

0   10   20   30   40   50 Miles

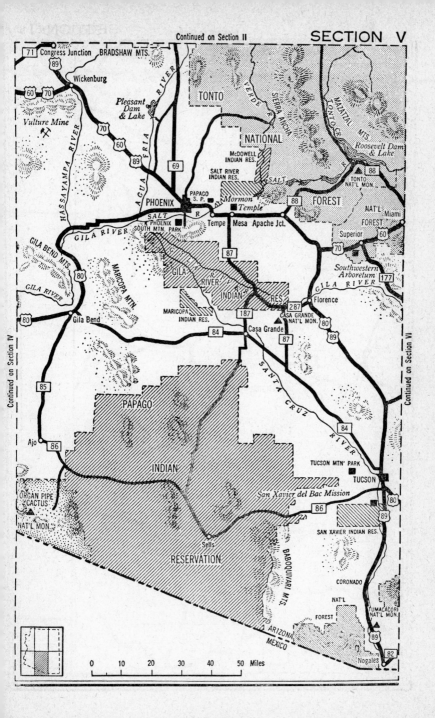

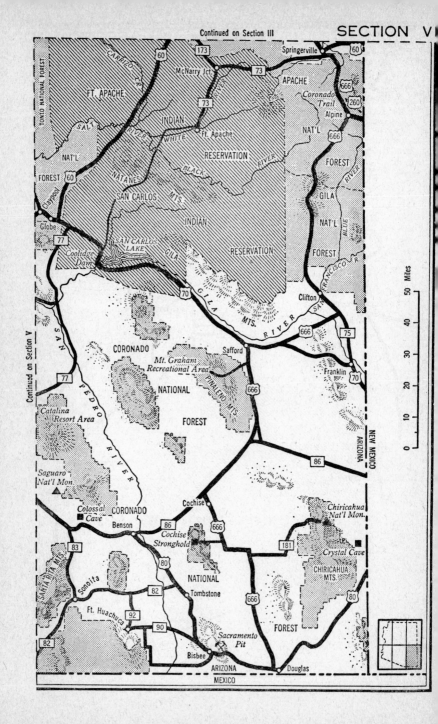

Continued on Section III

Continued on Section V

Index

523